New Essays on the Rationalists

# New Essays
# on the
# Rationalists

Edited by
Rocco J. Gennaro
and
Charles Huenemann

New York    Oxford
OXFORD UNIVERSITY PRESS
1999

Oxford University Press

Oxford    New York
Athens   Auckland   Bangkok   Bogotá   Buenos Aires   Calcutta
Cape Town   Chennai   Dar es Salaam   Delhi   Florence   Hong Kong   Istanbul
Karachi   Kuala Lumpur   Madrid   Melbourne   Mexico City   Mumbai
Nairobi   Paris   São Paulo   Singapore   Taipei   Tokyo   Toronto   Warsaw

and associated companies in
Berlin   Ibadan

Published by Oxford University Press, Inc.
198 Madison Avenue, New York, New York 10016

Oxford is a registered trademark of Oxford University Press

Library of Congress Cataloging-in-Publication Data
New essays on the rationalists / edited by Rocco J. Gennaro and
Charles Huenemann.
p.   cm.
Includes bibliographical references and index.
ISBN 0-19-512488-X
1. Rationalism — History — 17th century.   2. Rationalism —
History — 18th century.   3. Descartes, René, 1596–1650.   4. Spinoza,
Benedictus de, 1632–1677.   5. Leibniz, Gottfried Wilhelm, Freiherr
von, 1646–1716.   I. Gennaro, Rocco J.   II. Huenemann, Charles.
B833.N48   1999
149'.7'09032 — dc21       98-20454

1  3  5  7  9  8  6  4  2

Printed in the United States of America
on acid-free paper

*To our precious daughters*
Olivia Anne Gennaro
*and*
Hanna Rose Huenemann

# Contents

## Part Two: Freedom and Necessity

## Part Three: Mind and Consciousness

# Contributors

JONATHAN BENNETT, now retired, was for nineteen years professor of philosophy at Syracuse University. His work in early modern philosophy includes two books on Kant; one on Spinoza; and one on Locke, Berkeley, and Hume. He is currently rewriting the last book, as well as working on a companion volume on Descartes, Spinoza, and Leibniz.

CLARENCE BONNEN no longer pursues philosophy as a vocation but rather as an avocation. He currently lives with his wife, Susan, in Austin, Texas, and cares for Kate and Benjamin Bonnen, their eight-year-old daughter and five-year-old son. He also serves as the newsletter editor and president of the Austin Girls' Choir and the newsletter editor of St. Mark's Episcopal Church.

JOSEPH KEIM CAMPBELL is assistant professor of philosophy at Washington State University. His primary research is in the areas of free will, the history of skepticism, and the philosophy of David Hume.

J. A. COVER is associate professor of philosophy at Purdue University and specializes in early modern history of philosophy, metaphysics, and philosophy of science. He has published articles on Leibniz, causation, modality, and space and time. He has coedited *Central Themes in Early Modern Philosophy* (Hackett, 1990) and *Philosophy of Science: The Central Issues* (W. W. Norton, 1997). He is also co-author (with John O'Leary-Hawthorne) of *Substance and Individuation in Leibniz* (Cambridge, 1999).

EDWIN CURLEY is a professor and Nelson fellow in the Philosophy Department at the University of Michigan, Ann Arbor. He has written on Descartes (*Descartes against the Skeptics*), Hobbes (whose *Leviathan* he recently edited), and Spinoza (whose works he is in the process of translating).

MICHAEL DELLA ROCCA is associate professor of philosophy at Yale University. He is the author of *Representation and the Mind-Body Problem in Spinoza* (Oxford, 1996) and of articles on contemporary metaphysics and seventeenth-century philosophy.

DANIEL FLAGE is associate professor of philosophy at James Madison University in Virginia. His publications include *Berkeley's Doctrine of Notions: A Reconstruction Based on His Theory of Meaning, David Hume's Theory of Mind*, and numerous articles on the history of modern philosophy. He is currently working on a book on Descartes (with Clarence Bonnen).

DON GARRETT is Kenan Distinguished Teaching Professor in Philosophy at the University of North Carolina at Chapel Hill and has also taught at Harvard University and Johns Hopkins University. He is the author of *Cognition and Commitment in Hume's Philosophy* (1997) and of articles in early modern philosophy. He is also the editor of *The Cambridge Companion to Spinoza* (1996) and the coeditor of *The Encyclopedia of Empiricism* (1997) and the journal *Hume Studies*.

ROCCO J. GENNARO is assistant professor of philosophy at Indiana State University, Terre Haute. He is the author of *Consciousness and Self-consciousness: A Defense of the Higher-order Thought Theory of Consciousness* (John Benjamins, 1996) and *Mind and Brain: A Dialogue on the Mind-Body Problem* (Hackett, 1996). He has also published articles on the philosophy of mind, metaphysics, and applied ethics.

SUSANNA GOODIN is associate professor of philosophy at the University of Wyoming. Her areas of research include early modern history of philosophy with an emphasis on Locke and Leibniz. She has also published in the field of ethics and has an interest in environmental ethics.

GEOFFREY GORHAM is assistant professor of philosophy at Cornell College in Mt. Vernon, Iowa. His recent publications include "Mind-Body Dualism and the Harvey-Descartes Controversy" (*Journal of the History of Ideas*, 1994) and "Similarity as an Intertheory Relation" (*Philosophy of Science*, 1996).

CHARLES HUENEMANN is assistant professor of philosophy at Utah State University. His philosophical interests include the history of early modern philosophy, metaphysics, epistemology, and the philosophy of science. He has published articles on Spinoza, Descartes, and Kant, and he is currently researching the evolution of architechtonic from Kant to Wittgenstein.

SAMUEL LEVEY is assistant professor of philosophy at Dartmouth College. He is the author of various articles on metaphysics and on Leibniz's philosophy.

ERIC PALMER is assistant professor of philosophy at Allegheny College in Pennsylvania. His current work in the history of philosophy centers on the French and Italian sources of Descartes's method. His recent work has considered the development of the method through Descartes's career, from the *Rules for the Direction of the Mind* to the *Discourse on Method* and later works.

ERIC SOTNAK is assistant professor of philosophy at the University of Akron in Ohio. His research interests range over Leibniz, Kant, ethics, philosophy of religion, and East Asian philosophy.

MATTHEW STUART is assistant professor of philosophy at Bowdoin College, in Brunswick, Maine. He has written on Locke's metaphysics and the philosophy of science.

STEPHEN VOSS is professor of philosophy at Bogazici University in Istanbul, Turkey. He has edited *Essays on the Philosophy and Science of René Descartes* (Oxford, 1993); has written on philosophy of religion, metaphysics, and history of early modern philosophy; and is presently working on Descartes's original vision and later philosophy and on aspects of consciousness.

GREGORY WALSKI is a Ph.D. candidate in philosophy at the University of Michigan, Ann Arbor. He is interested primarily in seventeenth- and eighteenth-century philosophy and the philosophy of religion, and he is currently working on Descartes's doctrine of the creation of the eternal truths.

CATHERINE WILSON is professor of philosophy at the University of British Columbia, Canada. She is the author of *Leibniz's Metaphysics* (Princeton, 1989), *The Invisible World: Early Modern Philosophy and the Invention of the Microscope* (Princeton, 1995); and articles on Leibniz, Descartes, and Kant.

MARGARET D. WILSON was professor of philosophy at Princeton University, where she taught from 1970 to 1998. She was the author of *Descartes* (1978) and published many articles on seventeenth- and eighteenth-century philosophy. She was also involved in nature conservation and animal protection causes.

# Abbreviations for Commonly Cited Works

A = German Academy of Sciences, ed. G. W. *Leibniz: Sämtliche Schriften und Briefe*. Berlin: Akademie Verlag, 1923–. Citations include series, volume, and page.

AG = Roger Ariew and Daniel Garber, eds. and trans. G. W. *Leibniz: Philosophical Essays*. Indianapolis: Hackett, 1989.

AT = Charles Adam and Paul Tannery, eds. *Oevres de Descartes*, 11 vols. Paris: CNRS and Vrin, 1964–1976. Citations include volume and page.

Curley = Edwin Curley, ed. and trans. *The Collected Works of Spinoza*, vol. 1. Princeton, N.J.: Princeton University Press, 1985.

CSM = John Cottingham, Robert Stoothoff, and Dugald Murdoch, eds. and trans. *The Philosophical Writings of Descartes*, 2 vols. Cambridge: Cambridge University Press, 1985–1986. Citations include volume and page. In citing the *Principles*, the part and the article are separated by a colon; for example, *Principles* 2:18 refers to article 18 of part 2.

CSMK = John Cottingham, Robert Stoothoff, Dugald Murdoch, and Anthony Kenny, eds. and trans. *The Philosophical Writings of Descartes, vol. 3: The Correspondence*. Cambridge: Cambridge University Press, 1991.

E = Benedict de Spinoza. *Ethics*. Citations include part and then (as appropriate) definition, axiom, proposition, demonstration, corollary, or scholium; for example, IIP38C2 refers to the second corollary to proposition 38 of part II.

Ep = Spinoza's *Letters*. Citations include letter number and (sometimes) Geb page.

Essay = Locke's *Essay Concerning Human Understanding*. Citations include book, chapter, and paragraph number.

G = C.I. Gerhardt, ed. *Die Philosophischen Schriften von Leibniz.* 7 vols. Berlin: Weidmann, 1875–90. Hildesheim: Olms, 1962. Citations include volume and page.

Geb = Carl Gebhardt, ed. *Spinoza Opera,* 4 vols. Heidelberg: Carl Winter, 1925. Citations include volume and page.

KV = Spinoza's *Short Treatise.* Geb page is given.

L = Leroy Loemker, ed. and trans. G. W. *Leibniz: Philosophical Papers and Letters,* 2nd ed. Dordrecht: Reidel, 1969.

RB = Peter Remnant and Jonathan Bennett, eds. and trans. G. W. *Leibniz: New Essays Concerning Human Understanding.* Cambridge: Cambridge University Press, 1981.

TdIE = Spinoza's *Tractatus de Intellectus Emendatione.* Citations include bruder number and/or Geb page.

TTP = Spinoza's *Theological-Political Treatise.* Citations include chapter and then either Sigwart number or Geb page.

# Introduction

The seventeenth-century philosophers René Descartes (1596–1650), Baruch Spinoza (1632–1677), and Gottfried Leibniz (1646–1716) are clearly three of the most important figures in the history of Western philosophy. These so-called "rationalists" were united in the belief that the intellect and human reason are powerful tools in our ability to know about the ultimate nature of mind and matter. Although the contrast with so-called "empiricism" can sometimes be misleading, it is a belief in the power of human reason that often separated the rationalists from many of their contemporaries who believed that all knowledge can ultimately be traced to sense experience. Of course, we must be careful not to view the rationalists as believing that the unaided intellect is *always* able to understand the true nature of reality. They are, in many cases, also concerned to draw limits on what we can know or understand.

This idea for this volume grew out of our participation in Jonathan Bennett's 1995 National Endowment for the Humanties (NEH) Summer Seminar on Descartes, Spinoza, and Leibniz. We wanted to put together a collection of previously unpublished papers on the rationalists. Most of us who participated in the seminar agreed to write new essays, emphasizing metaphysics and epistemology. We then invited several other philosophers to contribute chapters to the collection (Michael Della Rocca, J. A. Cover, Edwin Curley and Greg Walski, Geoffrey Gorham, Don Garrett, Margaret D. Wilson, and Catherine Wilson). It has been a real team effort: each author commented on at least two other chapters before the final works were submitted. We thank everyone for his or her cooperation.

The book is divided into three parts. Part One contains papers on the nature of matter and substance, a topic dear to the hearts of all three rationalists. Jonathan

Bennett (chapter 1) attempts to sort out and evaluate Descartes's concept of empty space, whereas Eric Palmer (chapter 2), in a different way, also challenges the coherence of Descartes's attack on the possibility of vacuum. Michael Della Rocca (chapter 3) presents an analysis of body-body causation in the work of Descartes and argues that, contrary to the views of such commentators as Gary Hatfield and Daniel Garber, bodies do cause changes in motion in other bodies. Matthew Stuart (chapter 4) addresses the question "What counts as an extended substance for Descartes?" He rejects two traditional answers (that there is only one extended substance, that there are no individual material substances) and defends a third alternative. J. A. Cover (chapter 5) brings together all three rationalists and explores the issue of whether or not Spinoza's "extended substance" is anything like the item that Descartes and Leibniz disagreed about. Cover compares and contrasts the treatment of substance in the work of Descartes, Spinoza, and Leibniz. Samuel Levey (chapter 6) writes on the interplay between Leibniz's thesis that matter is actually infinitely divisible and Leibniz's constructivism about mathematical entities. Levey argues that Leibniz's analysis of matter is the basis for the philosopher's monadism about substance. Susanna Goodin (chapter 7) brings together the work of Leibniz and John Locke on their well-known dispute over the issue of species classification. She examines Leibniz's reaction to Locke's theory of essences and species and argues that Leibniz's response to Locke is inadequate.

Part Two includes four chapters on freedom and necessity. Joseph Keim Campbell (chapter 8) and Eric Sotnak (chapter 9) examine, respectively, Descartes's and Leibniz's theory of free will from a so-called "compatibilist" point of view. Charles Huenemann (chapter 10) and Edwin Curley and Gregory Walski (chapter 11) critically discuss Spinoza's necessitarianism. Huenemann argues that Spinoza did believe that all possibles are actual, whereas Curley and Walski do not think that Spinoza held such a strong necessitarianism.

Part Three covers the topics of mind and consciousness. Stephen Voss (chapter 12) examines the suspicion that a Cartesian soul must be isolated from this world in the way that a spectator is isolated from the action on a stage. Clarence Bonnen and Daniel Flage (chapter 13) attempt to explicate Descartes's implicit criterion of distinctness. They argue that an idea of $x$ is distinct only if it is subsumed under an eternal truth that specifies the conditions sufficient for the existence of $x$ (where $x$ is taken to be an entity of a particular kind). Geoffrey Gorham (chapter 14) attempts to relieve some of the embarassment that seems to follow from Descartes's beliefs that minds and bodies are very different kinds of substances, that minds causally interact with bodies, and that effects must be similar to their causes. Don Garrett (chapter 15) brings together Aristotle and all three rationalists while comparing and contrasting their respective positions on teleological explanation. He argues, for example, that it is not Leibniz but Spinoza who holds the position on teleology nearest to that of Aristotle. Margaret D. Wilson (chapter 16) criticizes the claim that Spinoza has a conception of animal mentality that is superior to Descartes's. She also argues that Spinoza fails to provide a coherent way of establishing what he considers to be our morally unconstrained "rights" with regard to brutes. Rocco J. Gennaro (chapter 17) argues that Leibniz held what has recently come to be known as the "higher-order thought theory of consciousness," that is, the view that what makes a mental state conscious is that it is accompanied by a higher-order thought (or awareness) that one is in that state. He then shows how this interpretation helps to make it clear why Leibniz did indeed believe that animals "apperceive" or are self-conscious to some extent. Finally, Catherine Wilson (chapter 18) argues that the notion that Leibniz had a coherent system is illusory mainly by calling attention to inconsistencies and other difficulties in his account of mental substance and perception.

We thank Jonathan Bennett for a wonderful 1995 Summer Seminar and the National Endowment for the Humanities for bringing us together and making this project possible. We also thank Cynthia Read of Oxford University Press for her guidance throughout our early work on this project.

Finally, the contributors share a sentiment expressed here by Jonathan Bennett: "Of the contributors to this book, many were pupils of Margaret Wilson's, some were personal friends of hers, and all were and are admirers. Her premature death in August 1998 has deprived students of early modern philosophy across the globe of a fine colleague and a shining example of how to combine scholarship with philosophical acuity, how to enter the fray without having or causing anger, and how to be professionally industrious without losing touch with many of life's other pleasures and values. We miss her and her example."

*Terre Haute, Indiana*                                                            R. J. G.
*Logan, Utah*                                                                   C. H.
*January 1999*

# PART ONE

# MATTER AND SUBSTANCE

JONATHAN BENNETT

# Space and Subtle Matter
# in Descartes's Metaphysics

## Space as Extended Nothing

Descartes's views about matter and space are more interesting, instructive, and problematic than has been generally realized. Let us start with his famous denial that there can be vacuum, or empty space:

> *It is a contradiction to suppose there is such a thing as a vacuum, i.e. that in which there is nothing whatsoever.* The impossibility of a vacuum, in the philosophical sense of that in which there is no substance whatsoever, is clear. . . . A body's being extended in length, breadth and depth in itself warrants the conclusion that it is a substance, since it is a complete contradiction that a particular extension should belong to nothing; and the same conclusion must be drawn with respect to a space that is supposed to be a vacuum, namely that since there is extension in it, there must necessarily be substance in it as well.[1]

Two things are going on here: one straightforward, the other not. Straightforwardly, Descartes is rejecting vacuum when it is understood as *extended nothing*, an instance of extension that does not consist in some thing's being extended.

The idea of vacuum as bulky nothing is fit to be rejected, but who has ever had it? Is not Descartes here tilting at a windmill? He thinks not. He writes, of something believed to be "an empty space," that "almost everyone is convinced that this amounts to nothing at all."[2] Elsewhere he makes a more fine-grained accusation: "People judge that so-called empty space is nothing; all the same they conceive it as a positive reality."[3] I like Descartes's subtle distinction between what people judge and how they conceive or represent things, but I shall not linger with it now. My concern is with the allegedly common opinion that space is extended nothing.

Surprisingly, there is a basis for this allegation. Descartes took care to reject that view of space because it had a place on the historical stage. I learn from Copleston that Leucippus, while holding that space is as real as body, referred to it as "what is not" and to body as "what is."[4] Similar views were mentioned by Aristotle and held by a number of medieval philosophers.[5] Echoes of this way of thinking linger on even today. After discussing early ideas about space purely in terms of "emptiness," Daniel Garber abruptly says: "Aristotle, of course, would have none of this nothingness. . . ."[6] This unheralded switch from emptiness to nothingness links Garber with the ancients and medievals whom Descartes was attacking.

Although Descartes is not making a historical mistake in thinking he needs to refute the thesis that space is a bulky nothing, he is philosophically wrong in thinking that this refutation is all he needs to establish his own view of space. There are two other lines for a non-Cartesian metaphysician of space to take; I shall discuss one in the following two sections and the other in a later section.

## Container Space

In *Principles* 2:16 Descartes notes that a body's being extended entails that it is a substance;[7] he generalizes this to the claim that anything's being extended entails that it is a substance; and then he purports to apply this to space. The natural way of applying it would be with this argument:

> Whatever is extended is a substance.
> Every region of space is extended.
> So every region of space is a substance.

That is not what Descartes says, however. He argues instead like this:

> Whatever is extended is a substance.
> Every region of space has extension in it.
> So every region of space has a substance in it.

If the first premise of that is equivalent to "Wherever there is extension there is a substance," then the argument looks valid; but its second premise is mysterious. What can it be for something to have extension in it? (i) It has been suggested to me that it means "Wherever there is a region of space, there is extension." What a bizarre meaning for that sentence! Anyway, the conclusion it yields is merely "Wherever there is a region of space there is substance," which is untouched by the notion of a-substance-*in*-it, which is my present topic. (ii) The second premise might mean that any region of space has extension in-it-as-subject, which is just to say that it is extended. That is a recognized way of speaking;[8] properties are often said to be "in" the things that have them; and Descartes's second premise on that reading of it is true. But those two premises yield only the conclusion that every region of space is a substance — not "has a substance in it," which is the conclusion of Descartes's that we want to understand. I conclude that Descartes reaches his thesis that every region of space has a substance in it through an argument that is plainly invalid or else has a perfectly obscure second premise.

In a later section I shall discuss what Descartes is up to in *Principles* 2:16. First, though, I present a metaphysic of space according to which regions of space can, strictly and literally, have substances in them — the regions being things or substances that have other substances in them. This is the theory that space is a container, an extended thing or substance whose parts (regions) can be colocated with or penetrated by extended substances of a different kind, namely, bodies. If there is a pebble at a certain place, according to this metaphysic, there are two things there: the pebble and a portion or region of container space.

(Do not confuse this with the peculiar way in which an object is sometimes said to be colocated with the portion of stuff of which it is composed. The *new* ring on my finger now coincides in space with an *old* portion of gold, from which some philosophers have inferred that these are distinct things that at present are colocated. Even if they are right, this differs from the colocation that container space involves. When a body is colocated with a region of such space, the two can part company: the body can move while the region stays, both continuing to stay in existence. My ring could not come apart from the gold that now constitutes it, with both remaining intact.)

If there is container space, it might all be full, so that nature is a plenum; or some might be empty, so that there are stretches of vacuum. Which of those obtains would be a contingent matter. Now, Descartes holds that there is matter everywhere, but nobody has ever credited him with holding that there is container space that is all full. He speaks of "spaces" as "full" rather than "empty" and as having bodies "in" them — we have just seen one example of this, and I shall explain that later. But it is perfectly clear that Descartes was no friend of container space.

Why? What did he have against it? Well, it might be thought to be ruled out by his doctrine that whatever is extended must be corporeal. (I shall call this doctrine Extension, for short.) Descartes seems to claim that he has argued against container space — or at least against empty container space — in that manner: "In *Principles* 2:18 I said expressly that I think the existence of a vacuum involves a contradiction, because we have the same idea of matter as we have of space."[9] In *Principles* 2:11 he explicitly says that we have the same idea of matter as we have of space; perhaps there and in 2:18 he can be seen as inferring from this that the existence of a vacuum involves a contradiction, though the argument is somewhat muffled. Anyway, let us consider the strength of this argument, whatever its status in the text.

If we demand Extension's credentials, Descartes has not much to say. His only argument for it, the discussion of the piece of wax in the Second Meditation, is not exact and scrupulous enough to support such a strong conclusion. But he has powerful reasons for wanting Extension to be true: its truth would mean that the basic concepts of physics are just those of geometry, together with the concept of time; and Descartes saw this as giving physics conceptually clear foundations, which would be threatened if we had also to admit, on the ground floor, some further concept such as that of force or mass. His physics failed, primarily because he tried to construct it with too few basic concepts; but the fact remains that he was indissolubly wedded to

Extension, so that we are entitled to put it into play when trying to understand why he rejected container space.

Is it much of a reason? Well, it is so if we assume that container space would have to be extended and incorporeal. "Portions of container space could not be bodies" — to your ears and mine that sounds right, but only because we do not accept Extension. If we did accept it, that would free us to allow that container space is one kind of matter or body. Why should we shrink from calling it "body" if all we meant was that it is extended?

If we adopt that option, however, we must allow that bodies can be colocated with other bodies — for example, pebbles with regions of container space. Is there anything wrong with that? Aristotle thought so: if two bodies could be colocated, he said, then all bodies could be colocated, in which case the entire world of matter would shrink to the size of a grain of wheat. This argument was offered against the thesis that any two extended items could be colocated, and in that form it was destroyed in the sixth century by John Philoponus, who pointed out that bodies might be colocatable with regions though not with other bodies. He held that space is not substantial (an extended nothing?), but that is not needed for his rebuttal of Aristotle. It seems not to have been involved when the same rebuttal was rediscovered and more clearly presented by Hasdai Crescas eight centuries later.[10] Both philosophers were relying, however, on the idea that extended items fall into two radically different kinds, with colocation possible between the kinds but not within either. The natural way to express this is

> Extended items are of two kinds, bodies and regions of container space.
> There can be colocation between the kinds but not within either.

We shall not word it like that, though, because we are going along with Descartes's resolve to describe everything extended as "corporeal." Still, we can stand against Aristotle's argument by saying instead:

> Extended items (bodies) are of two kinds. There can be colocation between
> the kinds but not within either,

and the difference between this formulation and the other may be merely verbal. If Descartes took this line, though, he would have to say more. Specifically, he would need to declare whether this difference between the two kinds of body is fundamental or derived; and each answer would be problematic for him. If the difference is basic, Descartes's physics loses its unity and conceptual spareness, for it now needs not only geometrical concepts and the concept of time but also the concept of what distinguishes the two basic kinds of body. If, on the other hand, the difference is derivative, supervening on differences involving only geometrical and temporal concepts, Descartes ought to tell us *how* this is so, as he tries to do with heat and color; and that is a patently hopeless task.

So perhaps we have here a reason why Descartes might keep container space at bay. We can, in the quick and shallow way of most of the secondary literature on this topic, express it as a simple appeal to Extension: container space would be extended and incorporeal; Extension says that what is extended must be corporeal, therefore and so on. Getting deeper into it, the reason is this: if there were container space with which (other) bodies could be colocated, either colocation could run riot as threatened by Aristotle or else there must be two fundamentally different kinds of extended substance, with colocation possible between them but not within each; and such a difference spells death for Descartes's biggest single ambition for his physics.

## Another Reason for Rejecting Container Space?

Descartes had a different and plainer reason for rejecting container space, embodied in an argument that rules it out by concluding that no extended item can penetrate, that is, be colocated with, any other:

> It is impossible to conceive of one part of an extended thing penetrating another equal part except by understanding that half of that extension is taken away or annihilated; but what is annihilated does not penetrate anything else; and so, in my opinion, it is established that impenetrability belongs to the essence of extension and not to that of anything else.[11]

Notice that Extension is not involved in this argument, which says nothing about the extended items being bodies. The argument concerns any pair of extended things — two bodies, two regions of space, or one of each. A little later, indeed, Descartes uses the argument to rule out More's suggestion that one part of space might be colocated with another.[12] I cannot find him applying it to a space-body pair, but he ought — and I think he would — be willing to do so. The quoted argument, if sound, shows that there cannot be container space since that would involve the possibility that one extended thing (a body) should be colocated with another extended thing (a region of space). Call the second extended thing a "body," too, if you like; but that has no effect on the argument, which owes nothing to Extension.

Garber reconstructs this "simple and ingenious" argument thus: "If a body is an extended thing, in the sense in which Descartes understands it, then take away extension and you take away body. But if two bodies could penetrate one another, then the total volume, and thus some amount of body itself, would be eliminated."[13] The confinement to "bodies" is unwarranted, but otherwise Garber clearly has it right. That clears the air, enabling us to see that the argument begs the question so openly as to be worthless. It assumes that the physical fusion of a body with volume $V_1$ and a body with volume $V_2$ must be a body with volume $(V_1 + V_2)$; but that is equivalent to assuming that there is no colocation. If bodies can interpenetrate, then it might be that one body has $V_1$ while another has $V_2$, though the two together occupy a total volume of less than $(V_1 + V_2)$; neither has lost any volume, but a part of one is colocated with a part of the other. Here is an analogue. Let the volume of a sound be that of the region throughout which it is audible; then it can happen that the shriek of a fire alarm has a volume of 550,000 cubic yards and the boom of an explosion one of 780,000 cubic yards, yet their combined volume is only a million cubic yards because throughout much of the city both are audible.

## Spaces and Places

Within a container-space metaphysic one can correctly describe regions of space as "empty" or "full," or as having bodies "in" them. For a region to have a body in it, in this metaphysic, is for all or part of the region to be colocated with a body. On no other basis is it strictly correct to speak of regions as either full or empty. Yet many of Descartes's commentators credit him with holding that no region of space is empty because all are full. He certainly does hold that there is matter everywhere — there's no doubt about that — but that is different from saying that matter completely *fills* something or other.

Descartes is partly to blame for this common misstatement of his position. We have already seen him writing of a space as having a body "in" it, and such turns of phrase occur often in his writings. Still, he does not believe that there is anything that the world's matter *fills* — there's no doubt about that either — so we have something to explain. Why does Descartes apparently misexpress his own views by writing of "spaces" as "full" and "empty"?

I say "apparently" because there must be more going on than appears on the surface. Whatever it is must also explain Descartes's writing this: "The subtle matter around a candle moves in a circle, and tends to spread out from there and to leave an empty space, that is to say, a space which would be filled only by what might come into it from elsewhere."[14] The original French makes it even clearer than does the CSM version that Descartes is saying only that the subtle matter *tends* to do this, not that it actually succeeds; but still the passage on the face of it tolerates the notion of container space. It is not credible that Descartes meant to do that; so something else must be going on. First I shall introduce a certain distinction in my own terms, then argue that Descartes was also employing it in a manner that helps to explain these puzzling passages.

We need to distinguish a (*region of*) *space* from a *place* or *location*. A place, in my sense of that word, is abstract: it is a complex relational property and thus differs *toto coelo* from a region of space. It is indeed a relational property that a region can have, just as a body may have it. If a body is colocated with a region of container space, then those two items have the very same place; that is, they are related in the same way to other bodies. It is vital to get clear about this concept of the *where* of a thing — its set of spatial relations to other things. When I use the word "place" it will be only to express that concept; that is one proper use of it, and whether it can also be acceptably used to mean the same as "region" does not matter.

If we are using "place" in this sense, it would be safer to say that bodies are "at" places rather than "in" them because the latter suggests containment, which invites confusion between places and regions. Still, we can rescue the "in" idiom by understanding a body's being "in" a place as being its possession of a certain relational property — just as we have a sense for "He is in a bad mood," which does not imply that he inhabits the mood or that it contains him.

With the concept of place in hand, let us look again at Descartes's extraordinary phrase "an empty space, that is to say, a space which would be filled only by what might come into it from elsewhere." Beneath the vexatious empty/full terminology, I suggest, Descartes is entertaining a thought about a *place*.

| *What Descartes Says* | *What He Means* |
|---|---|

The subtle matter tends to move in such a way as to

| move out of a region | lose a certain relational property |
| which would | |
| remain empty | no longer be possessed by anything |
| unless bodies from elsewhere | |
| moved into it. | came to possess it. |

This is still counterfactual: it says only how the matter tends to move, meaning how it would move if. . . . And I do not know how Descartes could make sense of the concept of a place — defining relational property that is once owned by something and later by nothing. But at least Descartes on this reading is not entertaining the thought of container space, which he so often declares to be absolutely, conceptually impossible.

In that passage, if I am right about it, Descartes is thinking of places while writing purely in terms of full/empty and "spaces" (regions of space). Elsewhere, however, he employs the "place" terminology. At the start of *Principles* 2:17 he uses the phrase "place or space" and then treats it as equivalent to "place." In 2:19 he alludes disparagingly to the common view that (parts of) "space" can be "empty," and then in 2:33 he reports that in 2:18–19 he has said "that every place is full of bodies." These turns of phrase provide some support for my conjecture — if, but only if, Descartes in them means "place" in the sense I have given it.

The best fairly direct evidence that he does mean it like that occurs in *Principles* 2:10–15. In these sections "place" and "space" are run in a single harness but treated as a pair; of Descartes's several ways of differentiating them, the most revealing is this:

> There is no real distinction between space, or internal place, and the corporeal substance contained in it; the only difference lies in how we are accustomed to conceive of them. For the extension in length, breadth and depth which constitutes a space is in reality exactly the same as that which constitutes a body. The difference arises as follows: in the case of a body, we regard the extension as something particular, and thus think of it as changing whenever there is a new body; but in the case of a space, we attribute to the extension only a generic unity, so that when a new body comes to occupy the space, the extension of the space is reckoned not to change but to remain one and the same, so long as it retains the same size and shape and keeps the same position relative to certain external bodies which we use to determine the space in question.[15]

The best way to understand this obscure passage, I submit, is by supposing that what Descartes is calling "space or internal place" is a complex relational property that may be possessed first by one body and then by another. That enables it to be true that first one body and then a different one is "in" (better: "at") a certain place, without there having to be some thing that literally contains first one and then the other.

I offer this proposal as a way of rescuing the things Descartes says about spaces and places. Still, he cannot have had this thought in a clear, explicit, and controlled manner because he thought of places as being extended. Places (in my sense, the sense relevant to Descartes) are not extended; complex relational properties do not have length, breadth, and depth. You might think that an item with no shape or size cannot contain bodies, but I remind you that places — in my sense — do not contain bodies. The "body in place" locutions that we freely use are an idiom that divorces "in" from all such notions as that of containment.

## Bodies as Adjectival on Space

John O'Leary-Hawthorne has suggested to me the following interpretation of Descartes's talk of "empty" and "full" and so on. Descartes might think that for there to be a pebble at a given place (in my sense of "place") is for there to be at that place a *pebbly region of space*. If a suitably constrained region of spatiotemporal zones is pebbly throughout, then we can describe that as a single pebble moving through space; and that makes it idiomatically all right to distinguish a region from a pebble that is "in" it. But really, strictly, there are only the regions of space that are sometimes pebbly and sometimes not; so that there is never a "real distinction" between any pebble and any region because that would be a distinction between things, and at the metaphysically basic level there are no such *things* as pebbles. We often say that there are, and this is idiomatic, convenient, and intelligible; but still it is only a shallow *façon de parler* which is, taken deeply and strictly, false. When we talk about pebbles that move, we do or ought to mean something about alterations in which regions are pebbly and which are not.

One way of handling the golden ring that I mentioned early is to say that strictly speaking there is only the portion of gold; it is idiomatically all right to say that there is a ring now because the gold is annular now; but a metaphysically deep inventory of the world's contents would include the portion of gold but not the ring. That is analogous to the suggested treatment of space and objects: a region being sometimes pebbly and sometimes not is comparable with a portion of gold being sometimes annular and sometimes not.

This view about bodies and space has been espoused by Plato, Newton, Spinoza, and some physicists in our own century. I ascribe it to Spinoza on the strength of many things in his *Ethics* — notably the doctrine that there is only one extended substance, of which finite bodies are "modes." If we take "mode" in its standard seventeenth-century sense, that means that finite bodies are states of the one extended substance and are adjectival upon it, relating to it as blushes do to faces. That implies that for there to be "a pebble in a region" is for the region to be pebbly, and that a pebble's movement through space is basically not the movement of a thing but rather an alteration in which regions are pebbly and which are not, comparable with the movement of thaw across a countryside.[16] (The strongest rival to my reading of Spinoza's monism about extended substance is Curley's, which is based on the premise — not independently defended — that Spinoza meant by "mode" less than half of what was commonly meant by it at his time.[17])

The case for this reading of Spinoza is strong, but Descartes's writings do not so well support an outright attribution of the same view of space and bodies to *him*. Just once, in the Synopsis to the *Meditations*, he seems to suggest that there is only one extended substance, which one naturally thinks of as the whole of space (CSM II, 10); but even that is not clear and straightforward, and nowhere does Descartes hint that finite bodies are adjectival upon space or the one extended substance. Perhaps he was starting to flirt with or move a little toward the Spinozist metaphysic of space and body, but I submit that he did not get close enough for it to much affect what he thought or wrote.

For my main purposes in this paper, however, it does not matter which way we choose to rescue what Descartes says about spaces as "full" and "empty." What does matter is to grasp firmly the fact that, although he frequently speaks of spaces/places as having bodies "in" them, there is no item of which Descartes believes that it can literally contain bodies. The humdrum sense in which a flask can contain tea is irrelevant to our topic. It involves one body merely surrounding another; Descartes would never say about the flask and the contained tea, as he does about the space or place and the body "in" it, that "there is no real distinction" between them.

## Space as a System of Relations

Descartes gave short shrift to container space, but he dismissed another time-hallowed metaphysic of space as though he had never even heard of it. I shall approach it through his attempt to "correct our preconceived opinion about absolute vacuum" by this argument:

> If someone asks what would happen if God were to take away every single body contained in a jar, without allowing any other body to take the place of what had been removed, the answer must be that the sides of the jar would in that case have to be in contact. For when there is nothing between two bodies they must necessarily touch each other. And it is a manifest contradiction for them to be apart, or to have a distance between them, when the distance in question is nothing; for every distance is a mode of extension, and therefore cannot exist without an extended substance.[18]

This argument deserves patient scrutiny. Descartes challenges us with this question: "What is there between the opposite sides of the jar?" He warns us against answering, "Only a distance": distances are modes, he says, meaning that they are adjectival upon things. You cannot have a sheer five inches between two things: it must be some third thing that measures five inches along one of its dimensions. "It is a complete contradiction that a particular extension should belong to nothing," we have seen Descartes saying; and he is right. This belongs to his proper denial that space could be a bulky nothing.

What is there between the sides of the jar after the air has been removed? Here is another possible answer: "Before God took action, there were two jar-shaped and -sized things in there — a portion of matter and a region of space — and after he had removed the matter the space remained." That is the container-space answer, and Descartes here offers no reason to reject it. All that he actually argues for is that the two noncontiguous sides of the jar must have some "extended substance" between them; but the conclusion he has announced is that the two sides must have some other "body" between them. This involves not merely a superficial verbal point but also, as we have seen, a deeper issue about colocation.

My topic in this section is a third possible answer to the question "What is there between the opposite sides of the jar?" It goes as follows. If when God removes the matter from the jar it does not collapse, then it follows that the opposite sides of the jar are apart. Now, Descartes assumes that if

(i)  Side $S_1$ is apart from side $S_2$,

that must be because

(ii)  Some thing is between $S_1$ and $S_2$.

That is, the obtaining of the seemingly dyadic fact about apartness must be an upshot of a triadic fact about betweenness. That snubs the possibility that (i) is a *basic* fact about how the two things are related, not one made true by an underlying fact about how the two relate to a third thing. That view was later endorsed by Leibniz in his famous correspondence with Clarke; it was also implicit in some earlier theories of space, but perhaps not clearly enough. At any rate, Descartes does not so much as hint at it.

I call this the theory that space is a system (or structure) of relations. Some other phrases might characterize it more aptly, for example, as the view that there is no space and that all our spatial concepts are concepts of spatial relations among bodies. But I need something brief, and shall stay with what I have chosen.

Descartes might challenge the Leibnizian:

> *If there is nothing between two things, they are contiguous.* That is so trivially obvious that someone who denies it does not deserve to be heard. And it entails, by contraposition, that if two things are not contiguous there is something between them.

The Leibnizian should reply that the "trivially obvious" thesis is false when taken strictly and philosophically and that it seems undeniable only when taken in a loose, colloquial fashion in which "There is nothing between them" merely means that they are contiguous.

Be warned: the relational view of space, which Descartes ignored and Leibniz defended, should not be confused with a relational view of *place*. Here is Locke taking a relational view of place:

> That our idea of place is nothing else but such a relative position of any thing . . . is plain . . . when we consider that we can have no idea of the place of the universe, though we can of all the parts of it; because beyond that we have not the idea of any fixed, distinct, particular beings in reference to which we can imagine it to have any relation of distance; but all beyond it is one uniform space or expansion, wherein the mind finds no variety, no marks.[19]

Our notion of the place of any body, Locke holds, must be a notion of how it is spatially related to other bodies. To cash it out instead in terms of which portion of space the body is in, we need a notion — not parasitic on bodies — of the separate identities of different portions of space; and we cannot have that because space is all "uniform."

Now this view of place is not, for Locke, a down payment on the theory that spatial concepts generally must be reduced to relational ones, that is, that space is a structure of relations. He is carefully agnostic about that theory,[20] and his working picture of space seems to view it as a substantial container, some parts of which are colocated with bodies.

My point is philosophical: someone who holds (i) that our only concept of place is a relational one is still free to affirm or to deny (ii) that space is not a thing but a system of relations. When Locke, having accepted (i), suspended judgment on (ii), this was an impeccable performance. It is similar for Descartes, who also accepted an odd version of (i) and silently turned his back on (ii).

## The Fourth View: Space Is a Separator

We have looked at Descartes's treatment or neglect of three views: that space is a bulky nothing, that space is a substantial container, and that space is a structure of relations. Descartes puts much energy into denying the first; his rejection of the second is silent, but there are reasons for it in his work; and he seems to ignore the third without giving or having good reasons for or against it. He does accept the much weaker thesis that our actual concept of place is relational, but that does not commit him to relationalism about spatial concepts generally.

We should consider just one other possible view, namely, that space is a separator, relating to bodies as water does to fish swimming in it. Water does not relate to fish in the "container" manner: no fish is colocated with any portion of water; rather, a fish swims among the portions of water, pushing them aside as it moves; fish and water compete for places. The portions of water, rather than "containing" the fish in my sense, surround the fish and separate them from one another. The separator metaphysic is analogous to that: there are regions of space and there are bodies, and the two kinds jointly exhaust all the locations there are; but no two particulars have the same position at the same time. Where body starts, space stops, just as where fish starts, water stops.

Portions of separator space would be, in Descartes's terminology, portions of *matter*; they would be *bodies*. He distinguishes portions of matter as more or less "subtle," less or more "dense"; and the items I have been calling regions of separator space are what he would call portions of *absolutely* subtle matter — bodies that can be divided and brushed aside by fish, pebbles, feathers, and so on without these being deflected, slowed down, or otherwise impeded. In what follows, I shall sometimes call separator space "absolutely subtle matter"; the phrase without that adverb will refer to all matter that is well out toward that end of the scale.

All portions of matter are movable, including portions of absolutely subtle matter. Also, none can be colocated with anything else; so all are perfectly impenetrable, and thus are solid. What marks off absolutely subtle matter from the rest is that it has no inertial resistance to being moved, so that no force is needed for any portion of it to be pushed aside by a portion of less subtle matter. Thus, you could not feel some absolutely subtle matter by swishing your hand through it, as you can feel pond water. You feel the water because it resists as your hand dislodges it, which absolutely subtle matter would not. Still, if we could arrange for your hand to be a piston moving into a cylinder containing absolutely subtle matter, with your hand fitting so perfectly that the matter could not escape between your hand and the piston wall, and if neither the piston wall nor your hand had fissures through which the absolutely subtle matter could leak away, then that matter — that portion of separator space — would be tangible to you, obdurately stopping your hand's motion into the piston and feeling, presumably, like steel.

Does Descartes allow that there is, or even that there might be, absolutely subtle matter? Sometimes he seems to stop short of that, apparently suggesting that any portion of subtle matter would, if studied minutely enough, be found to have properties of dense matter. He speaks of our careless tendency to think we have found empty space when confronted by regions in which "we do not perceive anything by sight, touch or any other sense,"[21] and he criticizes the supposition "that a space we call empty contains not just nothing perceivable by the senses but nothing whatsoever."[22] If Descartes is here referring strictly to the unaided senses, excluding what might be learned through artifice, he may be assuming that each apparently empty region would show up as granulated, striated, or the like, through powerful enough microscopes, or would impede the movement of other bodies by an amount that could be detected by sensitive enough measuring instruments.

He does not say that outright, however, and sometimes he seems to deny it. He comments on what we are apt to say "if we understand there to be nothing in a given place but extension in length, breadth and depth," apparently allowing that what "we understand" may be correct.[23] He explicitly declares to be "intelligible" the idea of "bodies which in no way hinder or assist the motion of other bodies."[24] He makes assertions about what happens when "a body moves through a space containing only matter which neither speeds it up nor slows it down."[25] He writes that "what is commonly called empty space is . . . a real body deprived of all its accidents," which he explains as meaning that the body is deprived of every property except determinates of extension.[26] In passages like those, Descartes seems to countenance extended items that will not affect sense organs or scientific instruments — ones whose existence as *things* depends purely on their geometrical properties together with abstract metaphysical argument against the notion of extended nothing.


## Smallness of Parts

It seems, therefore, that Descartes does not rule out there being portions of absolutely subtle matter, "bodies" lacking density, inertia, resistance, and any other properties through which they could be detected other than their merely geometrical ones of size, shape, and location. In the remaining four sections of this paper I shall consider whether his metaphysic permits this tolerance. Is Descartes entitled, on his own principles, to think that there could be absolutely subtle matter?

He cannot accept that absolutely subtle matter differs in a *basic* way from matter that is somewhat dense. If he allowed two fundamentally different kinds of matter, his physics would lose its unity and its conceptual parsimony — the features that he most prized in it. However, Descartes openly holds that some bodies are subtler than others, ranging all portions of matter on a long subtler/denser continuum; and for him this difference is not basic but derivative, like that between warmer and colder. Let us ask how Descartes explains this derived continuum, looking for an answer that could carry over to the absolutely "subtle" end of the scale. If we find one, then Descartes is free to believe in separator space.

One determinant of subtleness, Descartes holds, is smallness of parts. He contrasts "some very subtle and very fluid matter" with "the less fluid or coarser parts of the air," and this opposition between "subtle" and "coarse" indicates that subtleness depends on size of parts.[27] In later work, having introduced a theory about spherical particles, which are his "second element," Descartes proceeds to introduce his "first element," which he characterizes in the Latin version of the work as "other more subtle matter" and in the French as "other more tiny particles."[28] The link between subtleness and smallness of parts comes to the surface later:

> We have . . . two very different kinds of matter which can be said to be the first two elements of this visible universe. The first element is made up of matter which is so violently agitated that when it meets other bodies it is divided into particles of indefinite smallness. . . . The second is composed of matter divided into spherical particles which are still very minute when compared with those that we can see with our eyes, but which have a definite fixed quantity and can be divided into other much smaller particles.[29]

That subtle matter is finely divided is made clear elsewhere, too.

To make sense of the idea that bodies might differ in how small their parts are, Descartes must tread delicately. For him all matter is indefinitely divisible, not merely geometrically but physically: any portion of matter, he holds, can be split into subportions.[30] Every portion is made up of indefinitely small "parts" in this sense; so part size cannot differentiate subtle matter from dense. To get further with this approach, Descartes needs a different concept of "part" — let us say *discriminated part* — in terms of which bodies can differ in the sizes of their (discriminated) parts. It is the same concept that is needed when Descartes writes: "All the bodies in the universe are composed of one and the same matter, which is divisible into indefinitely many parts, and is actually divided into a large number of parts which move in different directions."[31] So a portion of matter may be divisible into parts into which it is not actually divided (*reipsa divisam*). What can Descartes mean by that?

For many metaphysicians, a discriminated part would be a physical part surrounded by (i) some empty container space or (ii) separator space. Descartes rejects (i) altogether. If he invoked (ii) to get differences of part size, he could not then use the latter as a basis for differences of subtleness, for that would make the whole procedure circular. Setting those two aside, then, what concept of discriminated part, or of actual division, *is* Descartes entitled to have en route to an account of subtleness?

Well, he clearly implies that if two portions of matter differ in the sizes of their discriminated parts, that must result from how the internal movements of one differ from those of the other:

> The matter existing in the entire universe is . . . one and the same, and it is always recognized as matter simply in virtue of its being extended. All the properties which we clearly perceive in it are reducible to the sole fact that it is divisible [*partibilis*] and that its parts can be moved, and its resulting capacity to be affected in all the ways which we perceive as being derivable from the movement of the parts. . . . Any variation in matter or diversity in its many forms depends on motion.[32]

That incidentally kills one plausible idea about how Descartes might explain discriminated parts, namely, with help from qualitative differences between portions of matter. Thus: if a corporeal sphere has core that is all F surrounded by a shell none of which is F, then that core is a discriminated part of that sphere. But the quoted passage rules that out as a basic explanation by implying that F/not-F differences in matter are never basic and must always supervene on differences in movements.

The quoted passage and others like it entail that the concept of discriminated part must be analyzed in terms of propositions about how portions of matter move. Although that conclusion does not emerge clearly in Descartes's writings, I think he saw and accepted it. I base this on his frequent conjoining of two ideas: that subtle matter is finely divided and that its parts move rapidly relative to one another. I have cited one example ("smaller and faster moving"), and we shall encounter others shortly. All I want at present is the sheer fact of relative motion of the parts; speed will come into play further down the line.

One might well object: "How can relative motions of parts help? Anything Descartes might say about how the (discriminated) parts of subtle matter move requires him already to have a concept of such parts; and that was our question. Your supposed 'clue' to solving our problem presupposes that it has already been solved." Well, I think that when Descartes talks about relative motions he is partly trying, albeit inexplicitly, to explain what discriminated parts are. I shall give this explanation more openly than he does, using a mild technicality. A portion of matter is *internally static*, I shall say, if there is no relative motion within it, all its subportions being in motion (or at rest) together in a block. The view that I think Descartes ought to take, and unclearly does take, is that a physical (= geometrical) part P of a body is a discriminated part of it just in case:

(a)  P is internally static, and
(b)  P is not a physical part of any larger internally static portion of matter.

On this account, the discriminated parts of any portion of matter are its largest internally static physical (= geometrical) parts. We can also now explain what it is for a portion of matter to be "actually divided": a particle is divided if some physical parts of it are moving relative to others; if all its physical parts are moving together but could begin to move relative to one another, the particle is undivided but divisible.[33]

(I am setting aside a more acute difficulty confronting Descartes. He maintains that all qualitative variety in the extended realm supervenes on differences in how portions of extended substance move; but that cannot be right if this is: *any content-ful notion of differences in how items move presupposes qualitative differences between them.* That was Leibniz's view, and I think that his arguments were good and their conclusion correct.[34] This is the deepest level at which Descartes's parsimonious physics fails. It is a fascinating topic of philosophical inquiry, but I have enough on my plate without it.)

## Subtleness and Size

Once he has in hand the account of discriminated parts that I have presented, Descartes might say that the subtleness of any portion of matter depends solely on how small its discriminated parts are, that is, on the size of its largest internally static physical parts. Then the question "is there any limit to how subtle matter can be?" is equivalent to "is there any limit to how small can be the largest internally static physical parts of a portion of matter?" Descartes's answer is negative: there is no limit to this. We have already seen him saying that matter of the first element "is divided into particles of indefinite smallness." On that view of subtleness, he has no reason to limit how subtle matter can be; so he has no grounds for denying that there is separator space, that is, matter that offers no resistance to being pushed around by other matter.

*Is* that Descartes's view about what subtleness consists in? Some texts favor yes, others no, but I can find no decisive evidence for either answer. Except for one thing that Descartes writes: "I conceive of subtle matter as a continuous liquid occupying all the spaces not taken up by other bodies, and not as something composed of disconnected parts such as the particles that make up dust."[35] That ought to mean that *all* subtle matter is actually divided into parts that are indefinitely small, from which it follows that part size cannot be what differentiates fairly from absolutely subtle matter. But I am not convinced that that is considered doctrine rather than an occasional opinion, so I am unwilling to place much weight on it.

The more interesting question, anyway, concerns what Descartes ought to say about this. Can he consistently explain, through differences in how finely portions of matter are "actually divided," their offering different amounts of resistance to being diverted by other bodies?

In *The World* he says that matter of the third element has parts that "are so large or so closely joined together that they always have the force to resist the motions of the other bodies."[36] The idea is that in a collision between one of those particles and a particle of first-element matter, the former wins. (When in the same paragraph Descartes writes that particles of the *first* element "move so extremely rapidly and are so minute that there are no other bodies capable of stopping them," he means only that these tiny, agile particles are unstoppable because they cannot be trapped: there are always cracks and crevices through which they can seep. He still holds that they could easily be stopped dead by stationary third-element matter that was crevice-free, if there were any such.)

So Descartes seems to hold that in a collision between a third- and a first-element particle, the former would be entirely unimpeded, not slowed down or redirected. That would clear the way to his admitting that there could be the absolutely subtle matter that I call separator space.

What makes the third-element particles impervious to interference from first-element ones is that the former are "so large or so closely joined together." It is hard to see what Descartes is up to here. One would have thought that two particles that are *jointes ensemble* must be parts of a single particle, in which case the "joined together" notion can be dropped from the story, leaving us only with size.

That is what the translators of the *Principles* say is the message of *Principles* 2:49f, two sections that "illustrate Descartes's view that . . . resistance to motion depends entirely on relative size. Quantity of motion plays no role whatever except that it must be conserved."[37] I cannot see that for myself in 2:49f, but apparently Descartes could. He later summed up and justified those sections to Clerselier thus:

> Here is the reason why I said that a motionless body could never be moved by an-
> other smaller body, no matter how fast this smaller body might be moving. It is a law
> of nature that if one body moves another, then the former must have more power to
> move the latter than the latter has to resist being moved by the former. But this sur-
> plus can depend only on the size of the body. . . . The reason is that if it is set in mo-
> tion by a body moving twice as fast as some other body, it must receive twice as much
> motion from it; but its resistance to this motion will also be twice as great.[38]

Now, one might try to get out of this a Cartesian explanation of subtleness, with all the work being done by size. A pebble is thrown into a stretch of subtle matter; it gives up speed to (i.e., is resisted by) any given particle of that matter in inverse proportion to how much bigger it is than the particle. The subtler the matter, the smaller its dis-criminated parts and so the smaller its effect on a large body that collides with it. At the limit — absolutely subtle matter, with "indefinitely" small parts — the effect on the colliding body is nil; the latter gives up none of its speed and does not change its direction, which is to say that the subtle matter has offered no resistance to its pas-sage, behaving instead like separator space. QED.

This adaptation of Descartes's rules of impact to yield an account of subtleness is a complete failure, for a reason that Descartes makes plain. The impact rules, he says, are offered subject to conditions that in fact are never realized. He introduces them thus:

> How much force to move or resist movement there is in each body . . . could easily
> be calculated if there were only two bodies colliding, and if they were perfectly hard
> and were separated from all others in such a way that their movements would be
> neither impeded nor aided by other surrounding bodies; for then they would observe
> the following rules.[39]

After stating the rules of impact, he acknowledges that they are hard to apply to ac-tual cases:

> Since no bodies in the universe can be so isolated from all others, and no bodies in
> our vicinity are normally perfectly hard, the calculation for determining how much
> the motion of a given body is altered by collision with another body is much more
> difficult than those given above. 〈So in order to judge whether the above rules are
> observed here or not, it is not sufficient to know how two bodies can act against one
> another on impact.〉 We have to take into account all the other bodies which are
> touching them on every side, and these have very different effects depending on
> whether they are hard or fluid.[40]

On that pivot he modulates into an account of how hard bodies differ from fluid ones. My problem arises just from the presence of other bodies, no matter what they are like; so I shall leave hard/fluid out of account and attend to the bare fact that Descartes's rules are stated subject to the condition that the colliding pair is in quarantine.

The difficulty this makes for the proposed account of subtleness is straightforward. The smaller a single particle is, the less it interferes with a body that hits it; but the smaller the particles in a portion of matter, the more of them there are; and the more there are, the greater (one would think) is their combined effect on the body with which they collide. So smallness and numerousness cancel out, so to speak, leaving the proposed line of thought quite empty. This criticism, I should add, applies to the use of *Principles* 2:49f to explain any degree of subtleness, not merely its use in explaining the absolute subtleness that defines separator space.

## The Integration Problem

This criticism needs to be sharpened, clarified, and deepened; but when I try to meet that need I slam into the brick wall of the *integration problem*, as I call it — the difficulty of bringing into a single coherent picture two utterly different Cartesian theories about events in the material world. They may well be consistent with each other, but I can find no clear, detailed, and unitary story incorporating both. I expect to return to the integration problem in later writings and shall merely sketch it here.

(a) *Movement loop theory*. Descartes is firm in rejecting container space, compression of bodies, and colocation of bodies with bodies. This triple-C denial entails that no portion of matter can travel unless other matter travels at the same time. An arrow's flight must be associated with two sets of other movements. (i) Its place must be taken by some matter, which must in turn be replaced by other matter, and so on. (ii) The arrow must displace some matter, which must move away and thus displace other matter, and so on. Set (i) is required by the denial of container space and of compression, set (ii) by those and the denial of the colocation of bodies with bodies.[41] Descartes meets these needs by supposing that the two sets of movements come together not only at the arrow but also somewhere else, creating a finite loop of moving matter: the arrow is replaced by air, which is replaced by air, which is replaced by . . . air, which replaces the arrow. The dependencies among movements within the loop are absolute, logical, conceptual, so they do not involve any lapse of time; a body in a loop is required to move as it does at time *T* by the movement *at T* of another body on the opposite side of the loop. (In his famous wine cask example, Descartes invokes loop theory to explain some empirical data in a manner that might be thought to generate predictions:

> When the wine in a cask does not flow from the bottom opening because the top is closed . . . the wine cannot leave the cask because outside everything is as full as can be, and the part of the air whose place the wine would occupy if it were to flow out can find no other place to occupy in all the rest of the universe unless we make an opening in the top of the cask through which the air can rise by a circular path into its place.[42]

Never mind whether this *does* promise to have predictive power; the argument as a whole is not worth discussing. Had he reflected on his usual account of vacuum pumps and barometers, Descartes would have seen that the wine cask argument was not available to him. In my next section I shall sketch his attempt to explain certain empirical data by applying loop theory to the propagation of light. That attempt is defective, though in different ways.)

(b) *Collision theory*. Descartes presents some "rules" that govern collisions between pairs of bodies.[43] This theory has predictive power: from the fact that two bodies are related *thus* and moving *so* a moment before they collide, Descartes's "rules" purport to let us infer where they will be, and how they will be moving, a few seconds later. In short, his physics of collisions aims to be time spanning and fertile with predictions, as one would expect of any branch of natural science, whereas the theory of movement loops is not time spanning and yields no predictions; it is essentially confined to single moments, telling us that if a particle is moving at T then such and such other things must be happening at T.

That (a) Descartes's movement loop theory is *toto coelo* different from (b) his collision theory can be brought out in other ways, too. For example, (b) can be used to explain why a body starts moving at T, whereas (a) cannot; and (b) embodies a direction from cause to effect, whereas in (a) there is only the symmetrical dependence of every part of the loop on every other.

The problem is to integrate these two parts of Descartes's account of the material world, bringing them together in a single coherent story about what happens when two moving bodies collide. That account would have to say exactly what happens *in* such a collision, showing how this can bring it about that *each* body is involved in a synchronous movement loop before the collision and in a *different* loop after it. I have tried long and hard to do this, and I have failed.

(Descartes handles physical transactions sometimes in terms of fluids and sometimes in terms of discrete relatively hard bodies. That is not the split that raises the integration problem, as I now show. First, if we conjoined our loop theory about fluids with a theory of collisions between portions of fluid, the integration problem would still arise. Conversely, if we conjoined our theory about colliding hard bodies with a hard-body form of loop theory — for example, likening a loop to the iron rim of a turning wheel — again the integration problem would stand untouched. Second, Descartes explains that fluids are aggregates of extremely small discrete bodies; and he could instead say, conversely, that a discrete body is a peculiarly coherent portion of fluid. Each explanation is at least plausible, whereas it would be a lunatic project to try to get collision theory out of movement loop theory or vice versa.)

In trying to drive deeper into my exploration of whether Descartes's collision theory permits separator space, I keep encountering considerations that involve movement loop theory. To get further, I need to solve the integration problem, learning how to keep these two balls in the air at once or showing that it cannot be done; I have failed to do either. Crucial as it is for the evaluation of Descartes's work, the integration problem seems to have been ignored in the secondary literature; it may be useful at least to have brought it to light as a problem.

## Subtleness and Speed

So much for trying to explain subtleness purely through the smallness of discriminated parts. Descartes, however, often speaks not only of the smallness of those particles but also of their speed relative to one another, treating smallness and rapidity as natural companions. "The first element surpasses all other bodies in speed," he says, and "The form I have attributed to the first element consists in its parts' moving so extremely rapidly and being so minute that there are no other bodies capable of stopping them."[44]

Speed might relate to subtleness in any of three ways. (i) It might be irrelevant to it. (ii) It might help to explain matter's subtleness by helping to explain the fineness of its division. In at least one place, Descartes takes that line: "The first element is made up of matter which is so violently agitated that when it meets other bodies it is divided into particles of indefinite smallness."[45] If either (i) or (ii) is right, then speed has no independent place in the explanation of subtleness, and this section would not be needed. (iii) However, the speed of the particles of subtle matter might somehow contribute directly to its subtleness. My present topic is the question of whether Descartes does or should hold that it does so.

In my discussion of whether subtleness could come from smallness, I was assuming that if it did, it would be on the principle *the smaller the subtler*; there seemed to be no other possible link between the two. When we now consider whether subtleness could come from speed, we cannot assume that this would have to involve the principle *the faster the subtler*. That would imply that absolutely subtle matter — separator space — must have particles moving infinitely quickly; and Descartes could not accept that. He clearly holds that no particle can move so fast. "No motion takes place in a single instant of time." "In order to conceive . . . any possible motion, it is necessary to consider at least two of its instants . . . and the relation between them." "No movement can happen in an instant."[46] There is also other evidence, less direct but more dramatic. The propagation of light is instantaneous, Descartes thought, but he likened that not to a projectile that travels infinitely fast but rather to the supposedly instantaneous production of an effect at one end of a stick by pushing on the other end.[47] In a 1634 letter to Beeckman, he describes empirical evidence that he thinks would show that light travels — that is, the effect travels — instantaneously.[48] The "evidence" depends on a stipulation about how fast light might move if it did take time (this being understood as resembling a thrown pebble rather than a thrusting stick). Descartes and Beeckman agree that if light takes time to travel it cannot go faster than about eighteen miles per second. This is not a man who thinks there is no limit to how fast matter can move!

Still, speed might help to explain subtleness in some way other than through "the faster the subtler" or its converse. Let us press on.

Some of what Descartes says about subtleness occurs when "hard" bodies, which cohere or "stick together," are contrasted with "fluid" ones, which easily fall apart. His attempt to explain cohesion seems to incorporate an attempt to explain why bodies differ in how much they resist being shouldered aside by other bodies. Sometimes, indeed, he explicitly gives cohesion a role in the difference between subtle and dense: "The only difference between this subtle matter and terrestrial bodies is that it is made up of much smaller particles which do not stick together and are always in very rapid motion."[49] Descartes seems to be assuming, naturally enough, that these two features of portion P of matter go together:

(i) The parts of P do not stick together; they are easily separated from one another.

(ii) P offers little or no resistance to being pushed aside by other matter.

Although it is plausible to think that (i) explains (ii), I am not satisfied that Descartes is entitled to hold that it does; but the reasons for that involve the integration problem, so I shall not pursue them here. Rather, I shall proceed on the assumption that Descartes does think that fluidity = noncohesiveness is intelligibly connected with fluidity = subtleness.[50] Let us then look at his treatment of the latter.

In common with every physicist who denies that there are attractive forces, Descartes cannot solve the cohesion problem, the problem of why the material world is other than perfectly fluid throughout, or of how things "stick together." In *Principles* 2:55 he strongly implies that cohesion is explained by the fact that the parts of the co-hering body are at rest with respect to one another: bodies cannot be held together by "any mode distinct from their being at rest. For what mode could be more contrary to the motion that separates them than their being at rest?" I agree with the commentators who wrote: "This is not, of course, an explanation of solidity but a *description* of the fact that the parts of a solid do not move relative to one another."[51] Descartes, however, seems to credit it with explanatory power.

Anyway, one section earlier he clearly offers to explain subtleness:

> The parts of fluid bodies easily move out of their places, and consequently do not resist the movement of our hands into those places; whereas the parts of solid bodies adhere to one another in such a way that, without sufficient force to overcome their cohesion, they cannot be separated. . . . [The reason for this difference is that] a body already in motion does not prevent another body's occupying the place which it is spontaneously leaving, whereas a body at rest cannot be expelled from its place except by some force ⟨coming from outside⟩.[52]

This is a terrible explanation! When I try to move my hand eastward, I am shoving it toward a multitude of little places: a tiny proportion of these, it is true, are just then independently being vacated by particles of subtle or fluid matter moving further eastward; but the great majority of the particles are moving into other little places that are still in the path of my hand, some indeed moving westward, directly against it. There is also a difficulty about speed: even particles that are independently heading east may be moving more slowly than my hand.

Descartes acknowledges the speed (but not the direction) trouble in a letter to Mersenne:

> When I conceive of a body moving in a medium which does not resist it at all, I am supposing that all the parts of the surrounding liquid body are disposed to move at

the same speed as the original body, both in giving place to it and in entering the place that it is leaving. Thus, every liquid is such as to offer no resistance to *some* movements; but to imagine some matter which did not resist *any* of the different movements of some body, you would have to pretend that God or an angel was moving its parts at various speeds to correspond with the speed of the movements of the body they surround.[53]

This implies that there is no absolutely subtle (= absolutely nonresistant) matter because such matter would require a miraculously ad hoc internal dynamics. The miracle that Descartes envisages has to be a double one: each particle must be caused to move at each moment and at the right speed *and in the right direction* for it not to impede the hard body that is moving through it.

Those problems for Descartes's explanation of subtleness, though probably fatal, are minor compared with this next one. Think about the adverb in this excerpt from the *Principles* 2:54 passage that I have quoted: "A body already in motion does not prevent another body occupying the place which it is spontaneously leaving." Descartes does not mean to attribute a will to the body that is "spontaneously leaving." He means only that when I put my finger into water it is not impeded by particles of water that are moving away from it *anyway*, that is, moving under some influence other than the push from my finger. That may seem safe enough, but I doubt that Descartes can say it because I doubt that he is entitled to distinguish matter that my finger pushes aside from matter that gives way to my finger for other reasons. That distinction implies that one body may *take x's place* while another *forces x out*; my finger has an easy time as place taker because something else is doing the forcing out. I can find in Descartes's physics and metaphysics no sound basis for separating these two roles. It is easy to see that getting to the bottom of this issue would require — yet again — solving the integration problem. The place-taker role belongs to loop theory, the forcer-out role to the physics of impact; and we do not know where or how those twain can meet.

In summary, Descartes has no halfway coherent explanation of subtleness in terms of speed. His quarter-coherent explanation supports the view that he is not entitled to believe that any matter is absolutely subtle, that is, to believe that there is separator space. It is not clear that he can use the concept of speed even to explain why some matter is subtler than some other matter.[54]

*Notes*

1. *Principles* 2:16; CSM I, 229f.
2. *Principles* 2:5; CSM I, 225.
3. Letter in 1641 to Hyperaspistes; CSMK 194.
4. F. C. Copleston, *A History of Philosophy*, vol. 1 (London: Burns Oates & Washbourne, 1950), p. 73.
5. For examples, see Edward Grant, *Much Ado About Nothing: Theories of Space and Vacuum in the Middle Ages to the Scientific Revolution* (Cambridge: Cambridge University Press, 1981), chap. 2.
6. Daniel Garber, *Descartes' Metaphysical Physics* (Chicago: University of Chicago Press, 1992), p. 127. The present work grew out of a conference paper that I expressed as a se-

ries of criticisms of Garber's treatment of these matters. His responses to those criticisms have helped me to improve my own treatment, and I owe him further thanks for comments on a draft of the present chapter.

7. Or replace "a substance" throughout by "substance." The difference between the mass and count uses of "substance," though often important, does not affect any issues discussed here.

8. Descartes uses it in sect. 2 of "Comments on a Certain Broadsheet"; CSM I, 294f.

9. Letter to the Marquess of Newcastle (1645); CSMK 275.

10. I take this history from Grant, *Much Ado About Nothing*, pp. 19f, 22.

11. Letter to More (1649); CSMK 372. I learned about this argument from Garber's book. Like Garber, I assume throughout that Descartes's "penetration" is exactly what I call "colocation."

12. See also Letter to [Unknown] (1645); CSMK 252.

13. Garber, *Descartes' Metaphysical Physics*, p. 147.

14. Letter of 1639 to Mersenne; CSMK 138.

15. *Principles* 2:10; CSM I, 227.

16. For details see Jonathan Bennett, *A Study of Spinoza's Ethics* (Indianapolis: Hackett, 1984), chap. 4.

17. Edwin Curley, *Spinoza's Metaphysics: An Essay in Interpretation* (Cambridge, Mass.: Harvard University Press, 1969).

18. *Principles* 2:18; CSM I, 231.

19. *Essay* II.xiii.10.

20. "Whether any one will take space to be only a relation resulting from the existence of other beings at a distance, or whether . . . [etc.], I leave every one to consider." *Essay* II.xiii.26.

21. *Rules* 12; CSM I, 48; see also *The World* 4; CSM I, 87; and *Meditation* 6; CSM II, 56.

22. *Principles* 2:17; CSM I, 230.

23. *Principles* 2:5; CSM I, 225.

24. *Principles* 4:21; CSM I, 268f.

25. Letter to More; AT II, 442. I learned of this passage from Garber. Could Descartes mean that (B) the moving body is not modified by (M) the matter it moves through because M gets out of B's way and thus does not collide with it? (If so, Descartes is not implying that M is so subtle that it does not affect B in a collision.) We shall see later that Descartes does try this "evasion" ploy, but that is a strained and insensitive reading of the present passage, and I mention it only because it has been suggested to me.

26. Letter in 1649 to More; CSMK 381.

27. *Optics* 1; CSM I, 154.

28. *Principles* 3:49; CSM I, 258.

29. *Principles* 3:52; CSM I, 258.

30. In *Principles* 2:34, Descartes supports this with an argument that Leibniz rightly called "beautiful."

31. *Principles* 3:46; CSM I, 256.

32. *Principles* 2:23; CSM I, 232. CSM puts "are reducible to its divisibility and consequent mobility in respect of its parts." The word "consequent," though Cartesian in its effect, has no basis in the Latin.

33. That is pretty much how Spinoza understood Descartes. "Matter that moves in various ways has at least as many parts into which it is actually divided as the different degrees of speed that are observed in it at the same time." Spinoza, *Descartes's Principles of Philosophy* 2, axiom 16; Curley 266. I suppose he says, "*at least* as many" because there may be differences that are not observed.

34. Leibniz, "On Nature Itself" 13; AG 163f.

35. Letter (1638) to Morin; CSMK 123.

36. *The World* 5; CSM I, 89.

37. V. R. Miller and R. P. Miller, eds., *René Descartes: Principles of Philosophy* (Dordrecht: Reidel, 1983), p. 66, n. 52.

38. Letter to Clerselier (1645); CSMK 246. Garber has suggested to me that when writing to Clerselier in 1645, when his ideas about impact were in a state of flux, Descartes was apt to have misrepresented his own thoughts of a few years earlier. See chapter 8 of Garber's book.

39. *Principles* 2:45; CSM I, 45. I have partly used the Millers' translation.

40. *Principles* 2:53; CSM I, 245. I follow CSM in using angle brackets to enclose material taken from the French version of the work.

41. Descartes makes it clear that he is pushed into movement loops by his rejection of compression and container space (*Principles* 3:51; not in CSM); but the denial of colocation of bodies with bodies, which he does not mention in this connection, is also required. For other statements of the movement loop theory, see *The World* 4; CSM I, 86; and *Principles* 2:33; CSM I, 237–239.

42. *The World* 4; CSM I, 87.

43. *Principles* 2:46–52, not in CSM.

44. *The World* 5; CSM I, 89.

45. *Principles* 2:52; CSM I, 258.

46. *Principles* 2:39; CSM I, 242; *The World* 6; CSM I, 96f; Letter to Morin (1638); AT II, 215; not in CSMK. I gathered these three references from Garber, *Descartes' Metaphysical Physics*, p. 174.

47. I was helped to understand this by correspondence with Richard Field. We now know that Descartes was wrong in his general view about this because no signal can be transmitted faster than the speed of light. As for his "stick" example, he wrongly envisaged the stick as perfectly rigid, when in fact nothing can be so. The push on the knob of the stick makes the ferrule move because shock waves pass down the stick, taking time to do so.

48. Letter to Beeckman; CSMK 46.

49. Letter to Vorstius (1643); CSMK 224.

50. The assumption receives the support from my next displayed quotation and from CSM I, 154; CSMK 21f, 52, 63, 121.

51. Miller and Miller, *René Descartes: Principles of Philosophy*, p. 70, n. 65.

52. *Principles* 2:54; partly in CSM I, 71.

53. Letter to Mersenne (1639), defectively rendered in CSMK 132. The italics are mine.

54. This chapter has benefited greatly from comments on drafts of it by Jan Cover, Daniel Garber, John Hawthorne, and Eric Palmer.

## 2

ERIC PALMER

# Descartes on Nothing in Particular

## Introduction: The Wine Cask and Vacuum in the Early *Principles*

How coherent, and how useful, is Descartes's conception of vacuum in the *Principles?* I will begin by backtracking: in the *World*, written most of a decade earlier, Descartes has much to say about macroscopic physical vacuum. He models the created universe as a finite container in which matter is situated, and his arguments are meant to indicate that the container is full to its boundaries in a continuously connected medium, so that no vacuum is present, and light can travel as pressure in the medium (AT XI, 32, 86).[1] Though he suggests his argument is not conclusive, Descartes's well-known treatment of the wine cask is a noteworthy prop: wine will not flow from an unstopped hole in a full cask unless a vent is provided to allow air to take its place since the universe is "as full as can be, and the part of the air whose place the wine would occupy if it were to flow out can find no other place to occupy in all the rest of the universe" (AT XI, 20).

As he does in the *World*, Descartes maintains in the second part of the *Principles* that "in every case of motion, there is a complete circle of bodies moving together," and he suggests that bodies that our senses cannot detect fill in the spaces as others separate. Descartes explains as much in his discussions of the empty jug (which is not empty but full of air) and of rarefaction, which is taken to be the process of a body enlarging by incorporating other matter, much as a dry sponge grows as it incorporates liquid (2:33, 17, 6). He argues that vacuum is unnecessary for motion in a non-atomistic universe and, as before, is a barrier to the passage of light (2:33, 3:53ff).

Physics in the two works is clearly similar, and so one would expect that Descartes would provide empirical arguments for the nonexistence of vacuum in the *Principles*, like those in the *World*. But such argument is not forthcoming in the *Principles*, and most notably, the wine cask is not evident. Why?

Part of the explanation for this change lies in a reconception of space that Descartes develops after the *World*. Space is no longer an absolutely full container, the bounds of which play their role in keeping wine within a cask: the argument in the *Principles* shifts to a fundamental reconception of matter as spatial, trumpeted in the claim "There is no real difference between space and corporeal substance" (2:11).

> If a stone is removed from the space or place where it is, we think that its extension has also been removed from that place, since we regard the extension as something particular and inseparable from the stone. But at the same time we think that the extension of the place where the stone used to be remains, and is the same as before, although the place is now occupied by wood or water or air or some other body, or is even supposed to be empty. (2:12)

Though we may remove a stone, nonetheless, in so doing we do not remove the extension of the stone from its place. But Descartes also holds that there is no evidence of an absolute place distinguishable from bodies within which those bodies lie: bodies simply take the places of others also in motion within the universe (2:13). So there is no need to posit space as an entity distinct from bodies: extension is a property of bodies, "which is thought of as being the same, whether it is the extension of a stone or of wood, or of water or of air or of any other body — or even of a vacuum, if there is such a thing — provided only that it has the same size and shape . . . " (2:12).[2]

Descartes's identification of extension with bodies explains the absence of the wine cask argument from his discussion in the *Principles*: no such argument is available because the universe is not a container, finite or infinite, that holds the wine in its place. What else follows from this metaphysics? Descartes comes quickly to one of the most puzzling sections of the *Principles*, his denial in 2:16–18 of vacuum. One part of that discussion is the following, which I think may take the palm for the very least appreciated argument in the *Principles*:

> 2:18. *How to correct our preconceived opinion regarding an absolute vacuum.* Almost all of us fell into this error in our early childhood. Seeing no necessary connection between a vessel and the body contained in it, we reckoned there was nothing to stop God, at least, removing the body which filled the vessel, and preventing any other body from taking its place. But to correct this error we should consider that, although there is no connection between a vessel and this or that particular body contained in it, there is a very strong and wholly necessary connection between the concave shape of the vessel and the extension, taken in its general sense, which must be contained in the concave shape. Indeed, it is no less contradictory for us to conceive of a mountain without a valley than it is for us to think of the concavity apart from the extension contained within it, or the extension apart from the substance which is extended; for, as I have often said, nothingness cannot possess any extension.

In the final sentence, Descartes suggests that there is a metaphysical dependence of space, as the shape or volume of the vessel, upon extension; and of extension upon something called "extended substance." Since it is abundantly clear that Descartes has written this passage as an argument against vacuum, it appears that the "extended substance" of concern would be what is not vacuum, that is, bodies — and this conception, of course, coincides with his previous identification of body with extension. So Descartes has argued that when we examine the matter carefully, we cannot clearly conceive of space without bodies, as a consequence of the sort of "wholly necessary connection" that also makes it clear to us that "nothingness cannot possess any extension." The idea of vacuum, then, would appear to be the product of inconsistent thought; and so, no vacuum could exist in nature.

It is evident that Descartes's argument is problematic, for it has supported diverging interpretations, most of which render the argument rather flat nonetheless. Are we to take seriously the suggestion that ideas of empty space are a "prejudice" and nothing more; or has Descartes merely invoked his definition of matter as extended substance (*Principles* 2:4) to argue the point?[3] Perhaps Descartes has an argument in the relation of "necessary connection" among concavity, extension, and substance;[4] an argument that we might give serious attention if we were to embrace Descartes's very parsimonious theory of corporeal substance, which attempts to account for all the properties of body strictly in terms of three-dimensional geometry and time (2:4). That conception is laden with problems for independent reasons, however.[5] It also seems that Descartes ought to rule out other possibilities: for we, and apparently some of his contemporaries, do not find a contradiction, or even a difficulty, in carefully conceiving of vacuum or void as a space without material bodies within it.[6] John Buridan did well enough long before Descartes when he wrote of vacuum as "a space distinct from the magnitudes of natural bodies, which does not have to give way in order to receive natural bodies . . . a volume [*dimensio corpora*] equal in length, width, and depth to the natural body that would fill it up if one placed it in this void."[7] Furthermore, beyond mere conceivability, the metaphysical point, at least in its ordinary seventeenth-century formulation, appears to have also been settled through physics: we know that a vacuum is possible since nothing stopped Torricelli from removing some of the mercury from a glass tube without replacing it with air.[8] Unfortunately for Descartes, and so for us, it appears that Torricelli did so just one month before the *Principles* were printed; and worse, Pascal's most important experiment and the growing body of experimental work on the vacuum were brought to Descartes's attention just after the later French edition of the *Principles* went to press.[9] Could 2:18 be an argument seriously intended to serve against such conceptions of vacuum, even though it preceded Descartes's survey of those empirical arguments taken to be in their support?[10]

Descartes has much more to say about vacuum, and I will argue here that his conception in the *Principles* is more coherent and more sophisticated than most critics have allowed. Though discussions of Descartes's treatment of vacuum in the *World* and in work after the *Principles*, such as the letters to More, are well covered,[11] critics make less frequent note of Descartes's earlier letters, and very few mention the discussion of vacuum contained in later portions of the *Principles*. In the latter source, Descartes makes little ado about considering the physical ramifications of "empty space," including a discussion of what the appearance of a star would be were an empty space to lie at the center of a celestial vortex; so indeed, some ideas about empty space don't strike Descartes as being in the least contradictory.[12] Descartes also addresses the experimental point in his discussions with Pascal late in 1647, and instead of suggesting conceptual incoherence on his junior colleague's part (which would seem to be an appropriate reply to a vacuist who expresses himself as Descartes suggests in 2:18), Descartes sets up his own experiments and may have suggested to Pascal "an experiment to see whether the mercury rises as high on the top of a mountain as at the foot."[13]

I would like to suggest that Descartes's arguments about vacuum in the *Principles* and other early writings have lately been misunderstood, and I hope to improve the general estimation of their coherence. They are difficult to read and to understand because the discussion of 2:4–33 and further work in *Principles* 3 and 4 contain many distinct arguments presented as responses to at least three distinguishable threads of discussion concerning void that were current at the time of writing. Though it has become difficult for us, at a historical distance, to distinguish the different lines of argument all put under the title "vacuum" by Descartes, to an audience familiar with the tradition of Albert of Saxony and with Galileo's work the different targets of many arguments should not have been difficult to sort out. Some of the arguments, such as II:18, may seem especially obtuse only because we cannot attend to their targets after having lost the historical thread. Several critics do acknowledge that Descartes's approach may be further illuminated by an investigation of his predecessors, and they make particular note of Edward Grant's helpful work on medieval conceptions of vacuum; but concerted efforts to explain the rationale of Descartes's approach and to explain his own conception of empty space have not been launched by these authors.[14] My main contribution, I expect, will be to separate two metaphysical strands that have received little careful attention, even though the first has received brief notice: the scholastic topic of annihilation of space and Descartes's serious consideration of the possibility of physical vacuum in the third section of the *Principles*, previously discussed in correspondence with Mersenne concerning Galileo's treatment of vacuum. Exposing the former thread should reduce puzzlement surrounding 2:18. The distinction between the two threads should clarify Descartes's odd habit of declaring vacuum "contradictory" in some contexts, "impossible" in others, and of arguing at length elsewhere to establish that none is present in our universe. Finally, in examining the latter thread, I will challenge the suggestion that Descartes ruled out vacuum conceptually or by definition and that he did not countenance vacuum as a possibility within the metaphysics and physical science of the *Principles*. I will begin with an effort to clear up 2:18 by discussing it in historical context, and in its context of argument, from 2:5–19. A short foray into the historical background will be beneficial to start, however, since Descartes's argument is set against an Aristotelian tradition and because his strategy of argument also shows specific parallels with that of Aristotle, whose approach may be easier to sort out.

## Two Arguments in Aristotle

That Descartes's discussion fits into a tradition is immediately apparent from a review of Aristotle's fourth book of the *Physics*, which provides arguments with some similarities to Descartes's own. The treatment by Aristotle that, on the face of it, most closely parallels Descartes's discussion in *Principles* 2:18 runs as follows:

The reason for thinking that between the limits of the container there is some kind of extension is that the distinct object contained often moves while the container stays still (think of pouring water out of a vessel), which makes it look as though there is something over and above the body which is being displaced. But this is wrong. What actually happens is that some other body — it could be anything, as long as it can be displaced and can fit the container — comes in to replace the original body. If place were some kind of extension which was capable of independent and permanent existence, there would be an infinite number of places in the same thing, because when water (or air) is being displaced, bit by bit, every bit behaves in the same way. . . . Also, place will not in fact be a stable entity, and so one place will occupy another place, and there will be a plurality of coincident places.[15]

Aristotle argues in this passage that because space is full of bodies, one body is replaced by another as the former is poured from a vessel. Descartes and Aristotle agree on this point as plenist physicists who hold that the physical universe is entirely filled with bodies. Descartes presents similar discussions of the flow of unperceived bodies into spaces vacated by others in his explanation of rarefaction (*Principles* 2:6) and his treatment of jugs, water, and air (2:16, 17). Aristotle's final two sentences in the passage above contain arguments in service of his claim that place is "the limit of the containing body" (212a4) rather than a thing itself: Aristotle is arguing for the claim that the place of an object, which he takes to be identical with the volume that it fills (216b12), is metaphysically dependent on body and is not itself a "stable entity." Once again, this aspect of Aristotle's view coincides nicely with Descartes's physics in the *Principles* (cf. 2:10, 45). Points of divergence between the two authors can be found further on, however, in *Physics* IV:5, where Aristotle's concept of place is developed further, both as an explanation of gravitation through natural motion and as a resource for absolute points of reference in space to which natural motions may be referred (211a21). Of course, Descartes's competing explanation of gravity (4:20) and his relativistic conception of motion (2:28) conflict with those Aristotelian explanations quite directly.[16]

Descartes's argument in 2:18 concerns void, however, and neither volume nor Aristotelian place. What Descartes may be attempting to defend, in Aristotle's words, is "that the only kind of extension there is is the extension of bodies, and that this cannot be separated from bodies or exist without them in actuality." (*Physics* IV:6, 213a32; cf. *Principles* 2:11, 46). The argument in Aristotle that most nearly approaches Descartes's treatment, then, is not the superficially similar discussion of the pitcher but, instead, the following:

If you put a cube in water, an amount of water equal to the cube will be displaced. . . . But this is impossible in a void, since a void is not a body. What must happen instead is that an already existing extension within the void, of equal dimension to the cube, must have penetrated the cube — as if the water or air were completely to permeate the wooden cube rather than being displaced by it. . . . So what will be the difference between the body of the cube and the void and place which are equal to it? And if two things can behave like this, why cannot any number of things coincide? (216a27–b10)

Aristotle suggests that one might as well maintain that void is everywhere as that it is in a particular extended space where no body is since it has similar properties — or similarly lacks properties — in either case. Clearly this alone wouldn't quite suffice as an argument to the conclusion "that the only kind of extension there is is the extension of bodies," and in fact, Aristotle is not arguing for that conclusion in this passage. Instead, he is only attempting to explain "what void is in its own right" (216a26), and his unsurprising suggestion is that if we consider it as distinct from all of place, extension, and impenetrability, spatial void would not be distinguishable from (any other) nothing, or as he may be taken to suggest in the final sentence, two or more voids in just the same spot! This discussion, then, is intended to point out a possible conceptual incoherence, and it would seem that Aristotle's argument against the existence of a physical vacuum must lie elsewhere, in fact, primarily in the passages of *Physics* IV:8 that precede this discussion. We will see shortly that Descartes is engaged in a similar effort of conceptual clarification in *Principles* 2:18.

A survey of those prior arguments reveals that Aristotle is concerned with showing the impossibility of the actual existence of void by reason of its incompatibility with the evidence presented by bodies in motion. Aristotle explains that his theory of motion implies that vacuum could not possibly have a place (214b17) nor coherently allow for the possibility of motion (214 b28–215a23).[17] Consequently, Aristotle's physics is plenist: matter must be everywhere that Aristotelian physics holds true, and so, wherever we find such a physics to hold, vacuum could not possibly be resident as well. Since Aristotle's discussion at 216a27ff is explicitly couched in terms of plenist physics, we must consider that argument, which is only meant to clear up a conceptual confusion, to be one carried out under the plenist assumption and not an attempt to establish the inconceivability of void *simpliciter*. Aristotle directly follows his discussion of the cube with the claim that the implication of the vacuist assumption, that two things may coincide, is an "absurd and impossible consequence." Again, I'd like to suggest that Aristotle does not argue here for the inconceivability of vacuum; rather, he indicates the incompatibility, the "impossible consequence," of a vacuum existing in a physical world that includes the motions of objects that we perceive, a world that he has explained in terms of plenum and place, based on independent justification. A separate void in an entirely empty universe has not been shown to be inconceivable; rather, in the world we experience, "it contributes nothing for there to be some other such extension, equal to the volume [of a material cube], but different from it" (216b19).[18]

What would the conceptions of vacuum that Descartes finds untenable be? For Aristotle, the coherent but physically incompatible position is presented in the void space of the atomists. Aristotle suggests that the impossible consequences engendered by conceiving of motion in a void show that the best arguments for vacuum, concerning motion, fail (216a21). Like Aristotle, Descartes will involve himself in two distinct tasks, clearing conceptual confusion and arguing that vacuum is ruled out empirically. Descartes will explicitly consider atomism in 2:20ff; so in 2:18, it seems reasonable that his target could be the same opponent or another, but Descartes leaves little trace to indicate just who his opponents are.[19] From the few clues that are present, however, and because the 2:18 argument seems to be a strong response to one position readily available for discussion at the time, I suggest that Descartes is arguing in passages 2:16–18 against a scholastic line of thought that may be found in Albert of Saxony and is also represented in Descartes's time in the work of André d'Abillon. I will argue that Descartes attempts to clear up arguments such as Albert's in the passage in 2:18 by arguing that Albert's position is a conceptual confusion, much as Aristotle approaches a different confusion at 216a27. Section 2:20ff, by contrast, represents a distinct response directed against a coherent conception of vacuum found in Galilean atomists in particular. Finally, discussion in parts 3 and 4 of the *Principles* covers yet another area of discussion of vacuum, this time a vacuum that Descartes suggests is physically possible but then dismisses because of the weight of further empirical evidence. I will take up each of these claims in the three sections that follow.

## Descartes's Arguments

### I: *Against Vacuum without Measure*

Though far from contemporary with Descartes, Albert of Saxony (ca. 1316–1390) stands as a particularly appropriate figure to consider because his texts, in their many printed editions, were the principal source of knowledge of the scholastics' positions at least until the beginning of the seventeenth century.[20] Though Albert largely follows John Buridan in his discussion of the void, his elaboration on the topic of annihilation of space shows significant changes and embellishments that are carried through and still taken as current thought in contemporary works that are similar in purpose to Descartes's *Principles*.[21] Descartes is not often one who identifies his opposition explicitly, however, and so Albert's text remains a useful focal point, as well as a particularly accessible one for us today.[22]

Albert begins his treatment of vacuum by arguing that, although vacuum can be defined as "a place not filled by body," this does not imply that any vacuum exists. That is, Albert notes that being able to define the term does not show that the thing defined exists. But a vacuum could exist, Albert suggests; and he is careful to explain how one might come about and what, then, it would be: "A vacuum is possible by means of supernatural power. This is obvious, because God could annihilate everything that is within the sides [or concave surface parts] of the sky, after which the sky would be a vacuum . . . " To this point, Aristotle might have agreed with Albert, were he to have accepted Albert's premise concerning divine powers. Albert's continuation, however, shows a remarkable further development:

> Either the sides of the sky would be distant [i.e., separated] or not. If they are not separated by a distance, they would be conjoined as two leaves of a book or an empty purse; but then it ought not to be conceded that the sky is a vacuum, because in the aforesaid case the sides of the sky would be immediate [i.e., in contact]. If, however, it should be stated in this case that the sides of the sky are yet distant [or separated], there would then be some dimension between them by which they would be distant [or separated]; hence there would be no vacuum. To this one might respond that the sides [or concave surface parts] of the sky are not distant [or separated] by a straight line, although they may well be separated by a curved line. But if it is said that then the sides of the sky would be conjoined, I deny this, for the sky would remain spherical, just as now; and its sides would not be in direct contact, even if not separated by a [rectilinear] distance.

Albert's claim, then, is that we could measure distance *around the periphery* of such a true vacuum, but we could not measure distance *across* it: we could circumscribe the vacuum but not measure it directly, as Descartes's contemporary André d'Abillon would suggest.[23] Though it could be a 'place', insofar as it would be the limit of the sphere of the moon as a containing body,[24] such a vacuum induced by God would not appropriately be called a space. I expect that Albert maintains that it could not be "a separate space in which there is no other body conjointly" because "a separate accident must not be assumed to exist without a subject." Albert's point, then, would be the plausible consequence of an Aristotelian metaphysics applied in a rather surprising situation: if God were to annihilate the region below the sphere of the moon, then no substance or *body* would be present; and so no bodily accident, such as length, could be present.[25]

With Albert's argument, and the plausible justification in Aristotelian metaphysics in view, I hope that Descartes's discussion in *Principles* 2:18 appears more an argument and less a simple confusion. That argument and the material leading up to it in 2:16–17 stand as Descartes's effort to show the incoherence attendant upon attempts to consider what he calls vacuum in the "philosophical sense," "i.e., that in which there is nothing whatsoever": a region that can be identified (e.g., circumscribed) yet is not measurable (2:16). Descartes's position appears to follow as a consequence of his own theory of extended substance, as Albert's did for Albert. Albert found there to be no bodily accidents without attendant substance, and Descartes's theory contains the principle that "there is no real difference between space and corporeal substance" (2:11). This appears to leave no room for vacuum in the sense that Albert suggests, for Descartes writes:

> For a body's being extended in length, breadth and depth in itself warrants the conclusion that it is a substance, since it is a complete contradiction that a particular extension should belong to nothing; and the same conclusion must be drawn with respect to a space that is supposed to be a vacuum, namely that since there is extension in it, there must necessarily be substance in it as well. (2:16)

Descartes continues in 2:17 to consider why we might be deceived concerning our ordinary use of the term 'empty,' and in 2:18 he produces the argument with which we began. He finishes that discussion by effectively contradicting what Albert has supposed true concerning a place in which substance is annihilated: "If God were to take away every single body contained in a vessel . . . the sides of the vessel would, in that case, have to be in contact. For when there is nothing between two bodies they must necessarily touch each other." The argument might be considered a mere quibble if we allow that all Descartes has done is invoke his definition of matter as extended substance (2:4) to argue the point. Descartes follows his conclusion with further support, however:

> For when there is nothing between two bodies they must necessarily touch each other. And it is a manifest contradiction for them to be apart, or to have a distance between them, when the distance in question is nothing; for every distance is a mode of extension, and therefore cannot exist without an extended substance.

This final clause might have been directed specifically at Albert or his followers, but the rest of Descartes's argument is more general. It might be well expressed by using a subject that Albert has touched on and that is especially dear to Descartes — geometry. Should the material inside the sphere of the moon be annihilated, then in Albert's account, basic geometric truths that Descartes would consider internal to the concept of a sphere would be violated, such as that any great circle over the sphere would be equal to $2\pi$ times the radius of the sphere (AT VII, 225): for in Albert's account, that sphere really would not have a radius.

Who has it right in this regard: Albert or Descartes? My imagination cleaves to Descartes's line, but I see only an argument about imagination in his discussion, not even the geometric argument I have proposed. Furthermore, whether or not Descartes might allow that God would nonetheless be able to create such a vacuum despite our inability to conceive such a possibility cannot, I think, be easily settled, for it would take us deep into a different area of Descartes's thought — the limits of God's power over contradictions and eternal truths.[26] Concerning Albert's proposal, the heart of the matter lies in a debate concerning the abilities of the God of the scholastics in relation to Aristotelian metaphysics and in a disagreement with John Buridan, and I have nothing to add to those discussions.[27] Adjudicating such points is not my purpose here; sorting out a puzzling passage of Descartes's writing is, and the puzzle appears to be solved. Descartes's discussion in part 2 of the *Principles* is not focused on a treatment of the power of God, whereas Albert's is. Descartes is not concerned with whether God could perform such an annihilation; rather, his point is that the only sensible conception of such an event occurring would include as a result the sides of the vessel lying against one another — a vessel no more — instead of the result that Albert envisions, which I suppose would allow what appears to be a vessel from the outside but nonetheless incapable of containing anything.[28] The two authors are at cross purposes, as one is focused on constructing a coherent theory of material substance, and the other is concerned with God's power; but at least Descartes's much maligned argument is an understandable one when directed to Albert or d'Abillon and is a response centered on the point at issue for Descartes, the coherence of one's theory of material substance.

It seems unlikely, then, that Descartes is attempting to argue incoherently against the conceivability of the sort of vacuum Buridan characterized as "a volume [*dimensio corpora*] equal in length, width, and depth to the natural body that would fill it up if one placed it in this void." That conception of space as a container, in which matter is to be placed, will demand a very different sort of treatment from Descartes, and indeed, Descartes marks the difference between opponents here by referring to only some of them as proponents of a "philosophical" conception of vacuum. Descartes's discussion of confused philosophical conceptions of vacuum is contained in *Principles* 2:16–18, and that discussion is nested within a larger discussion of a parallel philosophical conception of rarefaction that spans 2:5–19. From 2:20 forward, Descartes will argue in a different manner against what he takes to be a more sensible possibility, concerning a physical vacuum that lies in the interstices between atomistic particles of matter. Descartes will consider larger macroscopic spaces in parts 3 and 4. These opponents I will dub "physical vacuists," and to them we now turn. Before considering Descartes's discussion in 2:20, it will be worth jumping further ahead in the *Principles* to his discussion of macroscopic vacuum, where he makes it especially clear that he countenances a number of conceptions of vacuum, and that vacuum construed as a region without extension is the only conception among them that he takes to be a confused.

### II: On Space without Plenum: Against Macroscopic Void

The wine cask argument in Descartes's earlier work, the *World*, was intended to show that no macroscopic void, of the size of a drop of wine or larger, could exist in nature. Given Descartes's new metaphysical assumptions, however, space is not conceived as a container full of matter that holds the wine inside its cask. The wine cask argument against vacuum is unworkable, then, though we might still hope that Descartes will be able to explain the physical phenomenon by some other reasoning at some point. Not only is the argument unworkable; I believe that Descartes has reversed his views concerning the compatibility of macroscopic vacuum with the phenomenon of the wine suspended in the cask. Descartes no longer argues that physical phenomena are entirely incompatible with physical vacuum as reconceived according to his new account of space; instead, he is very clear, in his treatment of celestial mechanics in part 3 (62–64), about the possibility of vacuum existing, but he then rules out, in his treatment of terrestrial gravity in part 4 (21–22), the possibility of it forming under any ordinary circumstances. But what could vacuum be, in this reconception, and how to account for the wine cask?

In the *Principles* account, the physical universe is made up of three elements (3:52). In his efforts to elucidate his characterization of the second element, which populates most of nonterrestrial space, Descartes writes:

> I shall examine [the effect of] these globules separately, without considering the matter of the first element any more than if all the spaces which that matter occupies were empty [*vacua essent*]; that is, if they were filled by a material which neither contributed anything to the motion of other bodies nor in any way impeded it. For in accordance with what has already been said, there obviously can be no other correct idea of empty space. (3:60; cf. 4:21)[29]

Though Descartes plainly begins his discussion of this fine matter as a conceptual simplification to account for the finer matter of the first element, that he finds such a simplification coherent already suggests his assent to the coherence of the idea of physical vacuum (cf. also 2:12). Descartes goes on to develop the account by adding a discussion of a number of physical consequences that bring the concept of vacuum into its own. The vacuum, though it contains "bodies," as Descartes suggests, appears to contain bodies with no discernible properties except extension: a continuous medium with no discernible particle size. Would this do well enough as a sensible seventeenth-century conception of macroscopic physical vacuum, worth the attention of Torricelli and Pascal?

The vacuum Descartes considers can easily be distinguished from particles of both the first and second elements. If such vacuum were to surround the surface of the spinning earth, Descartes suggests, earthy bodies of the third element would fly *away* from the planet to fill the void (4:21). That is the opposite of the activity of the third element in the presence of the second, for the vortex of particles of the second element that shrouds the earth drives earthy objects to the center of that vortex, and so particles of the second element that are below earthy ones would flee from the center of the earth's vortex. For like physical reasons, bodies of the first element would move similarly in the presence of bodies of the third. Only in the presence of vacuum, then, would the third element move away from the vortex's center. It would not do so in the presence of finer particles of any size, even those of the first element, which are "divided into particles of indefinite smallness" (3:52).

There are other independent physical reasons for distinguishing vacuum from the first element. The first element "adapts its shapes to fill all the narrow parts" of space around larger particles (3:52), and for that reason plays the role of the connecting medium that allows for light transmission. It must be unlike the vacuum, however, because of consequences concerning motion in the celestial vortex, especially the motion that is light (3:64). Descartes suggests that were a vacuum of the sort that he envisions to be present in a celestial vortex, bodies of the second element would fill it, and a space would shortly appear at the center of the vortex as a consequence of the other bodies' tendency to move away from the center. A similar state of affairs would obtain between matter of the first and second elements, but Descartes closes by once again distinguishing between the first element and vacuum. Because bodies of the second element revolving in a vortex would strive away from the center, a universe with vacuum in place of the first element would be different from ours, but not by much: "if the body of the Sun were nothing other than an empty space, nevertheless, its light (which would admittedly not be as strong, but which would otherwise not differ from what it now is) would still be perceived by us" (3:64).

Descartes's view appears to allows for the following possible scenario. Imagine that God creates a vacuum of elements inside a pitcher on the earth's surface. This vacuum would not, of course, be appropriately characterized by the confused "philosophical" conception of vacuum dispensed with in the previous section: it would be body with no humanly detectable property except extension, and the sides of the pitcher would remain separate and ready to contain material, such as air, that would soon fall into its open cavity. As material falls in, vacuum would reappear in the place previously occupied by that material, were it not the case that other material is immediately present and moving just as quickly to fill the prospective gap. Because all of the elements within a Cartesian vortex strive away from the center of rotation (3:60), this would suggest as a consequence that a new vacuum would make its appearance at the center of the earth (as has been suggested two paragraphs above); but the celestial vortex also constricts the terrestrial one in its striving away from its own center, and so the entire dimension of the earth vortex would reduce by the volume of one pitcher. That constriction would be complemented by a similar adjustment in the ether that carries the earth vortex, and a vacuum would appear as quickly as one has disappeared, now at the center of the celestial vortex. The details of this scenario have been necessary to make the following point: the vacuum, it seems, would not be an entity that travels with a discernible path toward the center of the celestial vortex, as would a body composed of, say, a distinct fourth element still finer than the first that is chased away from its original place. Such a vacuum would have no intrinsic bulk, for as matter moves in (however fast) to fill the void in the pitcher, other matter would be in position to move just as quickly to fill any space as it became vacant throughout the terrestrial and celestial vortices, except at the center of the latter, where a new vacuum would simply appear. What I will call "Cartesian vacuum," then, does not occupy space as ordinary matter does: to the limits of human abilities to detect it, it is only space or extension, pure and simple, and in this most important respect it does not seem to diverge from what one would expect a physical vacuum to be.

Descartes's discussion of dim stars late in the *Principles* suggests that he did indeed mean to allow for the possibility of such a scenario despite the fact that this appears to conflict with one important tenet of his system. The tenet is plenist physics, the view that the universe is full of bodies and that all motion is merely circulation of bodies, with no gaps among them of the sort that I have characterized as Cartesian vacuum. Even after the shift to the new conception of space in the *Principles*, the tenet plays its role in many important explanations of phenomena, such as gravity and the transmission of light. The conflict is only apparent, however, because Descartes's physics does not require such plenism, even though he is under the impression that no vacuum exists (2:33). Though vacuum is not an impossibility, Descartes still has the plenum for most practical purposes anyway because vacuum is so readily removed from our ordinary local physical environment. Practically, the physical universe in which we move is full: whatever vacuum may arise at the birth of the universe, or because of divine action, quickly becomes isolated at the center of a hollow vortex that continues to press its inner boundaries outward by virtue of the naturalness of rectilinear motion (2:39, 3:58). The sun might change some characteristics, such as luminosity, but nothing else would be new under the sun, unless one were able by some means to oppose the pressure of the celestial vortex and recall vacuum from the center of the vortex — a topic that will be at issue in Descartes's discussion with Pascal in the next section. I will argue there that Descartes has good reasons for defending this conception against Pascal, even in the face of the experiments Descartes came to confront after the *Principles*, for Descartes can allow that such a vacuum might exist at the center of a star and nonetheless plausibly defend the claim that what Pascal discovered through his experimental manipulations was material of the second element and not such (nonbulky) vacuum.

The problem of the wine cask with which we began has, of course, been solved along the way: whether or not there is a physical plenum, the pressure imposed by the celestial vortex on the earth's atmosphere accounts for the wine's inability to flow. The wine cask argument, then, is displaced from Descartes's universe, not to reappear in the *Principles*. Container space vanishes also, but a sensible conception of vacuum remains, and vacua might have existed at the centers of Cartesian stars, though Descartes claims that they do not. He has not provided a clear argument to suggest that vacua do not reside there in our universe, however, for though stars with such holes at their centers might be dimmer than filled stars, Descartes has provided no argument to suggest that some (or all) of the stars we observe are not just such dim stars!

### III: On Rarefaction and against Galilean
### Interstitial Void

To this point, I have argued that Descartes considers two very different sorts of vacuist position and replies to them in two very different sorts of ways. He responds with conceptual analysis to those "philosophical" vacuists who argue that vacuum is truly nothing. To those who argue that space may contain extension devoid of any other properties of matter, Descartes proposes a physical argument concerning the physical consequences of such void space in a fluid medium of the elements. In this section I will introduce a final area of concern in the *Principles*, Descartes's focus on void and rarefaction. The discussion of rarefaction overlaps the other two treatments in that Descartes presents *both* conceptual clarification and physical argument, and I will suggest that the two sorts of arguments are again directed at different opponents. Clarification is once more used to respond to opponents — such as Albert, once again — who argue that matter itself may expand and contract. Descartes takes the other tack in his discussion of atomism and void in 2:21ff: a new set of physical arguments are necessary to respond to different opponents, his atomist contemporaries. Descartes's purpose is to show the irreconcilability of atomism with plenism; and in his letters to Mersenne, though not in the systematic exposition of the *Principles*, Descartes also responds to independent arguments from Galileo intended to deny plenism and support the hypothesis of a vacuum between atoms: an interstitial, microscopic void. I will consider these arguments in turn.

Descartes's first attack in the *Principles* on interstitial void concerns topics introduced by Aristotle (213b14), such as the apparent increase in size of an object without an apparent increase in quantity of matter, as wine, for example, behaves during fermentation. Aristotle's position is that expansion and diminution of matter itself does occur and that, consequently, such an example of rarefaction would not support claims concerning the existence of an interstitial void between particles (214a26ff). That matter may itself expand can be found in Albert as well,[30] and it should be no surprise that this constitutes what Descartes considers a conceptually confused philosophical position concerning the nature of matter. Descartes holds that rarefaction of such an object occurs much as rarefaction of a dry sponge does when it is placed in water, absorbing other particles from its environment: "its pores are open wider, so that it spreads over a greater space" (2:6). A quantity of matter cannot itself expand because matter can be clearly conceived of in terms of its extension only: more extension is just more matter (2:9). Descartes's argument on this topic concludes in 2:19, so it is clear that the clarification concerning the terms 'place' and 'space' and the examination of faulty conceptions of vacuum that we have considered above are intended to clarify misconceptions concerning the rarefaction of wine, as well as the space in the pitcher it occupies: Descartes effectively completes in 2:19 a discussion he has begun in 2:5, where he marks his concern with "preconceived opinions concerning [both] rarefaction and empty space." I will not, however, consider this argument further here: Descartes's argument is certainly flagged in 2:9 as an effort to clarify conceptual confusion; how much clarification results from his argument I will leave to others to consider[31] so that I may keep this paper focused on Descartes's account of vacuum.

From 2:20 forward, however, Descartes is not concerned with the preconceived opinions of the philosophical vacuist and matter theorist. His target, after making a conceptual point in 2:20, is of a different sort: the atomist who allows for the possibility of interstitial microvacuum between individual atoms in a solid or fluid body. Though (as I've suggested in the previous section and will support further below) Descartes could find such a conception of vacuum "intelligible," he nonetheless also holds that there is no such vacuum because "every place is full of bodies" (2:33). Descartes's treatment of atomism culminates in a response, in 2:33–35, in a thought experiment intended to demonstrate that motion is possible without recourse to vacuum for the plenist, whereas it would require vacuum of the atomist. In the argument, Descartes asks the reader to consider a collection of bodies flowing through a closed circuit of motion in a fixed volume and then to consider the consequences of including a continuously narrowing funnel within that circuit. The narrowing, he suggests, demands that the flowing material must be effectively continuous or composed of assorted sizes that diminish ad infinitum if the whole is to remain of constant volume, for as the passage narrows by infinitesimal degrees, the particles must reassort themselves in indefinitely many combinations of breadth to accommodate that narrowing. Under the assumption that the universe is in fact full, and so all bodies move in closed circles of constant net volume, Descartes suggests that such motion is possible only if there is no smallest particle — that is, no atom — for no vacuum can be created to allow the change in volume that would be required for atoms to assort themselves in order to pass through such a passage. If there were a smallest actual particle, then, we might expect that any such movement would be halted wherever it were to occur throughout the universe, as particles would jam at whatever continuously constricting spaces they were to encounter.

The atomist, therefore, cannot allow the scenario that Descartes envisions without an appeal to vacuum. Why not, then, appeal to vacuum, especially since Descartes suggests further on that vacuum is actually possible? He claims to have found earlier that the universe is full of bodies, but in the Latin text he does not claim to have provided a demonstration; and indeed, the previous argument hardly suffices to seal the case against the atomist. If he had shown previously that vacuum is impossible, the demonstration in 2:33 would also be quite redundant. Descartes claims to have shown the impossibility of the vacuum of atomists later, in 4:202, but that passage follows the discussion of macroscopic vacuum in parts 3 and 4 also, after which he might more justly (though nonetheless erroneously) conclude that he has constructed a demonstration. So the question remains: why not allow for the creation of such an interstitial vacuum, which is drawn from the center of a vacuous star, perhaps?

I can find no compelling evidence in the *Principles* to complete this argument, though some support may be found in other writings. Descartes finds a contemporary opponent for this portion of the *Principles* in Galileo, in *Two New Sciences*. Descartes certainly read Galileo's book, which he discusses in great detail with Mersenne in about a dozen letters over the course of a year, beginning in October 1638.[32] It will be worth a careful excursion into Galileo's text and Descartes's comments to determine how Descartes extended himself to reply to this sort of vacuist position in order to show that he did not find vacuum in this case to be an incoherent concept, as he does for philosophical vacuum at 2:18.

In one of the passages Descartes focuses on, Galileo notes that two marble plates, if well polished, will slide smoothly alongside one another but will momentarily resist lateral separation, even when great force is applied. Galileo applies this observation to philosophical effect by using it to call Aristotelian arguments concerning motion in a vacuum into question:

> Seeing the lower slab follow the upper when this is lifted with swift motion assures us that motion in the void would not be instantaneous despite the opinion of many philosophers, and perhaps of Aristotle himself. For if it were, the two surfaces would be separated without any resistance whatever, the same instant of time sufficing for their separation and for the running together of the surrounding air to fill the void that might [otherwise] remain between them. Thus, from the following of the upper slab by the lower, it is deduced that motion in a void would not be instantaneous.

Though this reply has significant affinities with the position Descartes develops in the *Principles*, at the next link in his chain of reasoning Galileo does not move as Descartes would; for on the basis of the phenomenon, he concludes that a vacuum exists:

> It is then further deduced that some void indeed does remain between the surfaces, at least for a very brief time; that is, for as long as the time consumed by the ambient air in running to fill this void. For if no void existed there, neither would there be any need on the part of the ambient air of running together, or of any other motion.[33]

Here Galileo proposes the existence of a small microlayer vacuum, providing an ingenious analysis of a phenomenon that stands as a plausible counterexample to Descartes's antivacuist position in 2:33–35. The separation of the plates, which approximates a separation of two planes, would require an infinite velocity of in-rushing air if the separation were to occur without pause.[34] The air particles, we might also note as a consequence of Descartes's analysis above, would have to begin their infinite rush at the first infinitesimal separation of the plates, to ensure that no vacuum existed in nature. But that a resistance to separation arises, and a pause is required before the marbles are separated, suggests to Galileo that a genuine vacuum is demonstrated by this phenomenon, one that exists at least for the space of time it takes for the in-rushing air, whether it is atomistic or infinitesimal in size, to flow between the plates and meet at their centers.

Galileo proceeds further with his analysis of the example and brings the discussion around to a theory of interstitial vacuum as he generalizes his conclusion about the marble surfaces in a hypothesis concerning the general characteristic of cohesion among the parts of solid and fluid bodies. Perhaps, he suggests, the vacuum force that holds the two marble plates together is the same force as the interstitial force that holds molecule to molecule in a body, each attracted to the other by a mutual resistance to a vacuum between each pair of particles. After proposing an experiment to measure the attractive power of vacuum, Galileo proceeds to a discussion of pumping devices; he notes the observation related to him by an expert that no suction pump will lift water in a column to a height greater than "18 Braccia" and concludes:

> Although I understood that a rope, a wooden staff, or an iron rod can be lengthened until its own weight breaks it when attached from above, it never occurred to me

that the same thing will happen, and much more easily, with a rope or rod of water. And that which is drawn up in a pump is nothing else than a cylinder of water which, having its attachment above and being lengthened more and more, finally arrives at that boundary beyond which it breaks, just as if it were a rope. (*Opere* VII, 64)

Galileo suggests, then, that vacuum provides a force of cohesion within solid and fluid bodies. His approach provides a surprising twist on Aristotelian metaphysics, for he allows that nature abhors a vacuum not absolutely but only to a limited degree: to a measure of force that correlates with a column the height of "18 Braccia" in the case of water, to a greater measure in the case of iron, and so on. Galileo completes his account of interstitial vacua with another hypothesis concerning the supposed effects of fire for breaking the vacuum that holds gold in its rigid shape:

Sometimes, in considering how heat goes snaking among the minimum particles of this or that metal, so firmly joined together, and finally separates and disunites them; and how then, the heat departing, they return to reunite with the same tenacity as before, without the quantity of gold being diminished . . . I have thought that this may come about because of very subtle fire-particles . . . these might, by filling the minimum voids distributed between these minimum particles [of metal], free them from that force with which those voids attract one [particle] against another, forbidding their separation. And being thus able to move freely, their mass would become fluid, and remain so until the fire-particles between them depart. But when these go, leaving the pristine voids, the usual attraction returns, and consequently the attachment of the parts. (66–67)

Galileo's hypotheses concerning the phenomena of the marble plates, interstitial vacua, and the action of fire, then, stand as a body of theory clearly opposed to Descartes's plenist physics. Do Descartes's replies to Galileo suggest that he did find such a conception of vacuum intelligible, even if false? Yes, but with some confusion that will require spelling out.

Descartes's easy dismissal of the problem of infinite speed of travel is that, try as one might to separate the marbles in a perpendicular line, one will nonetheless invariably pull them at some angle, separating one side first; and so one will not face the problem of infinite velocity in that case. He admits, however, that if one were able to separate them so, one would indeed create a vacuum for an instant; so Descartes once again hints at the coherence of the possibility of vacuum in this case.[35]

Concerning Galileo's discussion of the adhesion of the plates, Descartes writes: "What he ascribes to vacuum should only be ascribed to the weight of the air. If it were abhorrence of a vacuum that prevented two bodies from separating, there would certainly be no force capable of separating them."[36] What Descartes is after in the second of these sentences is not clear to me, and he does not elaborate. Perhaps he suggests that the phrase "nature abhors a vacuum," if it is to have any explanatory value, expresses an absolute law of nature that would prohibit the creation of a vacuum. Why that must be so is not evident, however, because other empirical phenomena, such as the particular constant rate of acceleration of gravity measured by Galileo, seem no less remarkable than a particular force of cohesive attraction. Descartes could also have been prompted by the historical connotations of the phrase to turn briefly to a mention of vacuum in the philosophical sense, as presented in Albert's treatment. If so, his reply is a bit cryptic as a reply to Galileo. Indeed, if the interpretation of the discussion of vacuum in the *Principles* that I have sketched is appropriate, and appropriate to his thinking at that time, he himself ought to have found it valueless.[37]

I would prefer to draw your attention to Descartes's first phrase, concerning the weight of the air as the cause of the adhesion of the plates. He continues in the letter to present a similar explanation of Galileo's water column in the pump and its incapacity to climb higher than eighteen yards. If the impediment is not attributable to mechanical shortcomings of the pump, he goes on to suggest, then it could be attributed "to the weight of the water, which counterbalances that of the air."[38] This account is the sort of explanation that Pascal would provide for the suspension of the mercury in the barometer ten years later in his *Récit de la Grande Expérience de l'Équilibre des Liqueurs* — of "an equilibrium of the weights of air and mercury."[39] Pascal, however, would go on to explain the equilibrium with reference to vacuum: the mercury would fall out of the tube into a mercury bath to a level that would support a similarly heavy column of atmosphere, and the space above the mercury in the closed tube would be a vacuum. How would Descartes explain the suspension of the mercury?

Descartes's plenist physics clearly would prohibit any explanation referring to vacuum; yet his approach to the water column problem could easily suggest a measure of the weight of the air. Descartes had no faith in the integrity of water pumps for such measurement, however, and it appears from Descartes' communication that Mersenne, in a letter now lost, had proposed an experiment to measure the weight of the air by measuring the force required to separate marbles laterally. This led Descartes to comment that one probably could not practically ensure that the marbles would be appropriately smooth nor that they would separate laterally instead of obliquely, even though the experiment, if successful, would create a void between the marbles. Such an admission would appear to run against Descartes's plenism,[40] but as Descartes proceeds in a brief space to discuss "subtle matter" in his letter, I expect that he would go on to suggest that matter of the second or first element would rush in to cancel out the formation of void through pores in the marbles (AT II, 481– 483). Thus, in raising the marble disc, one would be lifting the entirety of the column of the atmosphere above the disc and forcing subtle matter from above the air to descend through the air, so that some subtle matter in the loop of bodies would fill the space vacated by the marble. As the space opens enough to allow the passage of air, the subtle matter then returns to its previous place, and the force necessary to separate the marbles is relieved. Thus, what we might have expected to be a measure of the force of interstitial vacuum on Galilean principles, or of the weight of the atmosphere in a framework that countenances void, is smoothly converted to a measure of the weight of the atmosphere under pressure from the celestial vortex in a plenist Cartesian physics.[41]

After Descartes and Mersenne had discussed and then dismissed experiments to measure the weight of the air by using marble discs, Pascal argued for a reliable and convincing method for measuring the weight of the air with the mercury column and presented an especially important argument in October 1648, in the *Récit de la Grande Expérience*, as a result of the Puy de Dôme experiment, in which his cousin showed that mercury will fall further at the top of a mountain than at its foot. The experiment suggested to Pascal and others that differences in the weight of air above the two columns was the cause of the observed difference. In discussions that arose in the wake of Pascal's *Expériences Nouvelles Touchant le Vide* of the previous year, many others became involved in the debate concerning the nature of the material, or the lack of material, at the top of the tube. In this period, Descartes proposed several experiments to Mersenne concerning barometric pressure and tests of the composition of the transparent space. He also asked others about Pascal's progress in the light of his suggestions, and he watched his own column.[42] Upon hearing the results of Pascal's experiment and finding that it was not contrary to his expectations, confirming his hypothesis concerning subtle matter, Descartes awaited further challenges from Pascal: challenges that he presumably did not come across before his death. Descartes must have felt vindicated, for the Puy du Dôme experiment disagreed with the Galilean theoretical stance that Pascal held at the time of their last communication, and Descartes may have been unaware that Pascal had changed his theory since that time.[43] The experiment also supported his physics in one independent respect that ran contrary to both of Pascal's vacuist positions: Descartes, I expect, could see clearly through the substance at the top of the glass tube, and since light required a medium, in Descartes's account, there was reason to believe that something more than Cartesian vacuum remained there.

## Conclusion

Descartes, like Aristotle, presents two sorts of response in his treatment of vacuum, against two types of position: conceptual analysis of what he takes to be nonsense, and metaphysical explanation and physical argument against what he takes to be competing physical theory. The nonsense position that Aristotle dispensed with quickly was a view that was properly reducible to the position that vacuum is truly nothing, once abstracted from all of place, extension, and impenetrability. Similarly, the nonsense positions that Descartes dispensed with in 2:5–19 were the views that vacuum has no extension and that the extension of a given quantity of substance is alterable. The authors approach another set of opponents — in Aristotle's case, atomists — very differently, however. Much of Aristotle's argument attacks the possibility of motion in a void. We do observe motion, so void is ruled out: such an attack is intended to exclude physical possibility. Descartes goes further than Aristotle, in that he takes several opportunities to detail sensible conceptions of both macroscopic and interstitial vacuum as extended space, lacking in any other properties of matter, most notably, bulkiness. Late in the *Principles*, Descartes allows that this conception of vacuum would be compatible with his physics, except for the brightness of the sun, and so he returns to an empirical argument, a strategy that closely parallels Aristotle's. Descartes's conception is also suitable for formulating a response to atomists such as Galileo and for his later discussions of macroscopic vacuum with Mersenne and others, in material written after the French *Principles*. In each of these attempts to rule out the possibility of vacuum he was not entirely successful, but a reasonably coherent and sophisticated body of argument on vacuum can be ascribed to Descartes.[44]

Notes

1. Quotations from Descartes's works are from CSM unless otherwise indicated. References of the form (AT XI, 32) refer to the volume and pagination of AT; references of the form (2:18) refer to *Principles*, part 2, sect. 18. I include the latter convention because reference to Descartes's divisions will often be more illuminating than reference to pagination.

2. For further defense of the shift of position from the *World* to the *Principles*, see R. S. Woolhouse, *Descartes, Spinoza, Leibniz: The Concept of Substance in Seventeenth Century Metaphysics* (London: Routledge, 1993), p. 82. Some passages in the *World* suggest that a break from the container metaphysic is already in progress during its writing; see, for example, AT XI, 36.

3. These are taken to be the matter of the argument as expressed in John Cottingham, *A Descartes Dictionary* (Oxford: Blackwell, 1993), pp. 159–160.

4. Frédéric De Buzon and Vincent Carraud, *Descartes et les "Principia" II: Corps et Mouvement* (Presses Universitaires de France, 1994), p. 27.

5. See, among others, Margaret Dauler Wilson, *Descartes* (London: Routledge, 1978), p. 87; Daniel Garber, *Descartes' Metaphysical Physics* (Chicago: University of Chicago Press, 1992), pp. 179–180; Stephen Gaukroger, *Descartes: An Intellectual Biography* (Oxford: Oxford University Press 1995), p. 240; and Jonathan Bennett, this volume.

6. For one contemporary, see Charles Sorel, *Science Universelle*, Tome 1 (Paris: Pierre Billaine, 1634), pp. 38ff. For predecessors, see Garber, *Descartes' Metaphysical Physics*, p. 128, and for current conceptions, see Bennett's discussion of "container space," this volume.

7. Buridan, quoted in Pierre Duhem, *Medieval Cosmology*, Roger Ariew, ed. and trans. (Chicago: University of Chicago Press, 1985), p. 408.

8. For continuation of the metaphysical debate as a twentieth-century physical problem, for example, concerning vacuum fluctuations, see Simon Saunders and Harvey Brown, eds, *The Philosophy of Vacuum* (Oxford: Clarendon Press, 1991). Concerning Torricelli, see W. E. Knowles Middleton, *The History of the Barometer* (Baltimore: Johns Hopkins University Press, 1964), chap 2.

9. Torricelli's experiments probably occurred in June 1644 (see Middleton, *History of the Barometer*, 22), and the *Principia* were printed by 10 July. Descartes to Princess Elizabeth, 6 June 1647 (AT V, 60), mentions that the complete French *Principles* are already in press; his renewed engagement on the topic of the space above the mercury appears to have taken place in a meeting with Pascal in September 1647, for Descartes writes to Mersenne in December that "I am surprised that you have kept this experiment secret for four years, as has the aforementioned M. Pascal . . ." Mersenne had experimented on the vacuum over three years before, and Pascal just one year before their meeting. For a detailed account of the history of Descartes's study of the experimental phenomenon, see Garber, *Descartes' Metaphysical Physics*, pp. 136–143.

10. Such a view of 2:16–18 is expressed in Daniel Garber, "Descartes' Physics," in John Cottingham, ed., *The Cambridge Companion to Descartes* (Cambridge:Cambridge University Press, 1992), pp. 299–300, though with reference to Greek atomists rather than to Descartes's contemporaries.

11. See especially Garber, *Descartes' Metaphysical Physics*, chaps. 4–5.

12. 3:64. See the discussion and defense below.

13. Descartes to Mersenne, 13 December 1647, contains the quotation and briefly mentions Descartes's experiments. Jacqueline Pascal reports on the meeting with Blaise Pascal but does not clarify who proposed the experiment; see the note on p. 653 in Blaise Pascal, *Oeuvres Complètes*, Louis Lafuma, ed. and notes (Paris: Éditions du Seuil, 1963).

14. Desmond Clarke, *Descartes' Philosophy of Science* (University Park: Pennsylvania State University Press, 1982), Garber and Gaukroger refer readers to Edward Grant's *A Sourcebook in Medieval Science* (Cambridge, Mass.: Harvard University Press, 1974) or to his detailed study, *Much Ado About Nothing* (Cambridge: Cambridge University Press, 1981). Garber, *Descartes' Metaphysical Physics*, and Woolhouse, *Descartes, Spinoza, Leibniz*, have presented the most serious efforts to clarify some aspects of Descartes's approach in discussion of Descartes's intersection with Pascal and with the "container space" metaphysic, respectively. Footnotes should indicate that I am indebted to these authors and to Bennett (this volume) in my discussion.

15. Aristotle, *Physics*, Robin Waterfield, trans. (Oxford: Oxford University Press, 1994), p. 87: *Physics* IV:4, 211b14–24.

16. Descartes lays out his own more restricted conception of place in 2:13–15.

17. These arguments are supplemented by arguments for the necessity of a motive medium in 215a24–216a10.

18. On the conceivability of vacuum in an Aristotelian physics, see Roger Bacon's position in Grant, *Much Ado About Nothing*, p. 106.

19. Garber, "Descartes' Physics," p. 300, holds that Descartes positions himself against Greek atomist tenets in all of 2:16–20. Garber correctly identifies the strategy of attack, which I will detail below, but I suggest that he mistakes the range of the opponents addressed.

20. Ernest Moodey, "Albert of Saxony," *Dictionary of Scientific Biography*, vol. I (New York: Scribner's Sons, 1970), p. 95.

21. See especially the third book of André d'Abillon's *Nouveau Cours de Philosophie en François: La Physique des bons esprits, ou l'Idee et Abrege d'une Physique Familiere et Solide divisee en cinq livres* (Paris: S. Picquet, 1643), pp. 278ff.

22. Albert of Saxony, *Questions on the Physics of Aristotle*, book IV, question 8, translated by Grant, *Sourcebook*, pp. 325–326.

23. "Les deux poles seroient distans, mais que entre eux deux, il ny auroit point de distance, car il ny auraoit rien entre les deux poles." D'Abillon, *Nouveau Cours*, p. 304.

24. Albert sketches this distinction in his treatment, which Toletus refers to as "external place"; see Woolhouse, *Descartes, Spinoza, Liebniz*, p. 83.

25. *Albert of Saxony, Questions*, p. 325; reaffirmed in arguments on p. 326. Note that this interpretation of Aristotelian metaphysics does not allow for the possibility of an accident occurring independently of substance, and would perhaps be unsurprising if it didn't also contradict one of the Condemnations of 1277 and Buridan's interpretation, which both maintain that God could create an accident without a subject (see Duhem, *Medieval Cosmology*, p. 410, and Grant, *Sourcebook*, p. 325, n. 7). Albert allows only this single way of conceiving of supernatural created vacuum, however, and explicitly denies Buridan's alternative conception, that there is a *dimensio corpora* that might remain in God's creation of vacuum. Duhem and Grant dismiss this difference, perhaps as a neglected possibility, but neither offers any substantial support for the dismissal. Albert is also followed in this explicit claim that where no substance is, no accident can be, by Descartes's contemporary Pierre Du Moulin; but only the natural and not the divine case is considered in *La Philosophie Mise en Francois et diuisee en trois parties, Sçauoir. Elements de la Logique. La Physique, ou Science Naturelle. L'Ethique, ou Science Morale* (Paris: Thomas Blaise, 1644), p. 18.

26. On that topic, see Descartes (AT VII, 145), and Descartes's letters to More, 5 February 1649, and to Arnauld, 29 July 1648. In these letters, Descartes states that he would not pos-

itively claim that God *can* do what Descartes cannot conceive clearly (V, 272), implying, I expect, that he would not claim that God cannot do it either; yet he also explains that "no barrel can be conceived to be so empty as to have inside it not extension, and therefore no body" (AT V, 224). See also De Buzon and Carraud, *Descartes et les "Principia" II* pp. 27–29; Garber, *Descartes' Metaphysical Physics*, pp. 151–152.

27. For an account of the larger debate, see Duhem, *Medieval Cosmology*, pp. 369–430.

28. Cf. d'Abillon's characterization: "vn lieu, c'est a dire vne superficie concaue, dans laquelle il ny ait rien," which is entirely lacking in "espace, ou capacité" (*Nouveau Cours*, pp. 297, 304).

29. Quotations of *Principles* 3 and 4 are from the translation of V. Miller and R. Miller, *René Descartes: Principles of Philosophy*, (Dordrecht: Reidel, 1984).

30. Albert of Saxony, *Questions on the Physics of Aristotle*, book IV, question 12, translated by Grant, *Sourcebook*, 339.

31. See Bennett, this volume, and see Woolhouse's discussion of the views of some of Descartes's opponents in detail, in *Descartes, Spinoza, Leibniz*, pp. 84–86.

32. See most of the correspondence between Descartes and Mersenne to 25 December 1639, at which point the discussion of vacuum and pumps shifts to water-lifting devices based on other principles.

33. Galileo Galilee, *Opere* VII 60, *Two New Sciences* Stillman Drake, trans. (Madison: University of Wisconsin Press, 1974), p. 20.

34. The physical problem of the separation of planes, and a response similar to Descartes's (see below) can also be found in an abstract treatment in Francisco Suarez, *Disputationes Metaphysicae* 19.1.7. See F. Suarez, *On Efficient Causality: Metaphysical Disputations 17, 18 and 19*, Alfred J. Freddoso, trans. (New Haven, Conn.: Yale University Press, 1994).

35. Descartes to Mersenne, 9 January 1639 (AT II, 482). But see note 40 for a qualification of this claim.

36. Descartes to Mersenne, 11 October 1638 (AT II, 382); see also a near reprise of this comment in Descartes to Mersenne 15 November 1638 (AT II, 440).

37. Descartes's discussion would find a better target, once again, in André d'Abillon, who argues for a position very like Albert's, that void cannot be produced by less than supernatural means of annihilation of substance. He continues on to the odd suggestion that the problem natural beings would face, were they to try to produce a void, is that they would not be able to muster *enough force* to separate bodies. See *Nouveau Cours*, 298.

38. Descartes to Mersenne, 11 October 1638 (AT II, 382), my translation. The CSMK translation cuts this passage midsentence, and consequently leaves out the final hypothesis.

39. Pascal, *Oeuvres Complètes*, 221.

40. Victor Cousin's edition of Descartes's works presents a variant text, mentioning a vacuum "of air," not suggesting absolute vacuum. See Cousin, *Oeuvres de Descartes*, VIII (Paris: F. G. Levrault, 1824), 71–72.

41. Descartes suggests a similar explanation of a related phenomenon as early as 1631, though, of course, he countenances a different metaphysics of space at the time. Descartes to [Reneri], 2 June 1631 (AT I, 206–207).

42. Descartes to Mersenne, 13 December 1647, and several letters between the two for several months after contain various reports of findings on the barometer; Descartes to Carcavi, 11 June 1649 (AT V, 366) poses the question of whether Pascal had completed the experiment suggested by Descartes in 1647.

43. On the later history, and especially Descartes's own position, see Garber, *Descartes' Metaphysical Physics*, 138–143.

44. Many thanks to the editors of this volume, as well as to Jonathan Bennett and the Na-

tional Endowment for the Humanities Summer Seminar Program, which provided the opportunity for me to start work on this subject. Thanks also to Jonathan Bennett, George Gale, Charles Huenemann, and Matthew Stuart, who provided helpful comments, and to the Allegheny College faculty development committee, which funded the primary research presented in this chapter.

## 3

MICHAEL DELLA ROCCA

# "If a Body Meet a Body"

## Descartes on Body-Body Causation

Do bodies cause changes in motion in other bodies, according to Descartes? To many interpreters of Descartes, the answer has seemed to be no. On this view, despite Descartes's frequent use of causal language in discussing the relations between bodies, it is clear that he sees God and not bodies as the cause of changes in motion in other bodies. Presently I will give the evidence for this reading of Descartes, which dates back to some early occasionalists but which also has prominent present-day proponents, particularly Gary Hatfield and Daniel Garber.[1] One who endorses such an account of body-body interaction in Descartes may acknowledge that, for Descartes, *minds* can cause changes in bodies and may acknowledge even that bodies can cause changes in minds.[2] But what is, on this view, clear-cut and undeniable is that bodies are *not* genuine causes of changes in motion (or of any other changes) in bodies. Garber says, in fact, "It seems to me *as clear as anything* that, for Descartes, God is the only cause of motion in the inanimate world of bodies, that bodies cannot themselves be genuine causes of change in the physical world of extended substance."[3] This view of Descartes thus amounts to seeing him as embracing occasionalism insofar as body-body interaction is concerned, though not necessarily an occasionalism of the more general form found, for example, in Malebranche.[4]

Descartes's position, as Garber reads it, is a result of Descartes's rejection of the Aristotelian-scholastic picture of causation, according to which substantial forms are causes of bodily change.[5] Descartes rejects this view for various reasons having to do with his rejection of mentalistic explanations of physical phenomena and his related rejection of teleological explanations in physics.[6] Without the substantial forms as causes of changes in bodies, some other causal agent is needed. Garber says that

Descartes brings in God and his immutable will to do the causal work of the no longer available substantial forms.[7] This, for Garber, is a key feature of Descartes's break with scholastic philosophy.[8]

All this is elegant and plausible as an interpretation of Descartes, and Garber and Hatfield elaborate the view with much insight. However, although the kind of occasionalism in question may be, as Desmond Clarke puts it, "a natural development of fundamental assumptions which are at least implicit in Descartes's system,"[9] and although this view may seem to make sense of Descartes's position, I do not believe that Descartes holds this view, which Garber and others attribute to him. Despite Descartes's rejection of substantial forms and his explicit claim that God is the cause of motion, I think that there are strong reasons to support the view that he does nonetheless see bodies as genuine causes of motion.[10]

These reasons are of two rather different kinds. First, there are textual reasons. It is important to note that Descartes never says that bodies are not genuine causes of motion, although if he were an occasionalist in this case one would expect that he would at some point make such a claim. Furthermore, there are certain passages in which Descartes uses causal language to describe the relations between bodies that are most awkward for the occasionalist interpretation of Descartes. This is so because these passages occur in stretches of text in which Descartes is particularly concerned to give us his official views on causation. These passages do not occur in contexts that can be read as loose and nontechnical when it comes to the matter of causation. The fact that Descartes does speak of bodies as causing motion in other bodies in precisely these technical contexts must count heavily against the occasionalist reading. The second kind of reason in support of the nonoccasionalist reading stems from Descartes's overall system. A consideration of certain central features of his conception of God — features most prominent in his discussion of the creation of the eternal truths — makes it more plausible that he holds that bodies cause changes in motion and do so, indeed, not *despite* the fact that God causes changes in motion but *because* of that fact. These pressures, deriving from Descartes's overall metaphysical position, suggest that to deny that bodies cause motion would, for Descartes, be to limit God's power in a way that would be illegitimate. These pressures also suggest that in the end, despite Descartes's rejection of substantial forms, he does adopt a key part of the Aristotelian-scholastic picture of causation.

I will begin with the case for an occasionalist reading. Then I will present the textual evidence for a nonoccasionalist reading followed by a discussion of Descartes's views on force, which are, obviously, important in understanding his views on causation. I will then explore the ways in which his views on the creation of the eternal truths add crucial support to the nonoccasionalist interpretation of Descartes.

## The Case for the Occasionalist Reading

Let's begin then with Garber's reasons for thinking that Descartes is an occasionalist in the matter of body-body causation. Garber is, of course, aware that in many places Descartes speaks as if bodies cause motion in other bodies. But Garber holds that to see what Descartes's official views on causation are, we must turn to the passages in which he takes up this topic explicitly; we must not rely on casual or nontechnical passages in which the topic of causation is not the focus of the discussion. This methodological restriction is entirely appropriate since even the most fully fledged occasionalists slip into everyday language that attributes causal power to bodies and other finite objects; such occasionalists insist on distinguishing this talk from their more official pronouncements in which they give us the lowdown, as it were, on the real cause of changes.[11]

Thus Garber is not going to be swayed by Descartes's frequent use of causal locutions in passages in which he is not directly elucidating his conception of the causes of motion. Consider, for example, the following passage from a 1648 letter to Silhon: "When one body makes another body move [*fait mouvoir*], it loses as much of its motion as it gives to the other" (AT V, 135; CSMK 330). Here Descartes's use of the phrase *fait mouvoir* indicates that the first body has causal efficacy. But since Descartes is not in this context focusing on God's role in bringing about motion and is thus not dwelling on his own official account of causation, this passage cannot provide any real support for the view that he recognizes that bodies are genuine causes of motion. The passage here may simply be one of those in which Descartes is speaking according to common opinion.[12]

To decide whether or not Descartes is an occasionalist in this case, we must focus, as do Garber and Hatfield, on those passages that give us the lowdown on causation. These include *Principles* 2:36 to approximately 2:45 and the parallel passages in *Le Monde*. Some passages from Descartes's correspondence must also be taken into account, particularly his correspondence with More. I will focus for now primarily on what Descartes says in the relevant stretch of the *Principles*.[13] In *Principles* 2:36, Descartes says that the "universal and primary" cause of motion is God.[14]

> As far as the general cause is concerned, it seems clear to me that this is no other than God himself, who in the beginning created matter, along with motion and rest, and now, merely by his regular concurrence, conserves the same amount of motion and rest in the material universe as he put there at the beginning. . . . God moved the parts of matter in various ways when he first created them, and he now preserves all this matter in the same way and with the same laws with which he originally created them; and it follows from what we have said that this fact alone makes it most reasonable to think that God likewise always conserves the same amount of motion in matter. (*Principles* 2:36)

Descartes goes on to say that God's preserving activity accounts for changes in motion:

> When he created the world in the beginning God did not only move the different parts of the world in various ways, but also at the same time brought it about that some parts impel others and transfer their motions to the others. Thus, since God preserves the world by the same action and in accordance with the same laws as when he created it, the motion which he preserves is not something permanently fixed in the same parts of matter, but something which is mutually transferred from some to others when collisions occur. The very fact that creation is in a continual state of change is thus evidence of the immutability of God. (*Principles* 2:42)

In an important letter to More, Descartes accounts for motion in a similar way by saying that matter "is impelled by God, conserving as much motion or transference in it as he placed in it from the beginning" (AT V, 404; CSMK 381). Garber ("Descartes and Occasionalism," p. 14) sums up the picture that emerges from these passages in the following way (see also Hatfield, pp. 121–122):

> God stands behind the world of bodies and is the direct cause of their motion. In the old Aristotelian philosophy, the characteristic behavior of bodies was explained through substantial forms; in Descartes's new, up-to-date mechanism, forms are out, and God is in; in Descartes's new philosophy the characteristic behavior of bodies is explained in terms of an immutable God sustaining the motion of bodies.

Garber's interpretation up to this point is important and correct, and nothing I say will challenge it.[15] Where Garber's view becomes more controversial, however, is in turning from the topic of God as the universal and primary cause of motion to the question of whether there is any room in Descartes' system for bodies as causes of motion as well. It may seem that Descartes is leaving room for this when he introduces in *Principles* 2:36 and 37 the notion of the secondary and particular causes of motion.[16] But it turns out that by "particular causes" Descartes apparently has in mind only the rules or laws of nature: "From God's immutability we can also know certain rules or laws of nature, which are secondary and particular causes of the various motions we see in particular bodies" (*Principles* 2:37). These laws specify, for example, that "each thing, insofar as it is simple and undivided, always remains in the same state as far as it can [*quantum in se est*]"[17] and that a moving body tends to move in a straight line.[18] Hatfield sums up the causal role of the laws of nature:

> The laws of nature, then, are the 'secondary, particular causes' of various motions inasmuch as it is according to them that God finds reason to change the direction and speed of any given moving particle as it comes in contact (one might say 'upon the occasion of its contact') with one or more other particles. Or, if we focus upon the fact that God creates the universe anew at each instant, these laws provide the reason for God to create the particle at successive instants along one path rather than along another. (p. 127)

From these claims about the causal role of God and the laws of nature, it is quite natural to infer that Descartes denies that *bodies* are causes of motion: God moves bodies around according to certain rules, and this rule-governed activity seems to account fully for changes in motion. It seems as if there is no genuine causal role for bodies to play. Garber makes such a claim in the following passage: "Descartes' whole strategy for deriving the laws of motion from the immutability of God presupposes that God is the real cause of motion and change of motion in the inanimate world of bodies knocking up against one another."[19] Hatfield puts the point this way: "Descartes removed causal agency from the material world and placed it in the hands of God and created minds" (pp. 134–135). Fred Freddoso expresses (without endorsing) the line of reasoning that might lead to an occasionalist position like the one Garber and Hatfield attribute to Descartes: "It is impossible to give a coherent and theologically orthodox account of how an effect might be brought about directly or immediately by both God and a creature—i.e., an account that does not render one of those alleged causal contributions wholly redundant" (p. 93).[20]

## Textual Evidence against the Occasionalist Reading

I admit that it seems quite natural to infer from God's role in sustaining bodies and causing motion that bodies are *not* genuine causes of motion. Nonetheless, I want to argue that Descartes did not draw this inference, that he held that despite or rather because of God's causal activity, bodies themselves are also causes of motion. First, I will present the textual evidence supporting my claim and later in the paper I will try to indicate what might have led Descartes *not* to draw the conclusion it is so natural to draw from God's causal activity.[21]

To begin the textual case, I would like to point out one striking fact: Descartes *never*, as far as I am aware, denies that bodies are genuine causes of motion, although his views on God's causal activity might be thought to entail such a denial. This is significant because if Descartes were an occasionalist in the matter of body-body causation, one would expect him to say so at some point. One would, of course, expect an occasionalist to employ often loose or nontechnical language in which he apparently attributes causal power to bodies, but one would also expect him somewhere, sometime, to cancel the impression of such nontechnical passages by explicitly denying that bodies are genuine causes. But this Descartes never does.[22] This fact should make us cautious about attributing to Descartes an acceptance of the apparent implication of his views on God's causal activity.

This caution turns to alarm when we realize that not only does Descartes not deny that bodies are causes but he also says or implies that bodies *are* causes. He does this not just in nontechnical passages but even in those passages in which he is apparently carefully spelling out the causes of motion, in those passages in which he is giving us his official account of the causation of motion. If Descartes is an occasionalist, at the very least he must, in those passages in which he is laying out his true views on causation, be careful not to say or imply that bodies are among the causes of motion. But as I will now argue, in those very passages, he does precisely this.

First I want to consider a particularly revealing and sometimes mistranslated passage from *Principles* 2:40. There Descartes is stating his third law of motion. This law is especially important for understanding the *causes* of motion because the law spells out the conditions under which bodies change their motion or rest upon encountering another body. The law specifies that in such an encounter the same quantity of motion is maintained by virtue of God's immutability.[23] Since the third law thus covers all those cases in which for Descartes bodies are caused to change their motion (with the exception, as Descartes points out, of any cases in which changes in motion are caused by human or angelic minds), his discussion of this law can be seen as central to his official account of what causes changes in motion. It would be particularly important therefore, if Descartes is indeed an occasionalist in this matter, for him *not* to say in his discussion of this law that *bodies* are causes of these changes. But look at what he does say: "Atque omnes causae particulares mutationum, quae corporibus accidunt, in hac tertia lege continentur, saltem eae quae ipsae corporeae sunt." I translate this as follows: "And all the particular causes of changes which occur in bodies are covered by [contained in] this third law, at least those that are themselves corporeal."[24]

It seems that Descartes is here recognizing particular causes that are somehow distinct from the third law itself, though somehow covered by it. What particular causes does he have in mind? I believe he has in mind *bodily* causes of changes in motion, cases in which one body that is moving or at rest causes changes in the motion or rest of another body. To show this, let's focus on the last clause that I quoted — "at least those that are themselves corporeal." If Descartes means those *causes* that are themselves corporeal, then he would be explicitly saying that the third law covers corporeal causes, or bodily causes. So in addition to the third law as a cause of changes in motion, Descartes would also seem to be asserting here that bodies themselves are particular causes of motion.[25]

But does Descartes mean those *causes* that are corporeal?[26] There is strong evidence that he does. Let's look more closely at the Latin. The demonstrative pronoun (*eae*) is the feminine plural, and this could refer to *causes* (*causae*) or *changes* (*mutationum*) since both of these nouns in Latin are feminine and, in this sentence, plural. (The pronoun cannot grammatically refer back to bodies (*corporibus*) since that noun in Latin is neuter.) Now John Cottingham's translation in CSM I takes *eae* to refer to changes.[27] But this would be odd since, based on this reading, Descartes would in a single sentence inexplicably switch from saying that the law in question covers *causes* of changes that bodies undergo to saying that it covers the bodily changes themselves. On the reading I am suggesting, Descartes is concerned throughout this sentence with *causes* as covered by the law. This provides, I believe, a smoother reading of the sentence. Another oddity of the Cottingham reading is the following. This translation portrays Descartes as restricting his interest here to a subclass of the changes that bodies undergo, that is the corporeal changes. But such a restriction would be meaningless since, it seems, any change that a body (*corpus*) undergoes would *eo ipso* be a corporeal change. This also counts against the Cottingham reading.

Further evidence that Descartes is speaking of those *causes* that are corporeal comes from the sentence following the one we have been examining: "I am not here inquiring into the existence or nature of any power to move bodies which may be possessed by human minds, or the minds of angels." Descartes specifies that he is not here speaking of the power of human or angelic minds — incorporeal entities — to cause motion. That would fit in with his restriction in the previous sentence only if that restriction were a restriction to corporeal *causes*. If Descartes were saying, as Cottingham would have it, that the law covers all *changes* that are corporeal, then since changes in bodies brought about by finite minds are no less corporeal than any other changes in bodies, it would follow that he would be holding that the third law covers those changes in bodies brought about by finite minds. But it is clear from the next sentence that Descartes is bracketing the causes of bodily motion brought about by finite minds, so based on this reading Descartes's claim to be covering all corporeal *changes* would be too broad. But his claim to be covering all corporeal *causes* would fit in perfectly with the next sentence that brackets concern with incorporeal causes.

If we turn to Picot's French translation of the *Principles* (which met with Descartes's approval) the case for seeing Descartes as being concerned with those *causes* that are corporeal is made even stronger. The French reads: "Les causes particuliers des changemens qui arrivent aux corps, sont toutes comprises en cette re-gle, au moin celles qui sont corporelles." Here *celles* translates *eae* and, like *eae*, it is a feminine plural demonstrative pronoun. What does it refer to? In this case, the gen-ders of the French words for "change" and for "cause" help us out. The French *causes* is a feminine noun, so *celles* can refer to this word. But unlike the Latin *mutationum*, the French word *changemens* that Descartes (or Picot) uses is masculine. So *celles* cannot refer to this word. The French version of the *Principles* thus indicates very strongly that Descartes is speaking here of the third law as covering those causes of bodily changes that are themselves corporeal.

As I noted, this result shows that Descartes is stating in *Principles* 2:40 that there are bodily, particular causes of motion, that is, that bodies or their states cause mo-tion. As I also pointed out, if Descartes is an occasionalist in the case of body-body causation, this is precisely what Descartes should *not* say here because the discussion of the third law is one of the most important places in which he gives us his official view on the causation of motion. Thus it would be imperative for Descartes, if he were indeed an occasionalist in this matter, not to make such a claim. But he does make such a claim.

I want to argue now that Descartes's notion of tending or equivalently striving, a notion that plays a prominent role in his discussion of the causes of motion, also provides strong evidence for believing that he holds that bodies are genuine causes of motion.

Let's begin with Descartes's notion of striving, which is explained most clearly in *Principles* 3:56:

> When I say that the globules of the second element 'strive' [*conari, font quelque ef-fort*] to move away from the centers around which they revolve, it should not be thought that therefore I am attributing some thought to them from which this striv-ing proceeds. I mean merely that they are positioned and pushed into motion in such a way that they will in fact travel in that direction, unless they are prevented by some other cause [*si a nulla alia causa impediantur, si elles n'estoient retenues par aucune autre cause*].

This passage suggests the following Cartesian account of striving:

> What x strives to do is what x will do unless prevented by external causes.[28]

Descartes's notion of tending seems to be equivalent to his notion of striving.[29] Consider, for example, this passage from chapter 7 of *Le Monde*: a moving body "al-ways has a tendency to go in a straight line and . . . it goes in a circle only under con-straint" (CSM I, 96; AT XI, 44; see also AT XI, 84).[30] Descartes thus seems to be say-ing that a moving body tends to go in a straight line unless prevented by external causes. This view also seems to be at work in *Principles* 2:37. First Descartes says that if a body is moving it will not "lose this motion of its own accord [*sua sponte*] and without being checked by something else."[31] He contrasts this view with the Aristotelian-scholastic account, according to which "it is in the very nature of mo-tion to come to an end, or to tend [*tendere*] towards a state of rest."[32] On this ac-count, moving bodies will stop even without being checked by an external cause. Descartes seems to be saying here that on his own view, in contrast with the

Aristotelian-scholastic view, a moving body *tends* to keep moving. He explicitly makes such a claim about the tendency of moving bodies in the course of stating his second law of nature: "every part of matter, considered in itself, never tends to continue moving along any curved lines but only along straight lines" (*Principles* 2:39). Descartes's point in *Principles* 2:37 is that, on the Aristotelian-scholastic account, a body tends to stop because that is what it will do in the absence of external causes keeping it in motion, and on Descartes's own account, a moving body tends to move because that is what it will do unless prevented by an external cause. (Similarly, a body at rest, for Descartes, will continue to be at rest unless prevented by an external cause.)[33]

That Descartes is interested specifically in external *causes* as those in terms of which the tendency of a body is to be understood is evident from various passages. In articulating his principle of persistence early in *Principles* 2:37, Descartes says that each thing, insofar as it is simple and undivided, always remains in the same state, as far as it can, and never changes except as a result of external causes (*causis externis*). He then goes on to give (later in *Principles* 2:37) his account of the tendency of things to stay in the same state. Indeed, in *Principles* 2:43, Descartes restates the first law, which does not explicitly mention the *tendency* of bodies to remain in the same state, in a way that does invoke this tendency: "everything tends, so far as it can, [*tendat quantum in se est*] to persist in the same state, as laid down in our first law." Since the first law is explicated in *Principles* 2:37 in terms of a thing's independence of external causes, we can see that Descartes's notion of tendency also involves this kind of reference to external causes.[34]

So the general account of tending at work in the passages introducing the laws of nature (i.e., in the passages in which Descartes explicitly discusses the causes of motion) and elsewhere is this:

What x tends to do is what x will do unless prevented by external causes.

Now what external causes does Descartes have in mind when he talks here of external causes as relevant to his account of tending? It is clear that these external causes are, at least in some cases, external *bodies* and not God or laws of nature. In other words, I think that in his account of tending, when Descartes speaks of external causes, he means to bracket causes such as God and laws. To show that this is so, I will first argue that if Descartes is not bracketing causes such as God and the laws of nature here, then he would be forced to contradict some of his most fundamental claims about the tendency of bodies. I will then provide direct textual evidence for the view that the external causes Descartes is interested in in connection with his account of tending are indeed external bodies.

First, consider what Descartes must hold if, for him, God does count among the relevant external causes. As we know from Descartes's theory of divine sustenance, each body would go out of existence unless caused to continue in existence by God.[35] So each existing body would stop existing unless prevented by God from going out of existence. In this sense then, if God is indeed within the scope of the external causes invoked in the notion of tending, Descartes would be committed to saying that each body tends to go out of existence. But this clearly goes against Descartes's view that "nothing can by its own nature be carried toward its opposite, or towards its own destruction" (*Principles* 2:37; see also AT XI, 40; CSM I, 94).

Furthermore, putting aside the issue of divine sustenance of the existence of bodies, let's focus simply on God's activity of causing the motion of bodies.[36] If a moving body were not caused to continue moving by God's activity, what would it do? It would, I believe, stop moving. This is suggested by Descartes's claim in *Principles* 2:36 that God is "the general cause of *all* the motions in the world" (my emphasis). This seems to imply that when a body moves or continues to move, God's causal activity must somehow be at work. Thus, if this activity ceases to cause the motion of a body that is currently in motion, that body will no longer be in motion; that is, on the assumption that the body continues to exist at all, the body will stop moving. Descartes's letter to More of August 1649 suggests a similar conclusion: "I agree that 'if matter is left to itself and receives no impulse from anywhere' it will remain entirely still. But it is impelled by God [*impellitur a Deo*]" (AT V, 404; CSMK 381). This passage indicates that all moving bodies receive an impulse from God and that without this causal activity from God, a body will remain still.[37] Now, if we considered God's activity of causing motion as one of the external causes relevant to Descartes's account of tending, then we would have to say that a moving body would tend to stop moving. This is true because it will stop moving unless prevented from stopping by the external cause of God's activity with regard to motion. But to say that a moving body tends to stop moving is to affirm precisely the Aristotelian-scholastic view that Descartes is at great pains to reject. For this reason, I think we must see Descartes's account of tending as not including among the relevant external causes God's activity of causing motion. Furthermore, since the laws of nature are simply manifestations of the immutability of God's causal activity, we can, I think, also say that these laws are not included among the external causes Descartes has in mind. Thus I think that Descartes's account of tending can be presented more explicitly in the following way:

> What x tends to do is what x will do unless prevented by external causes other than God and the laws of nature.[38]

Read in this way, Descartes's account of tending is analogous to his account of substance. His account of tending brackets external causes such as God and God's activity. Bracketing these causes allows Descartes to say that, on his notion of tending, bodies in motion tend to stay in motion. But one can construct an unqualified notion of tending that does not bracket in this way the activity of God. On such a stronger notion, bodies in motion would not, as we have seen, tend to stay in motion. Although I have found no clear sign of this stronger notion of tending in Descartes's work, it parallels in some respects the stronger of his two notions of substance. For Descartes, a substance is "a thing which exists in such a way as to depend on no other thing for its existence" (*Principles* 1:51). Now, if "no other thing" is understood to include God, then, as Descartes notes, no finite thing would count as a substance since for him each finite thing does depend for its existence on God. But Descartes is willing to allow that certain finite things — finite minds and bodies — do count as genuine substances if they depend on no other thing *except God*, if, as Descartes puts it, "they need only the concurrence of God in order to exist" (*Principles* 1:52).[39] This weaker notion of substance allows one to bracket the activity of God in order to determine whether a thing has the independence required for being a substance; this notion is thus analogous to the weaker notion of tending that Descartes employs. The weaker notion of tending allows one to bracket the activity of God in order to determine what a thing will do unless prevented by the activity of external causes, and thus in order to determine what a thing tends to do. In a similar way, the stronger notion of substance is analogous to the stronger notion of tending.

Given that Descartes eliminates God and the laws of nature as the external causes relevant to his account of tending, what then are the external causes he has in mind? Descartes himself provides the answer. When he explicates his principle of persistence, and thus his account of tending, it's clear that he is speaking very often of external *bodies*. Consider, for example, the initial statement of this principle in *Principles* 2:37. In the Latin version, Descartes says that each thing, insofar as it can, always remains in the same state and never changes except as a result of external causes. In the French version, Descartes (or Picot) makes the reference to external causes more specific by saying this: ". . . never changes except through collision with others [*par la rencontre des autres*]." Presumably these others with which a body collides are not God or the laws of nature but rather other bodies. This provides strong evidence that Descartes sees the external causes relevant to the principle of persistence and thus relevant to the account of tending as external *bodies*. A comparison of the Latin and French versions of *Principles* 2:41 points to a similar conclusion. In the Latin version, Descartes says: "Everything that is not composite but simple, as motion is, always persists in bodies so long as it is not destroyed by an external cause." In the French version, the last clause reads: "so long as it is not forced to change by colliding with some other object [*jusques à ce qu'elle soit contrainte de changer par la rencontre de quelqu'autre*]."[40] Further evidence that the external causes Descartes is interested in are external bodies is found later in the French version of *Principles* 2:41. There Descartes speaks of the cause that makes a body lose its motion, and he specifies that this cause is "the resistance of the body which deflects its path [*la resistance du corps qui l'empesche de passer outre*]." Finally, consider *Principles* 2:38, where Descartes elaborates on his principle of persistence in the following way: "What is once in motion continues to move until it is slowed down by bodies that are in the way." Here again external bodies seem to be the causes relevant to the application of the principle of persistence and thus to determining whether or not a body will in fact do what it has a tendency to do.

I conclude that to make sense of Descartes's notion of tending, we must, for the reasons given in the last few paragraphs, see him as taking not God or the laws of nature but external bodies to be among the external causes in question, and thus, a fortiori, we must see Descartes as regarding bodies as causes. Since, as his examples indicate, the external causes cause changes in motion and rest, we must see Descartes as regarding external bodies as causes of changes in motion.[41]

Now, Descartes's account of tending is at work, and prominently so, in his discussion of the laws of nature, and this discussion itself is crucial to his presentation of his account of the causes of motion. Since the account of tending itself clearly involves the claim that bodies are causes of motion—and since, if Descartes were an occasionalist, we would expect him to avoid such a claim in those very passages in which he introduces and explains his views on the causation of motion — we have once again strong evidence against the occasionalist reading of Descartes and for the claim that he sees bodies as genuine causes of motion.[42]

For all the reasons given in this section, I believe, contra Garber and Hatfield, that there is good evidence that in the very passages in which Descartes is most directly concerned with the causes of motion, far from denying that bodies cause motion, he actually says or implies that they do.

## Force

Much of the debate about whether Descartes accepts the view that bodies are genuine causes of motion has centered around the issue of whether bodies genuinely have any force or power to produce motion. If they do not, then it is hard to see how bodies can be genuine causes; if they do have force, then it would seem that they can be genuine causes of motion. This connection betweeen force and causation is a natural one to make in interpreting Descartes for he does seem to identify forces and causes or at least to see them as intimately related. For example, he speaks of forces having effects in *Principles* 2:45, and as Gueroult notes, he seems to identify force and cause in *Principles* 1:21.[43]

Now, Descartes does say explicitly that bodies have force, that they have some kind of power. See, for example, *Principles* 3:57, where he speaks of "the force of moving which is in [the stone] itself [*vim motus quae in ipso est*]." He also speaks of a body's force of continuing in a straight line and of another body's force of resisting (*Principles* 2:40). In a letter to Mersenne of 28 October 1640, Descartes says: "It is certain that a body, once it has begun to move, has in itself for that reason the force to continue to move, just as, once it is stationary in a certain place, it has for that reason the force to continue to remain there" (AT III, 213, CSMK 155). All of these passages seem to take seriously the idea that bodies have force (and thus can be causes).

However, defenders of an occasionalist reading of Descartes would argue that these passages are not to be taken at face value. They would argue that for Descartes force is not, after all, really in bodies. One way to reach this conclusion is by developing a line of thought suggested in *Principles* 2:43. There Descartes explicitly takes up the question of what constitutes the force that he attributes to bodies. He says (in a passage quoted in part earlier) that this force "consists simply in the fact that everything tends, so far as it can, to persist in the same state, as laid down in our first law." So for Descartes the force of a body is nothing other than its tendency to persist in the same state. But this tendency stems directly and completely from God's activity of preserving the same quantity of motion in the universe. Bodies would not tend to stay in the same state were God not preserving things in accordance with his immutability (*Principles* 2:37). Thus for Descartes the force of a body, like its tendency, is somehow grounded in the causal activity of God.

Now, does the fact that the force that Descartes attributes to bodies is grounded in God's causal activity show that for Descartes bodies do not genuinely have force? Hatfield thinks that it does. He holds that since the tendency of bodies is grounded in "the immutable nature of the divine action that preserves bodies at each moment" ("Force (God) in Descartes' Physics," p. 126), the force attributed to bodies by Descartes in passages such as those cited above cannot be a real or legitimate force. Hatfield's point seems to be that because of God's role in the production of motion, bodies do not in fact have force.[44]

But this line of thought would show that for Descartes bodies do not have force only if Descartes would hold that the fact that God causes motion precludes it from being the case that bodies themselves can legitimately be said to cause motion. If bodies could still be causes, then, it seems, they could still have forces. But as we have already seen, it is far from clear that Descartes thinks that God's causal role is incompatible with a legitimate causal role for bodies to play. In fact, as I have emphasized, those very passages in which Descartes elucidates God's causal role contain a commitment to the view that bodies are indeed causes. So we can be confident that forces are not really in bodies because of the above line of thought only if we can be confident that for Descartes bodies are not legitimately causes. But as we've already seen, we cannot be confident of this: there are strong signs that Descartes sees bodies as causes even though God causes motion.

Thus the fact that, as Descartes says in *Principles* 2:43, a body's force consists simply in its tendency to stay in the same state, a tendency that in turn is simply a function of God's causal activity, does not clearly show that for Descartes this force is not really in bodies. I admit that one might find the claim that I am suggesting Descartes holds rather unnatural. Earlier I admitted that one might find it quite natural to infer from God's causal activity, as described by Descartes, that bodies are not genuine causes of motion. Similarly, I also grant that it is quite natural to infer from God's causal activity that bodies do not have any genuine force for causing motion. Nonetheless, there is no evidence, I believe, for the view that Descartes draws this inference; that is, there is no evidence that the force that Descartes attributes to bodies is, for him, anything other than genuine.

I think that for similar reasons, we must conclude that Garber's somewhat different argument for the claim that bodies do not possess force, according to Descartes, also does not succeed. Garber focuses not so much on *Principles* 2:43 as on the fact that, for Descartes, bodies are purely geometrical objects. As Descartes puts it, "I recognize no matter in corporeal things apart from that which the geometers call quantity, and take as the objects of their demonstrations, i.e. that to which every kind of division, shape and motion is applicable" (*Principles* 2:64; see also AT VI, 227, and Garber, *Descartes' Metaphysical Physics*, pp. 68–69). Garber holds that forces or counterfactual properties such as tendencies cannot be in things merely extended.[45] Now, surely a purely geometrical object cannot have a tendency or counterfactual property simply by virtue of its being a purely geometrical object. If that is what Garber means by saying that bodies do not have forces or tendencies for Descartes, then Garber is right: Cartesian bodies do not have forces of this kind.

This argument, however, leaves open the possibility that Descartes holds that a body can have force in some other way than simply by virtue of being a purely geometrical object. Descartes does hold, of course, that purely geometrical objects can stand in certain relations to God. (For Descartes, they are, after all, as Garber himself emphasizes, caused by God and set into motion by God.) Now, one of the relations a purely geometrical object may stand in to God is this: God and his immutability see to it that a certain purely geometrical object maintains its current state of motion or rest unless it encounters a certain other body, in which case God sees to it that the first body's state changes in such a way as to preserve the overall quantity of motion in the two bodies. By virtue of standing in this relation to God and his immutability, a purely geometrical object has certain counterfactual properties: it would undergo certain changes or remain in the same state in certain circumstances. Furthermore, in virtue of this relation, we can meaningfully speak of it as having a tendency of a certain kind: a tendency to remain in the same state. This is a tendency grounded not simply in its character as a purely geometrical object but also and crucially in its relation to God. Yet it is a tendency nonetheless, and it is a tendency that seems perfectly compatible with the body's character as a purely geometrical object. This tendency grounded in God's immutability is all that Descartes refers to, as I have claimed and as *Principles* 2:43 indicates, when saying that bodies have force.[46]

Now Garber, of course, agrees that bodies stand in these relations to God compatibly with their purely geometrical character. He denies, though, that bodies really have force for Descartes. Garber thus apparently holds that for Descartes the force or tendency grounded in God's immutability is not a genuine force. Again, in light of Descartes's claim that God causes motion, this might appear to be a reasonable conclusion. However, for reasons already given in connection with Hatfield's argument, I see no evidence that Descartes draws this conclusion from that claim that God causes motion. That is, I see no sign that for Descartes the fact that the force or tendency bodies have is grounded in God's causal activity makes that force not genuine or real.[47]

In suggesting that for Descartes bodies do have genuine force, I am in agreement with Martial Gueroult and Alan Gabbey.[48] However, I am not clear on the extent to which they hold, as I do, that this force is nothing but a tendency grounded in God's activity. I believe that I emphasize more than they do that this force or tendency is nothing but a body's standing in a certain relation to God. Cartesian forces, as Gueroult and Gabbey conceive them, seem to be less austere than this. Gueroult, for example, says that these forces are "immanent" in nature or extension ("Metaphysics and Physics of Force," p. 198). He also says that moving force "is nothing other than the power which — from within them — puts each one [body] in duration and consequently cannot be distinguished from their existence" (p. 220). I am not sure if these claims are compatible with the interpretation of Descartes's account of force I have developed.[49] In one sense, then, my view falls between that of Garber, on the one hand, and those of Gueroult and Gabbey, on the other. Like Garber, I emphasize that for Descartes bodies are purely geometrical objects and that whatever force or tendency they have is grounded solely in their relation to God. Gueroult and Gabbey, as Garber points out,[50] do not seem to take proper account of the purely geometrical nature of bodies. However, unlike Garber, I hold that for Descartes this force grounded in God's activity is a genuine force that a body possesses. In Descartes's view, as I interpret it, what it is for a body really to have force is for it to stand in a certain relation to God and his immutability. In saying that bodies do really have force for Descartes, my view, then, is in one respect more like Gueroult's and Gabbey's views than it is like Garber's.

Before leaving this section on force, it is important to discuss a passage that has been invoked both by proponents of the occasionalist reading of Descartes and by proponents of the nonoccasionalist reading. Writing to More in August 1649, Descartes explicitly takes up the topic of the force that is moving a body: "The moving force can be that of God conserving as much transference in matter as he placed in it at the first moment of creation or also that of a created substance, like our mind, or something else to which He gave the power of moving a body" (AT V, 403–404; CSMK 381). What is the "something else" to which God may give the power to move bodies? In particular, does Descartes mean to include bodies as among those creatures with power to move bodies? Some have claimed that Descartes does include bodies here.[51] Garber, however, emphasizes that bodies are not explicitly mentioned in this sentence, and he goes on to claim, in keeping with his occasionalist reading of Descartes in the matter of body-body causation, the following:

> If Descartes really thought that bodies could be causes of motion like God, us, and probably angels, I suspect that he would have included them *explicitly* in the answer to More; if bodies could be genuine causes of motion, this would be too important a fact to pass unmentioned.[52]

Now I agree with Garber here to the following extent: the sentence in question is not explicitly concerned with bodies as having force or power, and in the context of Descartes's correspondence with More, it seems more likely that Descartes has angels in mind as the "something else." Nonetheless, the sentence in question does not deny that bodies have such power; in fact, in the very next paragraph of the letter, Descartes seems to claim directly that bodies have a certain kind of force, the force of resistance. In response to some of More's questions concerning Descartes's notion of rest, Descartes writes:

> I think that what causes you difficulty in this matter is that you conceive of a certain force in a quiescent body by which it resists motion, as being something positive, namely as a certain action distinct from the body's being at rest; whereas in fact it is nothing but a modal entity. (AT V, 404; CSMK 381–382; cf. AT V, 348)[53]

I read this passage as saying, in part, that there *is* a force of resistance in a resting body. More mistakenly, according to Descartes, sees this force of resistance as an action over and above the rest itself, but Descartes is not denying that there is such a force of resistance. More has merely misconceived its nature. So here Descartes seems to be attributing a certain kind of force to bodies in the very letter to More in which he earlier was silent on whether bodies have force or power.[54]

Now Garber, of course, must read this passage differently, as one in which Descartes is not attributing a force of resistance to bodies. Garber says that the *it* that is ascribed to bodies as a modal entity is the positive something that More regards as being in bodies and not any force of resisting: "The 'positive something' that More imagines to be in resting bodies themselves is only the state of rest, and *that* is only a mode" (*Descartes' Metaphysical Physics*, p. 362, n. 29). If this reading is accepted, then Descartes would not in this passage be attributing any kind of force to bodies themselves. Garber's reading of the passage is grammatically legitimate since no explicit subject is given in the last clause.[55] However, I think that this is a rather strained reading of the passage (and Garber himself seems somewhat unsure of his reading). The sentence more naturally reads with the "it" of the final clause referring to force. The logical structure of the passage seems to be this: More conceives of X as if X were Y; whereas in fact (*cum tamen*) X is Z. On Garber's reading, the structure is this: More conceives of X as if X were Y, whereas in fact Y is Z. Although not, I suppose, absolutely impossible, this reading seems rather odd and for that reason I prefer the reading according to which Descartes is attributing some kind of force to bodies in this passage. For this reason also, I take the letter to More as in the end providing evidence for rather than against the view that for Descartes bodies have force and are causes of motion. This, however, is not my main textual argument for that view. The chief textual considerations are those I developed in the previous section. My primary purpose in discussing the letter to More is to show that at the very least it does *not* provide support for the occasionalist reading of Descartes.

## God's Causation of Motion and God's Creation of the Eternal Truths

I think I have provided strong textual evidence for the view that for Descartes, despite God's causal role with regard to motion, it is still true that bodies are causes of motion. Nevertheless, this interpretation still faces a major challenge: It may seem rather uncharitable to attribute this view to Descartes. As I mentioned at the beginning, given that Descartes holds that God directly moves bodies around according to certain rules, bodies themselves seem to have no causal role to play. As Malebranche would put it, they are merely occasional causes and not genuine causes. Such a conclusion seems so obvious and natural a one to draw from Descartes's claims about God's causation of motion that to fail to attribute it to Descartes would, it seems, be highly uncharitable and unfair. Even with supporting textual evidence of the kind I have presented, one should therefore be wary of attributing instead to Descartes the possibly incoherent view I have attributed to him, unless one can find in his thought as a whole systematic and principled reasons for holding such a view. The remaining challenge to the interpretation of Descartes I have developed is to find such reasons.

In this section, I want to go some distance toward meeting this challenge. I want to show why the view that God's causal role is compatible with that of finite bodies might have appealed to Descartes. It will emerge that considerations central to his conception of God's activity and most explicit in his doctrine of the creation of the eternal truths may be behind the views on causation that I have attributed to him. In fact, given this conception of God's activity, we can see that the view I find in Descartes is more genuinely Cartesian than the occasionalist alternative.

I will begin by drawing a certain analogy between Descartes's reasoning, as I have interpreted it, in the case of causation and his reasoning in the case of the creation of the eternal truths. To do this, I want to make more explicit the general structure of the view I have attributed to Descartes on causation. First note that for Descartes, as I have interpreted him, bodies have the power to move other bodies or the ability to cause changes in motion, and they have this ability purely in virtue of their tendency to remain in the same state.[56] Now, as Descartes makes clear and as I have emphasized, bodies have such a tendency simply in virtue of God's activity in causing motion in a way consonant with his immutability. So, on the view that I claim is to be found in Descartes, bodies have the ability to cause changes in motion in virtue of *God's* causing those changes in motion.

Let's take a particular case: body A moving in a certain way encounters body B and there follows a certain change in the motion of B. On Descartes's view, as I am interpreting it, God causes this change in B. Furthermore, A also can be said to cause the change in B *and* A causes this change in virtue of God's immutability, as reflected in part in his causing the change in B. So, in short, A causes a change in B in virtue of God's causing the change in B. But how can this be? Given that A does not, of course, cause God to cause the change in B,[57] it is hard to see how A is doing any causal work at all. The problem lies not simply in attempting to reduce A's causation of motion to some fact about God. Rather, the problem lies more specifically in the attempt to reduce A's causation of motion to a causal fact about an agent, that is, God, that acts independently of A. It is hard to see how a different and independent entity's causation of a certain motion can be that in virtue of which A's genuine causation of that very motion consists. In such a case, A would seem to have no genuine causal role to play. In other words, Descartes seems to succeed not in reducing A's causality to God's causality but rather in eliminating or denying A's causality.

The structure of the problem is this. Descartes holds that

(1) A causes B's motion to change.

Descartes also claims that (1) is true in virtue of

(2) God, in keeping with his immutability, causes B to move.

But given that

(3) God's activity is not dependent on A

(2) seems, contrary to what Descartes holds, incapable of grounding (1).

Now, compare the structure of Descartes's view here with the structure of his view concerning the creation of the eternal truths.[58] It is well known that for Descartes God somehow has power over the eternal truths. Thus Descartes says:

> You . . . ask what necessitated God to create these truths; and I reply that he was free to make it not true that all the radii of the circle are equal — just as free as he was not to create the world. (Letter to Mersenne, 27 May 1630; AT I, 152; CSMK 25)

> I turn to the difficulty of conceiving how God would have been acting freely and indifferently if he had made it false that the three angles of a triangle were equal to two right angles, or in general that contradictories could not be true together. It is easy to dispel this difficulty by considering that the power of God cannot have any limits. (Letter to Mesland, 2 May 1644; AT IV, 118; CSMK 235)

> I do not think that we should ever say of anything that it cannot be brought about by God. For since every basis of truth and goodness depends on his omnipotence, I would not dare to say that God cannot make a mountain without a valley, or bring it about that 1 and 2 are not 3. (Letter for Arnauld, 29 July 1648; AT V, 223–224; CSMK 358–359)

Thus, for Descartes, God's free will somehow made it true that, for example, squares have four sides. I will call the proposition that squares have four sides "p." Now, it might be thought that this freedom on the part of God precludes p from being necessary. But Descartes denies this. On the contrary, he holds that God not only willed p to be true but also willed p to be necessary, and that p is therefore necessary:

> I do not think that the essences of things, and the mathematical truths which we can know concerning them, are independent of God. Nevertheless I do think that they are immutable and eternal, since the will and decree of God willed and decreed that they should be so. (AT VII, 380; CSM II, 261)

> It is because he [God] willed that the three angles of a triangle should necessarily equal two right angles that this is now true and cannot be otherwise; and so on in other cases. (AT VII, 432; CSM II, 291)

In a similar vein, Descartes says in the letter to Mesland cited earlier that there are "things which God could have made possible, but which he has nevertheless wished to make impossible" (AT IV, 118; CSMK 235). Thus for Descartes, p is necessary in virtue of God's willing p to be necessary.[59]

Now, this might seem incoherent or at least bizarre. God's willing p to be necessary is free, just as any other act of God's will (if it were not, then even God's willing that p be true could not be free). So it seems that God could have willed that p not be necessary. Indeed, it seems that, given Descartes's claim that God's power has no limits, God could have willed that p be false.[60] But if God could have willed that p be not necessary and could have willed that p be false, how can p be necessary? If God had willed that p be false, then since God's will is, of course, always efficacious, p would have been false. Thus it seems that p is not necessary. Yet Descartes nonetheless clearly affirms that p is necessary. In light of his general views on the indifference and absolute freedom of God's will, it seems that God's willing that p be necessary is unable to ground the necessity of p. Yet Descartes asserts that it is able to do this. God's willing that p be necessary seems to be incapable of doing the job that Descartes assigns to it, that is, making p be genuinely necessary.

We can represent the structure of the problem in the following way. Descartes says:

(4)  p is necessary.

Descartes also holds that (4) is true because

(5)  God willed p to be necessary.

But given that

(6) God's will is absolutely free and has no limits

(5) seems incapable of grounding (4). Yet Descartes asserts that it does.

The similarities with the case of the causation of motion are obvious. In each case the independence of God's causal activity[61] (its lack of dependence on A, in the case of causation, or its lack of dependence on any external constraint whatsoever, in the case of the creation of the eternal truths) seems to render God's activity unfit to do what Descartes says it can and does do. In both cases, God's independent causal activity is said to underwrite a certain claim ("A causes B to move" or "p is necessary"), whereas in fact this activity might more naturally be thought to undermine that claim. Now, the fact that Descartes rather clearly holds such a view in the case of the creation of the eternal truths is enough by itself to make it more plausible to think that he holds such a view, as I have argued, in the case of the causation of motion. In light of Descartes's rather provocative and, some might say, outlandish views on necessity and God's activity, it may no longer seem so uncharitable and unfair to attribute to him strikingly analogous views in the case of the causation of motion.[62]

This good result of looking at Descartes's doctrine of the divine causation of motion in light of his doctrine of the divine creation of the eternal truths invites us to examine more closely the connections between the two. If we do, we will find even further reason for attributing to Descartes the nonoccasionalist account of causation, and we will get even further insight into why he might have held this unusual view.

Let's begin by stating in a somewhat different way the problem posed by Descartes's claims about the eternal truths. Given that God freely willed that p, that squares have four sides, it might seem that it is not part of the nature or essence[63] of squares to have four sides. After all, if God *freely* willed that p, then it is possible that squares do not have four sides and if this is possible then it cannot be part of the very nature of squares to have four sides.[64] However, despite the fact that it is natural to draw this conclusion about the nature of squares, Descartes does not draw this conclusion. Instead, he holds that it is not possible that squares do not have four sides and that it is part of the nature of squares to have four sides.[65] In fact, Descartes goes so far as to say that God's activity of willing p to be true and necessary *bestows*, as it were, an essence or nature on squares. In this regard, recall the passage from the Fifth Replies in which Descartes says that the essences of things are not independent of God (AT VII, 380; CSM II, 261). In the letter of 27 May 1630 to Mersenne, Descartes says that God "is the author of the essence of created things, no less than of their existence; and this essence is nothing other than the eternal truths" (AT I, 152; CSMK 25). Harry Frankfurt puts the point this way: "Asserting that the eternal truths are laid down by God is tantamount, then, to saying that God is the creator of essences."[66] Thus Descartes's view is that God's causal activity is capable of bestowing natures on things. The point holds not just for squares but also for anything with a nature.[67] In this way, we can see that Descartes's perhaps outlandish views on necessity can be described as outlandish views on the natures of objects. For Descartes, something can be or can follow from the nature of an object even though that nature has been imposed on the object by the free causal activity of God and thus even though God could have imposed a different nature on the object. To hold that it is not in God's power thus to impose natures on objects would, for Descartes, constitute an illegitimate limitation on God's power.

Now, in his views on the causation of motion, does Descartes make any analogous claims about God's activity bestowing natures on objects? Can we describe his problematic views on the causation of motion in terms of a problem that stems from God's bestowing natures on objects? Rather surprisingly, we can, as we can see by returning to his views on the tendency of bodies to persist in the same state. As I have noted, on my interpretation of Descartes, bodies cause motion in other bodies in virtue of their tendency to remain in the same state. For Descartes this tendency is closely bound up with the nature of a thing. A number of passages indicate that what a thing tends to do is what it does by its very nature. Consider first *Principles* 2:37, in which Descartes describes the Aristotelian-scholastic account of motion in this way: "It is in the very nature of motion to come to an end, or to tend towards a state of rest [*ex natura sua cessare, sive tendere ad quietem*]." Descartes here seems to be treating as equivalent the notion of what motion tends to do and the notion of what it does by its very nature. This indicates that Descartes holds the general view that what a thing tends to do is the same as what it does by its very nature.

Further support for attributing to Descartes this general view comes from the next sentence in *Principles* 2:37: "Nothing can by its own nature be carried towards its opposite, or towards its own destruction." This claim is clearly equivalent to the claim made by Descartes in *Le Monde* that nothing tends to destroy itself.[68] Thus once again he seems to treat as equivalent what a thing does by its own nature and what a thing tends to do.

Finally, a rather different source of evidence that Descartes holds this view is the following. As I have demonstrated elsewhere, what a thing tends or strives to do is, for Descartes, what it does *quantum in se est*.[69] This is indicated by the fact that his first law, which in *Principles* 2:37 includes the term *quantum in se est*, is often restated by Descartes in terms involving tendency. See, for example, *Principles* 2:43 and also the connection between *quantum in se est* and striving in *Principles* 3:55. Now, there has been much controversy over how to translate this term, which is also found prominently in Newton and Spinoza. Most literally the term means "insofar as it is in itself," and it is usually taken to indicate that there are limits on the ability of an object to do certain things. That is why I translated the first law earlier as "each thing . . . always remains in the same state, as far as it can." However, there is another dimension to the meaning of this phrase that is not captured by this translation. As I. Bernard Cohen shows in his classic study "'Quantum in se est': Newton's Concept of Inertia in Relation to Descartes and Lucretius," on the contemporary seventeenth-century understanding of the phrase, it could also be expressed by the terms *naturaliter, sua vi,* or *ex natura sua*. So, based on this understanding, what a thing does *quantum in se est* is what it does naturally, or by its own force or from its own nature. As Cohen demonstrates, this contemporary understanding of the phrase would probably have been known to Descartes.[70] Thus, given this understanding and given that for Descartes what a thing tends to do is what it does *quantum in se est*, we can say that for Descartes what a thing tends to do is what it does from its very nature. Here again we have evidence for attributing to Descartes the general view linking nature and tendency.

Now, as we have seen, on my interpretation of Descartes, the motions a body causes are a function of what it tends to do. As we have also seen, what a body tends to do is a function of its nature. Thus, on my reading of Descartes, what motions a body causes are a function of its nature.

In holding that a body's nature is the source of what it can do causally, Descartes, as I have interpreted him, is in agreement with the Aristotelian-scholastic tradition. On this tradition, a body's nature or form is the locus of causal explanations.[71] Now, for reasons mentioned earlier, these forms or natures, as they were traditionally conceived to be, were rejected by Descartes. But in rejecting this conception of the natures of physical objects, he did not reject the general view that we should turn to the natures of bodies in order to account for their causal powers. Cohen makes a similar point: "Both Newton and Descartes were using *quantum in se est* in a way that transformed into the language of the new inertial physics what had been conceived in the traditional physics as 'natural', or 'according to its nature', or 'by nature', or 'by its own force'" ("'Quantum in se est,'" p. 147). Here, despite Descartes's break with Aristotelian-scholastic philosophy, he adopts an important feature of the traditional view of causation.

Since, as we have seen, what a thing tends to do is what it does by its very nature, and since God's action of moving bodies in conformity with his immutability bestows a certain tendency on a body, we can see God's causal activity here as bestowing a certain nature on a body. Because, as we have also seen, what changes in motion a body causes are a function of the body's nature, we can see that God's activity in bestowing a certain nature on a body also bestows on it certain causal powers.

This way of characterizing Descartes's views allows us to describe in a somewhat different way the apparent incoherence facing his account of causation. We might be willing to allow that if certain motions follow somehow from the nature of a given body, then that body causes those motions. (This general insight is captured by the Aristotelian-scholastic account of causation.) But we might go on to object that Descartes is not entitled to say that certain motions follow from the *nature* of a given body. These motions seem rather to follow from the causal activity of *God*. The fact that the motions are brought about by God's activity seems to preclude the nature of a given body from having any causal bearing on those motions and thus seems to preclude the body itself from being a cause. Nevertheless, Descartes does say that bodies cause motion and that these motions somehow follow from the natures of those bodies. We are thus back at our initial puzzlement over Descartes's views on causation. The focal point of the puzzlement now, however, is this: how can God's activity in causing motion bestow a certain nature on bodies?[72]

This latest characterization of Descartes's position on the causation of motion brings out an even deeper connection with his views on the eternal truths. Not only is it the case that both in his views on the creation of the eternal truths and in his views on causation, Descartes appeals to God's causal power to ground a certain fact (the necessity of p; the fact that body A causes body B to move), that it might more naturally be thought to undermine, but also in each case God purportedly grounds the fact in question by bestowing a certain nature on objects. (In the case of the eternal truths, God bestows, e.g., a nature on squares whereby they have four sides; in the case of causation, God bestows a nature on bodies whereby they tend to persist in the same state in a way that can lead to changes in motion in other bodies.) And just as in the eternal truths case it might seem illegitimate to say that God's activity (of willing that p be necessary) can really impose a certain nature on squares, so, too, it might seem illegitimate to say that God's activity of moving bodies in accordance with his immutability can really impose a nature on a body whereby it can be said to tend to remain in the same state and thus to cause certain motions. In both cases, the problem is at bottom the same: how can God's causal activity impose certain natures on things?

These further connections between Descartes's views on the eternal truths and his views, as I have interpreted them, on the causation of motion make it even more plausible to see Descartes as holding these views on causation. In fact, the rival interpretation, according to which his views on body-body causation are more or less occasionalistic, now appears to be rather un-Cartesian. For Descartes to hold, as he does on Garber's interpretation, that God's activity in causing motion precludes any causation of motion by bodies would be tantamount to saying that God's activity in causing motion cannot endow bodies with a nature of a certain kind, a nature whereby they tend to stay in the same state in a way that can lead to changes in motion in other bodies. However, Descartes's views on God's ability to endow things with natures by means of his causal activity — a view most explicit in Descartes's discussion of the creation of the eternal truths — makes one suspicious of any claim (such as the one in effect made by Garber) that for Descartes God's causal activity with regard to motion cannot endow bodies with certain natures. Such a claim now appears as a perhaps illegitimate limitation on God's power over the natures of objects. And for this reason I think that the view Garber attributes to Descartes may actually be rather unpalatable to Descartes, who as we have seen, rejects limitations on God's power with regard to natures. So paradoxically, perhaps, a view such as that of Garber's Descartes — which holds that because God causes motion, bodies do not — limits God's power in a way that my reading of Descartes does not. By denying any causal role to bodies, Garber's view may seem to make God even more powerful, but I contend that, since this view denies that God's activity of causing motion can bestow a certain nature on bodies, Descartes may well see this view as placing an improper restriction on God's power.[73]

In this light, it seems likely that at least part of the source of Descartes's view that bodies cause motion in virtue of God's causation of motion is his view that God's activity enables God to impose natures on objects. To tie in this way Descartes's views on the causation of motion to this central aspect of his concept of God is to make is seem less uncharitable and unfair to attribute what we can now see as a rather Cartesian view to Descartes. Thus, I believe, I have gone at least some distance toward meeting the challenge raised at the beginning of this section.

I should point out that in meeting this challenge, I am *not* claiming that Descartes's views on the eternal truths *dictate* or *entail* his views on the causation of motion. My claim is rather that his views on the eternal truths can help us isolate certain aspects of his conception of God, which may in part be behind his views on the causation of motion and which add crucial support to the interpretation of his views on causation that I have outlined.[74]

Of course, this response to the challenge raises a number of further questions —

questions that I will not be able to address here. For example, (1) on the view I have attributed to Descartes, the nature of a body consists in or at least somehow involves its tendency to remain in its current state. It is not immediately clear how or if this view is compatible with his view that extension constitutes the nature of a body (*Principles* 1:53, 63; *Dioptrics*, AT VI, 227). The problem here is *not* one of seeing how a purely geometrical object could have qualities such as a tendency. I have already addressed that issue by pointing out that a purely geometrical object can stand in certain relations to God and that its tending to stay in the same state consists entirely in its standing in these relations. The problem I am raising here is a different one: given that an extended object genuinely has this tendency, how can its nature be constituted by extension and also somehow involve this tendency?[75] I suspect that Descartes may have been using the term "nature" in different senses, which he did not completely reconcile.

(2) The answer to the previous question may turn on the answer to the following question. What kind of necessity characterizes the claim that certain motions, in certain circumstances, follow from the nature of a certain body? How is the necessity here related to the necessity that characterizes the eternal truths? For example, does the claim that a body in motion will continue to stay in motion unless prevented by external causes hold with the same kind of necessity as the claim that squares have four sides? If the kind of necessity in question differs, exactly how does it differ? This is another matter that requires further exploration.[76]

(3) Finally, perhaps the most important questions arise in the following way. I have argued that Descartes holds that God's direct causation of motion does not undermine a body's causation of motion and that this view fits in quite well with Descartes's views on the eternal truths. But it is not yet clear *why* Descartes holds these views on causation and necessity. In particular, what is it about God's causal activity that makes it the case that that activity does not have the consequences one might expect it to have? Why doesn't the freedom of God's activity preclude him from bringing it about that certain truths are genuinely necessary? Why doesn't God's causation of motion undermine the claim that bodies are causes of motion? I believe that part of Descartes's answers to these questions would involve two related points: first, that God's activity is incomprehensible; second, that at least some predicates do not apply univocally to God and to creatures. Each of these points, though perhaps in different ways, might lead to the claim that we cannot draw the kinds of conclusions from God's activity that we might straightforwardly expect. But these are obviously quite large topics, which I cannot go into here.[77]

Nevertheless, even without answers to these questions, the textual evidence and systematic considerations I have presented have, I believe, gone a long way in defending the view that for Descartes God's causal activity grounds and does not undermine the causal activity of bodies. Although the occasionalist interpretation of body-body causation in Descartes is initially plausible, this plausibility is outweighed, I believe, by the various arguments I have presented here. Similarly, I would claim that that the interpretations according to which p is after all not necessary — interpretations that might be seen as the modal analogues of Garber's occasionalist reading — have some initial plausibility. Nonetheless, I would argue, they must be rejected for reasons similar to those behind my rejection of Garber's interpretation.[78]

The works of Garber and others have emphasized the role God plays for Descartes in the causation of motion, but we should not let this important fact blind us to the subtle and provocative ways in which, for Descartes, God's causal activity bears upon the causal activity of objects in the world. If we focus, as Garber and others do, on the occasionalist leanings in Descartes, we may miss some of what is most intriguing about his account of the causation of motion and, in particular, we may miss the way in which that account is surprisingly connected with Descartes's views on the creation of the eternal truths and his conception of God as the cause of the natures of things.[79]

## Notes

1. See Garber, "Understanding Interaction: What Descartes Should Have Told Elisabeth"; "How God Causes Motion: Descartes, Divine Sustenance, and Occasionalism"; *Descartes' Metaphysical Physics*, chap. 9, "Descartes and Occasionalism." See also Hatfield, "Force (God) in Descartes' Physics." My description of this view will tend to focus on Garber's version since his is the most detailed. I will, though, frequently refer to Hatfield's important work as well. Other recent authors who take Descartes to deny causal efficacy to bodies with regard to other bodies include Machamer, "Causality and Explanation in Descartes' Natural Philosophy," pp. 178–179; Nadler, "Introduction," in *Causation in Early Modern Philosophy*, pp. 3–4; and Nadler, "Occasionalism and the Question of Arnauld's Cartesianism" (see p. 133, where Nadler speaks of "the occasionalist account of the motion of inanimate bodies in Descartes"). Louis de la Forge was an early advocate of this reading of Descartes. De la Forge says that "It is God who is the first, universal and total cause of motion" (*Traité de L'Esprit de L'Homme* in *Oeuvres Philosophiques*, p. 241). He goes on to say that there is no doubt that "what I have said about the causes of motion and of its nature conform to the thought of Monsieur Descartes" (p. 244). Malebranche also seems to see Descartes as denying that bodies cause motion: "It is ordinarily supposed that bodies can move each other, and this opinion is even attributed to Descartes, contrary to what he expressly says in articles 36 and 37 of the second part of his *Principles of Philosophy*" (*The Search After Truth*, p. 677). On early readings of Descartes as denying causal efficacy to bodies, see Garber, *Descartes' Metaphysical Physics*, p. 365, n. 48, and Hatfield, pp. 136–137.

2. Garber does think that Descartes throughout his career allows that minds can act on bodies, but he sees Descartes as gradually becoming more occasionalistic in the case of body-to-mind causation. On the former point, see especially, "Mind, Body, and the Laws of Nature in Descartes and Leibniz." On the latter point, see especially *Descartes' Metaphysical Physics*, pp. 70–75.

3. Garber, "Descartes and Occasionalism," p. 12, my emphasis.

4. By the claim that Descartes's view would amount to a limited version of occasionalism, I do not mean to imply that the motivations for such a limited version of occasionalism would be similar to the motivations behind Malebranche's and other standard forms of occasionalism. As Garber has emphasized, Malebranche, de la Forge, and others come to their occasionalism out of the conviction that only an infinite thing can be a genuine cause. *If* Descartes is an occasionalist in the body-body case, he would *not* be so because of a concern to deny finite causation. This is because he does seem to allow finite minds to be genuine causes. (See Garber, *Descartes' Metaphysical Physics*, pp. 304–305; "Descartes and Occasionalism," pp. 24–26.) It is interesting to note that Berkeley, who does explicitly deny that bodies can have causal power and who thus approaches a limited form of occasionalism, does not

deny finite causation per se. Berkeley, like Descartes, holds that finite minds are genuine causes of certain changes.

5. See, for example, Aquinas: "The active quality, such as heat, although itself an accident, acts nevertheless by virtue of the substantial form, as its instrument" (*Summa Theologica* I, q115a1ad5). On this feature of the Aristotelian-scholastic account of causation, see Garber, "Descartes and Occasionalism," p. 12; *Descartes' Metaphysical Physics*, pp. 95–96, 274–275; "How God Causes Motion," p. 574. For a very helpful account of the subtleties of the Aristotelian-scholastic account, see Maier, *On the Threshold of Exact Science*, chap. 2, "Causes, Forces, and Resistance." Wallace, "Causes and Forces in Sixteenth-Century Physics," gives a useful description of some late scholastic views on causation.

6. For Descartes's rejection of substantial forms and their causal role, see AT III, 420–421; 503, 648–649, 667–668; VII, 439–447; CSM II, 296–301; CSMK 188, 208, 216, 219. See also Gilson's classic essay in *Etudes sur le Role de la Pensée Médiévale dans la Formation du Systeme Cartésien*, pp. 141–190, and Garber, *Descartes' Metaphysical Physics*, chap. 4. Strictly speaking, Descartes does not hold that *all* bodies lack substantial forms. In the special case of a living human body, Descartes claims that the mind is the substantial form of that body and thus can cause changes in it. On this facet of Descartes's account, see AT II, 503; III, 505; VII, 356; CSM II, 246; CSMK 207, 208; see also Garber, *Descartes' Metaphysical Physics*, pp. 89, 99, 104, 274–276, and "How God Causes Motion," p. 575. Despite the fact that Descartes recognizes these special substantial forms, I will sometimes speak in the text, loosely, of his rejection of substantial forms generally.

7. Garber, "Descartes and Occasionalism," pp. 12–14, 25; "How God Causes Motion," p. 576; *Descartes' Metaphysical Physics*, pp. 274–275.

8. Freddoso sums up well the general occasionalist transformation of an Aristotelian account of causation: "It is just God's steadfast adherence to certain arbitrarily chosen 'norms' that serves as the occasionalist surrogate for Aristotelian natures. That is to say, constant divine intentions provide the stability and regularity in the universe that the Aristotelians attribute to the natures of corporeal substances." "Medieval Aristotelianism and the Case against Secondary Causation in Nature," p. 103.

9. Clarke, *Occult Powers and Hypotheses*, p. 129.

10. Gueroult ("The Metaphysics and Physics of Forces in Descartes") and Gabbey ("Force and Inertia in the Seventeenth Century: Descartes and Newton") offer, perhaps, the best-known defenses of this interpretation of Descartes. I will discus their views briefly later.

11. For example, Malebranche explicitly acknowledges that he sometimes speaks "according to common opinion" with regard to causation and that it would be wrong to take such loose expressions as indicative of his considered views on causation (*The Search After Truth*, pp. 672–673; cf. Berkeley's claim, made in a related context, that we "ought to think with the learned and speak with the vulgar," *Principles of Human Knowledge*, sect. 51). Evidence that Garber wants to discount passages in which Descartes may be speaking less technically comes from the fact that in making his case for an occasionalist reading of Descartes in the case of body-body causation, Garber relies primarily on those passages in *Le Monde* and the *Principles* in which Descartes explicitly takes up the topic of the causes of motion. Furthermore, in his paper "Understanding Interaction: What Descartes Should Have Told Elisabeth," Garber says: "It is interesting that in the sections of *Principia* II that deal with the *causes* of motion, properly speaking, sections 36 and following, bodies are *never* mentioned as genuine causes" p. 32, n. 27. (We will see later that this claim about Descartes is false.) Hatfield also clearly embraces this strategy. He says that he will focus on those passages "in which Descartes sought to clarify the concept of force" (p. 120). He also makes the general claim that Descartes "quite often employed words according to the common usage throughout a work, only to indicate, when explicitly dealing with the concept in question, that some other reality lies behind the

common usage" (p. 137). Hatfield holds that this general claim applies to Descartes's conception of causation (see also pp. 127–128).

12.  Hoenen, "Descartes' Mechanicism," p. 359, and Prendergast, "Motion, Action, and Tendency in Descartes's Physics," p. 460, invoke this passage (unsuccessfully, in my opinion) to show that for Descartes bodies are causes of motion. Anderson ("Cartesian Motion," pp. 211, 212) invokes some passages from early in part II of the *Principles* to show that Descartes recognizes that bodies are causes of motion (*Principles* 2:25, 33). However, since these passages occur in the *Principles* before Descartes's official discussion of the causes of motion (which begins in *Principles* 2:36), Garber and Hatfield would argue, and rightly so, that these passages cannot be taken as showing that Descartes recognizes bodies as genuine causes of motion.

13.  Similar conclusions could be reached by looking at the parallel passages in *Le Monde*. See Hatfield, pp. 127–129.

14.  For some helpful reflections on the notion of universal and primary cause in Descartes and in previous philosophy, see Garber, *Descartes' Metaphysical Physics*, pp. 201–202, 353, n. 6.

15.  Although Garber's claim that God's causal activity is responsible for motion is correct, there is an important question about how to understand that activity that I will not take up here. For Descartes, God is continually re-creating bodies (see, e.g., AT VII, 110; CSM II, 79). Is God's causation of motion nothing over and above the fact that God re-creates a given body at different locations at successive moments? (This is how de la Forge understands God's causation of motion; see *Oeuvres Philosophiques*, p. 240, cf. Malebranche, *The Search After Truth*, elucidation 15, p. 678; *Dialogues on Metaphysics and on Religion*, 7, p. 117.) Or is God's causation of motion an activity somehow separate from his act of continual re-creation? The latter view is, as Garber points out, suggested by Descartes's talk (in the letter to More quoted above) of bodies continually receiving an impulse from God (AT V, 404; CSMK 381). As Garber shows, this latter view is important because it allows a way in which minds may be genuine causes of motion even if bodies are not. (On these points, see Garber, "How God Causes Motion," pp. 578–580; *Descartes' Metaphysical Physics*, pp. 273–280; "Descartes and Occasionalism.") I do not need to, and so will not attempt to, resolve this controversy about understanding God's causation of motion here.

16.  Other thinkers, including of course Aquinas and Suarez, certainly did hold that bodies are secondary causes of motion. See, for example, Aquinas, *Summa Contra Gentiles* III, chaps. 66–70; Suarez, *On Efficient Causality: Metaphysical Disputations*, 18, sect. 1. See also Garber, *Descartes' Metaphysical Physics*, p. 274 and the references there.

17.  *Principles* 2:37. See also *Le Monde*, AT XI, 38; CSM I, 93. For a discussion of the restriction to simple and undivided things, see Garber, *Descartes' Metaphysical Physics*, pp. 211–212. I will return to the puzzling and important phrase *quantum in se est* later.

18.  *Principles* 2:39. See also *Le Monde*, AT XI, 43–44; CSM I, 96.

19.  Garber, *Descartes' Metaphysical Physics*, p. 303 (this passage is repeated in "Descartes and Occasionalism," p. 19). See also "Understanding Interaction," p. 26. On p. 14 of "Descartes and Occasionalism," Garber goes from saying that God sustains the motion of bodies to saying that "in the material world, at least, God is the only genuine causal agent."

20.  This would, of course, be an argument for a full-blown version of occasionalism and not merely for the limited version of occasionalism that Garber and Hatfield see in Descartes. But the general form of the argument is the same. Similar thoughts are expressed by Suarez, (sect. 1, p. 38). It should be noted that at least one passage in *Le Monde* does explicitly seem to give bodies a causal role to play with regard to motion: "God alone is the author of all the motions in the world insofar as they exist and insofar as they are rectilinear; but it is the various dispositions of matter which render them irregular and curved" (AT XI, 46; CSM I, 97).

See also AT XI, 37; CSM I, 93: "There must be many changes in its [matter's] parts which cannot, it seems to me, properly be attributed to the action of God (because that action never changes), and which therefore I attribute to nature" (which Descartes here understands to be matter). Although I will ultimately defend a nonoccasionalistic reading of Descartes, I will not do so on the basis of these passages, which have no analogues in Descartes's more mature *Principles*. Anderson (pp. 207–208) wrongly, I think, makes much of the latter passage to support a nonoccasionalist reading. For different ways in which a defender of the occasionalist interpretation of Descartes might handle these passages, see Hatfield, p. 128, and Garber, *Descartes' Metaphysical Physics*, pp. 288–289.

21. One criticism of the occasionalist reading of Descartes that I am sympathetic to, but will not rely on here, is the following. Descartes does say that bodies cause sensations in the mind. This is a prominent theme in the Sixth Meditation. But if bodies are genuine causes in the body-mind case, why then can't they be causes in the body-body case? Kemp Smith presses this objection (*New Studies in the Philosophy of Descartes*, p. 214). Garber himself raises this difficulty in various places ("Understanding Interaction," p. 26; "Descartes and Occasionalism," pp. 19–24; *Descartes' Metaphysical Physics*, pp. 72–75), and he attempts to deal with it by suggesting that a shift toward a more occasionalist account of body-mind causation occurred gradually from the Sixth Meditation (1641) to the Latin version of the *Principles* (1644) to the French version of the *Principles* (1647). For a rather different reading, according to which, for Descartes, bodies are not efficient causes of mental events, see Nadler, "Descartes and Occasional Causation."

22. A fortiori, Descartes never explicitly *argues for* occasionalism. The Malebranchian arguments are nowhere to be found in Descartes. By contrast, Malebranche, a genuine occasionalist in the matter of body-body interaction, and in other areas as well, often explicitly makes and argues for such a denial (see, e.g., *Dialogues on Metaphysics and on Religion*, 7, p. 110, and *The Search After Truth*, book 6, part 2, chap. 3).

23. See the passage from *Principles* 2:42 quoted earlier.

24. Anscombe and Geach (*Descartes: Philosophical Writings*) have a similar translation, as does Garber in "Mind, Body, and the Laws of Nature," p. 116, and in *Descartes' Metaphysical Physics*, p. 303.

25. I am assuming that if Descartes means corporeal causes here, he has in mind causes that are themselves bodies (*corpora*) or states of bodies. I don't see how something that is not a body or a state of a body could be a corporeal cause. In particular, I find very implausible the idea that, for Descartes, corporeal causes could refer to the three laws of nature or, perhaps, to the rules subsidiary to the third law. As far as I can tell, Descartes never refers to these laws or rules as themselves corporeal. For some interesting comments on this term, see Descartes's letter to Hyperaspistes of August 1641 (AT III, 424–425; CSMK 190.)

26. Miller and Miller take it that he does, since in their translation, they include the word "causes" here. Their translation reads: "All the individual causes of the changes which occur in [the motion of] bodies are included under this this law, or at least those causes which are physical" (*Principles of Philosophy*, p. 62).

27. "All the particular causes of the changes which bodies undergo are covered by this third law — or at least the law covers all changes which are themselves corporeal."

28. I am relying here on my analysis of this passage in "Spinoza's Metaphysical Psychology," p. 195. In part I of that essay, I explore some of the connections between Spinoza's notion of striving and Descartes's notion; I also discuss their notions of tending.

29. For this equivalence, see *Principles* 3:57, where Descartes speaks of a body "tending or striving to go" (*tendere, sive ire conari*). See also Garber, *Descartes' Metaphysical Physics*, pp. 354, n. 10, 355, n. 29.

30. The French word Descartes uses here is, actually, *inclination*. However, since he

does use the verb *tend* earlier in this passage in conjunction with the word *inclination*, I take the sentence I have quoted as elucidating Descartes' notion of tending.

31. See the helpful note on the term *sua sponte* that appears in AT VIIIA, 350.

32. See also CSM I, 94; AT XI, 40.

33. See *Principles* 2:37, where Descartes says that if a body is at rest "we do not believe that it will ever be moved unless it is pushed into motion by some cause." The context here makes clear that Descartes has external causes in mind.

34. For other references to external causes in similar contexts, see AT III, 208, 619; XI 38, 84; CSM I, 93; *Principles* 2:41. In quoting this passage from *Principles* 2:43, I should correct an oversight in my discussion of Descartes's notion of tendency in my earlier paper, "Spinoza's Metaphysical Psychology." There I said that, as far as I was aware, Descartes does not use the term *quantum in se est* in conjunction with the terms for striving or, equivalently, tending (p. 198). In making this claim, I overlooked the passage just quoted from *Principles* 2:43.

35. See, for example, *Principles* 1:21; AT III, 429; CSMK 193.

36. As I explained in note 15, God's activity of sustaining the existence of bodies may or may not be separate from his activity of causing motion in bodies.

37. Garber interprets this passage in a similar way as implying that "were God to withdraw his continual impulsion, everything would stop" (*Descartes' Metaphysical Physics*, p. 227).

38. The account of striving can similarly be expressed in this more explicit way. Spinoza seems to have appreciated the point that for Descartes God at least is not among the external causes in question. In representing Descartes's views in his geometrical exposition of part of the *Principles*, Spinoza gives what is, in effect, a restatement of Descartes's first law: "If we attend to no external, i.e., particular causes, but consider the thing by itself, we shall have to affirm that insofar as it can it always perseveres in the state in which it is" (*Descartes' Principles of Philosophy*, part II, prop. 14, demonstration in Curley, p. 277). By "particular" causes, Spinoza means to exclude God, whom he described earlier as the general cause of all motion (part II, prop. 11, scholium). By "particular," Spinoza does *not* seem to mean the laws of nature, for in his account of Descartes's views, he never presents the laws of nature as particular causes. On this point, see the helpful comments in Curley, p. 276, n. 36.

39. See also AT III, 429; CSMK 193. On the issue of whether finite bodies or finite portions of matter are substances for Descartes, see Garber, *Descartes' Metaphysical Physics*, pp. 175–176.

40. Garber also comments on the differences between the Latin and French versions of *Principles* 2:37, 41 (see *Descartes' Metaphysical Physics*, pp. 214, 363, n. 37). He does not, of course, invoke these differences, as I am suggesting, to reach the conclusion that bodies are for Descartes causes of motion in other bodies.

41. Of course, finite minds also might be considered as among the external causes in question (see *Principles* 2:40), but this does not affect the claim that Descartes is, in the account of tending, taking bodies to be causes. It would not be plausible on Cartesian terms to think that finite minds are involved in the causation of *all* changes in motion.

42. It might be thought that my argument here, if correct, proves too much. I have argued that since Descartes specifies his notion of the tendency to persist in the same state in terms of the notion of external causes understood as bodies, he is in this account implicitly treating external bodies as genuine causes of motion and rest. But it might be thought that if this argument is correct, then a similar argument would show that Malebranche, the paradigmatic occasionalist, also accepts that bodies are genuine causes of motion and rest since he, too, discusses tending in terms of external causes (understood as external bodies). See, for example, *The Search After Truth*, book I, chap. 1, p. 4. However, a more detailed statement of my argumentative strategy shows that my strategy does not have the unfortunate implication

that Malebranche is not an occasionalist. The reason why Descartes's use of the notion of external causes in his account of tending indicates that he accepts bodies as genuine causes is that his explanation of his account of tending occurs in that stretch of the *Principles* where, as Garber and Hatfield emphasize, Descartes is particularly concerned to give us his true views on the causation of motion. Thus Descartes's use of the notion of causation here cannot easily be seen as loose and nontechnical.   By contrast, although Malebranche does speak of external bodily causes when he discusses tending, he is quite careful when he takes up the matter of the genuine causes of motion — that is, when he is speaking technically with regard to causation — to specify that these external bodily causes are *mere* occasional causes (see, e.g., *The Search After Truth*, elucidation 15, p. 664; *Dialogues on Metaphysics and on Religion*, 10, pp. 187–188). Any passages in which Malebranche speaks of external bodies as causes according to his account of tending, and in which he does not specify that the causation is merely occasional and not genuine, can thus easily be seen as invoking the notion of causation in a loose and nontechnical fashion. (See the passage quoted in note 11 of this paper.) I thank Charles McCracken for pressing me to be more explicit on this point.

43.  See Gueroult, p. 223, n. 26. See also Gabbey, p. 303, n. 40. See also AT XI, 11; CSM I, 85, where Descartes speaks of "the virtue or power of self-movement found in one body [*la vertu ou la puissance de se mouvoir soy-mesme, qui se rencontre dans un corps*]."

44.  For a similar argument, see Woolhouse, *Descartes, Spinoza, Leibniz: The Concept of Substance in Seventeenth-Century Metaphysics*, pp. 136–137. Jammer (*Concepts of Force: A Study in the Foundations of Dynamics*, pp. 103–105) also holds that bodies do not genuinely have force for Descartes. But Jammer does not emphasize, as Hatfield and Woolhouse do, the features of God's activity from which this conclusion might be derived.

45.  *Descartes's Metaphysical Physics*, p. 294. Cf. de la Forge, p. 238: after denying that the notion of "force comprises in its concept the idea of extension, as do the other modes of body," he says, "thus we have reason to believe that the force which moves is not less really distinct from matter than thought is." There are important differences here between Garber's and Hatfield's views on this matter, over and above the fact that they argue for the conclusion that bodies do not have force in different ways. Hatfield locates force in God. Garber denies that force is in God. For Garber's Descartes, force is neither in God nor in bodies: it is nowhere at all. See Garber, *Descartes' Metaphysical Physics*, pp. 297–299. I need not explore this difference between Hatfield and Garber here since I am interested only in their point of agreement — that force is not in bodies.

46.  Since I hold that bodies really have forces or tendencies for Descartes, one may naturally raise the question of how I see such features as fitting into Descartes's substance/mode ontology. I believe that his notion of mode is broad enough to encompass forces and tendencies as I see them. Here I would appeal to a distinction that Garber draws between modes in the narrow sense and modes in the broad sense. I grant that the tendency or the power a body has is not a mode of extension in the strict sense, that is, a way of being extended. (In this sense, of course, shape and size, for example, are modes of extension.) But as Garber emphasizes, not "all real properties of bodies are modes of extension in the narrowest sense" (*Descartes' Metaphysical Physics*, pp. 67–68). Garber gives the example of enduring through a certain period of time as a genuine accident of a body even though this feature is not understood through extension at all. Similarly, Garber claims, motion is not a mode in the strict sense since, unlike shape and size, motion presupposes time, as well as extension. Nevertheless, motion is, as Descartes emphasizes, a "mode" of a body (see, e.g., *Principles* 1:65, 2:36). Garber concludes that there is at work in Descartes a broader sense of 'mode' whereby a mode of extension is not just any way of being extended but also any way of being an extended substance (p. 68). Garber expresses this broader sense elsewhere as the notion of "a real thought-independent feature of the world of bodies" (p. 175). Although motion and duration are not purely geometrical fea-

tures (and thus not modes of extension in the strict sense), they are features that the "objects of geometry existing formally outside of our conception" (p. 175) can have. In the same way, I would argue that the relations these bodies — or existing objects of geometry — have to God constitute genuine, albeit relational, features of these bodies. Since bodies really have these relations to God, I see no reason to deny that in the broad sense of "mode," these relations and the powers or tendencies Descartes says are grounded in them are modes of bodies.

47. Malebranche, by contrast, seems to hold that this grounding of bodily forces in God's causal activity makes the bodily forces not genuine. He says: "We must give, if we can, the natural and particular cause of the effects in question. But since the action of these causes consists only in the motor force activating them, and since this motor force is but the will of God, they must not be said to have in themselves any force or power to produce any effects. And when in our reasoning we have come at last to a general effect whose cause is sought, we also philosophize badly if we imagine any other cause of it than the general cause" (*The Search After Truth*, elucidation 15, p. 662). Malebranche thus draws the conclusion that I am saying, that Descartes does not draw from God's causal activity.

48. See also Westfall, *Force in Newton's Physics: The Science of Dynamics in the Seventeenth Century*, chap. 2, and Prendergast, p. 460.

49. Another, related difference between my interpretation and those of Gueroult and Gabbey is that their readings, unlike mine, turn on the claim that somehow the force of a body is to be identified with its existence and duration.

50. *Descartes' Metaphysical Physics*, pp. 296–297.

51. Hoenen, p. 359; Prendergast, p. 460.

52. *Descartes' Metaphysical Physics*, p. 303 (also in "Descartes and Occasionalism," p. 19). See also Hatfield, p. 130, n. 73.

53. "Tibi autem puto ea in re parare difficultatem, quod concipias vim quandam in corpore quiescente, per quam motui resistit, tanquam si vis illa esset positiuum quid, nempe actio quaedam, ab ipsa quiete distinctum, cum tamen nihil plane sit a modali entitate diuersum."

54. There are subtleties in this passage that I am skipping over. In particular, I will not take up the issue of exactly what Descartes means by saying that the force of resistance is not an action distinct from rest and the issue of how this is compatible with his saying elsewhere in the letter that the resistance of a body is not itself its rest ("*etsi . . . res quiescens, ex hoc ipso quod quiescat, habeat illum renixum, non ideo ille renixus est quies.*" AT V, 403; not in CSMK). I think the point is that the force of resistance arises from the rest and could not exist without it. In this sense the force is not distinct from the rest (see Descartes's account of real distinction as it appears, e.g., in the Sixth Meditation, AT VII, 78; CSM II, 54). However, since the force arises from the rest ("*ex hoc ipso quod quiescat*"), they are not strictly identical: one gives rise to the other. For a different discussion of this issue, see Gueroult, p. 223, n. 26. Notice that, on my reading of this passage, Descartes is saying that the force in a body at rest is a modal entity. This suggests that he does recognize force as a mode of bodies, as I claimed earlier in note 46.

55. CSMK, however, takes the "it" to be force, thus agreeing with my interpretation of the passage.

56. See again *Principles* 2:43. See also AT I, 117, where Descartes says that the continuation of motion is the principal cause of the rebounding of balls. As he specifies, by the continuation of motion he is referring to the fact that "a thing that has begun to move, by this very fact, continues to move as long as it can." See also AT I, 107.

57. Descartes affirms that God is not acted upon in *Principles* 1:23. For some general discussion of this point, see Freddoso, pp. 87–88.

58. I should note that as will be obvious, I do not aim here to give a complete interpretation of this most problematic doctrine. I will, however, focus on passages that any interpretation must account for and suggest what I take to be natural readings of these passages. I will

also briefly consider rival interpretations of Descartes's creation doctrine.

59. On this point, see Beyssade, *La Philosophie Première de Descartes*, p. 112. Frankfurt and Plantinga adopt the contrary view that for Descartes claims such as p are, after all, contingent. Frankfurt: "The eternal truths are inherently as contingent as any other propositions" ("Descartes on the Creation of the Eternal Truths," p. 42). Plantinga: "*Every* truth is within his [God's] control; and hence no truth is necessary" (*Does God Have a Nature?*, p. 113).

60. In his "Descartes on the Creation of the Eternal Truths," p. 581, Curley implicitly denies this. He says that for Descartes, a claim such as p is necessary but not necessarily necessary. Since, in Curley's view, things are true only by virtue of God's will (p. 580), if it is necessary that p be true, then it is necessary that God wills that p be true. But this seems to place more of a restriction on God's will than Descartes would allow. Plantinga criticizes in this way the kind of position Curley adopts (pp. 112–113). Curley (p. 582, n. 23) alludes to Plantinga's objection but does not seem to respond directly. In his acount of the creation of the eternal truths, Bennett, like Curley, holds in effect that it is necessary that God wills that p be true ("Descartes's Theory of Modality," p. 657). This account is thus vulnerable to a criticism similar to the one to which Curley's account is vulnerable. I do not, however, have the space here to do justice to Bennett's subtle and provocative reading.

61. Descartes makes clear that God is the *efficient cause* of the eternal truths and their necessity. See AT I, 152; VII 436; CSM II, 294; CSMK 25.

62. I think another strikingly analogous set of views emerges in connection with the Cartesian circle. Descartes claims that God's activity of guaranteeing the truth of our clear and distinct ideas enables us to be certain that clear and distinct ideas are true. However, given that we have no way that is independent of our clear and distinct ideas to ascertain whether or not God is really seeing to it that our clear and distinct ideas are true, it may seem that we cannot be genuinely certain that clear and distinct ideas are true even if it is in fact the case that God is guaranteeing that those ideas are true. (I have discussed some of these points in my "Mental Content and Skepticism in Descartes and Spinoza.") God's activity (of seeing to it that our clear and distinct ideas are true) thus may seem incapable of grounding something (our certainty that clear and distinct ideas are true) that Descartes claims that God's activity does ground. In this respect, I believe, Descartes's views about God's activity in the epistemic case are analogous to his views on necessity and causation.

Of course, there are many controversies concerning Descartes's epistemology that are relevant here, and I do not have space to enter into them. I simply want to point out that there is at least a prima facie analogy between the case of the Cartesian circle, on the one hand, and the case of the creation of the eternal truths and the case of the causation of motion, on the other. I will explore this matter further in future work.

63. Descartes equates nature and essence in various places. See, for example, AT II, 367; VI, 33; VIIIB, 355; VII, 8, 64, 78, 104, 115, 240; CSM I, 127, 302; II, 7, 45, 54, 76, 83, 168; CSMK 121.

64. For example, Descartes says in his *Comments on a Certain Broadsheet*, "It would be quite foolish and self-contradictory to say that the nature of things leaves open the possibility that the essence of something may have a different character from the one it actually has" (AT VIIIB, 348; CSM I, 297). See also AT III, 423, 478; VII, 371; CSM II, 256; CSMK 189, 203.

65. See Descartes's discussion in the Fifth Meditation of the properties of a triangle that follow from its essence (AT VII, 64; CSM II, 45). Descartes says in the First Replies, "It belongs to the nature of a triangle that it consists of no more than three lines" (AT VII, 112; CSM II, 80).

66. Frankfurt, p. 38. See also AT VII, 435; CSM II, 293–294.

67. Or, perhaps, as the passage from the letter to Mersenne suggests, the nature of any *created* thing. This point bears on the issue of whether eternal truths that are in some way about God himself are exempt from the creation doctrine. For discussion of this point, see Wells, "Descartes' Uncreated Eternal Truths."

68. AT XI, 40; CSM I, 94. There Descartes says of Aristotelian motion, that "contrary to all the laws of nature, it strives of its own accord [*tache soy-meme*] to destroy itself." The key term here is *tache*, but this is equivalent in meaning, I believe, to "strives" or "tends."

69. See Della Rocca, "Spinoza's Metaphysical Psychology," pp. 194–197.

70. Gabbey endorses Cohen's reading of the phrase (p. 315, n. 175) and he points out, as I do, that a close reading of *Principles* 2:37 supports Cohen's claim (p. 320, n. 225).

71. For this claim about natures in particular, see Aristotle, *The Complete Works of Aristotle, Physics* II: 1: "Nature is a principle or cause of being moved and of being at rest in that to which it belongs primarily, in virtue of itself and not accidentally" (192b; see also *Metaphysics* IV, 1014b). Cf. Aquinas: "The word *nature* has been applied to every principle of movement existing in that which is moved" (I, q115a2). See also the other works cited in Gilson, p. 156, n. 2.

72. Malebranche also holds that God's immutable causation of motion bestows certain natures on things (*The Search After Truth*, elucidation 15, pp. 662, 668). But, unlike Descartes, Malebranche holds that such a nature is not a locus of causal power in bodies. So Malebranche does not face the problem I am here raising for Descartes.

73. Aquinas and Suarez would agree that it is more consonant with divine power for God to allow for genuine secondary causation than to eliminate all secondary causation. See Aquinas, *Summa Contra Gentiles* III, chap. 69; *Summa Theologica* I, q105a5; Suarez, *Metaphysical Disputations* 18, p. 43. I should note that Garber does not deny that God could have given bodies causal power; rather he denies, in effect, that God's regular activity of causing motion can be that in virtue of which bodies have such a power. Each of these denials, I would claim, limits God's power in a way that would be unacceptable to Descartes, but Garber makes only the second denial.

74. It would be quite interesting to explore the connection between these two views in the cases of other philosophers. For example, Malebranche holds that God does *not* create the eternal truths and that bodies are *not* causes. I suspect that these claims, which are the flip side of Descartes's claims, are importantly connected with one another, just as Descartes's claims are. I cannot, of course, explore this here.

75. A similar question arises concerning Spinoza, who says that the essence of each thing is its striving to remain in existence. Yet he also says that the essence of a body is its proportion of motion and rest and also that its essence is to have certain causes. It is not clear here how or if these claims are all compatible. For some discussion, see my *Representation and the Mind-Body Problem in Spinoza*, chap. 5.

76. On this topic, see Broughton, "Necessity and Physical Laws in Descartes's Philosophy"; Dutton, "Indifference, Necessity, and Descartes's Derivation of the Laws of Motion"; Normore, "The Necessity in Deduction: Cartesian Inference and Its Medieval Background."

77. Descartes explicitly maintains that God's activity of creating the eternal truths is incomprehensible (AT I 146; IV 118; VII 436; CSM II, 294; CSMK 23, 235). Beyssade has a very helpful discussion of the role of the incomprehensibility of God in Descartes's account of the creation of the eternal truths (pp. 111–113, 128). Marion emphasizes the lack of univocity of certain predicates insofar as they apply to God and to creatures and the bearing of this lack of univocity on the creation of the eternal truths (*Sur la Théologie Blanche de Descartes*, passim). Marion also has a thorough discussion of Descartes's rejection of univocity and its connection with earlier views on analogy. Descartes makes a general appeal to a lack of univocity in AT V, 347; VII, 137, 433; CSM II, 98, 292; CSMK 375. (Cf. his claim — discussed earlier in this paper — that there are two senses of "substance.") Descartes explicitly invokes the lack of univocity of a causal term in order to resolve a related problem concerning human freedom. Although he thinks that God determines everything — even human actions — this determination does not render human actions unfree. Instead, Descartes seems to maintain that human ac-

tions can still remain undetermined in a significant sense despite the determination of all by God. Descartes appeals to different kinds of determination in an important passage from his letter to Elizabeth of 3 November 1645: "The independence which we experience and feel within ourselves, and which suffices to make our actions praiseworthy or blameworthy, is not incompatible with a dependence of quite another kind, whereby all things are subject to God" (AT VII, 333; CSMK 277; for a related passage, see *Principles* 1:41).

78. Similarly, there are epistemological analogues of Garber's occasionalist reading. For example, some have argued that Descartes does not seek to argue that our clear and distinct ideas are certain, in the sense of certainty according to which we are rationally justified in believing clear and distinct ideas. In this view, espoused by Loeb, "The Cartesian Circle," and suggested by Bennett, "Truth and Stability in Descartes' *Meditations*," just as for Garber, Descartes denies that bodies genuinely cause motion in bodies; and just as for Frankfurt and Plantinga, Descartes denies that p is genuinely necessary. Descartes also denies that we are genuinely, that is, normatively, certain of our clear and distinct ideas (or at least, in this view, Descartes is not primarily interested in claiming that there we can have such certainty). I would argue that although this view may seem to capture a strand in Descartes's epistemological thinking, it is beset by problems that are analogous to the problems facing the occasionalist reading of Descartes. I will explore this matter elsewhere.

79. A version of this chapter was delivered at the Midwest Seminar on the History of Early Modern Philosophy at the University of Chicago in May 1997 and at Rutgers University and Yale University in January and February 1988. I would like to thank those present on these occasions, particularly Dan Garber, for their helpful comments and questions. I am also grateful to Steven Nadler for useful correspondence and to the editors of this volume, two anonymous referees, Robert Adams, Martha Brandt Bolton, and Carol Rovane for reading and commenting on earlier versions.

## BIBLIOGRAPHY

### Works by Descartes

Adam, Charles, and Paul Tannery, eds.) *Oeuvres de Descartes*, 12 vols. Paris: J. Vrin, 1964–1976. (Abbreviated AT.)

Anscombe, Elizabeth, and Peter Thomas Geach, eds. and trans. *Descartes: Philosophical Writings*. Indianapolis: Bobbs-Merrill, 1971.

Cottingham, John, Robert Stoothoff, and Dugald Murdoch, eds. and trans. *The Philosophical Writings of Descartes*, 2 vols. Cambridge: Cambridge University Press, 1984–1985. (Abbreviated CSM.)

Cottingham, John, Robert Stoothoff, Dugald Murdoch, and Anthony Kenny, trans. *The Philosophical Writings of Descartes*, vol. 3. Cambridge: Cambridge University Press, 1991. (Abbreviated CSMK.)

Miller, Valentine Rodger, and Reese P. Miller, trans. *Principles of Philosophy*. Dordrecht: Reidel, 1983.

### Other Works

Anderson, Wallace E. "Cartesian Motion." In P. Machamer and R. G. Turnbull, eds., *Motion and Time*, pp. 200–223. Columbus: Ohio State University Press, 1976.

Aquinas, St. Thomas. *Summa Theologica*. New York: Benziger, 1947.

——— . *Summa Contra Gentiles*, 4 vols., Vernon J. Bourke, trans. Notre Dame: University of Notre Dame Press, 1975.

Aristotle. *The Complete Works of Aristotle*, 2 vols. Jonathan Barnes, ed. Princeton, N.J.: Princeton University Press, 1984.

Bennett, Jonathan. "Truth and Stability in Descartes' *Meditations*." *Canadian Journal of Philosophy*, Supplementary vol. 16 (1990): 75–108.

——— . "Descartes's Theory of Modality." *Philosophical Review* 103 (1994): 639–667.

Berkeley, George. *A Treatise Concerning the Principles of Human Knowledge.* In A. A. Luce and T. E. Jessop, eds., *The Works of George Berkeley Bishop of Cloyne*, vol. 2, pp. 19–113.

Beyssade, Jean-Marie. *La Philosophie Première de Descartes.* Paris: Flammarion, 1979.

Broughton, Janet. "Necessity and Physical Laws in Descartes's Philosophy." *Pacific Philosophical Quarterly* 68 (1987): 205–221.

Clarke, Desmond. *Occult Powers and Hypotheses.* Oxford: Clarendon Press, 1989.

Cohen, I. Bernard. "'Quantum in se est': Newton's Concept of Inertia in Relation to Descartes and Lucretius." *Notes and Records of the Royal Society of London* 19 (1964): 131–155.

Curley, Edwin. "Descartes on the Creation of the Eternal Truths." *Philosophical Review* 93 (1984): 569–597.

Della Rocca, Michael. "Mental Content and Skepticism in Descartes and Spinoza." *Studia Spinozana* 10 (1994): 19–42.

——— . *Representation and the Mind-Body Problem in Spinoza.* New York: Oxford University Press, 1996.

——— . "Spinoza's Metaphysical Psychology." In Don Garrett, ed., *The Cambridge Companion to Spinoza*, pp. 192–266. New York: Cambridge University Press, 1996.

Dutton, Blake. "Indifference, Necessity, and Descartes's Derivation of the Laws of Motion." *Journal of the History of Philosophy* 34 (1996): 193–212.

Frankfurt, Harry G. "Descartes on the Creation of the Eternal Truths." *Philosophical Review* 86 (1977): 36–57.

Freddoso, Alfred. "Medieval Aristotelianism and the Case Against Secondary Causation in Nature." In Thomas V. Morris, ed., *Divine and Human Action: Essays in the Metaphysics of Theism*, pp. 74–118. Ithaca, N. Y.: Cornell University Press, 1988.

Gabbey, Alan. "Force and Intertia in the Seventeenth Century: Descartes and Newton." In Stephen Gaukroger, ed., *Descartes: Philosophy, Mathematics and Physics*, pp. 230–320. Sussex: Harvester Press, 1980.

Garber, Daniel. "Mind, Body, and the Laws of Nature in Descartes and Leibniz." *Midwest Studies in Philosophy* 8 (1983): 105–133.

——— . "Understanding Interaction: What Descartes Should Have Told Elisabeth." *Southern Journal of Philosophy* 21 (1983, supplement): 15–32.

——— . "How God Causes Motion: Descartes, Divine Sustenance, and Occasionalism." *Journal of Philosophy* 84 (1987): 567–580.

——— . *Descartes' Metaphysical Physics.* Chicago: University of Chicago Press, 1992.

——— . "Descartes and Occasionalism." In Steven Nadler, ed., *Causation in Early Modern Philosophy*, pp. 9–26. University Park: Pennsylvania State University Press, 1993.

Gilson, Etienne. *Etudes sur le Role de la Pensée Médiévale dans la Formation du Systeme Cartésien.* Paris: J. Vrin, 1930.

Gueroult, Martial. "The Metaphysics and Physics of Forces in Descartes." In Stephen Gaukroger, ed., *Descartes: Philosophy, Mathematics and Physics*, pp. 196–229. Sussex: Harvester Press, 1980.

Hatfield, Gary. "Force (God) in Descartes' Physics." *Studies in History and Philosophy of Science* 10 (1979): 113–140.

Hoenen, P. H. J. "Descartes's Mechanicism." In Willis Doney, ed., *Descartes: A Collection of Critical Essays*, pp. 353–368. Garden City, N.Y.: Doubleday, 1967.

Jammer, Max. *Concepts of Force: A Study in the Foundations of Dynamics*. Cambridge, Mass.: Harvard University Press, 1957.

Kemp Smith, Norman. *New Studies in the Philosophy of Descartes*. London: Macmillan, 1952.

la Forge, Louis de. *Oeuvres Philosophiques*. Pierre Clair, ed. Paris: Presses Universitaires de France, 1974.

Loeb, Louis E. "The Cartesian Circle." In John Cottingham, ed., *The Cambridge Companion to Descartes*, pp. 200–235. Cambridge: Cambridge University Press, 1992.

Machamer, Peter. "Causality and Explanation in Descartes' Natural Philosophy." In P. Machamer and R. G. Turnbull, eds., *Motion and Time*. Columbus: Ohio State University Press, 1976.

Maier, Annelise. *On the Threshold of Exact Science*. S. D. Sargent, trans. Philadelphia: University of Pennsylvania Press, 1982.

Malebranche, Nicolas. *The Search After Truth*. T. M. Lennon and P. J. Olscamp, trans. *Elucidations of the Search after Truth*. T. M. Lennon, trans. Columbus: Ohio State University Press, 1980.

———. *Dialogues on Metaphysics and on Religion*. Nicholas Jolley, ed.; David Scott, trans. Cambridge: Cambridge University Press, 1997.

Marion, Jean-Luc. *Sur la Théologie Blanche de Descartes*. Paris: Presses Universitaires de France, 1981.

Nadler, Steven. "Introduction." In Steven Nadler, ed. *Causation and Early Modern Philosophy*, pp. 1–8. University Park: Pennsylvania State University Press, 1993.

———. "Descartes and Occasional Causation." *British Journal for the History of Philosophy* 2 (1994): 35–54.

———. "Occasionalism and the Question of Arnauld's Cartesianism." In Roger Ariew and Marjorie Grene, eds. *Descartes and His Contemporaries*, pp. 129–144. Chicago: University of Chicago Press, 1995.

Normore, Calvin. "The Necessity in Deduction: Cartesian Inference and Its Medieval Background." *Synthese* 96 (1993): 437–454.

Plantinga, Alvin. *Does God Have a Nature?* Milwaukee: Marquette University Press, 1980.

Prendergast, Thomas L. "Motion, Action, and Tendency in Descartes' Physics." *Journal of the History of Philosophy* 13 (1975): 453–462.

Spinoza, Baruch. *The Collected Works of Spinoza*, vol. 1. Edwin Curley, ed. and trans. Princeton, N.J.: Princeton University Press, 1985. (Abbreviated Curley.)

Suarez, Francisco. *On Efficient Causality: Metaphysical Disputations 17, 18, and 19*. Alfred J. Freddoso, trans. New Haven, Conn.: Yale University Press, 1994.

Wallace, William A. "Causes and Forces in Sixteenth-century Physics." *Isis* 69 (1978): 400–412.

Wells, Norman J. "Descartes' Uncreated Eternal Truths." *New Scholasticism* 56 (1982): 185–199.

Westfall, Richard S. *Force in Newton's Physics: The Science of Dynamics in the Seventeenth Century*. New York: American Elsevier, 1971.

Woolhouse, R. S. *Descartes, Spinoza, Leibniz: The Concept of Substance in Seventeenth-Century Metaphysics*. London: Routledge, 1993.

## 4

MATTHEW STUART

# Descartes's Extended Substances

## Are Physical Objects Substances?

Descartes famously maintains that mind and body are distinct substances; he explicitly refers to several ordinary physical objects as substances; and in the *Principles* he tells us that "a body's being extended in length, breadth and depth in itself warrants the conclusion that it is a substance."[1] Despite all this, it is far from clear that ordinary physical objects — things like human bodies, tables, and planets[2] — really count as substances for Descartes. For one thing, he gives two different criteria for substancehood: one having to do with property ownership, and the other having to do with independent existence.[3] It is not immediately clear that the two criteria are coextensional or that ordinary physical objects satisfy either one. More difficulties are raised by a passage in his Synopsis of the *Meditations*. In this passage (henceforward, simply "the Synopsis passage"), Descartes is explaining why the *Meditations* contains no proof of the immortality of the soul. He says that a demonstration of the immortality of the soul must wait for the whole of physics, for two reasons:

> First, we need to know that absolutely all substances, or things which must be created by God in order to exist, are by their nature incorruptible and cannot ever cease to exist unless they are reduced to nothingness by God's denying his concurrence to them. Secondly, we need to recognize that body, taken in the general sense, is a substance, so that it too never perishes. But the human body, in so far as it differs from other bodies, is simply made up of a certain configuration of limbs and other accidents of this sort; whereas the human mind is not made up of any accidents in

this way, but is a pure substance. . . . And it follows from this that while the body can very easily perish, the mind is immortal by its very nature.[4]

It is clear that Descartes wants to argue for the immortality of the soul as follows:

(1) A human mind is a substance.
(2) Every substance is immortal by its nature.
(3) Hence, a human mind is immortal by its nature.[5]

However, he realizes that a parallel argument—one that treated human bodies as extended substances—would yield the absurd conclusion that human bodies are immune to destruction from natural causes. This prompts him to draw a distinction between "body, taken in the general sense," which is a substance, and a human body, which is not. And this invites a number of questions: what does Descartes mean by "body, taken in the general sense"? What is the relation between body in this sense — extended substance — and an ordinary physical object such as a human body? What is meant by the claim that the mind, in contrast with the body, is a "pure" substance?

Discussions of the Synopsis passage tend to gravitate around two interpretations. Some commentators maintain that Descartes is seriously committed to the existence of only one extended substance: the whole of the material universe.[6] Many of those who read Descartes as a monist about extended substance also go on to say that he regards individual physical objects as modes of the one extended substance.[7] Other commentators deny that he is committed to the existence of even one extended substance. They point to the ambiguities that arise because he wrote in Latin, a language that contains no definite or indefinite articles. Descartes's '*substantia*' can mean either "*a* substance," "*the* substance," or "substance" (mass term). This has led to the suggestion that whereas he countenances talk of individual, countable, thinking substances, Descartes's talk of extended substance is always talk about extended *stuff* rather than extended *things*.[8]

Our work toward an understanding of Descartes's account of extended substance will begin in the following two sections, with a closer examination of his two criteria for substance, keeping in mind the question of whether these criteria are satisfied by ordinary physical objects. Ultimately, I will argue that at least one of them — the so-called independence criterion — is not satisfied by ordinary physical objects. This accounts for Descartes's denial, in the Synopsis passage, that a human body is a substance. And it is the Synopsis passage we turn to next. In a later section I argue that neither of the two commonly proposed readings of that passage will do because each conflicts with Descartes's considered remarks about the individuation of material substances. Following that, I offer my own account of Descartes's extended substances. Drawing on his correspondence with the Jesuit Denis Mesland on the subject of transubstantiation, I show that Descartes distinguishes between an ordinary physical object and the quantity of matter of which it is composed. I argue that although he does not think that an ordinary physical object is a substance, he does accord that status to the quantity of matter that composes it. Finally, in the last section, I show how this solution avoids the difficulties faced by competing accounts, and I consider the possibility that Descartes thinks of ordinary physical objects as modes of the quantities of matter that compose them.

## The Subject Criterion

Descartes's first definition of 'substance' comes in the *Second Replies*, where he says that a substance is a subject of properties: "This term applies to every thing in which whatever we perceive immediately resides, as in a subject, or to every thing by means of which whatever we perceive exists. By 'whatever we perceive' is meant any property, quality or attribute of which we have a real idea."[9] This passage prompts two questions of interpretation. The first arises from the fact that properties can themselves be the subjects of properties: the color of an object can be bright or dull; the acidity of coffee can be pronounced or reticent. Descartes acknowledges as much, writing to Mersenne that "there is no awkwardness or absurdity in saying that an accident is the subject of another accident, just as we say that a quantity is the subject of other accidents."[10] This raises the question of whether Descartes means to count all subjects of properties as substances, or whether he instead restricts the class of substances to those subjects of properties that are not themselves properties — a class we may call *basic subjects*. If the first, more permissive, reading is correct, then individual physical objects undoubtedly qualify as substances, for physical objects certainly do possess properties. If the more restrictive reading is correct, and only basic subjects are substances, it is still quite possible that physical objects pass the subject criterion for substances — we do generally regard physical objects as being the subjects of properties and not as being properties themselves — but it would take more to establish this. There are metaphysical systems that treat physical objects as modes or properties, so before concluding that physical objects satisfy the subject criterion on the restrictive reading, we would need to know that Descartes did not endorse such a metaphysical system.

Although there are some passages in Descartes's writings that suggest the identification of a property with a substance,[11] the preponderance of the evidence suggests that he means to define a substance as a basic subject. He frequently contrasts substance and accident in a way that makes sense only if the two categories are mutually exclusive. For instance, in the *Second Replies* he writes that "a substance has more reality than an accident or a mode," concluding that it is a greater thing to create or preserve a substance than to create or preserve an accident or mode.[12] The notion that different things possess different degrees of reality is of course a dubious one; but if one supposes that all properties that possess properties are substances, then Descartes's degrees-of-reality doctrine loses even the barest semblance of coherence.

A second difficulty raised by the account of substance in the *Second Replies* has to do with the distinction between a basic subject and the properties that belong to it. The question is whether Descartes thinks of a basic subject as something that is distinct from the totality of those properties. If he does, this would seem to require that a basic subject be a substratum devoid of any intrinsic character, a so-called bare particular or bare substratum. This conception of substance — one that is often (and I think correctly[13]) attributed to Locke — is of doubtful coherence. The reason for possibly attributing it to Descartes is that there are a number of places where he seems to be saying that substances cannot be perceived, and that their existence must be inferred from the existence of properties, which can be perceived:

> We do not have immediate knowledge of substances, as I have noted elsewhere. We know them only by perceiving certain forms or attributes which must inhere in something if they are to exist; and we call the thing in which they inhere a 'substance'.[14]
>
> We cannot initially become aware of a substance merely through its being an existing thing, since this alone does not of itself have any effect on us. We can, however, easily come to know a substance by one of its attributes, in virtue of the common notion that nothingness possesses no attributes, that is to say, no properties or qualities. Thus, if we perceive the presence of some attribute, we can infer that there must also be present an existing thing or substance to which it may be attributed.[15]

These passages suggest that a substance is something distinct from the properties that inhere in it, and that our belief in the existence of a substance is justified by an inference involving the principle that properties must after all belong to *something*. An allegiance to the bare substratum conception of substance would explain his view that we know of the existence of a substance by inference rather than perception, and it is hard to see what else would do so.[16] Incidentally, it is widely thought that Descartes favors the representative theory of perception, the doctrine that we immediately perceive only our mental representations of objects, and not the objects themselves. If he does hold this theory of perception, then the passages above suggest that he regards our perceptions of substances as doubly mediate: first, we perceive only properties, justifying our belief in the substances to which they belong by inference; second, even when it comes to the properties, it is our own ideas of them — rather than the attributes themselves — that are the *immediate* objects of perception.

On the other hand, there is evidence from the *Conversation with Burman* that Descartes rejects the bare substratum conception of substance. Responding to Descartes's claim that it is greater to create a substance than to create the attributes or properties of a substance, Burman says: "But surely the attributes are the same as the substance. So it cannot be 'a greater thing' to create the substance." Descartes concedes the point: "It is true that the attributes are the same as the substance," he says, "but this is when they are all taken together, not when they are taken individually, one by one."[17] Here he seems to be endorsing a bundle theory of substance, a theory that identifies a substance with a collection of coinstantiated properties.[18] If Descartes does favor such a theory, what are we to make of the claim that properties are revealed by sensation, whereas substances are not? One possibility is that he believes substances to be collections of properties, some of which are observable and some of which are not. The collection as a whole cannot be observed, and its existence must be inferred from that of the observable properties that partly constitute it. However, this reading has its own difficulties. Why should Descartes believe that the perception of a property establishes the existence of a substance consisting of both observable and unobservable properties? Why should a bundle composed of observable properties alone be a metaphysical impossibility?

It is natural to suppose that the question of whether Descartes endorses the bare substratum theory or the bundle theory is crucial for determining whether or not physical objects satisfy his subject criterion. If a substance is a basic subject, and if a basic subject is a collection of coinstantiated qualities, then the case for physical objects being substances has at least some promise. On the other hand, if the bare substratum reading is correct, it would seem that we cannot identify a physical object and a substance, because a substance would be just one component of a physical object, the others being properties. (And note that if intrinsically featureless substrata *were* the only things that satisfied the subject criterion, then minds, too, would fail to qualify as substances, for just the same reason.)

In fact, the substratum debate is a red herring, at least as it relates to the question of whether ordinary physical objects qualify as substances. Even if Descartes does, or does sometimes, think of a substance as an intrinsically featureless substratum distinct from all of the properties anchored in it, he does not always use 'substance' to refer to *bare* particulars. He also speaks of thinking substance and extended substance. If properties must be supported by substrata that are devoid of intrinsic character, then a thinking substance consists of such a substratum *plus* the property of thought, and an extended substance consists of such a substratum *plus* the property of extension. Thus, on the substratum reading 'substance' is used to refer both to bare substrata, and to substrata clothed in properties.[19] And if a substratum clothed in properties is a substance, it would seem that minds and physical objects should qualify as substances after all. The only reason for hesitation about this is again the possibility that Descartes denies physical objects the status of basic subjects because he favors a metaphysic that treats physical objects as properties of something else. We shall return to this possibility later, but we may say that if an ordinary physical object is not a property of something else, then it qualifies as a substance on Descartes's subject criterion, whether basic subjects are conceived of as bundles of properties or as substrata devoid of intrinsic character.

## The Independence Criterion

In *Principles of Philosophy*, Descartes offers a second criterion for substance: "By 'substance', we can understand nothing other than a thing which exists in such a way that it needs no other thing in order to exist."[20] He says that only one thing satisfies this criterion for substance, and that this one thing is God. However, he is also willing to allow that this definition can be extended somewhat. In an extended sense, Descartes counts as substances those things that fail to satisfy the independence criterion on its strictest interpretation just because "they can exist only with the help of God's concurrence." A passage added to the French translation of the *Principles* contrasts substances in this secondary sense with the qualities or attributes of created things: whereas secondary substances need only the ordinary concurrence of God in order to exist, qualities and attributes "cannot exist without other things."

What sort of independence is Descartes requiring of substances? We shall consider three possibilities. The first is that he takes substances to be those things that are *logically* independent of other things. The second is that substances are those things that are *causally* independent of other things. The third possibility is that

Descartes holds a mixed view, one that requires of substances some degree of both logical *and* causal independence.

We might say that one thing, x, is logically independent of another, y, if the claim that x exists does not imply the claim that y exists. On a logical reading of the independence criterion, a substance in the primary sense is a thing whose existence implies the existence of no other thing. A substance in the secondary sense is a thing whose existence implies the existence of God, but of no other thing. A property fails to qualify as even a secondary substance, because the existence of a property instance implies the existence of a thing to which it belongs.

This reading of the independence criterion does square well with some of Descartes's remarks about the relation between properties and substances. Earlier in the *Principles*, for instance, he says that it is well known by the natural light that nothingness possesses no attributes or qualities. From this he says it follows that "whenever we find some attributes or qualities, there is necessarily some thing or substance to be found for them to belong to."[21] However, problems begin to arise as soon as we consider the case of divine attributes and their relation to substance. First, it would seem that God cannot be logically independent, because his existence must imply the existence of his properties (there can no more be a substance without properties than there can be properties without a substance).[22] And we cannot hope to circumvent this problem by supposing the independence criterion to be saying that a substance is a thing whose existence implies the existence of no other *substance*, for that would render the criterion viciously circular.[23] One possible line of response on Descartes's behalf would be to invoke the traditional doctrine of divine simplicity, according to which all of God's properties are identical with one another and with God. In fact, Descartes does seem to take this doctrine very seriously, writing that "the unity, the simplicity, or the inseparability of all the attributes of God [*les choses qui sont en Dieu*] is one of the most important of the perfections which I understand him to have."[24] If God is identical with each of his properties, then the fact that his existence implies the existence of his properties poses no threat to his logical independence. A second problem for the logical reading is that it seems to yield the conclusion that divine attributes qualify as substances in the secondary sense. For it is at least arguable that the existence of a divine attribute implies the existence of God and of no other thing. Here, too, Descartes could avoid the problem by calling on the doctrine of divine simplicity: if each divine attribute is identical with God, and God is a primary substance, then each divine attribute is the sole primary substance.

Although the logical reading of Descartes's independence criterion may survive these difficulties concerning divine attributes, there are other problems as well. To begin with, this reading has Descartes saying that the existence of any secondary substance implies the existence of God. Is there a Cartesian argument showing that the existence of each of his candidates for secondary substance implies the existence of God? If every created mind contains an idea of God innately, then the Third Meditation contains an argument that the existence of each created mind implies the existence of God. However, that argument depends on a number of causal principles, such as the principle that the cause of an idea must have as much formal reality as the idea has objective reality. If the existence of a finite mind "implies" the

existence of God only because of a causal principle such as this, then the logical reading of the independence criterion threatens to collapse into a causal reading of it.
What of extended substance? Is there a Cartesian argument showing that the existence of extended substance implies the existence of God? We have yet to discover
what Descartes means by 'extended substance,' but in the Third Meditation he does
argue for the claim that at each moment in the existence of *any* thing, there must be
some cause that preserves it. He deduces this from the fact that "a lifespan can be divided into countless parts, each completely independent of the others."[25] And in the
*First Replies*, he casts this as an argument — or at least the outline of an argument —
for the claim that the existence of each created body must at every moment be preserved by God.[26] When we examine the idea of body, he says, we do not find in it an
idea of the capacity for continual self-preservation. We must conclude that at each
moment a body derives its existence from something outside itself. Furthermore,
anything with the power to preserve a body would also preserve itself. By attending
to the idea of God, he says, we can see that God is self-preserving. Descartes says that
it can be easily demonstrated that God *alone* possesses the superabundance of
power that is necessary for a thing to be the preserving cause of its own existence.
Thus since whatever preserves a body must also preserve itself, and since only God
is self-preserving, it follows that it must be God who preserves the existence of each
created body from moment to moment.

Even if there were forthcoming a demonstration that God alone is self-preserving, Descartes's conclusion that bodies are logically dependent on God also depends
on a causal principle — this time the principle that the life span of any thing is composed of causally independent temporal parts. So again the logical dependence of
secondary substance on primary substance threatens to collapse into causal dependence. The logical reading of Descartes's independence criterion also faces two further — and I believe insuperable — problems. First, the existence of any candidate for
secondary substance will imply the existence of some properties belonging to it. But
a secondary substance is supposed to be a thing whose existence implies the existence of God and of no other thing. Hence nothing can qualify as a secondary substance. Second, and equally troublesome, is the fact that the logical reading leaves
Descartes with a notion of secondary substance that cannot do the metaphysical work
he requires of it. For there is no reason to think that things that are logically independent — things whose existence implies the existence of nothing else but God —
will be impervious to destruction by natural forces. And if a substance is not naturally immortal, then Descartes's intended argument for the immortality of the soul
is undermined.

The most obvious alternative is to construe the *Principles*'s definition of substance as involving causal, rather than logical, independence. I propose the following causal reading of the independence criterion: something is a substance in the
primary sense if it exists without ever being caused to exist by something else; something is a substance in the secondary sense if, at every moment of its existence, it is
causally dependent on God, and on God alone, for its existence.[27] In many respects,
this reading succeeds where the logical reading fails. Descartes does think of God as
causally independent. He also does think that created things are causally dependent

on God for their existence at every moment. We have seen him express the view that created minds and matter are dependent on God for their preservation at every moment. He also thinks that if we reflect on the nature of time, we will see that "the same power and action are needed to preserve anything at each individual moment of its duration as would be required to create that thing anew if it were not yet in existence."[28] This leads him to conclude that "the distinction between preservation and creation is only a conceptual one." Indeed, he does not hesitate to describe God as an "efficient cause" of the things he preserves.[29] Happily, the proposed causal reading of the independence criterion also has the implication that secondary substances are naturally immortal. For on this account, a secondary substance is at every moment of its existence being caused to exist by God. If anything other than the withdrawal of divine concurrence is to destroy a secondary substance, it must do so despite the fact that God is at that very moment willing that substance into existence. Because God is omnipotent, nothing could destroy a substance against God's will. Therefore, nothing but the withdrawal of divine concurrence can result in the destruction of a secondary substance.

Unfortunately, this reading of the independence criterion does not smooth out all of the bumps. Recall that in a passage added to the French edition of the *Principles*, a contrast is drawn between the independence of secondary substances and the dependence of qualities and attributes. Secondary substances are relatively independent because they depend only on God's concurrence for their existence, whereas qualities and attributes "cannot exist without other things."[30] Descartes draws the same contrast in a letter to Hyperaspistes:

> When we call a created substance self-subsistent we do not rule out the divine concurrence which it needs in order to subsist. We mean only that it is the kind of thing that can exist without any other created thing; and this is something that cannot be said about the modes of things, like shape and number.[31]

Whereas the Latin *Principles*'s definition of substance *is* best understood as requiring causal independence of substances, Descartes does seem to have logical dependence in mind when he contrasts the independence of substances with the dependence of properties. This leaves us to choose between two possibilities: either Descartes conflates the notions of causal and logical independence on at least two occasions, or else he is rather clumsily endorsing a kind of mixed view. On one possible mixed view, something is a substance in the primary sense if it is both logically and causally independent; something is a substance in the secondary sense if it is logically independent, but causally dependent on God; qualities and attributes fail to qualify as substances even in the secondary sense, because they are logically dependent (and presumably causally dependent as well).[32] This mixed reading is consistent with the texts, and has some of the virtues of the causal reading without implying that Descartes confuses logical and causal independence. However, it also retains a fatal shortcoming of the logical reading: nothing at all can qualify as a secondary substance according to it. Because the existence of any candidate for secondary substance implies the existence of some properties belonging to it, no candidate for secondary substance can meet the requirement of being logically independent. We should therefore adopt the straightforward causal reading of Descartes's independence criterion, and recognize that on occasion he confuses causal independence with logical independence.

Do human bodies, tables, and planets count as secondary substances on the causal reading of the independence criterion? It would seem that they do not. For even if each of them is causally dependent on God for its preservation, none is causally dependent on God *alone* at every moment of its existence. Human bodies are brought into existence by the sexual activities of human beings; tables are brought into existence by the labor of woodworkers; and, according to Cartesian physics, planets are brought into existence by huge, spinning vortices of celestial matter. Furthermore, there are occasions on which not only the creation but also the continued existence of a physical object depends on the activity of a created thing. For example, the continued existence of a fragile glass vase might depend on the exertions of a person who keeps a weight from crushing it. This result accords with Descartes's denial, in the Synopsis passage, that the human body is a substance.

There is one way of resisting this conclusion. One could argue that whether or not ordinary physical objects satisfy the independence criterion depends on Descartes's view of the division of labor between God and created things. Descartes is variously portrayed as an occasionalist, a quasi occasionalist (holding that minds have causal powers but that bodies do not), and as not endorsing any form of occasionalism. It could be argued that if he were a thoroughgoing occasionalist, then he should regard each human body, table, and planet as satisfying the independence criterion. He is already committed to the view that God is, at every moment, an efficacious cause of the existence of each physical object. Occasionalism implies that at each instant a physical object depends causally on God *alone*, because God is the only cause. By the same reasoning, if Descartes were a quasi occasionalist — believing that finite minds have causal powers, but that bodies do not — then he should not regard human bodies and tables as satisfying the independence criterion, but he should regard planets as doing so. In that case, human bodies and tables would have the activities of created minds in the causal ancestries, whereas planets — according to Cartesian physics — would not. It is only if Descartes believes that created things possess the causal powers we ordinarily ascribe to them that he should regard human bodies, tables, and planets as all failing to satisfy the independence criterion.

A full discussion of Descartes's view of the division of labor between God and created things is beyond the scope of this chapter, but a few remarks are in order. As Malebranche demonstrates in the seventh of his *Dialogues on Metaphysics*, a powerful argument for occasionalism (or at least occasionalism within the material realm, which is all that need concern us) can be constructed by using some familiar Cartesian premises.[33] Descartes holds that each created body must be preserved or re-created by God at each moment. Malebranche's spokesman, Theodore, adds that it is impossible to create a body at an instant without putting it at some definite location. Thus the Cartesian doctrine of divine concurrence seems to imply that at each moment, God is responsible for the existence of each body at its particular location. Theodore could have added that given Descartes's view that all of the other qualities of bodies supervene on the motions of their parts, it also follows that at each moment all of the qualities of each body are completely determined by God. There seems to be nothing left for finite causes to do in the material world. Of course, to show that an argument for occasionalism can be constructed by using Cartesian premises is not yet to show that Descartes was an occasionalist. It is possible, for instance, that in addition to genuinely Cartesian premises, Malebranche's argument also employs some that Descartes would have rejected.[34] Furthermore, even if Descartes's commitments do lead inexorably to occasionalism, it is possible that Descartes does not realize this.

If Descartes *were* an occasionalist, he certainly could have been clearer about this aspect of his metaphysical system. He often speaks of created things as having causal powers: for example, he says that the moon causes the ebb and flow of the tides, a kind of fire causes new wine to seethe when it is left to ferment, and changes in the brain cause dreaming.[35] To be sure, such talk does not by itself preclude a commitment to occasionalism: to preserve the truth of much ordinary talk, occasionalists do typically draw a distinction between true and genuine causes, on the one hand, and secondary or natural causes, on the other. To say that one event is the natural or secondary cause of another is simply to say that it is the sort of event that typically serves as the occasion for God to cause an event of the other sort. Thus occasionalists will permit talk about created things causally interacting with one another, as long as this is understood as talk about natural or secondary causes only. Perhaps this explains Descartes's talk of the moon's influence on the tides, and the brain's influence on our dreams. It is less easy to dismiss a passage in the *Fifth Replies*, where he draws a distinction between two kinds of causes, for there he is specifically addressing the nature of divine concurrence. Descartes says that there are causes of *coming into being*, and causes of *being itself*, and *both* God and created things appear in the examples he gives of *both* sorts of causes:

> Thus an architect is the cause of a house and a father of his child only in the sense of being the causes of their coming into being; and hence, once the work is completed it can remain in existence quite apart from the 'cause' in this sense. But the sun is the cause of the light which it emits, and God is the cause of created things, not just in the sense that they are the causes of the *coming* into being of these things, but also in the sense that they are causes of their *being*; and hence they must always continue to act on the effect in the same way in order to keep it in existence.[36]

While the occasionalist can allow some talk about causal interactions among created things, as long as this is understood properly, it is also true that the nonoccasionalistic theist typically concedes that there is *some* sense in which God is the ultimate or original cause of all there is. So the claim that God is the ultimate cause of all there is — and in particular the claim that God is the cause of all motion — cannot automatically be taken to preclude true finite causes. We have seen that in the Synopsis passage Descartes explicitly denies that a human body is a substance. Since a human body seems to satisfy his subject criterion for substance, and since a human body would also satisfy his independence criterion if he were an occasionalist (or a quasi occasionalist), this is another reason for thinking that Descartes is not an occasionalist (or a quasi occasionalist). However, there is another possibility; even if Descartes is an occasionalist (or a quasi occasionalist), there is a way of accounting for his denial, in the Synopsis, that a human body qualifies as a substance. For it is possible that the causal independence demanded by the independence criterion of secondary substances is causal independence in the natural or secondary sense. In what follows, I shall assume that Descartes holds that ordinary physical objects such as human bodies fail to satisfy the *Principles*'s independence criterion, but I shall not try to decide whether (i) he believes that human bodies and other ordinary physical objects fail to satisfy the independence criterion because they are dependent on true finite causes, or (ii) he is an occasionalist (or a quasi occasionalist) but frames the independence criterion in terms of independence from natural or secondary causes.

Let us briefly review where we are. We began by considering Descartes's subject criterion for substance, and we decided that something satisfies this criterion only if it is a *basic* subject, that is, a subject of properties that is not itself a property. Some support was found both for the contention that Descartes regards a basic subject as a bundle of properties, and for the opposing claim that he regards it as a substratum distinct from any properties. However, this dispute proved moot, since ordinary physical objects seemed to qualify as basic subjects whether they were conceived of as bundles of properties or substrata clothed in properties. The only reason for hedging was the possibility that Descartes favors a metaphysic that treats ordinary physical objects as being properties of something else. Next, we considered several interpretations of his independence criterion for substance. I argued that a causal reading of that criterion best captures his meaning, but conceded that he occasionally confuses causal and logical independence. I maintained that ordinary physical objects do not pass the independence criterion. If this is correct, then either (i) Descartes's two criteria for substance are not coextensive, or else (ii) he treats ordinary physical objects as properties of something else, so that physical objects fail to satisfy the independence criterion *and* the subject criterion. We shall briefly take up these possibilities later, but now we turn to the Synopsis passage and to two accounts of Descartes's view of the relation between physical objects and extended substance.

## Monism and Mass Terms

The notion of immaterial substance is central to Descartes's proposed demonstration of the Christian doctrine of the immortality of the soul. That demonstration, as we have seen, consists of the premise that the soul is a substance, together with the premise that all substances are naturally immortal. Although the idea that all substances are naturally immortal is therefore important for Descartes, it does raise a problem with the notion that there are substances in the material realm. Individual physical objects — such things as rolltop desks, wine glasses, and flowering plants — seem to come and go. This fact — together with Descartes's explicit denial, in the Synopsis passage, that human bodies qualify as substances — leads most commentators to assert that there is an asymmetry between his treatments of thinking and extended substance. However, they disagree about the nature of this supposed asymmetry, and about the meaning of Descartes's claim that "body, taken in the general sense, is a substance."[37]

A great many commentators have taken Descartes to be claiming, or at least implying, that there is only one material substance: the whole of the extended universe.

In fact, there is a tendency on behalf of those who regard Descartes as a monist about extended substance to simply assert, without the benefit of supporting argument, that the Synopsis passage commits Descartes to monism about extended substance. One assumes that this is so because the suggestion that Descartes is a monist about extended substance *does* supply an attractive set of answers to some of the puzzles raised by the Synopsis passage. For instance, it is clear why one might think the whole physical universe passes the independence criterion whereas individual physical objects do not. Individual physical objects can be made to go out of existence by the rearrangement or scattering of their parts, but the totality of the world's matter is invulnerable to destruction in this manner. The material universe does not go out of existence simply because its contents are reorganized, and on Descartes's view only God can annihilate matter. As for the relation between an individual physical object and extended substance, several different stories are compatible with the monist reading. Most of those who attribute monism about extended substance to Descartes also ascribe to him the view that individual physical objects are modes of the one extended substance. Some commentators also suggest that for Descartes there is an element of conventionality about which modes of the one extended substance are regarded by us as distinct physical objects.[38] Though none of these commentators tarries over the question of what sort of modes physical objects are, it is perhaps most charitable to interpret them as attributing to Descartes the view that physical objects are modes of *parts* of the one extended substance. This avoids the rather obvious problem of ascribing incompatible properties to the one extended substance whenever one physical object is hot and another is cold. However, it is also worth noting that the view that ordinary physical objects are modes is by no means forced on one who would read Descartes as a monist about extended substance. One who regards the totality of the world's matter as the only extended thing satisfying the independence criterion might seek, for example, to reduce physical objects to nonsubstantial parts of the one extended substance. Another possibility would be to reduce physical objects to series of temporal stages of nonsubstantial parts of the one extended substance, thus making room for the possibility that an enduring physical object might be composed of temporal stages of different nonsubstantial parts of the one extended substance. This innovation might be thought necessary to explain how an ordinary physical object could survive the replacement of some of its parts. It would be anachronistic to attribute such a view to Descartes in the absence of direct textual evidence. At the same time, I know of no direct textual evidence for the claim that Descartes regarded physical objects as modes (or as nonsubstantial parts) of the one extended substance either.

The suggestion that Descartes is a monist about material substance does make sense of the Synopsis passage, but it also flatly contradicts his considered remarks about the individuation of extended substances. There are a number of places where Descartes refers to extended objects smaller than the universe as substances. These items include a stone, particles, a hand, and articles of clothing.[39] Advocates of the monist reading will regard these as infelicitous references to things that Descartes really regards as modes of parts of the one substance (or as nonsubstantial parts of the one extended substance, or as series of temporal stages of nonsubstantial parts of the one extended substance). However, they cannot so easily dismiss the *Principles*'s account of what is meant by a "real distinction," an account that clearly commits Descartes to a plurality of material substances. Descartes says that a real distinction can hold only between two or more substances, and that "we can perceive that two substances are really distinct simply from the fact that we can clearly and distinctly understand one apart from the other."[40] It is a matter of considerable debate what exactly Descartes means by this last remark, but there is no doubt that he goes on to maintain that there are real distinctions between all of the parts of an extended substance. According to Descartes, we can be certain that if there is any extended or corporeal substance, then "each and every part of it, as delimited by us in our thought, is really distinct from all the other parts of the same substance."[41] Given that the *Principles* is arguably the most finished statement of Descartes's metaphysics, and that here he is explicitly addressing the issue of the individuation of extended substances, the burden of proof must surely lie with those who would deny that Descartes believes in a plurality of extended substances. Far from endorsing monism about material substance, he is committed to the existence of an infinity of material substances, since he believes not only that every part of an extended substance is itself an extended substance, but also that every extended thing can actually be divided into parts (at least by God).[42] His commitments to the infinite divisibility of matter and the plurality of extended substances are also explicit in a letter to Gibieuf, where he writes that "from the simple fact that I consider the two halves of a part of matter, however small it may be, as two complete substances . . . I conclude with certainty that they are really divisible."[43]

A second approach to the puzzle raised by the Synopsis passage is the suggestion that when Descartes is speaking of the extended realm—and when he is being careful—he uses 'substance' only as a mass term and not as a count term. Mass terms refer to stuffs, whereas count terms refer to things. Thus 'granite' and 'oxygen' are mass terms, whereas 'tree' and 'station wagon' are count terms. Some words can be used either as mass terms or as count terms, as in the case of 'coffee' and 'chili.' In English, the indefinite article serves as a grammatical marker, distinguishing count terms from mass terms; we say "a station wagon" but not "an oxygen." There are other clues as well. For example, plural count terms are used in conjunction with words like 'many' and 'few' and range over individuals. Mass terms are used in conjunction with words like 'much' and 'less' and when pluralized must be understood as ranging not over individuals but over *kinds* of individuals (so, for example, 'different granites' must be taken to refer to different varieties of granite, not different pieces of granite). The absence of articles in Latin means that we must rely on context rather than grammar alone to tell us whether Descartes is using *substantia* as a mass term or a count term. This second approach to the Synopsis passage says that whereas Descartes uses *substantia* as a count term when discussing the mental realm, he uses it only as a mass term in his discussions of the extended realm. Recall that the monist reading had portrayed the asymmetry between the mental and material realms this way: many individual things count as mental substances, but only one individual thing counts as a material substance. The mass term reading, on the other hand, says that while many individual things count as mental substances, *no* individual thing counts as a material substance. There may be portions of material substance (mass term), but none of these portions [including the totality of material substance (mass term)] is itself a substance (count term). On this reading, the contrast drawn in the Synopsis passage — the contrast between a human body and "body, taken in the general sense" — is the contrast between a human body and the kind of stuff of which it is composed. Descartes would be saying that while individual human bodies come and go — thus failing to satisfy the independence criterion — there continues to be extended stuff, and this extended stuff is causally dependent on God alone for its existence.

It might be doubted whether there can be extended stuff without there being at least one extended thing, namely, the totality of that stuff. The proponents of the mass term reading will point out that it is consistent with their reading that there be extended things, as long as these things do not qualify as substances. The difficulty is that if the totality of material stuff is a thing, it would seem to be a thing that Descartes should regard as satisfying his independence criterion. If Descartes does regard the totality of extended stuff as being a thing that satisfies his independence criterion, then the mass term reading collapses into the monist reading, inheriting its difficulties. However, even if the mass term reading does not collapse into the monist reading, the former does no better than the latter when it comes to accommodating the *Principles*'s account of what is meant by a "real distinction." If 'substance' were being used as a mass term when Descartes tells us that "a real distinction exists only between two or more substances,"[44] then he would be saying that real distinctions hold only between two or more different *kinds* of substances. But we know that for Descartes there are fundamentally only two different kinds of substances. If a real distinction could hold only between two or more kinds of substances, then there could be only one real distinction — the distinction between mind and matter. Yet as we have seen, Descartes says that each part of extended or corporeal substance is really distinct from every other part of that same substance.

## Transubstantiation and Extended Substances

Like the notion of immaterial substance, the notion of material substance has an important role to play in Descartes's philosophical theology. Just as the notion of immaterial substance plays the central role in his argument for the immortality of the soul, so the notion of material substance plays the central role in his account of the transubstantiation of the Eucharist.

As Descartes reports in the *Fourth Replies*, the Council of Trent taught that during the Mass "the whole substance of the bread is changed into the substance of the body of Our Lord Christ while the form of the bread remains unaltered."[45] Many of Descartes's contemporaries took this to imply that the substance of the bread departed while its accidents remained behind.[46] And this, in turn, was taken to require the doctrine of "real accidents," according to which "there are accidents which could by divine power exist apart from any subject."[47] It is this which prompts Arnauld, in the *Fourth Objections*, to say that the aspect of Descartes's thinking that is likeliest to give offense to theologians is his view that accidents are unintelligible apart from some substance for them to inhere in. As Arnauld sees it, if Descartes's philosophy is accepted, "the Church's teachings concerning the sacred mysteries of the Eucharist cannot remain completely intact."[48]

Descartes first responds by saying that he never positively denied the doctrine of real accidents; he merely found it unintelligible, and did without it. Moreover, he was careful never to deny that God can do what we find unintelligible. But after this defensive parry, Descartes goes on to offer an account of the transubstantiation that he regards as consistent with both the edicts of the Council of Trent, and with the rest of his own philosophy. This account requires, first, that we conceive of the surface of a body not as a part of it or as a part of the immediately surrounding corporeal substances, but as the boundary between these two. This boundary, he reminds us, will be different from that which is revealed by touch or our unaided vision: the surface of a body is determined by variegated clusters of particles too small to see. Moreover, since some of these particles may be in motion, the surface defined by them may be constantly changing. But whether in motion or not, Descartes says, the surface of a corporeal substance must be the locus of any contact with other corporeal substances. He then cites Aristotle as an authority for the further claim that all sense perception occurs only by contact. Descartes believes not only that all sense perception requires contact (mediate or immediate) between our sense organs and the bodies we perceive, but also that the opportunities a body presents for contact with our sense organs determine its observable qualities. That is, a body's observable qualities supervene on the disposition of its surface. Descartes therefore draws the conclusion that any corporeal substance that comes to replace another, filling exactly the same surface, must as a result acquire precisely the same observable qualities as those possessed by the original. And this in turn yields a new understanding of the council's claim that in the course of the Mass the substance of the bread is changed, while the form remains the same: the change of substance is the substitution of another substance of exactly the same dimensions, whereas the "form," which remains unaltered, is the boundary between the original bread and the surrounding particles. Descartes regards this account as being of great value to the Catholic faith, as it satisfies the letter of the Council of Trent's teachings while dispensing with the "gratuitous" and "incomprehensible" doctrine of detachable real accidents.[49]

In the *Fourth Replies*, Descartes does not say how we are supposed to understand the claim that a substance occupying a boundary that formerly contained a small piece of bread could be Christ's body. He deflects this question by saying that the Council of Trent teaches that the manner of Christ's presence is something that "we can scarcely express in words."[50] But later, in an important letter to the Jesuit priest Denis Mesland, he points out that the council's words fall short of a proscription against attempts to explain the manner of Christ's presence, and he makes just such an attempt himself. In the process of doing so, Descartes disambiguates the word 'body' and at the same time sheds considerable light on his conception of material substance:

> First of all, I consider what exactly is the body of a man, and I find that this word 'body' is very ambiguous. When we speak of a body in general, we mean a determinate part of matter, a part of the quantity of which the universe is composed. In this sense, if the smallest amount of that quantity were removed, we would judge without more ado that the body was smaller and no longer complete; and if any particle of matter were changed, we would at once think that the body was no longer quite the same, no longer numerically the same. But when we speak of the body of a man,

we do not mean a determinate part of matter, or one that has a determinate size; we mean simply that whole of the matter which is united with the soul of that man. And so, even though that matter changes, and its quantity increases or decreases, we still believe that it is the same body, numerically the same body, so long as it remains joined and substantially united with the same soul.[51]

Recall that in the Synopsis passage, Descartes distinguished between "body, taken in the general sense" and a human body, telling us that the former but not the latter is a substance. Here he has drawn the same distinction, but now his French makes it clear that the contrast is that between *a* body in the general sense and a human body.[52] And here he also identifies a body in the general sense with a determinate quantity of matter. Since a body in the general sense is an extended substance, if follows that a determinate quantity of matter is an extended substance. A human body, however, is not to be identified with any determinate quantity of matter: its matter changes over the course of its career. The identity of a human body, Descartes says, is determined by its union with a soul.

When Descartes identifies a body in the general sense with a determinate quantity of matter, he is using 'quantity' (*quantité*) in the sense that has more recently been given such careful treatment by Helen Cartwright.[53] In this sense, though your ring and my ring may contain the same *amount* of gold (being each of the same purity and weight), they cannot contain the same *quantity* of gold unless we are sharing a ring. Two rings are made up of precisely the same quantity of gold, in this sense of 'quantity,' only when one ring is melted down and another is made from the resulting liquid, with no gold added and no gold left over. Thus, sameness of quantity implies sameness of amount, but the reverse does not hold. That Descartes is using 'quantity' in this way, and not as meaning "amount," is shown by his account of transubstantiation. According to Descartes, transubstantiation involves the replacement of one extended substance with another, without any change in the surface of the bread. As Descartes identifies an extended substance with "a body, taken in the general sense," and a body in the general sense with a determinate quantity of matter, it follows that for him the transubstantiation involves the replacement of one determinate quantity of matter with another. At the same time, Descartes maintains that there is absolutely no change in the surface to be occupied, and hence no change in the *amount* of matter present.

When Descartes resists the identification of a human body with any determinate quantity of matter, his point is not just that human bodies sometimes increase and decrease in size, but also that each human body is composed of numerically different chunks of matter at different stages in its existence. Later in the correspondence with Mesland, he writes that "it is quite true to say that I have the same body now as I had ten years ago, although the matter of which it is composed has changed, because the numerical identity of a body of a man does not depend on its matter, but on its form, which is its soul."[54] A human body is not to be identified with the determinate quantity of matter that composes it at a time, because that human body and that quantity of matter have different identity conditions. A human body can persist without the determinate quantity of matter that once constituted it persisting; and as we shall see shortly, a determinate quantity of matter can persist without the human body it once constituted persisting. In the remainder of this section, we take a closer look at Descartes's remarks about the identity conditions of human bodies and of quantities of matter.

Descartes believes that the identity of a human body depends on its union with a human soul. In the first letter to Mesland, quoted from above, he explains that there are two ways in which this can take place. In the case of the Eucharist, particles of bread and wine become the body and blood of Christ because the soul of Christ becomes "supernaturally" joined with those particles through the power of words of consecration. This supernatural union does not require any particular organization on the part of the particles of bread and wine. But Descartes also writes, "The soul of Jesus Christ could not have remained *naturally* joined with each of these particles of bread and wine unless they were assembled with many others to make up all the organs of a human body necessary for life."[55] In the *Passions of the Soul*, he goes so far as to say that "death never occurs through the absence of the soul, but only because one of the principle parts of the body decays."[56] So although, strictly speaking, it is correct to say that union with a human soul is sufficient to render a quantity of matter a human body, in the natural course of things this union is possible only when the quantity of matter has a very particular organization. As he put it in the Synopsis passage, a human body is a particular "configuration of limbs and accidents."[57]

What Descartes tells Mesland about the identity conditions of a quantity of matter is that a quantity of matter cannot survive the removal of even the smallest amount of that quantity; if any particle of the matter were changed, he says, a numerically different body (in the general sense) would result. A great deal depends on what exactly Descartes means here by 'remove' (*ôter*) and 'change' (*changer*). Let us begin with three possible renderings of his claim that a quantity of matter cannot survive the removal of any of its parts:

   (i) A quantity of matter cannot survive the rearrangement of any of its parts.
  (ii) A quantity of matter cannot survive the separation of any of its parts.
 (iii) A quantity of matter cannot survive the annihilation of any of its parts.

If Descartes intends either (i) or (ii), then quantities of matter will not satisfy the independence criterion for substance, since causal interactions between finite bodies often do result in the rearrangement and scattering of their parts. On the other hand, if (iii) alone captures his meaning, then quantities of matter will pass the independence criterion, since Descartes holds that God alone can annihilate matter.

In fact, there is reason to think that (iii) alone does capture Descartes's meaning. Option (i) can be ruled out quickly. Descartes clearly maintains that a body in the general sense can survive changes in the arrangement of its parts. In the *Principles*, he says that "one and the same body, with its quantity unchanged, may be extended in many different ways."[58] This is an important point of contrast between a body in the general sense and an ordinary physical object, such as a human body. While a quantity of matter can survive being extended in many different ways, a human body must maintain a certain organization. One need only rearrange the parts of a human body in order to destroy it. "In the case of the human body," he tells us in the *Second Replies*, "the difference between it and other bodies consists merely in the arrangement of the limbs and other accidents of this sort; and the final death of the body depends solely on a division or change of shape."[59] And if the persistence of a human body depends on a quantity of matter being extended in a particular manner, this is even clearer in the case of inanimate physical objects, where the question of union with a soul (and the possibility of a supernatural union) does not arise: one can destroy a table or a planet simply by pulverizing it.

Option (ii), on the other hand, seems ruled out by Descartes's account of rarefaction. He says: "Rarefied bodies . . . are those which have many gaps between their parts — gaps which are occupied by other bodies; and they become denser simply in virtue of the parts coming together and reducing or completely closing the gaps."[60] Since Descartes takes a rarefied body to be a body with gaps between its parts, and since he evidently regards it as possible for there to be rarefied bodies, he evidently regards it as possible for there to be bodies whose parts are scattered. It makes no difference here that Descartes is a plenist and therefore believes that the gaps between the parts of a scattered body will be filled by other bodies.

If a quantity of matter can survive the rearrangement and scattering of its parts, but not their annihilation, what are we to make of Descartes's remark that a body in the general sense would cease to be numerically the same if any particle of its matter were "changed"? He cannot have in mind just any change, or else the mere arrangement of a body's parts would suffice to destroy a quantity of matter. Perhaps Descartes is saying that if one particle of a body were annihilated and replaced with a different particle, the body would no longer be the same. Or else he might be trying to make the point that if a particle belonging to an ordinary physical object were separated from the object, with a different particle assuming the place it had previously occupied, the quantity of matter constituting the object would no longer be the same quantity of matter as had previously constituted it.

## Conclusions

Descartes identifies extended substances with quantities of matter, things that can survive any rearrangement or scattering of their parts, but not the annihilation of any of them. Once we recognize this, a number of things fall into place. A quantity of matter in this sense satisfies both of Descartes's criteria for substancehood. It satisfies the subject criterion because it is a subject of properties but is not a property of something else. It satisfies the independence criterion because it is causally independent of everything but God. Ordinary physical objects come into and go out of existence with the rearrangement of quantities of matter — something that in the ordinary course of nature results from the action of finite causes, whether genuine or occasional — but quantities of matter themselves can be created or destroyed only by God. Since every part of a quantity of matter is itself a quantity of matter, we also get the desired result that every part of an extended substance is itself an extended substance. If Descartes sees an asymmetry between the mental and material realms, it does not have to do with the number of substances belonging to each.

The identification of extended substances with quantities of matter also makes sense of the Synopsis passage. Descartes's distinction between a human body and a body in the general sense is the distinction between an ordinary physical object and a quantity of matter. Although a human body is, at any moment during its career, composed of a quantity of matter, Descartes tells us that the human body and the quantity of matter that composes it have different identity conditions. For the persistence of a human body requires the persistence of "a certain configuration of limbs and other accidents,"[61] whereas this particular arrangement of limbs and accidents is merely an accidental property of the quantity of matter that composes that human body. Here Descartes draws a contrast between the realms of matter and mind. Unlike the human body, he says, "the human mind is not made up of any accidents in this way, but is a pure substance." He explains: "For even if all the accidents of the mind change, so that is has different objects of the understanding and different desires and sensations, it does not on that account become a different mind; whereas a human body loses its identity merely as a result of a change in the shape of some of its parts."[62]

On Descartes's view, the persistence of a human mind does not depend on the persistence of properties that are merely accidental to the substance that composes it. In fact, when it comes to the mental realm, Descartes does not even see a need to distinguish between a substance and the thing it composes, and *there* is the asymmetry between his accounts of matter and mind. He sees no need to distinguish between a thinking substance and a mind because he thinks that a mind's properties are all psychological, and he rejects the notion that any kind of psychological continuity is necessary for the persistence of a mind. No matter what modifications the substance that is my mind comes to have, it does not on that account cease to be the same mind.

Ordinary physical objects other than human bodies fail to qualify as substances for much the same reason as human bodies do: the persistence of a chair, like the persistence of a human body, requires that a quantity of matter be organized in a certain way, and in the natural course of things this requires the cooperation of other finite causes (whether genuine or occasional). Descartes must therefore be regarded as speaking lightly when he claims that stones, hands, and articles of clothing are substances. However, this bit of untidiness is not peculiar to the reading defended here: champions of the monist reading and the mass term reading must say the same thing. Furthermore, the reading defended here is able to make sense of a locution that on these other two readings is quite mysterious. Descartes sometimes speaks of "the substance *of* a brain"[63] or "the substance *of* the wax."[64] These phrases are not easily explained by the monist reading or the mass term reading. On the present reading, however, the substance of a brain is the quantity of matter that composes a brain; the substance of the wax is the quantity of matter that composes the wax.

As we have seen, the subject criterion seems more liberal than the independence criterion, since ordinary physical objects seem to satisfy the former but not the latter. There are several possibilities here. One is that Descartes's criteria for substance are not coextensive, but that he intends them to supply *jointly* necessary and sufficient conditions for being a substance. In that case, no particular problem would be raised by ordinary physical objects satisfying one criterion and not the other: failure to satisfy either of them would be sufficient grounds to exclude a thing from counting as a substance. A second possibility is that the criteria are not coextensive, that Descartes fails to provide us with a single, coherent account of substance, but that when he is doing serious metaphysics it is in fact the independence criterion that he relies on. A third possibility is that the two criteria are coextensive after all, and that Descartes regards ordinary physical objects as failing to satisfy even the subject criterion.

If ordinary physical objects fail to satisfy the subject criterion, it is presumably not because they fail to qualify as the subjects of properties, but because they are properties themselves. And if Descartes regards ordinary physical objects as properties, he presumably regards them as properties of quantities of matter. While I know of no direct, textual evidence that Descartes regards an ordinary physical object as a property of the quantity of matter that constitutes it, the relationship between an ordinary physical object and the quantity of matter that constitutes it does seem to fit his characterization of the relationship between substance and mode. For example, he says that "the nature of a mode is such that it cannot be understood at all unless the concept of the thing of which it is a mode is implied in its own concept,"[65] whereas "we can readily understand a substance apart from a mode."[66] One could certainly argue that the concept of an ordinary physical object includes the fact that such an object must, at any moment, be composed of some quantity of matter, whereas it does not follow from the concept of a quantity of matter that it must, at any moment, constitute some ordinary physical object. And in the letter to Mesland, which provided our clue to the identification of an extended substance with a quantity of matter, Descartes distinguishes a mode from a substance by saying that the mode "cannot be changed without a change in that in which or through which it exists."[67] The supervenience of the properties of an ordinary physical object on those of the quantity of matter that constitutes it could be seen as an instance of this principle. Finally, if Descartes did think of ordinary physical objects as modes of quantities of matter, this would dissipate any oddness resulting from the colocation of ordinary physical objects and quantities of matter. For there is nothing odd about a thing and its properties being at the same place at the same time.[68]

*Notes*

1. CSM I, 230.

2. I intend "ordinary physical objects" quite liberally, including not only human bodies, tables, and planets but also books, clouds, snails, mountains, telephones, wisps of smoke, and bubbling brooks. What is common to all of these things is that they come into and go out of existence because of the arrangement of material stuff. I qualify these physical objects as *ordinary* to distinguish them from quantities of matter, where this is understood in a sense explained below.

3. Peter Markie finds *three* distinct conceptions of substance in Descartes. See "Descartes's Concepts of Substance," in John Cottingham, ed., *Reason, Will, and Sensation* (Oxford: Clarendon Press, 1994), pp. 63–87.

4. CSM II, 9. To say that a substance is immortal by its nature is to say that because of its nature it is immune to destruction by any natural cause. This does not mean that a substance is invulnerable to destruction by a supernatural cause, and Descartes believes that God can annihilate any created substance at any moment simply by withdrawing his concurrence. According to Descartes, God annihilates a created substance by failing to sustain it, not by performing a positive, destructive act. To Gassendi he writes that it would be an imperfection in

God if he had to "tend towards non-being by performing a positive action whenever he wished to bring our existence to an end" (CSM II, 255). See also CSMK 193.

5.  Descartes apparently regards these matters as falling at least partly within the domain of physics and consequently outside the domain of the *Meditations*.

6.  See S. V. Keeling, *Descartes* (Oxford: Oxford University Press, 1968), pp. 129–130; B. Williams, *Descartes: The Project of Pure Enquiry* (London: Penguin, 1978), pp. 126–129; J. Cottingham, *Descartes* (Oxford: Blackwell, 1986), pp. 84–88; Georges Dicker, *Descartes: An Analytical and Historical Introduction* (New York: Oxford University Press, 1993), pp. 212–217; T. Lennon, "The Problem of Individuation among the Cartesians," in *Individuation and Identity in Early Modern Philosophy*, K. Barber and J. E. Gracia, eds. (Albany: State University of New York Press, 1994), p. 13; T. Lennon, "Descartes's Idealism," in *Philosophie et Culture*, Proceedings of the XVII World Congress of Philosophy (Montreal: Editions Montmorency, 1988), pp. 53–56.

7.  Of the commentators mentioned in the previous note, Cottingham is the sole exception.

8.  See J. Bennett, *Kant's Dialectic* (Cambridge: Cambridge University Press, 1974), sect. 13, "Cartesian Substances", pp. 42–44; R. S. Woolhouse, *Descartes, Spinoza, Leibniz: The Concept of Substance in Seventeenth Century Metaphysics* (London: Routledge, 1993), pp. 22–24.

9.  CSM II, 114.

10.  Letter of 21 April 1641 to Mersenne for Hobbes; CSMK 178.

11.  For instance, *Principles* I:63; CSM I, 215.

12.  CSM II, 117.

13.  For arguments supporting this claim, see J. Bennett, "Substratum," *History of Philosophy Quarterly* 4 (1987); 197–215.

14.  CSM II, 156.

15.  CSM I, 210.

16.  R. S. Woolhouse cites these passages, among others, as showing that the notion of a bare substratum "seems to be present" in Descartes (*Descartes, Spinoza, Leibniz*, pp. 17–18). In "Descartes's Concepts of Substance," Markie also attributes the bare substratum reading of Descartes to Louis Loeb (p. 76). I suspect that this attribution is not accurate, but finding Loeb's account, in *From Descartes to Hume: Continental Metaphysics and the Development of Modern Philosophy* (Ithaca, N.Y.: Cornell University Press, 1981), pp. 78–83, itself rather obscure, I cannot be sure.

17.  *Descartes' Conversation with Burman*, J. Cottingham, ed. and trans. (Oxford: Oxford University Press, 1976), p. 15.

18.  This reading of Descartes is defended by Markie in "Descartes's Concepts of Substance" and by Cottingham in *Descartes' Conversation with Burman*, pp. 77–79.

19.  To the extent that the notion of a bare substratum is even intelligible, Descartes could be charged with the mistake of treating the relationship between a bare substratum and the properties that inhere in it as like the relationship between two substantial things, such as a man and his clothes. When we are interested in distinguishing between a biological organism and its trappings, we can use 'man' to single out the creature beneath the clothing; nevertheless, a fully clothed man is also called a man.

20.  *Principles* 1:51. Here I deviate from CSM, using instead the translation of the *Principles* by V. R. Miller and R. P. Miller, *René Descartes: Principles of Philosophy* (Dordrecht: Reidel, 1983), p. 23, which translates *indigere* as "need" rather than "depend on."

21.  *Principles* 2:11, CSM I, 196.

22.  This objection is advanced by J. Hoffman and G. Rosenkrantz in *Substance among Other Categories* (Cambridge: Cambridge University Press, 1994), p. 54.

23. Descartes *does* say this at one point in the *Fourth Replies* (CSM II, 159), but it would be uncharitable to regard this as a careful expression of the independence criterion.

24. CSM II, 34; see also II, 98. I have doubts about the coherence of the doctrine of divine simplicity, but it does still have serious defenders.

25. CSM II, 33.

26. CSM II, 79–80. For other versions of this argument, see CSM II, 116–119, and *Principles* 1:21; CSM I, 200.

27. Loeb offers a different causal reading of the *Principles*'s criterion. He says that for Descartes x is a secondary substance if it is *possible* that x's existence does not depend causally upon the existence of any other entity except God (*From Descartes to Hume*, pp. 93–100). I ignore this reading because the "possible" in Loeb's formulation represents a departure from the text of *Principles* 1:51.

28. CSM II, 33.

29. CSM II, 33, 79.

30. *Principles* 1:51; CSM I, 210.

31. Letter of August 1641 to Hyperaspistes; CSMK 193–194.

32. Another possibility is that substance in the primary sense is logically and causally independent, whereas substances in the secondary sense are both logically and causally dependent on God alone. This view faces the same difficulty as the mixed view I consider.

33. *Dialogues on Metaphysics*, Willis Doney, ed. and trans. (New York: Abaris Books, 1980), pp. 145ff.

34. Daniel Garber (who portrays Descartes as a quasi occasionalist) argues that Malebranche's "divine sustenance" argument for occasionalism depends on a "cinematic" view of God as the cause of motion, a view that Descartes rejects in favor of an "impulse" view of God as the cause of motion. See "How God Causes Motion: Descartes, Divine Sustenance, and Occasionalism," *Journal of Philosophy* 84 (1987): 567–580.

35. Moon: CSM I, 133; wine: CSM I, 134; brain: CSM I, 139.

36. CSM II, 254–255.

37. CSM II, 10.

38. Williams, *Descartes*; Cottingham, *Descartes' Conversation with Burman*; Lennon, "Descartes's Idealism."

39. A stone: CSM II, 30; particles: CSM I, 246; a hand: CSM II, 157; clothing: CSM I, 299, and II, 297.

40. CSM I, 213.

41. Ibid.

42. See CSM I, 231, and II, 59.

43. CSMK 202–203.

44. CSM I, 213.

45. CSM II, 175.

46. See Arnauld at CSM II, 153.

47. CSM II, 281.

48. Ibid., 152–153.

49. See CSMK 88 and 177.

50. AT VII, 252. Here I depart from the translation in CSM II, which has "cannot express in words."

51. CSMK 242–243.

52. "Quand nous parlons d'un corps en general, nous entendons une partie determinée de la matiere . . . " (AT IV, 166).

53. "Quantities," *The Philosophical Review* 79 (1970): 25–42.

54. CSMK 278–279.

55. Ibid., 244 (my emphasis).
56. CSM I, 329.
57. CSM II, 10.
58. CSM I, 215.
59. CSM II, 109.
60. CSM I, 225.
61. CSM II, 9.
62. Ibid., 10.
63. *Principles* 2:5; CSM I, 100.
64. CSM II, 248.
65. CSM I, 301; cf. 213–214, 298.
66. Ibid., 298.
67. CSMK 241.
68. I wish to thank Scott Sehon and Margaret Wilson for instructive comments on an earlier draft of this chapter.

## 5

J. A. COVER

# Spinoza's Extended Substance

*Cartesian and Leibnizian Reflections*

Spinoza argues for the claim that there is exactly one extended substance, which he calls "God or Nature."[1] One way (there are many) of coming to grips with Spinoza's claim is to ask *what it is* that he believes the one extended substance to be — that is, to orient this bit of his metaphysics alongside other ontologies we take ourselves to understand reasonably well and to look for agreement or departure. More specifically, the historian of philosophy is invited to ask to what extent this item of Spinoza's ontology is recognizable as something accepted or rejected by his historical and intellectual neighbors. In what follows I want to set Spinoza's "there exists one extended substance" alongside familiar Cartesian and Leibnizian treatments of substance and extension (and existence, too, leaving questions of counting[2] aside).

## Preliminaries: Descartes and Leibniz

To suppose that Descartes's and Leibniz's views about extended substance are familiar isn't to pretend we're perfectly clear on all matters of detail. Thus:

(i) If it is generally agreed that Descartes believes that spatial extension is the whole essence of material or corporeal substance, I take it nevertheless to be a point of controversy whether Descartes believes there are many extended substances. Commentators have claimed that he does not; but passages from the Synopsis to the *Meditations* and part 2 of the *Principles* are suggestive at best.[3] Moreover the implication of *Principles* 2.18 — that "there is no body between spatially distant points $p_1$ and $p_2$" is equivalent to the necessarily false "the distance between $p_1$ and $p_2$ is a mode of extension but it measures no extended substance" — recommends the natural translation of 2.16: "a body's being extended in length, breadth and depth in itself warrants the conclusion that it is a substance" (AT VIIIA, 49: CSM I, 230). I shall in any case take it that Descartes is willing to reckon space (the whole of it) as extended substance, and perhaps as *an* extended substance. From this, together with the claim that the whole essence of body is extension, it follows that there can be no vacua, no regions of space devoid of material substance.[4]

(ii) If it is generally agreed that Leibniz's individual monads are unextended substances, his broadly "phenomenalist" account of body and his reductionist attitude about space remain issues of considerable debate. Suppose we read the Clarke correspondence to offer an eliminative reduction of extended absolute space, treating spatial claims as adjectival on relational facts about bodies otherwise said to be in it. The further phenomenalist account of bodies themselves, conducted elsewhere, looks nevertheless to make monads spatial if not extended: any individual monad is said to have "its own location [*locus*] in the order of coexistents, that is, in space" — to have "a certain kind of situation [*situs*] in extension" (G II, 253: AG 178). Moreover, we are left with Leibniz's repeated claims, in the Clarke correspondence and so many other mature texts, that space is an *ens rationis* or "ideal" — terms of art for the ontological status of what, in the present case, looks for all the world to emerge from an identificatory reduction of relational space to abstracta in the mind of God.[5] I shall in any case take it that Leibniz denies the existence of extended substantial space, and indeed denies that there are any extended substances whatsoever. His arguments against spatial vacua, serving their polemical role at a level of discussion shared by the Newtonians (where bodies are yet in the picture), do not figure at the deepest level of his metaphysic of unextended substances.

Here then is a standard way of viewing Descartes and Leibniz on this issue: Descartes affirms the existence of something — extended substantial space — whose existence Leibniz denies. Standard, received views can of course be challenged. To anticipate our discussion of Spinoza's extended substance, it is perhaps worth reflecting on the burden confronting one who rejects the standard view just sketched. The facts themselves look to serve well enough.

(i′) Descartes was taught and understood the traditional Aristotelian-Scholastic account of substance. Two core features of that account[6] are central to Descartes's own. (a) First, a substance "depend[s] on no other thing for its existence" (AT VIIIA, 24: CSM I, 210); substances are — dependence on God (notoriously) aside — able to "exist on their own" (AT VII, 222: CSM II, 156), are "capable of existing independently" (AT VII, 44: CSM II, 30). (b) Second, substances are the bearers of properties, properties standing to them in a way that they do not stand to anything. "Substance," says Descartes, applies to that in which a property, quality, or attribute immediately "resides as in a subject."[7] Among the properties any substance has is a special one: each substance has "one principal property which constitutes its nature and essence" (AT VIIIA, 24: CSM I, 210). Rejecting the hylomorphism of the schools, Descartes thus asserts that extension alone — spatial spreadoutness in length, breadth and depth — is the principal property (or often "principal attribute" or simply "attribute") of material substance. That is the fundamental Cartesian move toward a geometrical physics. From it follows the view that "there is no real difference between space and corporeal substance" (AT VIIIA, 46: CSM I, 227). The extension constituting the nature of a space (we might say "a region") is the same as that constituting the nature of a body. And extended space itself — the whole of it — is likewise an extended substance. Call it, as we did earlier, "extended substantial space." Descartes claims that extended substantial space is among the items of the created universe.

(ii') The conceptual background of seventeenth-century metaphysics, against which Descartes's account of extended substance is developed, is Leibniz's too; it is a background they shared. So it is implausible at best to suppose that writing a mere forty years after Descartes was composing the *Principles*, the mature Leibniz was unfamiliar with or misunderstood the deployment of core features (a) and (b) in Descartes's account of substance. Leibniz deploys them himself, claiming that (a') "each substance is a world apart, independent of everything outside of itself except God" (*Discourse*, sect. 14: G IV, 439: AG 47) and that (b') "when several predicates are attributed to a single subject and this subject is attributed to no other, it is called an individual substance" (*Discourse*, sect. 8: G IV, 432: AG 40). Famously, Leibniz is keen to highlight another feature of the traditional, Aristotelian concept of substance — viz. (c') "that most widely accepted principle of philosophy — that actions belong to substances" (*On Nature Itself*, sect. 9: AG 160). This feature, according to which substances contain within their nature or essence the source of activity and change, signals a consequence (decidedly not the origin) of the mature Leibniz's disagreement with Descartes — not about the basic notions of substance, essence, principal attribute, and extension themselves but about the adequacy of Descartes's physics.[8] Thus Leibniz argues (in "On the Nature of Bodies and the Laws of Motion," "A Specimen of Dynamics," and elsewhere) that if extension is the essence of body, we cannot salvage the correct laws of motion; furthermore he argues (in "On Nature Itself") that if extension is the essence of body, then the distinction between motion and rest cannot be properly made out, and indeed that we cannot ground any distinction among bodies (plural) at all. At the deeper level of his metaphysic of substance, Leibniz claims that extension is unsuitable for the role of principal attribute or essence of substance since it is not basic or primitive but presupposes, or is "resolvable" into, other, more fundamental notions of plurality, continuity, and coexistence.[9] Hence the extended world of experience, for Leibniz, can only be metaphysically derivative, not part of the basic furniture of the substantial world at all. Other, more direct routes completing his rejection of extended substance come in letters to Arnauld (e.g., of 28 November 1686 and 30 April 1687), where Leibniz claims that extended objects would have parts and that things figure as parts of something only insofar as they stand in certain relations. Such relations can only be accidental, not intrinsic to objects but "extrinsic" in the sense that they "reside in the way we conceive things." But an accidental unity is no unity at all: genuine substances are true unities, *unum per se* not *unum per accidens*. Moreover the existence of extended wholes would presuppose the existence of the parts composing them and so would fail the requirement that (created) substances are independent of other created things. There are no extended substances, for Leibniz, large or small. Whether or not Descartes claims that there exist extended substantial bodies in addition to extended substantial space, Leibniz denies the entire lot of it.

The point of rehearsing details is not to show how one would go about defend-ing a received view that scarcely needs defending but to emphasize how great is the burden of one wishing to deny the traditional view. Descartes claims that extended substantial space exists. In offering us sentences that clearly look to express the de-nial of a position Descartes affirms, Leibniz is not writing from a different meta-physical tradition; he gives us no evidence that his notion of existence or being, when affirmed or denied of a thing in the cited texts, is anything unusual; he espouses a traditional distinction between a substance, on the one hand, and the properties in-hering in it, on the other; he speaks of the essence or nature of a substance in a per-fectly ordinary way; his concept of extension, as a candidate for the principal attribute or essence of substance, is the received one. Indeed his fundamental concept of sub-stance is standard and familiar. What is at issue is not the notion of substance itself but the adequacy of a certain candidate for its essence or nature, and Leibniz argues that extension cannot do the job. Never mind whether his arguments fail or succeed: given that Leibniz was familiar with Descartes's views and the presumption that his readers are familiar with them, it would be strange at best if Leibniz were to depart so drastically from received conceptual foundations as to render his conclusions *con-sistent with Cartesianism* and yet remain perfectly silent about that departure.

## Spinoza and Descartes

Where does Spinoza fit into this picture? Here is the standard view. Like Descartes, Spinoza works with the traditional distinction between a thing and its properties — between substance, on the one hand, and its attributes and modes, on the other. Like Descartes, Spinoza agrees that substance is independent: substance is "what is in it-self and conceived through itself, that is, that whose concept does not require the concept of another thing" (E ID3). Like Descartes, Spinoza thinks in terms of prin-cipal properties or attributes, attributes "constituting the essence" of substance (ID4). Like Descartes, Spinoza claims that God exists and is a thinking substance. But un-like Descartes, Spinoza claims that there is just one thinking substance; indeed Spinoza claims that there is just one substance *full stop*, God or Nature, which is also extended. Spinoza's notion of extension, as a principal attribute or essence of substance, is the received one: it is spatial spreadoutness in length, breadth, and depth. The one extended substance is thus the entirety of space, of what has length, breadth, and depth, and so like Descartes (and unlike Leibniz), Spinoza believes that extended substantial space exists. Spinoza's one extended substance is Descartes's ex-tended substantial space.

That is the standard, traditional view. Like all standard views it can, of course, be rejected. R. S. Woolhouse rejects it, denying that Spinoza's one extended sub-stance is Descartes's extended substantial space.[10] Suppose, for what follows, that the only extended substance in Descartes's ontology is extended substantial space. According to Woolhouse's (let us call it) anti-Cartesian reading, Descartes and Spinoza diverge on the ways in which they take their respective extended substances to exist: "when Descartes says . . . '(an) extended substance exists' he means some-thing radically different from what Spinoza means when *he* says . . . '(an) extended substance exists'." (SDE 28) That there is logical space for this difference between them emerges from a distinction found in Descartes and Leibniz — and in Spinoza too. In the *Fifth Meditation*, Descartes claims that even if there were nothing existing outside him in the corporeal world serving as the object of his idea of a triangle or some other figure, nevertheless, corresponding to such nonfictitious ideas, "there is still a determinate nature, or essence, or form of the triangle which is immutable and eternal, and not invented by me or dependent on my mind" (AT VII, 64: CSM II, 45). The "essence or nature or form" of a triangle is not a mental idea but something else, something which exists in a way that instantiations of such natures — actually existing triangles in the corporeal world — do not. A similar distinction arises in Leibniz's claim that the word *ens* (entity) is ambiguous, one sense being equivalent to *existens* (actually existing thing), the other sense denoting whatever is abstractly possible.[11] A corresponding ambiguity infects *est*. Leibniz thus claims that propositions asserting the existence of a thing are either "existential" or "essential." "Pegasus is a winged horse" or "A figure that bears a constant relation to some one point exists" are false, read existentially, for there actually exist no such objects; but they are true, read essentially, since there are real or everlasting essences grounding their possibility. "Cover is a man" and "A philosopher who climbs mountains exists" are true existentially.

Here, then, is the proposed anti-Cartesian reading of Spinoza: when Descartes says "extended substance exists," he is to be understood as asserting an existential proposition, on a par with asserting that climbing philosophers exist; when Spinoza says "extended substance exists," *he* is to be understood as asserting an essential proposition, on a par with claiming that a figure bearing a constant relation to some one point exists. Descartes has asserted the existence of a thing instantiating a nature or essence, whereas Spinoza has asserted something more like the existence of a nature or essence itself. Spinoza's extended substance is not Descartes's.

The anti-Cartesian proposal is a genuine one — a possible way in which Spinoza's "extended substance exists" might depart in a very fundamental way from Descartes's tokening of that sentence. The pressing question is what grounds we have for believing that it represents an actual departure from Descartes — whether there are good reasons for rejecting the standard account in favor of an importantly new construal of Spinoza's relation to Descartes on extended substance.

On the anti-Cartesian proposal, Descartes's extended substance is the instantiation of an essence or nature, whereas Spinoza's extended substance is not: rather, it is modes that are instantiations of essences, and extended substance itself is rather more like a Cartesian immutable nature or a Leibnizian eternal essence. If that is in fact Spinoza's view, one might expect his account of the distinction between substance and modes to give some clear indication of it. Thus Woolhouse asks us to "consider what [Spinoza] says in various places where he warns us against falling into the supposition that the kind of existence substances have is the same as that of modes (which are, for him, instantiations of essences)" (SDE 33). Now, unless we are to beg the question against the standard reading here at the very outset, we shall have to allow for the possibility that even if modes are instantiations of essences and extended substance exists in a way that modes do not, extended substance nevertheless remains the instantiation of an essence. For two kinds of thing $x$ and $y$, it may be that $x$ "exists in different a different way" than $y$—and be different in kind for this reason—even if both $x$ and $y$ are instantiations of an essence: $x$ might be eternal or necessary, for example, whereas $y$ is not, even if both instantiate an essence. (Set Spinoza aside: God or angels might "exist in a different way" from human creatures, even if all alike instantiate the principal property of thought.)

It is worth noting that Spinoza does not use the terminology of "instantiation." Presumably the closest we come to it in our texts is the relation in which a thing stands to an attribute or property when that thing is said to "have" that attribute or property. That is close enough, shy of any evidence to the contrary: the metaphysical and conceptual background against which Spinoza writes is one he shares with Descartes, and Spinoza gives no explicit indication that his adoption of the standard substance-attribute taxonomy departs from the traditional thing-property distinction of which it is a species. Spinoza claims that God or Nature has all attributes, including the attribute of extension. On the face of it, then, extended substance instantiates—has—the attribute of extension. Indeed, Spinoza's claim of E IP7 that God's essence necessarily involves existence, and his resulting ontological argument of IP11, have all the marks of Descartes's own view that the existence of God *is* the necessary instantiation of God's nature or essence. Are there good reasons for thinking otherwise?

One might argue as follows: any entity P to which some $x$ is related when $x$ is said to "instantiate" or "have" P must by its very nature admit of multiple instances; must (in the contemporary taxonomy) be general, not singular; must be that by virtue of which things can share something in common. (Thus Scotus, in offering his "formal distinction" between the common nature of things and their individuating *haecceitas*, will insist that one cannot reckon haecceities as properties precisely *because* properties are the sorts of entities that can be shared, that things can have in common.) As far as I am aware, Spinoza never asserts this view or anything entailing it. Were he to have held the view, one might suppose a route to the claim that his extended substance is not an instantiation would be ready to hand: Spinoza argues (in E IP5) for a no-shared-attribute thesis—for the claim that in Nature it is impossible for two or more substances to have the same attribute. But this route seems unavailable in any case. For Spinoza's demonstration of IP5 clearly presupposes the *intelligibility*, if falsity, of multiple instantiation by substances. After claiming that differences in affections can be "put to one side" (apparently but mysteriously because these differences must be conceived through a prior difference of attributes[12]), Spinoza argues that two putative instances of an attribute by two substances cannot have any further qualitative differences among them and that qualitatively identical but numerically distinct substances could no longer be conceived through themselves.

So far then we have little reason for attributing to Spinoza the claim that extended substance cannot be, or is not, an instantiation of the attribute of extension. Descartes, following the tradition, adopts the explicit usage of attributes and properties inhering in or "residing in" a substance: to say that a substance is extended is to say that it has or instantiates that attribute. It would be strange linguistic behavior at best that Spinoza, in this same tradition, should have quietly adopted the received ways of speaking and been altogether silent about the radical departure an anti-

Cartesian reading attributes to him. Lacking anything like direct evidence that Spinoza is making the departure, the case rests on indirect evidence for his taking the anti-Cartesian route Woolhouse notes as a possibility.

One sort of indirect evidence for a nonstandard reading would come in its ability to clarify certain otherwise difficult texts. Here perhaps the anti-Cartesian may earn its keep. For might it be that insofar as one finds in Spinoza an apparent inclination to identify substance with its attributes [by such expressions as "substances, or what is the same thing, their attributes" (E IP4D) and "God or all of God's attributes" (IP19, 20C2) and others elsewhere (cf. IP14C2)], we *do* have evidence that Spinoza's one substance is rather more like an attribute or essence itself than a Cartesian instantiation of an attribute? Well, not unless one can establish that Spinoza's inclination to speak in this way is not simply inherited from Descartes's own view that there is no *real distinction* (in the received scholastic sense) between extension and extended substance, and not unless one can in addition establish that the resulting identification implies that substance is attributelike rather than that attributes are substancelike. The second gets little purchase without the first. And so it is worth noting (in connection with the first) that Descartes, too, immediately following his appropriation of the scholastic taxonomy of real, modal, and rational (conceptual) distinctions, will say that extension is to be reckoned "as nothing else than . . . extended substance itself" (AT VIIIA, 301: CSM I, 215). Never mind for the moment that this seems to make attributes rather more substancelike — an overtone not uncommon in various scholastic texts.[13] In the face of the fact that such talk is common to both Descartes and Spinoza, there is no plausibility to the idea of giving it the contemporary gloss of straight numerical identity in the case of Spinoza but withholding that gloss in the case of Descartes.[14]

There is little plausibility to giving such talk the contemporary gloss in any case. The syntactically challenged "Substance *is* its attributes" needs more than a grammatical rescue: straight numerical (contemporary) identity is one-one, not one-many. Consider four unhappy options for rendering it intelligible. (i) Construe "substance S" as a *plural referring term*, and say that God or Nature is not one but are many, as the British tell us (of their rock group) that "the Who are Pete, Roger, John, and Keith." (ii) Avoid the queerness of saying that God or Nature is one substance but many attributes by adopting a *relative identity thesis*, and say that extension and thought are attributes *and* are substances, but although they are the same substance S they are different attributes F and G. (iii) Back off the identity claim and say that substance S *is constituted by* its attributes: God or Nature is simple but nevertheless stands to extension and thought in some kind of one-many relation. (iv) Insist on an identity claim, but say that S is identical with extension and S is identical with thought.[15] Now, option (i) isn't a one-substance doctrine at all; option (iii) is mere handwaving in the direction of some relation or other with the right logical properties, and in any case offers no promise of yielding a view of Spinoza's God or Nature as rather more like the many attributes than a view of them as more like the one extended substance; and option (iv) — by the transitivity of identity — yields the hopeless conclusion that extension *is* thought. However unhappily the relative-identity option (iii) may sit with the contemporary mind (and its approach to early modern texts), Descartes's own deployment of the scholastic taxonomy — where traditionally weaker and stronger distinctions are seen to entail the denial of (respectively) stronger and weaker identities — invites something very like it.

That story, and its relevance for Spinoza as a commentator and successor of Descartes, requires a separate discussion of its own. But two elements of the story are worth emphasizing here. First, Descartes insists that the species of rational distinction (in the *Principles*, also later called *formal* in correspondence) he is prepared to accept is not *distinctio rationis ratiocinatae* but rather *distinctio rationis rationcinantis* (AT IV, 349–350: CSMK III, 280). Given its provenance in Suarez and Eustachius, we must understand the latter distinction between substance and attribute to "pre-exist in reality, prior to the discriminating operation of the mind, so as to be thought of as imposing itself, as it were, on the intellect, and to require the intellect only to recognize it, but not to constitute it."[16] There is no room here either for downplaying the distinction as something ontologically innocent or for glossing it as consistent with straight numerical (contemporary) identity. Second, Descartes believes that neither attributes nor modes are real in the technical scholastic sense that a real attribute or real mode would be a quality of a *res* that is itself a *res*. (Something can of course fail to be a *res* and still *exist*.) Given a commitment to degrees of reality (e.g., AT VII, 185: CSM II, 130), it is attributes that are more real so less (more weakly) distinct from substance than are modes for Descartes; and his willingness to say in the *Principles* that attributes are "only" or "merely" (*tantùm*) rationally distinct from substance underscores his view that attributes are rather more substancelike than substances are attributelike. Relative to scholastic predecessors, there is room in the early modern metaphysic for heightening the reality of attributes toward *res* but not for denigrating the reality of *res* toward something weaker. And here, I suggest, Spinoza agrees with Descartes.

We are still seeking indirect evidence for the anti-Cartesian reading of Spinoza's extended substance. Return again to Spinoza's view that extended substance exists in a way that modes do not. In his letter to Meyer of 20 April 1663 (Ep 12), Spinoza sets out to "explain these four [concepts]: Substance, Mode, Eternity, and Duration" (Geb IV, 53: Curley 201). As to the first pair, Spinoza claims that in the case of substance, "existence pertains to its essence, i.e. . . . . from its essence and definition alone it follows that it exists," whereas in the case of affections or modes, their definition "cannot involve any existence." Now *this* difference, between the ways in which substance and modes exist, even when conjoined with Woolhouse's claim that modes are instantiations of essences, scarcely entails that Spinoza's substance does not instantiate the attribute or essence of extension, for reasons noted earlier. The case for the anti-Cartesian proposal will in this context thus depend on Spinoza's connection of that first pair to the second — on the further claim that substance enjoys eternal existence whereas modes do not. More explicitly, Spinoza claims that the way in which substance exists is explained in terms of eternity, whereas the way in which modes exist is explained in terms of duration. And here Woolhouse reminds us (SDE 34), "eternal existence" is said by Spinoza to be existence that "follows necessarily from the definition alone of the eternal thing," one that "cannot be explained by duration or time, even if the duration is conceived as being without beginning or end" (E ID8).

What exactly is the force of this as evidence for the anti-Cartesian interpretation? If construed as an argument, it cannot be anything so simple and invalid as this: (a) the existence of finite modes is explained through duration, not eternity, and they instantiate essences; (b) the existence of substance is not explained through duration but through eternity; therefore (c) substance does not instantiate essences. The proposal is something less forceful than an argument, I think: the connection left implicit — between eternal existence versus (let me say) durational existence, on the one hand, and fitness for instantiating an essence or attribute, on the other — is not a connection so obviously there in Spinoza as to assert itself as a premise. We have rather an anti-Cartesian conjecture, an invitation to see that if according to Spinoza substance is eternal whereas modes are durational, then it is reasonable to suppose that Spinoza does not understand eternal substance to be like durational or temporal modes in respect of instantiating an essence or attribute. So at least three claims are at work here: the third of them has, as I say, been left implicit by Woolhouse and, while crucial to the anti-Cartesian position, is offered as *probably true*.

1. If substance is eternal, then it is not durational or temporal.
2. Modes, which *are* temporal/durational, instantiate the essence or attribute of extension.
3. Whatever is *not* durational/temporal does not instantiate the essence or attribute of extension.

The first claim can be resisted. Alan Donagan resists it, opting for the "Aristotelian" over the "Platonic" reading of eternity in Spinoza; and as Woolhouse notes, Jonathan Bennett resists it, too, claiming that for Spinoza being eternal is being necessarily sempiternal.[17] I don't want to enter that tangle here but simply note this commitment to a certain reading of "eternity" attending Woolhouse's proposal — a reading, it must be granted, less able than its Aristotelian alternative to make sense of Spinoza's occasional claim that substance and the infinite modes always (*semper*) exist.

Suppose we grant claim 1 above, agreeing that Spinoza's extended substance is not temporal in any way as are finite modes of extension. The third claim can be resisted.[18] In particular, I suggest that the force of Spinoza's withholding durational or temporal existence from substance is not implying or even suggesting that it fails to instantiate the attribute of extension. Two related considerations, one (A) textual or historical, the other (B) more broadly philosophical, recommend this.

(A) When Spinoza insists that the way in which substance exists is to be explained in terms of eternity (unlike the case of finite modes), what, in addition to "its essence or definition does not involve duration," is Spinoza withholding from substance? Given the work that Spinoza's concept of duration performs in his metaphysical system, *very little* — though the very little points us in a direction away from the anti-Cartesian reading. The force of Spinoza's point about duration is primarily to distinguish that whose existence follows from its essence from that whose existence is causally dependent, reaching outside its essence. This is clear enough in comparing Spinoza's claims in the letter to Meyer already noted with his account of duration in *Metaphysical Thoughts*, published the same year. For both the Scholastics and Descartes, *duratio* is the mode by which one conceives the perseverance (the enduring) of finite things.[19] In *Principles* 1:55 Descartes himself claims that duration is "a mode under which we conceive the thing insofar as it continues to exist" (AT VIIIA, 26: CSM I, 211). Following the Scholastic and Cartesian lead, Spinoza understands duration to be that by which "we conceive the existence of created things insofar as they persevere in their actuality."[20] The point of applying duration to the existence of certain things, but not to others, is manifest when Spinoza's goes on to claim that duration is not to be attributed to God since "duration is an affection of existence and not of the essence of things" (*Metaphysical Thoughts* II.1: Geb I, 250: Curley 316). Thus, for example, the duration of a finite extended body "does not depend upon its essence" but instead "is determined to exist and produce effects from other causes," and so "depends on the common order of Nature and the constitution of things" (E IIP30d). This connection between finite, causally dependent created things in the order of nature and duration is repeated in his claim that "there was no time or duration before creation" (Geb I, 269: Curley 334), where by "creation" Spinoza simply refers to the causal dependence of finite extended modes. To attribute duration to finite extended modes and withhold it from God or extended Nature is thus to distinguish what is finite and causally dependent from what is infinite and eternal.

Now one *could*, with Woolhouse, claim that according to Spinoza, whatever has nondurational or nontemporal existence cannot instantiate the attribute of extension. But this is not invited by the texts, and they do nothing to render claim 3 above probably true. All we can conclude is that extended substance is eternal, is not created, and has its existence follow from its essence. There may, of course, be things — essences or attributes themselves — whose existence is not explained by duration; but nothing Spinoza says about the difference between the ways in which extended substance and its modes exist recommends this. As far as the texts we have considered go, that is not what Spinoza has in mind.

There are other texts we have not yet considered, where the nature of essences themselves are under consideration. The anti-Cartesian will remind us that in the *Metaphysical Thoughts* Spinoza distinguishes between (among other things) the "being of essence" and the "being of existence."[21] The "being of existence," according to Woolhouse, is "the being of an instantiation of an essence; it is, says Spinoza, 'attributed to things after they have been created by God'" (SDE 37). Now, any supposed contrast here — implying that "being of essence" is inapplicable to instantiations — is not supported in the *Metaphysical Thoughts*: as Spinoza says, "*being of Essence* is nothing but that manner in which created things are comprehended in the attributes of God" (Geb I, 238: Curley 304). Nevertheless, Spinoza does emphasize, in responding to those inclined to confuse essences with ideas, that they must be conceived "outside the intellect," being "something different from the idea." Such essences "depend on the divine essence alone" (Geb I, 239: Curley 305); they "exist . . . insofar as they are comprehended in God's attributes" and not insofar as they have duration (E IIP8). Now, Woolhouse suggests that while Descartes and Leibniz must understand true and immutable natures or eternal essences as being in the divine mind, since Spinoza's God is not only a thinking substance but an extended substance, Spinoza must surely understand the essence of geometrical figures (of a triangle, say) as "contained in God insofar as he is extended substance" (SDE 39), not as thinking substance. Woolhouse continues: "Of course, if one's conception of corporeal substance were like Descartes's, the instantiation of an essence, it would be absurd even to flirt with the idea that essences of geometrical figures are in any way dependent on it. . . . All that could be dependent upon corporeal substance conceived in that way could be instantiations of those essences [not the essences themselves]" (SDE 39). The argument is apparently this: (1) Creaturely essences depend on God the extended substance; (2) If extended substance is an instantiation of an essence, then creaturely essences do not depend on God the extended substance; therefore (3) God the extended substance is not an instantiation of an essence. Both premises can be resisted, I think. Concerning (1), Spinoza does not *say* that creaturely essences are dependent on God or are contained in God, the extended substance, but rather that (above) creaturely essences "depend on the divine essence" or are "comprehended in God's attributes." (The anti-Cartesian may well insist that those are equivalent to "depend on God, are contained in God," but that equivalence is precisely what is here in question.) The essence of geometrical figures can be conceived as being dependent on or comprehended in one of the divine attributes, even if Spinoza's substance instantiates that attribute, that is, is extended substantial space.[22] Relatedly, concerning (2): affirming the dependence of creaturely essences on the divine essence doesn't entail denying their dependence of the instantiation of that essence. If, as the standard Cartesian reading would have it, the essence of extended substance is *necessarily instantiated* [if indeed God's essence and existence are "one and the same" (E IP20)], there is nothing at all implausible about the idea that by depending on the essence of extended substance, the essences of geometrical figures thereby depend on its necessary instantiation, that is, on extended substance itself.[23]

(B) Let me now wed the earlier textual points about duration with a picture of Spinoza's extended substance and its finite modes, taking seriously his claims that *duration has application only at the level of finite created things* (bodies) and that *duration or time exists only when created bodies do*. In particular, suppose that Spinoza, like (perhaps) Augustine before him and (certainly) Leibniz after him, reckons the temporal aspects of Nature to arise from the causal order of created enduring objects and causal interactions among them. The *conatus* of any finite created individual mode of extension "expresses, in a certain and determinate way, God's power, by which God is and acts" (E IIIP6); and it is by this power (which, viewed under the attribute of extension, is the immediate and infinite mode of motion and rest) that infinite substance differentiates itself in infinitely many finite *res particulares*. Duration and time figure only at this level of finite created modes and their causal order: duration and time have no application whatsoever to the whole of extended substance itself. Here is C. L. Hardin's version of the picture:

> I would propose to ascribe to Spinoza a causal theory of time. . . . To see how this works, let us for the moment abstractly represent "the face of the whole universe"

under the attribute of extension by means of a space-time diagram with three spatial axes and one directed "temporal" axis. Any two finite modal states A and B may be ordered with respect to one another according as A is a remote or proximate cause of B, B is a remote or proximate cause of A, or A and B either cause one another or have no causal relationship to one another. In the first case, we shall call A "earlier than" B, in the second we shall call A "later than" B, and in the third instance, we shall say that A is "simultaneous" with B. Our diagram will exhaustively represent all the kinematic [i.e., motion and rest] relationships among the modes. . . . Although sets of points within the continuum may be described as having temporal relations to one another, it would be downright misleading to describe the continuum itself as "existing in time" or as "existing at all times."[24]

What's wrong or strained about that? Despite the abstractness of the representation, it captures perfectly well Spinoza's claim that the existence of infinite extended substance is (as we have been calling it) nondurational or nontemporal, duration and time making their appearance only at the level of finite created modes of extension. Thus we do full justice to the distinction Woolhouse emphasizes between "eternal" and "durational" existence of substance and its modes (respectively), while easily reckoning Spinoza's one substance to be the whole of space, extended in length, breadth, and depth. Spinoza's God or Nature, nontemporal precisely *because* it is not created, is extended substantial space.[25]

Or so this picture, with the traditional view, has it. To suppose otherwise, in the absence of explicit or strong indirect evidence to the contrary, is to strain Spinoza's words beyond that which Descartes or Leibniz, or anyone in the tradition of our three philosophers, would have recognized. Spinoza claims — in just these words — that God is an extended thing (E IIP2). If the anti-Cartesian reading is correct, then Spinoza's words do not mean that there exists something spatially extended. What exactly they *do* mean is then somewhat obscure. For the anti-Cartesian Spinoza, extended substance is rather more like an attribute or essence or eternal and immutable nature than anything else. It can hardly *be* an attribute or essence or nature, in any normal sense, for this would have Spinoza claiming that substance itself can have multiple instances; moreover the traditional substance-attribute (more generally, thing-property) distinction would be badly obscured, and we would have to understand modes as ways essences or natures are, which is more obscure still. Woolhouse himself claims that substance "can be nothing like that of the instantiation of an essence but must be more like that of the essences themselves of which it is the substrate" (SDE 39), and when Spinoza asserts the existence of substance, he is "asserting the existence of a 'substrate' or 'support' for natures or essences, something on which they depend for their existence" (SDE 47). But — leaving aside the fact that Spinoza rarely if ever speaks of substance in that way —[26] what, then, exactly is the nature of this substrate? It is true that Spinoza, like Descartes and Leibniz, wants to ground eternal truths and essences in God in some way, and a virtue of Woolhouse's discussion is that it brings into sharp relief the importance and difficulty of understanding how Spinoza accomplishes this. Leibniz's own Platonic-Augustinian account makes eternal truths and essences dependent on the mind of God, on the divine intellect: they are divine ideas. But we can follow Woolhouse in reckoning essences of geometric objects to be grounded in the nature of God as extended (not as thinking) without having to view Spinoza's substance itself as a kind of Platonic object. Again, one does best to take Spinoza at his word when claiming that finite essences "depend on the divine essence" (Geb I, 239: Curley 305) or are "comprehended in God's attributes" (E IIP8 and Geb I, 238: Curley 304). If one inclines toward a Platonistic grounding for the essences of finite objects, why stretch for a Platonistic substance to play this role when the broadly abstract or Platonic attributes themselves are already near to hand? And again, one can in any case still reckon extended substance as an instantiation to be the "support" of creaturely essences, given that the essence of extension is necessarily instantiated.

We have, in any case, Spinoza's willingness to speak of (I) substance itself, and (II) extended substance in particular, in ways positively inviting the traditional, Cartesian construal of "extended substance" — ways not easily wedded to construing his one substance as rather more like an eternal essence or nature itself. Before moving to a final contrast of Spinoza with Leibniz, let me finish this section with a comment about each of those.

(I) In no crucial way does Spinoza depart from the medieval and Cartesian conception of substance; his primary departure from them is in applying it only to God or Nature, claiming that finite things are only modes of the one substance. This departure emerges in part from his rejection of a broadly Aristotelian-Scholastic dualism of matter and form,[27] which combine to form all substances (plural), a dualism that in its later incarnations underwrites the distinction between an immaterial thinking God, on the one hand, and a material world of extended bodies, on the other. In both the *Short Treatise* and the *Ethics*, Spinoza's project is thus to argue not only against those who believe that there are many substances but also against those who suppose that an immaterial, unextended God could be the cause of a world of extended bodies.[28] Rejecting the scholastic notion of God as pure form or intelligence, Spinoza is able to say in his own way that God *is* the cause of a world of extended material bodies, by claiming that God is extended (cf. E IP3 and IIP6). In this, Spinoza is explicit in ascribing to God a principle attribute that the tradition — and indeed his readers — reserved for the created world distinct from God: "Things which they because of their prejudices regard as creatures, I contend are attributes of God" (Ep 6, to Oldenberg: Geb IV, 36: Curley 188). That is, "extension is an attribute of God" (TdIE I.2, 18). And this is Spinoza's primary departure from Descartes, who held God to be a thinking substance distinct from extended substantial space. Spinoza denies the distinction; his extended substance is Descartes's extended substantial space.

(II) And so Spinoza must pause at great length to reply to those who "try to show that corporeal substance is unworthy of the divine nature, and cannot pertain to it" (E IP15s):

> They prove this best from the fact that by body we understand any quantity, with length, breadth, and depth, limited by some certain figure. Nothing more absurd than this can be said of God, viz. of a being absolutely infinite. . . . Meanwhile, by the other arguments by which they strive to demonstrate this same conclusion they clearly show that they entirely remove corporeal, or extended, substance itself from the divine nature. And they maintain that it was created by God. (Geb II, 57: Curley 421)

This item surely alludes to the traditional problem of creation noted above, for Spinoza goes on to say that "they are completely ignorant of that divine power by which [extended corporeal substance] is created."[29] In the rest of the scholium, Spinoza replies to two arguments against the incorporeality of God, both of which are found in the traditional Scholastic literature and in Descartes (at *Principles* 1: 23–24). The first is that corporeal substance must have parts and so be finite, which are limitations or imperfections;[30] the second is that God, being perfect, must be active, but corporeal substance, since divisible, is passive. Spinoza replies that these results do not follow from his supposition that the one substance has an infinite quantity but rather "from the fact that [these Authors] suppose an infinite quantity to be measurable and composed of finite parts." And this composition Spinoza denies. Earlier in E IP12 and P13 he had argued that "no substance, and consequently no corporeal substance, is divisible" (P13C). In the present scholium, Spinoza argues that divisibility would entail the possibility of a vacuum, which — with Descartes — Spinoza denies:

> For if corporeal substance could be so divided that its parts were really distinct, why, then, could one part not be annihilated, the rest remaining connected with one another as before? And why must they all be so fitted together that there is no vacuum? Truly, of things which are really distinct from one another, one can be, and remain in its condition, without the other. Since, therefore, there is no vacuum in nature (a subject that I discuss elsewhere) . . . it follows that . . . corporeal substance, insofar as it is a substance, cannot be divided. (Geb II, 59: Curley 423)

That is, infinite substantial space is simple.

As before (in the first section above), my point in rehearsing familiar detail is less to defend the traditional view than to emphasize how great is the burden of one wishing to deny it. The conceptual background of seventeenth-century philosophy, against which Descartes's account of extended substantial space is developed, is Spinoza's too. So in offering us sentences looking clearly to assert the existence of an infinite substance that is extended, Spinoza is not writing from a different metaphysical tradition; in speaking of God as extended he is scarcely *talking past* the traditional creation problem — of how God could be related to a world of material bodies; in replying to those who claim that extended corporeality is unworthy of the nature of God, Spinoza does not say that he is understanding corporeal substance differently than they; to those who claim that ascribing "a quantity with length, breadth and depth" to God or Nature must entail its possession of parts, Spinoza does not respond by denying the attribution of length, breadth, and depth to the one substance; in arguing that his one substance has no parts, he deploys the familiar Cartesian notion of a spatial vacuum; and so on. All of this fits smoothly into the Cartesian picture of extended substantial space, and none of it, taken at face value, can be intelligibly wedded to the construal of Spinoza's one substance as something like a Platonic attribute or an eternal and immutable nature. Granting the possibility of Spinoza's silent departure from that which his readers would have understood by familiar usage, a nonliteral rendering of Spinoza's words might be offered to accomplish the marriage. But it is strikingly unclear how such a rendering would go, and none has been offered.

## Spinoza and Leibniz

That bits of evidence weigh strongly in favor of a certain reading of some historical figure is, as the anti-Cartesian proposal makes clear, consistent with there being claims by that figure inclining in a different direction. To complete the historical comparison, I want to broach other views of Spinoza on extended substance, which when set alongside related views of Leibniz, look prima facie to weigh rather more heavily on the anti-Cartesian's side. The tack here is similar to Woolhouse's own: just as there are things Spinoza says about extended substance sharing certain features of Leibniz's eternal essences — whose existence is to be understood essentially not existentially — so there are other things Spinoza says about extended substance that seem to share certain features of Leibniz's anti-Cartesian account of space.

Among things Spinoza says which might incline one to suppose that by "extended substance" he cannot mean anything like Descartes's extended substantial space are his claims that "no attribute of a substance can be truly conceived from which it follows that the substance can be divided" (E IP12) and that "a substance which is absolutely infinite is indivisible" (IP13). According to Spinoza, substance has no parts. Leibniz agrees. And while their respective routes to this conclusion are fundamentally different, there remain important similarities in their views on the relation of parts to wholes — views that, for Leibniz at least, are of ontological significance. Let me get Leibniz into the picture first, via his rejection of extended substantial space.

We have noted already (in the first section) certain philosophical difficulties in coming to grips with Leibniz's views. There are others, of a broadly methodological sort; chief among them is Leibniz's willingness to conduct his discussions at various levels of metaphysical strictness. This is especially problematic in the case concerning us here, about extended substantial space. Sometimes (as in the letters to Arnauld and in the *Monadology*) Leibniz's views emerge from a deployment of his deepest metaphysical principles about the nature of individual substance, to the conclusion that substance cannot have parts; add the claim that whatever is extended has parts, and out rolls the denial of extended substantial space, leaving his "phenomenalism" about body to pick up the pieces. Other times, however (as in his exchange with the Newtonians), Leibniz is willing for the sake of argument to grant his opponent talk of "real extended bodies"; in such cases, Leibniz deploys other considerations (about extension itself) and different principles (about sufficient reason and the discernibility of nonidenticals) to argue for the conclusion that extended space is not among the furniture of the universe. Worse still, Leibniz sometimes (as in the letters to de Volder and Sophia) runs these levels of discussion together.

The intersection with Spinoza is most apparent if we limit our attention, in the first instance, to the less strict of Leibniz's accounts. It is sometimes claimed that Leibniz took space (and time) to be a well-founded phenomenon, on a par with bodies.[31] Were that his considered view, we should face the embarrassing difficulty of explaining why, in the Clarke correspondence, Leibniz is (on the one hand) willing to talk of "real" bodies and relations among them, while nevertheless (on the other hand) he argues at great length (cf. the Fifth Letter, sect. 47: G VII, 402–403) against allowing space to be among the furniture of the created world. In fact no such embarrassment faces us: the mature Leibniz did not believe that space is a well-founded phenomenon. I shan't review here the historical details of the transition from Leibniz's brief flirtation with that view in the early 1680s to his clear rejection of it thereafter.[32] The transition texts stretch from 1696 to 1709, including especially the de Volder correspondence. By the time we get to the *Metaphysical Foundations of Mathematics* (ca. 1715) and his exchange with Clarke (1715–1716), Leibniz already had firmly placed a sharp divide between the level of "real" or "actual" bodies and "ideal" space. The latter designation is one Leibniz reserves explicitly for what is *not* phenomenal — for *abstracta* broadly conceived, including other such items as the geometric and arithmetic continua, which like space and time are not judged part of the real created world of individual substances and phenomenal bodies supervening on them.

The distinction between the phenomenal and ideal levels, in Leibniz's system, is drawn along both epistemic and metaphysical lines. Among the former is Leibniz's insistence that, unlike the real world of perceived phenomenal bodies, the ideal world is accessible via abstraction or by thought alone (cf. G II, 249: L 523; G II, 249: L 529; G VII, 561, 564; A 6.6.110; G VI, 584: L 621). The emphasis of perceptual versus broadly conceptual features is implicit in other bits of Leibnizian nomenclature, where ideal things are reckoned *res mentalis* (G II, 268) or *entia rationis* (G II, 189; A 6.6.226–227), to be set off from the well-founded phenomenal level of *entia semimentalia* (G II, 304, 306) or *quasisubstantiae* (G II, 263: L 534). Along purely metaphysical lines, it is typically mereological and topological features that Leibniz highlights in distinguishing the ideal from the phenomenal. And here I want Leibniz to speak for himself:

> Matter is not continuous but discrete, and actually infinitely divided. . . . But space, like time, is something not substantial, but ideal, and consists in possibilities, or in an order of coexistents that is in some way possible. And thus there are no divisions in it but such as are made by the mind, and the part is posterior to the whole. In real things, on the contrary, units are prior to the multitude, and multitudes exist only through units. (G II, 278–279)

> The mass of bodies is actually divided in a determinate manner, and nothing in it is precisely continuous; but space, or the perfect continuity which is in the idea, represents nothing but an indeterminate possibility of dividing it however one likes. In matter and in actual realities the whole is a result of the parts, but in ideas or possibilities . . . the indeterminate whole is prior to the divisions, as the concept of unity is more simple that of fractions, and precedes it. (G VII, 562)

> Space is something continuous but ideal, mass is discrete, namely an actual multitude, or being by aggregation, composed of an infinite number of units. In actuals, single terms are prior to aggregates, in ideals the whole is prior to the part. (G II, 379)

> A continuum . . . involves indeterminate parts, while on the other hand, there is nothing indefinite in actual things, in which every division is made that can be made. . . . The parts are actually in the real whole but not in the ideal whole. (G II, 282: L 539)

This is quite enough Leibniz, for now, save for a couple of stray items we'll retrieve presently. What I want from him is the following schematic picture, lacking in details left purposely aside.[33] There is no such entity as Cartesian extended substantial space. Nevertheless, there is an ontological category distinct from that of the world of created extended bodies. To this ontological category belongs the abstract continuum we call "space." Crucial to this ontological distinction between kinds of beings is the following mereological fact. On the one hand, extended things are wholes properly so-called — dependent on logically prior parts out of which they are genuinely composed, divisible in the sense that there are actual divisions or distinctions among the parts in them. (For this reason — being neither unities per se nor independent of other created things — they are not genuine substances.) On the other hand, space contains no parts, strictly speaking: there exist no logically prior parts out if which it is composed, into which it is divisible. It is logically simple, noncomposite, indivisible.

The anti-Cartesian Spinoza should find all of that congenial; Spinoza himself might have believed it. The distance between Spinoza himself and Woolhouse's anti-Cartesian Spinoza seems to diminish in light of several parallels between Leibniz's ideal space and Spinoza's extended substance. In briefly discussing these parallels below, I am not arguing as follows: Leibniz said thus-and-so about his ideal space; Spinoza said thus-and-so about his extended substance; therefore Spinoza's extended substance is Leibniz's ideal space. The point is not about inductive evidence by analogy, which I'm prepared to accept,[34] but rather about historical provenance, which of course doesn't run from Leibniz to Spinoza; the strength of the parallels, as bits of inductive evidence for a shared view, is partly a function of the extent to which the points of intersection between Spinoza and Leibniz have historical antecedents, of which both philosophers are presumed to have been aware.

1. Spinoza's extended substance is simple, noncomposite, indivisible. His arguments at E IP12 (continued in P13 and P15S) for the conclusion that no substance "can be divided" are at once puzzling and suggestive. In the dilemma of P12, we are to see that a substance cannot have either substances or nonsubstances as parts. The latter would seem clear enough, for if a substance were divisible into *non*substances, such a division would be an annihilation of a substance, and that's ruled out by IP7. But the emphasis on nonsubstantial leftovers is a distraction: it is *being divisible* in the relevant sense, not being divisible *into nonsubstances*, that threatens annihilation. A substance is annihilated if it exists at $t_1$ and doesn't exist at $t_2$. If at $t_1$ substance S is a whole, composed of parts $x$ and $y$, then we've got three things at $t_1 - x, y$, and the substance S they compose; upon division at $t_2$ we've got two things — $x$ and $y$ but nothing they now compose. What has the (substantial vs. nonsubstantial) status of $x$ and $y$ got to do with it? Whether at $t_1$ we've got three substances (the whole and its substantial parts) or just one (the whole and its nonsubstantial parts), the composite S exists $t_1$ but not at $t_2$, and that's all Spinoza needs.

All this presumes that the composition relation, in which Spinoza is arguing that a substance never stands to parts, isn't simply a mereological sum relation — harmlessly presumes, I mean, that Spinoza isn't considering the view that so long as $x$ and $y$ exist, there is some whole S they make up. Surviving parts but annihilated whole is *conceptually* impossible in that case. But there's another supposition here, too: that Spinoza is thinking of parts $x$ and $y$ as existing at $t_1$ prior to S's division at $t_2$. Perhaps he is instead thinking that at $t_1$ we've just got S, and talk of divisibility is talk of sacrificing S in the formation of two new things $x$ and $y$. This whole-prior-to-part reading doesn't explain why Spinoza goes to more trouble than he needs in the second (annihilation) horn of the dilemma. But it does help to explain part of what he says against the first horn, where S is imagined as being divisible into substances. There, Spinoza argues that divisibility of S into substances $x$ and $y$ is ruled out — not because in that case we shall have envisioned one substance to be formed from many, but rather because in that case "many substances will be able to be formed from one," which by E IP6 is absurd. That rather sounds as if at $t_1$ we've got S (but not x and y, these not yet formed by division), and we're to imagine that division at $t_2$ forms two new substances $x$ and $y$, which Spinoza's "no substance can be produced by another" rules out. There is no work to which Spinoza can put IP6 if the scenario is one where substances x and y exist, and compose S, predivision at $t_1$; for if they exist before and after division, no new substance is formed by division.

Although I do not recommend the whole-prior-to-part reading of what is going on at E IP12, it seems to me clearly at work in Spinoza's thought about extended substance. The fundamental position from which his replies to opponents come at length in IP15S is a rejection of the claim that substance "consists of parts" (Geb II, 57/25) or is "composed of parts" (58/18), that it is divisible in the sense that "its parts are really distinct" (59/12) or, in the case of extended substance explicitly, that "infinite quantity is composed of parts" (58/22–25). The extent of agreement between Spinoza and Leibniz here emerges in part from the distinction between what can be said of the created world of real bodies, available to the senses or the imagination, and that of infinite quantity as it is conceived by the intellect. For Leibniz, in the former case the parts are prior to the whole and really in the whole, whereas in the latter case the whole is prior to the part and "not really in" the whole. Spinoza likewise distinguishes between quantity "as it is in the imagination," on the one hand, being "finite, divisible, and composed of parts," and quantity "as it is in the intellect," on the other hand, being "infinite, unique, and indivisible" (IP15S at 59/22–30).[35] The former would correspond to modes of extended substance; the latter would correspond to the eternal nature or attribute of extension — or, given Spinoza's claim that extended substance is not composed of parts, to extended substance itself. That is Woolhouse's anti-Cartesian view, or nearly so: extended substance is the substrate of objects instantiating extension, rather like the quantity itself.

So it is no surprise that in his account of extended substance, Spinoza is prepared to treat examples common to both Leibniz and their predecessors — of a geometrical plane or a mathematical line, for example (E IP15S 59/4–9), of a whole prior to its parts that is "divisible" in the sense Leibniz makes explicit, one implying that it is not genuinely composed of actual parts. Already Aristotle had asked whether the definition or form of a line (a continuous quantity) includes its possession of parts, claiming that even if a line when divided into two "passes away into its halves," it still "does not follow that lines are composed of [those halves] as parts of their substance" (*Metaphysics* VII: 10, 1035a17–21). That is, being divisible in the sense applicable to a line does not imply being a whole composed of logically prior parts making it up. Leibniz would later compare ideal space to "a mathematical line, whose parts are only possible and completely indefinite," claiming that "space . . . is ideal and consists in possibilities . . . thus there are no divisions in it but such as are made by the mind." In this he followed Aristotle's view that continuous quantities, though infinitely divisible, nevertheless permit another sense in which they are *indivisible* — meaning they have no actual parts: "Since, however, the term 'indivis- ible' has two meanings, according as a whole is not potentially divisible or [accord- ing as it] is actually undivided, there is nothing to hinder us from thinking an indi- visible [whole], when we think of length (that which is actually not divided)" (*De Anima* III: 6,430b6–8). Aquinas echoes this view when claiming that "the continu- ous is indivisible" since it actually has no divisions but is only "potentially divisible" (*Summa Theologica*, par. I, quaest. 85, art. 8). Crescas[36] soon thereafter would dis- tinguish corporeal extension from what he called incorporeal extension or space, existing outside the created universe and independent of it; the former is composed of actual parts, but the latter is not composed of actual parts and is only potentially divisible.[37]

Thus we are invited to see this sort of distinction implicit or explicit in Spinoza's predecessors and explicit in Leibniz — between extended concrete wholes composed of actual parts and something closer to abstracta ("continuous quantities," "incorpo- real extension"), containing no actual parts and indivisible strictly speaking — as in Spinoza, too, corresponding to extended modes, on the one hand, and to that which "cannot be divided into any parts, or cannot have any parts" (Ep 12), on the other. When Spinoza speaks of "substantial extension" in the *Short Treatise*, claiming that "extension is a substance," he has in mind something rather more like extension itself, an eternal essence or nature, in Woolhouse's view, which like the mathematical line is a whole prior to its parts. As Spinoza says of such a whole and its parts in the *Short Treatise*, they are "beings of reason" (KV I.2, sect. 19: Geb I, 24/19–20: Curley 71).

2. Let me recover a bit more of what Leibniz had in mind when calling the ab- stract continuum of space an "ideal" thing, among the *entia rationis*. One item we have already mentioned: unlike the real world of perceived phenomenal bodies, the ideal world is accessible via abstraction or by thought alone, by the intellect. The other item comes from Leibniz's inclination to combine his nominalist views about abstracta generally with sympathies for a broadly Platonic account of the contents of our ideas and the foundation of eternal truths. The benefits of Platonism are pre- served for the nominalist Leibniz by appeal to the divine mind. Thus in a letter to Hansch of July 1707, praising "*enthusiasmo Platonico*," Leibniz says that "many of the Platonic ideas are most beautiful . . . that there is an intelligible world in the di- vine mind, which I usually call the *region of ideas*.[38] Here Leibniz is following Augustine and other Christian theologians. In citing the scholastic debate of *de con- stantia subjecti* (about eternal truths whose subject corresponds to nothing in the cre- ated world), Leibniz says the following about the connections among ideas expressed in eternal truths:

> But it will be further asked what the ground is for this connection, since there is a reality in it which does not mislead. The reply is that it is grounded in the linking together of ideas. In response to this it will be asked where these ideas would be if there were no mind, and what would then become of the real foundation of this cer- tainty of eternal truths. This question brings us at last to the ultimate foundation of truth, namely to that Supreme and Universal Mind who cannot fail to exist and whose understanding is indeed the domain of eternal truths. St. Augustine knew this and expresses it pretty forcefully. (A 6,6, 447: RB 447)

The connection between this Platonistic "region of ideas" and "ideal" space emerges for Leibniz via a relationalist view of space as an abstract structure of possible orderings among objects: "space," recall, "is ideal, and consists in possibilities, or in an order of coexistents that is in some way possible." Thus Leibniz says, "Relations and orderings are to some extent 'beings of reason' . . . for one can say that their reality like that of eternal truths and possibilities, comes from the Supreme Reason."[39]

And here we do well to recall that — in addition to calling substantial extension conceived as a whole prior to parts a "being of reason" (above: KV I.2, sect. 19: Geb I, 24/19–20: Curley 71) — Spinoza, too, likens the nature of his extended substance to that of eternal truths. Unlike the existence of durational extended modes (finite bodies) accessible to perception or the imagination, the existence of the one eternal and extended substance conceived by the intellect, "like the essence of a thing, is conceived as an eternal truth" (E ID8). Moreover, the similarity of Spinoza's distinction between modes or bodies and extended substance to Leibniz's distinction between "real" bodies and "ideal" space is further suggested by IP8S2,[40] where in addressing confusions that might arise in connection with IP7, Spinoza indicates his awareness of the Scholastic debate concerning truths whose subject corresponds to nothing in the created world. Confusion about IP7 ("it pertains to the nature of a substance to exist") is likely to arise, says Spinoza, if one fails to distinguish "between modifications of substance and substance itself." One payoff to ridding ourselves of the confusion — by "attending to the nature of substance" itself — is an explanation of "how we can have true ideas of modifications that do not exist" (Geb II, 50/8–12). Leibniz would explain the possibility of truths whose subject does not correspond to anything outside our thought — figures bearing a constant relation to some point, or the winged horse Pegasus — in terms of everlasting essences in God, grounding the possibility of such objects. Spinoza does much the same, claiming "though [such modes] do not exist outside the intellect, nevertheless their essences are comprehended in another in such a way that they can be conceived through it." As Leibniz would say that "God is the source of possibilities and consequently of ideas," the latter construed ideally in God "which we participate in by our knowledge," so Spinoza will say that there are in God (qua extended, now, not thinking) the eternal and immutable essences of nonexisting but possible modes of extension, grounding truths about them. The ultimate grounding is something eternal, rather more like a Platonic abstractum in which modes can participate, rather more like essences or natures themselves. So far, so close: that is Woolhouse's anti-Cartesian view.

3. Finally, let me retrieve one last item from Leibniz's distinction between "real" bodies and "ideal" space — one suggesting a further parallel to Spinoza's durational extended modes, on the one hand, and eternal extended substance on the other, construed rather as an essence or immutable nature itself. In his fourth letter to Clarke, Leibniz claims that extension "must be the affection of some thing that is extended" and that space of the sort Clarke and the Newtonians had in mind, being distinct from bodies and admitting of vacua, would be "an attribute without a subject, an extension without anything extended" (G VII, 372–373). And in his fifth letter he says that Clarke has confused the extension or immensity of things with space and their duration with time. Here Leibniz is returning to a view held as early as 1704, according to which the ideal continua of space and time must be distinguished from

the extension and duration of bodies: "If you regard this mathematical body as *space*, it must be correlated with *time*; if as *extension*, it must be correlated with *duration*" (G II, 269: L 536). The same point is raised in a 1711 dialogue against Malebranche, where he concludes that "extension stands to space as duration stands to time; duration and extension are attributes of things, but space and time are taken by us to be outside of things" (G VI, 584: L 621–622). Thus "extension" so-called in the proper sense — that is, *space* — is, as he says to Clarke (G VII, 401) and Malebranche, outside of finite created bodies; it is ideal, in the realm of the eternal truths and immutable essences. But extension and duration apply to bodies themselves; they are, as Leibniz says, literally in them as in a subject.[41]

And here we are invited to recall again Spinoza's claim that the existence of infinite and eternal extended substance is different in kind from the existence of finite and durational modes. However untraditional as a reading of Spinoza, Woolhouse's distinction between "substantial extension" itself as an eternal nature (not an instantiation) and extended modes as durational bodies is nothing as remote as all that. In distinguishing between space as "ideal," at the level of eternal truths and immutable essences accessible to the intellect, and bodies that are extended and durational, at the level of "real" phenomena accessible by perception or the imagination, we have at the very least a near cousin to a distinction Spinoza himself may have had in mind, concerning the ontological status of extended substance. (There are of course huge differences: Leibniz's space is no substance. Might one say that, had Leibniz possessed Spinoza's courage to place equally within his one eternal and uncreated and ultimate cause (God) the foundations not only of thinking but also of extended creatures, his space would have been Spinoza's extended substance? Perhaps, though Leibniz was still thinking with the Cartesians when he supposed that extended creatures would be substances having real parts, which, with Spinoza, he rejects. But that cannot be the end of the matter, for it leaves unexplained why Leibniz should reject the view that bodies are modes — something he seems in any case to have entertained in the late Paris years.[42] I shall return briefly to Leibniz's rejection of Spinoza's extended substance below.)

We began this section by noting that certain of Spinoza's views about extended substance, when set alongside those of a prominent intellectual neighbor (Leibniz), give prima facie weight to Woolhouse's account. We have since been invited to acknowledge several important parallels between them as indirect evidence that Spinoza might have reckoned the ontological status of his extended substance to be rather more like that of Leibniz's ideal space than anything like Descartes's extended substantial space. In closing I want to suggest how the parallels can and in some cases should be resisted as evidence for Woolhouse's view.

1′. Spinoza's extended substance, like Leibniz's ideal space, is indivisible, a whole prior to its parts, not in any way composed of parts, strictly speaking. This shared mereological feature can count as indirect evidence for Spinoza's extended substance having an ontological status rather more like Leibniz's ideal space than Descartes's extended substantial space *only if* Descartes's extended substantial space lacks this feature. But Cartesian or Newtonian space itself is plausibly a whole prior to its parts. To whatever extent space (again in the more traditional, received sense of "space") can be said to have parts, they do not relate to the whole in a way threatening its status as a substance — as a genuine composite, conceptually dependent on prior parts from which it is built up. Indeed the E IP12 dilemma works just fine for the whole of extended space as traditionally conceived, no regions of which can be either separated from one another or conceived independently of the whole of which they are a part. It is presumably this fact that Leibniz had implicitly in mind when arguing against Descartes — that there are no natural divisions there to be marked out in his purely geometrical extension fit to ground the boundaries of whatever is said to be in motion, from which qualitative variety among bodies is said to arise (cf. Leibniz's arguments in *De Ipsa Natura*, sect. 13, against Descartes's *Principles* 2:23, noted in the first section).

2'. Spinoza's extended substance, the existence of which is "conceived as an eternal truth," "just like the essence of a thing," bears the marks of Leibniz's ideal space as an *ens rationis*, as among the quasi-Platonic objects in the region of ideas in God. But the texts are too slim to make much of this as evidence for Woolhouse's anti-Cartesian view, and the disanalogies are considerable. First, when replying to the objection that "since extension is divisible, the perfect being would consist of parts," Spinoza says, "That part and whole are not true or actual beings, but only beings of reason" (KV I.2, sect. 19: Geb I, 24/19–20). Here Spinoza is simply denying that extended substance is genuinely composed of parts; he is decidedly not placing his extended substance among the *entia rationis* properly so-called. Second, notice Spinoza's claim that beings of reason "are not true or actual beings" — something he would scarcely say of his one eternal and infinite substance.[43] That sentiment is implicit in Leibniz, too: of space itself he says that "being neither substance nor accident, it is therefore a mere ideal thing" (L 704). In Leibniz's case, the sentiment is a feature of his relationalism about spatial truths, and the construal of ideal space is a system of abstract relations among actual and possible objects. A standard thirteenth-century "*esse deminutum*" doctrine of relations understood them to have a "weaker being" as compared to other categories,[44] this emerging from Aristotle's own view (in book XIV of the *Metaphysics*) that relations, unlike substances, do not possess their own forms of generation and corruption, being instead dependent on the accidents in the related individual substances themselves. Thus, not only do we have in Leibniz a motivation for his ascribing to ideal space the ontological status he does (i.e., relationalism), to which there is no obvious corresponding motivation in Spinoza; we must also acknowledge that insofar as Spinoza and Leibniz alike would reckon beings of reason unfit as candidates for substance, Spinoza's view that the existence of extended substance is like that of essences and eternal truths can at most express a general epistemic feature of *entia rationis* — of being available to the intellect or of having a nature discoverable by the mind — and not a fact about ontological status sufficient for distinguishing Spinoza's substance from Descartes's extended substantial space.

3'. There remains the supposed parallel between Spinoza's claim that the existence of infinite and eternal extended substance is different in kind from the existence of finite and durational extended modes and Leibniz's distinction between ideal ("mathematical") space and genuinely extended durational bodies. The suggestion is that Woolhouse's Spinoza can be seen to anticipate the notion that modes or bodies are genuinely extended and durational, whereas substance (Spinoza's, qua "extended") or space (Leibniz's) does not, strictly speaking, instantiate extension. It is worth noting that Leibniz himself, perhaps the most well placed of any to recognize a parallel here between Spinoza's account and his own, did not in fact recognize any — in large measure because of the ontological difficulties noted above. We encountered earlier Spinoza's way out of the traditional creation problem — of explaining how a purely immaterial thinking God could cause the created world of extended material bodies: make extension an attribute of God. And we noted too (notes 28 and 29) Leibniz's agreement here but without noting his misgivings; to Spinoza's claim at E IP15S that adherents of the traditional account "are entirely ignorant" of that power by which an immaterial unextended God could create a world of extended material bodies, Leibniz says that "there is something true in this, but, I think, it is something not sufficiently understood" (AG 274). What Leibniz goes on to say is that it won't do to conceive of God as extended since to do so is either (i) to conceive of God as extended and material, composed of inhomogeneous parts, and hence not a substance at all but an aggregate, or else (ii) to conceive of God as homogenous extension but (thereby) incomplete, abstract, and purely passive — and so, again, not a substance at all. (i) refers to Leibniz's long-standing objections to extended substance as having only being *per accidens*, as *ens per aggregationem*; (ii) refers to Leibniz's mature critique of the Cartesian claim that extension is a principal attribute of substance.[45] Clearly in this context, Leibniz's interpretation of Spinoza is the traditional one, and the anti-Cartesian Spinoza, or any parallel suggesting Woolhouse's Spinoza, is altogether absent.

The closest one will come to seeing Leibniz recognize the suggested parallel is the following,[46] where it is mentioned and dropped: "It is also remarkable that Spinoza, as above (*On the Improvement of the Intellect* [Geb II, 33]) seems to have denied that extension is divisible into parts and is composed of parts, which is without meaning except, perhaps, in the sense that space is not a divisible thing. But space and time are orders of things, not things" (AG 275). That is tantalizing and nearly too short to work with. If Leibniz's concession to the meaningfulness of Spinoza's claim is a reference to his own ideal space, it points once again to the unfittingness of an ideal entity as any serious candidate for substance. Leibniz is right to drop it.

## Conclusion

The anti-Cartesian Spinoza is, I think, not Spinoza. We can resist the invitation to grant that if according to Spinoza substance is eternal whereas modes are durational, then he does not understand eternal substance to be like durational or temporal modes in instantiating an essence or attribute. One can do justice to that distinction of Spinoza's even if his one extended substance is Descartes's extended substantial space. We can, in addition, resist the temptation to put Spinoza's eternal substance on a par with essences of geometric figures, by seeing the latter not as grounded in a quasi-Platonic substance but (as Spinoza says) instead as comprehended by or contained in the relevant divine attribute of extension itself. Moreover, the quasi-Platonic construal of substance as more like an essence or eternal and immutable nature does nothing to explain Spinoza's effort to solve the traditional creation prob-

lem; more crucially, it cannot plausibly be wedded to—and so cannot explain—
Spinoza's lengthy defense of God as "corporeal substance," to which length, breadth,
and depth strictly apply. Nor is Spinoza's view that extended substance is indivisible
and partless evidence against the traditional Cartesian construal of his extended substance, in favor of something rather more like Leibniz's ideal space. For while it is
true that Spinoza's extended substance shares with Leibniz's ideal space the mereological character of a whole prior to its parts, the whole of Descartes's extended substantial space shares it as well. And as Spinoza explicitly recognizes, the ontological
status of *entia rationis*, among which Leibniz's ideal space is numbered, render them
unfit as candidates for genuine substances. So it is not surprising that Leibniz himself recognized in Spinoza nothing like his own ideal space; and in contexts where
such a reading would have most likely presented itself, Leibniz attributes to Spinoza
the traditional reading and rejects it right along with Cartesian extended substance.
Leibniz, I think, saw in Spinoza what was really there, and he didn't find what was-
n't there.[47]

### Notes

1. The claim summarizes well enough an entailment of E IIP2 together with IP11 and
IP14. In what follows, translations of Spinoza are those of Curley; textual citations adopt the
abbreviations of the present volume, to which are added the following: C = *Opuscles et fragments inédits de Leibniz*, L. Couturat, ed. (Paris: Presses Universitaires, 1903); DSR = *De Summa Rerum*, G. H. R. Parkinson, ed. and trans. (New Haven, Conn.: Yale University Press, 1992);
LH = *Die Leibniz-Handschriften der Königlichen Öffentlichen Bibliothek zu Hannover*, Ed-
uard Bodemann, ed. (Hannover: Hahn, 1889; reprint Hildesheim: Olms, 1966); PLP = *Leibniz: Logical Papers*, G. H. R. Parkinson, ed. and trans. (Oxford: Clarendon Press, 1966); VE
= *Vorausedition zur Reihe VI (Philosophische Schriften)*, Munster: Leibniz-Forschugsstelle
der Universistät Münster, 1982–.

2. I mean, leaving wholly aside (i) questions of how easily Spinoza's claim in Ep 50 (say,
that "nothing can be called one or single unless some other thing has first been conceived
which agrees with it") can be wedded with E IP14C1 and its deductive offspring IIP4D, and
leaving largely aside (ii) the question of whether "substance" is a mass- or count-noun for Spinoza and Descartes.

3. *Synopsis*: AT VII, 14: CSM II, 10; and *Principles* 2:23: AT VIIIA, 52: CSM I, 232.

4. That way of putting it makes the denial of vacua look rather like plain sailing. It isn't.
The reader is directed to Jonathan Bennett's "Space and Subtle Matter in Descartes's Metaphysics" in this volume. The claim that for Descartes the whole of space is (an) extended substance might not be plain sailing either; one subtlety is broached in the second section, below, this chapter (cf. note 14).

5. On the former problem of monads and spatial location, see J. A. Cover and Glenn A.
Hartz, "Are Leibnizian Monads Spatial?" *History of Philosophy Quarterly* 11 (1994): 295–316;
on the latter taxonomy of eliminative versus identificatory reduction, as it figures in understanding Leibniz's views of space and time, and on the notion of space and time as "ideal," see
J. A. Cover, "Non-basic Time and Reductive Strategies: Leibniz's Theory of Time," *Studies in
History and Philosophy of Science* 28 (1997): 289–318, and the third section of this chapter (below).

6. Two out of four. They are, in terms roughly hewn: (a) that which is independent of
other things; (b) that which is the subject of predication but is not predicated of another, (c)

that which contains within it a principle of activity, and (d) that which endures through change. The route from various Aristotelian pronouncements [see, e.g., (a) *Categories* 5, 2a34; (b) *Categories* 5, 2a12; (c) *Physics* 1, 193a–b; (d) *Categories* 5, 4a10], through scholastic thought into the early modern period, is an interesting and difficult one, the reconstruction of which I leave to more capable hands.

7. AT VII, 161: CSM II, 114. Presumably the asymmetry of "residing in" or "inhering in," relevant to feature (b), is not unconnected to the putative asymmetry of dependence holding between property and substance but not substance and property, relevant to feature (a) (cf. AT VIIIA, 24: CSM I, 210; AT VII, 87: CSM II, 54; AT VII, 222: CSM II, 156). The extent to which this connection can be made out is a measure of the extent to which (a) and (b) form a unified conception of substance.

8. Descartes himself acknowledged the need to account for change in the perceivable world of extended bodies, and motion was to do the job. In *Principles* 2:23, after claiming that "all the matter existing in the entire universe . . . is recognized as matter simply in virtue of its being extended" and that all variety in matter "is reducible to its divisibility and consequent mobility in respect of its parts," Descartes adds: "This seems to have been widely recognized by the philosophers, since they have stated that nature is the principle of motion or rest. And what they meant by 'nature' in this context is what causes all corporeal things to take on the characteristics of which we are aware in experience" (AT VIIIA, 53: CSM I, 232–233). Leibniz's reply is that this last concession in the direction of Aristotle and the Scholastics does not go deeply enough: if the nature or essence of substance must contain the causal resources for explaining all change, then the passive and purely geometric property of extension fails to account for even the most basic sort of change, motion itself, for "we must admit that extension, or that which is geometrical in bodies . . . has nothing in itself from which action and motion can arise" (G IV, 510; AG 161).

9. Cf. "Conversation of Philarete and Ariste" and the letters to the Cartesian de Volder of 24 March 1699 and 20 June 1704. Leibniz's implicit premise here — that some property P is suitable as the essence or principal attribute of substance only if other properties presuppose it but it does not presuppose others — is also implicit in Descartes's *Principles* 1:53, where it is argued that extension is fit for the principal attribute of corporeal substance on the grounds that "everything else which can be attributed to body presupposes extension."

10. In R. S. Woolhouse, "Spinoza and Descartes and the Existence of Extended Substance," in J. A. Cover and Mark Kulstad, eds., *Central Themes in Early Modern Philosophy* (Indianapolis and Cambridge: Hackett, 1990), pp. 23–48, and in his *Descartes, Spinoza, Leibniz: The Concept of Substance in Seventeenth Century Metaphysics* (London and New York: Routledge, 1993), pp. 45–50. For purposes of citation, I abbreviate the former as SDE. Edwin Curley has taken a somewhat different route than Woolhouse's to a related, anti-Cartesian conclusion (see note 15); I shall not be engaging Curley's efforts in this paper, nor his exchange with Jonathan Bennett (cf. note 15).

11. C 392: PLP 81.

12. "Mysteriously" since the difference between squareness and roundness, say, seems for all the world to represent a difference of affections not requiring a difference of attributes.

13. For example, prior to his main argument for the existence of God in the *Monologion*, Anselm suggests that God, who is a simple active substance, might be conceived as Justice no less than a just being.

14. One might aim to find in Descartes's reference to space or extension "considered in general" (*extensio consideratur in genere*, at *Principles* 2:12; AT VIIIA, 46: CSM I, 228) reason to go whole hog and apply the gloss in Descartes's case as well; extension considered in general would be an abstraction and not a singular, concrete existing substance. But Descartes is clear that space as a concrete extended substance must include the extension of particular ex-

tended bodies themselves, and the passage under consideration (from *Principles* 1:63), about the nature of body, can scarcely be given the suggested gloss of abstract extension or space considered in general — particularly given his emphasis that we have a more clear and distinct understanding of extension if we consider it as extended substance. As he says, "A concept is not any more distinct because we include less in it" (by abstracting the "substance" away from "extended substance").

15. Elements of both (iii) and (iv) figure in the anti-Cartesian reading of Edwin Curley, *Spinoza's Metaphysics: An Essay in Interpretation* (Cambridge, Mass.: Harvard University Press, 1969), pp. 16ff. Curley's reading and those elements of (iii) and (iv) are taken up by Jonathan Bennett, *A Study of Spinoza's Ethics* (Indianapolis and Cambridge: Hackett, 1984), pp. 64–65. The (iii)–(iv) mix reappears in Curley's sequel, *Behind the Geometrical Method* (Princeton, N.J.: Princeton University Press, 1988), pp. 27–30; the Curley-Bennett exchange, into which I shall not enter explicitly here, is continued in Yirmiyahu Yovel, ed., *God and Nature: Spinoza's Metaphysics* (Leiden: E. J. Brill, 1991).

16. Suarez, *Disputatio metaphysicae* VII.1.4.

17. See Alan Donagan, "Spinoza's Proof of Immortality," in Marjorie Grene, ed., *Spinoza: A Collection of Critical Essays* (Notre Dame, Ind.: University of Notre Dame Press, 1973), pp. 241–258; and Bennett, *Spinoza's Ethics*, pp. 204–205.

18. The second claim — that modes are instantiations of the attribute of extension — might be resisted, too, though I shall not press that either since doing so presupposes a picture already at odds with Woolhouse's. In the picture I'm referring to, bodies are modal in the sense that statements about the existence and nature of bodies are equivalent to statements predicating F or G or of extended space. In this view, we don't quantify over bodies at the end of the day, and so modes aren't, strictly speaking, items of our final and considered ontology to be properly reckoned instantiations of extension.

19. Time, which for Aristotle was the number or measure of motion or change (cf. *Physics* IV:11, 219b), later comes to imply a measure of the duration (from the Latin *durare*, eventually "to continue or to last") of persisting but changing things. Scholastics and early moderns differed in their views of the connection between time and duration; all alike reckoned duration to express the continued existence or succession in persisting things (changing and unchanging alike).

20. Geb I, 244; Curley 310. I leave aside the issue of why Spinoza here calls duration an attribute of finite created things and elsewhere calls it a mode (cf. Geb I, 250/13–14); a similar feature is there in Descartes (*Principles* I:55 and 56).

21. Though I hasten to note that the context in which this distinction arises in the *Metaphysical Thoughts* — indeed the reflections "from which one may clearly see" the distinction (Geb I, 238/9) — is one in which Spinoza has followed Descartes in reminding us that (from his earlier E IP16) "because . ·. an extended thing, by its very nature, is divisible, i.e., contains an imperfection, we could not attribute extension to God." That doesn't sound like the Spinoza of the *Ethics*. Whereas a proponent of the anti-Cartesian reading might reckon this grist for the mill (extension isn't instantiated by God but exists only eminently in God as a substrate for instantiations), a proponent of the standard reading would see that proposal as speaking rather against Woolhouse's account. Spinoza is clearly able to articulate a certain view when representing the Cartesian line on God and extension but doing quite otherwise when speaking for himself in E IP15S, arguing that the one extended corporeal substance isn't divisible.

22. For a discussion and defense of taking Spinoza at his word when claiming that essences (forms) of finite modes — geometrical figures, say — are comprehended in or depend on the attribute of extension, see Charles Huenemann, "The Necessity of Finite Modes and Geometrical Containment in Spinoza's Metaphysics," chapter 10 in this volume.

23. Thanks to Michael Della Rocca for helping me think more clearly (if not yet clearly enough) about these matters.

24. From C. L. Hardin, "Spinoza on Immortality and Time," in Robert W. Shahan and J. I. Biro, *Spinoza: New Perspectives* (Norman: Oklahoma University Press, 1978), pp. 130–131.

25. Note well that in the causal theorist's reading just proposed, it is not *facies totius Universi* but the extended continuum itself that emerges as nontemporal, as nondurational. Some helpful comments by Roger Woolhouse and Charles Huenemann (in correspondence) have convinced me that hereabouts one might fruitfully aim to locate in Spinoza an anti-Cartesian departure from the received, standard reading — by more carefully distinguishing the one (nontemporal) extended substance, conceived in itself apart from modal variegation into material bodies, from the (durational) infinite mode that is the physical universe in toto (cf. Ep 64 and lemma 7 of the physical digression following E IIP13). Pursuing this would require a more refined understanding than I now possess of the role of motion and rest in Descartes's and Spinoza's account of bodies and of their respective denials of the vacuum. (On the one hand, Descartes's denial is perhaps rather more a consequence of the Aristotelian concept of *place* than I represented; on the other hand, Spinoza's denial in E IP15S seems to serve as evidence that for him God is, so to speak, *materially* extended.)

26. There may be an exception in a textually suspect passage in the first dialogue of the *Short Treatise* (Geb I, 29/22–23; Curley 75).

27. And here by "dualism" I mean an ontological plurality, not a conceptual distinction.

28. Two things having different attributes have nothing in common with one another (E IP2); and if things have nothing in common with one another, one of them cannot be the cause of the other (IP3). No doubt Spinoza had Cartesian interactionism in mind, too; but the mind-body problem is, as Malebranche saw clearly, the problem of creation writ small. Leibniz would have agreed with Spinoza about the traditional creation problem. Where Spinoza can understand God as the cause of a created world of extended bodies by reckoning him as extended, Leibniz will say that God is thinking and that there are no genuinely extended bodies.

29. Here, recall (see note 28), Leibniz will concur. In his reading notes on Johann Wachter's *Elucidarius cabalisticus* (the latter of which includes the chapter "On the Agreement Between the Cabala and Spinoza"), Leibniz writes: "Spinoza also denies that God could have created any corporeal and material mass to serve as the underpinnings [subjectum] of this world, since, he says, those who disagree 'don't know from what divine power it could have been created.' There is something true in this" (AG 274).

30. As presented in the *Short Treatise* I:2, sect. 18, this argument concerns only simplicity, not (also) infinity (see Geb I, 24: Curley 70–71).

31. Nicholas Rescher explicitly says that space and time "are [well-founded] phenomena," in *Leibniz: An Introduction to His Philosophy* (Totowa, N.J.: Rowman & Littlefield, 1979), p. 84; Stuart Brown tells us in *Leibniz* (Minneapolis: University of Minnesota Press, 1984), p. 147, that "material substances are reduced to well-founded phenomena as also are space and time"; John Earman in "Was Leibniz a Relationist?" in P. French et al., eds., *Midwest Studies in Philosophy*, IV (Minneapolis: University of Minnesota Press, 1979), p. 263, sets out to "explain Leibniz's insistence that both bodies and space are well-founded phenomena."

32. The full story can be found in Glenn A. Hartz and J. A. Cover, "Space and Time in the Leibnizian Metaphysic," *Noûs* 22 (1988): 493–519.

33. Part of what I'm leaving aside are difficulties raised by Leibniz's view; among them is the problem of understanding how, strictly speaking, bodies should fail to instantiate geometrical properties.

34. I mean that there is nothing wrong with arguing as follows: if Leibniz said that ideal space is F, G, H, and (explicitly) P, and Spinoza said that extended substance is F, G, and H,

then we have inductive grounds for believing that Spinoza believes extended substance is P, to the degree we can find *in Spinoza* connections between P and F, G and H, and to the degree that disanalogies between Leibniz's claims about ideal space and Spinoza's claims about extended substance are weak or irrelevant.

35. In the TdIE (Geb II, 39/4–14; Curley 43–44), the former is what Spinoza describes as perceived through a cause, suggesting the relation of finite and created modes to infinite and eternal substance.

36. Chasdai Crescas (ca. 1340 — ca. 1410), Spanish rabbi and commentator on Maimonides in *The Light of the Lord (Or Adonai)*, especially in the first section on physics and the relation of God to the created world, was read by Spinoza (cf. Ep 12 at Geb IV, 62; Curley 205).

37. Here see Harry Austryn Wolfson, *The Philosophy of Spinoza* (Cambridge, Mass.: Harvard University Press, 1934; New York: Meridian Books, 1958), vol. 1, pp. 275–281.

38. L 592: *God. Guil. Leibnitii Opera Philosophicae quae exstant Latina, Gallica, Germanica omnia*, J. E. Erdmann, ed. (Berlin: Eichler, 1839–1840; Aalen: Scientia Verlag, 1974), p. 445. Leibniz was later (in a letter of 1715 to M. Remond, addressing du Tertre's attack of Malebranche) to say that "as God is the source of possibilities and consequently of ideas, the Father may be excused . . . in distinguishing [ideas] from notions and in taking them for perfections of God which we participate in by our knowledge. . . . It even seems that Plato, speaking of ideas, and St. Augustine, speaking of truth, had kindred thoughts, which I find very remarkable; and this is the part of Malebranche's system that I should like to have retained (pp. 735–738).

39. A 6.6.227: RB 227. In his notes on Temmik (LH IV 8, Bl. 60–61, watermark ca. 1715 or early 1716), Leibniz says that relations aren't created but "born by virtue of the divine intellect alone. . . . They are not beings — any being other than God is in fact a creature — but they are [eternal] truths" (cf. *Notationes quaedam ad Aloysii Philosophiam*, VE 1083).

40. See SDE 42–43.

41. That is, "bodies have extension" is true at the level of discourse we described earlier as the less strict of Leibniz's account. In this exchange with Malebranche and to the Cartesian de Volder, Leibniz goes on to say that in the strict and philosophical sense, extension cannot be the essence of anything substantial because it is incomplete, abstract, and presupposes something prior — something "diffused and expanded in a subject" — which Leibniz himself will identify with primitive active force.

42. Consider, for example, his willingness in 1676 to speak of "all possible modes, or things" (A 6.2.532: DSR 85) and this: "It can easily be demonstrated that all things are distinguished, not as substances (i.e. radically) but as modes. . . . The essence of all things is the same, and things differ only modally" (A 6.2.573: DSR 93–95). Judging from the mature *De Ipsa Natura* (sect. 8), we see that Leibniz's misgivings about this aspect of Spinozism are broadly theological.

43. Spinoza distinguishes real from fictitious being (*ens fictum*) and from being of reason (*ens rationis*) in the *Metaphysical Thoughts* (Geb I, 233/15ff), the latter explained as "nothing but a mode of thinking, which helps us to more easily retain, explain, and imagine the things we have understood." In a difficult pair of passages in the *Short Treatise*, Spinoza considers the relation of God as a whole to (I take it) modes as parts — a forerunner of the view in E IP14 that everything is in God. In the first Dialogue, Lust objects: "I think I see a very great confusion. For you seem to want the whole to be something outside of or without its parts, which is indeed absurd. For the Philosophers all say unanimously that *the whole is a second notion (tweede kundigheid), which is no thing in Nature, outside human thought (begrip)*" (Geb I, 30: Curley 75). The accusation seems to be that Spinoza's account of substance as a whole renders it what the Scholastics would have called a second intention (*intentio secunda*) or *ens*

*rationis*, rather like a universal (or a genus or species) under the nominalist conception. Spinoza first replies (in the voice of Reason) that the objection plays on an ambiguity (cf. Geb I, 20/17–18), and later in the second Dialogue, responding to Erasmus, he says that we must distinguish the sense in which a whole is a being of reason from that in which a universal is (Geb I, 32–33). Although I do not fully understand Spinoza's reply, it seems clear that his willingness here to designate the whole — his "One Unique being or Unity" — an *ens rationis* is of the sort encountered earlier in KV (sect. 19), construed now as characterizing simply the relation of whole as immanent cause to its effects, not as characterizing the ontological status of God as something other than an *ens reale*.

44. See Duns Scotus, *Super Praedicamenta*, quaest. 25, 10 ("Relatio inter omnia entia est debilissimum ens"), and Thomas Aquinas, *De potentia* quaest. 8, art. 1.4 ("Relatio habet esse debilissimum").

45. What is material and extended is "real," says Leibniz, "but it is not a substance, since it is an aggregate or the resultant of substances. I speak of matter insofar as it is secondary matter or extended mass, something that is hardly a homogeneous body. But that which we conceive of as homogeneous and call primary matter is something incomplete, since it exists merely in potency. On the other hand, a substance is something complete and active" (AG 274). The full critique of the Cartesian claim that extension is a principal attribute of substance, according to which it emerges as "incomplete, abstract, and purely passive," can be found in the Dialogue with the Malebranchians (G VI, 584: L 621–622) and in the 24 March 1699 and 30 June 1704 letters to de Volder. See also note 41.

46. Here we're still in the mature Leibniz's reading notes on Wachter's 1706 *Elucidarius cabalisticus*, where the discussion focuses on the TdIE. In his (ca.) 1678 reading notes on the *Ethics* (cf. G I, 139–150), the younger Leibniz makes no bones about E 1P12, P13, or P15S.

47. I am grateful to Jonathan Bennett, Michael Della Rocca, Charles Huenemann, Mark Kulstad, and especially Roger Woolhouse, from the caliber of whose help this chapter is, as a result, now less distant.

## 6

SAMUEL LEVEY

# Leibniz's Constructivism and Infinitely Folded Matter

Mathematics has long provided fuel for philosophy. Its capacities both to inspire and to frustrate philosophical inquiry have been familiar at least since Plato and are called on still today. But perhaps nowhere are both inspiration and frustration combined more pointedly than in the philosophy of Leibniz. In what follows I shall explore how Leibniz's views of mathematics play out in his philosophical engagement with a puzzle about matter that figures centrally in his early metaphysics. As I see it, his early theory of matter is seriously defective; in particular, his account of the way matter is divided into its parts is sharply at odds with his own metaphysical analysis of the nature of matter. I shall argue that whereas some of his views of mathematics, especially his views about infinity, encourage him to construct a particular sort of account of the structure of matter, others blind him to the problems infecting that account.

In the first three sections of this paper I shall develop the metaphysics of the puzzle and Leibniz's mathematical strategy for solving it. The following section spells out the metaphysical model of matter that Leibniz crafts, and the next two sections offer criticisms that detail the troubles with that model. In the final two sections, I shall bring to light a subtle constructivist strand in Leibniz's philosophical views of mathematics, which I believe leads him into error in his metaphysics of matter, and suggest how, as a further consequence, that strand of thought also contributes to the development of his monadism.

## How Matter Might Be Infinitely Divided

In 1676, nearly thirty years before the *New Essays* and forty years before the *Monadology*, Leibniz's metaphysics is already embroiled with the idea of the actually infinite division of matter. On the one hand, he accepts the Cartesian hypothesis that any portion of matter that circulates through irregular spaces in a plenum will divide into an actual infinity of parts.[1] But on the other hand, he flatly denies that matter could be composed either of indivisible points (what he often calls *minima*[2]) or of infinitesimal particles. Infinitesimals he writes off as mere "fictions" of his mathematics, with no claim to real existence (*De Quadratura Arithmetica*, 133), and points fare only slightly better. In his analysis points exist, but only as *modes* of extended things — that is, boundaries or *endpoints* (*extrema, termini*) — and never as *parts* of them (A 6.3.553–555). Whatever the parts of matter are, they must be finite and divisible, for the infinitesimal and the indivisible can never be parts of anything. Those claims about the properties of the parts of matter plus the Cartesian hypothesis that motion in the plenum requires infinite division into parts issue jointly in the thesis that a finite portion of matter might divide into an actual infinity of finite and divisible parts. Thus a puzzle arises right at the center of Leibniz's theory of matter: how it is even *possible* for a finite portion of matter to divide into an actual infinity of finite and divisible parts?

Leibniz's answer is that a portion of matter could be so divided, just as an infinite convergent series of numbers could consist entirely of finite and divisible terms but still have only a finite sum.[3] Take, for example, Zeno's "dichotomy" series, 1/2, 1/4, 1/8, 1/16, 1/32, and so on ad infinitum. Each term in the series is immediately succeeded by another term of half its value, so there is no last term in the series (it is unbounded) and no smallest term. Yet each term has only a finite value and is further divisible, and the combined sum of all the terms in the infinite series is equal to 1. In the same way, Leibniz contends, a finite portion of matter can be seen as dividing into an infinity of ever smaller but always finite and divisible parts. The existence of the infinite convergent series of numbers is supposed to establish the possibility that a finite portion of matter could dissolve into an infinity of finite and divisible parts.

This tactic of defending the coherence of his doctrine of the infinite division of matter by an appeal to the infinite convergent numerical series becomes a long-standing feature of his metaphysics of matter. More than twenty years later, for instance, he unlimbers precisely that defense to meet a challenge by John Bernoulli, who writes: "You admit that any finite portion of matter is already actually divided up into an infinite number of parts; and yet you deny that any of these parts can be infinitely small. How is this consistent?" (GM III, 529).[4] Leibniz responds:

> I do not think it follows from [the infinite division of matter] that there exists any infinitely small portion of matter. Still less do I admit that it follows that there is any absolutely minimum portion of matter. . . . Let us suppose that in a line its 1/2, 1/4, 1/8, 1/16, 1/32, etc., are actually assigned, and that all the terms of this series actually exist. You infer from this that there also exists an infinitieth term. I, on the other

hand, think that nothing follows from this other than that there actually exists any assignable finite fraction, however small you please. (GM III, 536)

The partition of a finite *extensum* into an infinity of parts — Leibniz's example here is a line and its subsegments, but it can be readily modified to fit the case of a body — can consist entirely of lesser *extensa*, all finite and divisible, arranged in a descending geometrical sequence. Contrary to the suggestion of Bernoulli's challenge, neither infinitesimal nor pointlike portions of matter have to be postulated to make sense of the idea of an actually infinite division of a finite magnitude.

Bernoulli's challenge has been met, but we should be careful not to infer too much from the infinite series model. What the existence of the infinite convergent numerical series establishes is this: no formal or mathematical inconsistency arises from the assertion that a finite magnitude can be resolved into an infinity of finite and divisible magnitudes. Can we advance to the still stronger claim that the existence of the infinite convergent series establishes that it really is possible for a finite extensum to divide into an infinity of lesser extensa none of which is infinitesimal or indivisible? Yes, if we uphold the further thesis — in my view both plausible and Leibnizian — that mathematical existence is *ontological possibility*. A full treatment of this thesis falls beyond the compass of the present chapter, but some remarks are in order.

On the Leibnizian account I have in mind, one would hold the following sort of view. The fact that 5 is a number is (or encodes) the fact that it is possible for there to be five *things*, say, five apples. Consider this: "There exists a natural number greater than 10 but less than 12"; that is, it is possible that there might exist some apples such that there are more than ten apples but less than twelve apples. The fact that 11 is a natural number is a first-order possibility: it is possible that eleven things might exist. The fact that there is an infinity of natural numbers is a second-order possibility: any of an infinity of *possibilities* might actually obtain in the real world.

If the natural numbers readily illustrate the thesis that mathematical existence is ontological possibility, it requires a bit more care to develop that thesis with respect to the infinite convergent numerical series. For any such series must necessarily include (infinitely many) fractions — that is, *rational* numbers — and their ontological significance is somewhat unlike that of the naturals. (The real numbers are yet a further matter, and for this chapter I shall simply leave them aside.) Before proceeding, though, it has to be said that my spin on the ontological significance of the natural numbers actually relies on the fact that each natural is also a *cardinal* number; roughly, it counts as an answer to the question "how many?" The rationals, by contrast, are not cardinal numbers. Rational numbers are ratios or integral proportions, as the standard notation $p/q$ suggests, and as such a rational number encodes ontological information about *measure* rather than about *number* or *cardinality* — about "how much" rather than "how many." Moreover, it encodes information about measure with respect to an *amount* of an unspecified *measurable quantity* and unspecified *unit* of measure.[5] The fact that 1/3 is a rational number is the possibility that for any given quantity and any (appropriate) unit of measure, there might be an amount of the given quantity whose measure is one-third that of the unit measure: there might be one-third pounds of clay, a line segment one-third inch in length, and so on.

Now, a *series* of rationals encodes two sorts of ontological information: information about number or cardinality and information about measure. *How many things there might be* is given by the cardinality of the series, and *what amount each thing has (its measure) of some quantity* is given by the particular rationals that the series contains. For example, the finite series of rational numbers 1, 1/2, 1/4, encodes the possibility that there might be three things of measures one, one-half, and one-fourth units of some quantity, respectively. And filling in the blanks, we might take the terms to represent three globes of weight one pound, one-half pound, and one-quarter pound. Filling in the blanks less determinately, we see that the existence of this small series of rationals yields the ontological possibility of three extensa such that one is the greatest of the three in respect of some measurable quantity and is twice the measure of a second in that respect and four times that of the third.[6] As a bonus, the small series of rationals also encodes a fact about the combined measure of all the extensa taken collectively: because this series has a rational number as its sum, we can infer that an extensum whose measure can be assigned by a rational number — and so a finite extensum — might exist and divide into three lesser extensa of the sort described.

We can now articulate precisely how the thesis that mathematical existence is ontological possibility applies in the case of the infinite convergent series of rationals. The cardinality of the series ensures that it is possible that there might be an infinity of things, the fact that the terms of the series are rationals ensures that those things might all be extensa of various finite sizes, and the fact that the series has a rational sum ensures that those extensa might be divisions of a greater but still finite extensum. Thus, the existence of the infinite convergent numerical series establishes that it is possible for a finite extensum to divide into an infinity of lesser extensa none that is infinitesimal or indivisible. Leibniz's example of a line divided into its 1/2, 1/4, 1/8, 1/16, 1/32, and so on fits this scheme perfectly.

Although his own remarks are far less detailed than those I have been offering, it is clear that Leibniz accepts the general thesis that mathematical existence is ontological possibility. He takes mathematics and geometry together to form "the science of continua, that is, of possible things"(G II, 282), and he persistently refers to mathematical entities — such as number, line, velocity, space, time, and so on — as possibles or as orders of possibility or as signifying what is possible.[7] "Number or time," he writes to de Volder, "are only orders ôr relations pertaining to the possibility and the eternal truths of things, ⟨orders ôr relations⟩ that are then to be applied to actual things as the circumstances arise" (G II, 268–269). And similarly, "space, like time . . . consists in possibilities, or in an order of coexistents that is in some way possible" (G II, 278–279). The most explicit single comment of Leibniz's that endorses the view of mathematical entities as ontological possibilities probably occurs in his 1702 reply to Bayle's *Rorias*:

> I acknowledge that time, extension, motion and the continuum in general, as one understands them in mathematics, are only ideal things — that is, they express possibilities just as do numbers. (G IV, 568)

However, there is one facet of our account of how to interpret the existence of the infinite convergent numerical series as an ontological possibility that, by

Leibniz's lights, must be sharply qualified. I said that the cardinality of a series of rationals encodes information about how many things there might be. But according to Leibniz, it is impossible that an infinite series should have a cardinality. For its cardinality would have to be an *infinite* cardinal number and, he holds, it is impossible for there to be such a number. I shall briefly discuss the basis for Leibniz's rejection of the infinite cardinal and his philosophy of the infinite and then see how our account of the ontological significance of infinite series can be qualified to mesh with Leibniz's philosophical commitments.

## Infinity and Paradox

Leibniz's case against the possibility of an infinite cardinal number descends from Galileo Galilei's discovery of the fact that the elements of an infinite collection can be put in one-to-one correspondence with those of some of its own proper subcollections (A 6.3.550f.). Each natural number, for example, has a unique square, and so there is a one-to-one mapping of the naturals onto the square numbers, each natural $n$ going to a unique $n^2$.[8] The existence of such a mapping satisfies a sufficient condition for the class of naturals to have the same number of elements as the class of squares, and so, in this sense, the class of naturals is "equal to" the class of squares. Yet the class of squares is manifestly only a part of the class of naturals, and a vanishingly small part at that. Thus it seems that there is a part of the class of naturals that is equal to the whole, a result that would contradict what Leibniz (and others) take to be axiomatic — that the part is less than the whole. This apparent failure of the "part-whole axiom" in the domain of the infinite is *Galileo's paradox*.[9]

Leibniz construes cardinal numbers (other than 1 and 0) as aggregates of "unities" or "ones" (e.g., $6 = 1 + 1 + 1 + 1 + 1 + 1$),[10] and he views them as applying to aggregates of things taken as a whole rather than to uncollected things taken as so many individuals. Where the number 1 or unity applies to an individual thing, the number 5 applies to an aggregate "whole" with five "parts" (what we would probably consider to be a *set* with five *members*). So in his view, the infinite cardinal number is bound up with the concept of an infinite aggregate or whole in two ways. First, an infinite number itself would count as an infinite whole; and second, such a number would apply to infinite aggregates or wholes. Consequently, the concept of an infinite number is also doubly bound up with Galileo's paradox: both the number and what it *numbers* would violate the part-whole axiom, if either were to exist.

The response that Leibniz offers to Galileo's paradox is to deny that there could be such a thing as an infinite aggregate. He writes,

> Therefore we conclude finally that there is no infinite multiplicity, from which it will follow that there is not an infinity of things, either. Or [rather] it must be said that an infinity of things is not one whole, ôr that there is no aggregate of them. (A 6.3.503)

Note that he distinguishes the claim that there are infinitely many Fs, or *an infinity* of Fs, from the claim that there is an infinite aggregate of those Fs. Only the second, he believes, jeopardizes the part-whole axiom and arouses Galileo's paradox. So, using that distinction, he aims to hold that there is an infinity of things without thereby being committed to the existence of an aggregate in which the part would be "equal to" the whole.

This solution to the paradox involves a flatly metaphysical claim about the unity of what we might neutrally call a *multitude* of elements.[11] Some multitudes perhaps may be true aggregates or wholes, but an infinite multitude of things — "an infinity" of things[12] — could only be so many separate elements. What it is for there to be an infinity of things is not for there to be an infinite number of them nor for there to be an infinite aggregate of them. Instead, what it is for there to be an infinity of things is this: there are more things than can be assigned by any (finite) number. Leibniz quite clearly intends his own use of "infinite" and its cognates in this way:

> By infinite I understand a quantity . . . greater than any that can be assigned by us or that can be designated by numbers. (1676. *De Quadratura Arithmetica*, 133)

> When it is said that there is an infinity [*dari infinita*] of terms, it is not being said that there is some specific number of them, but that there are more than any specific number. (1698. GM III, 566)

In the case of numbers, this means that despite the fact that there are infinitely many finite numbers, there is no aggregate of them all and there is no infinite number:

> I concede the infinite multitude of terms, but this multitude does not constitute a number or a single whole. It signifies nothing but that there are more terms than can be designated by a number. Just so, there is a multitude ôr complex of all numbers, but this multitude is not a number or single whole. (1699. GM III, 575)

Leibniz cannot allow that an infinite series of numbers has a cardinality in the strict sense of there being a specific number that says exactly how many terms there are in the series. Indeed, he cannot strictly allow that there are such things as infinite series of numbers at all since an infinite series, if taken to be a true unity (i.e., if it is taken truly to *exist*; cf. G II, 97) would be an infinite aggregate or whole. Leibniz's attitude toward the infinite series is most evident in his rigorous reformulation of the statements of mathematics that involve apparent reference to an infinite series. He reformulates loose mathematical talk of infinite series of numbers as rigorous talk about finite series of numbers related by a common rule. For example, he writes:

> Whenever it is said that a certain infinite series of numbers has a sum, I am of the opinion that all that is being said is that any finite series of the same rule has a sum, and that the error always diminishes as the series increases, so that it becomes as small as we would like. (A 6.3.503)[13]

"Infinite series" are thus construed as uncollected, or at most finitely collected, multitudes of numbers obeying a certain rule. Such a rule is what he will often refer to as "the law of the series."

Recall that our way of cashing out the ontological significance of the infinite convergent numerical series expressly calls on the cardinality of that series to encode information about how many things there might be if that series were actually to be instantiated in the world. Furthermore, by assuming that the infinite series has a cardinality, we thereby also assume that the infinite series itself is a true unity or whole, for cardinality is strictly a property of aggregates of things (i.e., sets) rather than of un-collected multitudes of things. As is now evident, Leibniz would reject both assumptions. This forces us to qualify that account of the ontological significance of the infinite series in order to comport with his views on the infinite.

We can effect the needed qualifications essentially by following Leibniz's lead. His use of "infinity" and its cognates allows us to say truly that there is *an infinity* of rationals in the infinite convergent series — that is, more rationals than can be specified by any number — without saying that the series has an infinite cardinality or that the number of terms in the series is an infinite number. And his concept of the rule or law of the series allows us to escape commitment to the infinite series taken as an infinite whole; such series are only infinities of uncollected individual numbers that obey the order of a certain rule. We finally nail down the ontological significance of the existence of infinite convergent series of rational numbers thus: there might be more extensa than can be specified by numbers, and those extensa can be arranged in a geometrically descending order according to their respective measures.

## The Continuous and the Discrete

Although we have proceeded rather slowly across some details of Leibniz's views about mathematics and the infinite, our route from a mathematical model of infinite division toward a coherent metaphysic of infinitely divided matter has so far been fairly plain sailing. The existence of an infinite convergent series of numbers is seen to establish the ontological possibility of an infinity of finite and divisible extensa whose collective measure is only finite. But now there is a fine point to be observed. Extensa come in two ontological kinds: the continuous and the discrete. And while the infinite series model, taken in its perfectly abstract form, is neutral between the two, Leibniz's metaphysics of matter very definitely is not. "Matter," he insists (in a typical refrain), "is a discrete being [*Ens discretum*], not a continuous one" (1676. A 6.3.474; cf. G II, 278–279, G VII, 562). The infinite division of matter is therefore the infinite division of a *discrete* extensum, and only a model that incorporates the ontological details connected with the discreteness of matter can possibly establish the coherence of Leibniz's account of its infinite division.

Leibniz often sums up the contrast between the discrete and the continuous with the terse remark that "in the continuum, the whole is prior to the parts" (A 6.3.502) but that in discrete things "the whole is not prior to the parts, but rather the converse" (A 6.3.520). While this mereological *priority thesis* does express a fundamental tenet of his metaphysics, it does not articulate the contents of his analysis of the difference between the discrete and the continuous very well. A more illuminating statement occurs in a 1669 letter to Jacob Thomasius, where Leibniz says of continuous quantity: It is *unbounded* . . . ôr indefinite; for so long as it is continuous, it is not cut into parts and therefore boundaries are not actually assigned in it" (A 6.2.435). Being "indefinite" and lacking "actually assigned" boundaries and parts are the critical elements of the Leibnizian analysis of continuity. A continuous magnitude does not consist of a determinate assemblage of parts, and no particular way of partitioning the whole into separate parts more nearly matches up with its actual component structure than any other, for it lacks the actual boundaries necessary for distinct parts to be actually assigned within it. Being instead intrinsically "unbounded," a continuum is indifferently divisible into parts in any number of ways.

On the other hand, matter (or more exactly, *secondary* matter) has boundaries actually assigned in it and is not continuous, for "in order for a variety of boundaries to arise in matter a discontinuity of the parts is necessary" (A 6.2.435). The parts of matter are discontinuous, each having its own separate boundaries, but the discontinuity of the parts is nonetheless consistent with the hypothesis of a material plenum. The boundaries of adjacent parts are always two and therefore strictly separate (A 6.2.435),[14] yet discrete bodies are always packed together in such a way that they are *contiguous;* that is, their boundaries touch, and no gaps arise between them (cf. A 6.2.435–436). Thus matter is a discrete quantity and does not form a true continuum; it is cut by the actual assignment of boundaries into an infinite mosaic of discrete but contiguous bodies.

Over the years Leibniz's take on the contrast between the continuous and the discrete is to remain essentially unchanged. A small sample of statements from his writings on matter, discreteness, and continuity of four decades later (and more) suffices to display this constancy of thought:

> Every repetition (or collection of things of the same kind) is either discrete . . . where the parts of the aggregate are distinguished, or [else] continuous, where the parts are indeterminate and one can obtain parts in an infinite number of ways. (1702. G IV, 394)

> Matter is not continuous, but discrete, and actually infinitely divided, though no part of space is without matter. (1705? G II, 278)

> The continuum . . . involves indeterminate parts, whereas in actuals [i.e., material bodies] there is nothing indefinite. (1706. G II, 282)

> In real things, namely, in bodies, the parts are not indefinite . . . but are actually assigned a certain way, in accordance with how nature has actually instituted divisions and subdivisions. (1704. G II, 268)

Also, Leibniz explicitly connects these differences between the discrete (i.e., matter) and the continuous — definite versus indefinite, determinate versus indeterminate, actually assigned versus assignable — with the contrasting claims of the mereological priority thesis:

> The mass of bodies is actually divided in a determinate manner, and nothing in it is precisely continuous. . . . In matter and actual things, the whole is the result of the parts, but . . . the indeterminate whole is prior to the divisions. (1705. G VII, 562)

> In the ideal or continuous the whole is prior to the parts, as the arithmetical unit is prior to the fractions that divide it, which can be assigned arbitrarily, the parts being only potential; but in real things [material bodies] . . . the parts are actual, are before to the whole. (1714. G III, 622)

As early as 1676, the priority thesis occurs in Leibniz's writing as the slogan for his analysis of the continuous and the discrete. But if the slogan does not advertise the contents of that analysis very fully, it nevertheless pinpoints a crucial feature of his metaphysics. The discrete whole, such as a material body, is always "a result of the parts." It is ontologically less basic than — ontologically dependent on — those things of which it is the aggregate. Continuous things, however, being prior to their parts, are not ontologically dependent on them. Indeed, continuous things *"are not really aggregated from parts,* since it is wholly indefinite how parts might wish to be assigned in them" (G II, 276; italics added).

## Three Ontological Models of Infinite Division: The Block, the Pennies, and the Folds

Having achieved a little clarity on Leibniz's metaphysics of the discrete and the continuous, I wish now to resume the task of evaluating his account of the infinite division of matter, an account that appeals to the concept of the infinite convergent numerical series to establish its coherence. The force of the appeal to an infinite convergent series of numbers lies in the fact that each term in such a series is finite and divisible. Despite the fact that the total combined magnitude of those terms is only finite — that the series of numbers has a finite "sum" — no term has to be either infinitely small or minimal. Likewise, the division of a finite quantity of matter into an infinity of parts does not have to entail the existence of infinitely small or minimal portions of matter. All that is necessary for it to be possible for a finite quantity of matter to decompose into an infinity of finite and divisible parts is that there be no *lower bound* on the possible size of a divisible part of matter. An infinity of finite and divisible parts can collectively "add up" to a finite quantity of matter if they can be ordered in a descending geometrical progression according to size (or, more generally, a monotonic decreasing or nonincreasing sequence converging to zero) so that successive parts of matter are proportionally smaller than preceding ones, and no part of matter is "smaller than all the rest, or at least no bigger than any other" (GM III, 536).

The infinite series model of infinite division is thus seen to trade on a respect of similarity between matter and the continuum; just as there is no lower bound on the size of finite fractions of the number 1 or of subsegments of the unit line, there is no lower bound on the possible size of a finite portion of matter. Matter has something of the mathematical character, so to speak, of the continuum. But as we have seen, it decidedly does not have the same metaphysical character. On the one hand, matter is discrete and determinate, its divisions are actually assigned, and its parts are prior to the whole; on the other hand, the unit line or the number 1, say, is continuous and indeterminate, its divisions are not actually assigned, and the whole is prior to the parts.

What lies in store is this: some ways of construing the infinite convergent numerical series *ontologically* as the infinite division of a finite extensum are inconsistent with Leibniz's metaphysics of matter. As I shall show presently, whereas some ontological construals appear to fit nicely, others positively clash with his metaphysical commitments. What is disturbing here is that Leibniz fails to see the difference and opts for the wrong construal. His resulting account of the infinite division of matter turns out to be incoherent. To show this I shall offer two ontological models of an infinite convergent series of numbers and explain how Leibniz's own model of the infinite division of matter lines up with the second of them. In the section that follows I shall level a few criticisms to display the clash between his model and his prior commitments in the metaphysics of matter.

Let's again take as our example of the infinite convergent series Zeno's dichotomy series, 1/2, 1/4, 1/8, 1/16, 1/32, and so on ad infinitum. Interpreted in one way, it represents an infinity of undivided finite *extensa*. We can picture this as a sequence of successively smaller bodies all packed into a finite space:[15]

> Imagine a glass jar halfway full of metal coins, say copper pennies. Resting squarely on the bottom of the jar, one coin is uniquely the largest of them all: this is the *alpha penny*. Otherwise like an ordinary penny, the alpha penny is one-half inch thick. Also inside the jar there is a penny, just one, which, like all the pennies in the jar, is ordinary in its width and circumference but which is exactly half as thick as the alpha penny; this second penny measures one-quarter inch in thickness. Further, there is within the jar a unique third penny whose thickness is only a quarter of that of the alpha penny and half of that of the second penny; this third penny measures precisely one-eighth inch in thickness. And so on, ad infinitum. For each and every penny in the jar, there is also, somewhere within the jar, a "successor penny" whose thickness is one-half that of its "predecessor's" thickness. So no penny is the thinnest — that is, the least thick — of all, and no penny fails to be thicker than some other penny in the jar. How many coins are there in our jar? Infinitely many. But while the pennies grow successively thinner and thinner without end, each one has yet some finite thickness to it and stands in some specifiable finite ratio to the thickness of the alpha penny. (There is no "omega penny," so to speak, of only infinitesimal thickness, to be found anywhere in the jar.)

As promised, there is an infinity of coins in the series, each of which is of finite size and undivided (though not necessarily indivisible), and the complete sequence of coins has only a finite thickness. If they were all pushed together, face to face in order of thickness, the pennies would occupy a space no more than a single inch thick (1/2 inch + 1/4 inch + 1/8 inch + etc.). Call this ontological model of the infinite convergent numerical series the "diminishing pennies" model.

On a second interpretation, however, Zeno's dichotomy series is seen to represent a very different ontological condition:

> Here's a block of stone one cubic foot in volume and regular in its dimensions: it measures one foot high by one foot long by one foot wide. On close inspection it is observed that the block is neatly divided down the middle by a hairline fissure into two equal slabs, each one foot high by one foot long but only half a foot wide. Still closer scrutiny reveals that each of the two slabs is also further divided lengthwise down the middle into equal halves, each one foot high by one foot long but only a quarter foot in width. Furthermore, these secondary "halves" (there are four), each a quarter of the original block, turn out also to be divided lengthwise into two equal parts. At this, now the third scale of inspection, we can see that the block is actually divided into equal eighths. And so on ad infinitum. As we progressively turn up

the power of the microscope, we observe that each of the nested halves (i.e., halves, fourths, eighths, sixteenths, thirty-secondths etc. of the original block) is itself divided into two further halves. Each and every slab is seen, in fact, to give way to two smaller slabs, without end.[16]

Call this the "divided block" model.

Unlike the diminishing pennies model of the infinite series in which every part of matter — that is, every penny — is finite and undivided, in the divided block model there are no finite and undivided parts of matter to be found. Each and every slab, however small, is divided into still smaller ones. That difference proves to be heavy with consequences for the Leibnizian program in the metaphysics of matter, as we shall see shortly. First, though, I want to show where Leibniz's own model of the division of matter stands with respect to the two models just outlined.

Leibniz's clearest and richest early thoughts on the infinite division of matter are to be found in his dialogue *Pacidius Philalethei* (1676); there his own model of matter's division surfaces in an inspired passage:

> The division of the [material] continuum must not be considered to be like the division of sand into grains, but like that of a sheet of paper or tunic into folds. And so although there occur some folds smaller than others infinite in number, a body is never thereby dissolved into points ôr minima. On the contrary, every liquid [i.e., all matter[17]] has some tenacity so that although it is torn into parts, not all the parts of the parts are so torn in their turn; instead at any time they merely take shape, and are transformed; and yet in this way there is no dissolution all the way down into points. . . . It is just as if we suppose a tunic to be scored with folds multiplied to infinity in such a way that there is no fold so small that it is not subdivided by a new fold. . . . And the tunic cannot be said to be resolved all the way down into points; instead, although some folds are smaller than others to infinity, bodies are always extended and points never become parts, but always remain mere extrema. (A 6.3.555)

I cannot attend to everything worth exploring here, but two details in these remarks are apposite for the purpose of placing Leibniz's model — hereafter, *the folds*[18] — within the framework provided by our first two. Matter, he says, is torn into parts, but "not all the parts of the parts are so torn in their turn." That perhaps initially suggests a likeness of the folds to the diminishing pennies model: at any given moment, there are some undivided, or *untorn*, finite parts of matter. But this suggestion is quickly wiped away as Leibniz goes on to say that the folds are "multiplied to infinity in such a way that there is no fold so small that it is not subdivided by a new fold." Thus the folds seem instead to resemble the divided block: at any moment, there are no strictly undivided finite parts of matter. Moreover, Leibniz's two claims appear to be in contradiction. Not all the parts of the parts are torn in their turn, and yet no fold fails to be further subdivided by a smaller fold. Is this consistent?

Indeed, it is. The key to seeing how it is consistent lies in Leibniz's theory of cohesion. A full treatment of his account of cohesion is, again, beyond the compass of this chapter, but a few details should dispel the appearance of contradiction in Leibniz's claims.[19] His early views on the topic of cohesion are intensely Cartesian, the most important similarity here being the thesis that matter is unified into cohesive bodies by *motion*. Adjacent parcels of matter form a cohesive whole in virtue of sharing a common motion (*motus conspirans*), but this is consistent with each parcel having a motion of its own that divides and distinguishes it from the others. Also there can be further differing motions within each parcel that distinguish *its* parts, and so on ad infinitum. The operative ideas in Descartes are visible in *Principles* 2:25: "By a 'body' or a 'part of matter' I understand everything that is transferred together, even though this may consist of many parts which have different motions relative to one another" (AT VIII, 53–54). Leibniz at least sometimes adheres closely to this definition, for example, when he writes:

> It is manifest that some body is constituted as definite, one, particular, distinct from others, by some motion of its own, or a particular endeavor [*conatus*], and if it is lacking this it will not be some separate body, but that by whose motion alone one continuous body coherent with it is moved. And this is what I have said elsewhere, that cohesion comes from endeavor or motion, that those things which move with one motion be understood to cohere with one another. (*Propositione Quaedem Physicae*, prop. 14; A 6.3.28)

The particular physical ontology of "endeavors" evident in this passage does not last long (it dries up well before the *Pacidius*), but the theory of cohesion that identifies a common motion as the basic source of cohesion, and differing motions as the cause of division, enjoys a fair tenure through Leibniz's early writings. And that theory is at work implicitly in the folds passage.[20] Each fold is further subdivided by the differing motions of the smaller folds within, but this does not require that all the parts of the parts be "torn" from the whole since they may nonetheless cohere to one another because of a *motus conspirans*.

In resolving the apparent contradiction in Leibniz's model of the folds of matter by noting how cohesion is compatible with division, it becomes clear that as an ontological model of matter's division, the folds are closely akin to the divided block rather than to the diminishing pennies. For each of the folds is strictly divided into smaller finite folds, just as each slab in the divided block is divided into smaller finite slabs without end. Some subfolds are not "so torn in their turn" into parts only in the sense that they are cohesive and retain some "tenacity," offering resistance to being torn apart (see note 15). But each fold is still actually divided into discontinuous parts that are actually assigned by their individual motions. As Aristotle might say, in the folds, as in the divided block, matter is divided "through and through." Borrowing a phrase of Leibniz's, I shall say simply that in his folds model "everything is subdivided" (A 6.3.566).

## Unity, Priority, and Infinity: Problems with the Folds

Now for the criticisms. In the folds model of infinite division, none of the parts of matter is both finite and undivided. But this should be impossible by the lights of Leibniz's metaphysics of matter. The folds model engenders a problem concerning *unity* that is not resolvable, given Leibniz's views of the part-whole relation, and a problem concerning the *dependency* that is absolutely intractable, given his analysis of the discreteness of matter. We'll consider them in turn.

The *unity problem* is this: if each and every part of matter is further divided into parts, and those parts into further parts ad infinitum, then any part of matter you specify will contain an infinity of parts. But this is impossible, on pain of Galileo's paradox. As we saw earlier, in Leibniz's view nothing can contain an infinity of parts without violating the axiom that the part is less than the whole; or, nothing that is truly *one* or a *whole* can have an infinity of parts. Leibniz's escape from the paradox, we recall, is to allow that there can be an infinity of "parts" as long as they are not actually parts of any one thing. In the present case, however, since *any* part of matter we specify would be subject to the precisely same infinite division into parts, it follows that *no* part of matter can truly be one or a whole. But to say that something is not truly one is to say that it does not truly *exist*. Thus in the folds model of matter's infinite division, since no part of matter can truly be one, *there can't be any matter*.

Although this problem with Leibniz's model of matter is not difficult to see, I find no evidence that Leibniz himself ever sees it. Across his writings he readily endorses both the part-whole axiom (with its attendant claim that there can be no infinite wholes) and the model of matter as actually divided into parts that are actually subdivided into further parts ad infinitum. It is worth noting, however, that a further assumption is tacitly being drawn on to generate the unity problem, that every *subpart* of a portion of matter is a *part* of it. This assumption is necessary because the model of infinite division, as stated, implies only that the division of a portion of matter into subparts proceeds ad infinitum. But the unity problem itself arises only if every portion of matter is taken to have an infinity of *parts*. Does Leibniz expressly discuss the thesis that subparts are parts, which I ascribe to him as an assumption? Well, no — not expressly. (That's part of why I say it's an *assumption*.) Might he escape the unity problem by denying that thesis? I think not. For although Leibniz does not expressly endorse it, he is nonetheless committed to it.

Two possible ways of being committed to the assumption that every subpart of a portion of matter is a part of it come immediately to mind, both of which would close the imagined route of escape from the unity problem. Leibniz probably would accept the one and certainly accepts the other.

First, one might accept as a general principle concerning parts and wholes the so-called *transitivity of parthood*: if *x* is a part of *y* and *y* is a part of *z*, then *x* is a part of *z*. Subparts of something, however remote in the hierarchy of parts and subparts, will count as parts of it by transitivity. Now, to my knowledge Leibniz never explicitly defends the transitivity principle, and I don't see that it does a great deal of work in his metaphysics. But I very much doubt he would willingly deny it, either. The transitivity of parthood seems *at least* as obvious as the part-whole axiom itself — indeed, perhaps far more obvious — and I find no reason to think that Leibniz would so vigorously defend the latter only to abandon the former. Quite probably Leibniz does (or would) accept the transitivity principle.

Second, one might adopt a substantive principle of parthood that would manage to identify every subpart of a portion of matter as a part of it by establishing a sufficient condition for being a part of the portion that every subpart actually satisfies. Leibniz explicitly does this when he insists that "to be contained in something is certainly to be a part of it" (A 6.3.551). Because every subpart of a portion of matter is *contained* in it — as the slabs are contained in the divided block, and the smaller folds are contained within the greater ones — every subpart is also a part of it. There is no escape from the unity problem for Leibniz by denying that all the subparts of a portion of matter are its parts.

The unity problem for the divided block model of infinite division is troubling, but it seems to be the less grave of the two difficulties I mentioned earlier. For although Leibniz's views on the part-whole relation don't, in fact, accord with the imagined escape from the unity problem, it doesn't seem to me that those views of the part-whole relation do a great deal of essential work in his overall metaphysics of matter. Even if he were to allow that only the primary "halves" or parts of any given whole count as its parts, and that subsequent halves or subparts technically are not parts of that whole, I don't see that any dire consequences for his general theory of matter would follow. By contrast, the really intractable difficulty for the folds model of matter's division draws on absolutely essential elements of Leibniz's metaphysics of matter. This problem is the *dependency problem,* and we'll turn to it now.

In ontological models of matter's infinite division, such as that of the folds or the divided block, no part of matter we specify turns out to be an undivided finite element of any given portion of matter. Each and every finite part itself divides into further finite parts and subparts without end. To spell out the problem I see arising from this fact, I shall use the divided block model, for it adds a little clarity and ease to the exposition. But everything I say here can and should be read in terms of the folds model as well.

Suppose the division of the block to be structured in levels, so that at level o we have the block itself, at level 1 we have the two primary halves into which the block is divided, at level 2 there are the four secondary halves, at level 3 there are the eight tertiary halves, and so on ad infinitum. No "half" occurring at any level fails to be further divided at the next level, and since there are infinitely many levels, no half fails to be infinitely further divided. There is no ultimate level of halves anywhere within the divided block. But it is of the essence of matter that the parts be prior to any whole that they should compose. A material whole is ontologically dependent on its parts; its reality consists in their reality, so to speak; and this dependency is not symmetric: the parts have priority.

The mereological priority thesis institutes a demand for ontological foundations for composite material wholes, for it is impossible that there should be something whose reality consists in the reality of other things, whose reality consists in the reality of other things, and so on without end. In Leibniz's view — and I think he's right about this — that would be a vicious regress. The idea of the existence of a composite material whole is coherent only if there are some undivided parts of matter invested with their own reality out of which the subsequent, dependent wholes are constructed. But because in the folds or divided block model of infinite division there are no undivided parts of matter, that account of matter's division, plus the priority thesis, triggers precisely such a vicious regress. And that, finally, is the dependency problem.

Obviously it is common to both the divided block and the folds, for on each there is no ultimate level of parts for any part of matter we specify. No fold ever resolves into a final multitude of smaller folds — "no fold is so small that it is not subdivided by a new fold." Yet the smaller folds are always the parts of the larger ones they subdivide; that is, the smaller folds are prior, and those larger folds they subdivide are dependent on them. The folds model, like the divided block, is incoherent, given Leibniz's metaphysics of matter.

Unlike the unity problem, the dependency problem has no hope of relief in the idea that not all the subparts contained in a given body count strictly as its parts. Even if Leibniz were to acknowledge that the subparts of the parts of a given portion of matter were not parts of it, the dependency problem would still arise. In virtue of the priority thesis, the dependency of a whole on its parts penetrates also to the subparts of its parts quite independently of whether those subparts are parts of it. For priority and dependency are transitive even if parthood is not; if $x$ depends on the $y$s and the $y$s depend on the $z$s, then $x$ depends on the $z$s.

I said before that Leibniz's metaphysics of matter would not be seriously jeopardized if his actual views about the part-whole relation were modified to allow for the possibility that some subparts contained within a material whole might not be parts of that whole. The same is not true of the aspect of his views of the part-whole relation that fuels the dependency problem — the priority of the part to the whole in matter. The priority thesis is supposed to reflect or encode the ontological differences between matter and the continuum: the discrete versus the continuous, the actual versus the potential, the determinate versus the indeterminate, and so on. Its place in Leibniz's metaphysics of matter could not be more central, and the disparity it fosters between that metaphysics and his own model of the infinite division of matter could not be more intractable.

Also unlike the unity problem, which goes forever unobserved by Leibniz, the dependency problem looms quite large in his later thinking about matter, as we shall see in the final section. But at the time of the *Pacidius*, and for a few years following, Leibniz evidently believes that he has finally arrived at a stable, coherent account of the composition of matter. In the *Pacidius* itself, he even proposes to extend the folds model to space, time, and motion, thus infecting them, too, with the unity and dependency problems.

> It will be worthwhile to consider the harmony of matter, time and motion. Accordingly I am of the following opinion: there is no portion of matter which is not actually divided into further parts, so that there is no body so small that there is not a world of infinitary creatures in it. Similarly there is no part of time in which some change or motion does not happen to any part of a body or point whatsoever. And so no motion stays the same through any space or time however small; thus both space and time will be actually subdivided to infinity, just as a body is. Nor is there any moment of time that is not actually assigned, or at which change does not occur, that is, which is not the end of an old or beginning of a new state in some body. This does not mean, however, either that a body or space is divided into points, or time into moments, because indivisibles are not parts, but the endpoints of parts; which is why, even though everything is subdivided, it is still not resolved all the way down into minima. (A 6.3.565–566)

This harmonious account of space, time, motion, and matter, according to which they are all discrete quantities, may come as surprise to fans of the later Leibniz. What we might call the "continua of nature" are not truly continuous at all but are discrete and actually assigned and divided into parts and further subparts ad infinitum. Only the abstract structures of mathematics and geometry, for example, the arithmetical unit and the unit line, count as true continua. The harmonious account, though, lives only in the flicker at the close of 1676. Almost immediately thereafter Leibniz will begin to pull this account apart, as space, time, and motion, for one reason or another, are each eventually to return to the sphere of the continuous, which for Leibniz is the *conceptual* sphere; there are no strictly continuous extensa in nature. Matter alone — more exactly, *secondary* matter alone — is to retain its status as a discrete extensum and constituent of the natural world.[21] But it is nice to have the harmonious account in hand: it marks the pinnacle of Leibniz's early thoughts on matter, a point at which, I think, his account of the structure of all reality is brilliantly, massively defective everywhere.

## A Final Problem: How Matter Resolves into Isolated Limit-sized Particles

At this point I shall offer a third and final criticism of the folds model, one that is logically independent of the first two. In offering this final criticism, I shall raise a classical perplexity about the infinite that faces Leibniz's account, and I shall do so in order to stage a dispute in the philosophy of the infinite in which Leibniz curiously appears to be on both sides. There is a deep tension in his philosophy of the infinite, and I wish to fetch it into the foreground.

It is the express purpose of the folds model to show how matter might be infinitely divided without thereby resolving into "a powder of points," or minima: the parts of matter are always to be divisible and of some finite size. Leibniz clearly believes it to accomplish this purpose. Take a second look at the end of the last passage quoted:

> This does not mean, however, either that a body or space is divided into points, or time into moments, because indivisibles are not parts, but the endpoints of parts; which is why, even though everything is subdivided, it is still not resolved all the way down into minima. (A 6.3.556)

Something is amiss here. Leibniz's metaphysical analysis of minima requires that they be only endpoints and not parts of things. Thus no proposed division of matter that would appear to resolve it into minima is truly possible as a division of matter. To point out as Leibniz does, however, that in fact matter cannot be resolved into minima does precisely nothing to show whether *it is a consequence* of his own proposed model of infinite division that matter be resolved into isolated minima. Similarly, consider whether an infinite partition of the sort specified by the folds model might perhaps reduce matter into a powder of infinitesimal particles. At this point in the dialectic, Leibniz takes the idea of an infinitesimal particle of matter no longer to be in play. But his earlier ground for ruling out the possibility that an infinite division of matter might resolve it into a powder of infinitesimals was simply the claim that infinitesimal quantities are impossible. Again, however, the claim that it is impossible for there to be infinitesimal parts of matter does not show whether it might still *be a consequence of the folds model of infinite division* that matter should be divided into infinitesimal particles.

The constraints imposed by Leibniz's metaphysics require that matter's parts always be divisible (and thus not minima) and of some finite size or other (and thus not infinitesimals). So the question facing his account of matter's infinite division is this: if indeed "everything is subdivided," as in the folds model, how could matter fail to be resolved into parts smaller than any finite part could be — whether into minima or into infinitesimals? Leibniz begs, or rather *evades*, the question. Let us frame it for him inescapably. To this end I shall adapt an example that dates back at least to Aristotle and has been offered as lately as 1964 by José Benardete. We begin with a fanciful story.

> Take a stick of wood. In 1/2 minute we are to divide the stick into two equal parts. In the next 1/4 minute we are to divide *each* of the two pieces again into two equal parts. In the next 1/8 minute we are to divide *each* of the four pieces (for there are now four equal pieces) again into two equal parts, &c. *ad infinitum*. At the end of the minute how many pieces of wood will we have laid out before us? Clearly an infinite number.[22]

Call our thought experiment a "Zeno procedure." One might reasonably argue that the imagined Zeno procedure presents a kinematic *im*possibility — as perhaps it does. But that is inessential to the basic point of the case. What matters here is that the resulting *state* of division this case invites us to consider perfectly mirrors the actual state described by the divided block model. So, too, it mirrors the actual state of the folds. If in the actual state of division that results the stick has been reduced into infinitesimally thin (or thinner) chips, then Leibniz's claim that matter's parts must always be finite in size is surely exploded. Thus we must at this point ask with some care whether in a folds-type model — one in which "everything is subdivided" — any of the resulting pieces of the stick *fail* to be finite in size. Are there any infinitesimal, or smaller, pieces before us? Benardete, for one, says that what results should be an infinity of actual infinitesimal parts: "If a stick should be successively divided into halves, quarters, eighths, &c. *ad infinitum* by our Zeno procedure, at the end of the minute we should have decomposed it into an infinite number of infinitesimal chips."[23]

Clearly this consequence would derail Leibniz's project. Does the consequence actually follow from his hypothesis that "everything is subdivided"? Perhaps one might deny that the resulting chips would be infinitesimals — but only to admit that they have thickness of measure zero or simply have no measure of thickness at all. The real issue turns on whether one can deny that any nonfinite chips would arise. The sequence of cuts successively whittles down the parts of matter so that their thicknesses approach a nonfinite limit (either zero or infinitesimal thickness). The classical perplexity is now at hand: is that limit measure of thickness actually reached?

I hasten to distinguish two questions. (1) Does any actual cut imposed on a part of matter immediately deliver a further part whose measure of thickness is the limit value? (2) Is the existence of a part whose measure of thickness is the limit value entailed by the actual sequence of cuts in the stick? The answers I should favor are *no* and *yes*, respectively, and this undoubtedly will appear paradoxical. The cuts do entail the existence of a nonfinite "limit chip" (indeed, an infinity of them), and so in that sense result in one, but no actual cut itself separates such a chip from any piece of the stick.

To feel the pull of this conclusion, concentrate on the status of the right-hand surface of the original stick during and after the process of division.[24] Suppose the letter Z were inscribed on this surface. The first round of cuts leaves the Z inscribed on a piece one-half inch thick. The second round of cuts leaves the Z inscribed on a piece one-quarter inch thick. After the third round of cuts, the Z appears inscribed on a piece only one-eighth inch thick. And so on ad infinitum. In the state of division that would obtain after the minute has fully elapsed, on what should we find our Z inscribed? It could only be on the surface of a chip whose measure of thickness is the limit value. As there was no last round of cuts, however, there is no actual cut that could separate the limit chip from any piece of the stick.

It will further be noticed that the fate of the Z-surface is also the fate of the left-hand surface of the original stick as well. Indeed, it is the common fate of each left- and right-hand surface of *every* piece of the stick that should be produced at *any* round of cuts. Each particular actual cut presumably results in a pair of adjacent surfaces.[25] Each such surface will be the surface of a limit chip in the actual state of division that results from the process. And since there is an infinity of cuts imposed during the process, there will be an infinity of limit chips in the resulting state. Once again, even if the process itself smacks of absurdity, its resulting state of division nonetheless is the mirror image of the state of the divided block and the state of the folds.

It should be noted that it is not generally true that a series of terms whose values approach a limit value entail the existence of a term that actually has the limit value. (Much less will the series itself contain the limit. Leibniz is absolutely right to insist that the infinite convergent series of numbers does not contain an infinitieth term of infinitesimal value.) Only under certain ontological conditions will the actual existence of the limit term be secured and not under others. For example, the diminishing pennies will contain coins whose thicknesses approach a limiting value that is not a positive finite number, but there is no limit coin — no "omega penny" — here.

The key difference between the diminishing pennies and the stick (or the divided block or the folds) can be seen in the fact that whereas the pieces of the stick form what we could call a *closed* sequence, the diminishing pennies form an *open* (or rather, *half open*) sequence.[26] I'll briefly explain what I mean by this.

Take the pennies lined up left-to-right in descending order of thickness. On the left-hand end of the sequence there is a first penny, a left-hand-most terminal element: the alpha penny. But there is no corresponding terminal element on the right-hand end of the sequence, no *last* penny to close that other end — the open end. Any object lying beyond the open end would not simply be faced with the outer surface of some penny or other in the sequence (displaying, say, heads or tails) but would rather be separated from each and every penny in the series by another penny. In fact, such an object would be separated from each penny in the series by an *infinity* of intervening pennies. Now, we might say that although the pennies have no terminal right-hand member, still the *space* occupied by the pennies itself has a limit at the right-hand end, a sort of super-thin terminal "limit space," which bounds the whole space on the right. *But none of the matter belonging to the pennies occupies that limit space.* Although the individual pennies approach closer and closer to that limit space, none is actually situated *in* it.[27] Impressionistically, the limit space is so thin that matter belonging to the pennies could manage to fill it only if the *surface* of some penny or other were to be situated in it. And if such a surface were in that space, then it would be the right-facing surface of the last penny in the sequence. As we mentioned, however, there simply is no such last penny in the sequence; hence there is no last boundary surface of any penny on that end to be situated in the limit space; and hence the limit space on that end is left unoccupied (or unoccupied by the pennies, at any rate).

The open right-hand end of the sequence of pennies is in various ways tantalizing, even paradoxical (there is a puzzle, for instance, about what one would *see* if looking into the open end). But it is precisely the "open-ness" of the open end that removes the worrisome possibility that in the actual state of infinite division the terminal surface might appear standing isolated from all the finite pieces of matter; *for there simply is no terminal surface on that end to be so isolated from all the pennies.*

By contrast, the original stick is *closed* on both ends. It fills the space in which it is embedded right to the limits, and its outer surfaces fill those limit spaces. Even the far end of the stick, where "most" of the infinity of cuts are located, is markedly closed by a definite last boundary: the Z surface. In the actual state of infinite division, a question will therefore arise about the status of the Z surface of the stick. Is it isolated from all the finite parts, or is it connected to at least one of them? That Z surface, like all boundary surfaces, is a minimum, a mode rather than a thing in its own right, so it must always be the *surface of* some piece or other; it cannot exist in isolation. In the actual state of infinite division that results, however, the Z surface could not belong to any small finite piece of the stick. The cuts have separated it from any such finite piece. It could therefore belong only to a limit piece whose size is smaller than any finite size you might mention—the infinitesimal limit chip— and likewise for every surface of every piece of the stick that gets separated from the rest at any stage of the division. Each cut into the stick results in a pair of adjacent stick pieces, each with its own boundary surface at the locus of the cut. In the actual resulting state of division, each of those surfaces (indeed an infinity of them), just like the Z surface, will still have to be the surface of some piece or other. In this "limit state" of division, however, only isolated limit chips could be available to support them.

I believe that any philosophy of the infinite that allows the hypothesis that *all* the cuts are *actually* effected and that everything is *actually* subdivided has to license the inference to the claim that there exists an isolated limit part of matter. At first glance, Leibniz's philosophy of the infinite certainly seems to be of that sort, so it seems that he should have to admit that the folds model would (*per impossibile*) resolve matter into infinitesimal (or smaller) parts—at first glance. But there is a complication.

## Leibniz's Constructivism

Leibniz's philosophical attitude toward the infinite in fact incorporates a diverse cluster of stances. In his ontology of matter, he assumes a distinctly *actualist* posture: matter divides into an actual infinity of parts each and every one of which is divided into further parts ad infinitum. Leibniz famously writes to Foucher: "I am so much in favor of the actual infinite that, rather than agree that nature abhors it, as is commonly said, I hold that nature affects it everywhere" (G I, 416).

In his mathematics, on the other hand, a very different attitudes about the infinite shows itself in his refusal to allow the existence of an infinite quantity or number. To restrict the concept of number to cover only terms of finite value (and to rewrite the techniques of mathematics so that reference to infinitary quantities may be systematically removed in favor of finitary expressions[28]) constitutes a sort of *finitism* about mathematics. As we saw earlier, Leibniz is able to balance his ontological actualism with his mathematical finitism by distinguishing the concept of an infinity of *F*s from that of an infinite aggregate (quantity, or number) of *F*s. There is an actual infinity of parts of matter but no aggregate or number of them.

There is another strand in his thought about mathematics, however, that threatens the stability of that carefully balanced account. And I think it may also explain why he formulates his picture of matter's infinite division on the model of the divided block rather than on the model of the diminishing pennies. What I have in mind is Leibniz's tendency—not a full-blown allegiance, just a tendency—toward a *constructivist* view of the infinity of numbers. He sometimes tends to think of numbers as forming an *indefinitely extensible* and *essentially incomplete* multitude rather than an actual and determinate infinity of terms. And to the constructivist cast of mind, the difference between the diminishing pennies and the divided block models may be indiscernible, or at least less vivid. In this section, I shall develop Leibniz's constructivism somewhat, and then in the next I explain why it might obscure the difference between those models from his view.

Leibniz confines numbers to the realm of *relations*, about which he famously holds some sort of mind-dependence, or *mentalism*. A close look at some remarks written in 1676 that express this mentalism also reveals the constructivist strand in his thought. For example, he writes on 10 April:

> It seems what should be said is this: there is no number of relations, which are true entities only when they are thought about by us: for example, numbers, lines or distances, and other things of that kind; *for they can always be multiplied by constantly reflecting on them,* and so they are not real entities, or possibles, except when they are thought of by us. (A 6.3.495; italics added)[29]

Numbers, in this view, have no existence independently of being applied to objects in mathematics or mathematical reasoning. Outside of such application they exist only potentially but not actually, and they come into being only through the constructive operations of the mind. Michael Dummett glosses this sort of view as follows: "Mathematical objects themselves are mental constructions, that is, objects of thought not merely in the sense that they are thought about, but in the sense that, for them, *esse est concipi.* They exist only in virtue of our mathematical activity, which consists in mental operations."[30]

Constructivism also takes a view of infinite series of numbers according to which they are finitely constructed but indefinitely extensible pluralities of terms. In the most familiar case, numbers are constructed in counting by the successive addition of "ones." But constructions can take less familiar forms as well. The key element in an "infinite" construction is the *rule* according to which successive numbers in a series are generated by recursive application. The terms $t_i$ of Zeno's series, for instance, may be generated by applications of the "rule" $t_n = 1/2^n$ as the value of $n$ successively increases by ones. No terminal element can be reached in the construction of this series. At any stage in the process of construction, the multitude of terms actually produced is only finite, but the process itself never reaches a stage at which no further term is constructable. More terms can always be reached; indeed, it is always possible to increase the multitude by a greater number of terms than it actually includes at the current stage. To the constructivist, infinity is always a merely *potential* infinity, never an actual one.

Leibniz's constructivist tendency can also be detected in a claim about the nature of the concept of number that he makes in the *Pacidius* and that becomes quite familiar in his later writings: "I believe it to be the nature of certain notions that they are incapable of *perfection* and *completion*, and also of having a greatest of their kind. Number is such a thing" (A 6.3.551). I believe that Leibniz is moved here by the idea that the infinite in mathematics is something essentially incomplete — a view favored in this century by *intuitionists* such as Brouwer and, again, Dummett:[31]

> All infinity is potential infinity; there is no completed infinity. This means, simply, that to grasp an infinite structure is to grasp the process which generates it; to recognise it as infinite is to recognise that the process is such that it will not terminate. In the case of a process which terminates, we may legitimately distinguish between the process itself and its completed output: we may be presented with the structure that is generated without knowing anything about the process of generation. But, in the case of an infinite structure, no such distinction is possible: all that we can, at any given time, know of the output is some finite initial segment of it. There is no sense in which we can have any conception of the structure as a completed whole save that we know the process by which it is generated.[32]

Now, intuitionism starts from the hotly empiricist design to attach content available from experience to mathematical statements in order to ensure their meaningfulness. Talk of actual or completed infinities is suspect precisely because of the implausibility that any mathematical (or other) experience could generate a concept to accompany it. While Leibniz does not worry over the source of meanings for mathematical statements, his constructivist philosophy of mathematics shares other distinctive features with intuitionism: the view of numbers as mental constructions, for example, and the view of the infinite as potential and essentially incomplete. The emphasis on knowledge aside, the content of Dummett's remarks is quite Leibnizian.

Numbers form at best an incomplete multitude, a merely potential infinity, because their ranks can always be increased by the mental construction of a further number. It is possible for there to exist a multitude that includes *some* numbers, but no multitude could include all numbers. Indeed, it is the classic position of the constructivist to deny that the phrase "all numbers" (where "all" has no other scope restriction) has a definite meaning. For use of the universal quantifier "all" is permissible in that context only if there is a determinate extension for "number." But if the multitude of numbers is indeterminate, as Leibniz holds, then "number" will lack a definite extension, and use of the phrase "all numbers" will be illegitimate. It is of no small interest, then, to see Leibniz walking the constructivist line on precisely this point as he grapples with a technical problem concerning incommensurable quantities:

> If this [ratio of the diagonal of a square to its side] is to be explicated by means of numbers, there will also be a need for an infinity of numbers — indeed, for *all* the numbers in the universe. But to say *all numbers* is to say *nothing*; and for this reason that ratio also signifies nothing unless it is something as close as desired. (A 6.3.502; italics added)

Either "all numbers" means nothing — as it would if we were mistakenly treating the domain of numbers as a determinate multitude — or else it must only signify "something as close as desired"; that is, it signifies a series of terms that can be extended according to a specified rule or law to contain as many terms as we like and whose "sum" can thus be brought as close as we desire (shy of absolute equality) to the actual value of the ratio in question.[33] Perhaps more than any other single piece of his writing, Leibniz's remarks about "all numbers" identify this strand of his thought unmistakably as the thinking of a mathematical constructivist.

In light of his constructivism, Leibniz's ontology of mathematics appears to stand in sharp contrast to his ontology of matter. Unlike numbers, the parts of matter cannot "always be multiplied in thought," and the multitude of them is not indefinitely extensible; rather, it is definitely given and it is an actual infinity. Constructivist and actualist philosophies of the infinite are quite opposed. And here at last is the dispute about the infinite in which Leibniz appears to take both sides. By taking one with regard to mathematics and the other with regard to matter, Leibniz's philosophy of the infinite in effect divides into two isolated accounts: one of the mathematical infinite, so to speak, and the other of the real infinite. Although there is an infinity of numbers and an infinity of material things, the two "infinities" altogether differ in stripe. To use Ryle's idiom, it would be a category mistake to say at once that the parts of matter and the natural numbers are infinite. Leibniz even claims explicitly that it is "impossible" that there should be "as many things as numbers" (A 6.3.495). The source of this metaphysical incommensurability?

> The multitude of things is something determinate, and that of numbers is not. (A 6.3.495)

With such a dualistic view of the infinite, it is critical that Leibniz keep his thinking about mathematical infinity well apart from his thinking about real infinity. I suspect, however, that he does not and that his constructivism spills over disastrously into his philosophy of matter.

## The Origin of Leibniz's Error and a Notable Upshot

Leibniz's main error arises in crafting a model of matter's division in which no fold of matter is so small that it fails to be subdivided by a further fold. Everything is subdivided. No doubt this feature of his model is meant to answer to the fact that a finite portion of matter may divide into an infinity of finite and divisible parts only if there is no lower bound on the sizes actually possessed by the parts of matter. Matter's division can mimic the structure of an infinite convergent series of numbers only if, for any part of matter, however small, there is another still smaller part. Leibniz's folds model accomplishes this in just the way that the divided block model does: it requires that every single part of matter itself actually divide into still smaller parts, ad infinitum. Each part of matter is surpassed in smallness by its own actual parts.

But this requirement ushers in three distinct problems. (1) The unity problem: any part of matter we specify will contain an infinity of actual parts, which violates the part-whole axiom, or else no part of matter is actually unified and thus no part of matter actually exists. (2) The dependency problem: the division of matter triggers an infinite regress of parts within parts, which turns out to be vicious in Leibniz's analysis of matter as a discrete quantity. The thesis that in the discrete the part is ontologically prior to the whole institutes the need for foundations out of which the aggregate wholes are constructed. By eliminating the possibility of ultimate parts, the regress of divisions guarantees that the world of matter will fail to contain such foundations. (3) The problem of limit parts: any finite portion of matter subjected to a partition in which everything is subdivided would, in the actual state of infinite division that results, be decomposed into infinitesimal (or smaller) parts.

But Leibniz is not *forced* into this trouble by the demands of the mathematical structure of the infinite convergent numerical series. It is possible to craft a model of the division of matter that satisfies the demand that every part of matter be surpassed in smallness by another part without requiring that everything be subdivided. The diminishing pennies model, for example, accomplishes this by the addition of successively smaller pennies to one end of an infinite series of pennies. No penny must be divided into further parts in order to secure the fact that there is no lower bound on the sizes that the parts of matter actually possess, for each penny is surpassed in smallness by another penny in the jar. Or, when we had the pennies all lined up in order of size, each penny was surpassed in smallness by its immediate right-hand neighbor. As there was no last penny on the right-hand end of the series (its open end), so, too, there was no last small size had by any penny — that is, there is no last small size had by any part in the infinity of matter's parts. Thus could the division of matter mimic the structure of the infinite convergent series of numbers without the troublesome thesis that everything is subdivided.

I conjecture that Leibniz fails to appreciate the difference between those two ontological construals of the infinite convergent numerical series, and he fails to recognize the difficulties with his folds model of matter's division, precisely because of the constructivist strand in his thought. At this point I make my accusation: the deep cause of the difficulty in Leibniz's theory of matter — what leads him into error and what prevents him from seeing it — is his constructivism.

Of the three problems, the first and the third — the unity problem and the problem of limit parts — come to view only if the infinite division of matter is conceived as a completed infinite. Again, take the infinite division encoded by the folds or divided block model to consist of ordered levels of cuts and parts. At the first level of division, there are two parts; at the second, there are four; at the third, there are eight; and so on ad infinitum. At no finite level does one ever encounter an infinity of parts. An infinity of parts comes to view only from the outside perspective, where the completed infinity can be seen all at once. This is what I have been calling "the actual state of infinite division." It is the limit state, and as it falls outside the series of finite levels but encompasses them all, we might call it the "omega level." Only at the omega level will it appear that any given part of matter occupying some finite level contains an infinity of actual parts; thus the unity problem is invisible until that level has been reached. And only at the omega level, with all the cuts actually in place, will the outer surfaces of the finite parts of matter be seen to belong to limit parts, for only when everything has actually been subdivided are the surfaces seen to be actually separated from any finite part. Hence the problem of limit parts, too, becomes clear only at the omega level.

To the constructivist about the infinite, however, *there is no omega level*. Infinity is always potential and incomplete (if indefinitely extensible). It is illegitimate to say that there might be a level at which "all cuts" are actually in place and "all resulting parts of matter" actually exist. The very idea of the omega level belongs only to the actualist. Thus the unity and limit-part problems simply disappear from the constructivist's field of vision. I said earlier that Leibniz's philosophy of the infinite divides into two isolated accounts: the actual infinity of nature and the constructive infinity of mathematics. I suspect that by looking back at the world of nature from the confines of the mathematics of infinite series, Leibniz lets his constructivism come between him and the parts of matter. By thinking in constructivist terms about the division of matter into parts, he loses sight of the omega level and the problems that should appear most vividly there.

The same cannot be said of the dependency problem, however. The fact that the priority thesis institutes a need for undivided parts to serve as foundations for material aggregates is evident quite independently of the actualist perspective. A constructivist has only to consult the rule for constructing (or unraveling) the folds of matter to see that no part of matter one specifies could be forever undivided. For any part of matter one likes, the series of cuts can be extended until that part, too, is divided into subparts. Each actual cut lies at some finite level within the division of matter that can actually be reached at some finite stage of construction. Thus even to the constructivist it is apparent that no true foundations for material aggregates are ever forthcoming. There is only an indefinitely extensible multitude of ontologically dependent parts of matter: a vicious regress even for the constructivist.

Perhaps unsurprisingly, then, it is uniquely the dependency problem of the three problems we discussed that eventually catches Leibniz's eye. Nearly forty years later he writes to de Volder:

> First, things which can be divided into many things are constituted by many things, ôr are aggregates. Second, whatever are aggregates of many things are not one except for the mind, and they have no other reality than what is derived, ôr belongs to the things of which they are aggregated. Therefore, third, those things that can be divided into parts have no reality unless in them there are things that cannot be divided into parts; indeed, they have no other reality than that of the unities which are in them. (21 January 1704. G II, 261)

And again:

> Anything that can be divided into many (actually existing) things is aggregated from many things; and a thing which is aggregated from many things is not one except for the mind, and has no reality except what is borrowed from its constituents. From this I have already inferred that there are therefore indivisible unities in things, since otherwise there will be no true unity in things, nor any reality that is not borrowed.

> And that is absurd. For where there is no true unity, there is no true multitude. And where there is no reality except a borrowed one, there will be no reality at all, since it must in the end belong to some individual subject. (30 June 1704. G II, 267)

Leibniz has not changed his mind on whether everything is subdivided: matter's parts are still imagined to divide part into part ad infinitum. The indivisible unities he speaks of here are neither made of matter nor are parts of matter. They are rather immaterial substances whose reality provides a metaphysical foundation for matter while residing outside of the endless regress of parts within parts. Leibniz calls these indivisible unities *monads*.

Thus the dependency problem infecting Leibniz's metaphysics of matter is seen later to evolve into an argument in favor of his monadism. His early theory of matter remains for the most part intact as a description of matter. Motion through irregular spaces in the plenum requires the actually infinite division of finite portions of matter into parts none of which are infinitesimal or indivisible; and this is accomplished in virtue of matter's being divided into parts just as an infinite convergent series of numbers resolves into its individual terms. This in turn is accomplished by the hypothesis that everything is subdivided ad infinitum. But now the principal defect pointed up by the dependency problem is recognized: there must be foundations for matter but those foundations cannot be parts of matter. The theory of matter then loses its status as a description of ultimate reality and yields to a metaphysics of monads.

These considerations about the structure of the infinite division of matter are not the only forces driving Leibniz to his monadism about substance. But they are perhaps the most powerful and profound. It is of some interest, then, to see that the hypothesis that everything is divided was not necessary to craft a model of matter's division that explains how a finite portion of matter could divide into an infinity of finite and divisible parts. If Leibniz's folds model had been fashioned in the image of the diminishing pennies rather than that of the divided block, that hypothesis might simply have been left aside. And if his constructivist tendencies are indeed responsible for his failure to recognize the ontological difference between those two models, then they are perhaps also responsible for his embrace of the ontologically defective one in his theory of matter. In that case, Leibniz's constructivism — the villain of our story — was instrumental in the emergence of the monads.[34]

## Notes

1. In a 1692 published criticism of the *Principles of Philosophy*, Leibniz recalls Descartes's argument for this hypothesis with uncharacteristically high praise, calling it "most beautiful and worthy of his genius"(L 393). For the argument itself, see *Principles* 11:33–35 (AT VIIIA, 57f.); for some critical discussion of Descartes and Leibniz on this score, see my "Leibniz on Mathematics and the Actually Infinite Division of Matter," *The Philosophical Review*, 107, no. 1 (January 1998). See also Richard Arthur, "Russell's Conundrum: On the Relation of Leibniz's Monads to the Continuum," in James Brown and Jürgen Mittelstrass, eds., *An Intimate Relation: Studies in the History and Philosophy of Science* (Dordrecht: Kluwer, 1989), pp. 171–201. Textual citations have the style of those of the present volume but also include the following: GM = *Mathematische Schriften von Gottfried Wilhelm Leibniz*, vols. 1–7. C. I. Gerhardt (ed.). (Berlin: A. Asher; Halle: H. W. Schmidt, 1849–1863); *De Quadratura Arithmetica*

= *De Quadratura Arithmetica Circuli Ellipseos et Hyperbolae cujus Corolarium est Trigonometria sine Tabulis*, annotated by Eberhard Knobloch, ed. (Göttingen: Vandenhoeck & Ruprecht 1993); EN = Galileo Galilei, *Opere*, Antonio Favaro, ed. (Florence: Edizone Nationale, 1898), pp. 70–80.

2. The class of minima actually includes points, lines, and planes, and the metaphysical story is the same for each. Each of them is a minimum in the sense that it cannot be divided into smaller parts. Planes are minimal in one dimension: they cannot be cut into thinner slices. Lines are minimal in two dimesions: they cannot be split into finer threads. And points are perfectly minimal: they are indivisible in every respect. But none of the three can exist as things in their own right or as parts of things. Rather, minima can exist only as boundaries of things: planes, lines, and points are the surfaces, edges, and vertices of extended bodies. This is, of course, not merely Leibniz's 1676 view of points but also his permanent view. Compare, just for example, a small sampling of passages: "Points are not parts but boundaries"(1686?. C 523); "Strictly speaking, points and instants are not parts. . . . They are only termini"(1704. A 6.6.152); "To what you have said about Zeno's points, I add that they are only boundaries, and so they can make up nothing" (1711. G II, 520); "Points, strictly speaking, are extremities of the extended, and not at all the constitutive parts of things; geometry shows this sufficiently" (1716. G VI, 627).

3. José Benardete is evdiently the first to notice this: cf. *Infinity: An Essay in Metaphysics*, (Oxford: Clarendon Press, 1964), p. 19; Arthur intelligently picks up Benardete's lead; cf. "Russell's Conundrum," p. 187. I discuss Leibniz's treatment of the analogy and his work on the foundations of the related mathematics in "Leibniz on Mathematics."

4. I am responsible for translations of Leibniz in this chapter, although I consulted Leroy Leomker, ed., *Gottfried Wilhelm Leibniz: Philosophical Papers and Letters* (Dordrecht: Kluwer Academic Publishers, 1969); Roger Ariew and Daniel Garber, eds., *G. W. Leibniz: Philosophical Essays* (Indianapolis: Hackett Publishing Company, 1989); for Leibniz's writings in A 6.3, I consulted manuscripts generously supplied to me by Richard Arthur of his splendid translation *The Labyrinth of the Continuum: Leibniz's Writings on the Continuum, 1672–1686*, forthcoming in the *Yale Leibniz Series*.

5. My use of "amount" is intended to walk the fine line of neutrality between taking amounts to be properties of concrete particulars and taking amounts to be, rather, the concrete particulars themselves. The philosophical spin on what I am calling amounts that has been fashionable since Helen Cartwright's work on the semantics of mass terms takes the latter view: amounts are things in themselves. Cf. "Quantities," *The Philosophical Review* 79 (1970); 25–42. Cartwright reserves the word "quantity" to talk of these supposed concreta (which certainly has more intuitive force as a name for concrete particulars than does "amount"), and unfortunately this could foster some confusion, given my use of "quantity."

6. Notice that the measurable quantity whose measure is given by the rational does not have to be taken as an *extensive* magnitude. It might instead be supposed to be *intensive*. Staying with the case of three globes, we might suppose three globes of the same diameter but of differing weights: one weighs one pound, another one-half pound, and the third one-fourth pound. Having pointed that out, however, in what follows I shall focus on examples in which the measurable quantity is an extensive magnitude: the size of an extended body.

7. Cf. G II, 282; G II, 276; G VII, 562–563; G II, 268. Most often Leibniz touches on the connection between mathematical existence and possibility in the course of *contrasting* the properties of mathematical objects with those of "real things" or material bodies. Thus, his remarks tend to be framed in the negative: "From the fact that a mathematical body cannot be resolved into first constituents we can, at any rate, infer that it isn't real, but something mental, indicating only the possibility of parts, not anything actual" (G II, 268); "number, hour, line, motion, degree of velocity, and other ideal quantities or mathematical entities of this sort

are not really aggregated from parts. . . . Indeed these notions must necessarily be understood in this way since they signify nothing but the mere possibility of parts" (G II, 276).

8. The relevant passages in Galilei read: "There are as many squares as there are their own roots, since every square has its own root, and every root its own square, nor is there any square that has more than one root, nor any root that has more than just one square" (EN 78); "if I were to ask how many roots there are, it cannot be denied that there are as many as all the numbers, because there is no number that is not a root of some number. That being so, it must be said that the square numbers are as many as all the numbers, because they are as many as their roots, and all numbers are roots" (EN 78).

9. Galilei explicitly draws out the paradox, stating at the start of his discussion that "all numbers comprising the squares and the non-squares are greater than the squares alone" (EN 78) and then arguing to the conclusion quoted in the last note: "it must be said that the square numbers are as many as all the numbers." His own response to the paradox is this: "In final conclusion, the attributes of equal, greater, and less have no place in infinities, but only in bounded quantities" (EN 79).

10. For example, at A 6.2.441, he writes: "I define number as one and one and one, etc., ôr as unities."

11. More carefully, we might simply talk in the plural about *the elements* themselves, without suggesting by the use of any singluar term (even a defanged phrase like "a multitude") that there is a *one* comprising the infinite *many*. Leibniz's strategy in defusing Galileo's paradox has not turned out to be the contemporary favorite. By later lights, the existence of infinite cardinals and infinite aggregates (i.e., infinite sets) has seemed worth the price of abandoning the part-whole axiom. But this is not to say that Leibniz's tactic of refusing to allow the formation of a unity out of an infinity of elements, and thereby refusing to admit that an infinity of elements strictly has a cardinality, is facile or antiquated. At most, it should be claimed that Leibniz's use of this tactic is premature, that Galileo's paradox might be solved by less extreme measures. But the tactic itself is hardly out of date. Mathematics has very much inherited this approach to cope with paradox. Resolution to various paradoxes of set theory — such as, say, the Burali-Forti paradox — is gained precisely by denying that various items in the set-theoretic "universe" are ever elements of any single set. For a nice discussion of some related issues, see Richard Cartwright, "Speaking of Everything," *Noûs* 28, no. 1 (1994): 1–20.

12. We shall codify Leibniz's talk of the "uncollected" infinite plurality with the phrase "an infinity," which we understand to stand in for an infinite *plural* term rather than to be a singular purporting to refer to a single entity. Leibniz does not observe this convention perfectly, sometimes saying outright that there is an infinite number of things, but it is always clear from context when he says no more than that there is "an infinity" of things in precisely our sense.

13. Leibniz here perfectly anticipates Cauchy's definition of the sum of an infinite series as the limit of its partial sums, as well as the essence of the delta-epsilon technique for defining the concept of the limit. The so-called rigorous reformulation of the calculus of the nineteenth century is thus fairly well in place in its author's seventeenth-century hands.

14. The relevant passage here is discussed, in a related connection, in a later section.

15. See also Benardete's vivid portrayal of this condition in *Infinity*, pp. 273f.

16. We might confirm this with a metaphysical microscope that can discern slabs of any finite thickness. It requires only a minute. In the first half minute, we detect the fissure that divides the block into two slabs; in the next quarter minute, we bring into focus the division of the halves into fourths; in the next quarter minute, we see the division into eighths; and so on. After the full minute has elapsed, we will have observed all the "halves" on every finite scale of inspection and satisfied ourselves that each and every one is further divided into two, there being no finest division into finite parts.

17. In the immediate background here is Leibniz's view that there is no absolute distinction between solid and liquid matter but rather that matter forms a "body that is everywhere pliant": "a body that is indeed pliant everywhere, but not without a certain and everywhere unequal resistance, still has cohering parts, although these are opened up and folded together in various ways" (A 6.3.555).

18. As Leibniz speaks of matter both as "folded up" (this in a line just before the passage quoted) and of the "folds" themselves, it is easy to slip into thinking of the folds as the crease lines or edges along which matter is being folded: as the *loci of division* rather than as *what is being divided*. But that slip would be a mistake. The folds are the finitely extended parts of matter themselves — as in the folds of a curtain, for example. (Leibniz's *plica* might alternatively be translated as "pleat." Perhaps, in some contexts, that rendering better preserves the idea that *plicae* are finitely extended parts of matter.)

19. For a good discussion of Leibniz on cohesion, see Richard Arthur, "Cohesion, Division and Harmony: Physical Aspects of Leibniz's Continuum Problem", forthcoming in the journal *Perspectives on Science: Historical, Philosophical, Social.* Indeed, it was Richard Arthur who first suggested to me this line of response to the appearance of contradiction in Leibniz's account.

20. In fact, in lines I omit, Leibniz explicitly links the motions of the parts of matter with their being distinguished and torn: "any point is distinguished from any other by motion"; "and yet in this way no point in the tunic will be assignable without its being moved in differing directions by its neighbors, although it will not be torn apart by them." The references to points introduce a special and for now distracting complication; I shall address them presently below.

21. For various interesting discussions of the development and maturity of Leibniz's metaphysics in this connection, see J. Cover and G. Hartz, "Space and Time in the Leibnizian Metaphysic," *Noûs* 22 (1987): 493–519; Robert Adams, *Leibniz: Determinist, Theist, Idealist* (New York: Oxford University Press, 1994), chaps. 9–11; Catherine Wilson, *Leibniz's Metaphysics* (Princeton, N.J.: Princeton University Press, 1989), chaps. 2, 3, and 6; and Daniel Garber, "Leibniz and the Foundations of Physics: The Middle Years," in Okruhlik and Brown, eds., *The Natural Philosophy of Leibniz* (Dordrecht: Kluwer, 1985), pp. 27–130.

22. Benardete, *Infinity*, p. 184.

23. Benardete, *Infinity*, p. 273.

24. Here, again, I am enlisting aid from Benardete; cf. *Infinity*, pp. 272–274.

25. See the following note.

26. In fact, for Leibniz, every *individual* part of matter is fully closed by its boundaries. This he takes to be a consequence of the discontinuity of matter's parts: "For by the very fact that the parts are discontinuous, each one will have its own separate boundaries (for Aristotle defines the continuous as *onta eskata ein*, those whose boundaries are one)" (A 6.2.435). Leibniz here presumably plays up the contrast with Aristotle's definition of continuous things thus: discontinuous things are those whose boundaries are *two*. I shall not pursue in this chapter whether he is right to insist that individual parts of matter have to be fully closed by their boundaries, for that line of inquiry would lead us too far afield into the philosophy of topology. I shall instead simply note that in Leibniz's view, no individual part of matter ever has an open end. He may still allow, of course, that an infinity of parts could be so arranged that no part occupies a terminal position in the arrangement. Again, the diminishing pennies provide a clear example: each penny may well be fully closed by its boundaries and yet the sequence of pennies (ordered, say, according to thickness) may be open on one end. But no *one* thing could itself have an open end. There is always a closing surface. (I should note here, however, that my use of the terms "open" and "closed" is meant in the present context to be fairly intuitive, rather than to pick up the contemporary topological concepts *open* and *closed* in a

rigorous way. In my present use, and roughly, an extensum is open if the outermost limits of the space it occupies are themselves *not* occupied by that extensum, closed if those limits *are* occupied by the extensum. Alternatively, an extensum is open if it lacks some boundary, closed if it does not. While it is possible and instructive to give a topologically rigorous presentation of Leibniz's views on matter, the details turn out to be labyrinthine, and it's not feasible to enter into them here. I defer discussion of those and some related topics arising in Leibniz's theory of matter to another occasion; see my "Discontinuity and the Structure of Leibnizian Matter," in progress.)

27. Note that if some alien object not belonging to the pennies were situated right *in* that limit space, it would be separated from each and every penny by an intervening infinity of pennies just as much as it would if it were lying out fully *beyond* the open end.

28. The rephrasal technique cited above for interpreting claims about the sums of infinite series in terms of rules and (infinities of) finite series is an example of this rewriting. For some related discussion of Leibniz's philosophical work in mathematics, see my "Leibniz on Mathematics."

29. In this passage Leibniz appears to suggest that he adopts mentalism about numbers *because* "they can always be multiplied in thought" and thus form an indefinitely extensible multitude. I suspect that his views are not actually ordered in that way, however, and that his mentalism and constructivism are simply bound up together, neither being more "basic" than the other. At any rate, it is important to note that the implication should *not* be seen as running in the opposite direction, from mentalism to constructivism. One can consistently assert that numbers are *res mentalis* without holding a constructivist view, that is, without holding that numbers form only an incomplete and indefinitely extensible multitude. One might believe that numbers are mind-dependent but nonetheless hold that they form a determinate and actual infinity. Presumably, the mature Leibniz holds just that view of possible worlds: they are *res mentalis*, but they do not form only an indeterminate plurality to be extended by the process of thought; rather, the infinity of worlds is fixed and definite. Young Leibniz, however, often maintains a decidedly constructivist mentalism about mathematical entities.

30. Michael Dummett, *Elements of Intuitionism* (Oxford: Clarendon Press, 1977), p. 7.

31. Cf. L. E. J. Brouwer, "Intuitionism and Formalism" and "Consciousness, Philosophy and Mathematics," both in Paul Benacerraf and Hilary Putnam, eds., *Philosophy of Mathematics: Selected Readings* (Cambridge: Cambridge University Press, 1983). For Dummett's version of intuitionism see his *Elements of Intuitionism*; and for a nice discussion of the infinite as an "indefinitely extensible concept," see his *The Seas of Language* (Oxford: Oxford University Press, 1993), pp. 428–445 ("What Is Mathematics About?").

32. Dummett, "Intuitionistic Mathematics and Logic," (Oxford Mathematical Institute, 1974), part i, p. 3.

33. The ratio Leibniz considers can be seen as the sum of an infinite series of terms, which is presumably what he has in mind here. But for the constructivist an infinite series of terms is only an indefinitely extensible series. Terms of the constructivist series may be pinned down successively so that its "sum" increasingly approximates the value of the ratio but never actually attains it. The series can be extended only so that its sum is "something as close as desired" to the actual value of the ratio. For any value we might specify as the difference between the series's sum at a given stage of construction and the actual value of the ratio — that is, for any "error" — the series can always be extended so that the difference is *less* than the value we specified. Thus, there is no "assignable" error.

34. I am very grateful to Christie Thomas, Jan Cover, and Jonathan Bennett, and to an anonymous referee for Oxford University Press, for their comments; and my thanks to Richard Arthur for helpful discussion of various topics treated in this chapter.

## 7

SUSANNA GOODIN

# Locke and Leibniz and the Debate over Species

Book III of the *New Essays* revolves around the issue of classification. Nicholas Jolley claims that this topic is one of the liveliest between Locke and Leibniz but also one of the most elusive.[1] This chapter is an examination of Leibniz's reaction to Locke's theory of essences and species, examining both his responses in the *New Essays* and his deeper views on species as developed in his other, more esoteric works. The central thesis here is that the responses Leibniz offers in the *New Essays* are inadequate as a refutation of Locke, and although Leibniz's account can be fleshed out by appeal to his more considered views, doing so requires metaphysical assumptions that if accepted do not allow Locke's original concerns even to arise. Leibniz can have a viable theory of species that avoids Locke's objections only by radically altering the terms of the debate.

## Locke's Theory of Essences

Over the last fifteen or so years, Michael Ayers[2] has developed an interpretation of Locke's theory of essences that has gained fairly wide acceptance.[3] According to this interpretation, Locke draws a distinction between the real essence and the inner corpuscularian structure. Ayers claims that Locke intended the term "real essence" to refer only to that aspect of the entire inner structure responsible for the qualities listed in the nominal essence. Thus if gold is defined as a metal that is yellow, the heaviest known, malleable, fixed, and soluble in aqua regia, the real essence would be that aspect of the entire corpuscularian structure that is responsible for only those essential or specific qualities, that is, its properties.[4]

An individual will have a number of qualities, but only some of those qualities determine it to be of a sort or species; that is, only some qualities are specific qualities, the essential properties. Whereas the corpuscularian structure is responsible for *all* the qualities, both specific and nonspecific, the real essence is only that part of the entire structure responsible for the specific properties.

Locke's basic point is that although the corpuscularian hypothesis (or something like it) works as an explanation for all the observable qualities a thing has, it will not do as an explanation for why a thing is the *sort* of thing it is since there is nothing in the structure itself (the physical arrangement of the corpuscles) to distinguish essential properties from nonessential accidents. Such an explanation takes place, for Locke, within the context of the nominal essence; a thing is the sort of thing it is because it has the proper characteristics, as set out by the nominal essence, essential for membership in the kind:

> He (Locke) held that what sets a boundary to the class is always what he calls the 'nominal essence', i.e. the abstract idea that embodies our criteria for the application of the kind-name or 'sortal'. What explains the properties of the species so defined, on the other hand, is corpuscularian structure (or, at least, something like it, if Boyle's theory is less than the whole truth). Those aspects of the structure of the individual members of a species which they have in common and in virtue of which they all possess the defining properties of the species, comprise what Locke called the 'real essence' of the species.[5]

Since individuals (or more likely, groups of individuals) will have different knowledge or different needs, the nominal essence of a species will vary. Because Locke sees nominal essences as variable, real essences, as the explanation for the properties in nominal essences, will also have to vary in accordance with that which needs to be explained. Therefore, in Ayers's reading of Locke, the real essence is not an independent or constant essence but one relativized to the nominal essence:

> Another part of Locke's argument denies the existence of objective specific essences at all. . . . The particular species and genera, horse, bird, gold, metal, and so forth, are each, Locke thinks, arbitrarily distinguished by us through a defining set of observable attributes which he calls the 'nominal essence'. The only serious candidate for the 'real essence' of a species is that *complex aspect* of its unknown material structure which is responsible for the concurrence of those observable attributes by which the species is defined. There is nothing truly substantial or distinct or permanent about a 'real essence' so conceived. It exists as something distinct only *relatively* to the arbitrary nominal essence through which it is indirectly picked out.[6]

The jeweler, the chemist, and the miner may all look upon the same piece of matter, but if they should have different criteria for gold, the real essence of gold would vary. The same piece of matter would, in this case, have three different real essences simultaneously even though the piece of matter remains unchanged in its corpuscularian structure.

> Locke thus suggests that the concept of a thing's real constitution is nonrelational, that constitution in no way depending upon our own mental activity, whereas the

concept of its real essence is relative, depending upon our construction of a nominal essence. There are real constitutions but no real essences apart from our own classificatory activity, and thus similarities but no species apart from the classificatory systems we produce.[7]

The role of the real essence is not to determine the species but to provide for the possibility of a mechanistic explanation for how a member of a species comes to have those qualities required for classification, however the qualities may come to be deemed essential. The structure is responsible for all the qualities, and there is nothing in the qualities themselves nor in the structure that suggests that some qualities are privileged or marked as specific qualities. The point Locke makes repeatedly is that the structure does not draw lines; it only provides any number of resemblances, and resemblances do not establish specific boundaries:

> The boundary marked is a precise one which owes its existence to our drawing it: reality itself simply could not, in Locke's view, supply such a boundary. Reality can supply resemblances, but resemblances do not constitute natural boundaries. Resemblances do not draw lines.[8]

Locke's theory is best (most easily) understood when one keeps in mind the issue Locke was addressing. Philosophers had long argued over the boundaries of species, most notably the boundary between man and beast. Scholastic philosophy had involved the search after the true nature and essence of things. Locke felt that such an endeavor was a waste of time.[9] While he championed corpuscularianism, he did not want people to think that if they were to see the internal structure of things they would be able to discover, finally, the real difference between man and beast. Locke's theory of essences and species was based on his insight that in a world made up solely of particles of matter arranged in different patterns, there is nothing that could do the task that traditionally had been assigned to specific essences. Corpuscularianism would not, because it could not, tell us how to draw the boundary. Nothing internal could provide such information. Just as nothing in terms of surface resemblances could settle the issue, since all it could do was suggest similarities here and there and allow us to choose between such similarities as we thought best, so, too, when we finally gained knowledge of the internal structure of all things (however skeptical Locke might have been that we would ever actually get this knowledge) we would find only more similarities—more stable similarities perhaps, but still only similarities, resemblances of inner structure. And these would be no more able to tell us where to draw species boundaries than were the macro-observable similarities:

> Contrary to Locke's expectations, we have now learned a great deal about the real constitution of many kinds of matter, and among their "insensible particles" we can now distinguish, among others, neutrons and protons. But what forces us to classify two lumps in the real constitutions of which there are the same numbers of protons but different numbers of neutrons as two different isotopes of the same substance rather than two different substances? . . . a choice for which we (or Mendeleyev) may have had very good reason, but which nonetheless remains a product of our own intellectual activity and is not simply forced upon us by objective similarities in nature.[10]

Locke was denying naturally existing specific essences, that is, essences out in the world that determine a thing to be a sort of thing independently of human input. It is true that Locke has often been read as if he argued for this claim by saying that we cannot be referring to the real essence when we make species claims because we do not have knowledge of the real essence. I do not wish to address that issue directly in this chapter, although I do think Locke said enough at various places in the *Essay* to justify much of the criticism he has received concerning it, but I do not think that the core of his objection to natural specific essences hinges on it. The reason we cannot refer to such essences is because there aren't any. And, given that there aren't any, it is true that we don't have knowledge of them; there is nothing there to know:

> On Locke's account, we cannot simply intend that our system of classification rigidly designate differences of microscopic real essence, not merely because we are — or were — largely ignorant of such differences, but because there are none.[11]

## Leibniz's Responses

In the *New Essays*, Leibniz gives two responses to Locke's theory of species and essences. The first deals with Leibniz's concern that Locke is misapplying the criteria for logical (or mathematical) species to his theory of physical species. Leibniz's second response is that, contra Locke, a common inner nature or structure does determine a species.

### Logical and Physical Species

At four points in book III of the *New Essays*, Leibniz raises the possibility that Locke makes the claims about essences and species that he does because he has confused the criterion for logical species with that for physical species.[12] The difference between logical species and physical species is that with logical (or mathematical) species any difference, even among accidents, is sufficient to make a new species; thus, except in cases of "perfectly alike" individuals, each individual would constitute a separate species. For physical species, a new species occurs only with a difference in essential properties:

> In mathematical strictness, the tiniest difference which stops two things from being alike in all respects makes them 'of different species.' . . . Two physical individuals will never be perfectly of the same species in this manner, because they will never be perfectly alike; and furthermore, a single individual will move from species to species, for it is never entirely similar to itself for more than a moment. (RB 308)

Leibniz does not want the criterion for logical (or mathematical) species to apply to physical species:

> Consistent with my own definition of species, I do not call this difference specific, for since I believe that no two individuals ever resemble each other perfectly, I should have to say that no two individuals belong to the same species, which would not be accurate. (L 581)

According to Leibniz, physical species are *real* when the boundaries of the species are drawn by nature. Real physical species have a common inner structure or nature, and it is in virtue of this common inner structure or nature that the boundaries of the species are marked off. Physical species are *provisional* when humans use similar appearances or resemblances to mark off the boundaries of the species. These are the species we make do with until such time as we come to know the species divisions actually found in nature. Leibniz suggests that the species boundaries for real physical species will be different, perhaps greatly so, from the provisional species boundaries. Accordingly, provisional species will be continually revised as we obtain new information about the actual divisions in nature.

Finally, physical species are *conjectural* when we intend that species divisions made by us match those found in nature. So, whereas provisional species are based solely on the similarities of appearances, with no claim of representing the true species boundaries, conjectural species, while still determined by humans, do involve a reference to the boundaries of real physical species, even though we might be wrong about the correspondence between conjectural species boundaries and real species boundaries:

> However in the physical sense, we do not give weight to every variation; and we speak either unreservedly, when it is a question merely of appearances [provisional], or conjecturally, when it is a question of the inner truth of things, with the presumption that they have some essential and unchangeable nature, as man has reason. (RB 325)

When Locke discusses his theory of nominal essences, he often says such things as "any two abstract ideas, that in any part vary one from another . . . constitute two distinct sorts . . . or Species" (*Essay* III.iii.14), which renders understandable Leibniz's concern that Locke is incorrectly applying the standard for logical species to the case of physical species. But Locke views the abstract idea as constituted by only those properties that are specific properties. He was not confused about the differences between logical and physical species. The change in property he was referring to *was* a change in specific properties, and Leibniz would agree that a change in specific properties makes a new species.

The real disagreement embedded in the discussion of logical and physical species occurs on a deeper level. One certainly hopes that Leibniz was aware that the differences in the nominal essence that Locke mentions are intended to be differences of specific essential properties. But Locke says that these differences, which occur whenever there is a difference in the ideas men have of a species, are all that is required to make a difference in species. Locke thus makes his nominal essence the sole criterion for the boundaries of a species. Leibniz objects because from his point of view, Locke's use of "essence" in this context is vacuous, especially if, as Locke seems to hold, this is the only legitimate use of "essence." From Leibniz's perspective, Locke's nominal essence fails to function as an essence.

For Leibniz, an essence must provide an explanation for the "ultimate reason of things":[13]

The objects of logic exist in the mind of God. Among these objects are mentioned possibilities or possibles, necessary or "eternal" truths, and essences or ideas. They are stratified. The essences are for Leibniz the most fundamental objects of logic. Possibilities depend on essences . . . and the eternal truths are said to depend on "ideas" (Mon 43), by which I believe essences are meant. The essences can be identified with ideas in God's mind, ideas of possible individuals, which constitute the possibility of such individuals, and which are concatenated to constitute the ideas, and the possibility, of possible worlds. And the necessary truths express, or follow from, facts about the essences and their relations.[14]

In Leibniz's metaphysics, an essence has to be able to explain why a thing is as it is. Locke says a thing is as it is because of its internal structure, and its internal structure is as it is because of the arbitrary will of God. Leibniz finds such an explanation inadequate and demands a reason for why anything, including the internal structure of a thing, is the way it is.[15] As will be discussed below, Leibniz provides a full account of why a thing is as it is through an appeal to both an individual's essence and the principle of sufficient reason.

In addition to their radically divergent views on essences, Locke and Leibniz also have very different understandings of the terms "real" and "nominal." From Leibniz's point of view, Locke's nominal/real essence distinction simply does not do any work. For him, Locke's nominal essence is just as real as Locke's real essence since all Leibniz requires for the condition of "real" to be satisfied is that the thing in question be grounded in reality; and since Locke's nominal essence is grounded in reality, being based on the observable similarities that are caused by the corpuscularian structure, Locke's nominal essence, for Leibniz, is real.[16]

Leibniz's response to Locke's division of essences into nominal and real is that Locke's "way of putting things constitutes a very novel mode of expression" (RB 293). Leibniz then presents the distinction between nominal and real *definitions*, suggesting that with definitions a distinction between nominal and real makes sense and is a common one, unlike Locke's.

In *Meditation on Knowledge, Truth, and Ideas*, Leibniz distinguishes nominal definitions from real definitions, claiming that a nominal definition is "nothing but an enumeration of sufficient marks" that allows one to distinguish the thing defined from other similar things. Real definitions are definitions that tell us that the thing is possible, that it contains no contradictions. The possibility of a thing can be known either a priori, by reason, "when we resolve a notion into its requisites, that is, into other notions known to be possible, and we know that there is nothing incompatible among them" (AG 26), or a posteriori, when it is known through experience that "a thing actually exists, for what actually exists or existed is at very least possible" (AG 26).

Leibniz is put off by Locke's use of "nominal" in connection with "essence":

> People have certainly spoken of 'nominal' definitions and 'causal' or 'real' ones, but so far as I know they have not until now spoken of *essences* other than real ones, unless a 'nominal essence' is understood to be a false and impossible one. (RB 293)

Given Leibniz's concept of an essence, a nominal essence makes little sense, but it should be clear to Leibniz that his use of "essence" differs from Locke's. Leibniz is here responding to Locke's remarks in III.iii.15, where Locke lays out three different uses of the term "essence."[17] Locke is quite clear that the word "essence" has different uses (even if how he intends those uses to be understood is not). Leibniz defines essence as "fundamentally nothing but the possibility of the thing under consideration" (RB 293) Given Leibniz's definition of essence, "nominal essence" is almost an oxymoron. But given its place in Locke's threefold definition of essence, the term is close to being redundant.

The term "nominal" for Leibniz is something of a derogatory term, and he uses it in this context to indicate a definition that is not fully reliable: "For we cannot safely use definitions for drawing conclusions unless we know first that they are real definitions, that is, that they include no contradictions" (AG 25). For Locke, "nominal," at least in "nominal essence" simply means "verbal." It isn't an essence in name only, as opposed to a "real" or genuine essence. Certainly Locke does not mean to imply that by calling one essence real and the other nominal that one essence really is an essence and the other isn't. If anything, Locke's nominal essence is more "really" an essence than is his real essence since all the work of sorting (Locke's view of what a specific essence does) occurs through the nominal essence. Locke's point is that the only essences that sort things into species are humanly determined lexical definitions. Herein lies an equivocation. Leibniz intends "real" to refer to the physical, that which is grounded in reality, but he often uses it to mean "genuine." Locke's use of "real" implies that the essence is physical, not that it is the more genuine or true essence. When Leibniz questions the usefulness of Locke's distinction between a real and a nominal essence, he understands "real" to mean "genuine," and in that sense, given Leibniz's views on phenomena, Locke's nominal essence is just as genuine as his real essence because it is just as grounded in the physical (in the phenomena) as is the real essence, and so it is just as real (genuine) as the real (physical) essence is real (genuine).

### Common Inner Natures

For Leibniz's objections to hold against Locke, it must be the case that there are real physical species. Locke repeatedly denies the existence of a "specific essence by means of which nature sets the boundaries" (*Essay* III.x.20). Leibniz claims that "both kinds of bodies, animate bodies as well as lifeless compounds, *will fall into species according to their inner structures*" (RB 318). When the inner structures are in common, says Leibniz, the commonality forms the boundary of a real species.[18]

A fairly natural reading of Leibniz's point is that these common inner natures determine the boundaries of a species. If common inner natures do in fact determine the boundaries of a species, then it would seem that Leibniz is right that there exist specific essences "by means of which nature sets the boundaries." However, when pushed, such an interpretation of Leibniz's claim falls into disarray. The first thing to note is that if "common inner natures" is taken to refer to just any commonality among inner natures, Leibniz is led into a view known as promiscuous realism, a position that, I will argue below, he would find most objectionable.

John Dupre is the originator of promiscuous realism, the theory that there are objective real species out in nature but that the species overlap and an individual belongs as much to any one of a number of species as it does to any other: "Certainly I can see no possible reason why commitment to many overlapping kinds of things should threaten the reality of any of them."[19] Dupre argues against the traditional essentialist doctrine of kinds in favor of a type of pluralism where "there are many equally legitimate ways of dividing the world into kinds."[20]

Would Leibniz accept promiscuous realism? He does accept, for theological reasons involving the principle of plenitude,[21] the concept of the gradation of species, that is, that there is no vacuum among forms. The gap between one species and another will be filled by intermediate species, which vary from each other so slightly as to be indistinguishable to the finite human comprehension. Although there appears to be a blurring of the species, it is a blurring in appearance only; each species is distinct from all other species.

Promiscuous realism, on the other hand, claims that any individual may be a member of a number of species at the same time. If any set of similarities is sufficient to determine the boundaries of a species, and if an individual may share similarities with members of group A and with members of group B, and the members of groups A and B do not share any similarities, then the individual is equally a member of A and B.

When discussing the gradation of species concept, which he accepts, Leibniz nevertheless pulls back from accepting its full implications. The species of man is separate, distinct from all other species. Rationality, the defining characteristic of the species, does not come in degrees and does not occur in any other species. Leibniz, then, can hardly be accepting of a theory that views the species man as just one of any of a number of equally valid ways of dividing up the world. In promiscuous realism, rationality would be just one basis of classification on equal footing with any other shared characteristic.[22]

The motivation for much of Leibniz's resistance to Locke's theory of species is his concern over the implications of Locke's views for the moral status of man. Although the line of attack is quite different, promiscuous realism also threatens the moral status of man with its implication that the class of individuals marked off by the property of rationality has no greater claim to represent the way nature is divided than does a class of individuals marked off by any other shared property. It seems clear, then, that Leibniz would reject promiscuous realism.

Not just any commonality will do, therefore, to determine a species, lest we are willing to accept the species red, which would include among its members both strawberries and blood. A commonality appropriate to species distinction, therefore, must be among specific properties only.

This condition has problems. Since Leibniz is insistent that a thing maintains its specific inner nature regardless of our knowledge of it, the distinction between specific properties and nonspecific accidents would seem to have to be a naturally occurring characteristic of the qualities themselves, independent of any human determination about what is to count as specific properties.

But the distinction between a specific property and a nonspecific accident does not seem to be inherent in the qualities themselves, as Leibniz allows that a quality that is accidental (nonspecific) for one species may be essential (specific) for another:

> Fluidity may, for example, be an accident of lead, for lead flows only in fire, but it belongs to the essence of mercury. Now the cause of fluidity is undoubtedly the free

curved figure of parts, whether they be spherical, cylindrical, oval, or spheroid. Therefore the curved figure of its subtle parts is an accident of lead but essential to mercury. (L 97)

Leibniz also claims that if a supposed member of a species should be discovered to lack what had been thought to be an essential quality of the species, this would count as evidence of the existence of a new species, rather than proof that what was thought to be an essential quality of a species really was not:

> Phil. For instance, if there were a body which had all the properties of gold except malleability, would it be gold? It is up to men to decide; so it is they who determine the species of things.
> Theo. Not at all; they would only determine the name. But this discovery would teach us that malleability has no necessary connection with the other qualities of gold, taken together. So it would show us a new possibility and consequently a new species. (RB 324)

Experience, therefore, can teach us that a particular quality is *not* necessarily connected to a cluster of other qualities; but what is there to tell us which qualities *are* necessarily connected? It would seem that the most experience can tell us is which clusters of properties are stable, that is, which properties are often or usually found together. But experience cannot tell us about necessary connections between properties, as there will always exist the possibility of a new discovery or test that could reveal that qualities thought to be necessarily connected were not, a fact that Leibniz himself realized:

> I reply that the body which is endowed with that inner constitution is also indicated by other outward signs excluding fixedness: it is as though one were to say that the heaviest of all bodies is also one of the most fixed. But all of that is merely provisional, for we might some day find a volatile body — such as a new mercury might be — which was heavier than gold, so that gold would float upon it as lead does on the mercury we have. (RB 312)

It seems, therefore, that Leibniz has no way of explaining how we are to know, through the study of objects out in nature, which properties are the essential properties, that is, which properties are necessarily connected to each other and thus form a species boundary. More to the point than just our inability to determine which properties are in fact the necessary ones is the problem of how nature itself must be in order to have necessarily connected properties. If Leibniz's theory of essences and species is to triumph over Locke's, Leibniz must have an account of necessity that allows him to make the claim that certain properties are essential and that this necessity is independent of humanly determined requirements for species membership.

On the level of phenomena, Leibniz seems in agreement with Locke that there is nothing that can do what specific essences are thought to do — thus his acceptance of provisional physical species when dealing solely with the appearances of things. He repeatedly agrees with Locke that the scholastic understanding of substantial forms as entities in things that cause them to have the specific natures they do must be discarded.[23] But as students of Leibniz are well aware, he has access to a level of explanation that Locke, restricted to a mechanistic materialism, does not. It is to Leibniz's deeper level of explanation that I now turn.

## Leibniz's Deep Theory of Species

Leibniz says little about species outside his debate with Locke in the *New Essays*. Of the few passages where he addresses this issue, perhaps the most important occurs in the *Correspondence with Arnauld*:

> I shall say a word about the reason for the difference that exists here between the concepts of species and those of individual substances with respect to the divine will rather than to simple understanding. This difference is that the most abstract concepts of species contain only necessary or eternal truths which do not at all depend on the decrees of God. . . . But the concepts of individual substances, which are complete and suffice to distinguish their subjects completely, and which consequently enclose contingent truths . . . must also enclose in their concept taken as possible, the free decrees of God, also viewed as possible, because these free decrees are the principal source of existences or facts. Essences, on the other hand, are in the divine understanding prior to any consideration of the will. (L 332)

Those qualities that are essential or necessarily connected to a species concept are necessary or eternal truths and, as such, depend on the principle of noncontradiction. To deny that man is rational would be to assert the contradiction that a rational being is not rational since, in Leibniz's account of species, it is an eternal truth, outside even the will of God, that rationality is part of the very nature of man.

God has a choice not only of which individual to actualize but also of which species to actualize.[24] Both decisions are the result of his free decrees based on the principle of sufficient reason; God brings into existence the greatest number of species compossible and the greatest number of individuals of each species compossible, with the aim of creating a world of maximal happiness.[25] But God does not have freedom in determining what will constitute the boundaries of the species he chooses to actualize. Which properties are essential to a species is established by the essence of the species itself, its nature, and the essence exists as an eternal truth in "the divine understanding." It is not necessary (logically necessary) that Socrates the man exists, but it is logically necessary that if Socrates the man exists, he must be rational.

As laid out in the first section, a major feature of Locke's theory of essences is that while individuals admittedly share qualities, these overlaps are not the boundaries of naturally occurring species. The reason for this position is that although Locke was aware that there are overlaps among the qualities of any of a number of individuals, he could not see that there was anything to justify the claim that some of those overlaps were naturally privileged as specific boundaries. In Locke's metaphysics, all there is is corpuscularian structure, and nothing in the structure can serve as an indication of which qualities are privileged as specific or necessary. When Leibniz is dealing with bodies as phenomena, he grants that there is nothing in the bodies to indicate qualities as being either specific or accidental; but he can still claim that certain qualities are specific properties and that this is part of the nature of the individual because, for Leibniz, all physical substances, including Locke's corpuscles, are actually well-founded phenomena and exist as substances only through the confused perceptions of the monads.[26] Monads are the only true existents and they come into existence complete, meaning that they are each created with their properties and accidents already determined. The properties are determined by the eternal essences and exist as possibilities for actualization in God's mind and determine the sort or species of each monad. The accidents are determined by God, based on the principle of sufficient reason, and are given to each monad to make it the particular individual it is.

Once the determination is made in the realm of possibilities of which individuals are to be actualized, a commonality among the specific properties can in fact indicate where the boundaries of a species are, since two members of the same species will have to have the same essential properties, but the commonality does not determine what the boundary of the species will be. Since the criteria of a species are an eternal truth, it is not the case that two things are members of the same species because they share a common inner nature; rather, they share a common inner nature just because they are, already, members of the same species. So it is not the case that "bodies will fall into species according to their inner structures" (RB 318), as Leibniz says in the *New Essays*; rather, things fall into their inner natures, that is, come to have the inner natures they do, according to the species to which they belong.

The problem for Leibniz, as laid out in the second section, was to explain or provide an account of how nature had to be in order for certain qualities to count as specific properties. On the level of phenomena, there seems to be no way to explain how this necessity could be implemented, especially if one accepts Locke's view of a nature composed of inert material corpuscles. Even if one accepts Leibniz's claim that certain properties are necessary or essential to a species because of the eternal essence of the species, it is still difficult, if not impossible, to see how the necessity inherent in the eternal nature of an essence could be imposed on inert corporeal matter.

Leibniz is able to resolve this difficulty precisely because his philosophy is one that reduces all physical phenomena to explanations on the level of monadic conceptions:

> The greatest threat to our understanding of this part of Leibniz's philosophy . . . [is the] assumption that conceptual connections cannot also be causal connections, that they impose necessity only on our thought, and cannot explain why anything occurs in reality. Leibniz certainly did not make this assumption, as is clear from his conceptual containment theory of truth and his use of it to explain the principle of sufficient reason. Leibniz thought that conceptual containments are precisely what do ultimately explain the existence of all real things and the occurrence of all real events.[27]

## Conclusions

Leibniz does have a viable theory of essences and species, one that is able to avoid both promiscuous realism and Locke's species nihilism. What he does *not* have is a theory of species that is able to engage Locke in debate on the terms of the issue that gave rise to Locke's position. Since Leibniz embraced an immaterialist metaphysics long before he tackled the *Essay*, this is not a major concern, but it does indicate a possible reason for the difficulty and apparent lack of focus for much of the discussion between Locke and Leibniz on essences. Jolley comments on the tone of exasperation and impatience one finds in Leibniz's responses to Locke, suggesting that the reason for Leibniz's mood is Locke's notorious lack of clarity.[28]

I wish to offer the admittedly speculative claim that Leibniz's frustration is due more to his own dissatisfaction with the partial account of species he offered in the *New Essays* than to Locke's lack of clarity. Repeatedly in the *New Essays*, Leibniz holds back from revealing his deep theories,[29] apparently preferring to engage Locke on Locke's own terms. But without his deep metaphysics and the full account of monads as conceptual entities, Leibniz has no way to validate his claim that some properties are specific or necessary. Until he secures that necessity, his responses fail to refute the points Locke makes against the possibility of naturally occurring species. Yet once Leibniz's claims about essences and species are fleshed out by his more considered views, the topic of the debate with Locke dissolves. It is only within the context (and confines) of the mechanistic corpuscularian hypothesis that Locke raises his concerns and denies the existence of naturally occurring specific essences. His fundamental claim is that in a world composed only of corpuscles (or something like them), one cannot give a coherent account of naturally occurring specific essences. I have argued that when Leibniz keeps to the purely phenomenal level, he, like Locke, has no way of accounting for such essences. He can refute Locke's denial of specific essences only by discarding Locke's materialist foundations.

If I may be permitted one final speculation, I would like to suggest that Leibniz is presenting what might be thought of as the groundwork for a reductio ad absurdum against materialism. He is willing to grant Locke's point that on the material level there are no naturally occurring specific essences and that provisional species do in fact determine species. But this account undercuts the crucial distinction between man and beast, which Leibniz finds absurd. Since there must be a real distinction between man and beast and since there is no way of maintaining this distinction in a purely materialistic metaphysics, the correct philosophical position to adopt, therefore, would be immaterialism. And, fortunately for him, Leibniz had just such a metaphysics, fully developed and waiting in the wings—but waiting, as it turned out, for an invitation from Locke that never arrived.[30]

*Notes*

1. Nicholas Jolley, *Leibniz and Locke* (Oxford: Oxford University Press, 1984), p. 145.

2. Michael Ayers, "Locke Versus Aristotle on Natural Kinds," *The Journal of Philosophy* 78, no. 5 (1981): 247–272; "Locke's Logical Atomism," in Anthony Kenny, ed., *Rationalism, Empiricism, and Idealism* (Oxford: Clarendon Press, 1986), pp. 6–22; *Locke: Vol. II, Ontology* (London: Routledge, 1991).

3. For a sample of various commentators who employ Ayers's interpretation, see Paul Guyer, "Locke's Theory of Language," in Vere Chappell, ed., *The Cambridge Companion to Locke* (Cambridge: Cambridge University Press, 1994); pp. 115–145; Pauline Phemister, "Real Essences in Particular," *Locke Newsletter*, 1990, pp. 27–55; David Owen, "Locke on Real Essences," *The History of Philosophy Quarterly* 8, no. 2 (April 1991); 105–118; and John-Michel

Vienne, "Locke on Real Essence and Internal Constitution," *Proceedings of the Aristotelian Society,* 1993, pp. 139–153. While the terminology differs among the commentators, the basic point of how to distinguish the real essence from the internal constitution is consistent.

4. For the scholastics and early moderns, "property" was a technical term, as was "accident." A property is an essential quality, a quality that an entity could not lose and still be the type of thing it is. Accidents, on the other hand, are qualities that a thing could gain or lose without a change in the type, or essential nature, of the thing. Although current use of these terms allows for both "essential property" and "nonessential property," for purposes of clarity I will adopt the following conventions in this paper: "quality" is any characteristic of a thing and is neutral in its essentiality; "property" is an essential quality, that is, a quality required for membership in a species. Thus, "property," "essential quality," and "specific quality" are used interchangeably. Similarly, an accident is a nonessential or nonspecific quality. For stylistic reasons, occasionally the term "nonessential property" will occur. This term should be understood to have the same status as the term "accident."

5. Ayers, *Locke,* pp. 67–68.

6. Ayers, "Locke's Logical Atomism," p. 14; emphasis added.

7. Guyer, "Locke's Theory of Language," pp. 133–134.

8. Ayers, *Locke,* p. 68.

9. For a discussion on this point, see J. L. Mackie, *Problems from Locke* (Oxford: Clarendon Press, 1976), pp. 86–88.

10. Guyer, "Locke's Theory of Language," p. 134.

11. Ibid., 140.

12. See RB 293, 308, 325, and 327.

13. Robert Adams, *Leibniz: Determinist, Theist, Idealist* (New York: Oxford University Press, 1994), p. 10.

14. Ibid., 177–178.

15. I am indebted to Charlie Huenemann for his suggestions on this point in an earlier version of the chapter. Any errors in the revised version, are, of course, solely my own.

16. I am indebted to Candice Goad for her help in sorting out my views in this section. Any errors are solely my own. For text where Leibniz makes this point, see RB 309.

17. For a clear account of how Locke intended the three uses of essence to be drawn, see Vienne, "Locke on Real Essence," footnote 3.

18. See RB 309–311.

19. John Dupre, *The Disorder of Things: Metaphysical Foundations of the Disunity of Science* (Cambridge, Mass.: Harvard University Press, 1993), p. 262.

20. Ibid., pp. 6–7.

21. For discussion on this point, see Donald Rutherford, *Leibniz and the Rational Order of Nature* (Cambridge: Cambridge University Press, 1995), chap. 2, "The Maximization of Perfection and Harmony," esp. pp. 29–31.

22. Just how Leibniz intended rationality to fit into his general scheme of species boundaries being determined by common inner natures or structures is not clear. Jolley notes the problems with claiming rationality as part of an inner structure; see his *Leibniz and Locke,* p. 155.

23. Leibniz often talks about his rejection of substantial forms. See RB 318, 322, and 323 and L 308.

24. See RB 307 for Leibniz's discussion on this point.

25. My presentation of this point is greatly influenced by David Blumenfeld's "Perfection and Happiness in the Best Possible World," in Nicholas Jolley, ed., *The Cambridge Companion to Leibniz* (Cambridge: Cambridge University Press, 1995), pp. 382–410.

26. For a rich discussion on this issue, see Adams, *Leibniz,* chaps. 9 and 10, and Donald

Rutherford's "Metaphysics: The late period," in Nicholas Jolley, ed. *The Cambridge Companion to Leibniz* (Cambridge: Cambridge University Press, 1995), pp. 124–175.

27. Adams, *Leibniz*, p. 78.
28. Jolley, *Leibniz and Locke*, pp. 144–145.
29. Ibid., pp. 159–160.

30. I wish to thank the National Endowment for the Humanities for funding the 1995 Summer Seminar on the Rationalists, directed by Jonathan Bennett. I am also grateful for the helpful comments and suggestions provided on various drafts by Mark Kulstad, Candice Goad, Eric Sotnak, Charles Huenemann, Jonathan Bennett, and the readers at Oxford. On a more personal note, I am very grateful to Mark Kulstad and Marcia Citron for graciously providing me with a place to live and work during the summer of 1996, when the majority of the work for this chapter was done.

# PART TWO

# FREEDOM AND NECESSITY

## 8

JOSEPH KEIM CAMPBELL

# Descartes on Spontaneity, Indifference, and Alternatives

In his writings on free will, Descartes notes three distinct, though possibly related, kinds of freedom. Two of them are mentioned in the 9 February 1645 letter to Mesland. Alluding to a passage from Meditation 4, discussed in detail below, Descartes writes:

> I would like you to notice that "indifference" in this context seems to me strictly to mean that state of the will when it is not impelled one way rather than another by any perception of truth or goodness. This is the sense which I took it when I said that the lowest degree of freedom is that by which we determine ourselves to things to which we are indifferent. But perhaps others mean by "indifference" a positive faculty of determining oneself to one or other of two contraries, that is to say, to pursue or avoid, to affirm or deny. I do not deny that the will has this positive faculty. (CSMK 245)

Indifference in the first sense — which I hereafter call simply "indifference" — is not, according to Descartes, essential to free will. However, indifference in the second sense — "a positive faculty" or power — is essential. I refer to the second, positive sense of indifference as "alternatives" since it is related to the more contemporary notion of *alternative possibilities*. Roughly speaking, a person has alternatives if and only if he is both able to perform some action and able to perform some contrary action.

The third kind of freedom discussed by Descartes is termed "spontaneity," and in several passages (CSM I, 296; CSM II, 40, 41; CSMK 234) he suggests that it, too, is essential to free will. Vere Chappell writes that "an action is spontaneous if it is performed by its agent entirely on his own, without being forced or helped or affected by an external factor, or by anything other than his very self."[1] Given what has been said so far, Descartes's theory of free will can be summarized as follows: alternatives and spontaneity are necessary for free will but indifference is not.

Philosophers have found fault with this theory, or even with the suggestion that Descartes endorses it, for two distinct kinds of reasons. First, some think that the view is *internally* problematic since an inconsistency, or at least a "logical tension," emerges when Descartes's assertions about free will are taken collectively. More specifically, commentators have made three related claims: (1) that the requirements of alternatives and spontaneity "appear to yield two different conceptions of freedom";[2] (2) that alternatives are essentially connected with indifference, so that Descartes cannot accept the former yet deny the latter as being necessary for free will;[3] and (3) that in certain passages (CSMK 246; AT VII, 57–58) Descartes even denies that alternatives are essential to free will.[4]

Second, there is the allegation that the above theory is *externally* inconsistent, that it conflicts with other claims held by Descartes. There is, for instance, his acceptance of what John Cottingham calls "the doctrine of the irresistibility of the natural light," or INL. According to INL, "When the intellect is confronted with a clear and distinct perception, the will is immediately and spontaneously compelled to give its assent to the truth of the relevant proposition."[5] The problem here is aptly expressed by Robert Imlay: "How can reasons be evidentially compelling and still leave us with genuinely open alternatives?"[6] There are similar criticisms, too, involving Descartes's assertions about God's foreknowledge or preordination, but I won't discuss them in this chapter since I think that what I do say applies to these cases as well.[7]

As the internalist criticisms suggest, the issue here is not simply the tenability of Descartes's theory but the proper identification of it. On the one hand, there are those, like myself, who think that Descartes holds a *two-way compatibilism*: he believes that free will is compatible with determinism, yet he also thinks that it requires alternatives, a *two-way* power "to pursue or avoid, to affirm or deny."[8] On the other hand, there are those who think that he adopts a *one-way compatibilism*. According to this view, Descartes either never really endorsed the requirement of alternatives or he later came to reject it, so he explains freedom in terms of spontaneity alone.[9] What's especially interesting is that nearly everyone who thinks that Descartes is a two-way compatibilist also believes that at least one of the above criticisms ultimately proves to be devastating to his account of free will. In general, then, either philosophers find Descartes's theory to be seriously flawed or they think that it is quite different from the prima facie sketch I provided in the opening paragraphs.

In this chapter, I argue in favor of the two-way compatibilist reading of Descartes. Not only do I think that this is the best way to understand him but also I believe that some form of two-way compatibilism is true. Thus, although Descartes's thoughts on the subject are no doubt abstruse, I think that he offers important insights about the nature of human freedom. The chapter is divided into four sections. In the first two, I define some preliminary notions and explain Descartes's two-way compatibilism in detail, providing textual support for my interpretation along the way. In the third section, I present and respond to the three internal problems noted above and explain, but then reject, the one-way compatibilist reading of Descartes. I believe that the charge of external inconsistency is related to the traditional problem of free will and determinism. In the space provided I cannot solve this problem, but in the final section I intend to show why Descartes's two-way compatibilism offers as good of a solution as we are likely, even at this time, to get.

## Descartes on Free Will: Some Preliminaries

According to the free will thesis, or FT, persons, at least sometimes, have free will.[10] Though much about Descartes's theory is debatable, it is beyond question that he endorses FT. In fact, he takes the radical view that "the will is by its nature so free that it cannot be constrained" (CSM I, 343). In the 25 December 1639 letter to Mersenne he writes that "God has given us a will which has no limits" (CSMK 141), and he makes similar remarks throughout his writings (CSM II, 39, 40, 42; CSM I, 204, 205). Descartes even goes so far as to say that although our will differs in important respects from the one that God possesses (CSMK 179; CSM II, 40, 291–292; CSM I, 203), in the "essential and strict sense" we are as free as God is (CSM II, 40; CSM I, 384). In the 1639 letter to Mersenne he adds: "It is principally because of this infinite will within us that we can say we are created in [God's] image" (CSMK 141–142).

That we have unlimited freedom is, for Descartes, a "primary notion" (CSMK 161), which is "innate" (CSM I, 205–206) and known by the "natural light" (CSM II, 134). Elsewhere Descartes claims that we know we have freedom by an "inner experience," "awareness," or "consciousness" (CSM II, 39, 40, 134, 259; CSM I, 194, 234, 314; CSMK 277, 296, 342). I take it that in making this last point Descartes is embracing a thesis, held by some twentieth-century philosophers, to the effect that our freedom can be established by introspection, by reflecting on our own inner states.[11] It is worth noting that the above comments are made throughout Descartes's writings on free will, from earlier letters (1639) to the *Passions of the Soul* (1649).

For Descartes, free will is a faculty that is designated by a variety of equivalent terms: "the faculty of assent," "the faculty of will," and "the faculty of choice or freedom of the will" (CSM I, 207; CSM II, 41, 39). Thus, according to Descartes, there is no difference between "the will" and "free will." Both designate the same faculty, most clearly noted as the faculty of choice. In *Comments on a Certain Broadsheet*, Descartes writes that "the term 'faculty' denotes nothing but a potentiality" (CSM I, 305). The potentialities relevant to the will I call "powers" or, synonymously, "abilities" or "capacities." A power is a potentiality in the sense that one might have it even if one does not use it.

Some may think that Descartes's definition is a bit of an understatement, for traditionally a faculty is thought of as "a collection of interrelated powers."[12] Others claim that calling the will a "faculty" suggests that there is a mysterious thing — the will — that has a certain property — being free.[13] But if we regard a collection as nothing over and above the things that make it up, then faculties are nothing more than their composite powers. Additionally, we cannot always distinguish between a collection of powers and a single power. We may speak, for instance, of the power of turning on the light (which I have in contrast to a chair) even though this is made up of other powers (e.g., the power to move my finger), which are at least interrelated enough to include the power of turning on the light. Hence, faculties need be no more mysterious than the sense we get from Descartes's definition. At least this is how I use the term: a *faculty* is merely a *power*; the faculty of *free will*, specifically, is the power to choose, allowing that it might also be a collection of other component powers.

As I see it, if one has the power — the potential — to choose something that one did not choose, then it must have been the case that one could have made another choice or, more simply, that one could have chosen otherwise. Thus, inasmuch as the will involves a power related to choice, someone who has free will also has the power of choosing otherwise. We could just as easily substitute "action" here for "choice" since, according to Descartes and myself at least, a choice is a kind of action (CSM II, 39ff., 270). Hence, having free will includes having alternatives; that is, anyone who ever had free will could have, in some relevant sense, chosen or done otherwise. This is an adequate way of understanding the concept, for generally we say that one is free to the extent that one can do other things. Free will is freedom in its pure form, so one has free will to the extent that one can do *at least one other thing* than what one happens to do.

The history of philosophy is nearly univocal in accepting that free will requires alternatives, as this quote from G. E. Moore might attest.

> The statement that we have Free Will is certainly ordinarily understood to imply that we really sometimes have the power of acting differently from the way in which we actually do act; and hence, if anybody tells us that we have Free Will, while at the same time he means to deny that we ever have such a power, he is simply misleading us. We certainly have *not* got Free Will, in the ordinary sense of the word, if we never really *could*, in any sense at all, have done anything else than what we did do.[14]

Though it is somewhat contentious, I claim that Descartes agrees with the above sentiment since alternatives turn out to be indifference in the positive sense, the one essential to free will. I discuss this point in more detail in the next section.

According to my interpretation, Descartes is a *compatibilist*; that is, he believes that FT is compatible with the thesis of determinism. Many confuse compatibilism with soft determinism but the two theories are not synonymous, as David Lewis nicely explains:

> Soft determinism is the doctrine that sometimes one freely does what one is predetermined to do; and that in such a case one is able to act otherwise though past history and the laws of nature determine that one will not act otherwise.
>
> Compatibilism is the doctrine that soft determinism may be true. A compatibilist might well doubt soft determinism because he doubts on physical grounds that we are ever predetermined to act as we do, or perhaps because he doubts on psychoanalytic grounds that we ever act freely. I myself am a compatibilist but no determinist.[15]

I do not claim that Descartes is a soft determinist. The suggestion is only that he thinks that one need not reject determinism in order to save free will, that he presents a theory of free will that is consistent with determinism or, in other words, that he is a compatibilist.

Certainly, Descartes never explicitly endorses the theory of determinism as we understand it today, but the same can be said for most other philosophers of his era. He does accept some related theses, such as the doctrines of divine foreknowledge, preordination, and grace. In fact, Descartes even believes that God is "the total cause of everything" (CSMK 272), which seems to entail that determinism is true.[16] Nonetheless, Descartes believes that each of these claims is consistent with FT (CSM II, 40, 134, 292; CSM I, 206, 380; CSMK 234, 277, 282). Thankfully, showing any connection between the above views and determinism is unnecessary since, as I explained above, Descartes need not be a determinist to be a compatibilist.

Compatibilism has long been the subject of controversy because, as some have argued, determinism entails that the world could not have been any different than the way that it is — that nothing could be otherwise — which would rule out our having any genuine alternatives and, thus, free will. *Determinism* claims that the past, together with the laws of nature, entails a single, unique future. The view that the world could not have been otherwise — that every true proposition is necessarily true — is called *necessitarianism*.[17] Thus, incompatibilists are usually motivated by the belief that determinism entails a kind of necessitarianism. Here is the *argument for incompatibilism*, which supports this view: "Given determinism, any future event is the consequence of the laws of nature and remote past events. But the laws of nature and remote past events are both necessary, in some sense. Therefore, all events — future as well as past — are necessary, in that same sense."[18] The laws of nature and remote past events — like the events that occurred prior to the existence of human beings — are necessary in the sense that "no one has (or ever had) any choice about whether" they are true.[19] According to the above argument, determinism spreads this necessity across all events, and, it seems, no one could ever do otherwise. Though it has received ample criticism, the argument still presents a challenge to any compatibilist theory.[20]

Important for my purposes is Descartes's assertion that FT is compatible with INL, which I noted above. This thesis is essential to the project of the *Meditations*, where Descartes must arrive at propositions that he is *unable*, in some sense, to doubt.[21] In Meditation 4, Descartes writes: "During these past few days I have been asking whether anything in the world exists, and I have realized that from the very fact of my raising this question it follows quite evidently that I exist. *I could not but judge* that something which I understood so clearly was true" (CSM II, 41; my emphasis). Strictly speaking, INL is much weaker than determinism since it is a doctrine that governs only beliefs and these only during times of clear and distinct perception. Still, INL entails a *local* determinism, in which, in at least some instances, our beliefs are necessitated in the same sense that all events are necessitated according to (global) determinism: holding *everything* fixed — the laws of nature and past events, including the particular reasons under consideration when a choice is made — the event could not have been otherwise. In such instances, our beliefs seem to be "compelled" by reason, and it is here where Descartes's assertions of our unlimited freedom become difficult to defend.

Nevertheless, Descartes is unwavering in his belief that there is no conflict between INL and FT. For not only are we free when our perceptions are clear and distinct but also we are "at our freest" when a "clear perception impels us to pursue some object" (CSM II, 292; see also CSM II, 40, 106; CSMK 245, 342). What is problematic, then, about Descartes's theory is that he believes that we have free will even when reason *compels* our beliefs and actions. The oddity of this view is brought out best by Descartes's own words: "The will of a thinking thing is drawn voluntarily and freely (for this is the essence of will), but nevertheless inevitably, towards a clearly known good" (CSM II, 117). How can something inevitable be, at the same time, free? This is precisely what I shall try to explain.

## Descartes's Two-way Compatibilism

I begin with a well-known quotation from Meditation 4. The sentences are numbered for easy reference.

> (1) The will simply consists in our ability to do or not do something (that is, to affirm or deny, to pursue or avoid); (2) or rather, it consists simply in the fact that when the intellect puts something forward for affirmation or denial or for pursuit or avoidance, our inclinations are such that we do not feel we are determined by any external force. (3) In order to be free, there is no need for me to be inclined both ways; (4) on the contrary, the more I incline in one direction — either because I clearly understand that reasons of truth and goodness point that way, or because of a divinely produced disposition of my inmost thoughts — the freer is my choice. (5) Neither divine grace nor natural knowledge ever diminishes freedom; on the contrary, they increase and strengthen it. (6) But the indifference I feel when there is no reason pushing me in one direction rather than another is the lowest grade of freedom; it is evidence not of any perfection of freedom, but rather of a defect in knowledge or a kind of negation. (7) For if I always saw clearly what was true and good, I should never have to deliberate about the right judgement or choice; in that case, although I should be wholly free, it would be impossible for me ever to be in a state of indifference. (CSM II, 40)

To a notable extent, unraveling Descartes's theory of free will requires nothing more than clarifying what is being said in this quotation, but that does not make the task any easier.

All of the kinds of freedom noted in the beginning of this essay are mentioned in this quotation. In passages (4)–(7), for instance, Descartes denies that mere indifference is essential to free will. He writes, in the 1645 letter to Mesland, that indifference is "that state of the will when it is not impelled one way rather than another by any perception of truth or goodness" (CSMK 244–245; see also CSM II, 40). In *Conversation with Burman* he adds that one "is more indifferent the fewer reasons he knows which impel him to choose one side rather than another" (CSMK 233). Thus I am indifferent to the extent that I lack reasons either in favor or against some choice. I might be indifferent either because I lack reasons altogether or because my reasons for alternative choices are of equal weight, as in the case of Buridan's ass as it sits between two equally appealing piles of hay.

What exactly, one may ask, is the connection between indifference and free will, according to those who disagree with Descartes? No one suggests that indifference is *sufficient* for free will. In at least one telling of the Buridan story the ass is indifferent yet still lacks the ability to make a choice, which is why it starves to death. The requirement of indifference, though, seems to ensure that one is not a slave to reason, that one can choose in spite of — or even, perhaps, against — the dictates of reason. As such, the requirement is in conflict with Descartes's acceptance of INL. In situations in which one's choices are based on clear and distinct perceptions, there is no indifference, according to Descartes.

This is precisely why Descartes must deny that indifference is necessary for free will, as indicated by his comments in (4)–(7). Thus, at (6) he regards indifference as "the lowest grade of freedom" and says that it is "a defect in knowledge or a kind of negation." And at (7) he claims that it is possible that "I should be wholly free" even if it is "impossible for me ever to be in a state of indifference," which suggests that one could have free will without indifference. Moreover, there are his comments in the *Sixth Replies,* where he unequivocally states that "indifference does not belong to the essence of human freedom" (CSM II, 292). Note that Descartes does not reject indifference altogether; he only claims that it is not a *necessary condition* for freedom of will. All of these observations are in accordance with comments made at (4) and (5) as well.

The meaning of (2), I think, is also clear. Descartes implies that in order to have free will there cannot be any immediate external causes of our choices. Now, what he actually says is that free will "consists simply in the fact that" when we make choices "our inclinations are such that *we do not feel* we are determined by any external force." Perhaps all that is required for free will is that we not *feel* an external force, not that such forces be absent. But if we couple this passage with Descartes's view that our freedom is known by an inner awareness, the stronger thesis follows. In other words, Descartes thinks that we can tell by introspection that we are free, so if "we do not feel we are determined by an external force" it would follow for him that *we are not determined* by such a force. As I noted earlier, this position is held by some contemporary philosophers as well.[22] I think that the view is incorrect, but I am merely noting that (2) suggests something stronger than it might at first seem to suggest, namely, that spontaneity is essential to free will.

Spontaneity is important to both *libertarians* — incompatibilists who endorse FT[23] — and compatibilists, and it is easy to see why. Neither indifference nor alternatives are, on their own, sufficient for free will, even if they are necessary. Think, for instance, of Buridan's ass. To have free will, the ass would need the ability to make a choice while in the state of indifference. Thus, it is believed by some that if indifference were combined with spontaneity, free will might be achieved. Likewise, alternatives are not sufficient for free will either since a person has alternatives even if his or her choices or actions are purely random. If we couple alternatives with spontaneity, however, concerns about the agent's lack of freedom might be dissuaded. This is why most philosophers regard spontaneity as essential to any freedom worth having. Not surprisingly, Descartes also links spontaneity with alternatives, as I show shortly.

There is a difference between most compatibilist theories of spontaneity and libertarian ones. Given determinism, the causal chains leading to our actions eventually trace back to events that occurred prior to our birth. According to incompatibilists, since we have no control over these events, we have no control over our actions. Thus, libertarians, like those who endorse the "agency theory,"[24] usually require that agents be the "sole and unique cause" of their actions. Most compatibilists, on the other hand, are content with saying that we are mere *adequate* causes of our actions, though not *original* ones.[25]

Passages (1) and (3) of the previous quotation are less congenial than the others. I offer two interpretations: my own, which I present here, and Michelle Beyssade's, discussed in the next section. I think (1) suggests that alternatives are essential to free will. Passage (3), on the other hand, merely repeats the claim made in passage (6): that indifference, in the *first* sense, is not essential to free will. It is repeated twice, I think, to ensure that one does not confuse alternatives with mere indifference. The significance of "or rather," at the beginning of (2), emphasizes that Descartes believes spontaneity and alternatives to be essentially linked, which is why he states — at (1) and (2) — that free will "consists" in each.

This last point is worth discussing in more detail. Consider, for instance, the following quotes from Descartes:

> You admit . . . that we can guard against error. Now this would be quite impossible unless the will had the freedom to direct itself, without the determination of the intellect, towards one side or the other. (*Fifth Replies*, written in 1641; CSM II, 260)

> That there is freedom in our will, and that we have power in many cases to give or withhold our assent at will, is so evident that it must be counted among the first and most common notions that are innate in us. (*Principles* 1:39, published in 1644; CSM I, 205–206)

> But perhaps others mean by "indifference" a positive faculty of determining oneself to one or other of two contraries, that is to say, to pursue or avoid, to affirm or deny. I do not deny that the will has this positive faculty. (Letter to Mesland, written 9 February 1645; CSMK 245)

Each of these passages can be used to support the claim that Descartes regards spontaneity as essential to free will. But in each it is difficult to miss the references to a two-way power: "towards one side or the other"; "to give or withhold our assent"; "to one or other of two contraries." Shortly after the second quote, at *Principles* 1:41, Descartes even refers to this power as a kind of "indifference": "Nonetheless, we have such close awareness of the freedom and *indifference* which is in us, that there is nothing we can grasp more evidently or more perfectly" (CSM I, 206; my emphasis).

In the context of this discussion, it might do well to repeat the first two passages from the *Meditations* quotation:

> The will simply consists in our ability to do or not do something (that is, to affirm or deny, to pursue or avoid); or rather, it consists simply in the fact that when the intellect puts something forward for affirmation or denial or for pursuit or avoidance, our inclinations are such that we do not feel we are determined by any external force. (CSM II, 40)

On both sides of the "or rather" are references to a two-way power. I suggest that according to Descartes, alternatives and spontaneity make up a single power — the power to determine oneself to either of two alternatives — which he identifies with free will. It follows that he thinks the individual powers that make up free will — alternatives and spontaneity — are both necessary for it and that he accepts a two-way compatibilism.

## Internal Criticisms of Descartes's Two-way Compatibilism

In this section I consider the three internal criticisms mentioned at the beginning of the chapter. I start with the contention that, in at least two passages, Descartes explicitly denies that alternatives are necessary for free will. Given this, it makes it implausible to think of Descartes as a two-way compatibilist, which renders the one-way compatibilist reading more probable. The first passage is claimed, by Beyssade, to be found in the original Latin text of the Meditation 4 quotation.[26] Here is a comparison of line (3) in the above translation with Beyssade's (3*):

> (3) In order to be free, there is no need for me to be inclined both ways
> (3*) In order to be free, there is no need for me to be able to go both ways.[27]

As I have already indicated, (3) denies that indifference is necessary for free will whereas (3*) says the same about alternatives since it rejects the need for a two-way power or ability. Thus, according to Beyssade's reading, Descartes puts forth the requirement of alternative possibilities provisionally in (1) but then later rejects it with (3*). It is (2) that signifies the essential feature of free will: spontaneity.

This, at least, is the view that Descartes held while writing the Latin version of the *Meditations*, published in 1641. By 1647, when the French version was issued, he had changed his mind. According to Beyssade, the turning point occurred sometime around the 1645 letter to Mesland. For convenience, I repeat the passage.

> I would like you to notice that "indifference" in this context seems to me strictly to mean that state of the will when it is not impelled one way rather than another by any perception of truth or goodness. This is the sense which I took it when I said that the lowest degree of freedom is that by which we determine ourselves to things to which we are indifferent. But perhaps others mean by "indifference" a positive faculty of determining oneself to one or other of two contraries, that is to say, to pursue or avoid, to affirm or deny. I do not deny that the will has this positive faculty. (CSMK 245)

Again, the first sense is what I have been calling simply "indifference," and Descartes is apparently alluding here to (6) from the *Meditations* quotation. He distinguishes this from the second sense of indifference, which I have been calling "alternatives" — "a positive faculty of determining oneself to one or other of two contraries" — using words reminiscent of passage (1). Here he seems to hold the position that I claim he held all along: alternatives and spontaneity are essential for free will but indifference is not.

However, according to Beyssade, the French edition of the *Meditations* "leaves it open for the reader to think that the two-way power *is* necessary for freedom —

something which the original Latin had explicitly denied."[28] She then suggests that even though "Descartes became more and more aware of the importance of the two-way power in freedom" he still held that "the essence of freedom does not amount to the two-way power" since "the greatest freedom consists in the spontaneous assent to the clearly known truth."[29]

Beyssade makes two claims in her interpretation which are important to distinguish: first, that Descartes's views on free will changed substantially from 1641 to 1647; second, that although Descartes became more appreciative of alternatives, he never believed them to be essential to free will. Given the second claim, Beyssade is led to adopt the one-way compatibilist reading of Descartes. Thus, her second contention is more important for my purposes. I want to say that Descartes is a two-way compatibilist, and I don't care very much when he came to hold this view. For this reason, I reply only briefly to Beyssade's first claim and then give a more extensive criticism of the one-way compatibilist interpretation.

I should confess that there is not much hope of my settling the textual question of whether (3) or (3*) provides a better translation of the original Latin. Beyssade herself admits that the issue is "far from easy" and notes that there are others who support the CSM II reading, given at (3).[30] But there are a few points I can make against Beyssade. For instance, there are the letters and essays written prior to 1645, in which Descartes claims that alternatives, as well as spontaneity, are fundamental to free will. Most notable are the above quoted passages from the *Fifth Replies* (CSM II, 260), written in 1641, and the *Principles* (CSM I, 205–206), published in 1644.

Moreover, Descartes seems to distinguish between the two senses of indifference in his 2 May 1644 letter to Mesland:

> Since you regard freedom not simply as indifference but rather as a real and positive power to determine oneself, the difference between us is merely a verbal one — for I agree that the will has such a power. However, I do not see that it makes any difference to that power whether it is accompanied by indifference. . . .
>
> As for animals that lack reason it is obvious that they are not free, since they do not have this positive power to determine themselves. (CSMK 234)

The comments here are very similar to those of the 1645 letter. There is the "positive power to determine oneself," which is essential to free will, and the *negative* power — indifference — which is not. It is true that in the 1644 letter, the power Descartes alludes to seems closer to spontaneity than alternatives, but as I've previously noted, there is good reason to think that Descartes believed the two to be essentially linked. Since there is no compelling reason to say that Descartes's theory of free will changed in any significant way from 1641 to 1647, I reject Beyssade's first claim.

The second passage in which Descartes apparently rejects the requirement of alternatives is also mentioned by Beyssade:[31] "But freedom  considered in the acts of the will at the moment when they are elicited does not entail any indifference taken in either the first or the second sense . . ." (CSMK 246). I wish I could say that Descartes is being merely ironic here, and if Descartes were Hume, perhaps I could. But it will take some doing to show that this quote is not damning. Let's see what immediately follows and try anyway: ". . . for what is done cannot remain undone as long as it is being done. It consists simply in ease of operation; and at that point freedom, spontaneity and voluntariness are the same thing" (CSMK 246).

When Descartes talks about "the acts of the will at the moment when they are elicited," he is referring to actions once they begin to take place. I suggest that the point he is making is that the question of whether one could have done otherwise makes sense only when referenced to some time prior to this time of action. Keith Lehrer writes: "Statements affirming that a person can do something have a double time index, one time reference being to the time at which the person has the capability, and the second being to the time of action."[32] Given the double time index noted by Lehrer, it makes sense to say that a person could have done otherwise, relative to some previous moment of time, even though, relative to the time at which the action was performed, the person could not have done otherwise.

An example might be helpful. A drunken driver cannot claim that his killing of a pedestrian was the result of an unfree act simply by pointing out that at the time of the accident, given his drunken state and the speed at which he was traveling, he could not have avoided hitting the victim. His act was freely done provided that there was some time prior to the accident when he could have done otherwise. Descartes believes (a) that to have free will, one must have alternative possibilities at some time but (b) that one can only have these alternatives prior to the time of action. The above passage is consistent with (a) and (b), yet (a) claims that alternatives are essential to free will. The passage does not provide evidence against Descartes's belief that alternatives are necessary for free will; it only places restrictions on when these alternatives take place.

Let me summarize the results so far. As difficult as it may be to explain how Descartes can consistently adopt two-way compatibilism, his acceptance of one-way compatibilism is even more untenable. The one-way interpretation relies on Descartes's belief that spontaneity is essential to free will, but roughly half of the passages that support this view indicate that our spontaneity is always conjoined with *some* two-way power. As for the two passages in which Descartes allegedly discards alternatives — CSMK 246 and AT VII, 57–58 — the latter refers, at most, to an early stage of Descartes's development, whereas the former is not damning so long as one pays careful attention to the logic of "could have" statements. Therefore, there is little reason to believe that Descartes endorses a one-way, as opposed to a two-way, compatibilism.

I turn now to the other claims of internal incoherence that have been leveled against my reading of Descartes: that alternatives and spontaneity "yield two different conceptions of freedom"[33] and that alternatives are essentially connected with indifference. Both claims involve a mistaken assumption about alternatives, namely, that alternatives cannot be adequately expressed in any compatibilist system. Though it is no fault of his, a famous quote of Hume's seems to be a major source of the difficulty. In the *Enquiry*, Hume writes: "Few are capable of distinguishing betwixt the liberty of *spontaneity*, as it is call'd in the schools, and the liberty of *indifference*; betwixt that which is oppos'd to violence, and that which means a negation of necessity and causes."[34] One problem with Hume's distinction is the implication that there are only two ways of thinking about free will: in terms of indifference and in

terms of spontaneity. If there is one thing that I could offer to historians who are study-
ing accounts of the will, it is that alternatives offer us a third way of understanding
freedom that allows for a broader spectrum of possible positions, one that is more
representative of the actual views put forth by philosophers.

Left with only Hume's dichotomy, it is not surprising that philosophers tend to
classify alternatives as a kind of indifference. For instance, Anthony Kenny writes:

> Throughout the history of philosophy there have been two contrasting methods of
> expounding the nature of human freewill. The first is in terms of power: we are free
> in doing something if and only if it is in our power not to do it. The second is in
> terms of wanting: we are free in doing something if and only if we do it because we
> want to do it.[35]

Later, after noting Hume's distinction, he adds: "Liberty defined in terms of wanting
is liberty of spontaneity; liberty defined in terms of power is liberty of indifference."[36]
This causes Kenny to classify alternatives as a *type* of indifference — for it is a "positive faculty" — which makes Descartes's theory seem blatantly inconsistent.[37]

William James is a good example of a libertarian who links alternatives with indifference. When illustrating his notion of free choice, James imagines himself to
come upon two streets, either one of which he could walk down to reach his destination. What does it mean to say that he has a genuine choice of which road to take?

> It means that both Divinity Avenue and Oxford Street are called; but only one, and
> that one *either* one, shall be chosen. Now I ask you to seriously suppose that this am-
> biguity of my choice is real; and then to make the impossible hypothesis that the
> choice is made twice over, and each time falls on a different street. In other words,
> imagine that I first walk through Divinity Avenue, and then imagine that the pow-
> ers that be annihilate ten minutes of time with all that it contained, and set me back
> at the door of this hall just as I was before the choice was made. Imagine then that,
> everything else being the same, I now make a different choice and traverse Oxford
> Street.[38]

The power that James is alluding to — the power to make different choices *in the exact same set of circumstances* — does require indifference, for inasmuch as actions are
attributable to agents, these circumstances will include the reasons one had for making those choices. If one's choices are compelled by reason — as INL suggests they
sometimes are — one will make the same choices, given the same set of reasons, and
will lack the power that James thinks is essential to free will. In a similar way, one
might argue that this power is incompatible with determinism. Thus, though the
compatibilist might claim that one can do otherwise, this is true only if we either
change some feature of the past or alter the laws of nature. For the libertarian like
James, though, free will requires *categorical* alternatives: one must be able to do otherwise in the exact same set of circumstances, with the same history and the same
governing laws.[39] Since categorical alternatives require indifference, they are incompatible with determinism and those events that are locally determined according to INL.

Alternatives, however, have historically been thought of in at least two different
ways: categorically, as James thinks of them, and hypothetically, as in the case of
Hume and twentieth-century compatibilists like Moore.[40] One way, though not the

only way, of understanding hypothetical alternatives is given by the *standard hypothetical analysis,* or SHA: a person, S, has alternatives if and only if "S could have done otherwise," where this simply means that "S would have done otherwise if S had wanted (or chosen or tried) to do otherwise."[41] Categorical alternatives are related to indifference but hypothetical ones are not. Here lies the kinship between Descartes's indifference and Hume's liberty of indifference: indifference is connected with categorical alternatives, which "means a negation of necessity." Hume saw that indifference entailed the falsity of determinism. For this reason, Descartes's rejection of indifference should lead us to think that he tends toward a compatibilist theory.

The distinction between categorical and hypothetical accounts of alternatives is one that philosophers like Kenny miss. I think it results in confusions about Descartes's theory, as well as Hume's. Hume, for instance, defines liberty as "a power of acting or not acting, according to the determinations of the will."[42] If we think only of spontaneity and indifference — as Kenny does — it is difficult to classify this definition because it describes freedom as both a *power* and a *wanting*. It is more accurate to classify Hume as a two-way compatibilist who claims that alternatives are essential to free will and puts forth a hypothetical account to spell this out. Likewise, some philosophers fail to even consider Descartes's endorsement of alternatives since they equate them with a form of libertarianism that goes against his acceptance of INL and his rejection of indifference. However, there are other accounts of alternatives that Descartes might offer instead.

The following table is useful in understanding the various kinds of freedom discussed in this chapter and how they relate, in general, to theories of free will:

| Freedoms | Two-way Compatibilism | One-way Compatibilism | Libertarianism |
|---|---|---|---|
| Indifference: | not essential to FT | not essential to FT | essential to FT |
| Alternatives: | hypothetical | not essential to FT | categorical |
| Spontaneity: | adequate causes | adequate causes | original causes |

Descartes, I have argued, is a two-way compatibilist. He thinks that indifference is not essential to free will but that both alternatives and spontaneity are.[43]

## Descartes's Compatibilist Account of Alternatives

In this final section, I consider the external problem. What is at issue here is whether Descartes can offer an explication of alternatives that is consistent with his endorsement of INL. The 1645 letter to Mesland holds some important clues:

> When a very evident reason moves us in one direction, although morally speaking we can hardly move in the contrary direction, absolutely speaking we can. For it is always open to us to hold back from pursuing a clearly known good, or from admitting a clearly perceived truth, provided we consider it a good thing to demonstrate the freedom of will by so doing. (CSMK 245)

Here Descartes makes a distinction between what we may call "moral alternatives" and "absolute alternatives." He admits that given the truth of INL, we sometimes lack the former, yet this does not preclude us from having the latter. But what does it mean to say that we have absolute alternatives, according to Descartes? I consider four options.

First, one might appeal to the remark made later on in the 1645 letter to Mesland, and noted above, that with regard to "the acts of the will at the moment when they are elicited" we have no alternatives of any kind (CSMK 246). Given what I've said, perhaps our freedom during moments of clear and distinct perceptions is contingent on our having alternatives at some prior moment, when we do not have compelling reasons before us.[44] There is a comment in Descartes's 1644 letter to Mesland that lends support to this interpretation:

> But the nature of the soul is such that it hardly attends for more than a moment to a single thing; hence, as soon as our attention turns from the reasons which show us that the thing is good for us, and we merely keep in our memory the thought that it appeared desirable to us, we can call up before our mind some other reason to make us doubt it, so perhaps suspend our judgement, and perhaps even form a contrary judgement. (CSMK 233–234)

This way of thinking of Descartes's theory of alternatives is dubious, however, for it goes against his insistence that we are "at our freest" when a "clear perception impels us to pursue some object" (CSM II, 292), which he seems to accept in this very same letter (see CSMK 233). It also suggests that some degree of indifference is necessary for our freedom, which Descartes emphatically denies in the letter (CSMK 233–235) and elsewhere.

Moreover, we can distinguish between the following three events: (a) the perception of evidentially compelling reasons, (b) the inclination of the will, and (c) the performance of some action. Given the way INL was specified at the beginning of this chapter, we might have to regard events (a) and (b) as occurring at the same instant,[45] but event (c) seems to be a slightly later event that we *can* "*hold back* from pursuing." This would suggest that according to Descartes, we have alternatives at the time (a) and (b) occur but not at the time (c) occurs. Hence, the later comments in the 1645 letter are unhelpful in trying to figure out the crucial difference between moral and absolute alternatives. They would only be worthwhile if (a), (b), and (c) occurred simultaneously, which does not seem to be the case.

Second, one might suggest that absolute alternatives are equivalent to categorical ones.[46] As I have shown in the previous sections, however, Descartes is too much of a compatibilist for this view to be taken seriously. Additionally, his remarks from the 1644 letter to Mesland rule out this option: "For it seems to me that a great light in the intellect is followed by a great inclination in the will, so that if we see very clearly that a thing is good for us, it is very difficult — and, on my view, impossible as long as one continues in the same thought — to stop the course of our desire" (CSMK 233).[47] Here, too, Descartes admits that when we are presented with a clearly known good, a contrary action — one in which we do not pursue the good — is impossible "as long as one continues in the same thought." Hence, categorically, we cannot do otherwise.

If we combine the information from the 1644 and 1645 letters to Mesland, it seems reasonable to suggest that the distinction between moral and absolute alternatives is *the same as* the distinction between categorical and hypothetical alternatives; that absolute alternatives simply are hypothetical alternatives. As I noted, the essential feature of categorical (or moral) alternatives is that one must be able to do otherwise *in the exact same set of circumstances*, with the same history and the same governing laws. On the other hand, what is essential to absolute (or hypothetical) alternatives is simply that they are *noncategorical*. Clearly, if INL — or determinism — is true, we sometimes lack categorical alternatives. Therefore, whether or not Descartes is able to escape the external problem comes down to whether we think categorical alternatives, as opposed to absolute ones, are *genuine alternatives* — the kind necessary for free will.

Since it is the best-known compatibilist theory of alternatives, it is reasonable to suppose that Descartes might offer an analysis like SHA in the 1645 letter to Mesland. The *Cartesian analysis*, as I call it, can be stated as follows:

> "S could have done otherwise" = df. "S would have done otherwise if S had considered it a good thing to demonstrate that he had free will."

This is the third option, and though it sheds some light on Descartes's theory, the illumination is not necessarily advantageous. For consider this counterexample to SHA. Suppose that Sam is a kleptomaniac and steals a piece of candy. It may be true that *if Sam had chosen not to steal the candy, then he would not have stolen it*, but our feeling that Sam lacks freedom is precisely due to our thought that he could not have *chosen* differently. The conditional is true, but he could not have done otherwise. Therefore, SHA is deficient. Similar remarks can be made about the Cartesian analysis, for we may ask: could S have considered it a good thing to demonstrate that he had free will? Descartes does seem to think that such considerations are "always open to us," but we might well wonder what reason there is for believing this. Since there is nothing to warrant that S *could* always consider a demonstration of free will a good thing, the analysis cannot guarantee that S has alternatives.[48]

It's important not to make too much of these observations. They should not, for instance, lead us to automatically reject all compatibilist theories of alternatives. Clearly there is room in logical space between SHA-type analyses and categorical alternatives, and a great deal, if not all, of this room is left for the compatibilist. At most we can only conclude that single conditional analyses of alternatives are defective. Of course, any noncategorical account of alternatives will involve conditionals of some sort. But it is incorrect to burden the compatibilist with single conditionals like the ones in SHA and the Cartesian analysis.[49]

This brings me to the fourth and final way in which Descartes might respond to the external problem. His comments should not be construed as putting forth an *analysis* — a set of necessary and sufficient conditions — for such a formal approach is not needed. I think he can rebut the external problem as long as he provides an opposing account of alternatives that is better than the one offered by the incompatibilist. That he has a different account is clear from his distinction between categorical (or moral) and absolute alternatives. What is essential to Descartes's theory is his endorsement of the following:

> S could have done other wise only if (1) S would have done otherwise if S had different reasons and (2) S would have had different reasons if certain aspects about the past had been different.

The claim that we can always "consider it a good thing to demonstrate the freedom of will" is, therefore, best understood as an *example*, one way in which we could come to have different reasons but not the only way. Statement (2) is meant to include this example but to include others, too. As such, the account offered by Descartes is not intended to provide sufficient conditions for having alternatives. For instance, it is logically possible for Sam, the kleptomaniac, to come up with a reason that would prevent him from stealing the candy, but this should not lead us to believe that he could have avoided stealing the candy. Still, (1) and (2) might make up necessary conditions.

Now, why should we think that Descartes's account provides a satisfactory understanding of genuine alternatives? Mainly because the incompatibilist cannot offer a better one. For instance, if we tried to construct a formal analysis of categorical alternatives, along the lines of SHA, we'd get the following:

> "S could have done otherwise" = df. "S would have done otherwise if the circumstances were exactly the same."

But this cannot be what is meant. A more accurate understanding would yield this:

> "S could have done otherwise" = df. "S could have done otherwise in the exact same set of circumstances."

Yet as an analysis, this is inadequate since what we want to know is what it means to say that one *can* do otherwise in the exact same set of circumstances.

If we suppose that there is no compatibilist analysis of alternatives, libertarians and compatibilists are on equal ground, for clearly the former has none to offer.[50] Of course, they both share certain pretheoretical conceptions and agree on at least *some* formal developments. Together these are helpful in determining that certain accounts — like SHA — are wrong. But none of this is sharp enough when it comes to choosing between categorical and absolute alternatives. Consider, for instance, the counterexample to SHA. We know that kleptomaniacs, like Sam, lack alternatives, but we do not know if they lack *categorical* ones. The example is not rich enough to tell us whether Sam has alternatives in the categorical or absolute sense. Now, if a formal analysis of alternatives cannot be given, we do not have a clear sense of what might be missing from the noncategorical accounts. So then, how could we know that these accounts lack something essential to free will? On what basis could we determine that absolute alternatives are, in some way, inadequate?

One might say that Descartes's theory is faulty because absolute alternatives are not genuine alternatives; categorical ones are. But this clearly begs the question, for how are we to know which alternatives *are* the kind that are necessary for free will? One could also point out that Descartes has not proven that absolute alternatives are genuine alternatives, so his claim is left unsupported. But as I noted, the incompatibilist is no better off in this respect. Presumably, such a justification would require an analysis of alternatives, and we are supposing that there is none available, categorical or otherwise.

Perhaps there is a difference between categorical and absolute alternatives in that the latter have been ruled out by the argument for incompatibilism, noted above. But if we look carefully, we can see that this is not so. According to the logic of the argument for incompatibilism, I cannot do otherwise, given determinism, unless I can alter either the past or the laws of nature. But a compatibilist can reject this. All that need be the case is that the past or laws of nature could have, in some absolute sense, been otherwise, not that I could have done anything to change either of them. This is the significance of clause (2) in Descartes's account. Following Lehrer and Lewis, we can distinguish between these two assertions:

> *Weak thesis*: I am able to do something such that, if I did it, the past would be different.
> *Strong thesis*: I am able to change the past.[51]

The compatibilist accepts the weak thesis, not the strong one. But it is the strong thesis that is needed for the argument for incompatibilism to be sound.[52]

So far I have suggested that categorical and absolute alternatives are on a par, but there is at least one important difference. When it comes to supporting our judgments of free will and moral responsibility, absolute alternatives have a distinct advantage. Consider, for instance, the case of Sam, the kleptomaniac. I cannot imagine how we could even begin to determine whether or not Sam lacks categorical alternatives, although I would hope that we can conclude that he lacks genuine alternatives and is, therefore, neither free nor morally responsible for his actions. After all, it is this judgment that caused us to reject SHA in the first place. Sam might well be a kleptomaniac even though he performs quite random acts that are not a consequence of the past and the laws of nature. That is, he might have categorical alternatives and yet be neither free nor morally responsible for his actions.

Here's where absolute alternatives are vastly superior. The judgment that Sam lacks alternatives is related to considerations of what Lehrer calls "circumstantial variety": "The greater the variety of circumstances under which we have seen the person perform an action, the more justified we are in claiming to know that he can perform it."[53] It is precisely because Sam tends *always* to steal — no matter what reasons he has before him or what situation he encounters — that we regard him as not having alternatives, not being free, and not being responsible for his actions. Of course, we can imagine situations where his actions might differ, but none of these are *accessible* to Sam. More important, the notion of accessibility seems unrelated to categorical alternatives.[54] It is not simply that Sam, as he is at this moment, with his past and the laws of nature tied to him, cannot do otherwise but also that Sam's actions would be no different even if we were to alter most of the circumstances surrounding them. We would have to radically alter Sam's past before we could gain the vari-

ability apparent in so-called "normal" cases. And it is these reflections about differing counterfactual situations — including those alterations of the past essential to absolute alternatives — that motivate our attributions of free will and moral responsibility. In this respect, determining what Sam could have done in the *exact same*
situation is of little help.

Of course, there is more to say on this issue. Ultimately one needs to completely
specify the difference between proper and improper alterations of the past in order
to determine whether or not Sam has genuine alternatives,[55] but there is little reason to think that categorical alternatives are required in order to do so. Thus, there
is good reason to think that Descartes offers a plausible solution to the conflict between two-way compatibilism and INL: INL deprives us of categorical alternatives
but not absolute ones, and only the latter are necessary for free will. Though
Descartes has not told us everything we need to know about the nature of the will, it
seems to me that he has not left anything out that an incompatibilist has more clearly
explained. More important, it is in those areas where Descartes's theory is lacking
that much of the work on free will is still taking place.[56]

## Notes

1. Chappell 1994, p. 180. See also Kenny 1972, p. 17; Cottingham 1993, pp. 65–66, 87;
Beyssade 1994, p. 194.

2. Chappell, p. 181. See also Kenny, p. 31; Cottingham, p. 65; Chappell, p. 189.

3. See Kenny, p. 31; Imlay 1982, pp. 91–2.

4. See Kenny, pp. 29–30; Beyssade, p. 205; Cottingham, pp. 64–65.

5. Cottingham 1993, 64–65.

6. Imlay, p. 89. See also Cottingham, 64–65. Imlay thinks that this inconsistency can be
resolved but at the cost of suggesting that INL is "in the final analysis incoherent as far as
Descartes is concerned" (p. 87; see also pp. 94–96). This doesn't strike me as much of a resolution.

7. For a discussion of these problems, see Chappell 1994, 184 and 190.

8. Two-way compatibilism is similar to that which I have previously called "strong compatibilism" (Campbell 1997). For examples, see Hume 1975, Moore 1912, Lehrer 1976, Lewis
1981, and Campbell 1997.

9. See Beyssade 1994. The name "one-way compatibilism" is derived, in part, from comments made to me by Stephen Voss and is similar to what I have previously called "weak compatibilism" (Campbell 1997). For examples, see Frankfurt 1971 and Fischer 1994.

10. Most of the definitions used in this section are taken from three sources: Lewis 1981;
van Inwagen 1983; Kane 1985.

11. See, especially, Campbell 1957.

12. Kane 1985, 19–20.

13. See van Inwagen 1983, 8, and Chappell 1995, 273.

14. Moore 1912, 87. Libertarians tend to embrace the requirement of alternative possibilities since this is the likely basis for their incompatibilism. Also many important compatibilists have done so (see Lehrer 1976; Hume 1975; Moore; and, I argue, Descartes). Even many
one-way compatibilists who think that free will is not essential to moral responsibility generally think that it requires alternatives, though some other, more relevant freedom might not
(see Fischer 1994). Spinoza, who denies FT, does so, in part, because free will requires alternatives (Curley; E IIP48).

15. Lewis 1981, 113. See also van Inwagen 1983, 13–14. At the suggestion of Bennett, I avoid use of the terms "hard" and "soft determinism" since they often mislead people into thinking that it is the *determinism* that is hard or soft, which is not the case.

16. See Chappell 1994, 189–190. See also CSM I, 201, 240.

17. This term is first used in Delahunty 1985 but appears in the appendix to Bennett 1984, and the references suggest that Bennett intended it to have the meaning I give it. See also Edwin Curley and Gregory Walski, in this volume.

18. This is a slightly altered version of "the Consequent Argument" in van Inwagen 1983, 16.

19. Ibid., p. 93.

20. For criticisms see Lehrer 1980, 199, and Lewis 1981.

21. Vere Chappell writes: "The inability of the mind to be mistaken when it affirms what it clearly and distinctly perceives is the ultimate basis of secure human knowledge" (Chappell 1994, 182). For a more detailed discussion of INL and its importance to the *Meditations*, see Kenny 1972, 19ff. and, especially, 29.

22. See Campbell 1957 and, for a criticism, see Lehrer 1966.

23. Note that this use of the term "libertarian," standard among contemporary writers on free will, is different from the meaning given to it in Chappell 1994.

24. See Campbell 1957, Taylor 1963, and Chisholm 1964.

25. See Lehrer 1976, 267, for an argument against this position, though it is generally accepted by both compatibilists and incompatibilists. The term "adequate cause" is from Spinoza (Curley; E IIID1ff.).

26. The Latin is "Neque enim opus est me in utramque partem ferri posse" (AT 57).

27. Beyssade 1994, 193ff.

28. Ibid., pp. 194–195.

29. Ibid., p. 205; see also 201.

30. See Beyssade 1994, 194, and Cottingham 1993, 65, for a translation similar to Beyssade's. See also Kenny 1972, 18–19, who advocates Peter Geach's translation, which is similar to the CSM II version. Interestingly enough, the CSM II translation of the *Meditations* is Cottingham's own, so by 1993 he seems to have changed his mind about this passage.

31. See Beyssade 1994, 203; Kenny 1972, 29–30; Imlay 1982, 93. It was Russell Wahl, however, who convinced me of the significance of this passage in his comments about a previous version of this chapter.

32. Lehrer 1976, 243.

33. Chappell 1994, 181.

34. Hume 1978, 407; see also Kenny 1972, 17; Imlay 1982, 88–89

35. Kenny 1972, 17.

36. Ibid., p. 17.

37. Ibid., pp. 28–29. See Cottingham 1993, 65, for a similar mistake.

38. James 1948, 44.

39. See Campbell 1957, 158–179.

40. See Hume 1975, 95, and Moore 1912, 84–95. Moore is often thought to be the father of the standard hypothetical analysis, which immediately follows. However, Moore's explication of alternatives is different in important respects from the more standard one, although the difference has often gone unnoticed. For Moore's account, see especially p. 94.

41. See Lehrer 1980, 187. Lehrer, of course, rejects this analysis.

42. Hume 1975, 95.

43. This table paints in broad strokes; I am not suggesting that it represents all views of human freedom. Consider, for instance, the theories of Spinoza and Keith Lehrer. Spinoza is a necessitarian of a sort that at least rejects free will in the traditional sense. Still, he gives

an account of freedom that is explicable in terms of adequate causes (Curley; E III, V). Lehrer is a compatibilist who hints at explaining freedom of spontaneity in terms of original causes (Lehrer 1976, 266–268). But even these detractors are best understood in light of the three kinds of freedom and the ways in which they diverge from more traditional paths.

44. This way of understanding Cartesian alternatives was first made clear to me by Russell Wahl, who attributed it to Jean-Marie Beyssade. See also Imlay 1982, 92ff. for a presentation, and then a rejection, of a similar line of thought, which he claims is held by Jean Lapport.

45. See Cottingham 1993, 64–65.

46. For an example of this mistake, see Imlay 1982.

47. Russell Wahl brought this quotation to my attention, though he thinks it does my view more harm than good.

48. See Lehrer 1976, 248–250. I thank Michael O'Rourke, Geoffrey Gorham, and Stephen Voss for convincing me that the Cartesian analysis is no better than SHA.

49. See Lehrer 1980.

50. For compatibilist analyses of alternatives that have not, to my knowledge, been refuted, see Lehrer 1976 and Campbell 1997.

51. See Lehrer 1980, 199, and Lewis 1981, 115.

52. According to the incompatibilist argument, alternatives are closed under entailment; according to the compatibilist, they are not. The issue of whether or not the incompatibilist argument is sound is indistinguishable from questions about the logic of "can" and its cognates.

53. Lehrer 1966, 175.

54. For more on accessibility, see Campbell 1997.

55. See Lehrer 1976 and Campbell 1997.

56. Much of the research for this project was completed while attending Jonathan Bennett's 1995 NEH Summer Seminar. I thank the National Endowment for the Humanities for support and Bennett and others attending the seminar for useful discussions. For written comments, I thank Bennett; Daniel Flage; Geoffrey Gorham; David Shier; Stephen Voss; Russell Wahl, who commented on a version of the chapter read at the 1997 Northwest Conference on Philosophy; and especially, Michael O'Rourke, who made extensive remarks on each of my many drafts. Finally, I thank the faculty and students of Washington State University and the University of Idaho who were in the audience for an earlier talk I gave on this subject.

## References

Bennett, Jonathan. 1984. *A Study of Spinoza's* Ethics. Indianapolis: Hackett.

Beyssade, Michelle. 1994. "Descartes's Doctrine of Freedom: Differences between the French and Latin Texts of the Fourth Meditation." In Cottingham 1994.

Campbell, C. A. 1957. *On Selfhood and Godhood*. London: George Allen and Unwin.

Campbell, Joseph Keim. 1997. "A Compatibilist Theory of Alternative Possibilities." *Philosophical Studies* 88: 319–330.

Chappell, Vere. 1994. "Descartes's Compatibilism." In Cottingham 1994.

Chisholm, Roderick. 1964. "Human Freedom and the Self." Department of Philosophy, University of Kansas. The Lindley Lecture: 3–15.

Cottingham, John. 1993. *A Descartes Dictionary*. Oxford: Blackwell Publishing.

——, ed. 1994. *Reason, Will, and Sensation*. Oxford: Clarendon Press.

Delahunty, R. J. 1985. *Spinoza*. London: Routledge and Kegan Paul.

Fischer, John Martin. 1994. *The Metaphysics of Free Will*. Oxford: Blackwell Publishers.

Frankfurt, Harry G. 1971. "Freedom of the Will and the Concept of a Person." *Journal of Philosophy*, 68: 5–20.

Hume, David. 1975. *An Enquiry Concerning Human Understanding*, 3rd edition, edited by L. A. Selby-Bigge, revised by P. H. Nidditch. Oxford: Oxford University Press.

———. 1978. *A Treatise of Human Nature*, 2nd edition, edited by L. A. Selby-Bigge, revised by P. H. Nidditch. Oxford: Oxford University Press.

Imlay, Robert A. 1982. "Descartes and Indifference." *Studia Leibnitiana*, 14: 87–97.

James, William. 1948. "The Dilemma of Determinism." In his *Essays in Pragmatism*. New York: Hafner Publishing Company.

Kane, R. 1985. *Free Will and Values*. Albany: State University of New York Press.

Kenny, Anthony. 1972. "Descartes on the Will." In *Cartesian Studies*, edited by R. J. Butler. New York: Barnes and Noble.

Lehrer, Keith. 1966. "An Empirical Disproof of Determinism?" In *Freedom and Determinism*, edited by K. Lehrer. New York: Random House.

———. 1976. "'Can' in Theory and Practice: A Possible Worlds Analysis." In *Action Theory*, edited by M. Brand and D. Walton. Dordrecht: D. Reidel.

———. 1980. "Preferences, Conditionals and Freedom." In *Time and Cause*, edited by P. van Inwagen. Dordrecht: D. Reidel.

Lewis, David. 1981. "Are We Free to Break the Laws?" *Theoria* 47: 113–121.

Moore, G. E. 1912. *Ethics*, chapter 6. New York: Oxford University Press.

Taylor, Richard. 1963. *Metaphysics*, first edition. Englewood Cliffs: Prentice-Hall.

van Inwagen, Peter. 1986. *An Essay on Free Will*. Oxford: Clarendon Press.

## 9

ERIC SOTNAK

# The Range of Leibnizian Compatibilism

## Introduction

Leibniz was a kind of determinist, and he believed that at least some created substances are free in their choices. He also believed that there is a sense in which God, too, is determined and is free in his choices. This makes Leibniz some sort of compatibilist. The aim of this chapter is to clarify just what sort of compatibilist Leibniz was and to examine the reasons for which he thought freedom and determinism compatible.[1] The picture is complicated by the fact that "determinism" is not univocal, and in some senses of the term Leibniz was not a compatibilist, although in other senses he was.

Incompatibilism cannot plausibly be defended simply by asserting that determinism implies absence of freedom. Arguments are required to show precisely why determinism implies such an absence. An examination of the structure of Leibniz's arguments regarding various deterministic threats to freedom turns up two basic forms of incompatibilist argument. The first is that determinism deprives agents of the power to perform alternatives to the actions they actually perform. The demand placed on the compatibilist, then, is to explain how the absence of such power fails to negate freedom. A compatibilist view that provides a satisfactory response to this concern may be said to meet the *alternatives requirement*. The second basic form of incompatibilist argument is that determinism renders all actions compelled. The challenge to the compatibilist is to explain why determinism does not constitute a form of compulsion. A compatibilist view that provides a satisfactory explanation along these lines may be said to meet the *no-compulsion requirement*.[2]

Determinism may be described very generally as the thesis that, given a set of initial conditions[3] for a world and a set of laws that governs all changes in that world from the set of initial conditions, there is only one possible future for the world. By specifying different characterizations of laws of change and initial conditions, it is possible to generate different varieties of determinism.

## Necessitarian Determinism and Compatibilism

Although it is not usually considered a form of determinism, it is possible to identify a position that we may call *necessitarian determinism*. According to necessitarian determinism (more commonly known simply as "necessitarianism"), the set of initial conditions encompasses all things in the universe (material or otherwise) and the laws of change are considered to be the only laws of change that are logically possible. If the set of initial conditions should prove to be logically necessary as well, there would then be only one logically possible future (indeed, only one logically possible history) for the universe. A philosopher[4] who took very seriously the thesis that God is a necessary being from whose nature all things follow with strict necessity would be classified as a necessitarian determinist.

Leibniz did not accept necessitarian determinism, nor was he a necessitarian compatibilist (that is, if necessitarian determinism *were* true, Leibniz would say that there would be no freedom). He insists that at one time he was at least close to accepting both necessitarian determinism and necessitarian compatibilism.

> I [once] found myself very close to the opinions of those who hold everything to be absolutely necessary; believing that when things are not subject to coercion even though they are to necessity, there is freedom, and not distinguishing between the infallible, or what is known with certainty to be true, and the necessary. (F de C 178; L 263)

Leibniz claims that he was persuaded to abandon necessitarian determinism because one can conceive alternate possible configurations of reality. That is, things can be conceived to have been otherwise than they actually are. Therefore (since whatever is conceiveable without contradiction is possible), things could have been otherwise than they actually are. Leibniz does not, however, provide a reason here for rejecting necessitarian *compatibilism*. That is, he never explains what is wrong with the view that a compatibilist need only satisfy the no-compulsion requirement and that the way to do so is to draw a distinction between what is both necessary and coerced and what is necessary but not coerced. Instead we find him arguing that *because* some truths are merely contingent, there is *therefore* an explanation for free events.

> I hold a notion of possibility and necessity according to which there are some things that are possible, but not yet necessary, and which do not really exist. From this it follows that a reason that always forces a free mind to choose one thing over another (whether that reason derives from the perfection of a thing, as it does in God, or from our imperfection) does not eliminate our freedom. (Gr 288; AG 20)

To this one might reply, glibly, that of course if it is a *free* mind that is so forced to choose, then *of course* that does not eliminate freedom since it has been stipulated that the mind is free. However, as we will see later, Leibniz often says that those minds are free that possess intelligence. Substituting "intelligent" for "free" nicely avoids the glib response. Having rejected the glib response, however, one is hard pressed to see just how it follows from Leibniz's notion of necessity and possibility that freedom is not eliminated by the mind's being forced to choose one thing over another by reason (more on this later). A reconstruction of Leibniz's argument in the foregoing text is as follows:

### Argument A

(1) A reason always forces an intelligent mind to choose one thing A over another thing B.
(2) In at least some such cases, B remains metaphysically possible even though A is chosen.
(3) Therefore, in at least some cases, intelligent minds make free choices.

Since this is clearly a non sequitur, it would be unfortunate if this were really the argument Leibniz intends to give. Contingency alone is not enough to establish freedom (other commentators have noted this as well).[5] Leibniz often writes as though he believes that contingency alone *is* sufficient to establish freedom, but it is also possible to interpret him as arguing only that contingency is a necessary, but not sufficient, condition for freedom.

A more charitable reconstruction would run as follows:

### Argument B

(1) For every choice there is a reason such that the reason determines (forces) the choice.
(2) At least some such reasons are contingent.
(3) Therefore, at least some choices are contingent (not metaphysically necessary).
(4) Freedom is impossible only if all choices are metaphysically necessary.
(5) Therefore, freedom is not impossible.

Reconstructed in this way, the argument aims only at rescuing the possibility of freedom. It might seem, however, that premise (4) is too strong. Surely there are conditions other than metaphysical necessity that render freedom impossible (such as compulsion or, perhaps, material determination). The problem with this objection, however, is that it hinges on a too weak understanding of "impossible." What is at issue is not whether freedom is possible under this or that set of circumstances but rather whether freedom is ever possible at all; what is at issue is the absolute (metaphysical) impossibility of freedom. Thus, by rejecting necessitarian determinism, Leibniz has rescued only the metaphysical possibility of freedom. Other conditions, perhaps, must also be met if freedom is to be not merely possible but also sometimes actual. If Leibniz does think that other conditions are necessary, he does not give us here any clear indication what they might be.

One still wishes to know the rest of the story concerning the connection between contingency and freedom. Even where such a story appears to be forthcoming, however, it often fails to satisfy. Having observed that there exist possible things that never become actual, Leibniz argues as follows: "Even if God does not will something to exist, it is possible for it to exist, since, by its nature, it could exist if God were to will it to exist" (Gr 289; AG 20). If Leibniz does wish contingency alone to establish freedom, this passage would seem to bring him perilously close to viciously circular reasoning. The circularity resides in the claims that God is free because what exists is contingent, and that what is contingent is so because God was free to have willed other things to exist instead. The best hope of escape from this circle is to hold that contingency does not depend on the divine will. We will see shortly that, in fact, this is what Leibniz does hold. Once contingency is defended, an argument for divine freedom is fairly easy to come by. On pain of heresy, Leibniz would have had to accept that God (being omnipotent) has the power to do whatever is logically possible. Since there are logically possible things that are not actual, it follows that God had the power to have created them instead of the things he actually did create. For example, although there is no planet Vulcan located between Mercury and the Sun, there could have been such a planet. God, in creating the universe, could have plopped in an extra planet if he had thought it a good idea.[6] Since Vulcan is possible and since God can do whatever is possible, God could have created Vulcan if only he were to will it. Since alternate possibilities exist for God, then, the alternatives requirement is satisfied, thus rescuing freedom from jeopardy in that respect.

Just when things seem to be going well for establishing the connection between contingency and freedom through alternate exercise of the will, however, Leibniz acknowledges that God cannot will the creation of anything other than what he has in fact willed to create, for his will is determined by his nature (moral perfection), and thus God cannot will otherwise than to create the best possible ordering of things:

> "But God cannot will [any nonactual possible thing] to exist." I concede this, yet, such a thing remains possible in its nature, even if it is not possible with respect to the divine will, since we have defined as in its nature possible anything that, in itself, implies no contradiction, even though its coexistence with God can in some way be said to imply a contradiction. (Gr 289; AG 20)

In other words, Leibniz defines the necessary as that whose contrary implies a contradiction, and the contingent (or possible) as that whose contrary does not imply a contradiction. Since God's choosing to create a given nonactual possible thing does not imply a contradiction, it is merely contingent that he does not choose to create it. Either nonactual possibilities exist but it is metaphysically impossible that God choose them, or God chooses from among the nonactual possibilities. The first alternative is heretical, so the second remains. Leibniz even thinks he can establish on independent grounds that the first alternative is false by arguing that only what implies a contradiction is metaphysically impossible, and it implies no contradiction to say that God might have chosen otherwise than he actually did (Gr 288; AG 20). In other words, although God *will not* choose some things because they would be imperfect, it still remains within God's power to choose them since God's power extends to anything that is logically possible. If this defense of God's freedom seems inadequate, perhaps it is because Leibniz's defense rests on a weak satisfaction of the alternatives requirement. Leibniz has argued that since alternatives are not logically impossible for God, there is therefore no threat to freedom.

One way to bolster Leibniz's argument here would be to argue that once necessitarian determinism has been refuted, there is no further obstacle standing in the way of divine freedom. That is, in the case of God, the only coherent threat to divine freedom is necessitarian determinism. If Leibniz did think that necessitarian determinism is the only coherent threat to divine freedom, it should no longer come as a surprise that his arguments for divine freedom appear more to be arguments for contingency. There is some small support for this reading of Leibniz. In *Theodicy*, section 235, Leibniz says: "For God chooses among the possibles, and for that very reason he chooses freely, and it is not compelled; there would be neither choice nor freedom if there were but one course possible" (G VI, 258; T 272). This passage shows clearly that Leibniz was committed to the view that freedom requires both absence of compulsion and the existence of alternatives. Since choice requires the existence of alternatives from which to choose, and necessitarian determinism denies the existence of such alternatives, necessitarian determinism implies the absence of choice, and where there is no choice, there is compulsion. Where there is compulsion, there is no freedom. Thus necessitarian incompatibilism is true. Fortunately, however, necessitarian determinism is false. Although I think the claim that only necessity could compel God in his choices requires more defense, I will not indulge in further discussion of that here.

Even if Leibniz has managed to defend divine freedom (or at the very least the possibility of it) by refuting necessitarian determinism, the same strategy seems wholly unhelpful for human freedom. It may be the case that the only coherent threat to divine freedom is necessitarian determinism, but the same cannot be said for human freedom. There are other forms of determinism that must be reckoned with.

## Material Determinism and Compatibilism

The most familiar variety of determinism is what I will here call *material determinism*.[7] According to material determinism, there is a set of initial conditions that comprise the material configuration of the universe and a set of laws of change that are laws describing the ways all material objects in the universe must behave under certain conditions — laws of nature. When applied to the initial conditions, the laws of nature permit exactly one material history for the universe.

Leibniz sometimes talks as though he accepted material determinism. He tells us that all changes in bodies "arise from each other according to the laws of efficient causality, that is, of motions" (L 637; G VI, 598). Since Leibniz also insisted that humans are capable of free actions and human bodies belong to the material world, he must, then, have been a material compatibilist. The problem for Leibniz is to answer the following incompatibilist argument:

*Argument C*

(1) If material determinism is true, then all human actions are compelled (by the determining conditions).
(2) If all human actions are compelled, no human actions are free.
(3) Therefore, if material determinism is true, then no human actions are free.

Things are not so simple as this, however. In Leibniz's view, bodies are mere phenomena; they do not constitute a metaphysically basic "level" of reality. This level of reality is made up of an infinite plurality of monads, or indivisible mental substances (G II, 517–520; AG 203–206),[8] some of which are intelligent minds. Material bodies, or phenomena, are in some manner founded on monads. The details of the relation between the metaphysically basic level of monads and the metaphysically derivative layer of bodies need not be hashed out for our present purposes. It is sufficient only to point out that monads and material bodies are different from one another in kind. To say that bodies are founded on monads is not to say that bodies are collections of monads. Monads are not material atoms but rather immaterial spiritual substances. What counts for our present purposes is that Leibniz thought that the framework of material causation was applicable only to bodies — not to monads and their perceptions: "It must be confessed . . . that perception and what depends on it are *inexplicable by mechanical reasons*, that is, by figures and motions" (*Monadology*, sect. 17; G VI, 609; L 644). Since choices depend on perceptions (the most basic states of monads), choices will be inexplicable for mechanical reasons (laws of material causation). That is, premise (1) of argument C is rejected on the grounds that the determining conditions do not apply to the choices of monads (throughout this chapter when I discuss the choices of monads, it should be clear that I am talking about intelligent and conscious monads, or what Leibniz calls "spirits" or "minds").

The reply to this defense is to insist on a distinction between human actions and the choices that motivate them. Human bodies are part of the material world, and the *actions* of human bodies (in contrast to the choices or decisions that we believe produce them) must be materially determined, along with the rest of the material bodies in the universe. If we are to think of the choices that produce human actions as free, the anti-Leibnizian argues, those actions cannot be materially determined. It won't do for Leibniz to insist that the actions are materially determined but the choices that produce them are not, for how can free choices possibly have any influence on what is materially determined? If material determinism is true with respect to human actions, then our choices must be causally impotent with respect to those actions.

Leibniz has at least two replies to this objection. The first is to deny that our choices really do influence bodily actions. The second is to deny that our actions are materially determined. I will examine each of these replies in turn. The denial of genuine influence of choices on actions is justified by Leibniz's doctrine of *preestablished harmony*. While the mind or soul belongs to the metaphysically basic level of monads and follows its own set of laws of appetition (discussed below), the body belongs to the level of phenomena and follows laws of material causation. The two levels run in parallel, so to speak, but do not actually influence each other:

> God has made each of the two substances from the beginning in such a way that though each follows only its own laws which it has received with its being, each agrees throughout with the other, entirely as if they were mutually influenced or as if God were always putting forth his hand, beyond his general concurrence. (G IV, 499; L 460)

Also:

> Nature has, as it were, an empire within an empire, a double kingdom, so to speak, of reason and necessity, or of forms and of the particles of matter. . . . These kingdoms are governed each by its own law, with no confusion between them, and the cause of perception and appetite is no more to be sought in the modes of extension than is the cause of nutrition and of the other organic functions to be sought in the forms or souls. But [God] . . . brings it about . . . that two very different series in the same corporeal substance respond to each other and perfectly harmonize with each other, just as if one were ruled by the influence of the other. (G IV, 391; L 409–410)

Since it is true that the mind does not causally influence the behavior of the body, it is no objection to point out that all the actions of the body are materially determined. God has ordained matters, from eternity, to be such that the mind freely makes the choices that it makes, and the body, materially determined though it may be, behaves just as if the choices of the mind exerted causal influence on it. The Leibnizian strategy here appears to be simply to grant argument C but to insist that even if no human bodily *actions* are free, human *choices* may yet be free, and presumably it is the freedom of choices that we should be concerned to preserve rather than freedom of actions.

The obvious anti-Leibnizian response here is to ask how it is possible for choices to be free yet still guaranteed to correspond to what has been materially determined. The Leibnizian answer is that such choices are also determined, though not materially determined. "There is just as much connection or determination amongst thoughts as amongst motions (since being determined is not at all the same as being forced or pushed in a constraining way)" (G II, 164; RB 178). At this point, the anti-Leibnizian will have to raise a new argument to show that the determinism that is operating at the monadic level is incompatible with freedom. A discussion of this must be postponed until later. There is another objection to the denial of choice-action influence that must be addressed here: if the two domains are really just *as if* they influenced one another, then might one not be able to predict the mind's free choices by appeal to material causes, and isn't this bad enough? For, one might claim, if it can be infallibly predicted that I will choose to perform some action, then I am not free in so choosing. Suppose that by appeal to the chain of material causes one predicts that my body will enter through the left of two doors. Then, might one not predict that my mind will freely choose to enter through the left door?[9] We can call this sort of prediction of choices by appeal to material causes *indirect prediction*. Although one might expect Leibniz simply to reject the argument from predictability to lack of freedom, he does not. Instead, he denies that such prediction is possible:

Free or intelligent substances . . . are not bound by any subordinate laws of the universe, but act as it were by a private miracle, on the sole initiative of their own power, and by looking towards a final cause they interrupt the connexion and the course of the efficient causes that act on their will. So it is true that there is no creature 'which knows the heart' which could predict with certainty how some mind will choose in accordance with the laws of nature; as it could be predicted . . . how some body will act, provided that the course of nature is not interrupted. For just as the course of the universe is changed by the free will of God, so the course of the mind's thoughts is changed by its free will: so that, in the case of minds, no subordinate universal laws can be established (as is possible in the case of bodies) which are sufficient for predicting a mind's choice. (C 20–21; MP 100–101)

A nice discussion of this is provided by R. Cranston Paull,[10] who extracts from this and similar texts what he calls the *theory of miraculous freedom*. The general idea here is this: according to Paull, the "subordinate universal laws" referred to are the laws of material causation. Now, not only are the choices of minds not determined by laws of material causation, but the laws that *do* determine their choices cannot be formulated as general universal principles, and such general universal principles are required for any creature to be able to make a genuine prediction (rather than a guess, however educated it may be). According to Leibniz, a miracle is an event that is not determined according to a subordinate law, but which is nevertheless determined: "Since nothing can happen which is not according to order, it can be said that miracles are as much subject to order as are natural operations, and that the latter are called natural because they conform to certain subordinate maxims which we call the nature of things" (G IV, 432; L 307). Each time a monad acts freely (acts on the basis of a free choice), that action cannot properly be subsumed under a subordinate law, or law of material causality, and therefore could not be predicted by any creature. It could be predicted only by God, and predictability by God is not incompatible with freedom (I will discuss Leibniz's reasons for holding this view later).

Several puzzles remain, however. First, why is predictability incompatible with freedom? Although the following argument does not seem to have much plausibility, it is an argument, I will argue, that Leibniz accepted.

### Argument D

(1) If it is possible for a creature[11] infallibly to predict an action, then that action is compelled.
(2) If an action is compelled, it is not free.
(3) Therefore, if it is possible for a creature infallibly to predict an action, then it is not free.

No justification is offered here for why one should accept premise (1) of this argument.[12] I will offer what I think is the reason in the section on psychological compatibilism. Even so, this will be an argument that must be extrapolated and is not explicitly given by Leibniz.

Second, Leibniz says that there are efficient causes that act on the will that are interrupted "by looking towards a final cause." What are these causes, and how are they interrupted? One possibility is that the efficient causes in question are the laws of material causation. Leibniz does say that all changes in bodies take place in accordance with "laws of efficient causality, that is, of motions" (L 637; G VI, 598). I have thus far been careful to speak of material causation to avoid presupposing that all efficient causation is material causation. I believe the most charitable interpretation of Leibniz's view is that *when dealing with bodies*, the efficient cause of a change in any given body is the motion of another body (or of several bodies). He does not intend to suggest that all efficient causation is the motion of bodies. It would seem very un-Leibnizian to maintain that laws governing material bodies also act on the will. The mind's ability to interrupt efficient causes pertains, rather, to psychological causes.[13] Further discussion of this and the ability to change the course of one's thoughts by free will are deferred to the section on psychological determinism.

A third puzzle is that the theory of miraculous freedom appears flatly inconsistent with the claim that all changes in bodies result from laws of material causation. Every time an intelligent monad performs an action based on a free choice, there will be a corresponding change in material bodies. That change cannot be explained by appeal to material causes since the free choice is miraculous; if prediction of the action were possible by material causes, then prediction of the choice would be possible (indirect prediction). Nor does it help to follow Paull in saying that miraculous actions of free creatures do not *break* the subordinate laws of material causality but are simply *above* them,[14] since Leibniz himself admits that miracles may be *contrary* to such subordinate laws (G II, 51; L 333), or that such laws may be "*repealed*" by God in cases of miracles (C 19; MP 99).[15] It is true that *choices* are above the laws of material causation since they belong to a distinct explanatory domain, but this does not help explain the changes in bodies (the actions) corresponding to such choices. This suggests a second way Leibniz might reply to argument C: he could deny that human actions (never mind choices) are materially determined at all.

If that were so, then what are we to make of Leibniz's explicit assertions that all changes in bodies are materially determined? It may be that Leibniz expresses his views in language that is stronger than he intends. Perhaps he would reply that when he says that the kingdom of bodies is governed only by laws of material causation, he simply omitted to add "except, of course, in the case of miracles, which, by the way, are as common as the performance of free actions by intelligent creatures." The world is chock-full of miracles. There is even some reason to think that this is Leibniz's intent:

> We do observe that everything in the world takes place in accordance with the laws of the eternal truths and not merely geometric but also metaphysical laws; that is, not merely according to material necessities, but also according to formal reasons. . . . [This] is true also when we descend to special cases and see the wonderful way in which metaphysical laws of cause, power, and action are present throughout all nature, and how they predominate over the purely geometric laws of matter themselves. (G VII, 305; L 488–489)

Perhaps, too, Leibniz's description of the two-layered metaphysic as a "empire *within* an empire*" (emphasis added) is meant to suggest that laws of material causality are to be considered a subset of the more general metaphysical laws of order, under which all phenomena, even the miraculous, are to be subsumed. And when Leibniz says: "I fully agree that all the particular phenomena of nature can be explained mechanically if we explore them enough and that we cannot understand the causes of material things on any other basis" (G IV, 391; L 409), he should be understood as claiming, really, that the only way in which *we* (lacking the acuity of the divine intellect) can understand the causes of material things is through the laws of material causation. It may also be that Leibniz is simply inconsistent on this point, claiming in some texts that all phenomena are materially determined and suggesting in other texts that human actions are not materially determined (though caution should be exercised in making allegations of inconsistency).

A final possibility is that Leibniz would deny the possibility of indirect prediction in the following way: although it is possible, in principle, to predict every human action by appeal to material causes, it is nonetheless impossible to predict the corresponding free choices. This is true because however complete one's knowledge of material causes may be, many possible mental states (at the level of monads) could correspond with the changes among phenomena (at the level of bodies), and nothing on the phenomenal level is sufficient to inform us which of these possibilities in fact obtains at the monadic level. Furthermore, not all such possible monadic states of affairs involve the free choice of the relevant monad. Therefore, indirect prediction of free choices from prediction of bodily behavior is impossible.

Leibniz thus has two primary options in answer to argument C. First, he can deny that human choices are compelled by material determinism since it applies only to bodies, and choices are made by monads. Second, he can deny that human bodily actions are materially determined. Human actions provide miraculous exceptions to laws of material causation. Strictly speaking, this evades the question of material incompatibilism. One may still ask whether freedom could exist if all human actions really *were* materially determined. We have seen that the same question can be asked about the argument for necessitarian determinism. And, as with necessitarian determinism, one may infer from the character of Leibniz's position that he accepts the truth of the conditional. That is, Leibniz would hold that universal material determinism (determination of choices, as well as actions) is incompatible with freedom. What is not yet clear is why this is so. In the case of necessitarian determinism, it is the absence of alternate possibilities that leads Leibniz to reject its compatibility with freedom. In the case of material determinism, however, such alternate possibilities do *not* appear to be absent. For even if it is materially determined that some action be performed, it is nonetheless metaphysically possible that the action not be performed. All that would have to be the case is that some alternate set of material causes obtains. For example, it may be materially determined that my body enters through the left of a set of doors, but it is surely metaphysically possible for it to go through the right door (all we need is to suppose a different set of causes, which determines the other possible action). What we will have to show is that although — as premise (4) of argument B states — freedom is *impossible* only where all choices are metaphysically necessary, there may be other conditions that render freedom absent.

The main reason, I think, that Leibniz accepts argument C is that, just as is the case under necessitarian determinism, material determinism (if it were truly universal) would leave no room for choice. But with the latter, it is not because alternate choices are metaphysically impossible that they are unavailable, nor is it even that they are unavailable, given the actual antecedent material conditions. Rather, material determinism is incompatible with alternate choices because it is incompatible with *any* choices at all. For Leibniz, I think, there is something about the nature of the mental that essentially precludes it from being even possibly subsumable under laws of material causes: "If we pretend that there is a machine whose structure enables it to think . . . one could think of it as enlarged . . . so that one could enter it as one does a mill. If we did this, we should find nothing but parts which push upon each other; we should never see anything which would explain a perception" (*Monadology*, sect. 17; G VI, 609; L 644). Since choices are based on perceptions, and thus irreducibly mental, material determinism, if true, would render all creatures (literally) mindless automata. And where there is no mind, there are no choices. Where there are no choices, there cannot be freedom.

## Divine Foreknowledge and Complete Concepts

Another potential threat to freedom comes from divine foreknowledge of future contingents. For example, God knew that Leibniz would choose to refuse communion on his deathbed. Since God's beliefs are infallible, God could not have been wrong in his beliefs about Leibniz's refusal of communion, and so Leibniz could not have failed to refuse communion. But if Leibniz could not have failed to refuse communion then it seems Leibniz was not free in refusing communion, since the alternatives requirement is not met.

Alvin Plantinga,[16] in defending the compatibility of divine foreknowledge and freedom, has pointed out that it is important not to confuse

(I) Necessarily, if God knows that S will do A, then S will do A.

with

(II) If God knows that S will do A, then, necessarily, S will do A.

Leibniz, too, was aware of the importance of this distinction[17] and also appeals to it in explaining why foreknowledge does not preclude freedom:

> Since every ordered series involves a rule for continuing, or a law of progression, God, by examining any part of the series whatsoever, sees in it everything that precedes and everything that follows. But this does not eliminate freedom in minds. For infallible certainty is different from absolute necessity, as St. Augustine, St. Thomas, and other learned men have known for a long time. (F de C 319; AG 132).

It is perfectly consistent to maintain that God knew infallibly that Leibniz would refuse communion and also that it was not absolutely (metaphysically) necessary that Leibniz do so. But, again, absence of metaphysical necessity alone is not sufficient for freedom. Leibniz has only shown that it is a mistake to take God's foreknowledge as necessitating what he foresees. That is, there is not yet any sound argument showing the incompatibility of freedom and foreknowledge.

Although both Leibniz and Plantinga begin their defense of the compatibility of freedom and foreknowledge in much the same way, their paths quickly diverge, and indeed, must do so. Plantinga endorses the alternatives requirement, and maintains that "if a person is free with respect to a given action, then . . . no antecedent conditions and/or causal laws determine that he will perform the action, or that he won't."[18] Leibniz, however, maintains that "there is just as much connection or determination amongst thoughts as amongst motions" (G V, 164; RB 178). Even more troubling, perhaps, is that according to Leibniz there is a unique complete concept of any given monad, constitutive of the essence of that monad, such that: "[this concept] once and for all includes everything which can ever happen to it and . . . in considering that concept, one can see everything which can truly be predicated of it, just as we can see in the essence of a circle all the properties which can be deduced from it" (G IV, 436; L 310).[19]

Just as one can give an argument for the incompatibility of foreknowledge and freedom, one can give an argument for the incompatibility of complete concepts and freedom. If it is contained in Leibniz's complete concept that he refuses communion, then Leibniz could not have failed to refuse communion, and so he was not free in doing so. Leibniz's response would be the same as to the foreknowledge argument, which is that there is no absolute necessity in his refusing communion. It is a mistake to think that Leibniz's complete concept *determines* him to refuse communion. Jonathan Bennett has pointed out to me that the complete concept doctrine is a semantic thesis and not a metaphysical thesis. This is quite right, just as divine foreknowledge is an epistemological rather than a metaphysical thesis. Even if this is so, however, an incompatibilist argument may still be made. The semantic thesis that each monad has a complete concept is inextricably bound up with a metaphysical thesis about all the different ways the world could be (just as is the epistemological thesis of divine foreknowledge). The metaphysical essence of a monad is expressed, in the mind of God, by a concept that describes that monad in such detail that all properties true of it may be deduced (by God) from the concept. Since refusing communion is contained in Leibniz's complete concept, and Leibniz has exactly one complete concept,[20] there is no possible world in which Leibniz exists and does not refuse communion on his deathbed. Unlike Plantinga, then, Leibniz cannot attribute to free individuals the ability both to perform and to refrain from performing an action. Instead, Leibniz simply sneaks freedom in the back door by stipulating that free choices/actions of monads are included in their complete concepts: "Adam sinning freely was seen of God among the ideas of the possibles, and God decreed to admit him into existence as he saw him" (*Theodicy*, sect. 231; G VI, 255; T 270). The mind of God contains the concepts of an infinite range of possible individuals, and God chooses, from eternity, to create a particular subset of these possible individuals. Once selected for creation, no monad has the power to change the properties it is determined to have.

It is of little help to appeal to a notion of other-world counterparts in explaining how individuals can be free. Although it is true that God could have created an individual very similar to Adam, except that the alternate possible Adam does not sin, this does not give the actual Adam the power to have refrained from sinning.[21] The following argument is apposite:

### Argument E

(1) If Adam had the power to refrain from sinning, then either Adam had the power to determine what was in his own complete concept or Adam had the power to cause God to choose to create some possible individual (a counterpart) instead of Adam.

(2) It is impossible for any created substance to cause God to have created in a way other than he did.

(3) No substance has the power to determine what is in its own complete concept.

(4) Therefore, Adam did not have the power to refrain from sinning.

Even if some counterpart theory could be defended that could explain how individuals might be said to have the power to behave otherwise than they do, Leibniz does not appear to appeal to counterparts in explaining human freedom. Rather, he seems more concerned to answer objections that his complete concept doctrine deprives God of the freedom to create the world as he saw fit (G II, 49–51; AG 71–73). Also, Leibniz insists that free actions are themselves contained in the complete concepts of substances. It is unlikely that in saying that free actions can be contained in complete concepts, Leibniz means to endorse something like this:

> A free action A is contained in a complete concept of a substance S if and only if there exists a counterpart of S, S*, whose complete concept contains S*'s refraining from performing A.

Rather, it seems likely that Leibniz thinks there are features intrinsic to actions themselves that render them free or unfree. In the section on appetitive determinism we will see what these features are.

Whether freedom is compatible, in Leibniz's views, with divine foreknowledge or the doctrine of complete concepts depends on the metaphysical foundation on which complete concepts and divine foreknowledge rest. Strictly speaking, then, the issue is whether or not freedom is compatible with Leibniz's metaphysical views on the nature of individual substances.

## Psychological Determinism and Compatibilism

Although Leibniz believed freedom to be compatible with divine foreknowledge, he did *not* believe freedom to be compatible with foreknowledge by any finite intelligence. This is somewhat peculiar considering his care to point out that divine foreknowledge does not impose an absolute necessity on actions. One would expect him to apply the same strategy to foreknowledge by finite intelligences. Instead, he maintains that just as there are no laws of material causation that would permit infallible prediction of free choices, so there are also no general psychological or metaphysical laws that would permit such infallible prediction. That is, if there were general psychological laws sufficient to determine the unique successor state for any given psychological state of a monad, a sufficiently intelligent creature would be capable of infallibly predicting the choice of that monad. If such predictability is incompatible with freedom, psychological determinism of this sort must, likewise, be incompatible with freedom. The threat of such general-law psychological determinism is eliminated by denying that any such prediction is possible.

Just as "there is no creature which 'knows the heart' which could predict with certainty how some mind will choose in accordance with the laws of nature" (C 20; MP 100), it is reasonable to suppose that infallible prediction in accordance with general psychological laws would be likewise ruled out. Most important, there is Leibniz's claim:

> The mind has this much physical indifference, that it is not even subject to physical necessity, far less metaphysical; that is, no *universal reason* or law of nature is assignable from which any creature, no matter how perfect and well-informed *about the state of this mind*, can infer with certainty what the mind will choose. (C 21–22; MP 102; my emphasis)

The term "physical necessity" here is misleading, for it suggests that Leibniz is speaking of what is necessary under material determinism. Indeed, Paull interprets "physical necessity" this way, arguing that "human freedom is [not compatible with] . . . physical/natural determinism," where physical/natural determinism is what I have called "material determinism."[22] If "physical necessity" means this, however, what are we to make of the following text?

> It is in a way a matter of physical necessity that God should do everything in the best way possible. . . . It is also a matter of physical necessity that those who are confirmed in the good—the angels or the blessed—should act in accordance with virtue, so that in certain cases, indeed, it could even be predicted with certainty by a creature what they should do. (C 21; MP 101)

If there is anything in the universe *not* governed by laws of material causality, surely it is God. Therefore we must not read "physically necessary" to mean "determined according to laws of material causation."[23] Fortunately, Leibniz explains what he does mean by the term: "Even if the world is not metaphysically necessary, such that its contrary would imply a contradiction or logical absurdity, it is nonetheless necessary physically, or determined in such a way that its contrary would imply imperfection or moral absurdity" (G VII, 304; L 488).

So Leibniz uses the term "physically necessary" as a synonym for what he elsewhere calls "moral necessity."[24] In saying that the mind has physical indifference in not being subject to physical necessity, then, Leibniz can mean one of two things. He might mean that the free choices of intelligent monads are not physically (morally) necessary at all, or he can mean that free choices of monads are not physically necessary relative to any general universal subordinate laws of the universe. He cannot mean the former, however. First, it would violate the principle of sufficient reason and the principle of the best. Second, in discussing the manner in which all free substances are predetermined in their choices, Leibniz says:

> All that is real in some ultimate determination of a free substance is necessarily produced by God, and I think that this fact covers what can reasonably be said about physical predetermination.[25] I understand a 'determination' to be produced when a thing comes into that state in which what it is about to do follows with physical necessity. (C 22; MP 102)

Since all free choices are predetermined in a manner that accords with physical necessity, it follows that all choices are physically necessary — necessary, that is, relative only to the ultimate designs of God. When Leibniz says that free minds are not subject to physical necessity, he can only mean that there is no general universal principle from which it can be demonstrated, and thus predicted with certainty by any finite intelligence, what such minds will choose. Only God can predict the free choices of minds with certainty, but not because he relies on general principles to make such predictions. Rather, God is able to see the very essence or nature of the creature, which is what properly determines its choices (even though the nature of the creature, in turn, ultimately derives from God).[26]

Then just why is predictability by a finite intelligence such a bad thing? That is, even if only God can infallibly predict choices of free minds, why would it bad if finite minds could do the same? One possibility is that if a mind's choices could be predicted by some general universal principle, such as a law of nature or a principle of psychological succession, such choices would then be *demonstrable*. And according to Leibniz, necessary truths are those that can be demonstrated by resolution into identities (Gr 302; AG 28; F de C 179; L 264). Therefore, if infallible prediction of choices were possible, they would be absolutely necessary, and as we have already seen, absolute necessity (necessitarian determinism) is incompatible with freedom.

This appears to be a bad argument, for it certainly seems possible to demonstrate or infallibly to predict some contingent truths. However, as the miraculous theory of freedom makes clear, truly infallible prediction is possible only when one is assured that no miracle will take place that will provide an exception to the general laws by means of which such a prediction must be made. Only God, however, ultimately has such assurance:

> When we present a choice to ourselves, for example, whether to leave or not to leave, given all the internal or external circumstances, motives, perceptions, dispositions, impressions, passions, inclinations taken together, there is a question as to whether . . . this true and determined proposition, that in all these circumstances taken together, I will choose to leave, is contingent or necessary. I reply that it is contingent, because neither I nor any other more enlightened mind could demonstrate that the opposite of this truth implies a contradiction. (G III, 401; AG 194)

In fact, however, the story is more complicated still. For not only are free choices not infallibly predictable by finite minds but also neither are natural phenomena.

> That this stone tends downwards when its support has been removed is not a necessary but a contingent proposition, nor can any such event be demonstrated from

the notion of this stone by the help of the universal notions which enter into it. . . .
For [God] alone knows whether he will suspend by a miracle that subordinate law
of nature by which heavy things are driven downwards. (C 20; MP 100)

Although it is true that infallible prediction by a creature would entail the demonstrability (and thus necessity) of the predicted choice, it is clear that Leibniz thinks choices are not predictable. Natural phenomena, however, are at least predictable "for the most part" since miraculous suspensions of the laws of material causation (the subordinate laws) are generally rare. Such "for the most part" prediction is impossible in the case of minds, however. The reason for this, I believe, is that if there were general psychological laws that would permit such prediction of choices by finite minds (in a manner analogous to the prediction of natural phenomena), the causes of such choices would have to rest outside the agent or else they would not be accessible to the predictor. And, as I will argue in the next section, freedom, for Leibniz, requires that the causes of those choices be internal to the agent. The primary source of freedom, then, is not so much the "miraculous" character of the choices made by intelligent creatures as it is the *spontaneity* of those choices, in the sense to be explained presently.

Necessitarian determinism, material determinism, and general-law psychological determinism are all incompatible with freedom. Since each of these varieties of determinism is false, however, there is no true threat to freedom, although Leibniz indicates that thoughts are determined.[27] It remains to specify precisely how thoughts are determined and how such determinism is compatible with freedom.


## Appetitive Determinism and Compatibilism

There is one form of determinism that Leibniz clearly accepted. For lack of a better term, I will call it "appetitive determinism." The basic states of monads are perceptions. The entire life of a monad is nothing but a series of continually changing perceptions. When a monad changes from one perception to another, the cause of such a change is entirely internal to the monad. Perceptual changes are not caused by anything outside the monad, except God, who is the ultimate cause of everything. However, God does not cause perceptual changes in monads on the fly, so to speak, but has rather set up the monad from creation so that the predetermined sequence of perceptions will unfold in perfect harmony with everything else in the universe. Leibniz calls this internally originated impulse of a monad to change from one perception to another "appetition" (G VI, 609; AG 215). Such appetitive changes are describable (at least in principle) by a law. Oversimplifying somewhat, let us say that for any given monad it is possible to specify a law that determines a unique sequence of perceptions for that monad. Let us call this the "appetitive law" for that monad.[28] Just as every monad has exactly one complete concept, so every monad has exactly one appetitive law. Appetitive determinism, then, is simply the thesis that the appetitive law for a monad determines only one sequence of perceptions for it.

The incompatibilist argument from appetitive determinism is straightforward. If all choices of a monad are determined by its appetitive law, then no alternative choices are possible for that monad; and without the power to make alternative choices, there can be no freedom (one might also argue that the appetitive law compels the choices of a monad).

A partial response to this argument is to define freedom in such a way that the existence of alternatives is not a requirement for freedom at all. Leibniz does, indeed, insist that free actions are contingent, rational, and spontaneous. The spontaneity requirement is likely to elicit some puzzlement[29] since, according to Leibniz, all perceptions of monads are spontaneous (*Theodicy*, sect. 291; G VI, 289; T 304). But Leibniz uses the term "spontaneous" in more than one way. In one sense, a monad acts spontaneously when all its perceptions derive from its appetitive law. In another sense, it acts spontaneously when the reason that may be said best to explain its perception is not found in conditions external to the monad. Wherever the reason that a monad performs an action is found in conditions external to the monad, that action is compelled. Of course, there is never any genuine external influence on any monad (*Monadology*, sect. 7; G VI, 607–808; L 643). Nevertheless, there are circumstances in which monads may be said to be active or passive with respect to each other. They are passive when their internal perceptual state is a mere response to what goes on in the world outside of them (G V, 195–196; RB 210). The perceptions of passive monads are thus spontaneous only in the first sense. But monads may also be said to be active when their perceptual state is not a mere response to or representation of the world outside them but is, instead, the product of rational activity. This is spontaneity in the second sense.

The spontaneity requirement, then, exists to satisfy the no-compulsion condition. A monad that is passive with respect to some external set of circumstances may be said to be compelled by those circumstances. Monads whose perceptions may be classified as active, however, are not so compelled, even though, in metaphysical strictness, the perceptions of all monads are spontaneous (i.e., in the first sense). In this way, the spontaneity requirement flows into the rationality requirement. A monad whose perceptions are rational may be said to be active rather than passive. And just as rationality admits of degrees, so, too, does activity. God, being supremely rational, is also supremely active, and since necessitarian determinism is false, God is supremely free. As long as a monad's perceptions are contingent, spontaneous, and rational, they are free from compulsion, and thus any choices such an intelligent monad makes are to be explained not by what is external to it but rather by what is internal to it. In this way Leibniz may be taken to hold a kind of agent-causation view of free actions; when changes in a monad's perceptions are best explained by conditions internal to it, it is the cause of its own actions.[30]

If Leibniz had taken contingency, spontaneity, and rationality to be jointly sufficient conditions for freedom, he would seem not to need to satisfy the alternatives requirement. Consider this argument:

### Argument F

(1) If appetitive determinism is true, then no one ever has the power to act otherwise than they do.

(2) If no one ever has the power to act otherwise than they do, then no one is ever free.

(3) Therefore, if appetitive determinism is true, then no one is ever free.

One would expect Leibniz to accept premise (1) of F and deny premise (2), relying on contingency, spontaneity, and rationality — again — to rescue freedom. Instead, Leibniz appears to accept premise (2) and seems to think he can give an account of how monads can have the power to do otherwise, even though doing otherwise is excluded by their complete concepts.

In *Discourse on Metaphysics*, section 30, Leibniz says: "In an absolute sense the will is in a state of indifference, insofar as this is the opposite of necessity, and *it has the power to act otherwise* or also to suspend its action entirely, since both alternatives are and remain possible" (G IV, 454; L 322; my emphasis).

This is a troubling passage, especially if we take very seriously Leibniz's assertion that alternatives not only are but also *remain* possible for a monad. For an alternative to "remain possible," one would think, the monad must have some sort of "access" to the possibility. Suppose that when Leibniz refused communion on his deathbed he had wondered whether it was possible for him to take communion instead. At that time, it was already specified in his appetitive law that he would refuse communion. Nevertheless, since God could have created a possible world in which Leibniz never existed, it is metaphysically possible that Leibniz might not have refused communion (although it is not metaphysically possible that Leibniz might have taken communion since a change in his complete concept or appetitive law would yield a metaphysically distinct individual).[31] But this does not establish that there is any sense in which refusing communion remains possible for Leibniz. Nor, again, does it seem helpful to appeal to a Leibniz counterpart in explaining how Leibniz might have had the power to accept communion.

It may be that Leibniz is simply inconsistent in his views on freedom, holding sometimes that all thoughts are determined by a unique appetitive law for each monad and sometimes that monads have a genuine power to make alternative choices to those they actually make. I do not think it is necessary to take this route, however. There is good reason to think that Leibniz believed he could hold both that appetitive determinism is true and that monads have the power to make alternative choices.

First, Leibniz insists that since the choices of intelligent monads cannot be demonstrated, they are contingent: "Now all the internal and external causes taken together bring it about that the soul is determined certainly, but not of necessity: for no contradiction would be implied if the soul were determined differently, it being possible for the will to be inclined, but not possible for it to be compelled by necessity" (*Theodicy*, sect. 371; G VI, 335; T 347). But for Leibniz, contingency is a strange thing. To say, for example, that there is no way to demonstrate that Adam sinned does not thereby imply that there is a possible world in which Adam does not sin. At best, there is some possible world where an individual *like* Adam does not sin. Nevertheless, intelligent monads may be said to act by their own power when their actions are spontaneous and rational. That is, to say that a monad acts by its own power is to say that the reason that determines it to act lies within the monad's own nature. Now, this seems to be an analysis of what it is for a monad to act by its own power, but it does not appear to be a satisfactory analysis of what it is for a monad to have the power to do otherwise. Nevertheless, Leibniz appears to think:

> A substance S has the power to do otherwise than x if and only if (i) there is no demonstration possible of S's doing x, and (ii) S's doing x is spontaneous and rational (i.e., S does x by its own power).

An account of power to do otherwise such as this appears indispensable if Leibniz is also to maintain, for example: "When God does leave it to a man [to determine and to be blamed for his own destruction], it has belonged to him since before his existence; it was already in the idea of him as still merely possible, before the decree of God which makes him to exist" (*Theodicy*, sect. 121; G VI, 175; T 195).

Second, if one is still troubled by the thought that one may be said to have the power to do something that one cannot really do, Leibniz will attempt to explain that this is not genuinely inconsistent. We have seen earlier that Leibniz believes that God chooses freely among infinite possible worlds which to create. Leibniz also maintains that it is physically (morally) necessary that God will create the best possible world, but there is no inconsistency here. There is a distinction between what is possible relative to God's will and what is possible relative to his power. God has the power to actualize every possibility. But his will infallibly determines him to choose only the best: "Power and will are different faculties, whose objects are also different. . . . All possibles are regarded as objects of [God's] power, but actual and existing things are regarded as the objects of his decretory will" (*Theodicy*, sect. 171; G VI, 216; T 233). Although God wills only the best through his nature, and thus could not will to create any world other than the one he has actually willed to create, it nevertheless remains within the scope of his power to create alternate worlds. From the standpoint of will, God cannot create alternate possibilities, but from the standpoint of power, he can. Possible things are possible by their own natures, but such natures have no existence independent of the divine intellect. Alternatives are possible for God because he chooses a particular series of contingent things from among an infinite range of possibles represented in his intellect. Such possibles cannot exist except through divine decree, and divine decrees are not necessitated. Thus each is within the scope of divine power. This is what I take Leibniz to mean when he says: "I set no limits on God's power, since I recognize that it extends *ad maxima, ad omnia*, to all that implies no contradiction" (*Theodicy*, sect. 227; G VI, 253; T 268). In other words, God has the power to do what he cannot will.

It may be that we can construe Leibniz's assertion that alternative choices are and remain possible for finite intelligences along analogous lines. Creatures also deliberate and choose from among actions that are represented to them in their own intellects as possible actions. That is, the intellect presents a set of putatively possible alternatives to the will, which then chooses among them. Of course, God knows which choices are truly possible relative to his own will, that is, which choices are predetermined in accordance with the monad's appetitive law, but the monad does not. Therefore, from the standpoint of the created intellect, there exist alternatives within the power of the creature to perform. Monads do not know which choices are appetitively determined until they make them, so from the standpoint of the finite intellect, they might as well be treated as though they are not determined:

> Could this soul, just before sinning, in good faith complain of God as if he determined it to sin? Since the determinations of God in such matters cannot be foreseen, how can the soul know that it is determined to sin unless it is already sinning in fact? . . . But can it be that it is assured from all eternity that I shall sin? Answer this for yourselves; perhaps it is not. (G IV, 454–455; L 322)

Although only one course of action is included in the complete concept or law of appetition of a monad, the monad does not know in advance which action is so included:

> If we do not always notice the reason which determines us, or rather by which we determine ourselves, it is because we are as little able to be aware of all the workings of our mind and of its usually confused and imperceptible thoughts as we are to sort out all the mechanisms which nature puts to work in bodies. (G V, 164; RB 178)

A monad that deliberates actively (spontaneously, i.e., determines itself) chooses from among a range of possibilities represented in its intellect, and in advance of such deliberation the will of the monad may be said to have the power to choose more than one alternative. That is, the will is appetitively determined to choose in a particular way, but the power of the monad extends beyond what is appetitively determined, to whatever is represented in the intellect as presumptively possible. For this reason, Leibniz thinks he can explain how appetitive determinism is compatible with having power to perform alternative actions. The sense in which alternative actions are and remain possible for a monad in a state of deliberation about an action is therefore epistemic possibility. Where it is epistemically possible that a monad choose not to do x, where it is contingent that the monad chooses to do x, where a monad is not compelled to do x, and where the monad consciously and rationally chooses to do x (i.e., does x by its own power), the monad is, in Leibniz's view, free in doing x.

Concern over the absence of *genuine* power to do otherwise, in the sense that there are alternate possible worlds where one does otherwise, is misplaced. One must remember and take comfort from the fact that God has elected to create the best world possible.

> The whole future is doubtless determined: but since we know not what it is, nor what is foreseen or resolved, we must do our duty, according to the reason which God has given us and according to the rules he has prescribed for us; and thereafter we must have a quiet mind, and leave to God himself the care for the outcome. (*Theodicy*, sect. 58; G VI, 134; T 154)

And "[thus] since we know nothing of what is foreseen, we should do our part without pausing over the useless question as to whether success is foreseen or not, all the more so since God is content with our good will when it is sincere and ardent" (Gr 364; AG 113). Furthermore, one may ask just what more one really wants in a theory of power to do otherwise. If one wants a sort of power that would allow the agent to choose either to do x or to refrain from doing x without any reason that determines the agent one way or another, one is asking for something impossible or, Leibniz thinks, incoherent (G II, 165; RB 180).[32]

## Summary

Leibniz rejected necessitarian, material, and psychological determinism (understood with respect to general universal psychological laws) and accepted necessitarian, material, and psychological incompatibilism. He also accepted appetitive determinism and appetitive compatibilism.

It only remains to assess the adequacy of Leibniz's compatibilist views, and I will restrict my remarks to just a few. It seems to me that Leibniz has done a fair job of addressing the no-compulsion requirement. Compulsion, for Leibniz, requires the absence of contingency, spontaneity, and rationality, so one's actions may be said to be caused by influences external to the agent. To the extent that one's actions originate from within one's own nature, one's actions are free. This is a Leibnizian brand of agent causation.

Leibnizian views on the alternatives requirement are another matter. He said he was once close to holding that "when things are not subject to coercion even though they are to necessity, there is freedom" (F de C 178; L 263). He had to abandon this view to avoid the heresy of depriving God of his liberty and power to create nonactual possibilities. It is substantially less clear, however, that the alternatives requirement needs to be satisfied in order to provide an account of human freedom. Still, Leibniz tries to satisfy it. Just as Leibniz distinguishes between God's will and power, holding that God has the power to actualize all possibilities but the will only to create the best, so Leibniz can maintain that finite intelligences have the power to perform actions that they are predetermined never to do. First, to say that some monad performs an action it is not determined to do is merely to express a falsehood; it is not to assert something contradictory (and therefore impossible). Second, monads do not know in advance what they are determined to do and choose. So just as God's power extends to possibilities represented in his intellect that his will prevents him from choosing, so the finite intellect may represent some actions to itself as possible even though its will is determined not to choose them.

Leibniz's account of power is not likely to be of much comfort to a sinner who suffers divine punishment. It is small consolation to be informed that although one was (appetitively) determined to sin and be punished, the sin and punishment are necessary components of a grand, divine scheme to create the best possible world. Nor is it much comfort to be informed that one could have avoided sinning because there is no way to *demonstrate* that one would sin. Finally, there is little solace in being told that one's sins are consequences of one's own nature and have not been imposed from without. Leibniz, I think, shares the discomfort at such thoughts, but when pressed he is simply unable to formulate an adequate response in terms permitted by his metaphysical commitments.[33]

## Notes

1. In addition to the editorial conventions for abbreviations adopted for this volume, I use the following abbreviations:

C = *Opuscules et fragments inédits de Leibniz.* Louis Couturat, ed. Paris 1903; Hildesheim: Georg Olms, 1966.

F de C = *Nouvelles lettres et opuscules inédits e* Leibniz. A. Foucher de Careil, ed. Paris: Auguste Durand, 1857.

Gr = *Textes inédits.* Gaston Grua, ed. Paris: Presses Universitaires des France, 1948.

MP = *Philosophical Writings.* Mary Morris and G. H. R. Parkinson, eds. and trans. London: Dent, 1973.

T = *Theodicy.* E. M. Huggard, ed. and trans. New Haven, Conn.: Yale University Press, 1952; Lasalle, Ill.: Open Court, 1985.

2. In presenting these two requirements, I do not intend to assert that either is in fact a necessary condition for freedom. It may be possible to argue successfully that one or the other requirement is not in fact a genuine requirement for freedom. However, I think it is fair to say that the no-compulsion and alternatives requirements fit most people's intuitions about what freedom involves. There may also be other conditions that a satisfactory compatibilist theory must meet. As far as I am able to determine, however, Leibniz's compatibilist arguments seem primarily intended to satisfy these two conditions, so I will use them as the primary touchstones for examining his compatibilism.

3. The initial conditions in question need not be *initial* in the sense that they represent the first temporal state of affairs for the world in question. As long as the laws that govern changes in that world are held constant, from any "temporal slice" of the world the laws of change will determine exactly one possible set of temporal successor states.

4. Spinoza comes to mind here (see *E* IP16, IP29). However, see chapter 11 in this volume by Edwin Curley and Gregory Walski, "Spinoza's Necessitarianism Reconsidered." Even should this prove not to be Spinoza's considered view, Leibniz appears to have thought it was (see, for example, L 195 or *Theodicy*, sect. 173; G VI, 217; T 234).

5. G. H. R. Parkinson, "Leibniz on Human Freedom," *Studia Leibnitiana*, Sonderheft 2 (Wiesbaden: Franz Steiner Verlag, 1970), p. 9; also, Pauline Phemister, "Leibniz, Freedom of Will and Rationality," *Studia Leibnitiana* 23, no. 1 (1991): 26.

6. The example here is merely to illustrate a point, so I will ignore the fact that in Leibniz's view, it seems one could not change *any*thing in the universe without, thereby, changing *every*thing in the entire universe. See, for instance, *The Principles of Nature and Grace, Based on Reason*, sect. 3 (G VI, 598–599; L 636–637).

7. For reasons that will become clear shortly, I will not use what would seem a more appropriate term — *physical determinism* — because it would create confusion in the context of the ensuing discussion of the Leibnizian notion of *physical necessity*.

8. To say that monads are mental substances is not to say that all monads are conscious or intelligent minds; some monads are completely unconscious. Monads are mental in the sense that their most basic states are perceptions (*Monadology*, sect. 14; G VI, 608).

9. Assuming one also takes note that, for example, I will not try and be unable to open the right door, there is no gunman standing by having uttered the sound "go through the left door," and so on.

10. "Leibniz and the Miracle of Freedom," *Nous* 26; no. 2 (1992): 218–235. See also

my doctoral dissertation "Leibniz on Contingency and Freedom," University of Rochester, Rochester, New York, 1994.

11. There are reasons, I will argue, for why it is acceptable that God be able infallibly to predict free actions but unacceptable that any creature be able to do so.

12. Paull, "Leibnitz and Freedom," correctly attributes to Leibniz the position that the miraculous theory of freedom ensures unpredictability, but he does not discuss why unpredictability is a requirement for freedom in the first place.

13. It is possible that the efficient causes acting on the will *are* motions of bodies, provided we understand causation in terms of Leibniz's account of activity and passivity of monads (discussed below). In this respect, efficient causes act on the will when the mind is passive concerning its perception of such motions. To say that the mind can interrupt the chain of such causal influences, then, is just to say that no universal psychological laws framed in terms of such influences will be adequate for predicting all choices. This is discussed further in the section on psychological determinism.

14. Paull, "Leibnitz and Freedom," pp. 222–223.

15. Indeed, Leibniz's claim here is stronger — even the primary metaphysical laws of order for the universe are within God's power to repeal. There is some reason to doubt the coherence of this claim, for God chooses everything that ever happens in the universe from eternity and cannot change any one thing in the universe without changing everything else. For more on the nature of God's primary decrees, see my "Primary and Secondary Divine Decrees in the Leibniz- Arnauld Correspondence," *Studia Leibnitiana* 27, no. 1 (1995): 85–103.

16. *God, Freedom, and Evil.* (Grand Rapids, Mich.: Eerdmans, 1974), p. 67.

17. See, for example, Gr 306; AG 30.

18. *God, Freedom, and Evil*, p. 29.

19. When Leibniz says, "*one* can see, etc.," he really means "only God can see, etc." See, for example, F de C 180; AG 96.

20. I have defended this claim in "Leibniz on Contingency and Freedom."

21. David Blumenfeld provides a very nice discussion of this point in "Superessentialism, Counterparts, and Freedom," in Michael Hooker, ed., *Leibniz: Critical and Interpretive Essays* (Minneapolis: University of Minnesota Press, 1982), pp. 103–123.

22. Paull, "Leibnitz and Freedom," p. 222.

23. It is for this reason that I use the term "material determinism" in preference to "physical determinism."

24. See also G V, 164; RB 178; G II, 38; AG 70.

25. The context in which this text is embedded shows that Leibniz is using "physical predetermination" here in contrast to "metaphysical predetermination."

26. See G VII, 305; L 488. I discuss this point more fully below in connection with Leibniz's distinction between divine will and divine understanding.

27. See G V, 164; RB 178.

28. Leibniz sometimes suggests that a perceptual change may be the result of a number of appetitive forces acting in concert on a monad (G V 174: RB 192). Although this complicates the picture somewhat, I think that Leibniz would accept the possibility (for God) of grasping or constructing a "master" law of appetition for a monad. Perceptual succession in monads is a thoroughly deterministic process; the exact sequence of perceptions a monad will undergo can be read off from its complete concept or from its (master) appetitive law.

29. See Phemister, "Leibniz," especially pp. 26–27.

30. The view here might seem to be more of a soft determinism. However, it is important to emphasize that there is no further ultimate cause of a monad's internal states than its own nature, which belongs to it from eternity. God only chooses whether or not the monad will exist.

31. I am presupposing here that the superessentialist reading of Leibniz is correct. If one wishes to maintain that Robert Sleigh's superintrinsicalist reading is somehow preferable, it should serve equally well since Sleigh, too, accepts that individuals have only one complete concept. See Sleigh, "Response to Benson Mates," *Leibniz Society Newsletter and Review* (December 1992): 9. Don Lodzinski argues explicitly against the superessentialist reading on the grounds that it is at odds with Leibniz's views on the power of individuals to make alternative choices. "Leibnizian Freedom and Superessentialism," *Studia Leibnitiana* 26, no. 2 (1994): 161–186. I will argue that when Leibniz's views on such power are suitably interpreted, there is no further threat to the superessentialist reading.

32. Lodzinski's argument in "Leibnizian Freedom" that both God and intelligent monads have a genuine power to do otherwise is that such "real power" is required if intelligent monads are to be held responsible for their actions. I believe I have shown that Leibniz thought he could account for freedom, responsibility, and power without accepting the "real power" view attributed to him. The real power thesis may, I think, be expressed as follows:

> S has the power to do x at T only if there is a possible state of affairs where, at T, S has all the properties she now has at T, except that instead of the property of choosing not to do x, S has the property of choosing to do x, and where S furthermore does x.

Perhaps the most telling reason not to accept the real power thesis is that if Leibniz accepted it, why then does he not employ it straightforwardly as part of his theodicy? One would expect him to assert that God bears no responsibility for evil because the real power of creatures prevents God from guaranteeing that the world that we get is the best possible. Instead, Leibniz maintains that the evil that God permits is outweighed by the greater good that is made possible in creating the possible world containing the evil. The real power thesis is also deeply problematic, considering Leibniz's theory of preestablished harmony, since bodies are perfectly regulated in advance to correspond perfectly to what takes place in monads. I conclude, therefore, that Lodzinski has not provided sufficient grounds for the real power thesis and, thus, for rejecting the superessentialist reading of Leibniz.

33. I am grateful to Alan Hart, Jonathan Bennett, and Joseph Keim Campbell for comments on an earlier version of this chapter.

## 10

CHARLES HUENEMANN

# The Necessity of Finite Modes and Geometrical Containment in Spinoza's Metaphysics

## Introduction

Midway through part I of the *Ethics*, Spinoza announces that

> I think I have shown clearly enough (see P16) that from God's supreme power, or
> infinite nature, infinitely many things in infinitely many modes, i.e., all things, have
> necessarily flowed, or always follow, by the same necessity and in the same way as
> from the nature of a triangle it follows, from eternity and to eternity, that its three
> angles are equal to two right angles.[1]

And later he boasts: "I have shown more clearly than the noon light that there is absolutely nothing in things on account of which they can be called contingent."[2]
These certainly sound like the words of a strict necessitarian, and Spinoza's commentators agree that Spinoza thought all things were necessary, *in some sense*. But
they disagree in their attempts to explicate that sense.

All agree that three entities or groups of entities in Spinoza's metaphysics should
be reckoned necessary in the strongest possible sense. First, it is clear that Spinoza's
God enjoys absolutely necessary existence since for Spinoza God is the one substance, the only entity that exists in itself and is conceived through itself (E IPP11,
14). Second, since God is defined as consisting of an infinity of attributes (E ID6),
each of God's attributes is also absolutely necessary; there is no possible universe lacking extension, thought, and whatever other attributes God has. Third, Spinoza
demonstrates that from God's absolute nature there follow certain modes that are
"eternal, infinite, and necessary" (E IPP21–23). Some of these infinite modes follow

immediately from "the absolute nature of God's attributes," whereas others follow only mediately; but *all* infinite modes, whether mediate or immediate, are entailed necessarily by things that exist with absolute necessity. Thus God, God's attributes, and God's infinite modes all exist with the strongest possible necessity; and in this all commentators are agreed.

Commentators disagree, however, about the status of finite modes. The disagreement stems from Spinoza's apparent vacillation between (a) treating finite modes as absolutely necessitated by God's nature and (b) treating them as relatively necessitated by the conjunction of God's nature and other finite modes. Here is a small sampling of that apparent vacillation:

(1) Spinoza claims in E IP16 that "from the necessity of the divine nature there must follow infinitely many things in infinitely many modes (i.e., everything which can fall under an infinite intellect)." Finite modes, it seems, can fall under an infinite intellect. So it seems that finite modes should follow from God's nature with the same necessity that infinite modes do.

(2) But then Spinoza demonstrates in E IP22 that "whatever follows from some attribute of God insofar as it is modified by a modification which, through the same attribute, exists necessarily and is infinite, must also exist necessarily and be infinite," which might be thought to entail that if there is only God, God's attributes, and God's infinite modes, then nothing necessary and finite will be produced: no finite modes. And when Spinoza finally does provide an account of the generation of finite modes in E IP28, he offers only a deterministic story that places each finite mode at an infinite distance, it seems, from God's nature:

> Every singular thing, or any thing which is finite and has a determinate existence, can neither exist nor be determined to produce an effect unless it is determined to exist and produce an effect by another cause, which is also finite and has a determinate existence; and again, this cause also can neither exist nor be determined to produce an effect unless it is determined to exist and produce an effect by another, which is also finite and has a determinate existence, and so on, to infinity.

> Spinoza's ensuing demonstration makes it clear that every finite mode demands another finite mode for its existence; but since no account is ever given of how a single finite mode can follow from God, God's attributes, or God's infinite modes, it is not clear why there should be any finite modes at all, let alone why they should be said to be necessary. So, from E IP16, taken in conjunction with E IP28, one might conclude that finite modes are not absolutely necessitated by God's nature alone, but each is only relatively necessitated by that nature together with other existing finite modes.

(3) Finally, at the end of E I, Spinoza returns to the theme that God's nature necessitates all things: both in E IP29 ("*all things* have been determined from the necessity of the divine nature to exist and produce an effect in a certain way"; emphasis added) and in the appendix to E

I ("*all things* have been predetermined by God, not from freedom of the will *or* absolute good pleasure, but from God's absolute nature, *or* infinite power"; Geb II, 77; emphasis added).

As a result, some commentators believe that finite modes in Spinoza's metaphysics are only relatively necessary, and they understand the passages that make finite modes sound absolutely necessitated to be exaggerated and misleading, whereas others try to find some way of making finite modes necessary despite E IP22, 28; still others despair of making sense of Spinoza on this issue.[3]

In this chapter I shall argue that Spinoza believed finite modes to be *overnecessitated*, that is, necessitated in more ways than one (compare "overdetermination"). Specifically, Spinoza believed that each finite mode is absolutely necessitated by God's nature and also relatively necessitated by God's nature in conjunction with other existing finite modes. I shall first critically examine two recent accounts of the issue. Each account rightfully emphasizes a crucial aspect of Spinoza's view, but it will be seen that any comprehensive account must go beyond them and into the heart of Spinoza's monism.

## Making Finite Modes Necessary

### Necessity: Relative and Absolute

In *Spinoza's Metaphysics*, Edwin Curley accounts for the necessity of finite modes through a distinction Spinoza himself makes in E IP33S (Geb II, 74):

> A thing is called necessary either by reason of its essence or by reason of its cause. For a thing's existence follows necessarily either from its essence and definition or from a given efficient cause. And a thing is also called impossible from these same causes — viz. either because its essence, or definition, involves a contradiction, or because there is no external cause which has been determined to produce such a thing.
>     But a thing is called contingent only because of a defect of our knowledge. For if we do not know that the thing's essence involves a contradiction, or if we do know very well that its essence does not involve a contradiction, and nevertheless can affirm nothing certainly about its existence, because the order of causes is hidden from us, it can never seem to us either necessary or impossible. So we call it contingent or possible.

The distinction is between necessity by reason of one's essence and necessity by reason of one's cause. Curley calls the first "absolute necessity" and the second "relative necessity." If a thing is absolutely necessary, then its definition (or essence) entails that it exists; in Spinoza's metaphysics, only God meets this criterion. If a thing is relatively necessary, then its definition does not entail that it exists, but the existence of another thing entails that it does. Infinite modes, for example, are only relatively necessary because it is God (or, more precisely, the absolute nature of God's attributes) that ultimately entails their existence (E IP23). Finite modes, it is clear, are also relatively necessary, for their essence does not involve existence (E IP24); but they are nevertheless necessitated by other relatively necessary finite modes, each of which is the result of an infinite sequence of causes (E IP28), a sequence too complex for us to know completely.

A finite mode is relatively necessitated by another finite mode only in conjunction with the laws of nature, which Spinoza regards as necessary truths. In fact, in his interpretation of Spinoza's metaphysics, Curley identifies God, God's attributes, and God's infinite modes with entities that are responsible for making various laws of nature true; their ontological order mirrors a logical order of the laws from most basic to most derivative. Finite modes, similarly, are entities responsible for making particular claims true. The elegant outcome of this nomological interpretation is that just as it is impossible to infer a statement of particular fact from the general laws of nature alone, so it is impossible for a finite mode to follow solely from God, God's attributes, or God's infinite modes. And just as one needs laws of nature together with antecedent conditions before one can derive a statement of particular fact, so one needs God together with other finite modes before another finite mode is produced (this series of finite modes is the "order of causes" mentioned in the preceding passage). In Curley's words, the laws of nature and the antecedent conditions are "separately necessary and only jointly sufficient" causes for any given finite thing.[4]

By making every finite mode only partially dependent on God, Curley's interpretation compromises Spinoza's monism, at least as it has been construed traditionally. Monism has been understood generally as the view that somehow all things (or apparent things) owe their existence and essence ultimately and exclusively to a single thing, and Spinoza has been understood generally as such a monist.[5] But according to Curley, Spinoza does not claim that finite modes owe their existence *exclusively* to God. God's nature plays a part in their existence, to be sure: it grounds the laws of nature, which are necessary for the generation of any finite mode. But the laws alone are not sufficient for a finite mode's generation. There must also be an independent causal chain of finite modes, a chain whose links are again governed by the laws of nature, but which (again) do not owe their existence exclusively to God. The independent causal chain of finite modes is, according to Curley, of mixed origin, being partly of God and partly not of God; hence Spinoza cannot be a traditional monist. Furthermore, the totality of finite modes cannot be understood as following from God's nature or God's attributes or God's infinite modes, according to Curley, since this would mean that each finite mode does so, and E IPP21–23, 28 rule this out. Thus there is no final explanation, in Curley's account, for the existence of the totality of finite modes other than the individual explanations for the existences of particular members of that totality.

Now it might be suspected that Spinoza thought that was sufficient; that is, he may have thought that by showing everything to be either relatively or absolutely necessary, he had explained how all things are as necessary as any geometrical fact. Jonathan Bennett, for instance, suggests that "Spinoza tended to think that something whose necessity is not inherent but only conferred by something else is still as strongly, completely, absolutely necessary as something inherently necessary."[6] But many passages show that Spinoza is aware of the difference in strength between relative and absolute necessity, and furthermore that he feels the need to account for the existence of finite modes by something stronger than relative necessity. Three examples may suffice.

First, in chapter 4 of book I of the *Short Treatise* (Geb I, 38–39), Spinoza argues that "if God had from eternity created all things in a different way, or had ordered or predetermined them differently than they are now" then he would not be equally perfect; for "because we have also shown that what makes [God] do something can be nothing other than his own perfection, we conclude that if it was not his perfection which made him do it, the things would not exist, or could not have come to be what they are now." In other words, it is not enough to show that each thing is relatively necessitated by some other thing; some account must finally be given that explains why all things exist and why they are not ordered or predetermined in a different way. God's perfection is supposed to ground this account.

Second, in chapter 3 of part I of the *Metaphysical Thoughts* (Geb I, 240–244), Spinoza distinguishes necessity with respect to a thing's essence (absolute necessity) from necessity with respect to a thing's cause (relative necessity); but then he further claims that "since nothing is more necessary in its existence than what God has decreed would exist, it follows that a necessity of existing has been in all created things from eternity." (In Balling's 1664 translation of the work, it is added that "the necessity of really existing is not distinct from the necessity of essence.") Thus relative necessitation is not sufficient; Spinoza appeals to "God's decree" in order to bring the proper strength of necessity to created things ("a necessity of existing has been in all created things from eternity").

Third, in E IP29, Spinoza demonstrates that "there is nothing contingent, but all things have been determined from the necessity of the divine nature to exist and produce an effect in a certain way"; and in his demonstration, when he comes to prove that the existence of finite things is not contingent, he does not appeal to the causal determinism of E IP28. He appeals instead to E IP24C, which states that "God is the cause of the being of things" and that *only* God can be the cause of the existence and duration of things since existence pertains only to God's nature. Again, relative necessitation is not sufficient for Spinoza's account; he appeals again to God's nature.

These three passages show, at the very least, that Spinoza is aware of the difference in strength between relative necessity and absolute necessity and that he believes that some ultimate explanation — beyond the explanation given through relative necessity — must be given for the existence and determinate nature of the totality of finite modes: God's perfection or necessity of existing *somehow* produces necessarily the totality of finite modes.

This means that Curley's account cannot be sufficient. In addition to the relative necessitation of finite modes by other finite modes, there must be some bridge from God's nature to the determinate character of the totality of finite modes. There must be, in other words, some feature of God that answers the question of why this totality of finite modes is actual and no other totality could be actual.

### God's Absolute Nature

In "Spinoza's Necessitarianism," Don Garrett provides a way in which God's nature may necessitate the totality of finite modes. Garrett agrees that E IPP21–23 rule out the possibility of finite modes following from the *absolute nature* of God's attributes. But he observes that this does not mean that finite modes do not follow from the *na-*

*ture* of God's attributes. According to Garrett, that which is manifested pervasively through an attribute — for example, what is found everywhere in the extended world, such as obedience to the laws of motion — follows from the absolute nature of an attribute; everything else follows from the nature of the attribute (and not specifically the absolute nature). In particular, finite modes, precisely because they are not found everywhere and at all times, follow from the nature, and not the absolute nature, of God's attributes. In Garrett's words:

> An attribute, if it is to have any internal diversity or change, must be qualified in different ways at different places and times. Now, some things about an attribute [namely, the infinite modes] will follow from the very nature of the attribute regardless of *how* it is qualified or "affected." . . . Other things, however — those local and temporary features that actually constitute the attribute's diversification and change — cannot similarly follow from the nature of the attribute *without regard* to how it is qualified or "affected"; otherwise, they would be necessarily pervasive and permanent as well.[7]

Thus, according to Garrett, whatever exists everywhere and at all times follows from the absolute nature of God's attributes, and whatever exists only somewhere and at some time follows from the nonabsolute nature of those attributes. This means, specifically, that finite modes *can* follow from the nature of God's attributes, without contradicting E IPP21–23, since those propositions claim only that no finite modes can follow from the *absolute* nature of God's attributes.

Now, for Garrett's account to be complete, it must explain precisely *how* the nature of God's attributes necessitates finite modes. Garrett offers two possible explanations. The first is to understand the nature of God's attributes just as the absolute nature of those attributes but limited by an additional constraint: namely, the constraint that God produce the best possible world, that is, the world exhibiting the greatest perfection.[8] Thus "the series of finite modes does *not* follow from the absolute nature of an attribute, but only from that nature *together with* this additional necessary constraint."[9] But there is a textual problem with this explanation. In the appendix to E I, Spinoza writes that "*all things have been predetermined by God*, not from freedom of the will *or* absolute good pleasure, but *from God's absolute nature, or* infinite power."[10] Garrett's first explanation, however, requires that the totality of finite modes specifically does *not* follow from God's absolute nature.

Garrett's second possible explanation avoids this problem. Suppose that from the absolute nature of God's attributes there follow not only the modes that exist everywhere and at all times but also the totality of finite modes.[11] Furthermore, let this totality include all possible things, not just the most perfect collection of them.[12] Suppose finally that this *totality* follows from the absolute nature of God's attributes, but *the individual members of that totality*, considered alone, follow only from God's nature and not from God's absolute nature. Then it follows that "all things" — including the totality of finite modes — follow from the absolute nature of God's attributes; but no finite thing (considered apart from that totality) does. This second explanation squares with both E IPP21–23 (which preclude finite modes from following from the absolute nature of God's attributes) and Spinoza's remark in the appendix to E I (which demands that *all things* follow from the absolute nature of God's attributes). More important, it seems that *some* such explanation is required in order to make Spinoza's claims consistent with each other.

But a problem arises: how might Spinoza intelligibly maintain that the totality of finite modes follows from the absolute nature of God's attributes whereas the individual members of that totality do not? Or, as Jonathan Bennett puts the question, "The truth about 'the whole series [of finite modes]' is presumably a long conjunction; how can that be necessary if no one of its conjuncts is necessary?"[13] Anticipating this question, Garrett writes that

> each finite mode would follow from the nature of an attribute, but *only in virtue of its membership as part of the . . . series of finite modes.* As a result, it would follow from an attribute *only insofar as the attribute is considered to be affected by particular finite modes* — just as E IP28 asserts.[14]

Thus each finite mode would follow from the nature of God's attributes only when it is seen as a member of the totality of finite modes; this, suggests Garrett, is what E IP28 asserts, and furthermore this is what it means to follow from the nature (but not the absolute nature) of God's attributes. The totality of finite modes itself, however, is an infinite mode (according to Garrett) and therefore would follow necessarily from God's absolute nature (E IP23). Again, each finite mode, considered individually, does not follow from the absolute nature of God's attributes; but it does follow when it is considered as a member of the totality of finite modes — a totality that does follow from the absolute nature of God's attributes — and this is why an individual finite mode is said to follow from the nature (but not the absolute nature) of God's attributes.

But the question may be pressed: if X follows from the absolute nature of God's attributes, and Y is a member of X, does Y not also follow from the absolute nature of God's attributes? Garrett answers this question in a note:

> Of course, the absolute nature of the attribute would "entail" the existence of each individual finite mode, in the sense that there would be no possible world in which the attribute had that absolute nature and yet the finite mode did not exist; but . . . Spinoza requires more than this of the "following from" relation. In his view, a finite mode can be said to "follow from" an attribute "considered" in one way, but fail to "follow from" it when it is considered in another, more restricted, way — a distinction that makes good sense when taken as expressing a finite mode's dependence for existence on its membership in the . . . infinite series of such modes, but a distinction for which the modern entailment relation makes no allowance.[15]

But it is hard to see how this answer is to be understood.[16] Perhaps a finite mode can follow from an attribute when the attribute is considered in one way and fail to follow when the attribute is considered in another way (suppose, by analogy, the finite mode is the number 7 and the attribute is considered alternately as "the set of primes less than 10" and "Adam's favorite set of numbers"); and perhaps a finite mode can follow or not follow from an attribute depending on how the finite mode itself is considered (suppose the attribute is "the set of primes less than 10" and the number 7 is considered alternately as "the number 7" and "Adam's favorite number"). But to answer the question that has been posed, Garrett must explain how a finite mode can follow from an attribute when the finite mode is considered as a member of the totality of finite modes, and can fail to follow from the attribute when it is considered alone and not considered as such a member. By analogy, this would be similar to explaining how the number 7 can follow from the attribute "is a prime less than 10" when 7 is considered as a member of the set including 2, 3, 5, and 7, but can fail to follow from the same attribute when 7 is considered alone and not considered as a member of that set. It is difficult to see how such an explanation might proceed. Moreover, there also needs to be an explanation of why "following insofar as it is a member of a totality" means the same as "following from the nature (but not the absolute nature) of God's attributes," and why "not following insofar as it is considered as an individual" means the same as "not following from the absolute nature of God's attributes." On the surface, the paired locutions are quite dissimilar. Finally, since Spinoza apparently identifies (by using *sive*) the absolute nature of God's attributes with God's infinite power, in the appendix to E I (Geb II, 77), it seems that somehow the relevance of God's power to the foregoing problems should be made clear.

Despite these problems, it is clear that Garrett is right to overcome E IP22's barrier by distinguishing the nature of God's attributes from the absolute nature of God's attributes; and it is clear that *some* distinction must be drawn in order to make Spinoza's claims in E IPP21–23 and the appendix to E I consistent with each other. What is finally required, then, is a comprehensive account that (1) explains how "all things" can follow from the absolute nature of God's attributes in one way (as the appendix to E I says), and yet finite modes can fail to follow from the absolute nature of God's attributes in some other way (as E IP22 says) and (2) encompasses both the causal determinism evident in Curley's account and the necessitation evident in Garrett's account. Providing this account requires a deeper exploration of the nature of Spinoza's monism.

## Geometrical Containment and Spinoza's Monism

### The Geometrical Containment of Formal Essences

An important clue for understanding the nature of Spinoza's monism is found in an analogy used to clarify E IIP8: "The ideas of singular things, or of modes, that do not exist must be comprehended in God's infinite idea in the same way as the formal essences of the singular things, or modes, are contained in God's attributes."

Before proceeding to Spinoza's analogy, two clarifications must be made. First, it is clear that by "things that do not exist" Spinoza means things that do not exist now but have existed in the past or will exist in the future.[17] Here is why: E IP30 states: "An actual intellect, whether finite or infinite, must comprehend God's attributes and God's affections, and nothing else." In his demonstration for this proposition, Spinoza asserts that "what is contained objectively in the intellect must necessarily be in nature." Next, E IIP4 identifies God's idea as the sole idea [*unica tantum*] in God's intellect — presumably, the grand idea of the totality of all existent things. Thus an idea of a singular thing that does not exist but which is comprehended in God's infinite idea can only be an idea of a singular thing that does not happen to exist now but did or will exist at another time. There can be no ideas in God's intellect of things that never exist.

The second clarification regards "formal essences." Spinoza uses the term about a dozen times throughout his works, and in no context (except one) is it even marginally clear whether by the formal essence of a thing he means (i) the actual existence of the thing (what Descartes calls "formal reality") or (ii) the form (or true and immutable nature) of the thing.[18] The second meaning seems to be implied by a remark made in the second appendix to his *Short Treatise* (Geb I, 117):

> The most immediate mode of the attribute we call thought has objectively in itself the formal essence of all things, so that if one posited any formal things whose essence did not exist objectively in the above-named attribute, it would not be infinite or supremely perfect in its kind.

This remark has its share of obscurities, to be sure, but when read carefully it seems to presume a distinction between "formal things" — that is, presumably, things that have formal reality, as opposed to mere objective reality — and their formal essences ("formal" simply because these essences are contained in the attribute that contains objectively in itself the formal essences of all things). At any rate, Wolfson is confident that Spinoza understands the formal essence of a thing to be the thing as a potential being — that is, the particular form (or true and immutable nature) that becomes instantiated when the thing comes into existence — and Wolfson's confidence will be presumed here.[19] So understood, E IIP8 states that God's intellect contains ideas of things that have existed or will exist in the same way that God's attributes contain the forms of those things.

Spinoza tries to clarify this proposition with an analogy. He recalls the geometrical fact that whenever two chords, AC and FG, intersect at point B within a circle, then the rectangle with base AB and height BC is equal in area to that with base BG and height BF.[20] Thus, writes Spinoza:

> In a circle there are contained infinitely many rectangles that are equal to one another. Nevertheless, none of them can be said to exist except insofar as the circle exists, nor also can the idea of any of these rectangles be said to exist except insofar as it is comprehended in the idea of the circle. Now of these infinitely many [rectangles] let two only, viz. [those formed from the segments of lines] AC and FG, exist. Of course their ideas also exist now, not only insofar as they are only comprehended in the idea of the circle, but also insofar as they involve the existence of those rectangles. By this they are distinguished from the other ideas of the other rectangles.

The analogy illustrates the sense in which a circle contains an infinite collection of rectangles, even if no chords or rectangles are actually drawn: the rectangles can be said to exist because the circle has such a nature as to allow for their construction. In an analogous way, Spinoza suggests, God's intellect contains the ideas of all possible things, and God's attributes contain the forms of all possible things, because God's intellect and God's attributes have such natures as to allow for the production of all possible things and their ideas. In other words, ideas lie *virtually* in the nature of the infinite intellect, just as the forms of things lie *virtually* in the nature of God's attributes.

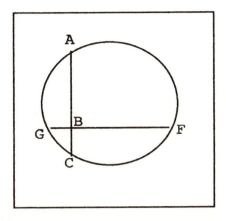

The virtual containment illustrated by Spinoza's analogy is not the same as logical entailment, for certainly the existence of a circle does not *logically* imply the existence of any rectangle; the rectangles do not exactly lie implicitly in the circle as conclusions reside in premises. Nor is it overt spatial containment since the rectangles need not actually be drawn within the circle. The containment is instead *geometrical*, in an old-fashioned sense of the term. For whereas post-Hilbertian geometers provide demonstrations in a logical-mathematical format, earlier geometers provided demonstrations in terms of "recipes" for constructing various figures. For example, in Euclid's own demonstration of Spinoza's example (in book III, proposition 35 of the *Elements*), Euclid begins with the circle and its intersecting chords; he then draws lines from the circle's center that bisect those chords; and he proceeds to explain how to construct a series of equal-area rectangles until, in the end, he has shown that the rectangles that could be constructed from the original chords are equal in area to one another (in virtue of being equal to equals). The force of the demonstration is in the general applicability of the "recipe" Euclid offers: it supposedly can be performed given any circle and any two intersecting chords. Although Euclid does appeal to propositions he has already demonstrated, those appeals are not sufficient for the proof; appeal must be made also to what can be constructed from what is given. Thus, when X geometrically contains Y, it means that X has sufficient features for producing Y, in accordance with sanctioned means of construction.

A simple broadening of this example takes Spinoza's point to a much deeper level. For just as a given circle may be said to contain geometrically an infinity of pairs of rectangles of equal area, an infinitely extended region can be said to contain all possible geometrical figures undergoing all possible motions. That is, from infinite extension, coupled with motion, the forms of all possible finite modes can be constructed; extension, in other words, contains the forms of all possible finite modes.[21] The means of construction employed, in this case, are those provided by the infinite modes, such as motion and rest, and the laws that govern motion and rest. Again, the containment is not logical entailment, and so it cannot be said that the forms of finite modes are *logically* necessitated by the nature of infinite extension; nor is the containment meant to be merely spatial, though of course the actual constructions will have to occur in the infinite extension, if that is the only extension there is. Instead, the containment is geometrical, in the sense described above, and this means only that all possible finite modes can be constructed from the features of extension and the laws of motion. The case is analogous for the other attributes.[22]

So far, this account only illustrates the sense in which all possible forms of finite modes are implicitly contained within God's attributes, as E IIP8 claims. Proceeding from possible, virtually contained *forms* to actual, necessitated *things*, however, requires an appeal to God's power, for God's power demands that absolutely anything possible be actual:

> But to those who ask "why God did not create all men so that they would be governed by the command of reason?" I answer only "because he did not lack material to create all things, from the highest degree of perfection to the lowest;" or, to speak more properly, "because the laws of his nature have been so ample that they sufficed for producing all things which can be conceived by an infinite intellect" (as I have demonstrated in P16).[23]

Because of God's supreme power, perfection, or reality, absolutely all possible things — "infinitely many things in infinitely many modes" — must be produced. This means that *all* of the formal essences contained in God's attributes must become instantiated. The "force of instantiation" is God's power; for, as Spinoza hints in Letter 83 to Tschirnhaus, the variety of things cannot be explained through extension alone, but that variety must be explained through some attribute that expresses "eternal and infinite essence." This eternal and infinite essence is presumably God's essence, which is the same as his power (since, by E IP34, "God's power is his essence itself"). Thus it becomes clear why Spinoza should claim that "from God's supreme power, or infinite nature, infinitely many things in infinitely many modes, i.e., all things, have necessarily flowed, or always follow, by the same necessity and in the same way as from the nature of a triangle it follows, from eternity and to eternity, that its three angles are equal to two right angles" (E IP17S) — or, indeed, just as it follows from the nature of a circle that a pair of equal-area rectangles can be constructed from any two intersecting chords.

The account provided so far explains how the totality of finite modes follows from God's nature. Moreover, it explains why the totality follows specifically from God's *absolute* nature; for the account makes crucial appeal to God's power, and God's power is identified as God's absolute nature: "All things have been predetermined by God, not from freedom of the will *or* absolute good pleasure, but from God's absolute nature, *or* infinite power" (appendix to E I; Geb II, 77). It remains to be seen, however, why finite modes, considered individually, do *not* follow from the absolute nature of God's attributes (as E IP22 forbids) and, furthermore, why they nevertheless follow from God's attributes insofar as they are affected by other finite modes, in just the way E IP28 describes.

### Efficient Causation of Singular Things

The key to providing such an explanation lies in Spinoza's distinction between two ways of conceiving things:

...either [1] insofar as we conceive them to exist in relation to a certain time and place, or [2] insofar as we conceive them to be contained in God and to follow from the necessity of the divine nature. But the things we conceive in this second way as true, *or* real, we conceive under a species of eternity, and to that extent they involve the eternal and infinite essence of God. (E VP29S)

The first way of conceiving things is to conceive them in their particular circumstances, that is, as singular, actual things embedded in a real order of efficient causation. The second way is to conceive them (more abstractly) as formal essences, for they are viewed as eternal objects and as "contained in God and to follow from the necessity of the divine nature." Objects conceived in the first way, as existing in a certain time and place, are conceived as having accidental and extrinsic properties; for example, Isaac is conceived as existing with a certain stature, as a son of Abraham, father of Jacob, and so on. The formal essences of those objects, however, lack such accidental and extrinsic properties; Isaac, in particular, is conceived in isolation from his particular surroundings, circumstances, ancestors, and descendants. Isaac conceived as a formal essence, it is clear, is necessitated by God's nature, for, as seen above, *all* formal essences are necessitated by God's infinite power of creation. But Isaac conceived as a singular, actual thing is not necessitated in this way. The only way to account for the actual Isaac, with all of his accidental and extrinsic properties, is by appeal to those objects and events that are responsible for Isaac having those properties; and, again, those objects and events must be accounted for by appeal to other objects and events, and so on ad infinitum. Thus the only way of accounting for Isaac's existence as a singular thing is the way suggested by E IP28, that is, through relative necessity.

This distinction between the two ways of conceiving things is important in Spinoza's philosophy in a number of ways. Its epistemological significance is demonstrated in Spinoza's *Treatise on the Emendation of the Intellect*, whose main purpose is to prompt the mind to discover ideas that are entirely clear and distinct, and to compound them only in clear and distinct ways, until an adequate idea of the whole of nature has been gained:

> The aim, then, is to have clear and distinct ideas, i.e., such as have been made from the pure mind, and not from the fortuitous motions of the body. And then, so that all ideas may be led back to one, we shall strive to connect and order them so that our mind, as far as possible, reproduces objectively the formal character of nature, both as to the whole and as to the parts. (Geb II, 34)

Spinoza's advice in this passage is not to catalogue observations and experiences of the natural world, for that, given Spinoza's account of the imagination, could provide only a catalog of ideas gained from "fortuitous motions of the body." Instead, his advice is to connect and order one's clear and distinct ideas so that the mind gains a representation of nature's "formal character." Indeed, Spinoza disparages efforts to catalogue the causal sequences found in the world:

> For it would be impossible for human weakness to grasp the series of singular, changeable things, not only because there are innumerably many of them, but also because of the infinite circumstances in one and the same thing, any of which can be the cause of its existence or nonexistence. For their existence has no connection with their essence, *or* . . . is not an eternal truth. (Geb I, 36)

But human weakness in this regard is no cause for serious concern since the "order of existing . . . offers nothing but extrinsic denominations, relations, or at most, circumstances, all of which are far from the inmost essence of things" (Geb I, 36). Spinoza thinks we should seek instead the essences of finite things from the "fixed and eternal things, and at the same time from the laws inscribed in these things, as in their true codes, according to which singular things come to be, and are ordered" (Geb I, 37). Spinoza's advice, in short, is to emend the intellect by confining one's attention to formal essences and not to be distracted by the fortuitous impacts of actual bodies on our senses. For Spinoza it is inconceivable that the intellect should adequately conceive something that God is unable to bring into existence; and it is equally unthinkable that God does not do all that he is able to do. The presumption is that the intellect contains within itself the ideas of all existent things, just as a circle contains an infinity of equal-area rectangles.

This distinction between ways of considering finite things explains why a finite mode, considered as a singular thing, does not follow from the absolute nature of God's attributes. For when the finite mode is considered as an individual located in space and time, it cannot be divorced from its particular circumstances or its accidental and extrinsic properties — and this requires an account of causal determinism as outlined in E IP28. On the other hand, if the finite mode is considered instead as a formal essence, and so is divorced from its particular circumstances, then it can be seen to follow from God's absolute nature; although when it is considered in this way, the account given for its necessity is the same as the account given for the necessity of any formal essence (namely, "This individual must exist because it is possible and God must actualize all possible things"). Thus Spinoza can claim both that finite modes (considered as singular things) do not follow from God's absolute nature and, at the same time, that all things (considered as formal essences) do follow from God's absolute nature.

Such an account of Spinoza's necessitarianism, relying so heavily on "ways of considering," might seem hopelessly subjective. But in fact Spinoza's distinction between the two ways of considering things captures a deep truth about understanding the existence of objects in the universe. If a particular object comes under study, there are two kinds of answers to the question "Why must this object exist?" The first answer involves an account of the object's efficient causes; and, indeed, this is the more common way of answering such a question. The question, so understood, demands a historical answer. But the second answer involves a far deeper story about the nature of the universe; it understands the question "Why must this object exist?" as asking, "What is the nature of the universe such that this object has come to exist in it?" Today the answer might involve grand cosmological theories, which in the end give statistical, thermodynamic answers that (ideally) would lead one to expect that such an object should eventually exist at some place and time or other. The question, so understood, demands a conceptual, theoretical, or scientific answer — at any rate, something deeper than the historical answer provided through efficient causation. Spinoza's own answer to this deeper question is particularly theological, invoking the infinite productive power of God: God must create everything creatable. This, finally, renders each thing to be necessitated by God's nature, *insofar as* it is considered as a formal essence in the order of geometrical containment; but the finite thing is only relatively necessary *insofar as* it is considered in the order of efficient causes.

It follows that if it is asked what makes a particular finite mode necessary, Spinoza has two answers to give. The first answer is that the finite mode is necessary in virtue of instantiating a formal essence that must be instantiated given God's absolute nature (i.e., God's power). The second answer is that the finite mode is relatively necessary in virtue of an infinite chain of efficient causes governed by the laws of nature that produces the finite mode. If it is further asked why that infinite chain of efficient causes, and no other, is actual, Spinoza's answer is that no other chain is possible; the totality of all possible formal essences must be instantiated, in virtue of God's absolute nature. If it is asked whether the infinite chain could exist in a different arrangement, Spinoza's answer is that the laws governing the arrangement of the totality of finite modes are no less necessitated by God's nature. Thus Spinoza's God necessitates finite modes in multiple ways, and Curley's and Garrett's accounts each rightfully emphasize one or another of those ways.

This "overnecessitarianism" can be seen readily in Spinoza's demonstration of E IP29: "In nature there is nothing contingent, but all things have been determined from the necessity of the divine nature to exist and produce an effect in a certain way." Spinoza demonstrates this proposition by calling on three claims he takes himself to have demonstrated already, displayed here in outline form for convenience:

1. God is necessary (and so in no way contingent) (E IP11).
2. The modes of God follow from God's nature necessarily (E IP16), either
   A. insofar as God's nature is considered absolutely (E IP21) or
   B. insofar as God's nature is considered to be determined to act in a certain way (E IP28).
3. God is the cause of modes both A. insofar as they exist (E IP24C) and B. insofar as they are determined to produce effects (E IP26).

"So," Spinoza writes, "all things have been determined from the necessity of the divine nature, not only to exist, but to exist in a certain way, and to produce effects in a certain way." The modes that follow necessarily from God's absolute nature (2A) are infinite and eternal (as E IP21 states); and the mode that is the totality of formal essences of finite modes must be included in this category.[24] The modes that follow necessarily from God's nonabsolute nature (2B) are the singular, actual things, *with finite and determinate existence*, as described in E IP28. (The italicized phrase indicates the distinction of singular things from their formal essences.) Thus, so far, each finite mode is necessitated as a formal essence (which, because of God's nature, must be instantiated at some time or other), and is also relatively necessitated as a singular, actual thing. But singular things are not merely relatively necessitated, for God is the cause of the existence of modes (3A). E IP24C states that *only* God can cause things to exist since God is the only being that requires no other thing for its existence.[25] Furthermore, once a thing exists, it necessarily acts as it does, for God determines all things to produce effects in a certain way (3B) since, as E IP26D states, effects are produced only from something positive, and God is the only source of positive things. Thus finite modes are necessitated in multiple ways: (i) "from above," meaning that God's nature generates an infinity of formal essences that must all be instantiated through God's power (E IP16); (ii) "from the side," meaning that each thing is relatively necessitated to exist by other things that owe their existence to God (E IPP24C, 28); and (iii) "from within," meaning that God determines each thing to produce the particular effects it does (E IP26). Well might Spinoza boast that "I have shown more clearly than the noon light that there is absolutely nothing in things on account of which they can be called contingent."

## Conclusion

By way of conclusion, it should be noted that this account also provides an intriguing perspective upon the true character of Spinoza's monism. For it is not sufficient to conceive Spinoza's God as the ground for the laws of nature; nor is it sufficient to conceive his God as some grand corporeal entity that spatiotemporally contains all things. Instead, Spinoza's God is understood as an infinite power with sufficient resources to allow for the production of all possible things; a power that, in a metaphor overworked by Spinoza himself, geometrically contains all things, just as a triangle's nature contains the fact that its angles are equal to two right angles. Anything that exists or occurs is explained ultimately through the nature of God, which is just to say, as Spinoza does, that all things are in or are conceived through God.[26] Spinoza's God, in other words, lies beyond the known universe and yet contains the known universe in his nature; it is a superstructure within which the universe locates itself. Spinoza's own example in E IIP8S is provocative enough: for if the rectangles described there could believe, the Spinozists among them would take the circle that geometrically contains them to be their God.[27]

*Notes*

1. E IP17C2S (Geb II, 62).

2. E IP33S1 (Geb II, 74).

3. See, respectively, Edwin Curley, *Spinoza's Metaphysics: An Essay in Interpretation* (Cambridge, Mass.: Harvard University Press, 1969) (hereafter Curley 1969); Don Garrett, "Spinoza's Necessitarianism," in Y. Yovel, ed., *God and Nature: Spinoza's Metaphysics, vol. 1, Spinoza by 2000: The Jerusalem Conferences* (Leiden: Brill, 1991) (hereafter Garrett 1991); and Jonathan Bennett, *A Study of Spinoza's Ethics* (Indianapolis: Hackett, 1984) (hereafter Bennett 1984).

4. Curley 1969, p. 70

5. See Roland Hall, "Monism and Pluralism," in Paul Edwards, ed., *The Encyclopedia of Philosophy*, 8 vols. (New York: Macmillan, 1967; reprinted 1972).

6. Bennett 1984, p. 123.

7. Garrett 1991, p. 196.

8. "Perfection" of course must be understood in some nonanthropomorphic sense, perhaps as the greatest possible qualitative diversity. John Carriero, in "Spinoza's Views on Ne-

cessity in Historical Perspective," *Philosophical Topics* 19, no. 1 (1991), also argues that Spinoza's God does not actualize all possibles but only the most perfect collection of them.

9. Ibid., p. 198.

10. Geb II, 77; emphasis added.

11. Garrett makes this supposition without noting the stark contrast between the totality of finite modes and that which is found pervasively throughout an attribute. It may be true that the totality of finite modes "occupies" all of extension, but that is entirely different from claiming that it — the totality itself — is found everywhere in an attribute. Nevertheless, as Garrett suggests, the totality itself is very likely supposed to be an infinite mode, and if so it must then follow from God's absolute nature (by E IP23). And perhaps, as Garrett hints, there is something about the totality — perhaps the way in which it stays the same, even though its parts are in constant change (if it is to be identified with the example given in Letter 64 of a mediate infinite mode, the *facies totius universi*) — that exists pervasively through extension.

12. Garrett leaves this supposition optional, but it must be made if the previous argument about the infinite intellect is correct.

13. Notes for NEH Summer Seminar: Central Themes in Descartes, Spinoza, and Leibniz, 1995 and 1996, p. 201. "Necessary," of course, should be understood as shorthand for "entailed by the absolute nature of God's attributes."

14. Garrett 1991, p. 198.

15. Ibid., p. 216, n. 11.

16. The problem may be that Garrett's note seems to presume his suggestion that Spinoza's God actualizes only the most perfect totality of finite modes, a suggestion rejected above.

17. For further discussion of this issue and an argument for an alternative reading of E IIP8S, see Carriero, "Spinoza's Views."

18. Those contexts are Geb I, 117–118; I, 238; II, 17–20; II, 63; II, 90; and II, 122.

19. H. A. Wolfson, *The Philosophy of Spinoza*, vol. 2 (Cambridge, Mass.: Harvard University Press, 1934; reprinted 1962), pp. 29–30.

20. This is Curley's helpful annotation; see Curley, p. 452, n. 15.

21. This may provide a clue for making sense of intuitive knowledge in Spinoza's epistemology: intuitive knowledge "proceeds from an adequate idea of the formal essence of certain attributes of God to the adequate knowledge of the [NS: formal] essence of things" (E IIP40S2).

22. In the *Treatise on the Emendation of the Intellect*, Spinoza provides an account of the "construction" of adequate ideas, from simple, intuited ideas to more complex ones.

23. Appendix E I (Geb II, 83). In their chapter in this volume, Curley and Walski suggest that in this passage, Spinoza means only to claim that there have been a great many antecedent conditions to produce a grand variety of things (although not all possible things). I believe it is telling, though, that Spinoza does not refer to antecedent conditions in this passage but instead to the amplitude of laws. The passage seems to say that the laws of nature are broad enough to allow for the actual production of absolutely every (logically and nomologically) possible thing.

24. This is a plausible candidate for the *facies totius universi*.

25. The sense of E IP24C seems to be that God "supports" the existence of things in each moment, just as Descartes suggests toward the end of the Third Meditation. This, together with E IP26, raises potentially interesting questions about the relation of Spinoza's thought to occasionalism.

26. A modern day, Spinozistically minded philosophy might understand all things to be and to be conceived through the three ultimate forces of nature: the electro-weak force, the strong force, and gravity. For it is out of these that all things are made, in contemporary cosmology. Or, more likely, such a philosophy would be counted among the physicists of super-

symmetry who maintain that these three forces will be subsumed finally under a single force in a Theory of Everything. See Paul Davies, *Superforce: The Search for a Grand Unified Theory of Nature* (New York: Simon & Schuster, 1984).

27. Jonathan Bennett, Edwin Curley, and Don Garrett are gratefully acknowledged for their rich, thought-provoking commentaries on Spinoza's metaphysics (see note 3). The National Endowment for the Humanities is also gratefully acknowledged for supporting Jonathan Bennett's 1995 Summer Seminar on the Rationalists, which aided the work for this chapter. Utah State University provided a University Research Grant, which also helped the work. Jan Cover, Edwin Curley, Diane Steinberg, Greg Walski, and an anonymous reader have all provided helpful comments on various drafts.

## 11

EDWIN CURLEY AND GREGORY WALSKI

# Spinoza's Necessitarianism Reconsidered

Everyone will agree that Spinoza is, in some sense, a necessitarian. After all, it is a theorem of the *Ethics* that "in nature there is nothing contingent, [that] all things have been determined from the necessity of the divine nature to exist and produce an effect in a certain way. (E IP29). And in the scholium to IP33, Spinoza claims to have shown "more clearly than the noon light that there is absolutely nothing in things on account of which they can be called contingent." But how much is Spinoza committed to by this denial of contingency?

Some interpreters of Spinoza have thought that because he acknowledges two different ways in which a thing may be necessary — either by reason of its essence or by reason of its cause (E IP33S1) — he is committed to allowing that some things (specifically, finite modes) are, in relation to their essence, contingent, and that as a consequence, there is a sense in which any particular finite mode might not have existed.[1] Arguably, this is implicit in IIA1: "The essence of man does not involve necessary existence, i.e., from the order of nature it can happen equally that this or that man does exist, or that he does not exist." This seems to imply that in addition to the actual world, in which we exist, there are, in Leibniz's language, other possible worlds in which we do not exist — presumably because in those possible worlds our finite causes, which stretch back into the infinite past (IP28), also do not exist. It is part of this view, of course, that the actual world *is* the only possible world if that means merely that, given a complete description of the world at any one time, the state of the world at any later time is determined by the laws of nature. Call this the *moderate necessitarian* interpretation of Spinoza.

Other interpreters, emphasizing such propositions as E IP16 — "From the ne-cessity of the divine nature there must follow infinitely many things in infinitely many modes, i.e., everything which can fall under an infinite intellect" — have taken Spinoza's necessitarianism more strictly, as implying that "each actual state of affairs is logically or metaphysically necessary," with the result that there is exactly one pos-sible world, the one which is actual.[2] Call this the *strict necessitarian* interpretation.

Still others have offered compromise positions of one kind or another: that Spinoza inconsistently commits himself both to strict necessitarianism and to its de-nial[3] or that the texts are too ambiguous to permit a decision concerning what he is committed to.[4]

In this chapter we will defend the view that Spinoza is committed to allowing for the existence of a plurality of possible worlds, that his necessitarianism is merely moderate, not strict enough to exclude the possibility of other worlds (in the Leibnizian sense of the expression, which requires that a "world" include all the things existing at all times and not merely all the things existing at some one time). We think this ought to be the default interpretation of Spinoza. It is, as Bennett says,[5] "tremendously implausible" that this is the only possible world. We operate on the methodological principle that views which are tremendously implausible should not be attributed to the great, dead philosophers without pretty strong textual evidence. To show that such evidence is lacking in this case, we shall concentrate on Don Garrett's article, "Spinoza's Necessitarianism," in the conviction that his case for at-tributing strict necessitarianism to Spinoza is the strongest one available.

## The Correspondence with Oldenburg

Garrett begins his article by citing an exchange between Oldenburg and Spinoza in their correspondence from 1675. In Letter 62 Oldenburg had written to Spinoza urg-ing him not to include in his *Ethics* anything which might seem to undermine the practice of religious virtue. In Letter 68 Spinoza asked what doctrines Oldenburg was advising him not to include. In reply (Letter 71) Oldenburg enumerated three doctrines which readers of the *Theological-Political Treatise* had found objection-able, though he did not explicitly claim that they might be harmful to the practice of virtue. In Letter 73 Spinoza pressed him to name a doctrine which would run that risk. In his reply (Letter 74) Oldenburg said that what had caused his friends the most distress was that Spinoza seemed "to build on the fatal necessity of all things and ac-tions; but they say that once that has been granted and asserted, the nerves of all laws, of all virtue, and of all religion, are cut, and all rewards and punishments are in vain. They think that whatever compels, or imposes necessity, excuses, and therefore, they think that no one will be inexcusable in the sight of God" (Geb IV, 310). In his re-sponse (Letter 75) Spinoza writes:

> At last I see what it was you were asking me not to publish. But because *that very thing is the principal foundation of all the things contained in the Treatise which I had determined to publish* [*Ethics*], I want to explain briefly in what way I maintain the fatal necessity of all things and actions. For I do not subject God to fate in any way, but I do conceive that all things follow with inevitable necessity from God's na-

ture, in the same way that it follows from God's nature that he understands himself. (Geb IV, 311–312)

Garrett emphasizes the phrase we have put in italics because he thinks he can show that interpreting Spinoza as a strict necessitarian, and treating strict necessitarianism as foundational in the *Ethics*, helps us to understand both Spinoza's monism and his doctrine that all adequate ideas must be true (in the sense that they correspond with their objects). And he treats IP29 and IP33 as key steps in the development of this foundation in the *Ethics*.

Garrett's use of this exchange sets the stage for his interpretation of the *Ethics*,[6] and ultimately his interpretation must be judged on the basis of the evidence he cites from that text. But it is worth pausing for a moment, before we get to the *Ethics*, to ask if there is anything in the *Theological-Political Treatise* which might suggest that in that work Spinoza commits himself to *strict* necessitarianism (as opposed to merely *moderate* necessitarianism). After all, it was from reading that treatise, not from reading the *Ethics*, that Oldenburg got the idea that Spinoza was committed to some objectionable form of necessitarianism. Garrett does not explore this issue, and Oldenburg does not say what texts made him think this. So we can only speculate. But we can find nothing in the *Theological-Political Treatise* more necessitarian than the following passage:

> Since nothing is necessarily true except by the divine decree alone, it follows quite clearly from this that the universal laws of nature are nothing but decrees of God, which follow from the necessity and perfection of the divine nature. Therefore, if anything were to happen in nature which was contrary to its universal laws, it would also necessarily be contrary to the divine decree, intellect and nature. (TTP vi, Geb III, 82–83)

There are two main claims here: first, that everything which happens in nature instantiates some universal law of nature; this is just determinism, which yields moderate necessitarianism but not strict necessitarianism; second, that the laws of nature follow from the necessity and perfection of God, that is, that they are themselves (absolutely) necessary truths (and not merely truths which are necessary in relation to other truths).

This second doctrine is not one which modern determinists normally hold; so what we have here is something more than just garden variety determinism. But it's not clear why the second doctrine would entail that the actual world is the only possible world in the Leibnizian sense. What generates the possibility of other worlds, on the moderate necessitarian interpretation of Spinoza, is the fact that laws alone will not determine what happens in the world. To explain any particular event it is necessary, on this interpretation, to know not only the laws of nature, but also the particular circumstances of their operation — what a modern philosopher of science would call the antecedent or initial conditions. If the state of the world at any given time is determined by the laws of nature in combination with the state of the world antecedent to that state, and both the laws and the antecedent state are required for the deducibility of the given state, neither being sufficient by itself, there will be an infinite regress of causes at the level of the antecedent states of the world. Spinoza apparently recognizes this in E IP28. And recognizing this seems to make acknowledging the possibility of other worlds (other instantiations of the laws) inescapable. For if the antecedent state was necessary, to make the given state what it is, then had the antecedent state been different, the given state would have been different. And if it should be suggested that the antecedent state (call it AS-1) was itself necessary absolutely, and not merely in relation to the state of the world antecedent to it (AS-2), this will be inconsistent with the implication of P28, that AS-1 was partially determined by AS-2.[7] Note also that it seems to be the determinism which is upsetting Oldenburg, not this eccentric thesis about the status of scientific laws. The objections he offers to the teaching of the TTP are the standard objections people make to determinism.

When Spinoza replies, he does so in a way which suggests a kind of soft determinism: the inevitable necessity of things does not make rewards and punishments pointless; the good which is offered as an incentive for good conduct will be no less desirable if the necessity of God's nature causes him to bestow it than it would be if he bestowed it as a judge might (i.e., in the popular conception, according to which a judge acts from free will and might, consistently with all antecedent circumstances, have acted otherwise); similarly, the evils which prospective criminals fear as a possible consequence of their bad conduct are no less evil if they follow necessarily from those actions (than they would be if God inflicted them by an act of free choice). If anything, they are more to be feared. If the criminal understands the necessity of the connection between wrongdoing and evil, he cannot hope to escape punishment by any contingency affecting his judge, such as a spontaneous act of mercy (cf. TTP iv; Geb III/63). Unlike a modern determinist, Spinoza focuses on the necessity of God's actions, not on the necessity of human actions. But what the necessity of God's actions makes necessary in the finite world is a connection between two events involving a finite being: his criminal action and the punishment (or his virtuous action and the reward). It does not make either the criminal action or the punishment intrinsically necessary.

## Garrett on IP16

Let's turn now to the *Ethics* and begin by looking at IP16. This is the first proposition in the *Ethics* which raises problems for our view. Garrett contends that P16 commits Spinoza to strict necessitarianism in two ways. First, he argues, Spinoza is committed to each of the following claims:

(1) Everything which falls under an infinite intellect follows from the necessity of the divine nature.
(2) "The necessity of the divine nature" is something necessary.

Proposition (1) is a paraphrase of P16 and seems unobjectionable as far as it goes. We'll have more to say about this later. Proposition (2) evidently means that the presence of the word "necessity" in (1) indicates that Spinoza thinks God's nature or essence is necessarily what it is. If anything is certain in Spinoza, it is that he holds (2), so interpreted. We add only that the necessity here attributed to God's nature should be understood in the strongest sense available. God's nature is necessary, not by reason of any external cause, but because of its intrinsic character (cf. IP33S1). We can call this strong notion of necessity "absolute (or unconditional) necessity" and use the phrase "relative (or conditional) necessity" for that species of necessity which holds when an object is only necessary given its cause. It is at this point an open question how "necessary" should be understood in its other occurrences in this argument.

(3)  Whatever follows from something which is necessary is itself necessary.

This is an axiom in any sensible modal logic, at least when "necessary" is understood as the logical necessity of modern modal logics. But recognizing that Spinoza does allow two ways in which a thing may be necessary, we think there may be some need for acknowledging that distinction in the way we formulate this proposition. More of this later.

(4)  Everything which is actual falls under an infinite intellect.

This is equivalent to saying that an infinite intellect must understand everything actual. Garrett argues that, given his understanding of "infinite," Spinoza would have to accept this. We agree, though it may emerge that we interpret (4) somewhat differently than Garrett does. But (1) through (4) entail this:

(5)  Everything which is actual is necessary.

And (5) is apparently equivalent to necessitarianism in the strict sense (the doctrine that every actual state of affairs is logically or metaphysically necessary, or that the actual world is the only possible world), or rather it is equivalent to strict necessitarianism if "necessary" is used throughout the argument in the sense of absolute necessity and if "actual" means what we might naturally suppose it does.

## Response to Garrett

Before we proceed to the second of Garrett's two routes from E P16 to strict necessitarianism, let us consider what we should say about this first argument. First, we accept (1) as a paraphrase of P16, only subject to the following interpretation:

(1′)  Everything which falls under an infinite intellect follows *in some way* (*either conditionally or unconditionally*) from the necessity of the divine nature.

The intent here is to make explicit that there may be more than one way for one thing to follow from another. Garrett apparently assumes that "follows" must mean "follows unconditionally," that is, without the aid of any other propositions. But this seems doubtful, for reasons which will emerge as we proceed. For now, let us simply note that the sequence of propositions IPP21–28 explains two different ways in which modes may follow from the necessity of the divine nature. PP21–23 deal with modes which follow from the *absolute nature* of one of God's attributes, or, in the language we used above, follow unconditionally from the necessity of the divine nature. P28 recognizes that not all modes follow from the absolute nature of one of God's attributes (cf. IP28D), or in the language we're using, that some follow from God's nature only conditionally, that is, with the aid of propositions which do not describe features intrinsic to God's nature. Accordingly, we would modify Garrett's (3) as follows:

(3') Whatever follows unconditionally from something which is absolutely necessary (i.e., necessary by reason of its essence) is itself absolutely necessary; but if something follows only conditionally from something which is absolutely necessary, then it is not itself absolutely necessary but only conditionally necessary (i.e., necessary by reason of its cause).

Given these amendments, Garrett's argument leads only to the harmless conclusion that

(5') Everything which is actual is either absolutely necessary or conditionally necessary.

This is harmless (for the purposes of this chapter) because it is consistent with moderate necessitarianism. It might not be harmless if our goal were to determine whether any finite being is morally responsible for his or her actions, for it certainly raises the problems Oldenburg was worried about. But if our concern is whether Spinoza thinks the actual world is the only possible world, it does not commit him to that.

Garrett anticipates a reply like this, though he does not anticipate quite this response. He notes that someone who thinks the series of finite modes is intrinsically contingent might seek to evade the implications of (3) by arguing that finite modes follow only *partially* from the nature of the divine attributes (p. 206), thereby invoking the distinction Spinoza will later draw between an adequate cause and a partial cause (E IIID2). But, says Garrett, if Spinoza *meant* that finite modes follow only partially from the divine attributes, and if he had the language available to make this distinction, why didn't he make it in Part I? Why did he leave us to read it back into his earlier discussion, after he explained this distinction to us in Part III?

There are various possible answers to this question. One is that Spinoza seems sometimes to deliberately violate the requirements of logical order which his geometric method might be thought to impose. For example, the demonstration of E IP21 assumes that thought is an attribute of God, but the proof of this proposition does not appear until IIP1. Another example occurs in the Scholium to IIP11C, which asks readers to abstain from judgment about the counterintuitive IIP11C ("the human mind is part of the infinite intellect of God") until they have read through everything Spinoza has to say. We take this disclaimer to be a general warning, applying to other propositions in the *Ethics* as well. More important, however, is the fact that Spinoza does, in the very neighborhood of E IP16, invoke a distinction equivalent to that between adequate and partial causes when he contrasts the things which follow from the *absolute nature* of a divine attribute with those which follow (as everything must) from the *nature* of a divine attribute but do not follow from the *absolute* nature of any divine attribute.

Garrett seems content to accept the account of God's causality offered in *Spinoza's Metaphysics*: "Finite modes follow from other finite modes *by means of* the laws of nature governing them. And these laws, at least—laws contained in the attribute or its infinite modes—do follow from the absolute nature of the attribute, whether there could have been a different total series of finite modes or not" (p. 206; Garrett's emphasis). But suppose it is allowed, as it seems to be here,[8] that the attributes and infinite modes contain laws of nature, and that we explain, adequately, the existence of a particular finite mode only by adducing both attributes and infinite modes, on the one hand, and prior finite modes, on the other, each kind of mode being only a partial cause when considered by itself. This is essentially the interpretation of IP28 offered in chap. ii of *Spinoza's Metaphysics*, an interpretation which seems to be gaining some acceptance in the literature.[9] This concession made, it is difficult to see how Garrett's Spinoza can escape the conclusion that there is more than one possible world (cf. *Spinoza's Metaphysics*, pp. 101–104).

We should say, at this point, that Garrett should have no problem with our interpretation of Spinoza's distinction between modes which do and modes which do not follow from the absolute nature of an attribute of God as equivalent to the distinction between adequate and partial causes. Spinoza defines adequate and partial causes as follows: "I call that cause adequate whose effect can be clearly and distinctly perceived through it. But I call it partial, or inadequate, if its effect cannot be understood through it alone" (E IIID1). Garrett argues that Spinoza employs the notion of following from the absolute nature of an attribute of God as a way to distinguish between things which follow from an attribute "without regard to how it is affected" and things which follow from an attribute "only where and when the attribute is qualified or affected in some particular way" (p. 196). Now, to say that a thing follows from an attribute without regard to how it is affected seems to imply that we need knowledge of nothing more than the attribute from which it follows in order to understand it. And to say that a thing follows from an attribute only when we consider the attribute to be affected in some way seems to imply that in order to understand that thing, we need not only general knowledge of the attribute from which it follows but also particular knowledge of the attribute's other affections. Hence, there should be no disagreement between Garrett and ourselves about the equivalence of these distinctions. But if the distinctions are equivalent, then Spinoza did not keep us waiting until Part III before he gave us the distinction we need to understand IP16. He introduced it within the next few propositions of Part I.

We find confirmation of our reading of E P16 in a crucial passage: the demonstration of P29, which aims to establish that in nature there is nothing contingent. Here is the key sentence: "The modes of the divine nature have also followed from it necessarily and not contingently (by P16)—either insofar as the divine nature is considered absolutely (P21) or insofar as it is considered to be determined to act in a certain way" (P28).[10] This seems to us to make it as clear as the noon light that Spinoza thought of the series of propositions between P16 and P29 as explaining the alternative ways in which a thing might follow from "the necessity of the divine nature."

There is, however, a problem about our restatement of (3) which needs to be acknowledged, even if it does not ultimately affect the issue between Garrett and ourselves. According to us, (3) should read:

(3′)  Whatever follows unconditionally from something which is absolutely necessary is itself absolutely necessary; but if something follows only conditionally from something which is absolutely necessary then it is not itself absolutely necessary, but only conditionally necessary.

This raises a problem about the status, not of the finite modes, but of the infinite modes.

According to (3′), the infinite modes should be necessary in precisely the same sense that the attributes are necessary. If we equate "absolute necessity" with the logical necessity of modern modal logics, and if we equate "follows from" with the entailment relation in those logics, this is inescapable. Accordingly, the author of *Spinoza's Metaphysics* sometimes said that, whatever Spinoza may have wanted to say, he *ought to have said* (given his view that God's existence and actions are logically necessary) that the infinite modes are necessary in whatever sense the attributes are necessary (cf. *Spinoza's Metaphysics*, pp. 107, 93, 98–99). And other authors on Spinoza have taken a similar line (cf. Bennett, *Study*, p. 111).

But this thesis about the infinite modes has its problems, both philosophically and textually. If the infinite modes are eternal in the same sense that God (or his attributes) is (are) eternal — that is, if their existence follows necessarily from their definition (E ID8) — then the infinite modes are *causa sui* (ID1). And this seems inconsistent with their status as modes (cf. ID5). Accordingly, in some passages in *Spinoza's Metaphysics* the author took a different line. In commenting on chap. v of part II of the *Short Treatise*, he argued that there Spinoza seemed to say that the infinite modes are only conditionally necessary (though conditionally necessary in a way very different from the way finite modes are conditionally necessary, since their necessity is conditional — ultimately, at least — only on the existence of something which is absolutely necessary). The passage which prompted this remark reads:

> Some objects are corruptible in themselves; others, through their cause, are not corruptible; but there is a third [object] which, solely through its own power and capacity, is eternal and incorruptible.
>
> The corruptible, then, are all the singular things, which have not existed from all time, or have had a beginning. The next are all those [universal] modes which we have said are the cause of the singular modes. But the third is God, or what we take to be one and the same thing, the Truth. (KV II, Geb I, 62–63)

The corruptible, singular things are clearly the finite modes of the *Ethics*. The universal modes, which Spinoza characterizes as the cause of the singular modes, are clearly the infinite modes of the *Ethics*,[11] which function as a kind of bridge between God and finite modes. Like God, the universal modes are incorruptible. But unlike God, they do not owe their incorruptibility to their own nature; they owe it to their cause, God. So they occupy an ambiguous status. If we take "incorruptibility" as a surrogate for "necessity," we cannot place them happily in either of the two categories of necessity which the *Ethics* recognizes in IP33S.[12] Perhaps what this shows is that Spinoza's "necessity by reason of the essence of the thing" should not be equated with the logical necessity of modern modal logics since a proposition which possesses this kind of necessity does not transmit the same kind of necessity (even) to its (unconditional) logical consequences.

## Garrett's Anticipation of Our Response

Anticipating something like our interpretation of E IP16, Garrett also contends that the demonstration of this proposition makes it clear that the relation between the divine nature and the infinitely many things supposed to follow from it "is to be understood as the relation between a scholastic essence and its properties" and that TdIE 96 shows that "the properties of a thing are all deducible from the essence of the thing *alone*" (p. 206; Garrett's emphasis). But Spinoza regularly oversimplifies the relation between the essences of things and their properties, as when he suggests in IP17S1 that it follows simply from the nature of a triangle that the sum of its three interior angles is equal to the sum of two right angles, as if the definition[13] were the only assumption needed to derive that theorem. If we look at the proof of the theorem in Euclid's *Elements* (book I, proposition 32) and trace its deductive ancestry back to the initial assumptions, we find — what should not surprise us - that not only must we assume the definition of a triangle in order to prove the theorem, but we must assume other propositions as well, such as the definitions of a right angle and of parallel lines and (what's much more serious since it involves an assumption which is neither definitional nor plainly axiomatic) the famous parallel postulate.[14]

    Why does Spinoza regularly *misrepresent* the geometrical situation in this way? We don't know. Perhaps he (and others who speak this way) do so because they think (correctly) that the proof of this theorem in Euclid requires no other substantive assumption about *triangles*, apart from the definition. Or perhaps Spinoza thought that a more rigorous geometry could dispense with the parallel postulate and rely only on definitions and common notions. Proclus seems to have thought that.[15] But if Spinoza did actually *misunderstand* the geometrical situation, then it was a mistake he apparently shared with Descartes, no mean geometrician, but also a philosopher who speaks in the Fifth Meditation as if it were possible to deduce Euclid I, 32, simply from the definition of a triangle (cf. AT VII, 64). We hypothesize that Spinoza may have understood the geometrical situation perfectly well, but misdescribed it because there had developed, by the time he wrote, a tradition among philosophers of speaking carelessly about these matters.[16]

## IP16 Again

The second way in which Garrett contends that E IP16 commits Spinoza to strict necessitarianism concerns the relation between actuality and possibility. First, Garrett argues that Spinoza is committed to the following claims:

(6) Everything which falls under the infinite intellect is actual.
(7) Everything which is possible falls under the infinite intellect.

We agree that Spinoza is committed to these two claims. He affirms the latter in IIP8, and as Garrett points out, the former is directly entailed by IP16 itself and confirmed in IP30. But from (6) and (7), it follows that

(8) Everything which is possible is actual.

Garrett claims that (8) is equivalent to strict necessitarianism, but we disagree.

To see why, we must understand the two senses in which Spinoza thinks a thing can be actual. In E VP29S, he writes:

> We conceive things as actual in two ways: either insofar as we conceive them in relation to a certain time and place or insofar as we conceive them to be contained in God and to follow from the necessity of the divine nature. But the things we conceive in this second way as true, *or* real, we conceive under a species of eternity, and to that extent they involve the eternal and infinite essence of God (as we have shown in IIP45 and P45S).

This is a somewhat mysterious Scholium, but we can make sense of it in connection with IIP8 and IIP8S. Let's divide it into two parts, dealing with the first part now.

Take any individual thing, say, Spinoza himself. We can conceive him as standing in spatiotemporal relations to other individuals, such as the other finite modes necessary to bring him into existence, or we can conceive him in abstraction from such relations. When we conceive him in the former way, we have an idea of an existent singular thing; and when we conceive him in the latter way, we have an idea of a nonexistent singular thing. Now, according to E IIP8, the abstract idea of Spinoza (which we should perhaps think of as the idea of a type of individual, which might be realized in a number of particular spatiotemporal situations) is comprehended in God's infinite idea in the same way as the formal essence of that type is contained in God's attributes.[17] Thus, when we think of the type, we are having an idea of a *nonexistent* singular thing, a thing which is nevertheless *actual* insofar as its formal essence is contained in God's attributes.[18]

The second part of E VP29S states that when we conceive things insofar as they follow from the necessity of the divine nature (which, in this context, means in abstraction from their spatiotemporal relations), "we conceive [them] under a species of eternity, and to that extent they involve the eternal and infinite essence of God." And IIP9 says: "The idea of a singular thing which actually exists has God for a cause not insofar as he is infinite, but insofar as he is considered to be affected by another idea of a singular thing which actually exists; and of this [idea] God is also the cause, insofar as he is affected by another third [NS: idea], and so on, to infinity." These two passages suggest that it is only abstract types which follow from the absolute nature of an attribute, that when we embed an instance of such a type into a network of spatiotemporal relations, we are thinking of a singular thing which has spatiotemporal existence but does not follow from the absolute nature of an attribute. This should come as no surprise, for E IIP9 makes the same point as IP28, only under the attribute of Thought. Where IP28 asserts that *singular things* do not follow from the absolute nature of an attribute of God, but from God insofar as he is considered to be affected by another singular thing, IIP9 makes the same assertion about *ideas* of singular things. Expressing the general point in the language we're using, we say that abstract types follow unconditionally from the necessity of the divine nature, whereas existent singular things follow only conditionally from the necessity of the divine nature, that is, given an accommodating prior series of finite causes.

Insofar as we agree with Garrett that Spinoza is committed to the claim that all possibilities are actual — Garrett's (8) — but have explained what we think is the correct interpretation of that claim, we have already addressed his second argument from E IP16 to strict necessitarianism. That being the case, it may seem superfluous to address the additional argument he offers for Spinoza's commitment to the claim that everything possible falls under the infinite intellect — Garrett's (7).[19] But because that argument contains an implicit attack on a moderate interpretation of Spinoza's necessitarianism, we feel it warrants attention.

As we have explained, Garrett points out that Spinoza's commitment to the claim that everything falling under the infinite intellect is actual, (6), is entailed by E IP16 and reinforced in IP30. That Spinoza held (6) is quite certain, as is the fact that (6) and (7) entail (8), which Garrett claims is equivalent to strict necessitarianism. It may appear, therefore, that the only way to avoid the alleged necessitarian conclusion is to deny that everything possible falls under the infinite intellect. As Garrett points out, however, if we explore the possible explanations for how Spinoza could have thought that, we see quite clearly that Spinoza could not accept any of those explanations without falling into inconsistency. This gives the impression (although Garrett does not say this explicitly) that a moderate interpretation of Spinoza's necessitarianism requires assigning to him a claim which is inconsistent with the text and, therefore, a bad interpretation.

As our arguments make clear, however, that impression is misleading, for it is based on a failure to acknowledge the two senses in which Spinoza thinks a thing can be actual (E VP29S). If we don't take this aspect of Spinoza's philosophy into account when evaluating the claim that all possibilities are actual, we are then naturally led to assume that actuality implies spatiotemporal existence. And because it is clear that Spinoza thought everything contained in the infinite intellect is actual, we are also led to assume (again, quite naturally) that if Spinoza does allow for possible but nonexistent finite modes, the infinite intellect must lack ideas of them. But by reading Spinoza's claim that everything falling under the infinite intellect is actual in the light of VP29S, we clearly see that a moderate interpretation of his necessitarianism does not require denying that the infinite intellect contains ideas of everything possible. Instead, attention to that scholium yields an alternative, *more complete* understanding of what Spinoza's commitment to the claim that all possibilities are actual amounts to. Contrary to what we might intuitively think it means, we are to understand it as asserting that all possible singular things are actual features of reality insofar as their formal essences are contained in God's attributes.

Thus, the fact that all possibilities are actual for Spinoza does not commit him to strict necessitarianism. His realism about laws — that is, his insistence that general truths have a basis in reality which transcends their exemplification in particular

things—means that the notion of actuality in his philosophy does not imply existence at some particular point of space and time.

## Garrett on IP29

The next proposition which Garrett argues commits Spinoza to strict necessitarianism is IP29, which states: "In nature there is nothing contingent, [that] all things have
been determined from the necessity of the divine nature to exist and produce an effect in a certain way." Because IP16 serves as the central premise of the demonstration of IP29, and because Garrett believes that he has established that P16 implies
strict necessitarianism, he thinks he can show very quickly that P29 implies strict necessitarianism: "If, as I have argued, the necessity of EIP16 must be construed as logical or metaphysical necessity, and not as mere "inevitability in light of antecedent
conditions," then the denial of contingency in EIP29, which is derived from and para-
phrased in terms of that proposition, must be understood in the same sense" (p. 209).
Now, there's certainly a strong case for interpreting "the necessity of EIP16" as logical or metaphysical necessity. For the reference to necessity in P16 is to a feature possessed by the divine nature, that is, God's infinite attributes, which are *causa sui* in
the sense of D1: their essence involves existence; they cannot be conceived except as
existing. There may be a problem about equating the unconditional necessity possessed by the divine attributes with the logical necessity of modern modal logic since
the infinite modes show that this necessity is not transmitted by entailment. But this
is a problem all interpreters must face, not a special problem of the strict necessitarian interpretation.[20]

Suppose we grant that God's nature is what it is necessarily, in the strongest sense
of necessity available in Spinoza's system (however precisely we understand that notion of necessity). Why should it follow *from that* that when Spinoza says *everything
else* in nature is necessary, he must be claiming that those things, too, are necessary
in the strongest possible sense and not merely inevitable in the light of their antecedent conditions (i.e., conditionally necessary)? If the attributes are not, by themselves, a sufficient condition for particular finite modes (as Garrett generally seems
willing to concede)—that is, if finite modes require for their explanation an infinite
series of prior finite modes as their causes, in addition to the attributes and infinite
modes—then why should we expect them to share the absolute necessity of their *partial* cause? More especially, why should we expect this when E IIA1 explicitly tells us
that the essences of particular finite things do not involve existence? That's a reasonable expectation in the case of the infinite modes, which follow unconditionally
from the attributes. But why should it be a reasonable expectation in the case of the
finite modes, which follow only conditionally from the attributes?

Garrett concedes that Spinoza holds that individual finite modes do not follow
from the absolute nature of the attributes.[21] But he thinks that this doctrine can be
understood in a way which does not commit Spinoza to allowing for a plurality of
possible worlds:

> Spinoza nowhere denies that the whole *series* of finite modes follows from the ab-
> solute nature of the attributes. His claim is only that no *individual* finite mode fol-

lows from it. Indeed, if the total series of finite modes as a whole series were *itself* an infinite mode — not an implausible suggestion, given its pervasive and permanent extent — then it would *necessarily* "follow from" the absolute nature of the attributes, by EIP23. (p. 198; Garrett's emphases)

Garrett is here tempted by Letter 64 to identify the individual described in E L7S, following E IIP13 — that is, "the whole of nature" — with the mediate infinite mode under the attribute of extension. This is probably a bad idea since that individual cannot serve his purposes, even if it is an infinite mode.[22] But Garrett wisely does not commit himself to this "suggestion":

> The crucial point is that no finite mode would follow, *considered independently of its membership in this series*, from the nature of an attribute. For if the mode followed *independently*, it would have to be necessarily pervasive and permanent throughout the attribute, i.e., it would have to be an infinite mode. Instead, each finite mode would follow from the nature of an attribute, but *only in virtue of its membership as part of the one consistently constructible or maximally perfect series of finite modes*. (p. 198; Garrett's emphases)

We find a number of difficulties with this reading. First, we do not see why we should suppose that there is exactly one consistently constructible series of finite modes, and we consider it question begging to assume that there will be — particularly in view of the argument in *Spinoza's Metaphysics* (pp. 101–104), which still seems to us to show that if you admit that finite modes are only conditionally necessary, you must admit a plurality of consistently constructible series of finite modes.

Second, suppose we emphasize the phrase "maximally perfect." Garrett seems to think that, just as the *ens realissimum* must have all possible attributes (E IP9), so it must express itself in the series of finite modes which has the highest degree of reality and perfection (p. 197). But how are we to understand the idea that the actual series of finite modes has the highest degree of reality and perfection without comparing its degree of reality and perfection with those of other possible series? And doesn't that bring in precisely the idea of a plurality of possible series, which Garrett's interpretation was supposed to avoid? If there's only one possible series, the claim that it has more reality and perfection than any other doesn't seem to say much.

Garrett acknowledges that the identity of the series of finite modes is constituted by the identities of each of its members[23] and that none of the members follows from the absolute nature of the attributes. But he still wants to say that the series as a whole follows from the absolute nature of the attributes because the series as a whole has some unique property. To us, this seems impossible. If you think of the series as having a first member and of the members of the series being so related that once the first member is given, the rest follow, then you can see how *causing the first member* would *cause the series as a whole*. That's the way the relation between God and the world is often conceived in traditional theology. But in this case there is no first member of the series, and the ultimate cause is supposed to produce (be a sufficient condition for) the series as a whole *without causing any individual member of the series*. We have yet to see how that is possible.

Garrett argues, however, that the series of finite modes *can* follow from the absolute nature of the attributes, even though no finite mode considered individually does. He admits: "Of course, the absolute nature of the attribute would 'entail' the existence of each individual finite mode, in the sense that there would be no possible world in which the attribute had that absolute nature and yet the finite mode did not exist." But he points out that "Spinoza requires more than this of the 'following from' relation" (p. 216, n. 11). And he explains that for Spinoza, "to speak of *x* [*sic*] as following from *y* [*sic*] is to locate *x* specifically as a necessitating *cause and ground* of *y* within a causal order of the universe that is at once dynamic and logical" (p. 194; Garrett's emphasis).

We have no doubt that Spinoza understood the causal relations between attributes and modes in the manner Garrett suggests.[24] But it is unclear how that might answer our question; it seems only to rephrase it. Now, we should ask: "If the absolute nature of the attributes is the cause and ground of the series of finite modes, wouldn't that entail that it is also the cause and ground of each finite mode within that series?"[25] Garrett suggests that it would not, apparently because for Spinoza "a finite mode can be said to 'follow from' an attribute 'considered' in one way, but fail to 'follow from' it when it is considered in another, more restricted way" (p. 216, n. 11).

But this distinction does not license Garrett's move. It *does* allow Spinoza to hold that whether a finite mode follows from an attribute depends on how the *attribute* is considered, and of course Spinoza makes heavy use of this distinction: infinite modes follow from the *absolute nature* of the attributes, and finite modes follow from the attributes only when the attributes are considered *with their affections*. But nowhere does he suggest that whether finite modes follow from the attributes depends on whether the *finite modes* are considered *individually or collectively*. And that would be what Garrett's reading requires.

We conclude, therefore, that E IP29 should not be understood as asserting strict necessitarianism.

## Garrett on IP33

The third and final proposition of the *Ethics* on the basis of which Garrett argues that Spinoza is committed to strict necessitarianism is IP33: "Things could have been produced by God in no other way, and in no other order than they have been produced." The difference between IP29, on the one hand, and IP33, on the other, is subtle. Whereas P29 is concerned to show that everything is determined, by the necessity of the divine nature, to exist and produce effects, P33 is concerned to show that the divine nature could not have determined things to exist and produce effects in any other way.

Garrett's contention that this proposition commits Spinoza to strict necessitarianism rests heavily on his analysis of Spinoza's use of the locution "the order of Nature" in the demonstration, which reads as follows:

> For all things have necessarily followed from God's given nature (by P16), and have been determined from the necessity of God's nature to exist and produce an effect in a certain way (by P29). Therefore, if things could have been of another nature, or could have been determined to produce an effect in another way, so that the order of Nature was different, then God's nature could also have been other than it is now, and therefore (by P11) that [other nature] would also have had to exist, and con-

sequently, there could have been two or more Gods, which is absurd (by P14C1). So things could have been produced in no other way and in no other order, and so on, q.e.d.

He claims that "of Spinoza's many uses of this term ["order"], in the *Ethics* and elsewhere, nearly all at least suggest that the order of nature includes particular finite modes as parts, and several imply it more directly" (p. 210).[26] Taking the finite modes to be part of the order of nature, a change in which leads to the absurdity that establishes IP33, and noting that IP33 says that things could have been produced in no other "order," Garrett concludes that the proposition must be understood as eliminating the existence of a plurality of possible worlds thus committing Spinoza to strict necessitarianism.

Now we certainly agree with this much of what Garrett says about Spinoza's use of "the order of nature": it is at least true that *frequently* Spinoza uses that expression in such a way that finite modes are clearly included in the order of nature. This is undoubtedly true of two of the three passages Garrett cites, E IP11D and IIP24D, and probably true also of three others which he does not cite: I/243, I/266, and II/213.

However, Garrett had good reason not to make a universal claim about Spinoza's use of this expression. For there are clear cases in which the order of nature does not include finite modes, most notably E IIA1, where Spinoza writes that "the essence of man does not involve necessary existence, i.e., from the order of nature it can happen equally that this or that man does exist or that he does not exist." This must mean that it is consistent with the laws of nature that any particular man should not exist, that the existence of any particular man requires (in addition to the laws of nature) the antecedent conditions which those laws specify; it cannot mean that it is consistent with the laws of nature and the past history of the world that a particular man who does exist should not exist. Otherwise Spinoza would give up (what everyone agrees he held) determinism.

Another case which seems equally clear (and quite interesting in its own right) occurs in the *Metaphysical Thoughts*: "There is the *ordinary* power of God, and his *extraordinary* power. The *ordinary* is that by which he preserves the world in a certain order; the *extraordinary* is exercised when he does something beyond the order of nature, e.g., all miracles, such as the speaking of an ass, the appearance of angels, and the like" (CM [*Cogitata metaphysica*] I, ix; Geb I, 267) Here an act "beyond the order of nature" is a violation of a law of nature. To the extent that Spinoza suggests that such violations occur, he is speaking as the expositor of Descartes, as the continuation of the passage makes clear enough for the perceptive reader:

> Concerning [God's extraordinary power] there could, not without reason, be considerable doubt. For it seems a greater miracle if God always governs the world with one and the same fixed and immutable order than if, on account of human folly, he abrogates the laws which (as only one thoroughly blinded could deny) he himself has most excellently decreed in nature, from sheer freedom. But we leave this for the Theologians to settle. (CM I, ix; Geb I, 267)

This is a reminder that Hume did not invent irony. But it also reminds us of what might have seemed to Spinoza to be at stake in the debate about necessity. It is a central theme in Spinoza's philosophy — a central point of difference between him and

Descartes — that God did not institute the laws of nature the way a king might ordain laws for his kingdom, as an act of free will. We think that all Spinoza is claiming in E IP33 is that the laws of nature are necessary truths which flow from God's very nature, not contingent truths which flow from an act of divine free will. In his day, and perhaps in ours, too, this is a bold thesis, which does not lack philosophic interest. It was certainly a thesis Spinoza emphasized in the passage from TTP which we discussed in the first section.

The argument from Spinoza's allegedly typical use of the phrase "order of nature" is a weak one. There are several passages in which it seems that Garret is clearly right; the phrase refers to the finite modes, as well as to the laws of nature. There are a number of other passages in which it seems to us to refer simply to the laws of nature; in addition to the two clear cases just cited, we would add the following as at least probable cases: Geb II, 75, 90, and 137. And there are quite a few cases in which the context simply does not suffice to fix Spinoza's meaning. In this category we would put I, 241; II, 16, 21, 28, 276; and (though this may be controversial) II, 25 (TdIE 65). So there doesn't seem to us to be enough consistency in Spinoza's usage to permit any inference about what he must mean in E IP33. What he means there must be decided, if it can be, by the particulars of that context. Since there is a perfectly sensible interpretation of P33 which is consistent with our reading of Spinoza as a moderate necessitarian, one which makes P33 intelligible as a contribution to his debate with Descartes (and any other theologian who thinks that the laws of nature depend on the arbitrary will of God), we see no need to regard P33 as a difficulty for our reading. The change in the order of nature which would ensue were things "of another nature" or "determined from the necessity of God's nature to exist and produce . . . effect[s] in a certain way" should be understood as the result of a change in the *causal laws which necessitate the existence and effects* of finite modes — not as the result of an *alternative series* of finite modes.

## Conclusion

In conclusion, we want to discuss briefly two passages not discussed by Garrett, which might seem to support his interpretation of Spinoza's necessitarianism. The first occurs in the scholium to E IP17.[27] Spinoza's opponents held that if God had created everything he understood, he would not have been able to create anything more, which they took to be contrary to his omnipotence. Spinoza argues, in response, that his opponents' position actually denies God's omnipotence since it implies that God understands things which he is unable to create, on pain of exhausting his power. Hence, he suggests that "all the things [God] actually understands exist" (Geb II, 62).[28] Garrett would presumably read this as implying that God has created everything in his intellect, that is, that there are no unrealized possibilities. It seems to follow that unicorns, for example, either are impossible or existent at some point in space or time. And that seems an unwelcome consequence. Prima facie, unicorns are possible but don't exist at any point in space or time. At any rate, before we attribute to Spinoza the view that their logical possibility guarantees their existence, we should ask if this is the only possible way to read what he says.

We suggest that the notion of an "unrealized possibility" deserves some scrutiny, that it might mean one or the other of two very different things. When we say, for example, that a unicorn is an unrealized possibility, we *might* mean that although such a being is logically possible, it is inconsistent with the laws of nature that there should be such a thing. On the other hand, we might mean that a unicorn is an unrealized possibility because, though consistent with the laws of nature, the sufficient conditions for the occurrence of a unicorn have never been realized (cf. E IA3: "If there is no determinate cause, it is impossible for an effect to follow"). Now, clearly, Spinoza wouldn't say that unicorns are an unrealized possibility on the ground that, while logically possible, they are inconsistent with the laws of nature; he thinks the laws of nature are logically necessary; it can't be the case that something logically possible is inconsistent with something logically necessary. So, in that sense, there are no unrealized possibilities; that is, everything that God understands exists. Our claim that there are unrealized possibilities for Spinoza, then, should be understood in the latter sense, as asserting that there are things which are possible insofar as they are consistent with the laws of nature, although they are not possible *simpliciter* since they are not provided with antecedent conditions sufficient to instantiate their existence. So we can admit that there is a sense in which a unicorn is an unrealized possibility: such a thing is (we assume) consistent with the laws of nature but unrealized because there is no accommodating series of finite causes for such a thing. In this sense, God does *not* create everything he understands; that is, there *are* unrealized possibilities. And that seems to be as it should be.

The other passage we would like to discuss — because it might seem to commit Spinoza to strict necessitarianism — occurs in the appendix to part I of the *Ethics*. Spinoza is arguing that "men judge things according to the disposition of their brain, and imagine, rather than understand them." (Geb II, 83) He suggests that someone who "imagines" things rather than "understands" things might ask "why God did not create all men so that they would be governed by the command of reason." Spinoza responds as follows: "I answer only 'because he did not lack material to create all things, from the highest degree of perfection to the lowest'; or, to speak more properly, 'because the laws of his nature have been so ample that they sufficed for producing all things which can be conceived by an infinite intellect' (as I have demonstrated in P16)" (Geb II, 83).

We find it rather suggestive here that Spinoza speaks of God as "not lacking material to create" all kinds of things. We read this as a tacit acknowledgment that God, insofar as he is infinite, is not an adequate cause of finite things, that he produces them only with the aid of other finite things, which provide, as it were, the material for his creation. But we don't think that we should press the language about "all things, from the highest degree of perfection to the lowest," as if Spinoza were committed by that language to the existence of everything which is logically possible (or even consistent with the laws of nature), including unicorns. We take the reply more narrowly, as saying simply that the "reason" there are both rational men and irrational men is simply that sufficient conditions for realizing both kinds were available (though they might not have been had the history of the world been different). If the material is there, God must "create" both kinds of men.

This talk of creation, of course, is "improper." That is why Spinoza corrects himself and rephrases his answer by producing a paraphrase of E P16, which emphasizes the causal role of the laws of God's nature. But if, as we have argued previously, P16 does not imply strict necessitarianism, then neither should this paraphrase.

We conclude, then, that the passages which have seemed to provide the strongest support for a strict necessitarian interpretation of Spinoza — both those which Garrett focuses on and others which he might have appealed to — do not do so, that they are, in fact, open to a more moderate interpretation. There is no compelling textual reason to think that Spinoza is committed to the claim that the actual world is the only possible world, nor, so far as we can see, is there any plausible philosophical explanation of how he might have thought that would be true.

## Postscript

In commenting on an earlier version of this chapter, Charles Huenemann objected that "your Spinoza cannot explain why one possible universe is actual and another is not. That this universe, and no other is actual is, I take it, a brute fact, true independently of any fact about God." And this might be thought to be inconsistent with what Bennett calls "the demands of explanatory rationalism" and what others might call "Spinoza's understanding of the principle of sufficient reason."[29]

It might help to see why the existence of this universe is not properly characterized as a "brute fact," if we set Spinoza's view, as we interpret it, in the context of some recent discussions in the philosophy of religion, specifically the work of Richard Swinburne, in his book *The Existence of God*.[30] We might put Swinburne's argument for the existence of God in the following way: there are certain facts about the world which science, in virtue of the logical form of scientific explanations, cannot explain. Scientific explanations take two forms, depending on the kind of fact to be explained. If the fact is a particular one (say, that this planet is at this point in its orbit at this time), then scientific explanation takes the form of deduction from certain general facts called laws of nature (say, Kepler's laws of planetary motion) in conjunction with other particular facts (in this case, for example, facts about the planet's positions at earlier times). If the fact is a general one, such as a law of nature itself, then scientific explanation takes the form of deduction from higher-level, more general laws.

On this picture of scientific explanation there are two kinds of facts which are, for logical reasons, not susceptible to scientific explanations: the totality of particular facts and the most general facts of all. The totality of particular facts cannot be explained because, if the totality really does contain all the particular facts (past, present, and future), the only facts available for explaining that totality are those wholly general facts described by the laws of nature, and you cannot deduce any particular facts from general facts alone. Again, the most general facts cannot be explained scientifically because if they really are (as the hypothesis assumes) *the most general* facts, there are no more general facts which could be adduced to explain them. So here are two kinds of facts which science cannot explain, not because it hasn't advanced sufficiently yet, but because, given the nature of scientific explanation, and the nature of those facts, it could *never* explain them. But we ought to try to explain whatever we can explain. If scientific explanations are necessarily unavailable, then we should seek a personal explanation, one which postulates as the cause a person, who has certain goals and has brought about the phenomena in question in order to realize those goals. This person, whom we conceive to be supremely perfect, we call God.

Now Spinoza, as is clear from the Appendix to Part I of the *Ethics*, does not think that a being who has the attributes traditionally ascribed to God can have goals. Broadly speaking, people have two kinds of goals: either they wish to achieve a future state different from their present state, and so far as they can see, better than their present state; or they wish to maintain their present state, which they judge to be better than some other possible future state which they think they might be in. But a supremely perfect being cannot have goals of either kind. If it is supremely perfect, then it cannot conceive any future state which it might be in as better than its present state. Nor if it is supremely perfect can it be threatened by the possibility of deterioration into a state which it judges to be inferior to its present state. One of the perfections a perfect being must have is immutability.

So the theistic hope that we might be able to explain by a personal explanation what we cannot explain scientifically is a chimera. A being which had the properties God would have to have, to serve as an explanation for the phenomena he is invoked to explain, could not have goals of the kind required for personal explanation. The only possible kind of explanation is scientific explanation. Once we understand that scientific explanations are necessarily unavailable for such phenomena as the existence of the totality of finite things and for the existence of the most general laws governing finite things—necessarily unavailable because of the nature of thosephenomena—then we understand that we have as much explanation as we can reasonably dersire. So we see why, for logical reasons, we ,ust seek no further explanation. In these circumstances it is inappropriate to speak of "brute facts." The facts in question, by their nature, are not the kind of facts for which an explanation is even conceivable; and the nature of the facts themselves explains why we—and Spinoza—should seek no further explanation for them.

*Notes*

1. One of the authors of this chapter argued for this position long ago. See E. M. Curley, *Spinoza's Metaphysics: An Essay in Interpretation* (Cambridge, Mass.: Harvard University Press, 1969), chap. 3. Alan Donagan also adopted this interpretation of Spinoza's necessitarianism in his *Spinoza* (Chicago: University of Chicago Press, 1988), pp. 113–116.

2. The most recent and elaborate defense of this interpretation is in Don Garrett's article, "Spinoza's Necessitarianism," in Yirmiahu Yovel, ed., *God and Nature in Spinoza's Metaphysics* (Leiden: Brill, 1991), pp. 191–192. But a similar interpretation can be found in Stuart Hampshire's *Spinoza* (New York: Penguin, 1951), and in A. O. Lovejoy's *The Great Chain of Being* (New York: Harper, 1960), pp. 151–157.

3. See Jonathan Bennett, A *Study of Spinoza's* Ethics (Indianapolis: Hackett, 1984), chap. v.

4. See R. J. Delahunty, *Spinoza* (London: Routledge & Kegan Paul, 1985), pp. 155–165.

5. In "Spinoza's Metaphysics," in *Cambridge Companion to Spinoza* (Cambridge: Cambridge University Press, 1996), p. 75.

6. We might say that it prejudices the discussion in his favor since the passage clearly indicates that Spinoza is committed to necessitarianism of some sort, and Garrett simply uses the term "necessitarianism" to mean the doctrine we are calling strict necessitarianism, as if what we are calling moderate necessitarianism did not deserve to be recognized as one form necessitarianism might take. The propriety of calling our "moderate necessitarianism" a form of necessitarianism may be seen by reflecting that it clearly entails what Hume calls "the doctrine of necessity" in his essay "Of Liberty and Necessity," *Inquiry Concerning Human Understanding*, sect. 8. (Hume's doctrine of necessity is the view that human actions, even when voluntary, are subject to the same laws of nature as the operations of matter.)

7. For a quasi-formal demonstration of this, see Curley, *Spinoza's Metaphysics*, pp. 101–104. Charles Huenemann has suggested in correspondence that *if* Spinoza holds (a) that the laws of nature are necessary, and *if* he holds also (b) that it is necessary that a certain quantity of matter (1) must exist and (2) undergo changes, and *if* he holds also (c) that every possible configuration of matter is actualized at some time or other, then Spinoza would be both a determinist and an absolute necessitarian. Perhaps so. We assume that in this set of views hypothetically attributed to Spinoza, "a certain quantity of matter" means "a finite quantity of matter." On that interpretation, we would concede that (a) and (b) entail (c), yielding a strict necessitarian reading of Spinoza. But we question whether, on that interpretation, Spinoza held (b1).

8. The passage quoted occurs in a context in which Garrett is simply imagining something someone might say, if that person wished to evade the force of his argument. So perhaps he is not speaking *propria persona*. But when he replies to that reply, he does not reject this part of it.

9. See, for example, Bennett, *Spinoza's Ethics*, p. 113; Michael Della Rocca, *Representation and the Mind-Body Problem in Spinoza* (New York: Oxford University Press, 1996), pp. 6–7; and (in its essentials, at least) Donagan, *Spinoza*, pp. 102–107. By the essentials of that interpretation we mean the doctrine that the attributes (insofar as they are infinite) are an adequate cause of the infinite modes but not of the finite modes, of which they are only a partial cause, and that they are an adequate cause of finite modes only insofar as they are also considered as modified by finite modes. (But finite modes are not themselves an adequate cause of other finite modes either.) When we add that the attributes and infinite modes are associated with laws of nature and that their causal role is to be understood in terms of a deductive-nomological theory of causal explanation, we add something inessential for the purpose of determining Spinoza's doctrine of necessity (though it may be illuminating in other ways).

10. The OP (*Opera posthuma*) has "P27" where we read "P28." Gebhardt thought that reading was correct, and it is supported by the NS (Nagelate Schriften), for what that's worth. Gueroult suggested "P28," which seems to us obviously right. See Martial Gueroult, *Spinoza*, vol. 1 (Paris: Aubier-Montaigne, 1968) p. 343n.

11. This is clear from our earlier introduction to them in part I, chaps. viii–ix, of the *Short Treatise*, where they are said to be "eternal" and "immutable." Presumably, though, they are not by themselves an adequate cause of the singular modes. Cf. KV I, 2nd dialogue, especially sect. 10.

12. Though the KV clearly has, in "incorruptibility," something analogous to the necessity of the *Ethics*, and though it also seems to have the doctrine that God, insofar as he is infinite, is only the partial cause of finite modes, the discussion of necessity in KV I, iv–vi, does not seem to reflect these distinctions.

13. We assume here that when Spinoza says that this property of a triangle follows from its nature, that implies that it follows from its definition since it is the function of a good definition to state the nature or essence of the thing being defined. See TdIE 95 and Geb III, 57/28, for a coupling of *natura* and *definitio* by *sive*.

14. In Euclid the proof of P32 depends on the proof of P29, which invokes the parallel postulate. So you don't have to trace the deductive ancestry of P32 back very far to get to a substantive assumption. Charles Huenemann reminds us, in comments on an earlier draft of this chapter, that it's clear from TdIE 95 that Spinoza does not approve of the Euclidean definition of a triangle, precisely on the ground that it does not suffice for a deduction of the properties of triangles. But it's hard to see how the alternative definition he proposes there would escape the same objection if we were to take very strictly the requirement that the definition should suffice all by itself.

15. See *Euclid: The Thirteen Books of the Elements*, T. L. Heath, trans. and intro. (New York: Dover, 1956), vol. I, pp. 321–322. This was still a live project in Spinoza's day. See Imre Toth, "Non-Euclidean Geometry Before Euclid," special issue on the Origins of Technology, *Scientific American*, 1997.

16. The oversimplification did trouble some of Spinoza's more mathematically sophisticated correspondents; cf. Letter 82, from Tschirnhaus. Spinoza's reply is interesting, but not, we think, helpful to Garrett's case.

17. By saying that a thing's formal essence is "contained in God's attributes," Spinoza means, roughly, that the essence of that thing is an actual feature of an attribute of God, insofar as the possibility of the existence of a thing with that essence is implied by the nature of the attribute. For a fuller explanation, see Curley, *Spinoza's Metaphysics*, pp. 138–142.

18. Spinoza refers to this point in E IP8S2: "This is how we can have true ideas of modifications which do not exist; for though they do not actually exist outside the intellect, nevertheless their essences are comprehended in another in such a way that they can be conceived through it."

19. See II1C: *"Parallelism and causal independence,"* pp. 207–209.

20. Perhaps the solution is to deny that when Spinoza says that one thing follows from another, he means that the one thing is deducible from the other in the sense in which deducibility is understood in standard contemporary modal logics. Garrett suggests this in one place (p. 194), for reasons having nothing to do with the present problem.

21. He could hardly deny it. But conceding that individual finite modes are not unconditionally necessary does seem inconsistent with the account he offers of strict necessitarianism, according to which it holds that "every actual state of affairs is logically or metaphysically necessary" (pp. 191–192).

22. The whole of nature in L7S is an individual which maintains its identity through time, in spite of the changes it is undergoing, because its parts (all bodies) maintain a constant relation to one another. It is not spread out over the whole of time in the same way as the total series of finite modes. The series consists of the totality of temporal "slices" constituted by the totality of bodies and their states existing at any given moment. So the series is a totality of the second order, whose members are first-order totalities. We propose to identify the *facies totius universi* with the features of the whole of physical nature which remain constant over time, not with the whole of nature itself.

23. E-mail correspondence, 26 July 1996.

24. See *Spinoza's Metaphysics*, chap. I.

25. We are not claiming that on Garrett's reading, individual finite modes would "follow from" the series of finite modes, in which case a particular finite mode not only would be caused by subsequent finite modes but also would be the cause of itself. Rather, we are arguing that if the absolute nature of the divine attributes were the cause of the series of finite modes, then it necessarily would be the cause of each finite mode within that series as well.

26. See II3: *"EIp33: The order of nature,"* pp. 210–211. Garrett cites P11D, IIP24D, and TdIE 65 in support of his interpretation of "the order of nature" in Spinoza.

27. Garrett does mention IP17S twice, but only parenthetically, on pp. 195 and 207.

28. In this same scholium, Spinoza writes that "from God's supreme power, *or* infinite nature, infinitely many things in infinitely many modes, that is, all things, have necessarily flowed, or always follow, by the same necessity and in the same way as from the nature of a triangle it follows, from eternity and to eternity, that its three angles are equal to two right angles" (Geb II, 62). But insofar as Spinoza refers us to IP16 for the demonstration of this claim, we have already addressed this passage.

29. Cf. Bennett, *Cambridge Companion*, pp. 75–76; Henry Allison, *Benedict de Spinoza* (New Haven, Conn.: Yale University Press, 1987), pp. 76–77.

30. Oxford: Clarendon Press, 1979. There is a convenient summary of Swinburne's argument in "The Justification of Theism," published in *Truth Journal*, available on the Web at http://www.leadershipu.com.

# PART THREE

# MIND AND CONSCIOUSNESS

## 12

STEPHEN VOSS

# A Spectator at the Theater of the World

In his early twenties Descartes announces, "So far, I have been a spectator in this theater which is the world, but I am now about to mount the stage" (AT X, 213). His program is participatory from the moment he formulates it. He means his intellectual labors to support a life of engagement in the world: "It was always my most earnest desire to learn to distinguish the true from the false in order to see clearly into my own actions and proceed with confidence in this life."[1] But I shall identify here certain pressures in his dualism and in his strategies for gaining certainty and security, which impel him in the end to get off the stage, join the audience, and become a spectator.

This conclusion is reminiscent (though its premises are not) of certain radical critics of Descartes — Vico, Schopenhauer, Marx, Nietzsche, Dewey. It makes contact with (but does not endorse) the anti-Cartesianism rampant in recent anglophone philosophy: "It is widely granted these days that dualism is not a serious view to contend with, but rather a cliff over which to push one's opponents."[2] The conclusion proposes an amendment to an orthodoxy painstakingly won by the great Descartes scholars of the last half century, who, approaching him neutrally, historically, and respectfully, argue that his dualism is compatible with a morals of engagement.[3] Their methods are models of what scholarship can be, and they jointly establish much of the orthodox position beyond serious dispute. Still, that position conceals one of the sources of the confused anglophone discontent with Descartes.

My aim in this chapter is to clarify the sources of one venerable strand in the deep philosophical distrust of Descartes: the suspicion that a Cartesian soul must be isolated from this world in the same way a spectator is isolated from the action depicted on the stage. Descartes himself spotlights the image of a spectator at a tragedy, and the suspicion turns out to be well founded. But the reasons are more subtle and also more complex than is traditionally assumed, and philosophically more interesting than the conclusion itself. When we expose the sources of the image of the spectator, we preserve Descartes's worldview as a philosophy worthy of serious criticism — not simply a resource for reductio arguments. All the same, the sources of that image impose restrictions on the place of the Cartesian soul in the Cartesian world not yet acknowledged in recent scholarship.

To be a spectator at a drama is to engage in one form of activity. There is no such thing as a purely passive spectator. As a spectator, one attends interpretively to the drama and, in consequence, through imagination identifies with its characters and feels analogues of their passions. Alongside the spectating, one continues to engage in other activities: adjusting one's seat, whispering to a companion, jotting notes. One continues to participate in life off the stage.

But a spectator is in one specific way entirely passive. As a spectator, one does not participate in the events of the drama: they are sealed off from one's activity and accessible only to imagination. One attends to real events on a stage, events which are easy enough to disrupt. But one interprets them as dramatizations of entirely different events, not located on a stage, events which, because they are fictional, are not accessible to one's intervention. One's concern is not to watch something real but to imagine what one knows is not. One may attend to what is real — an actor's gaffes, the poor acoustics, one's own passions or actions — but spectating is attending to what is not real. One understands that one's passions are generated by one's imagination of fictional events, and takes both the events and the passions less seriously than those of life off the stage. One can always reassure oneself with the correct thought that it's only a play. Knowing that, one regards the drama as falling into a category distinctly less important than life beyond the stage.

Descartes himself employs various comparisons to a spectator at a tragedy, revealing something of his own conception of the spectator. He draws the comparisons late in his career, for reasons which will become apparent below, in five letters to Elisabeth in 1645–1646, and in the *Passions of the Soul* in 1649.[4] It will be useful to sketch the conception of the spectator that he displays in these passages. When we watch a tragedy, says Descartes, we see an action "represented on a stage" (passages a, f, g, h); what we see is not a murder, for example, but the representation of one. It is given to the senses and imagination (a, g, h), but insofar as we know that the tragedy is an imaginary fable, it will not touch the intellect (b). It will arouse passions in us, which may cause discomfort (d) and even harm the health (b). But these passions do not penetrate deeply into our soul (e, h), because the represented action is imaginary (b), does not matter much to us (e, h), and cannot harm us (f). Even passions like sadness and hatred, aroused by a tragedy, can give pleasure and joy (a, c, f, g), first because we naturally take pleasure in feeling our passions (f, g), when we remain in control of them (c), and second because at times we have the impression that our passion is virtuous (c). Our pleasure is an intellectual joy, which in contrast with those passions penetrates deeply into the soul (g).

I will sometimes call attention to Descartes's comparisons with the experience of a spectator. But my aim is to draw comparisons of my own, between the position

I conceive a spectator at a drama to adopt and the position of anyone who accepts Descartes's strategic priorities and his dualism. I'll mention his comparisons only to illuminate the ones I want to draw.

Descartes's epistemology, morals, and metaphysics each contain reasons to look on most of real life as a spectator looks on a drama. The reasons derived from his epistemology are the least serious and can be defused without much distortion. But the impulse to view the world as a play is inherent in his morals and is still more deeply rooted in his metaphysics. I will discuss each of these kinds of reasons in turn.

## The Epistemological Spectator

Even though Descartes experiences a spontaneous impulse to believe he is sitting by the fire in a winter dressing gown with a piece of paper in his hands, it strikes him in the First Meditation that he might be lying undressed in bed. His apparent knowledge of his own actions is his first defense against the skeptical assault: "Yet at the moment my eyes are certainly wide awake when I look at this piece of paper; I shake my head and it is not asleep; as I stretch out and feel my hand I do so deliberately, and I know what I am doing. All this would not happen with such distinctness to someone asleep" (AT VII, 19). He soon finds reason for uncertainty about his own actions, and transforms them from actions into particulars to be known: "Suppose then that I am dreaming, and that these particulars—that my eyes are open, that I am moving my head and stretching out my hands—are not true. Perhaps, indeed, I do not even have such hands or such a body at all." A moment later his thought of these actions has entirely dissolved into the abstract conception of the kinds of bodily parts they involve: "At least these general kinds of things—eyes, head, hands and the body as a whole—are things which are not imaginary but are real and exist" (AT VII, 19–20). At this point, bodily actions are replaced by kinds of bodily parts. The meditator no longer attends to his own actions. He is entirely preoccupied with the epistemic credentials of his beliefs about his body. Watching his body move as though in a dream, he no longer knows what he is doing.

Suppose now that I have established that there is a nondeceiving God. If I set out deliberately to move my body and to attend to the way my action appears to me, I might be able to get evidence that I am not dreaming. Being able to act and to observe attentively how my action looks and feels may help. But Descartes does not include these capacities when in the Sixth Meditation he enumerates the faculties God gives me to gain knowledge and distinguish waking from sleeping. He does not include deliberate action I can attend to as I act, but only the faculties of sense, memory, and intellect (AT VII, 89; the list is repeated on 90). The last paragraph of the *Meditations* ignores the meditator's capacity for (i) deliberate movement of his body and engagement with physical things and (ii) attentive observation of the way his action and its consequences appear to him. It depicts a being who has imaginatively transformed and alienated his own actions, as a spectator might transform an actor's performance into the slaying of Agamemnon.

We find something similar in the Fourth Meditation. Descartes analyzes erroneous judgment as the joint product of intellect, a passive faculty, and volition, an active one.[5] His conception is often interpreted in this way: intellect apprehends a proposition as being more or less likely to be true and presents it as such to the will, which then executes an act of judgment on the presented proposition. That is not accurate. Descartes asks intellect to do much more work than that — far too much, it seems to me, for a faculty that he defines as entirely passive and incapable of judgment. Here are some of the things this passive faculty does:

(1) Intellect *enables me* not simply to have ideas but *to perceive my ideas* (AT VII, 56).[6]
(2) Intellect *enables me to perceive the truth*. I should refrain from judgment when I do not perceive it with sufficient clarity and distinctness (59, 61).
(3) Intellect sometimes *makes the truth clear*. It *reveals things* to me. And I should judge only when intellect makes the truth of a matter clear (62).
(4) Intellect *lets me understand things*. It is the faculty of understanding (57). Using it, I can understand things clearly and distinctly (61). I should make judgments about things only after I have understood them (58, 60, 61).
(5) Intellect *operates infallibly*. It is incapable of error, not on the conceptual ground that intellect is prior to judgment, but because its origin is divine: "The cause of my errors is not . . . the power of understanding, for since my understanding comes from God, everything I understand I undoubtedly understand correctly, and it is not possible that I am deceived here" (58; also *Principles of Philosophy* 1:30, 43).

In short, intellect is the faculty of knowledge (56). Since error requires volition and judgment, and knowledge does not, knowledge is simpler than error. Intellect is something like a passive homunculus, which can do nearly every epistemic task without judgment or volition and never err in doing it. With such a robust faculty of knowledge, one might wonder why we need a faculty of judgment at all.[7]

The doctrine is not new. Rule 12 of the *Rules for the Direction of the Mind* distinguishes "the faculty of the intellect by which it intuits and knows things from that by which it judges in affirming and denying" (AT X, 420). The premise of the rules of method in the *Discourse on Method* is that knowledge of the truth is prior to the judgment in which we receive it as true: "The first [rule] was never to receive anything as true that I did not know evidently to be so: that is, carefully to avoid precipitousness and prejudice; and to include nothing more in my judgments than what presented itself so clearly and so distinctly to my mind that I would have no occasion to put it in doubt" (AT VI, 18).

When Descartes's meditator sets out in search of knowledge, his passivity goes far beyond that of the usual spectator. In the First and Sixth Meditations, he ceases to examine the results of his efforts to move his own body, but any spectator can do that. In the Fourth Meditation, his faculty of knowledge is entirely passive, but a normal spectator attends and interprets, affirms and denies, and in general makes use of active faculties. The meditator is a radically and implausibly passive spectator.

If I ignore the consequences of my attempts to move my body, I place a very large obstacle in the way of gaining knowledge. Attentive observation of the way my actions and their consequences appear to me is the essential core of any experimental program. And if I use only passive faculties, I cannot possibly gain knowledge. The terms "knowledge" and "understanding" and "perception" are particularly unfortunate labels for any passive faculty. If intellect is the faculty of knowledge, it incorporates active, as well as passive, functions (though perhaps not always acts of will, or voluntary acts). Just as there cannot be a purely passive spectator, there is no such thing as a purely passive knower.

But Descartes is not deeply committed to modeling the knower after a radically passive spectator. True, in the First Meditation he questions the reliability of observation, and as we shall see in the next section he has already questioned whether bodily movements count as actions. But after he restores some of the credentials of observation in the Sixth Meditation, he might easily enough have recalled that God renders the soul-body union reliable for generating bodily movement and licensed observation of my own attempts to move my body.

It is also true that the Fourth Meditation requires Descartes to analyze judgment into passive and active components. But he might have done better to speak of passive and active intellect than to treat intellect as wholly passive. He creates the materials he needs for the passive aspect in the Second Meditation: "I am now seeing light, hearing a noise, feeling heat. But I am asleep, so all this is false. Yet I certainly *seem* to see, to hear, and to be warmed. This cannot be false" (AT VII, 29). On the one hand, it strikes me that there is light: I am passive. On the other hand, I judge that there is light: I am no longer passive. Descartes introduces the distinction into sense perception, but it is at home in nonsensory judgments too: on the one hand, Cantor's set theory and Pascal's wager strike me as plausible; on the other hand, I take them to be flawed. There is all the difference in the world between being given something and taking it. When light is given, I need not accept the gift. And only if I accept it — only if I take it that there is light — will I see or perceive or know or understand that there is light. Knowledge, as well as error, requires the judgment in which I take what is given. Without much difficulty, and without much violence to the *Meditations*, Descartes might have acknowledged the active aspect of intellect in the making of judgments both true and false.[8] He could have confined intellect's passive function to the presenting of (i) propositions to me, together with (ii) an epistemic indicator of their apparent truthfulness — the likelihood, as it seems to me, that those propositions are true. He could then have denied the possibility of knowledge prior to judgment.

For these reasons, the passages I have cited from the *Meditations* do not license the common variety of reflexive Descartes bashing. Descartes's epistemology does not require either a knower who cannot attend to his own attempts to take action or a faculty of knowledge that is entirely passive. One way in which I think it is possible to preserve Descartes's philosophy as worthy of serious criticism is to show that it is not deeply committed to the image of the hyperpassive spectator.

Nevertheless, the legacy of the radically passive epistemological spectator for three and a half centuries has been deep and disastrous. Clarity about that antique model is still valuable philosophically, since even today our recovery is incomplete. Here are two examples of what I mean.

First, we are inclined to confront skeptical challenges as beings incapable of attending to our own actions. A few decades ago, philosophers bruited about a new version of an old skeptical hypothesis. Inspired by the first generation of computers — but also by the First Meditation — they floated the possibility that my sensations may be generated by a machine that electrically stimulates my sensory nerves, on the basis of a program entirely insensitive to my wishes or volitions or motor nerve impulses, and thereby provides me with a simulacrum of a world.[9] This machine is simple and easy to conceive, for it is not interactive and has no capacity to receive signals from me. These philosophers thought that a machine incapable of responding to my attempts to take action could give me a representation of what it is like to live in a real world.

Years passed before anyone realized that there is a simple and devastating reply to the skeptical challenge posed by the simple machine.[10] My own sensations are affected by my efforts at physical activity. I attempt to close my eyes: my visual field darkens; to shake my head: my visual field shifts; to stretch out my hand: I feel new objects. I could be deceived by that machine only if my experience were that of a total paralytic whose sensations do not depend on attempts to move his body, that of a dreamer unable to act, or that of a spectator so caught up in the drama that it does not occur to him to take action. My sensations are a function of two independent variables: not only the state of the world poised to stimulate my nerves, but also the movements by which I intervene in the process. Once philosophers noticed the fact, they set about designing an interactive, second-generation machine. I do not mean here to evaluate their success. My question is not philosophical but historical: why did it take them so long to notice that the simple hypothesis need not be taken seriously? Part of the explanation is that we have learned from Descartes to regard ourselves as onlookers at the epistemological theater of the world: spectators of the process of acquiring our own knowledge.

Second, we have learned from the Fourth Meditation that we have a passive faculty of knowledge. We have allowed ourselves to suppose that while error requires judgment, knowledge and understanding need not. The Fourth Meditation encourages the mischievous idea that there is a kind of knowledge prior to judgment. That is one root of the disastrous notion of knowledge by acquaintance, an apprehension of "the given" that requires no taking, a kind of knowledge so simple as to be immune from error. It was Descartes who called the play: "The light of nature or faculty of knowledge which God gave us can never encompass any object which is not true in so far as it is indeed encompassed by this faculty" (*Principles* 1:30). He flipped the ball to Spinoza: "All ideas, insofar as they are related to God, are true" (*Ethics* IIP32), and on the next play lateraled to Leibniz: "Since God's view is always true, our perceptions are always true; it is our judgments, which come from ourselves, that deceive us" (*Discourse on Metaphysics* 14). But it was Bertrand Russell who caught the touchdown pass and electrified the crowd. The idea of knowledge by acquaintance is not dead. It lives on in the entirely unproductive and fundamentally incoherent cottage industry that nurtures discourse concerning raw feels or qualia. What gave that industry its first big boost, and supports it still, is Descartes's thesis that it is possible to "perceive ideas" without employing the apparatus of judgment.

The image of the hyperpassive epistemological spectator is, in part, the shadow cast by a more formidable spectator, generated by the dualism of soul and body and by the dream of security from error and regret. Descartes's metaphysics and morals may require a gap between thought and extension like that between the audience and the stage. They may require that we value the extended world less than we do. In metaphysics and in morals, the role of spectator may be harder to shake off.

## The Moral Spectator

The second maxim of Descartes's provisional morals in the *Discourse on Method* was "to be as firm and resolute in my actions as I could." The third was "to try always to master myself rather than fortune, and change my desires rather than the order of the world" (AT VI, 25). Descartes intends singlehandedly to establish a "practical philosophy" that will make possible great new achievements in mechanics and medicine (AT VI, 61–62), but he does not want to risk disappointment if he fails. As Ferdinand Alquié puts it: "Descartes desires success and domination of nature, and counsels abstention and resignation."[11] How can he act firmly and decisively without risking disappointment? How can he make himself, as it were, a "master and possessor of nature" without trying to master fortune?

Corneille will have three years to ponder these two maxims before he puts in the mouth of Auguste words that will epitomize Descartes's century: "Je suis maître de moi comme de l'univers: Je le suis, je veux l'être" (*Cinna* V, 3). Marion underscores the tension: "The 17th century orders: it orders contraries, under the ascetic pressure, if you will, of a will all the more imperious for mastering the I before the world, all the more firm for officiating under the title and in the name of reason."[12] Descartes will risk all of his beliefs about the world in order to find an Archimedean point from which to move the world from the scholastic gloom of occult qualities into the thin, bright Galilean light of reason. He will risk all of his hopes for mastery of the world of nature in order to master himself. In the end, he will claim each time to secure definitively all he has risked. Now, in the name of reason, he begins to seek a way to resolve the apparent conflict in his morals, so that he may yet master nature as well as himself.

His approach is twofold: first, to consider that what he has failed to achieve, after he has done all he can with external matters, is absolutely impossible in relation to him; second, to recommend that we consider all external goods as equally beyond our power. For then we shall cease to desire them, and for that reason we shall not regret our failure to obtain them. Observe his reasoning (AT VI, 25–26):

(1) We should believe that "what we fail to achieve, after doing our best with things external to us, is absolutely impossible with respect to us."
(2) It is (1) alone that will suffice to prevent us from desiring in the future anything we are not going to get[13] and from regretting our failure to get it.[14]
(3) For our will naturally tends to desire only what our intellect represents to it as somehow possible.
(4) Unstated reflection: all external goods depend at least in part on external conditions that we cannot control or be sure of beforehand. So even

in the case of those external goods we manage to achieve, we cannot be sure beforehand that we will achieve what we desire. Therefore, if the aim is to forestall unsatisfied desire, (1) does not in fact suffice.

(5) More strongly, then, we should "consider all external goods as equally beyond our power."

(6) That will indeed protect us from unsatisfied desire. When the sages whom Descartes emulates "perfectly persuaded themselves that nothing was in their power but their own thoughts . . . this alone was sufficient to keep them from having any affection for other things." If we follow (5) and consider all external goods as beyond our power, then given (3) we will no longer be naturally inclined to desire them.

But now antinomy results.

(7) Unstated corollary: when we cease to desire any external goods, nothing will move us to do our best with them. But (1) presupposes that we are so moved, and the second maxim requires it.

Descartes deals with the antinomy by proposing two extraordinary new doctrines. Each of them leads him to regard events beyond the soul as a spectator regards the action in a play.

His first extraordinary response, aroused in 1638 by Pollot's allegation that (5) is a "fiction,"[15] is to assert that none of the activities of the body can be morally attributed to the human being: no bodily activities are actions performed by a human being. Here are his words:

> It does not seem to me a fiction, but a truth nobody should deny, that there is nothing entirely in our power except our thoughts, at least when the word 'thought' is taken as I do. . . . In philosophical language there is nothing at all properly attributable to man apart from what is covered by this word; for as for the functions that belong to the body alone, they are said to take place in the man rather than to be done by the man. (AT II, 36)

Descartes's motivation is clear enough. He seeks a strategy that will forestall regret. Now regret results from reflection on actions we have done or could have done. If a human being understands that nothing but thoughts can be attributed to him, he will be immune from regret over activities that belong to the body, since such things are not his actions. In fact, if he regrets only what is attributable to him, and if something is attributable to him only if it is entirely in his power, then it will be entirely in his power not to suffer regret.

What is extraordinary is the path Descartes takes to stave off regret. The actions human beings do will now be confined to their souls. Such actions will include no bodily movements at all — neither involuntary functions like the beating of the heart (that much Pollot would have granted) nor the movements that occur when we move our head or stretch out our hands or (AT VI, 26) treat our illnesses. The bodies of human beings will be sealed off from their action in the same way the world beyond is: nothing a human being does will take place in the body. If we take "doing our best with things external to us" to designate the action of a human being, it will be a thought internal to the soul.

Once human beings have carried out such thoughts, they must now regard the things that take place in their bodies much as a spectator regards the events depicted on the stage. For what happens in our body and what happens beyond it are (to use the words of AT VI, 26) "equally beyond our power." And, as Descartes will tell Elisabeth eight years later,

> I think we should take little account of all the things outside us that do not depend on our free will, in comparison with those that do depend on it. Provided we know how to use our will well, we can make everything which depends on it good and thus prevent the evils that come from elsewhere, however great they may be, from penetrating any further into our soul than the sadness which actors arouse in it when they represent before us certain fateful actions. (AT IV, 355)

If Descartes holds that the functions that belong to the body are not done by the human being, we can perhaps see one reason why, in the First Meditation, he will regard moving my head and stretching out my hands not as actions but as particulars to be known.

In the words of 1638 I have quoted above, Descartes can also be seen as taking the first step on a tortuous journey that will lead him first to abandon the principle that soul and body constitute a composite entity — a "true human being," in the words from the *Discourse*, whose ink has so recently dried (AT VI, 59) — and then in consequence to devalue the life of the body. This journey takes him squarely into metaphysics and saddles him with the deepest reason for adopting the outlook of the spectator.

The body is one part of a human being, the soul another. We can perhaps understand why a bodily movement that occurs because the soul wills it might not be attributed to the *soul*; the movement takes place in the *body*. But why should Descartes deny that that movement, which also takes place *in the human being*, can be *attributed to* the human being? We have seen the moral motivation for the denial. But observe the metaphysical consequences. What happens in the human being can still be *predicated of* the human being; it still "takes place in" that being. But it cannot be attributed morally to, and is not performed by, the human being. Agency in a human being is restricted in this way to thought. Here begins the metaphysical erosion of the nature of the human being.

The metaphysical ground for adopting the position of a spectator is the most fundamental, and I shall consider it in the next section. I turn now to a second moral ground, which results directly from Descartes's second singular response to the antinomies of the third maxim. That extraordinary response takes place only in 1649. Allow me a moment to set the stage.

Pleasure and pain may or may not be related in the obvious way to antecedent desire. They sometimes enter our lives unanticipated and reflect no preexisting desire to gain the pleasure or avoid the pain. I learn with surprise that a dreaded conversation is enjoyable; I learn with surprise that the stove burns my hand. I had not sought pleasure in the conversation or wished to avoid pain in touching the stove. Our desires are crude instruments for obtaining pleasure and avoiding pain, and must forever scurry to keep up with the actual sources of pleasure and pain.

But if we learn wisely, we come increasingly to desire what will give pleasure and stave off pain. Consequently pleasure will increasingly result from getting something we desire. Insofar as we care about our own pleasure and are good judges of what will produce it, more of life's pleasures will derive from desire satisfied, and more of its pains from desire thwarted.

Now in the *Discourse*, and as late as 1645 (AT IV, 265–266), Descartes advises us to desire only what is entirely within our power. Suppose that I am planning a trip and think it would be good to avoid being robbed. I know one of the two routes is more dangerous than the other. Avoiding robbery is not entirely within my power. So I should not desire to avoid it. Instead, I should desire to do two things to the best of my ability: (i) to reason about which route to take and then (ii) to will to take the route that reason dictates. And I should strictly confine my desire to these two things.

This advice is problematic. If you do not have the desire (iii) to avoid being robbed, what reason would you then have to do all that is entirely in your power that might conduce to *that* end? If I confront a task which like (iii) depends partly on me and partly on other causes,[16] why should I desire to do the part of *that* task that is in my power? It certainly seems that I will desire to do the part that is in my power — (i) plus (ii) — only in virtue of *somehow* desiring to do (iii), the entire task.

Descartes never explicitly acknowledges this difficulty, but it may explain why, in two successive articles of the *Passions of the Soul*, he amends his advice that we should cease to desire things that do not depend entirely on our free will. He says now that we "should never desire them with passion" (art. 145). This suggests that there are two varieties of desire — common desire and something we can call "desire without passion." Language employed both in this article and in the next suggests that what is characteristic of desire without passion is that it does not "occupy" our thought.

Desire is by definition a passion (art. 86), so it may seem that desire without passion is like a square without shape. But this, too, is no occasion for hasty Descartes bashing. For twelve years Descartes has struggled with an antinomy, and in the next article of the *Passions* he gives significant substantive content to his new language.

Desire without passion has two distinctive features (art. 146). First, like common desire, it moves us to act: it does not leave us "indifferent to choosing," and hence it remains "instrumental in regulating our actions." Second, if we fail to get what we desire in this way, we feel no disappointment and our satisfaction is not reduced. Descartes says that if we do all in our power to avoid being robbed and simply have desire without passion for that outcome, "our desire . . . must be fulfilled"; and desires so regulated "always give us complete satisfaction." If such a form of desire is indeed possible, its understanding and nurture would be a great good; such desire has, it would seem, the benefits of common desire without its drawbacks.

But the doctrine has a striking and perhaps disturbing corollary. We will gain no *further* satisfaction from achieving things we desire, in case those things depend on causes outside of us. For example, Descartes tells Burman that he wants both Turks and Europeans to accept his philosophy (AT V, 159), but if they do, that will give him no more pleasure than if they reject it. Among the pleasures and pains of the life of the body, there will remain to us only those that are innocently unrelated to our desires.

To the extent that our pleasure in things beyond our soul is truncated, Descartes's morals further encourage the model of the spectator. The spectator reminds himself, "It's only a play," and qualitatively alters his passions. Descartes re-minds himself, "It's not in my power," and qualitatively alters his desire. Each may then remind himself, "It cannot harm me." In each case the result is that events matter less than they would have and are not taken with such seriousness. The fictional actions represented on the stage give a spectator distinctly different varieties of pleasure and pain. The objects of "desire without passion" give no pleasure or pain at all.

## The Metaphysical Spectator

According to part V of the *Discourse* and the Sixth Meditation, the soul and the body are joined so closely that they form a composite entity—the human being (AT VI, 59; VII, 81). But I believe that in about 1642, a year after the *Meditations* was published, Descartes ceases to hold that soul and body make up a larger whole, though they remain closely united. I believe that his metaphysics of soul and body forces him to this position. And I shall argue that the rejection of the human being on metaphysical grounds is what impels him most forcefully toward the position of spectator.

I shall sketch two reasons why his own metaphysics leads Descartes to cease to accept the existence of the composite human being. The first is a *problem of predication*. A theory of human beings must specify the kinds of properties that can be predicated of them. But it is difficult to square the resulting anthropology with his dualistic metaphysics. The second is a *problem of meaning*. What is meant when one predicates something of a human being?

Consider first the problem of predication. It is natural to suppose that

(1) There are human beings who are five feet, nine inches tall and re-member meeting Isaiah Berlin.

Nevertheless, this statement contradicts Descartes's metaphysics of soul and body. For according to that metaphysics,

(2) What is five feet, nine inches tall is extended,
(3) What remembers meeting Isaiah Berlin thinks, and
(4) Nothing that is extended thinks.

At those moments when Descartes sets out to convince his reader of the real distinction between soul and body, he frequently raises the question whether as a thing that thinks he could possibly be a body, or an extended thing.[17] What does he mean by "body" in this context? Of course he does not mean, as he will by the end of his discussion, "thing that is extended and lacks thought"; that would trivialize his question. He means simply "extended thing"; he has in mind in particular the human body; and he is concerned above all else to refute the panoply of Aristotelian scholastics who maintain that what thinks is not the soul but the ensouled and extended human body.[18] If he cannot rule out the attribution of thought to bodies so conceived, he has signally failed.

The fulcrum of his argument for the real distinction is often a defense of proposition (4): a thinking thing cannot be a body. In particular, a thinking thing cannot be an extended and ensouled human body. Of course, on the Aristotelian view, the ensouled and extended human body is the human being. Descartes means to rule out the view that the human being as conceived by Aristotelians exists, if it both thinks and is extended. It seems to me likely, for reasons that will emerge in a moment, that it was in the course of writing the Sixth Responses that he began to understand that his answer also ruled out the position that the human being as conceived in the Sixth Meditation both thinks and is extended.

Proposition (4) is, in fact, Descartes's principal support for the thesis that there is a real distinction between thinking things and extended things. It is absolutely central to his metaphysics. We should not expect him to give it up. To the contrary, I believe that it was precisely his ruminations on (4) that led him to give up propositions like (1) — and in the process to give up human beings themselves.

In 1638, Descartes had written that thoughts can be attributed to a human being, although bodily movements cannot, and only take place in a human being. It seems reasonable to interpret his assertion that movements cannot be attributed to, and are not performed by, a human being as a moral-cum-metaphysical thesis: a denial of moral responsibility to the human being on the grounds of a denial of agency. And it seems reasonable to interpret his assertion that they take place in a human being as a purely metaphysical thesis: an affirmation that movements can be predicated of human beings. But that thesis, in conjunction with the thesis that thoughts can be attributed to human beings, brings us very close to (1) and the clash with (4).

Descartes returns to the question with a difference, in the Responses to the Sixth Objections to the *Meditations*. He observes that some philosophers "might even affirm that it is one and the same being that thinks and moves from place to place" (AT VII, 423). And he attacks the scholastic interpretation of the affirmation: the thesis that there is a "unity of nature" between the thinking thing and the extended thing, so that the thing that thinks and the thing that is extended are one and the same in virtue of an "affinity or connection" between thought and extension. "When they are said to be 'one and the same,'" he asks, "is this not rather in respect of unity of composition, in so far as they are found in the same man?" (AT VII, 424).

Toward the end of the Sixth Responses, Descartes denies that he has ever seen that human bodies think; all he has seen is that there are human beings, who have both bodies and thought. But the crucial question is how human beings can "have" both. Here is his explanation: "This occurs by a thinking thing's being combined with a corporeal thing" (AT VII, 444). Descartes might mean to explain his thesis that human beings have bodies and thought in one of two ways. He might continue his explanation either by saying (i) "and that is what makes it true that a human being is in fact thinking and extended" or by saying (ii) "and this does not involve a human being's itself thinking and being extended." According to (i), a human being thinks and is extended because it has a part that thinks and one that is extended. According to (ii), the way a human being "has" thought and a body is *not* by itself thinking and being extended but rather by having thinking and extended parts.

If we let the first passage elucidate the second, we may plausibly interpret Descartes as maintaining a more radical position than he had in 1638. It seems to me that the most sensible interpretation of the second passage is (ii) — that there is nothing that both thinks and is extended. In particular, it is false that thought and extension can be predicated of human beings. For surely one thing that disturbs Descartes in the unity-of-nature position — that "it is one and the same being that thinks and moves from place to place" — is the idea that the same thing can think and be extended. "Do we find between thought and extension the same kind of affinity or connection that we find between shape and motion, or understanding and volition?" (AT VII, 423). The rhetorical question suggests that human beings have bodies and thought, not because thinking and corporeality are predicable of them, but because they are composed of two distinct things, of which one thinks and the other is corporeal. That is tantamount to refusing to countenance (1), and it directly raises the problem of predication. If we cannot predicate thought and extension of human beings, what can we predicate of them?

When Descartes reflected on the conflict between statements like (1) and (4), did he immediately excise human beings from his world? Perhaps the problem of meaning intervened, for perhaps his first response was to recall his remarks to Pollot (AT II, 36) and hold that only thoughts are predicable of human beings. That idea, though, might naturally lead him to reflect on what such a predication actually means. If thoughts and thoughts alone take place equally in souls and in human beings, what does the predication of thoughts to the human being *add* to the predication of thoughts to the soul? *On what grounds* do we decide that human beings have thoughts but not extension? What is *meant* by predicating something of a human being?

If we can predicate joy, for example, of some human being, it is because the soul of that human being possesses joy. If we say that a human being is joyous, we must add that what it is for that human being to be joyous is simply for his soul to be joyous. In other words, what it is for the human being to be joyous is *nothing but* his soul being joyous. But if the whole truth is simply that his soul is joyous, it isn't really the case that the human being is joyous. The truth is simply that the soul is joyous. That is *all* the truth. "That human being is joyous" is a misleadingly expressed predication of joy to a certain soul; as a predication of joy to a human being, it has no meaning. For that reason, and in that manner, predicating joy of a human being is frivolity, not serious philosophy.

Understanding what it is for a building to be dangerous, we might well judge that a certain edifice is dangerous because part of it is dangerous — its radon-filled cellar, its asbestos-lined ducts, its crumbling supports. Our judgment about the building is serious business. But if we had no such understanding and sought to make up for our incomprehension by stipulating that (for example) a building is dangerous if and only if some part of it is, our affirmation that the edifice is dangerous would become empty and frivolous. If the whole truth is that the ducts are dangerous, that is really all the truth. I believe that Descartes came to understand that judgments about soul-body compounds are empty in just that way.

If you say that a human soul is material or that God exists everywhere, and really *mean* that the soul is material and that God exists everywhere, Descartes will deny what you say. He does not believe that a human soul is material. Still, he will let you say that the soul is material — if by "material" you agree to mean "united with the body" (AT III, 691, 694). Similarly, he does not believe that God exists everywhere, but he will let you say that — if you mean "exerts his power everywhere" (AT

V, 342–343). And I believe that he might let you say that there are joyous human beings — but on his own principles he should allow you to say this *only* on the condition that you agree to mean by it *simply* that there are joyous souls that are united to
bodies. It follows that if you happen to mean by it that there are certain composite
joyous entities — if you mean that there are joyous human beings — he ought to deny
what you say.

There is a difference between the question of the human being's joy and the
questions of the soul's materiality and God's omnipresence. In the latter cases, we
understand the nature of the substance in question, and that is enough to support
the denials of materiality and omnipresence. The difficulty with a joyous human being is more fundamental. We understand nothing about a human being's nature.
What supports the denial that the human being is joyous is simply that no content
attaches to the affirmation.

We can use proposition (1) to clarify the meaning problem. I think that the heart
of the problem is that, given Descartes's metaphysics of soul and body, the relevant
facts are exhausted when we have said that the soul remembers meeting Berlin; the
body is five feet, nine inches tall; and the two are closely united. There is no *further*
fact that a certain human being who is five feet, nine inches tall remembers meeting Berlin. The robustness of the predications that Descartes makes about human
souls and human bodies has extracted all there was from our pre-*Meditations* predications about human beings. Literally nothing remains of them. Whereof one cannot speak, one must keep silent. And that is what Descartes does. In the *Meditations*
of 1641 he begins to develop a theory of the composite human being; after 1642 he
drops the theory.

I think that the problems of predication and meaning explain why, in the
*Principles* (part I, arts. 48 and 53), Descartes spells out a metaphysics of souls and bodies, indicating their characteristics and principal attributes, but does not breathe a
word about the nature or principal attribute of human beings. I think they explain
why, in the *Passions*, he replaces his Sixth Meditation discussion of what is harmful
to the human being (AT VII, 83–89) by discussion of what is harmful to the soul or
to the body (arts. 137–146), with no mention at all of harm to the composite human
being. I think they explain why Descartes virtually ceases after 1642 to speak of the
soul and body as composing a whole, though there is abundant discussion of the intimate union that links them; why he makes no reference after 1642–1643 to the principle that this union is intimate enough to constitute an entity of the linked elements;
and why he speaks of the soul as the form of the *human being* in 1641–1642 but only
as the form of the *body* or its *matter* thereafter.[19]

Finally, I think that these two problems explain the most tantalizing fact of all.
In 1645, Descartes characterizes the human being in a way that he firmly disowned
in 1641. The alternatives between which he moves during these years are clearly
mapped in well-known texts from Augustine:

> What, then, shall we say man is? Is he soul and body together, as a pair of horses or
> a composite beast like a centaur is one thing? Or shall we say that he is a body only,
> albeit a body used by a soul which rules it? — just as we call a clay lamp a 'light': we
> do not say that the clay vessel and the flame together make up a light; we call the
> lamp a light, but we do so on account of the flame. Or, finally, shall we call the soul

alone man, and do so on account of the body which it rules? — just as we call a man a knight, not the man and his horse together, but we do so on account of the horse he rides.[20]

In the Fourth Replies, having defined the human being in the Sixth Meditation "as composed of mind and body," Descartes emphatically rejects Arnauld's attempt to tag him with "the Platonic view" that a human being is "a soul which makes use of a body" (AT VII, 88, 203, 227–228). Four years later, though, he characterizes the human being as "the mind insofar as it is united with the body" (AT IV, 284). The philosopher who invented modern soul-body dualism is not likely to be slipshod in defining the human being, and his words suggest that he has seen more implications in his dualism than we have. And if he does conclude that thoughts, and thoughts alone, take place in the human being, identifying the human being with the mind would elegantly explain the fact.

I cannot repeat the details of the case I have made elsewhere for the thesis that Descartes's Sixth Meditation anthropology, the theory of the human being composed of body and soul, expires in 1642–1643. What I hope to do here is to trace the connection between the reasons for its demise and one of its important consequences. Human value ought to appear profoundly different if Descartes's dualism forces human beings off the stage. And we shall now see that his understanding of value after 1642 indeed shifts in the ways that might be predicted. I'll focus on value in medicine, since he says that the preservation of health has always been the principal goal of his studies (AT IV, 329; cf. AT VI, 62).

The fundamental aim of medicine is to preserve life. If there are no human beings, we can no longer say that life is *a good for a human being*. But perhaps it is a good *for the soul* to be united to a living body. Still, the soul will possess this good only extrinsically — that is, in virtue of being united to something beyond it. Being united to a living body will therefore be good for a soul in a fundamentally different way than being alive would be good for a human being.

Is the preservation of "the machine of our body" like the maintenance of a machine? The repairman aims simply to preserve a machine as long as it is useful, knowing that its owner will survive it. Descartes counsels Elisabeth against suicide (AT IV, 314–315, 333), but does he have good reasons? In a letter of 1646 to Chanut he writes that "our soul would have no reason to want to remain joined to its body for a single moment, if it . . . could not feel [the passions]" (AT IV, 538). His point is that it is only the passions that give the soul the slightest reason to remain joined to the body. And he will soon attenuate the reason the passions provide, both by the restriction on satisfaction that desire without passion generates and by the restriction on pleasure that I discuss in the next few paragraphs. When only the soul and not the human being is involved, the question whether it is good to preserve life gains new legitimacy.

Again, consider the joy I take in the soundness of my body. In 1649 Descartes says, as he had much earlier, that "titillation of the senses"

> consists in the fact that objects of the senses are exciting some movement in the nerves which would be capable of harming them, if they did not have enough strength to withstand it or the body were not well disposed. This produces an impression in the brain which [is] instituted by nature to testify to this sound disposition and this strength.[21]

But he now adds that this impression leads to joy by representing the body's sound-ness as an *extrinsic* good of the soul — "as a good which belongs to it, insofar as it is united with the body." And then, in what would otherwise be an astonishing com-parison, he assimilates it to the pleasure of watching a play.

> For nearly the same reason one naturally takes pleasure in feeling moved to all sorts
> of passions, even sadness and hatred, when these passions are caused only by the un-
> usual adventures one sees represented on a stage or by other similar matters, which,
> not being able to harm us in any way, seem to titillate our soul in affecting it.[22]

As Descartes presents it, the joy we derive from a sound body is perhaps a species of pride.[23] And if Hume is right, the strength of pride is proportioned to the intimacy I conceive between myself and the cause of my passion.

> A beautiful fish in the ocean . . . that neither belongs, nor is related to us, has no
> manner of influence on our vanity. . . . It must be some way associated with us in or-
> der to touch our pride. Its idea must hang in a manner, upon that of ourselves . . .
> every change in the relation produces a proportionable change in the passion. (*Trea-
> tise* II.I.ix)

In particular, when I no longer conceive that the body and I form a composite be-ing, the pleasure I take in the body's soundness will be weakened.

Descartes indeed plays down pleasure in the body's soundness in his later writ-ings. His assimilation of the pleasure of titillation to that of a spectator finds a nat-ural place in his later understanding of all the pleasures and miseries of this life. We have seen him tell Elisabeth, in 1646, how we can prevent evils that arise externally "from penetrating any further into our soul than the sadness which actors arouse in it when they represent before us certain fateful actions" (AT IV, 355). In the same vein, in 1645 he denigrates "servile and common" souls who "are happy or unhappy only according as things that befall them are pleasing or displeasing," and he char-acterizes "the greatest souls" in these words:

> Considering themselves as immortals and as capable of receiving profound con-
> tentments, and . . . considering that they are joined to mortal and fragile bodies, sub-
> ject to many infirmities and inevitably perishing in a few years, they do everything
> in their power to render Fortune favorable in this life, but they nevertheless esteem
> it so little in relation to Eternity that they come close to considering the events of
> [this life] as we do those of a play . . . as the greatest prosperities of Fortune never
> make them conceited and do not make them more insolent, so the greatest adver-
> sities cannot cast them down.[24]

My belief that I am immortal, supported by dualism, massively enlarges the scope of life beyond the career of my body through the world of nature and makes it that much easier for me to look on that career with the eyes of a spectator. And then when I cease to believe that my body and I compose a human being, the pleasure I take in the life of my body is conceptually transformed and attenuated: it comes to resem-ble the disinterested pleasure of a theatergoer.

The same conclusion follows not only from Hume's theory of pride but also from Descartes's own theory of love. Love leads the soul to consider itself as joined with what it loves, in such a way that the soul imagines a whole of which it thinks itself to be one part and the beloved another (*Passions*, arts. 79–80). Insofar as I resist thinking that I and my body are parts of a larger whole, I shall resist feeling love for my own body. When Descartes's dualism leads him to cease to believe that soul and body compose a human being, the soundness and even the life of the body matter less, and differently, to him.

We have seen that for years Descartes esteemed medicine as the most valuable of the applications of his philosophy. But by 1646 morals comes to rival medicine in his esteem. In a famous letter he writes that he has found it "much easier and surer" not to fear death than to preserve life (AT IV, 442). How can this be easier? These words are not just empty piety or the wisdom of middle age. For he attributes his discovery to "certain foundations in morals," and he hints that "knowledge proper to the nature of the human being, of which I have not yet treated," has helped establish them (AT IV, 441). We have, I think, discovered part of the explanation. Once human beings have disappeared and human goods have become goods for the soul alone, the preservation of his own life is not, after all, such an important good. That is one more reason why, from the vantage point of the soul, he comes to regard his life on earth almost as a spectator looks on a drama.

## Conclusions

Into his fifties Descartes promotes a "practical philosophy" for the understanding and mastery of nature. But as his morals and metaphysics shift, the motivation available for pursuing such ends shifts as well. The texts of the 1640s exhibit with increasing frequency praise for the goods of the soul over the goods of fortune. The tension between the program of engagement and the grounds for spectating becomes increasingly evident.

The denigration of the body, as a source of error and regret, encourages Descartes to regard his own bodily movements as particulars he can observe rather than as actions he is performing. The denigration of volition, as a source of error, encourages him to hold that a passive faculty can provide him with knowledge of the world.

The aim of preventing regret leads first to the thesis that the actions of human beings are confined to the soul, so that the body is sealed off from human activity, and second to the cultivation of "desire without passion," an emotion that both reduces our interest in things outside our soul and strips us of most of the pleasure we once took in such things.

The dualism of soul and body threatens predications of human beings with metaphysical falsity, and finally with lack of meaning, and leads Descartes for such reasons to abandon the compound human being. Its demise gives the soul new grounds for devaluing the life of the body.

Descartes dreams pervasively of security, both epistemic and emotional.[25] Judgment is most free from risk of error when its object is internal to the soul. Desire is most free from risk of regret when its object is internal to the soul. But he dreams as well of risk-free varieties of judgment and desire when their objects are external to the soul. The avenue he discovers to this end is a pair of analogues of the faculties of judgment and desire: intellect prior to judgment, desire without passion. Intellect perceives the truth about things and understands them clearly and distinctly without risk of error. When the soul has done its best, desire without passion is always fulfilled and always gives complete satisfaction.

But the price he pays for making these modes of engagement with the external world risk-free is to thin them so that they are more like modes of spectating than modes of true engagement. Intellect is like a homunculus that refrains not only from putting nature to the question but even from those internal acts of interpretation and judgment that any spectator carries out. Desire without passion takes little note of whether its object is attained, reminding us of the impassable spectator who understands that the events represented on the stage cannot harm in any way and matter very little. In the epistemic and emotional spheres alike, Descartes seeks complete security when the external world is in question. But real epistemic and emotional engagement with the world entails risk; risk is avoided only by becoming, as it were, a spectator at a play.

The real distinction between body and soul is indispensable to the project of securing judgment and desire from risk. But Descartes himself may have been surprised when it led him to abandon the thesis that soul and body compose a human being. Human actions will now be supplanted by actions of the soul, and human goods by goods for the soul. In this way, both moral agency and moral subjecthood are confined to the soul. The outcome of the project of securing desire from risk may also have surprised the philosopher who began his career hoping to become, as it were, master and possessor of nature. For he will now confine agency to the thoughts of the soul, and transform desire to minimize pleasure and pain arising from events external to the soul. The soul is now not only the sole moral agent and the sole moral subject but also very nearly, though not entirely, the sole moral arena. The soul is finally disjoint from the body and nature in such a way that it comes close to considering the life of the body as a theatergoer looks on a drama.

A well-known portrait of Descartes bears the inscription "Mundus Est Fabula" — "the world is a play." Perhaps the reference is to a literary device he tries out in *The World*, where he asks the reader to let his thought wander to "another world — a wholly new one which I shall bring into being before your mind in imaginary spaces" (AT XI, 31). Descartes means the device to reveal the nature of the real world which engages his intellectual activities, and to convince the reader that it is the world of scholastic physics that is imaginary and fictional. Ironically, he increasingly comes to look on the real world beyond the soul as a spectator regards the imaginary world represented in a drama. For epistemological reasons, but above all for moral and metaphysical reasons rooted in the dualism of body and soul, that is where his thought leads.[26]

Notes

1. AT VI, 10. See Louis Millet, "Man and Risk," *International Philosophical Quarterly* 2(1962): 417–427.

2. Daniel Dennett, "Current Issues in the Philosophy of Mind," *American Philosophical Quarterly* 15 (1978): 249–261, at 252.

3. I have in mind such classics as Ferdinand Alquié's *La Découverte métaphysique de*

*l'homme chez Descartes*, 2nd ed. (Paris: PUF, 1966); Martial Gueroult's *Descartes selon l'ordre des raisons*, 2nd ed. (Paris: Montaigne, 1968); Henri Gouhier's *Essais sur Descartes*, 3rd ed. (Paris: Vrin, 1973); and Geneviève Rodis-Lewis's *L'Oeuvre de Descartes*, 2 vols. (Paris: Vrin, 1971).

4. In this paragraph only, I refer to these texts simply by letter: (a) AT IV, 202–203; (b) IV, 219–220; (c) IV, 309; (d) IV, 331–332; (e) IV, 355; (f) *Passions of the Soul*, art. 94; (g) art. 147; (h) art. 187. Text (a) does not appear in CSMK, but I translate it in my edition of the *Passions of the Soul* (Indianapolis: Hackett, 1989), pp. 120–121, n. 25.

5. Intellect and perception are passive, volition active. The doctrine is stated most explicitly in the Fourth Meditation, the letter to Regius of May 1641 (AT III, 372), and *Passions* (arts. 17–19, 41–46), but Descartes maintains it consistently throughout his writings.

6. "Nam per solum intellectum percipio tantum ideas de quibus judicium ferre possum, nec ullus error proprie dictus in eo praecise sic spectato reperitur" (56, 15–18). The French translation of 1647 spoke of conceiving ideas rather than of perceiving them: "Car par l'entendement seul je n'assure ni ne nie aucune chose, mais je conçois seulement les idées des choses" (AT IX, 45). But the damage had been done.

7. For one answer and an illuminating discussion, see Hiram Caton, "Will and Reason in Descartes's Theory of Error," *Journal of Philosophy* 72 (1975): 87–104.

8. In "Descartes' Natural Light," *Journal of the History of Philosophy* 11 (1973): 169–187, at 174–175, John Morris agrees that understanding is a passive faculty, but he locates passages in which Descartes marks off a "quasi-active role" for it, under the title "the power of conceiving." He cites AT X, 415; III, 454–455; IX, 29, 45–46, 58 (cf. VII, 38, 57–58, 72–73); *Passions*, art. 1. The doctrine Morris thinks he sees still calls for correction; Descartes owes us an explanation of how a passive faculty can play a quasi-active role, and in Morris's interpretation, it is still in its purely passive role that understanding enables us to recognize truth or falsehood (AT VII, 56–57, in particular).

9. From a large literature in the 1960s and 1970s, see Jonathan Harrison, "A Philosopher's Nightmare, or, The Ghost Not Laid," *Proceedings of the Aristotelian Society* 67 (1967); and Peter Unger, *Ignorance: A Case for Skepticism* (Oxford: Clarendon Press, 1975).

10. Here are a few milestones. Hilary Putnam, in *Reason, Truth and History* (New York: Cambridge University Press, 1981), p. 6, observes that if a machine is to raise a skeptical problem effectively, it must be "so clever that if the person tries to raise his hand, the feedback from the computer will cause him to 'see' and 'feel' the hand being raised." In papers I read during the past decade, I argue that a simple machine cannot succeed and also that the new generation Putnam envisages is doomed to fail ("Taking Action against the Skeptic," University of Massachusetts at Amherst, 1989; Windsor University, 1994; European Congress for Analytic Philosophy, Leeds, 1996). Daniel Dennett defends the latter point in *Consciousness Explained* (Boston: Little, Brown, 1991), pp. 5–7.

11. *Oeuvres philosophiques de Descartes*, 3 vols. (Paris: Editions Garnier Frères, 1963–1973), III, p. 1059, n. 1.

12. Jean-Luc Marion, "The Exactitude of the 'Ego,'" *American Catholic Philosophical Quarterly* 68 (1993): 561–568, at 563.

13. CSM wrongly translates "pour m'empêcher de rien désirer à l'avenir que je n'acquisse" (AT VI, 25, 29–30) as "to prevent me from desiring in future something I could not get" (CSM I, 123–124). Donald A. Cress, in his translation of the *Discourse on Method* and *Meditations on First Philosophy*, 3rd ed. (Indianapolis: Hackett, 1993), gets it right: "to stop me from desiring anything in the future that I would not acquire."

14. Failing to get what you desire may not always lead to regret. In that case, Descartes's strategy should be geared to forestalling regret, not unfulfilled desire. His difficulties stem in part from conflating the two.

15. "The third rule is a fiction for giving oneself illusion and deception rather than the resolution of a philosopher, who ought to scorn possible things, if that is expedient for him, without pretending that they are impossible; and a man of common sense will never convince himself that nothing is in his power but his thoughts" (AT I, 513). In this interchange both Descartes and Pollot (as represented by Reneri) subtly vacillate between the distinct theses in (1) and (5). Something may be in my power though not entirely in my power.

16. This is the way article 146 of the *Passions* classifies (iii).

17. See, for example, AT X, 518–521; II, 38; VII, 78, 85–86, 121, 131–132, 423–425, 440–445; III, 247–248; and *Principles* 1:8.

18. See Aristotle, *De Anima* I:1, 403a3–b19.

19. I have defended the assertions this paragraph takes for granted in "Descartes: The End of Anthropology," in John Cottingham, ed., *Reason, Will, and Sensation* (Oxford: Clarendon Press, 1994). For the three points mentioned in this sentence, see, respectively, texts P, U, and F enumerated in the appendix to the article.

20. Augustine's answer is the "Platonic" one: a human being is "a rational soul using a mortal and earthly body." *De moribus ecclesiae catholicae et de moribus Manichaeorum* I 4.6, 27.52: Migne, *Patrologia Latina* 32.1313, 35.1553, as quoted in A. H. Armstrong, ed., *The Cambridge History of Later Greek and Early Medieval Philosophy* (Cambridge: Cambridge University Press, 1967), pp. 356–357.

21. *Passions*, art. 94, repeating the analysis of the *Treatise on Man* (AT XI, 144) and *Principles* 4:191.

22. The comparison is suggested earlier, at AT IV, 202–203, though not so explicitly.

23. In article 160 of the *Passions*, Descartes says that "because pride and generosity consist only in the good opinion we have of ourselves, and differ only in that this opinion is unjust in one and just in the other, it seems to me that they can be referred to a single passion — excited by a movement composed of those of wonder, joy, and love, both that which we have for ourselves and that which we have for the thing making us esteem ourselves." See Alexandre Matheron, "Psychologie et politique: Descartes: la noblesse du chatouillement," *Dialectiques* 6 (1974): 79–98.

24. AT IV, 202–203. Later in 1645 Descartes will link for Elisabeth the pleasure Christian charity affords, "even while weeping and deeply distressed," to "the contentment which [the soul] finds in weeping at some pitiable and fateful episode in the theater" (AT IV, 309); and he will ultimately sanctify the assimilation of virtuous contentment to the pleasure of the theatergoer in articles 147–148 of the *Passions*.

25. See note 27 to part I and note 78 to part II of my edition of the *Passions*.

26. Work on this chapter was supported by Jonathan Bennett's 1995 summer seminar, sponsored by the National Endowment for the Humanities. In 1996 I read part of it to the conference "L'esprit cartésien" of the Association des Sociétés de Philosophie de Langue Française, and versions of it to the British Society for the History of Philosophy and Istanbul University. I am grateful to NEH for its support and to all four audiences for valuable comments. Anne Andronikof-Sanglade, Joseph Campbell, Pınar Canevi, John Cottingham, Edwin Curley, Charles Huenemann, Matthew Stuart, Feyza Tulga, Kazuko Uchida, Serenity Voss, Catherine Wilson, and Margaret Wilson made helpful contributions. I am particularly indebted to Jonathan Bennett and to Arda Denkel for a profusion of critical comments.

## 13

CLARENCE BONNEN AND DANIEL FLAGE

# Distinctness

> So I decided that I could take it as a general rule that the things we con-
> ceive very clearly and very distinctly are all true; only there is some diffi-
> culty in recognizing which are the things that we distinctly conceive.
>
> Descartes, *Discourse on the Method*

This remark is one of the few places, if not the only place, where Descartes recognizes some difficulty with his clarity and distinctness rule.[1] Unfortunately, he
provides no explicit criterion for determining when a perception is distinct. Is there
an implicit criterion? Even if Descartes's texts allow us to answer this question, we
must also ask whether his concern is with perceptions as objects, that is, ideas (AT
VII, 53, 78, 387, 476; CSM II, 37, 54, 265, 321) or with perceptions as acts (AT VII,
25, 36, 43, 119, 245, 379, 519; CSM II, 24, 25, 29, 85, 171, 260, 353). And if Descartes
takes both perceptions as objects and perceptions as acts to be clear and distinct,
which is primary? Once one has an answer to these questions, the rule itself leads us
to ask what Descartes meant in claiming that clear and distinct perceptions are
"true"?

In this paper we argue that an idea of $x$ is distinct only if it is subsumed under
an eternal truth that specifies the conditions sufficient for the existence of $x$, where
$x$ is taken to be an entity of a particular kind. To show this, we examine Descartes's
claim that clear and distinct perceptions are true. Following Margaret Wilson,[2] we
argue that clear and distinct ideas are *materially* true, that they show only that the existence of a thing of a certain kind is possible. This notion of material truth provides
the basis for our argument that the sole plausible ground for deeming an idea distinct is that it can be subsumed under an eternal truth. Given our interpretation, one
would expect to find alternative distinct ideas of a thing $x$ corresponding to alternative descriptions of $x$. We show that this is precisely what one finds in the *Meditations*.
Along the way, we attempt to explain what Descartes means when he assumes that
there are degrees of distinctness.

## Metaphors

The doctrine of clear and distinct perception plays a central role in Cartesian thought. Yet Descartes says remarkably little about clarity and even less about distinctness. His most detailed discussion is in the *Principles of Philosophy*:

> A perception which can serve as the basis for a certain and indubitable judgement needs to be not merely clear but also distinct. I call a perception 'clear' when it is present and accessible to the attentive mind — just as we say that we see something clearly when it is present to the eye's gaze and stimulates it with a sufficient degree of strength and accessibility. I call a perception 'distinct' if, as well as being clear, it is so sharply separated from all other perceptions that it contains within itself only what is clear. (*Principles* 1:45; AT VIIIA, 22; CSM I, 208)

Clarity is a visual metaphor, but unless one looks at other discussions of clear and distinct ideas, Descartes's claim that "a perception [is] 'clear' when it is present and accessible to the attentive mind" tells one nothing. His other discussions show that one has clear and distinct ideas of *what* something is. His paradigms of clear and distinct ideas include the idea of the self as a thing that thinks (AT VII, 27; CSM II, 18); ideas of mathematical entities (AT VII, 36, 63–64; CSM II, 25, 44–45); and his idea of God as a supremely perfect being, an idea that is "utterly clear and distinct" (AT VII, 46; CSM II, 32). Clear and distinct ideas are logically prior to and provide the basis for (formally) true judgments (AT VII, 58; CSM II, 40–41; *Principles* 1:43; AT VIIIA, 21; CSM I, 207) since "according to the laws of true logic, we must never ask about the existence of anything until we first understand its essence" (AT VII, 107–108; CSM II, 78). If one clearly perceives what something is, one discerns the several properties exemplified by a thing of a certain kind, just as to visually recognize an object as an object of a certain kind one must discern its several properties.

There is an additional point to notice. When Descartes introduces clarity and distinctness as the criteria of truth, he often claims that "whatever I perceive *very* clearly and distinctly" (AT VII, 35; CSM II, 24; our emphasis) or "the things we conceive *very* clearly and *very* distinctly are all true" (AT VI, 33; CSM I, 127, our emphasis)[3] suggests that, like visual clarity, conceptual clarity (and distinctness?) is a matter of degree. Just as a myopic philosopher might literally take steps to increase the clarity with which he or she visually perceives the properties of an object, there is a process that can be undertaken to clarify one's ideas. As we show below, this is precisely what one finds.

But even if one can unpack the visual metaphor with respect to clarity, Descartes's remarks on distinctness are less helpful. What does it mean to claim that an idea is distinct only if "it is so sharply separated from all other perceptions that it contains within itself only what is clear"? While this comment makes it look as if clarity is a necessary condition for distinctness, it offers no precise understanding of distinctness. Nonetheless, the allusion to "sharply separated from all other perceptions" implies that a perception is distinct insofar as it is distinguishable from perceptions of all other kinds. His remark in *Principles* 1:63 bears out our interpretation. There Descartes states that the distinctness of a perception "simply depends on our carefully distinguishing what we do include in it from everything else" (AT VIIIA, 31; CSM I,

215). But if the distinctness of a perception of $x$ consists of our ability to distinguish $x$ from all other things (or kinds of things) in virtue of the properties we clearly perceive in it, how does one determine that the perception is distinct? Does one continue to follow the visual metaphor and suggest that one compares the idea of the kind in question with ideas of all other kinds of things, as Locke seems to suggest one does in his account of abstract ideas and nominal essences? Or, since Descartes seems not to draw a real/nominal essence distinction,[4] is there some other means by which one can determine that a perception represents a distinct kind of thing?

To answer this question, we must examine an apparently separate issue, namely, what Descartes means in claiming that all clear and distinct perceptions are true. As we shall see, in answering that question we shall find the clue to understanding the grounds for deeming a perception distinct.

## Truth

Descartes claims that all clear and distinct perceptions are true (AT VI, 33; CSM I, 127; AT VII, 35; CSM II, 24; *Principles* 1:43, AT VIIIA, 21; CSM I, 207). He also claims that clear and distinct perceptions provide the basis for judgments that are formally true (AT VII, 56; CSM II, 39), that formal truth is limited to the domain of judgment (AT VII, 43–44; CSM II, 30), and that error is most properly identified with formal falsehood (AT VII, 7, 43–44; CSM II, 30). So, clear and distinct perceptions cannot be *formally* true; that is, they cannot be taken to represent existent objects. In what sense, then, can they be true?

Descartes provides no explicit answer to that question. Although he consistently claims that ideas that are *not* clear and distinct are *materially false* (AT VII, 43–44; CSM II, 30; see also AT VII, 232–235; CSM II, 162–164), he never introduces a definition of "material truth." Indeed, the expression "materially true" appears only once in the Cartesian corpus. Replying to Mersenne's objection to the ontological argument (AT VII, 127; CSM II, 91), he writes:

> I now turn to the argument which you compare with my own, *viz.*, 'If there is no contradiction in God's existing; therefore' etc. Although materially true, this argument is formally a sophism. For in the major premise, the term 'contradiction' applies to the concept of a cause on which the possibility of God's existence depends; in the minor premise, however, it applies to the divine essence and nature itself. (AT VII, 151–152; CSM II, 107–108)

Mersenne's original objection was that critics of the argument "If there is no contradiction in God's existing, it is certain that he exists; but there is no contradiction in his existing" attacked the second premise: "there is no contradiction in his existing." Either they held that the truth of the second premise cannot be known or they denied its truth (AT VII, 127; CSM II, 91). In his reply, Descartes distinguishes between the material truth of the premises and the formal invalidity of the argument based on them. He suggests that an idea (or proposition) is materially true if and only if it represents or could represent an entity whose existence is possible, that is, not self-contradictory. Margaret Wilson also reads Descartes in this way. She argues that an idea is materially true if and only if it represents an object whose existence is possible.[5] So understood, an idea is materially true if and only if it is internally consistent.[6] Whereas internal consistency guarantees that an idea *might* represent an object, as such it does not guarantee that *anything* is represented by the idea, whether that "thing" be an existent object, a nature or essence, or an idea in the mind of God. But is there any hard evidence that Descartes entertained a concept of material truth according to which an idea of something *t* is materially true if and only if it guarantees that the existence of *t* is possible?

Yes. The evidence is of two sorts. On the one hand, as Harry Wolfson has acknowledged, a tradition exists among the ancients and medievals according to which an idea or concept is materially true just in case the existence of the object conceived is possible.[7] On the other hand, a consistent theme emerges from the Cartesian corpus according to which the clarity and distinctness of a perception guarantees nothing more than the *possible* existence of an object so conceived. In the Sixth Meditation, the point is made this way: "I know that everything which I clearly and distinctly understand is capable of being created by God so as to correspond exactly with my understanding of it" (AT VII, 78; CSM II, 54). In the *Comments on a Certain Broadsheet,* one finds this:

> We should note that even though the rule, 'Whatever we can conceive of can exist',
> is my own, it is true only so long as we are dealing with a conception which is clear
> and distinct, a conception which embraces the possibility of the thing in question,
> since God can bring about whatever we clearly perceive to be possible. (AT VIIIB,
> 352–353; CSM I, 299; see also *Principles* 1:60; AT VIIA, 28; CSM I, 213)

Insofar as a notion of material truth was entertained by the medievals and such a notion pertained only to the possibility that a thing could exist, and insofar as Descartes claims that acknowledging the clarity and distinctness of an idea guarantees only that a thing so conceived is possible — that it could be created by God as it is conceived — we may reasonably conclude that all clear and distinct ideas are materially true. But if we are concerned only with the possible existence of a thing corresponding to a clear and distinct idea, how does one demonstrate such possible existence? In what follows we argue that the proof of possible existence occurs by subsuming a clear idea under an eternal truth.

## Proving Possible Existence

Descartes does not directly discuss how one proves possible existence; however, some evidence suggests that one has a distinct idea of a thing of a certain kind — and therefore recognizes the possible existence of such a thing — if one recognizes that a clear idea falls under an eternal truth of the form, "Everything that has the property *p* exists as a thing of kind **Φ.**" Before turning to that evidence, we shall dispel a possible objection to the effect that such a position proves too much.

Some might hold that the *Cogito* cannot be reconstructed as a syllogism with the suppressed premise "Everything that thinks exists" since, in the Aristotelian interpretation of categorical logic, the assumed universal premise has existential import and therefore begs the question at hand.[8] But if the *Cogito* cannot be an en-thymematic argument, our suggestion that the mark of an idea's distinctness is the subsumption of the idea under an eternal truth of the form "Everything that has prop-erty $p$ exists as a thing of kind $\Phi$" would prove too much. It would show that there is at least one actual existent of kind $\Phi$; it could not show that the existence of a thing of kind $\Phi$ is merely possible. Hence, our proposed interpretation must be rejected. Such is the objection.

This objection is sound only if Descartes accepted the Aristotelian interpreta-tion of categorical logic, and there is incontrovertible evidence that he did *not* ac-cept that interpretation. In *Principles* 1:10, Descartes discusses what he can know prior to knowing his own existence:

> And when I said that the proposition *I am thinking, therefore I exist* is the first and most certain of all to occur to anyone who philosophizes in an orderly way, I did not in saying that deny that we must first know what thought, existence, and certainty are, and that it is impossible that that which thinks should not exist, and so forth. But because these are very simple notions, and one which on their own provide us with no knowledge of anything that exists, I did not think they needed to be listed. (AT VIIIA, 8; CSM II, 196)

As Bernard Williams has acknowledged, Descartes's contention that the principle "it is impossible that that which thinks should not exist" is assumed by the *Cogito* and that this provides "us with no knowledge of anything that exists" is sufficient to show that Descartes rejected the Aristotelian interpretation of categorical logic.[9] Nor should one find this surprising. Had Descartes assumed that universal propositions have existential import, that would have conflicted with his principle that "we must never ask about the existence of anything until we first understand its essence" (AT VII, 107–108; CSM II, 78), for in the Aristotelian account, that principle would en-tail that knowledge of the essence of a thing of kind $\Phi$ and knowledge of the exis-tence of at least one thing of kind $\Phi$ occur at the same logical moment. Insofar as one must know *what* something is before one knows *that* it is, knowledge of essence must be logically (and temporally?) prior to and distinct from knowledge of existence. And Descartes's practice shows that except in the case of the idea of God as a perfect being, knowledge of the essence of a thing does not immediately entail knowledge of the existence of a thing of that kind. But what does one claim to know in knowing that the essence of a thing of kind $\Phi$ is $p$?

To have knowledge of the essence of a thing is to know those properties that a thing of a certain kind would have if it existed. It specifies the noncausal conditions under which the existence of a thing of a certain kind is possible. To claim that a hu-man is essentially a thing that thinks, for example, entails that if there is something that thinks, then a human being exists; but this does not entail that there is a thing that thinks. Since the distinctness of an idea of a kind pertains to its distinguishabil-ity from ideas of all other kinds (*Principles* 1:63; AT VIIA, 31; CSM I, 215), and since knowledge of the essence of a thing pertains to those properties a thing of a certain kind must have in order to exist as a thing of that kind — it pertains to the conditions under which it is possible for a thing to exist as a thing of a certain kind — one may assume that the reason for deeming a perception a distinct perception of $\Phi$ is the recognition of an eternal truth of the form "Everything that has property *p* exists as a thing of kind Φ." But is there any evidence for this?

Though we find no explicit evidence, the circumstantial evidence tends to support our interpretation. First, the structure of *Principles*, part I, implies a close conceptual connection between clear and distinct perceptions and eternal truths known by the natural light. Beginning with section 43 to the end of *Principles*, part 1, Descartes's overriding concern is with concept formation and the adequacy thereof. After discussing clear and distinct perceptions in sections 43–47, Descartes turns to the objects of conception in section 48 and explicitly to eternal truths (common notions or axioms) in sections 49–50. His examples of eternal truths include "*Nothing comes from nothing*"; "*It is impossible for the same thing to be and not to be at the same time; What is done cannot be undone; He who thinks cannot but exist while he thinks*; and countless others" (*Principles* 1:49; AT VIIIA, 24–25; CSM I, 209). Of these, only the last complies with the general form of an eternal truth that shows the conditions necessary and sufficient for the existence of a thing of a kind, namely, the existence of a thinking thing. Yet the passage provides some evidence that other eternal truths exist that correspond to the essences of other kinds of things.

Second, the light of nature guides us to knowledge of eternal truths. Already in section 30, Descartes ties clear and distinct perception to the light of nature: "It follows from this that the light of nature or faculty of knowledge which God gave us can never encompass any object which is not true in so far as it is encompassed by that faculty, that is, in so far as it is clearly and distinctly perceived" (AT VIIIA, 16; CSM I, 203). Similarly, in section 50 Descartes links common notions to the doctrine of clear and distinct perception: "In the case of common notions, there is no doubt that they are capable of being clearly and distinctly perceived; for otherwise they would not be called common notions" (AT VIIIA, 24; CSM I, 209).

Although both of these passages connect clarity and distinctness with knowledge by the light of nature, some might suggest that they cannot support our interpretation. The first passage, they would say, suggests that the light of nature perceives clearly and distinctly, and the second passage indicates that eternal truths are themselves clearly and distinctly perceived. Such an objection, however, is misleading. As we indicated at the beginning of the chapter, an ambiguity runs through Descartes's discussions of clear and distinct perception: he sometimes writes as if the object of perception — the idea — is clear and distinct (AT VII, 78, 387, 476, 532; CSM II, 37, 54, 265, 321), while at other times clarity and distinctness seem to be properties of the mental act in virtue of which an idea is clear and distinct (AT VII, 25, 36, 43, 119, 245, 379, 519; CSM II, 24, 25, 29, 85, 171, 260, 353). These two passages indicate that clarity and distinctness are properties of the act. So understood, an idea is clear and distinct in virtue of the clarity and distinctness of the act of perception (conception). Thus, one conceives an object as an idea of a distinct kind, the components of which are clearly perceived, whenever one recognizes an eternal truth of the form "Everything that is p is Φ." It follows that clarity and distinctness are epistemically primitive as properties of mental acts. Distinctness as a property of an idea is parasitic on the clarity and distinctness of a mental act, and an element of such an act is an eternal truth that specifies the necessary and sufficient conditions for a person to recognize an object as an object of a certain kind.

Finally, some structural elements of Descartes's philosophy support our interpretation. Clear and distinct ideas are true, where "true" alludes to the possibility of real existence as conceived. Principles known by the light of nature — including eternal truths — hold in all possible worlds.[10] If distinctness were a discernable property of an idea of a kind, then one would expect that it could be discovered by simple inspection. But the Descartes of the *Discourse on Method* warns that "there is some difficulty in recognizing which are the things we distinctly conceive" (AT VI, 33; CSM I, 127). Therefore, a simple inspection of an idea present to the mind will not yield the idea's distinctness. Nor does it seem likely that distinctness can be determined by a comparative inspection of all ideas clearly conceived, for such a comparative inspection might involve an indefinitely great number of ideas. Furthermore, a comparative inspection would provide no grounds for the strict differentiation of things into kinds, a position that seems inconsistent with Descartes's doctrine of true and immutable natures (see AT VII, 64; CSM II, 44–45). Hence, there must be something separate from the ideas themselves that provides the basis for the strict differentiation of ideas into kinds, some nonideational basis for deeming an idea distinct. If the eternal truths include principles specifying the conditions necessary for the possibility that a thing of a certain kind exists, this would provide grounds for deeming an idea not merely clear but distinct as well. Descartes's contention that the principle that anything that thinks exists is an eternal truth known by the natural light shows that at least some eternal truths specify such a condition. We can find no other plausible account of how distinctness is recognized. If we are correct, then the clarity and distinctness of an idea is parasitic on the clarity and distinctness of a perception qua mental act, and an essential element of that act is the recognition of an eternal truth specifying the properties necessary and sufficient to be a thing of a certain kind.

## Counting Clear and Distinct Ideas

Although we can cite no passage in which Descartes explicitly delineates clear and distinct ideas in the manner we suggest, collateral evidence supports our interpretation. First, if one assumes our interpretation, then in principle one can conceive of a given object *x* under more than one clear and distinct idea. In what follows we show that Descartes offers multiple clear and distinct ideas of the self and God. Second, our account will explain why Descartes could claim that both clarity and distinctness are matters of degree.

The metaphysical question of the *Meditations* is what exists, rather than what are the necessary and sufficient conditions for the possible existence of an object of a certain kind. Nonetheless, since claims of actual existence entail corresponding claims of possible existence, this difference need not concern us. We predicate our discussion on the assumption that Descartes takes seriously his principle "that we must never ask about the existence of anything until we first understand its essence" (AT VII, 107–108; CSM II, 78) since knowledge of the essence of a thing of a kind specifies the conditions necessary and jointly sufficient for the possible existence of a thing of that kind. So let us turn to Descartes's concepts of the self in Meditations II and VI. We shall notice that several concepts of the self are operative.

In the third paragraph of Meditation II, the so-called "*Cogito* paragraph," Descartes proves his own existence. We are *not* concerned with the structure of the argument to the existential claim; rather, we are concerned with the several conceptions of the self found in the paragraph:

> I have convinced myself that there is absolutely nothing in the world, no sky, no earth, no minds, no bodies. Does it now follow that I too do not exist? No: if I convinced myself of something then I certainly existed. But there is a deceiver of supreme power and cunning who is deliberately and constantly deceiving me. In that case I too undoubtedly exist, if he is deceiving me; and let him deceive me as much as he can, he will never bring it about that I am nothing so long as I think that I am something. So after considering everything very thoroughly, I must finally conclude that this proposition, I am, I exist, is necessarily true whenever it is put forward by me or conceived in my mind. (AT VII, 25; CSM II, 16–17)

Descartes proves his existence three times under three different concepts of himself: (1) I am a thing that convinced myself of something; therefore I exist; (2) I am a thing that thinks I am something; therefore I exist; (3) I am a thing that entertains the proposition "I exist"; therefore I exist. Each of these concepts specifies a condition that if realized is sufficient to prove his actual existence. In each case, Descartes conceives of himself as a thing of a distinct kind prior to claiming he exists. If one must have knowledge of what something is before one has knowledge that a thing of that kind exists, each of the three related proofs is based on a different clear and distinct idea of himself. This shows that already in the *Cogito* paragraph, Descartes has conceived of himself under multiple clear and distinct ideas.

Famously, however, Descartes is not satisfied with the concepts of himself that are implicit in the *Cogito* paragraph and he attempts to clarify them. He rejects the Aristotelian-Scholastic concept of the self as a rational animal on the grounds that neither the notion of rationality nor the notion of animality is clear.[11] He then turns to the equally ancient conception of the self as a combination of body and soul, and he whittles away and clarifies the several component concepts until he reaches the conclusion:

> I am, then, in the strict sense only a thing that thinks; that is, I am a mind, or intelligence, or intellect, or reason — words whose meaning I have been ignorant of until now. But for all that I am a thing which is real and which truly exists. But what kind of a thing? As I have just said—a thinking thing. (AT VII, 27; CSM II, 18)

Notice the relationship the conception of the self as a thing that thinks bears to the earlier conceptions of the self: the notion of thinking subsumes the three previous conceptions of the self as instances. The conception is simpler — more general — than the previous conceptions. Given the role he ascribes to simplicity, we may reasonably claim that the degree of clarity increases as the simplicity (generality) of the concept that provides the basis for the conception increases.[12] Yet we do not mean to imply that one should assess the clarity of an idea solely on the basis of simplicity.

The notion of a "thing" is ambiguous. The word "thing" can be ascribed to either a substance or a mode. The Descartes of Meditation II does not use the word "substance"; the Cartesian notion of substance as a thing that can exist independently is not introduced until Meditation III (AT VII, 43; CSM II, 29). Once he has introduced his notion of substance, Descartes describes himself in terms of a thinking *substance*. This shift constitutes a further clarification of the idea of the self as mind. But just as the shift from the idea of a self as a thing that entertains the proposition "I exist" is conceptually distinct from the idea of a self as a thing that thinks insofar as the differentiating kind is simpler, so the idea of a self as a thinking thing is conceptually distinct from the idea of the self as a thinking substance insofar as the latter idea is a clearer and more precise idea of the genus.

If our account of the clarification of the idea of the self is correct, this indicates that in spite of his critical remarks on the Aristotelian approach to definition by genus and difference (see, for example, AT VII, 25; CSM II, 17), Descartes retains that model. Just as Arnauld later distinguished a description that allows one to delineate a kind in terms of multiple properties from a real definition by genus and difference, contending that the latter is the preferred model of a real definition,[13] accordingly the successive ideas of the self qua mind are clearer insofar as they tend to approach the model of a definition by genus and difference. The difference from the Aristotelian definition is in the degree of clarity (universality and precision) ascribable to the component ideas. If this is correct, we should notice other instances in which the "clarification of an idea" — more precisely, a succession of increasingly clear ideas — of a thing involves a conceptual move from a collection of ideas (concepts) that provides the basis for the differentiation of one kind from all others to an idea that corresponds to a definition by genus and difference. This conceptual move is precisely what we will find upon examining Descartes's ideas of God.

In Meditation III we find a succession of ideas of God.[14] Initially, Descartes describes "the idea that gives me my understanding of a supreme God, eternal, infinite, ⟨immutable,⟩ omniscient, omnipotent and the creator of all things that exist apart from him" (AT VII, 40; CSM II, 27). Later, the description of the idea is modified to "a substance that is infinite, ⟨eternal, immutable,⟩ independent, supremely intelligent, supremely powerful, and which created both myself and everything else (if anything else there be) that exists" (AT VII, 45; CSM II, 31). Here one might reasonably suggest that the differences between the two descriptions of the idea of God are minimal: "omnipotent" and "omniscient" become "supremely powerful" and "supremely intelligent," and in the second Descartes explicitly introduces the notion of substance.[15] Are these ideas clear and distinct? Descartes does not explicitly say, but since (1) they provide the basis for a proof of the actual existence of God, (2) actual existence entails possible existence, (3) they are ideas of the essence of God, and (4) the essence of a thing must be known before its existence, they would seem to be clear and distinct. But these are not the only descriptions of the idea of God found in the Meditation. Later, after entertaining the possibility that the idea of God is materially false, Descartes introduces a third idea of God, that of a supremely perfect and infinite being. This idea is "utterly clear and distinct, and contains in itself more objective reality than any other idea" (AT VII, 45; CSM II, 31): "This idea of a supremely perfect and infinite being is, I say, true in the highest degree" (AT VII, 45; CSM II, 31). Nonetheless, the idea is redundant since "supreme perfection" entails infinity, a point Descartes seems to have acknowledged by the Fifth Meditation, where the idea of God is reduced to a "supremely perfect being" (AT VII, 65; CSM II, 45). Notice that the idea of perfection subsumes the ideas of the several perfections mentioned in the earlier ideas of God, and it is therefore simpler. Notice also that Descartes shifts from an idea of God that corresponds to what Arnauld called a description to an idea that corresponds to a definition by genus and difference.[16]

If our interpretation is correct, there are several clear and distinct ideas of God in Meditation III. An idea is distinct as long as it allows one to differentiate a thing of a kind from things of all other kinds. Each of the ideas of God allows one to do so. Nonetheless, since distinctness is parasitic on clarity (*Principles* 1:45; AT VIII, 22; CSM I, 208), it is plausible to suggest that even distinctness occurs in degrees. An idea is distinct insofar as it provides the basis for the division of the world into kinds. But just as one can conceive of a single thing under a number of alternative descriptions — for example, just as one can conceive of Sir Walter Scott under the descriptions "the author of *Waverly*" and "the author to whom a large monument is erected in Edinburgh" — there are several clear and distinct ideas of God. Because the ideas differ in the degree to which the component ideas are clear, one can talk of some ideas being more distinct than others.

## Conclusion

In this chapter we examined Descartes's doctrine of clear and distinct perception. We argued that a clear and distinct idea is materially true if it shows the possible existence of the thing conceived. Focusing on how one would know the possible existence of a thing, we argued that clarity and distinctness are primarily characteristics of perceptions as mental acts and that only when one recognizes an eternal truth does the perception qua act become distinct, or, in other words, in the recognition of an eternal truth, one knows the possible existence of the object conceived. This implies that one can have alternative distinct ideas of a single thing. By examining Descartes's alternative ideas of the self as mind and his alternative ideas of God, we showed that this is precisely what one finds in the *Meditations*.[17]

### Notes

1. Whereas Descartes formulates the rule in the *Discourse on Method* in terms of conception, in the Third Meditation he reformulates it in terms of perception: "Whatever I perceive very clearly and distinctly is true" (AT VII, 35; CSM II, 24). It is beyond the scope of this chapter to ask whether one should attach any significance to the terminological shift.

2. Margaret Dauler Wilson, *Descartes, The Arguments of the Philosophers* (London: Routledge & Kegan Paul, 1978), pp. 107–115; see also Daniel E. Flage and Clarence A. Bonnen, "Descartes and the Epistemology of Innate Ideas," *History of Philosophy Quarterly* 9 (1992): 20–23.

3. It is, perhaps, worthy of notice that this variability in degree is *not* found in the *Principles*, where he says, "We will never mistake the false for the true provided that we give our assent only to what we clearly and distinctly perceive" (*Principles* 1:43; AT VIIIA, 21; CSM I, 207).

4. Although Descartes does not exemplify the nominalistic/conceptualistic strains common among the British empiricists insofar as he claims that there are true and immutable natures (AT VII, 64; CSM II, 44–45), his discussion of "How universals arise" in *Principles*, part 1, section 59 (AT VIIIA, 27–28; CSM I, 212–213), is not unlike discussions of abstraction in

Locke, Berkeley, and Hume. However, to examine the compatibility of Cartesian conceptualism vis-à-vis universals and his doctrine of true and immutable natures is beyond the scope of this chapter.

5. Wilson, *Descartes*, pp. 107–115; Flage and Bonnen, "Descartes and Epistemology," pp. 20–23.

6. Thus we disagree with Gewirth, who claimed that "Truth . . . is an external quality since it consists in a relation of 'conformity' between and idea or thought and an extra-ideational thing or object." Alan Gewirth, "The Cartesian Circle Reconsidered," *The Journal of Philosophy* 67 (1970): 680. Although Gewirth's claim may be correct for formal truths, it does not apply to material truths. Furthermore, by recognizing the distinction between material and formal truth, it is possible to construct an answer to the problem of the Cartesian circle — an answer that is based on truth rather than certainty — although to develop such an account is beyond the scope of the present discussion.

7. Harry Wolfson, *The Philosophy of Spinoza: Unfolding the Latent Processes of His Reasoning*, 2 vols. (New York: Schocken Books, 1934), vol. 2, pp. 98–99. See also AT VII, 235; CSM II, 169.

8. This is not the only kind of objection that might be raised. Some would find stronger evidence in the third reply to the second set of Objections, where Descartes seems to deny that there could be such a suppressed premise (AT VII, 140–141; CSM II, 100). While we are not convinced that such an objection is sound — see Daniel E. Flage, "Descartes's *Cogito*," *History of Philosophy Quarterly* 2 (1985): 163–178 — we wish to stress that our current objection is distinct from exegetic issues germane to that passage.

9. Bernard Williams, *Descartes: The Project of Pure Enquiry* (Harmondsworth, England: Penguin, 1978), p. 91.

10. The most notorious example of a principle so known is "that there must be at least as much reality in the total and efficient cause as in the effect" (AT VII, 40; CSM II, 28).

11. A more complete discussion of the grounds on which Descartes rejects the Aristotelian conception of the self can be constructed on the basis of the several possible trees of Pophery, but such a discussion is beyond the scope of this chapter.

12. As we shall see below, this is particularly noticeable with regard to the ideas of God.

13. Antoine Arnauld, *The Art of Thinking: Port-Royal Logic*, James Dickoff and Patricia James, trans. (Indianapolis: Bobbs-Merril, Library of Liberal Arts, 1964), pp. 164–166.

14. Nor are the ideas of God that are explicitly mentioned in Meditation III the only ideas of God Descartes entertains. In his reply to Hobbes, Descartes claims one forms an idea of God by "extending" the idea of one's own understanding and other attributes (AT 7:188; CSM 2:132). This idea is less clear than any of those mentioned in Meditation III. For a more complete discussion of the relation of this idea of God to those mentioned in Meditation III, see our "Descartes's Factitious Ideas of God," *The Modern Schoolman* 66 (1989): 197–208.

15. This second idea, of course, is redundant insofar as the notion of substance includes the notion of independence.

16. See Arnauld, *Art of Thinking*, pp. 164–166.

17. We wish to thank Steven Voss, Joseph K. Campbell, Charles Huenemann, and an anonymous reader for Oxford University Press for their helpful comments on an earlier version of this chapter.

## 14

GEOFFREY GORHAM

# Causation and Similarity in Descartes

## Introduction

From a rationalist perspective, causal connections ought to be intelligible. It is not enough to learn that events like the effect have regularly followed events like the cause; one would also like to understand what makes the cause capable of bringing about its effect. Descartes believed that causation is intelligible only if the cause and effect are similar since it is impossible to understand how the reality of an effect could owe anything to the reality of its cause if the two have nothing in common: "For where, I ask, could the effect get its reality from if not from the cause? And how could the cause give it to the effect unless it possessed it?" (CSM II, 28) Purely mechanistic explanations of natural phenomena are to be preferred over traditional scholastic models for precisely this reason. For although we understand quite well how the size, shape and motion of one body can produce properties of the same type in another body, yet "there is no way of understanding how these same attributes (size, shape, and motion) can produce something else whose nature is quite different from their own — like the substantial forms and real qualities which many philosophers suppose to inhere in things" (CSM I, 285)

Despite its importance for Descartes, the requirement of causal similarity has been, in at least three distinct ways, a source of embarrassment for his admirers. First, since the requirement plays a crucial role in the Third Meditation arguments for God's existence, when the hyperbolic doubt is in full force, it stands in need of a very strong justification. Yet all Descartes offers is a weak pragmatic defense together with casual assurance that the similarity condition is just the old axiom that nothing can come from nothing. Second, Descartes's account of what is needed for similarity seems to render the causal condition practically trivial: just about any two things are sufficiently alike to cause one another. Third, if the requirement has any teeth at all, then it would appear to be incompatible with the doctrine of mind-body interaction. After all, minds do not have the features of extended things and bodies do not have the features of thinking things.

My goal is to relieve some of the embarrassment in each of these areas. I will offer a formulation of the similarity condition that is nontrivial and for which Descartes had a reasonably strong justification. So understood, the condition is perfectly compatible with Descartes's late view of the causal connection between mind and body. Indeed, there are surprising features in his late view of interaction, which can be explained only if he relied on something very close to the formulation of the similarity condition that I present.

## The Similarity Condition

In his late (1648) conversation with Burman, Descartes declares it "a common axiom and a true one that the effect is like the cause (*effectus similus est causae*)" (CSMK, 339). Let me briefly explain what Descartes thinks is required for causal likeness. He holds that effects must be like their causes in a very strong sense: "There can be nothing in an effect which was not previously present in the cause" (CSMK, 192). Usually, he says that the cause must itself *contain* whatever reality or perfection is produced in the effect.[1] There are two ways in which a cause may contain the perfections it is responsible for. First, the perfections of the effect may exist *formally* in the cause, that is, "in a way which exactly corresponds to our perceptions of it" (CSM II, 114). In other words, a cause actually exemplifies the perfections that it contains formally. Second, even if a cause actually exemplifies none of the perfections in its effect, it may still contain those perfections *eminently*. In this case the cause must contain the perfections in such a way that it can "fill the role" of objects that contain the perfections formally (CSM II, 114). To meet this condition, the cause must be of at least as high a degree of reality or perfection as the perfections in the effect.[2] For example, something that does not actually exemplify heat may still be a cause of heat as long as it is at least as real or perfect as heat (CSM II, 28). In Descartes's ontological hierarchy, substances are of a higher order of reality than accidents or modes, and infinite substances are more real than finite substances (CSM II, 117, 130). Thus, I may eminently contain extension, shape, and motion since these are simply modes of bodies whereas I am a thinking substance (CSM II, 31). Likewise, if God is the cause of my ideas, he will contain eminently all that belongs to my ideas since he is an infinite substance whereas my ideas are merely modes of thought (CSM II, 55). Of course, since I am finite, I contain neither formally nor eminently the infinite perfections contained in God and in my idea of God (CSM II, 31).

One last wrinkle: a perfection contained formally or eminently in a cause may be contained merely *objectively* in the effect, that is, in the manner of a representation (CSM II, 28, 113). For example, the perfections contained formally in my cat (e.g., furriness) exist objectively in the sensory ideas she produces in me. If it turns out that God is the true cause of those ideas, then he contains the same perfections eminently (CSM II, 55). The ontological hierarchy described above holds firm at the level of objective reality: the idea of a substance has more objective reality than the idea of a mode, whereas the idea of an infinite substance has more objective reality than the idea of a finite substance (CSM II, 28, 117).

With these technical terms defined, we can now state Descartes's causal similarity condition: "*Whatever reality or perfection is contained objectively or formally in a thing is contained formally or eminently in its total and efficient cause.*"[3] The provision that the cause is "total" is intended to rule out mere contributing causes. Thus, it is not required that the sun or rain contain all that is in the animals they nourish since they are not the total cause of the animals (CSMK, 166), that is, the cause of their "very being" (CSMK, 340). Furthermore, Descartes applies the condition strictly to efficient, rather than material, causes. He finds it "unintelligible" to suggest that such things as "perfection of form" could ever preexist in a material cause (CSM II, 252).

## Justifying the Similarity Condition

In the geometrical exposition of the *Meditations*, Descartes offers a kind of pragmatic defense of the similarity condition:

> IV. Whatever reality or perfection is in a thing is present either formally or eminently in its first and adequate cause.

> V. It follows from this that the objective reality of our ideas needs a cause which contains this reality not merely objectively but formally or eminently. It should be noted that this axiom is one which we must necessarily accept, since on it depends our knowledge of all things, whether they are perceivable by the senses or not. (CSM II, 116–117)[4]

The first thing to notice about this sort of defense is that it concerns only the cause of ideas. So it could not justify the general version of the similarity condition (IV). Nevertheless, Descartes's limited claim about our knowledge depending on the similarity condition is quite correct in the context of his system since the principle is a key premise in the argument for the existence of an epistemically benevolent God. Of course, this in itself hardly justifies the similarity condition; no one who was skeptical of that principle to begin with would agree that Descartes's proof establishes a secure foundation for knowledge.

In any event, Descartes suggests that the similarity condition is implicated in every specific belief we have about the external world, not just in the proof of God's existence. Consider his own illustration of the pragmatic defense. We judge that the sky exists only because we have an idea of the sky, and "the only reason why we can use this idea as a basis for the judgment that the sky exists is that every idea must have a really existing cause of its objective reality" (CSM II, 137). The illustration does not seem to support Descartes's point about the indispensibility of the similarity condition. For notice that what we need to suppose is simply that our idea of the sky has a "really existing cause," not that this cause must itself contain every perfection in our idea of the sky. In fact, it is this much weaker principle that seems to underlie what Descartes says about empirical knowledge in the *Meditations* themselves. For example, he there strongly cautions us against the assumption that our ideas of bodies exactly resemble the bodies themselves. Such beliefs, he says, are "acquired not from nature, but from a habit of making ill-considered judgments" (CSM II, 56). So there is no reason to suppose that there is anything in the fire that is similar to the feelings of heat and pain it causes in me; "there is simply reason to suppose that there is something in the fire, whatever it may eventually turn out to be, that produces in us the feelings of heat and pain" (CSM II, 57). But if, as this passage suggests, we can know that the perfections of our ideas are caused by external bodies, regardless of whether the bodies resemble those perfections, then the pragmatic defense of the similarity condition is worthless.[5]

Fortunately, Descartes preferred a metaphysical justification for the similarity condition: "The fact that 'there is nothing in the effect which was not previously in the cause, either in a similar or higher form', is a primary notion which is as clear as anything we have; it is just the same as the common notion 'nothing comes from nothing' (*a nihilo nihil fit*)" (CSM II, 97). It is tempting to interpret this "common notion" as the familiar principle of universal causation: everything must have a cause.[6] But although Descartes accepted and relied on this principle, he did not use it to justify the similarity condition.[7] Furthermore, it seems very unlikely that he regarded the principle of universal causation as equivalent to the similarity condition, given they are in fact very different. On the one hand, "everything must have a cause" does not require that every cause contains the perfections of its effect. On the other hand, the similarity condition does not imply that everything has a cause. Nor is the principle of universal causation presupposed by, *pace* Frankel (1986, 325), or derived from, *pace* Dicker (1993, 102), the common notion. As Descartes formulates it, "nothing from nothing" is silent on the question of whether all things actually have causes. It holds that a thing must exist in order to have causal power: "It is impossible that nothing, a non-existing thing, should be the cause of the existence of anything, or of any actual perfection in anything" (CSM II, 116). But this does not preclude uncaused things.

Still, there must be more to the "nothing from nothing" axiom than the truism that a thing must exist if it is a cause, for this would hardly justify the similarity condition. Descartes's view seems to have been that the axiom is violated when a putative cause brings its effect into existence *out of nothing*. For example, we doubt that the magician is a genuine cause of the rabbit, not because we doubt the magician exists, but rather because it is impossible to produce something out of thin air. This reading of "nothing from nothing" makes clearer how it might support the similarity condition. The reason we think that the magician would have to bring the rabbit into existence out of nothing is that neither the magician himself nor any of his incantations have anything in common with the rabbit. By contrast, there is nothing miraculous about ordinary reproduction: the rabbit and its parents have a good deal in common. Thus, Descartes holds that a cause would have to produce the perfections of its effect out of thin air unless it already contained them: "For if we admit that there was something in the effect which was not previously present in the cause, we shall have to admit that this something was produced from nothing (*a nihilo factum*)" (CSM II, 97).[8]

But this last inference can still be questioned: why couldn't the newly emergent perfections in the effect be produced out of the very different perfections in the cause?[9] Descartes's answer seems to be that the perfections in one thing do not genuinely *come from* another thing unless those very perfections originate there. Suppose we are following a putative cause through to its effect and a perfection emerges that was not previously present. But then the effect did not come from the putative cause any more than a person who boarded the transcontinental train in Chicago came from New York. Indeed, if we rule out contributing and intermediate causes (stops along the way), then in this case the perfections in the effect do not come from anywhere; they simply appear. So, if an effect truly receives its perfections from a cause, then the cause must have those perfections to give. Descartes writes: "Now it is manifest by the natural light that there must be at least as much reality in the efficient and total cause as in the effect of that cause. For where could the effect get that reality from, if not from the cause? And how could the cause give it to the effect unless it possessed it?" (CSM II, 28). Thus, Descartes's view is that a cause is genuinely responsible for an effect only if the perfections of the effect literally originate in the cause. Otherwise, the cause would have to do what is impossible: bring perfections into existence out of nothing.

Recall that Descartes thinks that the similarity condition and the "nothing from nothing" axiom are equivalent. We have just seen why he thinks dissimilar causation would imply creation from nothing. As for the other half of the equivalency, Descartes says: "The reason why nothing cannot be the cause of a thing is simply that such a cause would not contain the same features as are found in the effect" (CSM II, 97). The point seems straightforward enough. And yet Bernard Williams has charged that the argument is circular because it assumes universal causation:

> For even granted that causes have as much reality as their effects, this will apply only to cases in which there are causes, and to argue from this that it is impossible for something to proceed from nothing, because what is nothing has no reality, is to assume that everything must proceed from something, and must have a cause; which was what was supposed to be proved. (Williams 1978, 141)

Two things should be said about this charge. First, even if Descartes's inference assumed universal causation, this would not make it circular. For, as was argued above, Descartes does not attempt to derive the principle of universal causation from either the similarity condition or the "nothing from nothing" axiom. Second, it would not violate Descartes's "nothing from nothing" axiom for something to "proceed from" nothing if this meant simply that the thing had no cause at all. The axiom is violated when causal power is attributed to nothingness since "nothingness cannot be the efficient cause of anything" (CSM II, 115); but if we believe a thing has no cause, then no causal power is attributed to anything.[10]

## Is the Similarity Condition Trivial?

The similarity condition is satisfied as long as the cause contains either formally or eminently what is in the effect. For one thing to contain another thing eminently, the first must be of at least as high an order of reality as the second. But if this is all that is required for eminent containment, then the similarity condition is extremely weak. It does rule out modes as causes of substances and finite things as causes of infinite things. Otherwise, anything is sufficiently similar to anything else to cause it. In particular, the similarity condition is completely uninformative about the most common variety of causal interaction, that among finite substances.[11]

This complaint assumes that one thing will eminently contain another thing just in case the first is of at least as high an order of reality. This would imply not only that any finite substance can cause any other finite substance but also that all finite substances contain every one of each other's perfections. Fortunately for the similarity condition, Descartes does not appear to hold that relative order of reality is sufficient for eminent containment. For example, when considering the possibility that I am the cause of my ideas of corporeal things, he says:

> As for all the other elements which make up the idea of corporeal things, namely extension, shape, position, and movement, these are not formally contained in me, since I am nothing but a thinking thing; but since they are merely modes of a substance, and I am a substance, *it seems possible* that they are contained in me eminently. (CSM II, 31; emphasis added)

The qualification suggests that Descartes did not believe things *necessarily* contain eminently all things of an equal or lower order of reality. Furthermore, there is some reason to suppose that Descartes thought bodies were altogether incapable of eminent containment. In none of the passages discussing eminent containment does Descartes consider the possibility of eminent containment by material things. For example, after concluding in the Sixth Meditation that his ideas of corporeal bodies must be produced by a substance other than himself, he says:

> This substance is either a body, that is a corporeal nature, in which case it will contain formally ⟨and in fact⟩ everything which is to be found objectively ⟨or representatively⟩ in the ideas; or else it is God or some creature more noble than a body, in which case it will contain eminently whatever is to be found in the ideas. (CSM II, 55)[12]

He disregards here a possibility that should be left open if relative order of reality is sufficient for eminent containment, namely, that our ideas of bodies are caused by finite material things that contain the objective reality of those ideas eminently but not formally. But in fact the passage strongly suggests that bodies could only cause the perfections of my ideas by formally containing them ("in which case . . . ").

I suggest that Descartes thought that thinking things (God and us), but not material things, are capable of eminent containment. If this is right, then the similarity condition does not imply that any finite substance is a possible cause of any other finite substance. Minds can cause perfections in bodies or other minds since they can contain those perfections either formally or eminently. But bodies, since they are incapable of eminent containment, can cause perfections in minds or other bodies only if they already actually exemplify those perfections.[13]

Before turning to the consequences of this view for Descartes' interactionism, I would like to address one other worry about the similarity condition itself. Notice that the condition could be met by things that actually exemplify complete dissimilarity, as long as the cause at least eminently contains the perfections it brings about in its effect. But then it may be argued that what I am calling the "similarity condition" is actually inconsistent with the common and true axiom "that the effect is like the cause (*effectus similus est causae*)" (CSMK, 339).[14] However, this objection assumes something that Descartes denies, namely, that two things can be alike only because they share formally contained perfections. Thus, in illustrating the common axiom, he says that even pebbles have a likeness to God, inasmuch as he is their cause. Of course, they have no likeness to God in the sense of a picture (*depictum*) or effigy (*effigatum*) "but in the broader sense of something having some resemblance (*similitudenum*) to something else" (CSMK, 339).

## The Problem of Interaction

It is usually assumed that Descartes believed throughout his life that mind and body produce effects in each other despite having different essential natures. But it has not gone without notice, even in Descartes's own time, that such interaction appears to be precluded by the condition of causal similarity.[15] I will shortly argue that Descartes himself recognized the problem and preferred to solve it by rejecting efficient body → mind causation rather than the similarity condition. There is evidence that he came to believe late in his philosophical career that bodies cannot be the total and efficient cause of our sensory ideas because bodies cannot possess any genuine features of ideas. On the other hand, he never questioned mind → body causation since he believed that minds can, in a very special sense, possess corporeal features.

Of course, Descartes might have resolved the inconsistency between his causal principle and his interactionism by abandoning the similarity condition. Indeed, he seems to do exactly this in a 1646 letter to Clerselier, who had expressed some concerns about mind-body interaction:

> These questions presuppose amongst other things an explanation of the union between the soul and the body, which I have not yet dealt with at all. But I will say, for your benefit at least, that the whole problem contained in such questions arises simply from a supposition that is false and cannot in any way be proved, namely that, if the soul and the body are two substances whose nature is different (*deux substances de diverse nature*), this prevents them from being able to act on each other. (CSM II, 275)

It is crucial to notice that what Descartes rejects in this oft-cited passage is not the similarity condition but rather the assumption that substances cannot causally interact if they have different natures or essences. The similarity condition does not require essential likeness, merely likeness with respect to the perfections that the cause produces in its effect. Nor does Descartes imply here that substances of different natures must be fully dissimilar. Indeed, he immediately goes on to say that there is *less* difference between different substances, such as mind and body, than between real accidents and substances.[16] Notwithstanding Clerselier's false supposition, minds and bodies can interact just to the extent that they can share perfections of the sort they produce in each other.[17] I now want to consider the extent to which this was possible for Descartes.

## Mind → Body Causation

What are the causal powers of minds? Consider first the infinite mind of God, the ultimate cause of all things. There is no difficulty concerning his creation of us since all of the perfections we possess formally as thinking substances are already contained in God either formally (e.g., knowledge and power) or eminently (e.g., number and length).[18] Indeed, Descartes frequently cites God's creation of us as reason to suppose we bear a likeness to him.[19] God is also the cause of material things. He does not, of course, possess formally the various perfections of bodies, such as shape and motion. But since he is infinite substance, God may contain these perfections eminently.[20] Thus, as we have seen, Descartes is prepared to accept that even such things as pebbles have a "very remote, minute and indistinct" similarity to God (CSM III, 340).

So the similarity condition is satisfied in God's causal power. Despite this, Descartes says in at least one place that God does not resemble bodies:

> Nothing that we attribute to God can have been derived from external objects as a copy (*exemplari*) is derived from its original, since nothing that is found in God resembles what is to be found in external, that is corporeal, things. Now any elements in our thought which do not resemble external objects manifestly cannot have originated in external objects, but must have come from the cause which produced this diversity in our thought. (CSM II, 132)

Descartes here attacks specifically the notion that our idea of God could be a copy of external objects. Presumably, a copy must actually exemplify some of the same features as its original. For example, if a thing contained redness merely eminently, it could not, at least in that respect, serve as a copy of things that actually exemplify redness. So to secure the point that our idea of God could not be a copy of external objects, it is sufficient to assume that nothing exemplified, or "found," in God is exemplified, or "found," in external objects. And this assumption is clearly correct since God does not formally contain length, shape, and so on. That Descartes is here concerned strictly with resemblance in the copy-original sense explains why he would say in the second sentence of the passage that bodies cannot in *any* way be the cause of perfections in our ideas — because bodies can contain perfections only formally (or so I have argued). So if they do not actually resemble a thing in the copy-original sense, they cannot be the cause of it at all, according to the similarity condition. None of this prevents God from causing perfections in bodies since he can contain those perfections eminently.

Nor is there any problem about the action of finite minds on material things.[21] The primary power of our minds on bodies is to produce motion in the pineal gland (CSM I, 340). Minds do not possess motion formally, of course. But given that human minds are substances, they can eminently contain motion, or indeed any of the typical modes of corporeal things (CSM II, 31). Thus, Descartes is prepared to admit that human minds are extended, "but only in virtue of their power," since they can act on things that are extended in substance, that is, bodies (CSMK, 375).[22] Now, I do not mean to suggest that Cartesian mind → body causation is actually intelligible, only that it is not prevented by lack of similarity in Descartes' technical sense.

### Body → Mind Causation

Bodies do not contain formally any of the perfections that minds exemplify. That is, bodies do not think, understand, will and so on. And I have already argued that bodies do not contain eminently any perfections at all. It follows, according to the similarity condition, that if bodies cause any perfections in minds, those must be perfections that the mind contains objectively. The objective perfections of minds are the perfections of its ideas. The question, then, is whether bodies contain formally the objective perfections in our ideas. If not, then in accordance with the similarity condition, Descartes would be forced to reject body → mind causation. In particular, bodies could not be the efficient and total cause of our sensory ideas.

In the *Meditations*, Descartes argues straightforwardly that external things must be the cause of our ideas of them and must, therefore, contain formally the objective perfections in our ideas since otherwise God would be a deceiver (CSM II, 55). And yet he immediately goes on to question whether corporeal things actually exemplify the perfections we find objectively in our sensory ideas. The causes of our sensory ideas, he says, may not exist in a way that "exactly corresponds to our sensory grasp of them" (CSM II, 55).[23] So, we have "no convincing argument" for supposing that there are things in fire that resemble heat or pain; we can only conlude that there is "something in the fire, whatever it may eventually turn out to be, which produces in us the feelings of heat or pain" (CSM II, 57).[24] I can see no way of reconciling comments like these with the similarity condition.[25] For one would have supposed that there was a perfectly convincing argument for assuming a resemblance between our ideas and their causes: "If an idea contains something which was not in the cause, it must have got this from nothing" (CSM II, 29).

There is significant evidence that Descartes finally resolved this conflict by abandoning the assumption that our sensory ideas are in any simple and direct sense caused by external bodies. For example, in a letter to Mersenne (22 July 1641), he offers the following account of the source of sensory ideas: "Altogether, I think those which involve no affirmation or negation are innate in us; for the sense organs do not bring us anything which is like the idea which arises in us on the occasion of their stimulus, and so this idea must have been in us before" (CSMK, 187). The similarity condition is clearly at work in this argument. Our sensible ideas are not caused by whatever stimulates our sense organs; they merely "arise in us on the occasion" of that stimulation.[26] And the reason the ideas must be innate (and "in us before") is that nothing the sense organs deliver is anything like the ideas themselves. The domain of the sense organs, namely, external bodies, is simply too dissimilar from our sensory ideas to be able to cause them.[27]

The same reasoning is presented in more detail in the *Comments on a Certain Broadsheet* (1647). In the following passage Descartes is concerned to undermine the view, expressed in the *Broadsheet*, that supposedly innate ideas could arise from sensation. His answer is that all of our sensory ideas are themselves innate:

> Nothing reaches our mind from external objects through the sense organs except certain corporeal motions, as our author himself admits in article nineteen, in accordance with my own principles. But neither the motions themselves nor the figures arising from them are conceived by us exactly as they occur in the sense organs, as I have explained at length in my *Optics*. Hence it follows that the very ideas of the motions themselves and of the figures are innate (*innatas*) in us. The ideas of pain, colours, sounds and the like must be all the more innate, if on the occasion of certain corporeal motions, our mind is to be capable of representing them to itself, for there is no similarity (*similitudinem*) between these ideas and the corporeal motions. (CSM I, 304)

Just as in the letter to Mersenne, Descartes argues that our sensory ideas are innate in the mind and do not originate from external bodies. The reason is simply that our ideas and external things are too dissimilar. And although it is true that we are wont to refer our sensory ideas to things outside us, this is only "because they transmit something which, at exactly that moment, gives the mind occasion (*occasionem*) to form these ideas by means of the faculty innate to it" (CSM I, 304). The mind alone has the power of genuinely causing perfections in ideas.[28]

I believe these passages strongly suggest that Descartes came to regard body → mind causation in sensation as problematic because it would violate his similarity condition.[29] But I will conclude by considering two recent interpretations that conflict with my own. Margaret Wilson (1991) argues that the lack of similarity referred to in the *Comments* passages is not directly connected with the similarity ("non-heterogeneity") condition itself:

> Note that the lack of "likeness" between idea and brain state with which Descartes is here concerned is different from that at issue in the heterogeneity problem. The issue here is not the heterogeneity of mental *qua* mental from physical *qua* physical, otherwise Descartes could not indicate that certain mental states are more like the exciting brain state than others ('so much the more'). (Wilson 1991, 304)

From the persepective of the similarity condition, the problem of interaction does not arise from the heterogeneity of the mental and physical as such. The condition does not prevent minds from acting on bodies, for instance. Nevertheless, Wilson is right that the *Comments* passage seems to imply that our ideas of colors and pains are *more* dissimilar from external bodies than our ideas of motions and figures, which in turn suggests that the latter have something in common with bodies. But according to my interpretation, which invokes the similarity condition, our ideas must all be innate because none of their perfections are contained in external bodies.

Presumably, Descartes allows that our ideas of motions and figures are not wholly dissimilar from external bodies for the simple reason that bodies really do formally contain motion and figure. So these ideas share with bodies certain types of perfections, though not any exact instances of those types.[30] If this were sufficient to satisfy the similarity condition, then it would have to be admitted that this condition cannot be at work in the *Comments* passage. But in fact the similarity condition seems to require that a cause contain the particular perfections it brings about in the effect, not merely perfections of their general type. Consider one of Descartes's examples: all the intricacy in my idea of a machine must be contained formally or eminently in its cause, whatever that cause may turn out to be (CSM I, 198–199) Elsewhere he says: "If someone possesses the idea of a machine, and contained in the idea is every imaginable intricacy of design, then the correct inference is clearly that this idea came from some cause in which every imaginable intricacy exists" (CSM II, 76). Now, the intricacy of a machine is presumably a function of its various motions and figures. But a simple lever, though it formally contains motion and figure, could not be the cause of our idea of the machine since it clearly would not contain every intricacy that the idea contains. Simply having a figure and motion is not sufficient to produce the particular, highly intricate motions and figures objectively contained in our idea. Similarly, in the *Comments* passage, Descartes requires that the cause of our ideas of figures and motions contain perfections that are "exactly as they occur" in the ideas themselves.

Daniel Garber has suggested that in the *Comments* passage, Descartes is concerned about the dissimilarity between sensory stimuli and sensory ideas, but not about the causal connection between them. Just as one would not want to conclude from the dissimilarity between a sequence of computer keystrokes and the picture it illicits that the keystrokes do not genuinely cause the picture, so, says Garber, Descartes's main point is simply that sensory ideas "cannot come directly from the motions that cause them" (1993, 23). The computer analogy is imperfect, however, since Descartes does not assert, either in the *Comments* passage or in the letter to Mersenne, that external motions are the cause of our sensory ideas. On the contrary, he is careful in these contexts to describe sensation in strictly occasionalist terms. Furthermore, if Descartes thought that external motions were the direct cause of our sensory ideas, in spite of their dissimilarity, he would have said that those ideas are adventitious rather than, or as well as, innate. On my view, it is not at all surprising or improbable that Descartes would make the inference from dissimilarity to innateness, for he took it to be a common axiom and a true one that the effect is like the cause.

*Notes*

　1. In Descartes's terminology, "realities" and "perfections" simply refer to specific individual properties. In what follows, I will normally use only the latter term.

　2. Just as "reality" and "perfection" are used interchangeably by Descartes to mean property, so he also seems to equate "degree of reality" and "degree of perfection." Thus he says: "What is more perfect — that is, contains in itself more reality — cannot arise from what is less perfect" (CSM II, 28).

　3. In various formulations, the similarity condition is found in the following places: CSM I, 128, 198–199; CSM II, 28–29, 76, 97, 116, 252; CSMK, 166, 192, 339.

　4. Descartes makes essentially the same claim earlier in the Second Set of Replies, where he says that the similarity condition is "the sole basis for all the beliefs we have had about things located outside of us" (CSM II, 97).

　5. In the end, Descartes rejected the notion that external bodies, even though they do

not resemble ideas, could nevertheless be the total and efficient cause of our sensory ideas. Or so I will argue in the final section.

6. Kenny (1968, 138) seems to read it this way, for example.

7. "What does seem to me self-evident is that whatever exists derives its existence from a cause or derives its existence from itself as from a cause" (CSM II, 80).

8. "For if we suppose that an idea contains something which was not in its cause, it must have got this from nothing; yet the mode of being by which an idea exists objectively ⟨or representatively⟩ in the intellect by way of an idea, imperfect though it may be, is certainly not nothing and so it cannot come from nothing" (CSM II, 29).

9. See Cottingham (1986, 51).

10. Jonathan Bennett faults Descartes for here treating "nothing" as "the name of an item so impoverished that it cannot cause anything" (1996, 128). But Descartes's derivation of the "nothing from nothing" axiom from the similarity condition can be stated without doing this: (i) causes must contain the perfections of their effects; (ii) perfections must be contained in something; (iii) perfections in effects must be produced from their causes; (iv) therefore, the perfections in effects must be produced from something.

11. Clatterbaugh (1980, 394).

12. See also CSM II, 29, 31, 97.

13. Margaret Wilson (1991, 300) suggests that bodies cannot eminently contain the perfections of minds, not because bodies are altogether incapable of eminent containment, but rather because bodies do not happen to contain "more excellent" things than minds contain. However, Descartes does not anywhere say that bodies could not contain "more excellent" things than the perfections of minds. In any case, as far as the ontological hierarchy goes, it seems to be enough for eminent containment that the cause be at least as real or perfect as the perfections it brings about in the effect. Thus, Descartes says explicitly that I may contain eminently the perfections of bodies "since they are merely modes of a substance and I am a substance" (CSM II, 31). This does not in itself require that I contain more perfect things than bodies contain, only that I am more real than the perfections of bodies. Therefore, since bodies are substances and my ideas are merely modes of a substance, there must be some other reason why bodies cannot eminently contain modes of thought.

14. This objection is made by O'Neill (1987, 240).

15. For a comprehensive survey of how Cartesians dealt with the problem, see Watson (1987). Daise Radner (1985) provides a very thorough defense of the view (shared by Leibniz) that Descartes was unable to resolve this inconsistency.

16. "And yet, those who admit the existence of real accidents like heat, weight and so on, have no doubt that these accidents can act on the body; but there is much more of a difference between them and it, i.e. between accidents and a substance, than there is between two substances" (CSM II, 275–276.)

17. So I disagree with Bennett's (1996, 125) reading of the Clerselier response, that "the idea that causes must resemble their effects is here flatly rejected." In his book, Richard Watson (1987, 51) assumes that Cartesian metaphysics holds to this principle: "There must be an essential likeness between cause and effect." I do not see how such a principle is supported by the causal similarity condition that Descartes actually defends. Radner (1985, 38) and O'Neill (1987, 228) also seem to think that "essential likeness" is what is at issue for Descartes; cf. Loeb (1981, 138).

18. CSM II, 55, 99, 118–119.

19. CSM II, 35, 98, 256–257; CSMK, 340.

20. CSM II, 55, 99.

21. For evidence that Descartes believed (to the end) that minds cause perfections in bodies, see Garber (1993, 15–19).

22. Cf. CSMK, 372, 381. For a fuller discussion of the sense in which Descartes was prepared to allow that minds are extended, see Bedau (1986, 494).

23. In Descartes's opinion, this failure of resemblance is not confined to our ideas of the so-called secondary qualities. He points out that distant bodies do not have the same size or shape as in the sensory ideas they cause (CSM II, 57). See also the discussion of size and shape perception in the *Optics* (CSM I, 172).

24. In the *Principles*, Descartes says that despite the complete difference between the local motions of a sword and the sensation of pain, there is no question that the former can produce the latter (CSM I, 284). In the *Optics*, he says bluntly: "There need be no resemblance between the ideas which the soul conceives and the movements which cause these ideas" (CSM I, 167).

25. And elsewhere the inference from causation to similarity is clear-cut, even syllogistic: "Now God is the cause of me, and I am an effect of him, so it follows that I am like him" (CSMK, 340); "Now any elements in our thought which do not resemble external objects manifestly cannot have originated in external objects" (CSM II, 132).

26. Garber (1993, 21–22) has noted various other places in which Descartes prefers a noncausal, apparently occasionalist description of the relation between sensory stimulation and sensory ideas. Wilson (1991, 295–297) provides further examples, although she opposes the occasionalist reading.

27. So Radner (1985, 42) is correct that bodies could not be the total cause of sensations since the perfections of sensory ideas could not exist formally or eminently in bodies. But she is too quick in assuming "that a similar argument against the mind's causation of motion in the body would complete the problem of interaction," for as we have seen, Descartes thinks it is possible for minds to (eminently) contain motion. As far as Descartes's views on causation are concerned, the problem of interaction is strictly one way.

28. Baker and Morris (1996, 155–156) have recently defended a similar conclusion: "Lack of resemblance between thoughts and movements amounts [for Descartes] to a denial of *efficient* causation." Unfortunately, they do not surport their conclusion with reference to Descartes's explicit constaints on efficient causation, such as the similarity condition.

29. It would be too strong to claim that Descartes entirely abandoned body → mind causation, for he says in *The Passions of the Soul*, which was written even later than the *Comments*, that sensory perceptions are caused by external motions (CSM I, 333, 337).

30. Descartes frequently observes that the perfections of bodies, including their motions, figures, and so on, do not "exactly correspond" to or "resemble" what we find in our ideas (CSM I, 165, 172; II, 55, 57).

*Bibliography*

Baker, Gordon, and Katherine J. Morris. *Descartes' Dualism*. New York: Routledge, 1996.
Bedau, Mark. "Cartesian Interaction." *Midwest Studies in Philosophy* 10 (1986): 483–502.
Bennett, Jonathan. Notes for NEH Summer Seminar: Central Themes in Descartes, Spinoza, and Leibniz, 1996.
Clatterbaugh, Kenneth. "Descartes' Causal Likeness Principle." *Philosophical Review* 89 (1980): 379–402.
Cottingham, J. *Descartes*. Oxford: Blackwell, 1986.
Dicker, Georges. *Descartes: An Analytical and Historical Introduction*. New York: Oxford University Press, 1993.
Frankel, Lois. "Justifying Descartes' Causal Principle." *Journal of the History of Philosophy* 24 (1986): 232–341.

Garber, Daniel. "Descartes and Occasionalism." In Steve Nadler, ed., *Causation in Early Modern Philosophy*. University Park: Pennsylvania State University Press, 1993.

Kenny, Anthony. *Descartes: A Study of His Philosophy*. New York: Random House, 1968.

Loeb, Louis. *From Descartes to Hume: Continental Metaphysics and the Development of Modern Philosophy*. Ithaca, N.Y.: Cornell University Press, 1981.

O'Neill, Eileen. "Mind-Body Interaction and Metaphysical Consistency: A Defense of Descartes." *Journal of the History of Philosophy* 25 (1987): 227–245.

Radner, Daise. "Is There a Problem of Cartesian Interaction?" *Journal of the History of Philosophy* 23 (1985): 35–49.

Watson, Richard. *The Breakdown of Cartesian Metaphysics*. Atlantic Highlands, N.J.: Humanities Press International, 1987.

Williams, Bernard. *Descartes: The Project of Pure Inquiry*. London: Penguin, 1978.

Wilson, Margaret. "Descartes on the Origin of Sensation." *Philosophical Topics* 19 (1991): 293–323.

## 15

DON GARRETT

# Teleology in Spinoza and Early Modern Rationalism

Roughly speaking, a *teleological explanation* explains why something is so by indicating what its being so is *for*. Somewhat more precisely, a teleological explanation is one that explains a state of affairs by indicating a likely or presumptive consequence (causal, logical, or conventional) of it that is implicated in the state's origin or etiology. Such consequences often, if not always, take the form of ends, goals, or goods. All of the following are examples of possible teleological explanations: a sapling draws nourishment from the soil because doing so is likely to contribute to the end of its becoming a mature tree; a human being constructs a house because it is supposed that doing so will help to achieve the goal of protection from the rain and cold; and an arrangement of sharp teeth in front and flat teeth in back occurs in an animal's mouth to serve the animal's goods of strength and continued life by allowing it to tear and chew food efficiently. *Teleology* is the phenomenon of states of affairs having etiologies that implicate, in an explanatory way, likely or presumptive consequences of those states of affairs.[1] No proposed teleological explanation, no matter how appealing or compelling, can be correct unless it cites an actual example of teleology.

A *mechanical explanation*, in contrast, explains a state of affairs by indicating how it arises from a previously existing physical structure and the distribution of forces within it. Thus, one possible explanation for the rising of one end of a seesaw might be that the seesaw constituted a lever and that the weight of the individual on the other side exerted a force in a downward direction on that side. *Mechanism* is the phenomenon of states of affairs having etiologies that implicate, in an explanatory way, the previous arrangement and distribution of forces within an extended physical structure. No proposed mechanistic explanation, no matter now appealing or compelling, can be correct unless it cites an actual example of mechanism.

Teleological explanations — typically expressed in the terminology of "ends" and "final causes" — played central roles in Aristotelian and scholastic conceptions of natural philosophy (that is, of what we would now call *natural science*). However, the growing prominence of mechanistic explanation in seventeenth-century natural philosophy demanded a complete rethinking both of the role of teleological explanation in scientific methodology and of the nature and scope of teleology itself. In the vanguard of this rethinking were Descartes, Spinoza, and Leibniz — each of them a defender, in his own way, of the importance of mechanistic explanation in natural science.

Descartes famously rejects teleological explanation in natural philosophy, asserting that "it is not the final but the efficient causes of created things that we must inquire into" (*Principles* 1:28; CSM I, 202), that "we shall entirely banish from our philosophy the search for final causes" (*Principles* 1:28; CSM I, 202), and that "the customary search for final causes (is) totally useless in physics" (Meditation IV; CSM II, 39). Spinoza evidently rejects at least some kinds of teleological explanation, writing: "Nature has no end set before it, and . . . all final causes are nothing but human fictions" (E IAP; Geb II, 80). Leibniz, in seeming contrast, insists that "all existent facts can be explained in two ways — through a kingdom of *power* or *efficient causes* and through a kingdom of *wisdom* or *final causes*" (A *Specimen of Dynamics*; AG 126). He defends "the way of final causes" as often useful in "divining important and useful truths which one would be a long time in seeking by the other, more physical way." As an example, he offers his observation that Descartes's attempt to derive the laws of refraction "by way of efficient causes" is "not nearly as good" as Snell's derivation of the same laws through "the method . . . of final causes" ("Reconciliation of Two Ways of Explaining Things"; AG, 55). Furthermore, he criticizes Descartes for "eliminating the search for final causes from philosophy" (Letter to Molanus, "On God and the Soul"; AG 242) and writes of himself as "cured" of his previous leanings toward "the Spinozist view which . . . dismisses the search for final causes and explains everything through brute necessity" (RB 71). Indeed, he charges that Descartes has "made himself suspect" of de facto Spinozism by, among other things, "rejecting the search for final causes" ("Two Sects of Naturalists"; AG 282).

Following Leibniz's lead, historians of philosophy often portray Descartes and Spinoza as staunch enemies of Aristotelian teleological explanation and portray Leibniz — enthusiastic conciliator between ancient and modern that he so obviously was — as seeking to rehabilitate Aristotelian teleology by reconciling it with the modern mechanistic philosophy. I believe that this common portrayal, while not entirely baseless, is largely misleading. Accordingly, I will try to provide a more accurate, if somewhat more complicated, account of the relations among Aristotle, Descartes, Spinoza, and Leibniz on the nature and scope of teleology and teleological explanation. The three points that I want to emphasize are (i) that although Spinoza maintains a certain rhetorical distance from the Aristotelian vocabulary of final causes, he fully and consistently accepts the legitimacy of many teleological explanations, at least as I have defined them; (ii) that in two of the most important respects, Leibniz's position on teleology is not more, and is perhaps even less, Aristotelian than

Descartes's; and (iii) that overall, among the three seventeenth-century philosophers under discussion, it is not Leibniz but Spinoza who holds the position on teleology and teleological explanation nearest to that of Aristotle. This is not to deny, of course, that Spinoza's doctrines about teleology are embedded — like those of Descartes and Leibniz — in a metaphysical system very different indeed from Aristotle's.

In the first section of this chapter, I will try to establish claim (i). My approach will have three parts. First, I will summarize the reasons for interpreting Spinoza as accepting the legitimacy of at least some teleological explanations. Second, I will try to rebut each of five reasons usefully surveyed by Jonathan Bennett (1983; 1984, chap. 9; 1990) for interpreting Spinoza as rejecting all teleological explanations. Third, I will appeal to Spinoza's distinction among three kinds of knowledge to indicate how teleological explanations can be accommodated within his mechanistic worldview.

In the second section, I will try to establish claims (ii) and (iii). My method will be to explore the answers given by Aristotle, Descartes, Leibniz, and Spinoza to four basic questions about the nature and range of teleology and teleological explanation. To the first of these questions — the question of whether there is teleology not dependent on thought — Aristotle and Spinoza give an affirmative answer, whereas Descartes and Leibniz give a negative one. To the second question — whether there is teleology through divine will or purpose — Aristotle and Spinoza give a negative answer, whereas Descartes and Leibniz give an affirmative one. To the third and fourth questions — whether there is subhuman teleology, and whether there is a substantive role for teleological explanations in natural philosophy — Leibniz sides with Aristotle against Descartes in giving affirmative answers; however, Spinoza also sides with Aristotle against Descartes on these questions, and does so in a rather more Aristotelian way than does Leibniz.

## Teleology in Spinoza

### Evidence that Spinoza Accepted Teleology

*Uses of Teleological Explanation.*    There are at least four related textual reasons for concluding that Spinoza accepted the existence of teleology and endorsed the legitimacy of at least some teleological explanations. The first lies in the many perfectly ordinary teleological explanations that Spinoza offers for various human activities throughout his philosophical and political writings and correspondence. For example, he begins the *Treatise on the Emendation of the Intellect* by explaining much of human activity as performed for the "ends" of attaining "wealth, honor, and sensual pleasure," and he goes on to explain his own philosophizing activity as the consequence of his desire to achieve a love whose object will be eternal, taking as "the end I aim at" the acquisition of a nature that will be "much stronger and more enduring" than the one he then has (*Emendation*, sects. 1–14; Geb II, 5–9).

*Human Ends.*    The second reason lies in Spinoza's general remarks about human ends in the appendix to *Ethics*, part 1. Although he emphatically denies that the one substance, God-or-Nature, has any ends or purposes through which its actions can be explained, he appears to contrast this with the case of human beings:

> All the prejudices I here undertake to expose depend on this one: that men commonly suppose that all natural things act, as men do, on account of an end. (E 1AP; Geb II, 78)

> Men act always on account of an end, namely, on account of their advantage, which they want. (E 1AP; Geb II, 78)

These statements strongly imply that the actions of human beings can be explained by reference to desired ends involving what is (or is presumed to be) advantageous to them. Such explanations would be teleological in the sense that I have defined.

*The* Conatus *of Singular Things.*   The third reason lies in Spinoza's doctrine of universal *conatus* (usually translated as "striving" or "endeavor"): "Each thing, as far as it can by its own power, strives to persevere in its being [*in suo esse perseverare conatur*]" (E 3P6; Geb II, 146). As Spinoza's demonstration of this proposition makes clear, its intended scope is all "singular things." He has already defined "singular things" as "things that are finite and have a determinate existence" (E 2D7; Geb II, 85). *Ethics* 3P6 therefore implies not merely that finite *human beings* strive to preserve themselves; it implies more generally that *every* finite thing," whether "organic" by ordinary standards or not, strives to exert some power to preserve itself.

   Curley (1990) rightly notes that the terms *conatur* and *conatus*, which he translates as "strives" and "striving," can mean simply "tends" and "tending" and need not be understood to involve *conscious* effort. Nevertheless, according to E 1P36 every singular thing has some power and produces some effects (Geb II, 77); and according to E 3P7D, the "power of each thing, or the striving by which it . . . does anything (is) the power, or striving, by which it strives to persevere in its being" (Geb II, 146). Hence, Spinoza seems to hold that each thing has at least some causal power whose exertion is a striving or tendency of the thing to persevere in its being.[2] This doctrine provides an obvious avenue for explaining the behavior of singular things by appeal to the self-preserving tendency of that behavior. These explanations may apply not only to humans, animals, and plants but even to such "inorganic" things as books and rocks; for in Spinoza's metaphysics, even objects not usually considered to be living can be understood to have some causal resources for resisting dissolution in the face of external forces.[3]

   It may be questioned whether the acceptance of teleology for all singular things implied by the *conatus* doctrine of E 3P6 is consistent with Spinoza's just-cited explicit denial in the appendix to *Ethics*, part 1, of the "prejudice . . . that all natural things act, as men do, on account of an end." To this there are two replies. First, Spinoza himself seems to treat his denial that "all natural things act . . . on account of an end" as interchangeable with his denial that *nature as a whole* "has no end set before it" (at Geb II, 80 of the appendix, for example), and his attempts to explain the origin, and establish the falsity, of this "prejudice" are directed entirely toward this latter doctrine.[4] Thus, it seems likely that he means in the appendix to deny only that nature as a whole acts for a unitary end, not to deny that each singular thing in nature acts for its *own* self-preservation. (There is, of course, no inconsistency between an affirmation of teleology for all singular things — as implied by E 3P6 — and a rejection of teleology on the part of God-or-Nature. This is because singular things are by definition finite, whereas Spinoza's God-or-Nature is an infinite thing and hence does not fall within the scope of the *conatus* doctrine of E 3P6.) Second, although Spinoza writes in the *Short Treatise on God, Man, and His Well-being* that bees making honey have "no other end in view than to provide a certain supply for the winter" (II.xxiv.6; Geb I,105), the *Ethics* uses the terms "end" and "final cause" only in application to human beings. Thus, it may well be that he has made a decision to withhold the term "end" from nonhuman nature in the *Ethics*; but such a terminological decision — motivated, presumably, by a desire to tie "ends" more directly to conscious intentions — would not by itself settle the question of whether the actions of nonhuman things exhibit *teleology* in the sense in which we are using that term. For example, Spinoza's own definition of "end" in E 4D7 reads as follows: "By the end for the sake of which we do something I understand appetite." On the one hand, this suggests that his use of the *term* "end" is being restricted to the case of human beings because he defines only the phrase "end for the sake of which we do something"; but on the other hand, it simultaneously suggests that the underlying phenomenon of action for ends is itself nevertheless pervasive throughout nature, for according to E 3P9S human "appetite" is simply human *conatus*, and *conatus* itself belongs to each singular thing in nature.

*Human Striving.*    The final reason for interpreting Spinoza as a committed teleologist lies in the many generalizations concerning human striving that Spinoza makes in *Ethics*, parts 3, 4, and 5. Here are just a few examples:

> We strive to further the occurrence of whatever we imagine will lead to Joy, and to avert or destroy what we imagine is contrary to it, *or* will lead to sadness. (E 3P28; Geb II, 161)

> When we love a thing like ourselves, we strive, as far as we can, to bring it about that it loves us in return. (E 3P33; Geb II, 165)

> A free man who lives among the ignorant strives, as far as he can, to avoid their favors. (E 4P70; Geb II, 262)

Each of these claims seems intended to license teleological predictions and explanations of human actions. Furthermore, since these generalizations — as well as claims in part 4 about the pursuit of objects under "the guidance of reason" — all trace their deductive ancestry to the *conatus* doctrine of E 3P6, there is further reason to interpret E 3P6 as providing a general basis for teleological explanation.

### Did Spinoza Reject All Teleological Explanation?

While fully aware of this evidence for Spinoza's acceptance of teleology — indeed, he acknowledges, cites, and discusses much of it — Jonathan Bennett (1983; 1984, chap. 9; 1990) argues that there is also very substantial evidence of opposition to all teleology and teleological explanation in Spinoza's *Ethics*. He thus regards Spinoza as involved in at least some inconsistency in his treatment of teleology. Bennett surveys five different considerations as evidence of opposition to teleology in Spinoza: (i) a statement in the appendix to *Ethics*, part 1, rejecting "final causes"; (ii) Spinoza's first argument in defense of this statement, concerning "necessity" and "perfection"; (iii) Spinoza's second argument in defense of this statement, concerning "the order of nature"; (iv) a deeper, unstated argument against all teleology for which there appear to be premises in part 2 of the *Ethics*; and (v) Spinoza's treatment, in part 3, of the concept of "appetite."[5]

*Final Causes as Human Fictions.*   In the appendix to Ethics, Part 1, Spinoza writes that "not many words will be required now to show that Nature has no end set before it, and that all final causes are nothing but human fictions" (Geb II, 80). Bennett reads the second clause of this statement, naturally enough, as a denial of the reality of all final causes and hence of all teleology. Curley (1990) emphasizes, however, that the second clause also admits of another natural reading, according to which it is merely restating the main idea of the first clause and hence is implicitly restricted to the denial of final causes considered as ends *that are set before God-or-Nature.* Curley notes that this reading has the advantage of greater consistency with the apparent endorsement of human teleology that occurs only two pages earlier in the same appendix, in passages already cited. It is also, of course, more consistent with the further evidence of commitment to teleological explanation later in the *Ethics* and elsewhere in Spinoza's writings. Thus, Curley's less radical reading of Spinoza's claim concerning "final causes" is to be preferred unless support for the more radical reading is forthcoming from other features of Spinoza's texts.

*Necessity and Perfection.*   Immediately after stating that "not many words will be required now to show that Nature has no end set before it, and that all final causes are nothing but human fictions," Spinoza goes on to say that he has "sufficiently established" this claim "both by the foundations and causes from which I have shown this prejudice to have had its origin, and also by P16, P32C1 and C2, and all those (propositions) by which I have shown that all things proceed by a certain eternal necessity of nature, and with the greatest perfection" (E 1AP; Geb II, 80). The proposition and two corollaries that Spinoza cites by number in this passage read as follows:

> From the necessity of the divine nature there must follow infinitely many things in infinitely many modes (i.e., everything which can fall under an infinite intellect). (E 1P16; Geb II, 60)

> God does not produce any effect by freedom of the will. (E 1P32C1; Geb II, 73)

> Will and intellect are related to God's nature as motion and rest are, and as are absolutely all natural things, which (by P29) must be determined by God to exist and produce an effect in a certain way. (E 1P32C2; Geb II, 73)

How does Spinoza intend these citations to support his claim about final causes? Bennett's (1984, chap. 9) answer to this question is straightforward: Spinoza cites these three claims in order to infer a denial of teleology from his strict causal determinism. Bennett rightly judges the inference itself to be weak, on the grounds that teleology does *not* in fact require causal indeterminism; however, he justly emphasizes that what matters most directly for purposes of interpreting Spinoza's conclusion is not the strength of his argument but its intended scope. Since a supposed purely *general* incompatibility between teleology and universal strict determinism would apply equally to divine and human teleology, Bennett suggests that Spinoza's ambiguous claim about final causes should be interpreted as a denial of all teleology.

However, as Curley (1990) notes, the three claims that Spinoza cites by number specifically concern only God and the *divine* nature. Although E 1P32 itself concerns freedom of will in general, Spinoza conspicuously does not cite it; instead, he limits his citation to the two corollaries concerning God that he draws from it. Furthermore, the only "prejudice" whose "foundation and causes" he has explained at this point of the appendix is the one that we have already noted: namely, the "prejudice . . . that men commonly suppose that all natural things act, as men do, on account of an end . . . [and] that God himself directs all things to some certain end, for they say that God has made all things for man, and man that he might worship God" (E 1AP; Geb II, 78).[6] The "foundation and causes" he cites for this prejudice do not call into question whether humans act for ends. Instead, they simply explain — as an overhasty extrapolation by human beings from their own case — the common opinion that God shares this mode of activity with them. In light of these facts, plus the evident weakness of the inference from general determinism to the denial of all teleology, it is reasonable to wonder whether Spinoza is concerned instead with a more specific — and perhaps more plausible — objection to divine ends in particular, an objection founded in the specific necessity of the divine nature.

Although he does not spell out such an objection explicitly, we can see how Spinoza might be thinking. The teleological functioning of an "end" or "final cause" arguably requires at least that something be *selected from alternatives* in a way that essentially involves some kind of *goodness or fitness of its likely or presumptive consequences* relative to those of other alternatives. For the actions of singular things, including human beings, the idea of such selection makes sense. Singular things have some causal power, for Spinoza, but their causality is not entirely self-sufficient (E 4A1; see also E 4P4). What they do is absolutely causally necessitated, but it is necessitated only by the nature and state of the singular thing *together with* the nature and state of the surrounding objects in the whole order of nature. *Relative to the power of the surrounding objects*, therefore, a variety of alternative actions are possible, depending on the nature and the present state of the singular thing — just as *relative to the power of the singular thing* various outcomes of its action are possible, depending on the nature and state of the surrounding objects. Since singular things naturally pursue their own self-preservation — according to the *conatus* doctrine of E 3P6 — we can appeal to a specified action's (likely or presumptive) beneficial consequences in order to explain why the singular thing "selected" *that* course of action over the alternatives that were equally possible relative to the power of the surrounding objects. In the special case of God, however, this teleological mode of explanation is doubly inappropriate. Because God is causally self-contained and self-sufficient, his actions are absolutely necessitated by his own nature; there is no surrounding context relative to whose powers various divine actions are possible. Indeed, when things are considered as divine actions, there are no unactualized possibilities (Garrett 1991). God's action, therefore, does not select *among possible al-*

*ternatives*. Furthermore, God's necessary existence and perfection entail that nothing can be helpful or hurtful to God, because nothing can destroy him or make him less perfect. Hence, there is *no divine "good" or "advantage"* to serve as a principle of selection for God.

In the appendix to part 1 of the *Ethics*, Spinoza is not yet in a position to elaborate the foregoing *contrast* between God and individuals because he has not yet provided his theory of individuation (beginning in the Physical Excursus following E 2P13), his account of the endeavor of singular things for self-preservation (beginning with E 3P6), or any suggestion of a sense of "possibility" that is relative to limited powers (as suggested, for example, at E 3P6, 4D4, and subsequent discussions of human choice). He has, however, said enough to support his denial of divine ends. Spinoza's reference to "P16, P32C1 and C2, and all those (propositions) by which I have shown that all things proceed by a certain eternal necessity of nature, and with the greatest perfection" can easily be understood as invoking his cumulative description of the divine nature from E 1P16, 1P22C1, 1P22C2, and elsewhere in part 1 to indicate that divine teleological explanation is inappropriate in both of the respects we have considered: the reference to "a certain eternal necessity of nature" concerns the absence of alternatives for selection, and the reference to "the greatest perfection" concerns the absence of a divine good or advantage to serve as a principle for selection.[7] We need not interpret Spinoza as rejecting all teleology on the basis of this argument.

*Reversing the Order of Nature.* In further defense of his remark that "Nature has no end set before it, and ... all final causes are nothing but human fictions," Spinoza writes that "this doctrine concerning the end turns the order of Nature completely upside down. For what is really a cause, it considers as an effect, and conversely. What is by nature prior, it makes posterior. And finally, what is supreme and most perfect, it makes imperfect" (E 1AP; Geb II, 80). At least the *third* point of this compound objection — the point concerning perfection and imperfection — appears to be concerned only with *divine* ends. For Spinoza goes on to defend it by making two observations specifically about God: (i) that the things God immediately produces are more perfect than things God produces only mediately, whereas the existence of divine ends would entail the reverse; and (ii) that God cannot act for the sake of an end unless he wants something that he lacks. Furthermore, there is no indication in the wording of the text that Spinoza intends his *first* two points of objection — which he says are "manifest through themselves" — to have any broader scope than the third. On the contrary, Spinoza's further remarks about the ways in which the "Followers of this doctrine" seek to defend it are likewise concerned exclusively with divine purposes. Nevertheless, as Bennett (1994, 216–217) observes, at least the first point of objection — namely, that the doctrine of ends at issue reverses the proper relation of cause and consequence — could in principle be raised against *all* teleology.

How compelling a reason is this to interpret Spinoza as rejecting all teleology, non-divine as well as divine? Both Bennett and Curley (1990) recognize that human teleology would escape the first point of objection *if* it could be understood as a species of efficient causation; and they both agree that at least one way of so understanding human teleology would be to locate the cause of human action in the *present representation* of a future effect. (This is *not* to say that there might not also be ways to avoid the objection by appealing to efficient causes that do not involve representation at all, as we shall see later.) Furthermore, Curley emphasizes that Spinoza seems to endorse precisely this sort of saving efficient-cause account of at least some human teleology in a passage from the preface to *Ethics*, part 4:

> What is termed a final cause is nothing but human appetite in so far as it is considered as the starting-point or primary cause of some thing. For example, when we say that being a place of habitation was the final cause of this or that house, we surely mean no more than this, that a man, from thinking of the advantages of domestic life, had an urge to build a house. Therefore, the need for a habitation in so far as it is considered as a final cause, is nothing but this particular urge, which is in reality an efficient cause. (E 4PR; Geb II, 207)

For Bennett (1984: 224), either (i) this latter passage is not intended (contrary to appearances) to explain the existence of a house teleologically by appeal to a process of efficient causation involving its imagined consequences, or (ii) it simply constitutes an inconsistency on Spinoza's part. It is clear, however, that we are still not compelled to interpret Spinoza as rejecting all teleology.

*The Causal Inefficacy of Representative Content.*    Although the passages that we have considered thus far can be interpreted quite naturally as limited to a denial of divine ends or purposes, they can also be interpreted — at the cost of attributing some inconsistency to Spinoza — as denying all teleology whatsoever. Bennett prefers the more radically antiteleological reading, partly because he attributes to Spinoza a further, deeper argument concerning teleology, an unstated argument whose premises he thinks Spinoza must nevertheless have accepted and whose universally antiteleological conclusion he believes Spinoza must, at least at some level, have grasped.

This deeper argument is roughly as follows. Teleology can exist only if some properties that have causal efficacy "map onto" representative properties — properties, that is, of *representing* something. (Presumably properties "map onto" others if and only if they can be related by identity, coextensivity, or a similar systematic correlation relation; "mapping onto" is thus a symmetrical relation.) But such properties of representative content are determined largely by causal origin, as Spinoza appears to recognize in E 2P16 (plus its corollaries), and in 2P40S1 as well.[8] Representative properties are therefore not intrinsic but merely relational, and relational in such a way that intrinsic properties cannot be mapped onto them. The universality of mechanism within the physical or extended realm — which requires that all causally efficacious physical properties be intrinsic properties such as shape or velocity — thus dictates that any *physical* properties whatever that *can* be mapped onto representative properties are of the wrong kind to have causal efficacy. From this and Spinoza's doctrine of the causal parallelism between the attributes of extension and thought (i.e., the physical and the mental), it follows that no *mental* properties that can be mapped onto representative properties are causally efficacious either. Hence, there are no causally efficacious physical or mental properties that map onto representative properties, and there is therefore no teleology. Bennett thus sees Spinoza as anticipating the concerns of many contemporary philosophers who doubt the causal efficacy of representative properties on the grounds that they do not map onto causally efficacious physical properties — all of which, they maintain, are nonrepresentative.

Somewhat more precisely, the argument that Bennett ascribes to Spinoza and the grounds that he cites for them may be outlined as follows (drawing on the presentations in Bennett 1983 and 1984 and on their defense and elaboration in Bennett 1990):

(1) The causally efficacious properties of things under the attribute of extension are all intrinsic geometrical and dynamic properties, such as shape and velocity (inference from Spinoza's so-called "Physical Excursus," the set of axioms and lemmas following E 2P13).

(2) Whether an entity with a certain complete set of intrinsic properties counts as having this or that *content* or *representative* property depends on when its bearer got it, in what circumstances, in association with what other items, and so on (inference from E 2P16, 2P16C1, 2P16C2, 2P40S1).

(3) No intrinsic property can be mapped onto any representative property [inference from (2)].

(4) Any properties of things under the attribute of extension that can be mapped onto representative properties lack causal efficacy [inference from (1) and (3)].

(5) The order and connection of ideas is the same as the order and connection of things [Causal Parallelism, as stated in E 2P7).

(6) Any properties of things under the attribute of thought that can be mapped onto representative properties lack causal efficacy [inference from (4) and (5)]

(7) All teleology requires that some causally efficacious properties map onto representative properties.

(8) There is no teleology [inference from (4), (6), and (7)].

Throughout this argument, the phrase "representative properties" must be understood to refer only to properties of what Bennett calls "indirect representation" (see Bennett 1984, 219). In Spinoza's metaphysics, every mode of extension is represented primarily — "directly," in Bennett's terminology — by a mode of thought with which it is *identical*. This doctrine entails that any versions of steps (2) and (3) concerned with direct representation would be false: for every intrinsic property of a mode of extension, there would be a corresponding idea *directly representing* precisely that property. Hence, a version of step (4) concerned with direct representation would have to be false as well: for any causally efficacious property under the attribute of extension, there would be a corresponding idea directly representing that property under the attribute of thought.

However, in the passages from *Ethics*, part 2, that Bennett (1990, 54–55) cites as support for step (2), Spinoza is considering a metaphysically secondary, or "indirect," way in which ideas can represent things with which they are *not* identical. In

Spinoza's example in E 2P17S, for instance, what directly represents Peter's body is simply Peter's mind; but an idea in Paul's mind — an idea that directly represents a state of Paul's body — can indirectly represent Peter's body. It will do so, according to Spinoza, to the extent that the state of Paul's body has been caused by Peter's body, and so owes some considerable part of its nature to the nature of Peter's body as well as part of its nature to Paul's body. This would occur if, for example, the state of Paul's body in question involved a physical image of a shape that corresponded to and was caused by the shape of Peter's body. This is the kind of representation that occurs when human beings *imagine* other bodies; and Bennett plausibly assumes that it is the causal efficacy of *this* kind of representation that Spinoza would think relevant to teleology in step (7). Hence, the argument univocally concerns indirect, rather than direct, "representative properties" throughout.[9]

Is Spinoza likely to have grasped and been motivated by this deeper argument against all teleology? Two of its key premises are the nonmapping doctrine of step (3) and the efficacy of representation requirement of step (7). It is not obvious, however, that Spinoza would accept either of them.

Michael Della Rocca (1996, 252–257) notes that Spinoza gives no textual indication of possessing a key distinction that is needed to grasp the efficacy in representation requirement of step (7): namely, the distinction between the causal efficacy of a *thing or state*, on the one hand, and the causal efficacy of the thing's or state's *representative properties*, on the other hand. Furthermore, we may add, there is a strong prima facie reason to suppose that Spinoza would *reject* this efficacy of representation requirement. All parties, including Bennett (1983, 1984, 1990), freely acknowledge that Spinoza often uses the general *conatus* doctrine of E 3P6 to underwrite teleological explanations. (Bennett regards this as inconsistent dealing on Spinoza's part; although the argument is much too long to repeat here, I have argued elsewhere[10] that Spinoza *consistently* construes the doctrine teleologically, both in his argument for it and in the consequences he derives from it.) Although most of his applications of the *conatus* doctrine are to human beings — which is understandable, given the primary purposes of the *Ethics* — at no point does Spinoza explicitly require that *conatus* operate only through indirect representation. On the contrary, the scope of E 3P6 is "singular things" generally, and the presence of *conatus* is essential to his account of the individuation of all finite things.[11] Yet many things (e.g., rocks, trees, and individual bodily organs) do not appear to have any indirect representations at all — or at least none beyond rudimentary and obscure traces of impacts on their external surfaces. Even higher animals, which *do* have developed indirect representations, perform many self-preservatory activities — the pumping of blood, involuntary respiration, perspiration, and so on — that do not utilize indirect representations. If Spinoza allows even one instance in which an individual's activity can be explained through its striving to persevere in being in a way that does not employ indirect representations, then he is obliged to reject step (7).

It is also doubtful whether Spinoza would be willing to infer the nonmapping doctrine of step (3) from the relational character of indirect representation that is postulated in step (2) (derived from *Ethics*, part 2). For the nonmapping doctrine of step (3) requires not merely that *some* representative properties resist mapping from causally efficacious physical properties; it also requires that *no* causally efficacious properties be mappable onto *any* representative properties. Philosophers of mind now often distinguish between *narrow* and *broad representative content*. Whereas the latter can involve representations of specific individuals or natural kinds and depends essentially on relational (including causal-history) properties of the representer that do not map onto intrinsic properties, the former is qualitative and may be supervenient on the intrinsic nonrelational properties of the representer. Adapting this distinction to Spinoza's case of Peter and Paul, we might say that when Paul has an idea whose broad content is "Peter's body," he also has an idea (perhaps even the same idea) with a narrow content that captures only a certain size, texture, and arrangement of physical parts, some of which pertain to Peter. Even if the broad representative content property were disqualified from causal efficacy by its dependence on causal history, it does not follow that a narrow representative content property of the kind indicated is also causally disqualified.

Whether there are in fact completely narrow representative contents that are completely independent of the representer's external relations remains a disputed question and need not be settled here.[12] But it should be emphasized that Spinoza's psychology is particularly congenial to narrow content, inasmuch as indirect representation is for him ultimately a matter of having *images*, embedded in a particular causal framework, that *resemble* and often even *reproduce* particular features of their originals. (Such images also, of course, have some features that are contributed by the nature of the representer.) This conception of representation — which is potentially both mental and physical, thinking and extended — makes it very plausible to suppose that, for Spinoza, indirect representation operates in the first instance to represent *by resemblance* the copied *properties* of objects and only more derivatively to represent the particular external objects themselves.[13] Once again, we are by no means forced to the conclusion that Spinoza rejected all teleology.

*The Concept of Appetite.* In E 4D7, Spinoza defines "end" in terms of appetite: "By the end for the sake of which we do something I understand appetite" (Geb II, 210). Bennett (1984, 222) writes that this definition "announces flatly that (Spinoza) will have no truck with the language of final causes unless it is construed in terms of his harmless (i.e., nonteleological) notion of appetite." Bennett interprets E 4D7 in this way — that is, as a rejection of all teleology — because he interprets Spinoza's concept of "appetite," first introduced in E 3P9S, as intended to provide a nonteleological *substitute* for the ordinary teleological concept of "desire."

Is Spinoza's concept of "appetite" nonteleological? He introduces the concept in the course of his main discussion of *conatus*:

> When this striving ("by which each thing strives to persevere in its being," i.e., *conatus*) is related only to the Mind, it is called Will; but when it is related to the Mind and Body together, it is called Appetite. This Appetite, therefore, is nothing but the very essence of man, from whose nature there necessarily follow those things that promote his preservation. And so man is determined to do those things.

> Between appetite and desire there is no difference, except that desire is generally related to men insofar as they are conscious of their appetites. So *desire* can be defined as *appetite together with consciousness of the appetite*.

From all this, then, it is clear that we neither strive for, nor will, neither want, nor desire anything because we judge it to be good; on the contrary, we judge something to be good because we strive for it, will it, want it, and desire it. (E 3P9S; Geb II, 147–148)

Bennett offers two reasons for interpreting this account of appetite as nonteleological. The first lies in his reading of Spinoza's claim that an appetite or desire for persevering in being is "the very essence of man." Bennett interprets this to mean that appetite is "causally potent only when construed in intrinsic rather than representational terms" (1990, 55; see also 1984, 221–222). He interprets Spinoza's claim in this way — that is, as appealing to a distinction between intrinsic and representational properties, considered as mutually exclusive — because he interprets "the essence" of a thing as consisting of all of its intrinsic, nonrelational properties. Accordingly, he holds that, for Spinoza, the proper notion of "appetite for *x*" is not the notion of a representative state but rather the notion of any *intrinsic* state "that causes one to move towards *x*" (1984, 221).

As noted in connection with the "deeper" eight-step argument that Bennett attributes to Spinoza, however, there is good reason to doubt whether Spinoza accepts the nonmapping doctrine expressed in step (3) (i.e., that no intrinsic property can be mapped onto any representative property). Hence there is good reason to doubt whether Spinoza would make the inference Bennett proposes from the *intrinsic* character of appetite to the *nonrepresentative* character of appetite. Furthermore, even if Spinoza were to grant this inference, we have also found reasons to doubt whether he accepts the efficacy of representation requirement expressed in step (7) (i.e., that all teleology requires that some causally efficacious properties map onto representative properties). Hence there is also reason to doubt whether he would allow the further inference from the alleged *nonrepresentative* character of appetite to the *nonteleological* character of appetite. Both proposed inferences are particularly dubious in the present context, where the object of the appetite in question is simply a general perseverance in being.

Fortunately, it is not necessary to see Spinoza as appealing to a radical distinction between intrinsic and representative properties in order to understand his remark at E 3P9S that appetite is "the very essence of man." As the context of that remark indicates, he is referring specifically to the appetite of each human being *to persevere in being,* and this appetite is identical, in his view, with the *striving* to persevere in being, or *conatus,* of each human being. Hence, his claim in E 3P9S about the "essence of man" is simply an application to human beings of the more general doctrine of 3P7 that "the striving by which each thing strives to persevere in its being is nothing but the actual essence of the thing." The essence of a thing, for Spinoza, is that which makes it what it is (so that its presence is necessary and sufficient for the existence of the thing) and from which follows everything that can be understood fully through the nature, power, or activity of that thing (E 2D3; Geb II, 84).[14] Hence, to say that the appetite for self-preservation is the essence of man is simply to say that its presence is necessary and sufficient for the existence of the man and that whatever activities can be understood through the nature of the human being at all are to be understood through this appetite or striving. For Spinoza, particular human desires are simply particular conscious aspects — that is, conscious directions onto more specific objects — of this general appetite for self-preservation.

Bennett's (1984, 223–224) second reason for interpreting Spinoza's concept of "appetite" as nonteleological concerns Spinoza's doctrine about the causal priority of desire over judgments of goodness, as stated in the final paragraph of E 3P9S. More specifically, it concerns Spinoza's remark that the causal priority doctrine follows "from all this" — that is, from the previous two paragraphs of the scholium. Bennett suggests that only his own nonteleological interpretation of "appetite" can explain this remark. In Bennett's nonteleological construal of "appetite," *all* representative states — including, therefore, those about goodness — are merely derivative from the *intrinsic* states that are identified as appetites or desires. It is for this reason, he suggests, that Spinoza affirms that judgments *about* (i.e., representing) goodness do not *explain*, but rather are *explained by*, our appetites or desires in the Spinozistic sense.

However, Spinoza's doctrine in E 3P9S that the appetite to persevere in being is the "actual essence" of each human being — that is, the explanatory essence from which the various actual properties and actions of the human being follow — provides the basis for a simple and plausible explanation of Spinoza's remark that is entirely consistent with a teleological conception of appetite. For if appetite is the *essence* of each human being, it must causally explain, rather than be causally explained by, such other properties of the person as judgments about the good, regardless of the representative or teleological character of the appetite.

### Teleology and the Second Kind of Knowledge

If the foregoing analysis is correct, then (i) Spinoza is committed to the existence of teleology in the behavior of human beings in particular and of singular things in general and (ii) nothing in his writings warrants the conclusion that he rejected all teleology. Yet the Physical Excursus following E 2P13 (Geb II, 96–103) presents a theory of nature in which the individuation, form, and behavior of bodies is evidently determined entirely by their motion and rest.[15] In light of this apparent commitment to mechanism for extended things and his clear doctrine of the causal parallelism of the attributes of extension and thought, we may still wonder whether there is any positive basis in his metaphysics and epistemology for teleological explanations.

The answer to this question lies in Spinoza's doctrine of three kinds of knowledge or cognition (*cognitio*), a doctrine presented in E 2P40S (Geb II, 122) and, in a slightly different form, in *Emendation*, sections 18–24 (Geb II, 9–12).[16] The first kind of knowledge is opinion (*opinio*). This kind of knowledge is based either on mere random experience (*experientia vaga*; see Gabbey 1996, 172–175, for a fuller explanation of this term) or on words or other signs; it is based on the imagination and hence is "inadequate." The second and third kinds of knowledge, in contrast, are based on the intellect and are entirely "adequate." The second kind of knowledge, reason (*ratio*), is based on inference from "common notions and adequate ideas of the properties of things," and the third kind of knowledge, intuitive knowledge (*scientia intuitiva*), "proceeds from an adequate idea of the formal essence of certain attributes of God to the adequate knowledge of the essence of things." These definitions appeal to the distinction between the essence of a thing and its properties. The *essence* of a thing, as we have seen, constitutes the thing's nature, makes it what it is, and is the basis for an adequate understanding of the thing itself and its activities. A *property* of a thing is any other characteristic of the thing that *follows* from its essence; a property may be shared in common with other things, and it can be understood by understanding only *enough* of the essence of a thing to allow us to see that the property does follow.

As Spinoza's examples show, the same fact can be known through different kinds of knowledge by different people. His examples also illustrate a fundamental difference between the second and third kinds of knowledge: whereas the second kind of knowledge allows one to understand, correctly and with certainty, *that* something is so (by inferring it from some general property that one knows a thing must have), knowledge of the third kind allows one to understand, correctly and with certainty, *how and why* something is so (by allowing one to infer it from an adequate knowledge of a thing's own essence). Although the distinction between the second and third kinds of knowledge is not itself a distinction between teleological and mechanistic modes of explanation, it does help us to understand how teleological explanation is possible and how it is related to mechanistic explanation.

Mechanistic explanation of an effect can produce knowledge of the second kind. This occurs when, by knowing *common properties* of bodies pertaining to motion and rest, we can infer the production of the effect in the given circumstances. Such common properties play a central role in the epistemology Spinoza presents throughout *Ethics*, part 2. However, teleological explanation of an effect can *also* produce knowledge of the second kind. This occurs when, by knowing *common properties* of bodies or minds pertaining to their endeavor to persevere in being, we can infer the production of the effect in given circumstances. Such common properties play a central role in the psychology of emotions that Spinoza presents throughout *Ethics*, part 3.

Consider, for example, a man who gives his beloved a beautiful and expensive gift. Striving to persevere in being is a property that (by E 3P6) we know all singular things to possess, despite the differences in their individual essences. One general consequence of this striving, in the case of all those singular things capable of love [defined in E 3PCS (Geb II, 151) as "joy with the accompanying idea of an external cause"], is demonstrated in E 3P33: "When we love a thing like ourselves, we strive, as far as we can, to bring it about that it loves us in return." Using this knowledge, we may explain the man's gift-giving teleologically: it is an action performed to bring it about that the beloved love him in return, in circumstances in which the giving of the gift constitutes the greatest effort to bring about the return of love that is within the man's power. The fact that the man strove to bring about a return of love explains his action teleologically because that likely or presumptive consequence is involved in the etiology of the action; were it not for its relation to that consequence, it is far less likely that he would have performed it. Thus far, however, our resulting understanding of the action is nevertheless only knowledge of the second kind, for we know only through a common property of lovers, rather than through the essence of the particular man, that such an action must occur in those circumstances.

Knowledge of the third kind, we may suppose, must combine and integrate both teleological and mechanistic explanation in cases where we seek to understand the effects of singular things under the attribute of extension. For in understanding the *essence* of a singular thing, we must understand that essence as a specific force, striving for its own specific self-preservation (by E 3P7). To understand in detail *how* a given extended thing strives for self-preservation, however, we must understand how its various parts interact mechanistically to constitute a mechanism that tends to produce its own perseverance in being through the variety of self-preservatory operations that it has within its own power or behavioral repertoire. We must, that is, understand how an extended thing's teleological strivings are implemented or realized mechanistically. In the case of the lover and his gift, we must understand the essence of the particular man well enough to be able to understand not only *that* a gift must be given but also *how* the giving of the gift will be brought about through the specific mechanistic nature of this (extended) man.

To understand fully by the third kind of knowledge how this mechanistic interaction occurs, however, we must in turn understand the nature of the divine attribute of extension itself, a nature that constitutes the essence of God; and this is why Spinoza writes in E 2P40S that knowledge of the third kind "proceeds from an adequate idea of the formal essence of certain attributes of God to the adequate knowledge of the essence of things." Spinoza is a pivotal figure standing squarely between an older conception of natural philosophy that aims to understand *things* through their *essences* and a more modern conception of natural science that aims to understand *events* through their instantiation of *laws*. He combines these two conceptions in a distinctive way. The fundamental purpose of natural philosophy or science, he holds, is to understand in greater detail the one substance, God; but this proves to require, if it is to be done properly, an understanding of the general laws of nature that constitute the essence of each divine attribute. These general laws of nature give rise to particular kinds of singular things, each with its own nature or *essence* — an essence that can, in turn, be understood in terms of what he sometimes calls the *laws* of that thing's *own* nature. Understanding these essences of singular things is a matter of understanding them as systems tending toward self preservation, and understanding their behavior is a matter of understanding how that behavior results from the self-preservatory, law-governed systems that they embody. In the ideal case of knowledge of the third kind, this knowledge of individual essences results from knowledge of the attributes and their most general laws as those laws give rise to particular essences. For Spinoza, understanding individual things and their behavior through their own essences is thus partly a teleological enterprise, but a teleological enterprise perfectly compatible with the mechanistic nature of extension. In fact, given the doctrine of the causal parallelism of the attributes, something analogous and parallel to mechanism must also be true in the attribute of thought.

## Teleology in Early Modern Philosophy

### *Is There Any Unthoughtful Teleology?*

Teleology requires that the etiology of a fact be correctly explainable by its likely or presumptive consequences. If consequences cannot directly produce their own antecedents, then it seems that teleology requires what may be called a *teleological selection process* — that is, a process capable of selecting and producing states of affairs on the basis of their typical or presumptive consequences. We may say that an example of teleology is *thoughtful* if the selection process through which the consequences of a state of affairs explain the existence of that state of affairs is or essentially involves thought. We may call an example of teleology *unthoughtful*, in contrast, if the selection process neither is nor essentially involves thought.[17]

Aristotle would grant that some teleology is thoughtful — as when one feeds oneself with the intention to be nourished. However, it is an important part of his metaphysics that much teleology is unthoughtful — as when an animal's development of an arrangement of teeth is explained by that arrangement's serving the ends of tearing and chewing. For Aristotle, there is no sense in which the development of an arrangement of teeth is caused by thought or intention. It was partly in response to the felt need to provide an unthinking teleological selection *process* in individual substances that Aristotle's scholastic followers elaborated a theory of substantial forms — that is, forms that are specific to each kind of substance, are present in individual substances, and help to determine the course of a substance's behavior and development in accordance with its natural ends.

The denial of substantial forms is a hallmark of Cartesian natural philosophy, and it evidently leads Descartes to reject all unthoughtful teleology. Will, operating through acts of volition, is the only teleological selection process that he acknowledges. Although he does not specifically deny the existence of other teleological selection processes, he does deny that we should look for final causes in natural philosophy, and he explains the seemingly teleological workings of animals as resulting from divinely preprogrammed mechanisms specific to each animal operation, rather than by postulating any teleological selection process located in the animal itself or anywhere else within the natural world. Since the workings of nature in general, and those of animals in particular, constitute the most likely places to look for unthoughtful teleology, Descartes's universal rejection of unthoughtful teleology seems evident.

In fact, Descartes's ontological dualism of extended and thinking substances seems to be reflected in a dualism of types of explanation. Extended substances, he implies, cannot themselves produce effects directly through teleological selection, whereas thinking substances cannot directly produce effects mechanistically. Because thinking substances and extended substances can interact causally, in Descartes's view,[18] a given state of matter may be explained teleologically (as when a muscle moves in order to move an arm), whereas a given state of mind (such as a physiologically induced passion) may be explained mechanistically. Of course, the alleged unintelligibility of Cartesian mind-body causal interaction may call into question the ultimate adequacy of these explanations. But in any case, whereas each kind of Cartesian substance may participate in either or both kinds of *explanandum*, each can evidently participate only in its own proper kind of *explanans*, each grounding or originating only its own proper kind of explanation. Minds, but not bodies, can have ends, goods, or purposes; and bodies, but not minds, can have physical structures and distributions of forces.

Leibniz's reputation as a friend of Aristotelian teleology depends largely on his attempted rehabilitation of the scholastic theory of substantial forms. But this attempted rehabilitation should not obscure the fact that Leibniz follows Descartes in requiring that all teleology be thoughtful. Indeed, his commitment to this doctrine is even clearer than Descartes's. Although Leibniz finds loci of teleological selection pervasive throughout nature, this is only because he also finds thought itself to be pervasive throughout nature. Rather than conceiving of the universe in Cartesian fashion — as divided into two distinct substantial realms, each having its own principal attribute — Leibniz makes the realm of thinking substances metaphysically and ontologically primary, so that all of the simple substances that give rise to material nature are understood as more or less rudimentary thinking souls. Whereas the activity of these simple substances may not always warrant such terms as "desire" and "intention" (which properly belong to souls at the higher end of the scale of perfection), all substances achieve their successive states by striving after them through *appetition*, and so "act according to the laws of final causes, through appetitions, ends, and means" (*Monadology* 79; AG 223). Even in their most rudimentary forms, appetition and perception are, for Leibniz, aspects of thought.

Spinoza is committed, as we have already seen, to the existence of teleology in the behavior of human beings and of all other singular things. Given that human beings are known only as modes of thought and of extension, the conjunction of this commitment with his doctrine of causal parallelism between the attributes of thought and extension (E 2P7) entails that teleology exists equally within both the attributes of thought and extension. But he also endorses, in E 2P6, a doctrine of explanatory dualism: "The modes of each attribute have God for their cause only insofar as he is considered under the attribute of which they are modes, and not insofar as he is considered under any other attribute." That is, aspects of extension can only be caused and explained through extension and not through thought, whereas aspects of thought can only be caused and explained through thought and not through extension. Hence, Spinoza is committed to the existence of unthoughtful teleology; indeed, he is committed to the existence of a parallel instance of unthoughtful teleology for each instance of thoughtful teleology involving ideas of extended things.

Since (by E 3P7) each singular thing must have an actual essence that consists in a striving to persevere in existence, the continued existence of each singular thing with its own actual essence constitutes, in itself, a general teleological selection process. From the various effects permitted by the force or power of surrounding objects and circumstances, this process selects those within its own power that are likely or presumed to be conducive to self-preservation. For Spinoza, as for Aristotle, this general teleological selection process involves various more specific processes that depend on the nature of the particular singular thing. In Spinoza's metaphysics, these processes operate unthoughtfully under the attribute of extension and, in a parallel way, operate thoughtfully under the attribute of thought. Some of these specific teleological selection processes involve *imagining* objects of desire through indirect representation, but some do not. For there is equal room, among the class of such processes, for the hunting of prey by a predator and the molecular cohesion by which a crystal resists dissolution.

### Is There Teleological Selection Through Divine Will or Purpose?

One obvious candidate for a teleological selection process is *will* or *intention*, for it is difficult to deny that voluntary or intentional actions are selected on the basis of their expected consequences. Such a will or intention may, in principle, be that of a divine, angelic, human, or subhuman being.

Although Aristotle finds teleology to be pervasive in nature, he does not judge any of it to involve divine will or purpose as a selection process. Aristotle's Divinity, although it is thinking, does not act through will or intention at all (*Metaphysics* XII.ix). Whereas the Christian scholastics certainly invoked the concept of divine purpose in accounting for teleology in nature, Aristotle himself did not.

According to Descartes, however, God creates and sustains all of nature through his divine will. Indeed, according to Descartes, God even creates the eternal truths of mathematics and logic through his will and determines what is good by willing that it shall be good. Although Descartes denies that God's purposes or plans are knowable by human beings, he regularly allows that such purposes and plans do exist and that God chooses what to create. It appears, therefore, that Descartes's God performs one or more creative (and sustaining) acts on the basis of his choice of what objects and truths to create (and sustain). If this is correct, then divine creative activity is an example of teleology for Descartes, and the divine actions themselves will have teleological explanations insofar as they are aimed at, and selected in order to produce, their objects. Indeed, since the divine will is, for Descartes, the source of all of nature, the divine will must also be the source of at least the existence of — if not also the determinant of foreordained outcomes of — whatever teleological selection processes might exist in nature, including those of the human will.

Nevertheless, for Descartes the teleological selection process of the divine will is — unlike that of the human will — an entirely *indifferent* one, not based on the perceived goodness of any consequences (Sixth Objections and Replies; CSM II, 291). In his view, God does not choose things because they are good; rather, things are good because God chooses them to be so. Moreover, God's original creative choices are not ultimately limited or directed even by principles of logical consistency, for these principles themselves are true only in consequence of God's choosing them to be. Hence, although Descartes's God evidently performs creative acts so that what he has chosen shall exist, these choices themselves do not occur for the sake of anything else. Although God's creative acts of will evidently have teleological explanations, his choices of *what* to create evidently do not.

Leibniz, too, holds that divine will is the source of all of nature. While not extending this doctrine of volitional creation to include the eternal truths, Leibniz does go beyond Descartes in holding that every contingent truth has a teleological explanation in terms of God's choice. If anything, Leibniz is much *more* insistent on the non-Aristotelian doctrine of teleological divine will than is Descartes. For although he recognizes that Descartes formally acknowledges divine will, Leibniz doubts, in effect, whether a genuine will *can* operate with a truly indifferent selection process — as opposed to one that is responsive to the perceived good, as Leibniz takes God's will to be. As we have seen, Leibniz accuses Descartes of not *wanting* "his God to act in accordance with some end" (Letter to Molanus; AG 242). Accordingly, he suggests that "Descartes's God is (really) something approaching the God of Spinoza, namely, the principle of things, a certain supreme power or primitive nature."

Spinoza's God, in contrast to the God of Descartes or Leibniz, acts not through a divine will but solely through the necessity of the divine nature. Spinoza emphasizes — as does Aristotle — that any doctrine of divine will is incompatible with the divine perfection. For example, he writes in the appendix to part 1 of the *Ethics* that "this doctrine (of divine ends) takes away God's perfection. For if God acts for the sake of an end, he necessarily wants something which he lacks" (Geb II, 80). He resolutely attacks the doctrine that "God himself directs all things to some certain end" (Geb II, 78), arguing instead that "Nature (i.e., God) has no end set before it."

Still, in the *Ethics*, Spinoza quite clearly accepts teleology — in the form of *conatus* and appetite — for non-human singular things without explicitly attributing will or ends to them.[19] Furthermore, he often implies that God produces the greatest possible reality and perfection. Hence, we may ask whether Spinoza does not after all accept some divine teleology even while he refrains from characterizing it in terms of will or ends.

In E 5PP35–36C (Geb II, 302), Spinoza recognizes a sense in which God emotionlessly "loves" both himself and human beings — even though, more strictly speaking, God cannot love because he cannot have joy, which implies a change in degree of power and perfection that is incompatible with his eternal and infinite existence (E 5P17; Geb II, 291).[20] Similarly, although he does not say so, Spinoza might be willing to recognize a sense in which God "strives" effortlessly to persevere in being — even though, more strictly speaking, God cannot strive to persevere in being because he necessarily exists eternally. Nevertheless, there can be little question that Spinoza rejects the idea that the perfection of God's modes *explains* God's action of creating them in any way, just as he rejects the idea that the perfection of God's modes explains God's existence. It is the very essence of God both to exist necessarily and to be the infinitely perfect and real being, and hence only one set of divine modes is so much as possible (E 1P16, 1P33, 1AP; Geb II, 60, 73, and 83, respectively); there is no sense to the supposition that God might have *selected* or created another set of modes if they had been more perfect.[21] Thus he elaborates his reasons for affirming that "Nature does nothing on account of an end" in the preface to *Ethics*, part 4:

> That eternal and infinite being we call God, or Nature, acts from the same necessity from which he exists. For we have shown (1P16) that the necessity of nature from which he acts is the same as that from which he exists. The reason, therefore, or cause, why God, or Nature, acts, and the reason why he exists, are one and the same. As he exists for the sake of no end, he also acts for the sake of no end. Rather, as he has no principle or end of existing, so he also has none of acting.

Of course, Spinoza holds that everything is in God (E 1P15; Geb II, 56), and hence he must also hold that whatever teleological selection processes exist must exist "in God." However, these teleological selection processes can be located only in the natures of the various individuals or singular things that constitute modes of God, not as teleological selection processes *of* God himself considered as an infinite whole.[22] For Descartes and Leibniz, we may say, all of nature is ultimately the product of teleology. For Aristotle and Spinoza, in contrast, all teleology is ultimately the product of nature.

### Are There Any Subhuman Teleological Selection Processes?

Aristotle, Descartes, Leibniz, and Spinoza all accept — what is difficult for anyone to deny — the existence of teleological selection through human will and desire. Descartes and Leibniz also accept, wheres Aristotle and Spinoza deny, teleological selection through divine will. We can now consider the question of whether any tele-ological selection processes exist within the subhuman realm.

For Aristotle, the answer to this question is obviously affirmative. His examples of unthoughtful teleology are at the same time examples of subhuman teleology. Not only does he hold that animals and plants develop and act so as to achieve their nat-ural ends or goods, but he also holds that even inanimate objects move in order to attain their natural place in the universe.

For Descartes, in contrast, the answer is evidently negative. While he regards di-vine will and its human counterpart as teleological selection processes, he holds that animals and plants are mere machines, the products ultimately of external divine de-sign. Had he wished to make any allowance for unthoughtful teleological selection at all, he might have theorized that God creates mechanical animal bodies with their own intrinsic unthoughtful teleological selection processes. Instead, however, he writes of the apparent fitness of any animal's action to its situation as resulting simply from "a par-ticular disposition [of its organs] for each particular action" (*Discourse on the Method*, part 5; CSM I, 140), with no suggestion of a view that any kind of striving or teleologi-cal selection — mechanically realized or otherwise — occurs within the animal itself.

Like Aristotle, Leibniz answers the question of subhuman teleology in the affir-mative, holding that loci of teleological selection operate throughout nature. For Leibniz, nature is composed of organic substances, each of which exhibits at least rudimentary teleology through appetition. Only those composites — such as rocks and tables — that are not themselves organisms fail to exhibit teleology of their own, and even those composites are entirely composed of organisms.

Although the *Ethics* does not use the terms "end" and "final cause" in applica-tion to subhuman nature, we have seen that Spinoza is committed by the *conatus* doctrine of E 3P6 to allow a pervasive teleology in nature. Neither E 3P6 nor its demonstration is in any way restricted to human beings; on the contrary, it is in-tended as a general truth about all singular things, one that follows from the nature of individuality, or "thinghood," itself. In Spinoza's view, something is an individual thing only to the extent that it has some nature or essence through whose genuine activity effects can be understood to follow. But that nature, he argues, can only be understood as a system endeavoring to persevere in its being.[23] Hence, all individu-als are active to some extent; and to whatever extent they act, they produce effects whose etiology must be understood through the tendency of those effects to con-tribute to the self-preservation of the individual who acts. As we have observed, the very existence of a singular thing with its actual essence constitutes a teleological se-lection process for Spinoza. Even inorganic objects such as rocks and tables that lack powers of imagination and indirect representation have, through the mechanistic laws of motion and rest, rudimentary ways of persevering and preventing their own dissolution in the face of external forces.

### Should Natural Philosophy Pursue Teleological Explanations?

Thus far, we have considered questions concerning the nature and scope of teleol-ogy itself. Equally important, however, is the question of the methodological role of teleological explanations in natural philosophy.

The prominence of final causes among Aristotle's four kinds of causes leaves no room for doubt that teleological explanation plays an essential role of his conception of the methods of natural philosophy. It is equally obvious, from passages already quoted, that Descartes aims to purge "final causes" from the methodology of natural philosophy and that Leibniz self-consciously seeks to reinstate them.

Yet beneath this sharp rhetorical opposition between Descartes and Leibniz lies a surprising amount of room for agreement. To appreciate the agreement, let us distinguish two main kinds of states of affairs that natural scientists might seek to explain teleologically: (a) specific or localized states of affairs and (b) general laws. Consider first the more specific or localized states of affairs. Descartes's oft-repeated reason for avoiding final causes in natural philosophy is that we "cannot guess God's purposes."[24] His doctrine of the indifference of God's will does indeed provide him with good reason to be skeptical of claims to know the divine purpose behind specific states of affairs. Yet Leibniz, too — who regards God's choices not as indifferent but as directed by independent knowledge of the good — cannot help but be extremely modest in his own claims to be able to provide detailed teleological explanations for specific or localized states of affairs in nature, such as earthquakes or even the development of specific kinds of teeth. Knowledge of such explanations would have to appeal either to knowledge of the appetition of other (usually quite rudimentary) substances or to knowledge of divine purposes. But our direct perception of the appetition of most other substances is highly confused and obscure, in Leibniz's view, and our confidence concerning God's more specific purposes must surely be substantially weakened by the realization that God must compare infinitely many facts about infinitely many mutually perceiving possible substances in infinitely many possible worlds in order to choose the best world to actualize. It is not surprising, therefore, that Leibniz's examples of "the way of final causes" in natural philosophy are *not* explanations of particular events in the natural world, such as earthquakes or the development of specific kinds of teeth. Rather, his prime example of using teleological explanation in natural philosophy is the deduction, by Snell, of the law of refraction from considerations of "ease" and "determinacy" for the passage of rays of light.

Leibniz regards these considerations as relevant — and teleological — because they are related to the unity of principle and reliance on sufficient reason that he regards as characteristic of divine concern for the best, and he suggests that other uses of teleology in natural philosophy will be similarly concerned with explaining general laws rather than more particular facts. But Descartes, too, is willing (*Principles* 2:36–42; CSM II, 240–243) to appeal to aspects of the divine nature — particularly immutability and simplicity — to explain general laws of nature (not the law of refraction, as it happens, but the basic laws of motion). Moreover, these aspects of the divine nature are said to govern God's "creation," "operation," and "works." Since Descartes presumably thought it within God's absolute power to create other laws of motion instead of the actual ones, it is difficult to see why Descartes should not regard his derivation of laws of motion as a discovery *and teleological explanation* of the laws of nature on the basis of knowledge about God's *willing* to exhibit his immutability and simplicity in creating the laws of nature.

Unlike Leibniz, Spinoza never writes of using a "method of final causes" in natural philosophy. Yet he maintains that a striving for self-preservation constitutes the actual essence of each singular thing, and his regular explanation of effects through this striving is, as we have seen, a teleological method. Bennett (1983, 147–149) remarks provocatively that because Spinoza regards the causal order of the attributes of thought and extension as the same, he should be embarrassed to know so much of mechanics but so little of the corresponding psychology. In fact, however, Spinoza does not claim to present very much mechanical physics; indeed, in one of his last letters (*Correspondence*, Epistle 83; Geb IV, 334), he admits that he has been unable to "arrange these matters in proper order." His hypotheses about the specific mechanisms of the human body (in the Physical Excursus immediately following E 2P13) are tentative at best. In contrast, he provides in parts 3 and 4 of the *Ethics* a fairly detailed psychology of human beings as teleological, self-preservation-seeking entities, a causal account that directly suggests a parallel account of human bodies as teleological, self-preservation-seeking entities. What Spinoza primarily lacks is not so much knowledge of psychology in comparison to knowledge of physics but rather the kind of knowledge of the inner workings of the essences of singular things — under either the attribute of thought or the attribute of extension — that would allow him to supplement his schematic (but still "adequate") teleological knowledge of the second kind and his schematic (but still "adequate") mechanistic knowledge of the second kind with the integrated knowledge of the third kind, which would combine both kinds of considerations into a coherent whole. But as the *Ethics* illustrates, for Spinoza — as for Aristotle, in contrast to Descartes and Leibniz — it is specific features of organic and nonorganic behavior, rather than general or mechanistic laws of nature, that are the appropriate objects of teleological explanations in natural philosophy. Spinoza's individual actual essences, understood as systems for producing self-preservatory behavior, replace the substantial forms of the scholastics as the loci of teleological selection.

## Conclusions

On the questions of subhuman teleology and the methodological role of teleological explanations in natural philosophy, Leibniz sides with Aristotle and against Descartes — although in the latter case, the difference between Descartes and Leibniz is perhaps not as substantive as it first appears to be. In two other important respects, however, Leibniz's theory of teleology is not *more* but perhaps even *less* Aristotelian than Descartes's. For whereas both Descartes and Leibniz appear to reject unthoughtful teleology, it is arguable that Leibniz does so more explicitly and definitively than Descartes. Whereas Descartes and Leibniz both accept teleology through divine will, Leibniz does so more enthusiastically and with a much broader scope than does Descartes, providing teleological explanations for divine choices of what to create, as well as for the creative acts of will themselves.

In fact, close examination shows that it is not Leibniz but Spinoza — whose acceptance of teleology I have tried to establish — who holds the position on teleology and teleological explanation nearest to that of Aristotle in each of the four respects surveyed. Unlike Leibniz, Spinoza accepts unthoughtful teleology. Unlike Leibniz, he denies teleology through divine will. Spinoza allows teleological selection even more pervasively within the subhuman realm than does Leibniz, recognizing even inorganic teleological selection. Finally, far more thoroughly than Leibniz, Spinoza makes teleological explanation of particular events and features of nature part of the methodology of natural philosophy.

I have not tried to determine whose account of teleology, among the four considered here, is closest to the truth. It is worth noting, however, that the recognition of biological evolution as a teleological selection process has produced a contemporary philosophical consensus concerning the answers to each of the four questions about teleology that we have considered. That consensus strongly suggests that it is Aristotle and Spinoza, rather than Descartes and Leibniz, who emerge — on these four questions, at least — as the more "modern" philosophers of teleology.[25]

*Notes*

1. I make no attempt to define the concept of "an explanatory way." My purpose is only to set out my conception of which explanations are teleological, not to undertake the more difficult task of analyzing the concept of "explanation." I will assume that the latter is clear enough for present purposes.

2. The phrase that Curley translates "as far as it can by its own power" in E 3P6 is *quantum in se est* — more literally, "as far as it is in itself." Spinoza's definitions of "substance" and "mode" (E 1D3, 1D5), combined with his claim at 1P4D that everything is either a substance or a mode, make it clear that something is "in itself" exactly insofar as it is "conceived through itself." But according to E 1A4, effects must be conceived through their causes. Hence, for Spinoza, something is "in itself" just to the extent that it is both conceptually and causally self-contained, as opposed to being understood through and causally produced or affected by other things. Accordingly, E 3P6 implies that each thing tends to act to persevere in its being just to the extent that it is causally and conceptually self-contained. I discuss Spinoza's conception of the "being in" relation and its bearing on the *conatus* of finite individuals more fully in "Spinoza's *Conatus* Argument" (Garrett, forthcoming).

3. For further discussion of the *conatus* of "inorganic" things, see Hampshire (1951, 121–125); Bennett (1984, 246–251), and Garrett (1994).

4. Spinoza's full description of the prejudice in question is as follows: "Men commonly suppose that all natural things act, as men do, on account of an end; indeed, they maintain as certain that God himself directs all things to some certain end, for they say that God has made all things for man, and man that he might worship God" (Geb II, 78).

5. Extremely helpful correspondence with Bennett concerning an earlier draft of this chapter has impressed on me that it is necessary to address all five considerations directly in order to establish Spinoza's consistent acceptance of teleology.

6. Lines 7–12 of Geb II, 78 make it unmistakable that Spinoza intends to discuss *other* prejudices only in the third section of the appendix, well after Geb II, 80.

7. For Spinoza's conception of perfection as absolute reality and power and his discussion of the good for each thing as that which is useful to it for self-preservation, see E 4PR and 4D1 (Geb II, 205–209).

8. *Ethics* 2P16 and its corollaries read as follows:

P16: The idea of any mode in which the human body is affected by external bodies must involve the nature of the human body and at the same time the nature of the external body.
Cor. 1: From this it follows, first, that the human mind perceives the nature of a great many bodies together with the nature of its own body.

> Cor. 2: It follows, second, that the ideas which we have of external bodies indicate the condition of our own body more than the nature of the external bodies. I have explained this by many examples in the Appendix of Part 1.

I take it that the reference to "many examples in the Appendix" concerns his claim there that people disagree in applying such notions as "*good, evil, order, confusion, warm, cold, beauty, ugliness*" because these terms relate directly to the effects that things produce in us, which differ from person to person, and only indirectly relate to the things themselves. At 2P40S1, Spinoza again refers to this doctrine, noting that "these notions are not formed in all in the same way, but vary from one to another, in accordance with what the body has more often been affected by, and what the mind imagines or recollects more easily."

9. Della Rocca (1996, chapter 3) argues that the distinction between direct and indirect representation does not involve two senses of "representation." This does not, however, affect the present point.

10. I present the argument in "Spinoza's *Conatus* Argument," forthcoming.

11. Bennett (1984, chap. 10) suggests that E 3P6 applies to all "individuals." I have argued (Garrett 1994, where I also try to explain how *conatus* contributes to individuation) that "individuals" include "inorganic," as well as organic, things for Spinoza. Bennett suggests that Spinoza generally restricts "individuals" to organic things, but he allows that these include organs and cells of larger organisms — and most of these do not appear to have their own indirect representations.

12. But see, for example, Jackson and Pettit (1993).

13. Furthermore, while an image resembling some individual $i$ may obviously be produced by a variety of objects other than the individual $i$ itself, it is much more debatable whether an image possessing certain specific properties can — as a matter of natural law — be produced without any causal contribution from an individual possessing those very properties. This is so particularly in the context of a Spinozistic conception of causation, in which effects must in some sense already be contained in their causes. Note, too, that in Spinozistic psychology, if individual $i$ is beneficial to individual $j$, then whatever *shares the same nature as* individual $i$ is also, to that extent, beneficial to $j$ (E 4PP29–31; Geb II, 228–230). This makes it even more plausible to say that, for Spinoza, a desire for object $i$ is also, more narrowly construed, a desire for anything sufficiently $i$-like.

14. The "properties" of a thing, in Spinoza's technical sense, follow from the thing's essence. Properties themselves are not parts of the essence of the thing, however, since they must be conceived through the essence, which is therefore causally prior. For further discussion of the relation between essences and properties, see Garrett (1991 and forthcoming).

15. For further discussion of the nature of motion and rest in Spinoza's philosophy, see Garrett (1994).

16. The *Emendation* distinguishes four kinds of "perception." The first two of these become subcategories of what the *Ethics* calls "knowledge of the first kind." What the *Emendation* classifies as the third kind of perception becomes "knowledge of the second kind" in the *Ethics*, and the fourth kind of perception becomes "knowledge of the third kind."

17. The term "thoughtful teleology" is due to Jonathan Bennett (1990), although this formulation of its meaning is mine rather than his. As noted earlier, the present definition of "teleology" appeals, with intentional vagueness, to the etiological role of "consequences," without specifying whether these must be causal consequences or may be consequences of another kind. Whatever kind of consequences are at issue, however, it seems fair to say that they cannot directly produce their antecedents and that therefore some kind of selection process, in at least a broad sense of "process," must be involved.

18. Indeed, at least in the case of God — who is, in a rather special sense, a thinking substance for Descartes — a thinking substance can even create an extended substance.

19. As noted previously, the *Short Treatise* does refer to the "ends" of bees. The *Ethics* affirms that horses, insects, fish, and birds have their own appetites and lusts (3P57S; Geb II, 187), but does not mention will or ends.

20. See Garrett (1996) for further discussion of this topic.

21. See Garrett (1991).

22. Such processes would be, in Spinoza's terminology, in God only insofar as God constitutes the nature of this or that particular thing. For some examples of this distinction of ways in which things can be in God, see E 2PP20D–25D (Geb II, 108–111), 2P36D (Geb II, 118), and 3P1 (Geb II, 140).

23. See Garrett (forthcoming) for a much fuller account of the argument.

24. This is a perfectly natural remark, of course, for someone seeking to replace the well-scaled and religiously intelligible Ptolemaic cosmology with the apparent religious indecipherability and disproportion of Cartesian Copernicanism in an indefinite space.

25. I have benefited greatly from discussion of previous drafts of this chapter with Jonathan Bennett and Nicholas White. An earlier version of this paper was presented at a conference organized by Kuno Lorenz under the auspices of the University of the Saarland in Saarbrücken, Germany, and I am indebted to those in attendance for their helpful questions and comments.

*Bibliography*

Bennett, Jonathan. 1983. "Teleology and Spinoza's Conatus," in *Midwest Studies in Philosophy, Volume VIII: Contemporary Perspectives on the History of Philosophy*, 143–160. Minneapolis: University of Minnesota Press.

——. 1984. *A Study of Spinoza's* Ethics, Indianapolis: Hackett Publishing

——. 1990. "Spinoza and Teleology: A Reply to Curley," in *Spinoza: Issues and Directions*, 53–57. Leiden: E. J. Brill.

Curley, Edwin. 1990. "On Bennett's Spinoza: The Issue of Teleology," in *Spinoza: Issues and Directions*, 39–52. Leiden: E. J. Brill.

Della Rocca, Michael. 1996. "Spinoza's Metaphysical Psychology," in *The Cambridge Companion to Spinoza*, edited by Don Garrett, especially 252–257. Cambridge: Cambridge University Press.

Garrett, Don. Forthcoming. "Spinoza's *Conatus* Argument," in *The Philosophy of Spinoza*, edited by John I. Biro and Olli Koistinen. New York: Oxford University Press.

——. 1996. "Spinoza's Ethical Theory," in *The Cambridge Companion to Spinoza*, edited by Don Garrett, especially 252–257. Cambridge: Cambridge University Press.

——. 1994. "Spinoza's Theory of Metaphysical Individuation," in *Individuation in Early Modern Philosophy*, edited by Kenneth F. Barber and Jorge J. E. Gracia, 73–101. Albany: State University of New York Press.

——. 1991. "Spinoza's Necessitarianism," in *God and Nature: Spinoza's Metaphysics*, edited by Yirmiyahu Yovel, 191–218. Leiden: E. J. Brill.

Jackson, F., and J. Pettit. 1993. "Some Content Is Narrow," in *Mental Causation*, edited by J. Heil and A. Mele, Cambridge, Mass.: MIT Press.

Parkinson, G. H. R. 1981. "Spinoza's Conception of the Rational Act," *Studia Leibniziana Supplementa* 20: 1–19.

Rice, Lee C. 1985. "Spinoza, Bennett, and Teleology," *The Southern Journal of Philosophy* 23.2: 241–251.

Spinoza, Benedict de. *The Collected Works of Spinoza, Volume I*, edited and translated by Edwin Curley, Princeton: Princeton University Press. 1985

## 16

MARGARET D. WILSON

# "For They Do Not Agree in Nature with Us"

*Spinoza on the Lower Animals*

I

Spinoza is often praised for maintaining an anti-Cartesian conception of "the mind" that conforms, at least in some respects, to certain mainstream, present-day philosophical positions. The human mind, for Spinoza, is not an absolute, simple entity radically distinct from the natural order (as Descartes held) — an autonomous substance lodged within the bodily machine and capable of intervening in the material world through free acts of will with causal impact on the body. On the one hand, Spinoza maintains that all physical phenomena whatsoever, including (one must suppose) what we think of as "intelligent behavior," are susceptible of explanation within the realm of physical causes exclusively. Mental "determination" of anything material is, according to his system, inconceivable. (And, likewise — and perhaps less attractively from a present-day perspective — he holds that material explanation of mental occurrences is ruled out.)[1] On the other hand, the mental aspect of finite things is, like the material, a "part of nature": minds themselves belong to "nature's order." Minds, like the bodies of which they are the "ideas," are compounds of subunits; and the changes of the ideas that compose minds are subject to deterministic explanation in some way parallel to an explanation of material change according to the laws of matter-in-motion. This notion of the mental seems to allow for a domain of psychological explanation that, while no less rigorous than the material, can proceed according to a distinct form of conceptualization — without implying that minds somehow function independently of their material substrata.

Spinoza himself draws from his position the conclusion that one mind is "superior" to another, just insofar as its body has certain superior capacities. In one or two passages he suggests that relatively superior minds possess a higher degree of consciousness than others. But he seems by implication further committed to the modern view that even within the most superior minds, many of the components are unconscious. For he holds that the human mind includes ideas of "whatever happens in" the human body (and *surely* wouldn't hold that even the most superior human mind is *conscious* of everything that happens in its body).[2] Besides, his theory of the affects or passions is bound up with the contention that many of our attractions and aversions are dictated by past encounters, which leave their mark without our having noticed.

Apart from Spinoza's conception of the human mind specifically, his related views about the minds of nonhuman animals may seem to represent a major improvement over Descartes. According to Descartes's rather notorious position, humans alone operate (in part) through the activities of an immaterial, intelligent mental substance, which contains no states of which we are not "in some manner conscious."[3] Other animals are purely material, mechanical entities, lacking any form of conscious "thought."[4] But both "common sense" (from Descartes's time to our own) and Darwinian ethological theories tend to reject the notion that there is a radical ontological chasm between humans and nonhuman animals, inferable from their respective behaviors. Spinoza's unequivocal assertion (in E IIIP57S) that "brutes feel," together with *certain aspects* of his conception of the pervasiveness of mentality in nature, can well seem a useful corrective to the stringent Cartesian position.

I have small inclination to defend Descartes's claims about the strictly "mechanical" nature of beasts. But I do wish to question some prominent accounts of Spinoza's views about animals that generally seek to portray his position in a favorable light. Apologetic commentators tend to play down Spinoza's truly ruthless conception of our "rights" with regard to other animals, *in the face of* his acknowledgement that they "feel." And on this issue, the problem is not *only* his ruthlessness but also (what seem to me) insufficiently acknowledged theoretical unclarities in his reasoning. However, even before one considers the ethical issues, one needs to try to understand Spinoza's *systematic grounds* for opposing Descartes on the mental status of animals. I think that some interpreters have been too quick to interpret Spinoza as presenting a clear, coherent, and commonsensical position on the topic of animal minds in the *Ethics*.

I begin the next section with an example of recent philosophical treatment of animal mentality, which — although not directly concerned with Spinoza — provides a sympathetic contemporary background for evaluating his position. I go on to cite several commentators' favorable accounts of his views on the mentality of brutes. In section III, I will argue that the theoretical basis for Spinoza's assertion that "brutes feel" is not as straightforward as some have supposed. And I will raise a question — relying on considerations I presented in an earlier paper — of whether Spinoza is entitled, given tenets laid down in part II of the *Ethics*, to distinguish human from bestial nature on the basis of the possession of "reason" (as he may seem implicitly to try to do in part IV). In the last main section, I critically assess Spinoza's defense of the view that we are entitled to treat the beasts in any way convenient to us, despite the fact that they "feel."

## II

In a recent book pervaded by anti-Cartesian themes (to take one prominent example), Daniel Dennett argues that much can be inferred by empirical considerations — anatomical, behavioral, and evolutionary-ecological — about the "phenomenology" of languageless animals: about what sorts of things they are conscious of or "what it is like" to be them.[5] Dennett maintains that we can be sure that such creatures lack "many of the advanced mental activities that shape our minds," that their minds differ greatly in "structure" from ours. "Does this mean," Dennett asks, "that languageless animals 'are not conscious at all' (as Descartes insisted)?" Dennett thinks that this question rests on an outdated assumption:

> It presupposes something [he says] that we have worked hard to escape: the assumption that consciousness is a special all-or-nothing property that sunders the universe into two vastly different categories: the things that have it (the things that it is like something to be . . . ) and the things that lack it. Even in our own case, we cannot draw the line separating our conscious mental states from our unconscious mental states. The theory of consciousness we have sketched allows for many variations of functional architecture, and while the presence of language marks a particularly dramatic increase in imaginative range, versatility, and self-control . . . these powers do not have the *further* power of turning on some special inner light that would otherwise be off. (p. 447)

Spinoza's conception of mentality, in opposition to Descartes's, seems to lend itself readily to an understanding of the "difference between men and brutes" along the lines proposed by Dennett. This suggestion receives support from accounts of his position offered by several of his most prominent interpreters. Edwin Curley, for instance, approaches Spinoza's position on the brutes by first sketching Spinoza's view of the physical world as consisting of increasingly complex individuals (beginning with the simplest particles and progressing through compounds, including the human body whose individuality depends on their maintaining a constant proportion of motion and rest, up to "the whole of nature"). Curley continues:

> One moral of this picture seems to be that man's distinctive mental capacities are a reflection of the great complexity of the body that is associated with them (E2P14). But the intellectual difference between man and the 'lower' animals appears to be a function of the differences in the complexities of their respective bodies, not of man's possessing an immortal soul radically different from any soul 'beasts' might be thought to have.[6]

Genevieve Lloyd, noting that Spinoza explicitly attributes feelings and affects to beasts, comments:

> Spinoza thinks, contrary to Descartes, that animals are sentient beings. This follows from his account of minds as ideas of bodies. Any idea of a body with a requisite de-

gree of complexity will be for him a sentient mind. But being of a different nature from ourselves — being, that is, ideas of bodies of a different structure — their emotions are different from ours.[7]

R. J. Delahunty asserts, wrongly, that Spinoza differs from Descartes in attributing "life" to beasts. (As Descartes points out to such contemporary critics as Henry More, he by no means denies that beasts are alive; rather, he understands "life" itself as a condition to be understood in mechanistic terms.[8]) But Delahunty further observes, more accurately, that Spinoza disagrees with Descartes in holding that animals "feel and sense, that they are to some degree rational or 'sagacious'": "In many respects, their sagacity even exceeds ours (*E* III, 2S); nor can we doubt that they have sensation — even insects, birds and fish experience lust and appetite, and live contentedly, taking pleasure in their own natures (*ibid.*)."[9] Spinoza's views on the beasts, Delahunty adds, "are in many respects an improvement over Descartes': in particular, it is encouraging to see him returning to the animals many of the features of which Descartes had stripped them" (p. 210).

Curley, Lloyd, and Delahunty all note (with varying degrees of apparent regret) that Spinoza's conception of the "mindedness" of brutes does not lead him to the conclusion that we owe them special consideration in our treatment of them. On the contrary, Spinoza maintains that we are fully entitled to use the beasts — and indeed all nonhuman parts of nature — according to our pleasure and convenience. Thus, Spinoza's view of man as "part of nature," and of nonhuman animals as possessing various mental capacities at least analogous to those of humans, does not lead Spinoza himself to espouse an ecological ethics, a position that would (in Curley's words) "recognize that non-human nature has either rights which must not be violated, or at least some intrinsic value, some value which does not derive merely from its being instrumental to human needs."[10] The efforts of some writers (especially Arne Naess), to construe Spinozism as a sort of protoecologism, collapse before Spinoza's own interpretation of the implications of his metaphysical position on our dealings with nonhuman nature.[11] Similarly, Spinoza's relatively positive views on the mentality of beasts are detached from recent efforts to derive moral restraints on our treatment of nonhuman animals from claims about their mental capacities.[12]

I will return to Spinoza's position on our unrestrained "rights" with regard to the treatment of nonhuman animals later on. Although his conclusion is certainly unequivocal, the reasoning he offers in support of it is not very clear (or so I'll suggest). But first I want to consider more closely the status of animal minds in Spinoza's system. The main questions I'll take up in this connection are the following. First, what is the theoretical basis for Spinoza's assertion that "brutes feel"? Is Lloyd right in thinking that this claim reflects a conception of the "complexity" of brute bodies?[13] (I will suggest that her interpretation, attractive as it may seem, lacks direct textual basis and in fact seems to be undermined by textual considerations.) Second, how, specifically, does Spinoza see the human mind as differing from that of brutes? In the possession of "reason"? *Does* the *Ethics* present a coherent position on the question of whether human minds alone are "rational"? I will claim that it does not; while also arguing that Delahunty's apparently supportive reading of Spinoza on the rationality of beasts rests on a misconstrual of the cited text.

## III

Is it true that Spinoza stakes out a view about the "sentience" of animal minds, grounded in the "sufficient complexity" of animal bodies, of which their minds are ideas? I don't think so. Of course it *is* an important part of Spinoza's conception of the mind-body relation that one mind is superior to another mind, just insofar as its body is superior to that of the other. For, after asserting that "all [individuals] are animate, though in different degrees" (E IIP13S), Spinoza adds:

> However, we also cannot deny that ideas ["minds"] differ among themselves, as the objects themselves do, and that one is more excellent than the other, and contains more reality, just as the object of one is more excellent than the object of the other and contains more reality. And so [he continues], to determine what is the difference between the human Mind and the others, and how it surpasses them, it is necessary for us . . . to know the nature of its object, i.e., of the human Body.

He goes on to indicate that a body which is more able than others to act and be acted on in many ways at once, and to act in a way more dependent on itself alone, will be a body with a superior mind.

But these observations about relative "excellence" and "reality" evidently do not amount to, or directly entail, an assertion that "sentience" is correlative with "requisite degree of complexity" in a given "idea's" body. And, in fact, Spinoza's praised conclusion that "brutes feel" involves no mention at all of bodily "complexity." In one of his two direct statements on this subject in the *Ethics* (in connection with an observation about the "difference in nature" between the "affects" of humans and brutes), he merely observes, parenthetically, that "after we know the origin of Mind, we cannot in any way doubt that brutes feel" (*bruta enim sentire nequaquam dubitare possumus, postquam Mentis novimus originem*) (IIIP57S). I take this aside to refer to the general account of "mind" offered in part II — of which the title is "Of the Nature, and Origin, of Mind." But, according to the early propositions of part II (leading up to IIP13), *all* modes of extension have corresponding "minds," or "ideas," which express the nature of God, conceived under the attribute of Thought. For (by the argument of part I, especially IP16), everything conceivable follows from God's essence; and, by IIP3, "In God there is necessarily an idea, both of his essence and of everything that necessarily follows from his essence." The specific issue of "origin of Mind" is most directly addressed in IIP5:

> The formal being of ideas recognizes God as cause only in so far as he is considered as a thinking thing . . . that is, ideas, both of God's attributes and of singular things recognize as their efficient cause not the objects themselves [*ideata*], nor the things perceived . . . but God himself, in so far as he is a thinking thing.

One notion that the early reasoning of part II certainly conflicts with is that minds have their "origins" — assuming that this term is to be understood in a causal sense — in *any* physical state or circumstance, including, obviously, the "complexity" of a body. But, as we've seen, Spinoza cites his account of the "origin" of mind in sole support of his assertion that "brutes feel." Thus, I think that his position on the "feeling" of beasts must be construed as *independent of* his further remarks on what explains the "superiority" of one mind over another. And if Spinoza's claim that beasts are sentient is indeed grounded in his *general* account of the origin of minds, it utterly fails to distinguish beasts from presumably less "complex" entities — even rocks or tennis balls, let alone plants — with regard to the presence of "feeling." It is not, in other words, something about *beasts* that is said to show that they feel — nothing about their specific types of behavior or physiological structure. If this interpretation is right, Spinoza's position has no genuine relation to the kind of considerations that make issues of animal cognition so intriguing today. Rather, his account of "the origin of mind" seems to have the implication that *every* individual "feels"; he merely draws the conclusion specifically with regard to beasts.[14]

One passage in the *Ethics* that does definitely link degree of consciousness — and hence, perhaps, "feeling" — to the capacities of a mind's body occurs much later, in the scholium to VP39:

> He who, like an infant or child, has a Body that is capable of very few things, and very greatly dependent on external causes, has a Mind which, considered solely in itself, is conscious of almost nothing of itself, of God, or of things; and on the other hand, he who has a Body capable of very many things, has a Mind which considered solely in itself, is very much conscious of itself, of God, and of things.

In an earlier work I observed that this tying of levels of consciousness to bodily autonomy (and, by implication, to the possession of adequate, or clear and distinct, ideas) is not easy to reconcile with Spinoza's statement, in proposition 9 of part III, that the mind *is conscious of* the "endeavor to persist in being" that constitutes its "nature," *both* "in so far as it has clear and distinct ideas, and in so far as it has confused ideas."[15] But even apart from that issue of textual consistency, it does *not* appear that VP39 tells us that sentience is *restricted* to ideas of bodies, or minds, possessing a "requisite degree of complexity."

It may seem comfortably commonsensical to attribute to Spinoza the view that beasts must be regarded as sentient just because they have appropriately complex bodies (whatever exactly that may be taken to mean).[16] But I see no clear basis in the *Ethics* for ascribing that position to him; and Lloyd does not offer directly supporting textual citation. Again, the wording leading up to the claim that brutes feel seems to hark back to the account of the "origin of mind" in part II, which is bound up with Spinoza's *general* attribution of "minds" to natural things.

Still, we *are* left with the result that "brutes feel," even if it is presented against a panpsychist background unlikely to be favored by Dennett or other philosophers who try to take account of the recent ethological and animal behavioral literature in arriving at theories about the minds of beasts.[17] The view that beasts do feel has, unsurprisingly, been favored throughout Western history, despite such striking exceptions as Descartes and some of his followers. A more consistently contentious issue is whether beasts differ from humans in lacking the faculty of "reason." This question, of course, can mean different things to different people. Again, unsurprisingly, many who are prepared to attribute reason to beasts do not claim that there is *no difference between* brute reason and human reason.[18] Leibniz, whose position on the subject was more than usually precise, attributes to brutes a "shadow of reason" but not the genuine thing. That is, he holds (especially in the *New Essays*) that brutes can make a sort of inference on the basis of past experience of repeated sequences of events; even humans, he thinks, rely on such purely empirical "inference" three-quarters of the time. But, he says, brutes have no access to necessary truths, as we humans do.[19]

As far as I can see, Spinoza presents no *explicit* position on the question of whether "brutes reason," under any natural interpretation of it.[20] Delahunty, as I mentioned, cites the scholium of E IIIP2 in support of his claim that Spinoza opposed Descartes in recognizing the "reason" of brutes. But, in fact, Spinoza's remark about brutes in this scholium is quite in line with Descartes's position. The proposition (IIIP2) itself asserts: "The body cannot determine the mind to think, nor can the mind determine the body to motion or rest, or to anything else (if there is anything else)".

The issue of the "sagacity" of brutes comes up in support of *the causal efficacy of the merely material*. Spinoza writes:

> Nobody has as yet determined what the body can do; that is, nobody as yet has learned from experience what the body can and cannot do, without being determined by mind, solely from the laws of its nature in so far as it is considered as corporeal. For nobody as yet knows the structure of the body so accurately as to explain all its functions, not to mention that in the animal world we find much that far surpasses human sagacity, and that sleepwalkers do many things in their sleep that they would not dare when awake; — clear evidence that the body, solely from the laws of its own nature, can do many things at which its mind is amazed.

The message here is, clearly, that animal "sagacity" can be explained wholly by material principles. Descartes, quite similarly, remarks in the *Discourse* that beasts "show more skill than we do in some of their actions" (AT VI, 58–59; CSM I, 141). He goes on to claim that such superior skills, restricted as they are to very limited types of behavior, show that brutes act from material "dispositions of their organs," rather than mind or intelligence. For (he says) if their superior skills derived from mind or intelligence (*esprit*), "they would have more intelligence than any of us and would excel us in everything." In later writings Descartes continues to maintain that he can explain, for instance, "the astuteness and cunning of dogs and foxes . . . as originating from the structure of their bodily parts" (AT V, 276; CSMK III, 365). The major differences between Spinoza and Descartes on this issue have to do not with "animal sagacity" but (to a considerable degree) with issues of explanation. Spinoza, that is, differs fundamentally from Descartes in apparently holding, first, that all *human* physical behavior whatsoever is susceptible of thoroughly materialist explanation; and, second, that the issue of "mindedness" is a separate one, having to do not with the explanations of behavior considered physically but with the status of Thought as an attribute, through which everything in nature can be conceived. (Additionally he denies "free will" to all minds without exception.)

Certain propositions of part IV (especially E P35–P37) seem to be trying to suggest a close connection between reason and *human* nature; and since Spinoza goes on at the end of scholium 1 to P37 (to be discussed below) to allude to differences between human nature and the nature of brutes, one might conclude that he does mean to hold that brute minds differ essentially from human minds in lacking reason. But the passages are (I think) pretty murky and do not unequivocally support this reading. And perhaps Spinoza has a particular systematic reason for being vague, relating (again) to the panpsychist implications of part II.

Above I cited Spinoza's claim that *all* "individuals" are animated as the basis for his conclusion that "brutes feel." But Spinoza seems to be committed (in part II) to much stronger panpsychic tenets as well. In particular, it seems that even nonhuman minds must, within the logic of his system, include *adequate* ideas, that is, ideas of "reason," in a special honorific sense.[21] For according to E IIP45, "Every idea of any body or singular thing existing in act necessarily involves the eternal and infinite essence of God," and according to IIP46, "The knowledge of the eternal and infinite essence of God which each idea involves is adequate and perfect." So, Spinoza's ensuing claim in IIP47 that "the human mind has adequate knowledge of the eternal and infinite essence of God" must be understood to apply to minds generally. (The proposition underlying this phase of his argument is IIP38: "What is common to all can only adequately be conceived."[22]) Similarly, every consideration that supports the intriguing corollary of IIP11 — "The human mind is part of the infinite intellect of God" — equally supports the conclusion that *every* body has a "mind" that is "part of the infinite intellect of God" and is therefore, presumably (in some sense), *intelligent*. (And indeed, this corollary falls within the scope of what IIP13 *explicitly decrees* to be "completely general."[23])

Further, Spinoza's very definition of "idea," combined with the notion that every body has its corresponding idea ("mind"), seems in another sense to commit him to acknowledging that "reason" is not restricted to humans (among finite modes).[24] For an idea is just a "conception of Mind, which Mind forms because it is a thinking thing" (*propterea quod res est cogitans*) (IID3). And, he explains, the term "conception" is meant to connote activity; as he later maintains, ideas are not images, or "dumb pictures on a tablet," but affirmations or denials — in other words, *judgments* (IIP49S). So, it seems, animal minds (actually, minds of *all* bodies) not only "feel," in the sense of passively receiving sensations, but also judge (affirm and deny).[25]

In what, then, do "man's distinctive mental capacities" consist, according to Spinoza? Well, first, the lines already quoted from E VP39S show that the question, so phrased (following Curley), is somewhat misleading insofar as it suggests that all human minds possess the *same* distinctive mental capacities, in an all-or-nothing way. Not only does Spinoza represent "the human mind" as *improving* from infancy to normal adulthood; he also particularly stresses that it is vitally important for adult men to strive to increase their understanding of things ("under a species of eternity"), thereby continuing to increase the "perfection" or "excellence" of their minds. In this way, and this way only, a human being can enlarge the portion of his (or her?) mind, which is itself "eternal."[26]

I mentioned earlier that Leibniz distinguishes the "shadow of reason" — an empirical association that he thinks wholly governs brutes' inferences — from the access to necessary truths that he takes to distinguish human grasp of natural processes (in about one-quarter of our thinking). In Spinoza's *Ethics* there is no sign of such a sharply conceptualized distinction between human and brute mental capacities, "reason," or "knowledge." But, still, Spinoza's implicit comparisons of minds with regard to adequacy of knowledge perhaps foreshadows Leibniz's. In the scholium to IIP29 Spinoza writes:

> I say that . . . the Mind has, not an adequate, but only a confused [and mutilated] knowledge, of itself, of its own Body, and of external bodies, so long as it perceives things from the common order of nature, i.e., so long as it is determined externally, from fortuitous encounters with things, to regard this or that, and not so long as it is determined internally, from the fact that it regards a number of things at once, to understand their agreements, differences, and oppositions. For so often as it is disposed internally, in this or another way, then it regards things clearly and distinctly.

External determination from fortuitous encounters with things seems to be something very much like the kind of "inference" based on past experience of the conjunction of events that Leibniz attributes to brutes. Internal determination — based on understanding agreements, differences, and oppositions, and (I suppose) their necessary consequences — involves a grasp of necessary truths. Spinoza's system (I've suggested) implies a less sharp distinction between brute and human cognitive capacities than we find in Leibniz's late work. Still, Spinoza seems to advance a notion similar to Leibniz's, that minds differ according to how many of their "thoughts" are based on insights into necessities, as opposed to mere "confused" association. That is, even if the minds of brutes, like those of all singular things, cannot *wholly* be denied some perceptions that are "adequate," *their* conceptions are much more extensively "inadequate" or "confused" than ours.[27] I stress, though, that this is a very speculative interpretation. I do not deny that it is very unclear exactly what Spinoza *meant* to say about the cognitive capabilities of brutes (or, for that matter, other nonhuman minds) and unclear also that he had considered views on the subject to anything like the extent that Descartes and Leibniz, among other early modern figures, did.

My suggestion, at any rate, is that Spinoza does not draw an absolutely sharp line between humans and nonhumans with regard to various attributions of cognitive capacities (even *apart from* bare "sentience"). But within the human race, and across nature, there are very great differences in the degree of adequacy of the minds' conceptions, which are directly related to the differences in the capability of their bodies.[28]

I now turn to my final topic: Spinoza's conclusion concerning our "rights" with regard to the brutes, in relation to their sentience, nature, and "affects."

## IV

Aside from a couple of definite indications that "brutes feel," Spinoza's most direct assertions in the *Ethics* about the mentality of the beasts are focused on their "affects." In one particularly evocative passage he writes:

> The affects of animals which are called irrational . . . differ from men's affects as much as their nature differs from human nature. Both horse and man are driven by a Lust to procreate, but the one is driven by an equine Lust, the other by a human Lust. So also the Lusts and Appetites of Insects, fish, and birds must vary. Therefore, though each individual lives content with its nature, which constitutes it, and rejoices in it, nevertheless that life with which each is content and that joy are noth-

ing but the idea or soul of the individual, and so the joy of the one differs in nature from the joy of the other as much as the essence of the one differs from the essence of the other.[29]

This passage occurs in the scholium to proposition 57 of part III: "Each affect of each individual differs from the affect of another as much as the essence of the one from the essence of the other." Spinoza's theory of the affects in fact ties them to the conatus, or the endeavor to persist in being, that he takes to constitute the essence of any individual. Thus, strictly, the affects, such as the "joy," of *any* two individuals must "differ." No doubt Spinoza supposes it to be clear that the essences — and hence the affects — of two humans are in some significant way much more *alike* than the essence of any human and the essence of any horse. But beyond that he does write, in more realist-sounding terms, of "human nature" in contrast to the "natures" of brutes.[30] In the first scholium to proposition 37 of part IV, he seems to draw a severe conclusion in part from this contrast:

> The law against killing brutes is based more on empty superstition and womanish compassion than sound reason. The rational principle of seeking our own advantage teaches us the necessity of joining with men, but not with brutes, or things, whose nature is different from human nature; but the same right that they have against us, we have against them. Indeed, because the right of each one is defined by its virtue, *or* power, men have a far greater right against the brutes than they have against men. Nevertheless I do not deny that the brutes feel (*bruta sentire*); but I deny, that we are therefore not permitted to consider our own advantage, use them at our pleasure, and treat them as is most convenient for us. For they do not agree in nature with us, and their affects are different in nature from human affects (see IIIP57S).

It is rather difficult to work out what exactly the pattern of reasoning is supposed to be in this associative and allusive passage.[31] Clearly, the "principle of seeking our own advantage" plays the *dominant* role in Spinoza's drive to the conclusion that we are permitted to treat brutes as we please. But there seem to be two other notions somehow involved in the argument (if such it is) in a kind of intermediate way. First, the principle requires us to join with other men but not with brutes. Second (and more perplexingly, I think), the fact that their *affects* are different in nature from ours — as argued in IIIP57S — has some important bearing on the lack of moral constraint on our behavior toward them.

But how, exactly, is the "difference in nature" between men and brutes supposed to contribute to the argument that brutes fall wholly outside of the constraints of human moral consideration? And why is the difference in "affects" so important specifically? I would like to pursue these questions a bit further, beginning with the introduction of one later passage from part IV: a passage that draws the same conclusion as the scholium to IVP37 just quoted but which adduces some more straightforward claims about the potential of human-animal association. In the appendix to part IV, section xvi, Spinoza asserts:

> Apart from men we know no singular thing in nature whose Mind we can enjoy, and which we can join to ourselves in friendship, or some kind of association. And so whatever there is in nature apart from men, the principle of seeking our own

advantage does not demand that we preserve it. Instead, it teaches us to preserve or destroy it according to its use, or to adapt it to our use in any way whatever.[32]

The basic idea, I take it, is that the "principle of seeking our own advantage" "demands" that we "preserve" just those things whose minds we can enjoy and to which we can join in friendship or "some kind of association." Otherwise, it "demands" that we preserve or destroy any given thing according to our convenience. Now, the claim that beasts never satisfy the exempting conditions specified here is bound to be roundly disputed. (And of course there seems to be a spread of *different* conditions offered. For instance, I believe that I have surely joined myself in "some kind of association" with several beasts, though I would not strictly count any of them among my "friends"; and I am unsure how to answer the question of whether I enjoy their minds — though I lean to saying yes.) But, even extending a lot of charity to Spinoza on these points, one can still press on with this question: how exactly does "difference in nature" between human and brutes help to underpin the conclusion that we need observe no moral constraints on our treatment of them?

What I am getting at is this. It really does not seem surprising that an ethics grounded on the principle of seeking our own advantage would fail to yield moral constraints on the treatment of beasts, or of nonhuman nature generally. (Perhaps it would be *unenlightened* to limit constraints on destruction or harmful treatment to *short-term* advantage, where conditions of friendship and the like do not apply. And Spinoza's statements, while of course not opposing this observation, may be considered not sufficiently to address it. Furthermore, Spinoza does not address the issue of *sharp conflicts* among human advantages: the bird-watcher's versus the land developer's, for example. But these are separate matters.) People who think that certain kinds of behavior toward nonhuman animals are clearly morally unacceptable (and I am one) are entitled to consider the conclusion Spinoza draws with regard to our treatment of the brutes at least a prima facie reductio of his general ethical position, insofar as it is based on the principle of seeking our own advantage. (We should just not be *surprised* that it turns out to have this particular consequence.) But I am not really concerned here with ethical criticism. I am, rather, interested in the question of how far Spinoza's position on our "rights" with regard to beasts connects with what we can discern of his views about the relation of brute and human minds, *beyond* the bare appeal to "seeking our own advantage."

The passage from the appendix just quoted suggests that one consideration Spinoza wants to convey is this: the difference in nature between the minds of humans and nonhumans *disqualifies the former from bonds of friendship (and the like) with humans;* so the brutes fail to be exempt from human exploitation according to the principle of seeking our own advantage. (The fact that they "feel" is beside the point.) But what, exactly, do claims about "difference in nature" turn on? And how, exactly, do they help undershore, or give added depth to, the conclusion that our unlimited "rights" over animals derive from the principle of seeking our own advantage?

Over the centuries, as Richard Sorabji, in *Animal Minds and Human Morals*, has shown in detail, many philosophers who concede sentience to brutes still maintain that we are justified in exploiting them *ad libitum*, on the grounds that we are "rational" and they are not. (It seems that sometimes the alleged impossibility of "friendship" or the like with a nonrational being is implicated in the argument; and sometimes not.[33]) I've suggested that Spinoza's position on "the mind" does not permit an entirely sharp line to be drawn between humans and brutes with regard to "rationality." But, in anyone's interpretation, he does emphasize that there are *at least* large differences in understanding, or possession of adequate ideas, both among humans and across species. And in fact there is considerable emphasis, in E IVP37 and preceding propositions, on common adherence to "the guidance of reason" as the grounding of positive human relationships. So it seems quite likely that in his mind *part* of the relevant "difference in nature" that deprives the brutes of any "right" to restraint on our part is connected with the deficiency (if not complete lack) of "reason" in them because of its implications for "friendship" or other relevant "association."[34]

What seems most striking about Spinoza's position, however, is his explicit appeal, at the end of the passage from E IVP37S1, to his remarkable observations in IIIP57 concerning the *affects* of brutes, together with his stress on "friendship, or other association" in the appendix to part IV. We are, he says in IVP37S1, entitled to use brutes at our pleasure, *"for they do not agree in nature with us, and their affects are different in nature from human affects (see IIIP57S)"* (emphasis added). And in the appendix passage, he also seems to signal an inference to a moral conclusion from a claim about enjoyment of minds and the possibility of "joining in friendship, etc: *And so* whatever there is in nature apart from man. . . ." My question is whether these allusive references to the difference of affects and the possibility of "friendships and other associations" between men and beasts contribute in any clear and credible way to Spinoza's position about our unlimited "rights" with regard to the treatment of nonhuman animals. Here is one way of explaining why I think they do not.

It seems to me entirely plausible that an "essential" difference in affects between two beings, as well as differences in "rationality," should have bearing on the question of what kind of "associations" the two can form. Thus, insofar as our unlimited "rights" with regard to nonhumans depends on a supposed impossibility of "friendships" or other relevant associations between them and us, it makes sense that any essential difference of affects should be considered relevant to the case. But in a way this concession makes it even more mysterious why issues of "friendship" (etc.) should be regarded as so crucial with regard to our "rights" over beasts.[35]

Why *should not* my belief (after Spinoza) that a squirrel in my yard or an osprey over the water — or for that matter a centipede in the bathtub — experiences joy in the life that it has inhibit me from eliminating that life, even *if* I think that its joy is "different in nature" from mine and that, accordingly, I cannot be "friends" with it? Why shouldn't my perception of the affection that my dog or cat has toward me rationally enlist a sense of responsibility toward the creature, even *though* I acknowledge that "its essence is different from mine" and *agree* that therefore its affection toward me is different in nature from mine toward it? (Why, that is, apart from the naked principle of seeking my own advantage, as distinct from the more abstract issue of difference in nature, and specifically of affects, across species?)

The very evocativeness of Spinoza's own account of "the affects of animals which are called irrational" seems to undercut rhetorically his dismissal of their claim to any kind of moral consideration from us. And it reinforces the sense of a peculiar *argumentative* gap in Spinoza's inference from the lack of certain kinds of "association" between man and beasts — even supposing he is right about that — to the absence of moral constraints on our treatment of them.[36]

## V

In conclusion, among the aspects of Spinoza's view of "mind" likely to seem attractive within the context of present-day philosophy is his anti-Cartesian conception of the mentality of brutes. I have argued, however, that his explicit attribution of sentience, and affects, to brutes is grounded in his general panpsychism, rather than any particularities of their bodies and behavior. In this important respect his position can hardly be seen as an antecedent of contemporary interest in animal cognition, bound up as that interest tends to be with evolutionary, ethological, and behavioral approaches. In passing, I have tried to assess what implications Spinoza's position might have with regard to the traditionally more controversial issue of the intelligence and rationality of beasts. Despite seemingly contrary implications of E IVP35–37, it appears to me that he is committed to attributing some degree of understanding and reason to "other" minds, again on grounds deriving from his general panpsychism. Spinoza, in any case, explicitly opposes the view, often advanced today, that the mental capacities of nonhuman animals dictate moral restraints on our treatment of them. I have tried to sort out, to a degree, the reasoning he offers on behalf of this negative claim. Largely it derives, no doubt coherently, from the "principle of seeking our own advantage," which is fundamental to his general ethical position. But it is involved as well with notions about the limits of human association, which can be disputed to some extent. Additionally, Spinoza seems to aim at a distinct metaphysical grounding in the "difference in nature" between humans and beasts, particularly with regard to the affects. I have suggested that this line of thinking is unclear and probably lacking in force.[37]

## Notes

1. See, especially, E IIP6 and IIIP2.

2. E IIP12. Below I cite and discuss Spinoza's specific statements about the "superiority" of minds and consciousness.

3. See, for instance, AT VII, 160 ("First Replies").

4. Descartes's main assertion of this position — backed up in several of his *Replies to Objections* — occurs in part V of the *Discourse on the Method*.

5. *Consciousness Explained* (Boston: Little, Brown, 1991), chap. 14, sect. 2.

6. "Man and Nature in Spinoza," in Jon Wetlesen, ed., *Spinoza's Philosophy of Man* (Oslo: Universitetsforlaget, 1978), p. 22.

7. "Spinoza's Environmental Ethics," *Inquiry* 23 (1980): 295. For related discussion, see her book *Part of Nature: Self-knowledge in Spinoza's "Ethics"* (Ithaca, N.Y.: Cornell University Press, 1994), pp. 155–158.

8. This is not to deny that Spinoza's "conatus" theory provides the basis for a conception

of a living being different from Descartes's. Still, Delahunty's bland repetition of More's error, persisting through his discussion of the beast-man issue, amounts to a serious flaw. *Spinoza* (London: Routledge & Kegan Paul, 1985), chap. 6, sect. 6.

9. Ibid., p. 208. The second internal reference should actually be to E IIIP57S.

10. "Man and Nature," pp. 22–23.

11. Naess does not ignore Spinoza's comments on our rights over beasts and other non-human individuals, but he tends to play them down. Among his several papers on the subject is "Spinoza and Attitudes Towards Nature," in Nathan Rotenstreich and Normal Schneider, eds., *Spinoza — His Thought and Work* (Jerusalem: Israel Academy of Sciences and Humanities, 1983).

12. See, for instance, Tom Regan, *The Case for Animal Rights* (Berkeley: University of California Press, 1983), p. 243; and Richard Sorabji, *Animal Minds and Human Morals* (Ithaca, N.Y.: Cornell University Press, 1993), p. 212. Sorabji also provides detailed information about a wide range of older — especially ancient and medieval — views about the moral implications of beasts' mentality.

13. In the comments mentioned in my final note, Curley seemed to endorse this view, too.

14. Curley observes, in a footnote to E IIP13S (in his translation of the *Ethics*), that Spinoza's statement that all individuals are animate, though in different degrees, is "open to very different interpretations." Many would deny that Spinoza is committed to "feeling" throughout nature. While I make no apology for my own interpretation on this point, I want to stress that the *main* question at issue in the preceding paragraph is simply how to understand Spinoza's brief remark in support of the claim that brutes feel.

15. "Objects, Ideas and 'Minds': Comments on Spinoza's Theory of Mind," in Richard Kennington, ed., *The Philosophy of Baruch Spinoza* (Washington, D.C.: Catholic University of America Press, 1980).

16. Perhaps a natural interpretation is that Spinoza has in mind *brain* complexity (as Rocco Gennaro has suggested in comments on an earlier draft of this chapter). Maybe so; but, again, it needs to be explained what exactly "complexity" is supposed to mean if this suggestion is to help much in illuminating a distinction between the sentient and the nonsentient — even supposing that Spinoza *does* intend to accommodate such a distinction in the face of his panpsychism. (I touch on a related point in note 28.) Incidentally, one needs to be careful about reading twentieth-century notions about the "complexity" of, say, mammalian or specifically human brains into seventeenth-century work — as I believe the briefest look at Descartes's account of the human brain in the *Treatise on Man* will show.

17. Even if I am right about Spinoza's grounds for this attribution, it is still the case that Spinoza offers a *reasoned* position against Descartes, unlike a surprising number of other philosophers of the period who opposed him. (See my "Animal Ideas," *Proceedings and Addresses of the American Philosophical Association* 69, no. 2 (November 1995).

18. See Sorabji, *Animal Minds and Human Morals*, and Wilson, "Animal Ideas."

19. Leibniz addresses the issue, for example, in the preface to the *New Essays on Human Understanding* and elsewhere in that work. (I provide fuller citations in "Animal Ideas.") See also Rocco Gennaro, chapter 17 in this volume. The issue of the "rationality" of brutes has surfaced again in recent times in, especially, Donald Davidson, "Rational Animals," in Ernest LePore and Brian P. McLaughlin, eds., *Actions and Events* (Oxford: Blackwell, 1985). Davidson, like certain ancient thinkers, as well as Descartes, maintains that the legitimate attribution of rationality to beings is tied up with the beings' possession of linguistic capabilities. Spinoza, however, does not directly relate rationality to linguistic competence.

20. In comments on an earlier version of this chapter (see final note), Edwin Curley observed that "unfortunately [for my argument] Spinoza does deny that brutes possess reason."

The texts he cited are from TTP (Geb. III, 8; III, 124) and concern the opinion that the end of the state is not to change men "from rational beings into beasts" (or "automata"). The remarks relate to the role of the state in ensuring human freedom. I would hesitate to put much weight on them in interpreting the logic of the *Ethics* with regard to the assumption of "adequate ideas" throughout nature or more subtle questions about the cognitive capacities of brutes. (See also note 27.)

21. Cf. E IIP40S2#3.

22. Here again (I think) I disagree with Lloyd, who seems to suppose that a mind's capacity to form the common notions of reason requires its being the idea of a body "of a sufficiently complex structure" (*Part of Nature*, p. 159). Compare her comment on the previous page: "Reason is an expression of human nature, and it arises from the complexity of bodily structure that distinguishes human bodies." Here, as in the case of her remarks on sentience, I think she is too free with the term "complexity" and not sufficiently precise about textual support.

23. It is, of course, possible to argue that some of the implications of the *Ethics*, particularly with regard to the issue of "panpsychism," are unintended; that they should be dismissed as mere spinoffs of an overly optimistic pretension to argumentative rigor. I concede that Spinoza, unlike most other major figures of the period, makes no specific assertions about whether beasts lack or possess "reason" or "understanding." Still, it seems to me that on this particular issue the implication that I take his system to yield—that beasts have some degree of understanding—is neither more implausible, prima facie, than its denial nor uniformly opposed by his contemporaries.

24. See, again, E IIP40S2#3.

25. This conclusion can also easily be reached from Spinoza's remarks on the affects of beasts, which I discuss below.

26. It seems to be widely agreed that Spinoza is quite derogatory in what he states and implies about the mentality of women. Ruth Barcan Marcus and Anne Jaap Jacobson have both suggested to me that it is worthwhile to consider the relations between major philosophers' views about nonmale humans and their views about nonhuman animals. I think they are probably right, but here I am only concerned with seeing what can be established about Spinoza's position on the difference between man and beast. So, for one thing, I deal more casually with certain translation issues than I would have if questions of the mental significance of gender differences had been central to my concern.

27. It would follow that a tiny, but only a tiny, portion of brutes' minds is "eternal." (As much or more as in the case of human babies? Who can tell?) I doubt that this is what Curley had in mind in remarking that, for Spinoza, humans are not distinguished from brutes by having an immortal soul; but it is not necessarily an awkward consequence for a reading to yield. The issue of the "immortality" of beasts', as opposed to human, souls was a live one in seventeenth-century philosophy. Leibniz, for instance, seems rather proud of being able to affirm—against the Cartesians—the "natural indestructibility" of the souls of brutes, as well as humans (though only the latter are granted admission into the Kingdom of Grace). Although Spinoza's concept of "eternity of mind" is different from the generality of seventeenth-century conceptions of immortality, I think there are enough affinities for this comment to be relevant.

28. It might be objected that Spinoza's correlation of the superiority of a mind to its body's "capacity to do and suffer many things" does not straightforwardly yield the result that even a brilliant human mind, let alone an average one, is "superior" to the minds of all beasts. Consider a paralyzed theoretical physicist, who while unable to feed or clothe himself or walk or even speak, can still function mentally at a high level. Is it right to attribute to such a person a "body capable of very much," a *more capable body* than, say, that of a physically unimpaired

eagle, wolf, or whale? I think that Spinoza's sympathetic commentators tend to assume that when he writes of more capable bodies, he has in mind primarily the physical substratum of theoretical understanding, as opposed to (say) ability to move the limbs. I have no real problem with this particular sympathetic reading; but there does seem to be something rather perverse about his phrasing if that is what he intends.

29. Note the "*are called* irrational" in connection with note 20.

30. I here set aside the issue, touched on by Lloyd in *Part of Nature*, of how to reconcile such realist-sounding talk about "natures" with the nominalist vein in Spinoza's thought, as expressed (especially) in the first scholium of E IIP40.

31. After citing this passage, Mary Midgeley observes "Many people today would, I think, simply echo this, including all the evident confusions. What principles are involved here?" *Beast and Man: the Roots of Human Nature* (Ithaca, N.Y.: Cornell University Press, 1978), p. 352. Midgeley goes on to suggest that Spinoza is trying to acknowledge the importance of emotions in love, despite holding that the moral restraints we owe to other humans are based on our common possession of reason. Or at least, that's how I understand her. She observes that Spinoza's ethical position has very attractive features, while deploring the results of his "egoism."

32. According to the next paragraph (xvii): "The principal advantage which we derive from things outside us — apart from the experience and knowledge we acquire from observing them and changing them from one form into another — lies in the preservation of our body."

33. As Descartes observes to More, his denial of thought to beasts is not so much cruel to them as indulgent to humans since it absolves us from the suspicion of crime when we kill and eat them (AT V, 278–279; CSMK, 366).

34. Curley, Lloyd, and Delahunty all place emphasis, in connection with the issue of "association," on the fact that beasts are unable to enter *political* associations with men — which may be tied to the lack of "reason." (They also cite remarks from TTP.) I don't deny that this is a relevant aspect of the issue, but to me it seems clearly not to fully accommodate the main passages on beasts in the *Ethics*, especially the comments about "difference of affects" and "friendship." Sorabji, incidentally, sketches a variety of historical views about the possibilities of natural association, "belonging," or community between humans and brutes (*Animal Minds and Human Morals*, especially chap. 10).

35. See also Midgeley, *Beast and Man*, pp. 351–335.

36. In *A Study of Spinoza's Ethics* (Indianapolis: Hackett, 1984), Jonathan Bennett offers a detailed and rather scathing critique of Spinoza's effort to move from the principle of seeking one's own advantage to "conservative," "collaborative" moral principles governing *interhuman* conduct through an appeal to "likeness" among humans (sect. 69). In a way my discussion here is (as far as I can see) complementary to his, in that I question Spinoza's movement from nonlikeness between man and beast to a dismissal of moral constraints on human treatment of the animals.

37. Edwin Curley provided detailed comments on an earlier version of this chapter — with which he indicated total disagreement — at an American Philosophical Association (Pacific Division) symposium in 1995 on Spinoza and contemporary philosophy of mind, arranged and chaired by Don Garrett. Although in general I have not been converted to Curley's views on Spinoza on animals, his comments have led to fairly substantial revisions in presentation; and I cordially thank him. Other improvements have been made in response to comments by Jonathan Bennett, Michael Della Rocca, Rocco Gennaro, and Charles Huenemann, for which I'm also very grateful. I'm only too well aware of not having been able to reflect all of their perceptive criticisms and suggestions adequately in the revised version.

This chapter was also presented at colloquia at Union College and Carleton College in the spring of 1997. On both occasions the discussions were imaginative and stimulating. The lack of a written record of them has resulted, unfortunately, in my losing track of some of the points that impressed me at the time; but I thank the contributors for reinforcing my interest in the subject and apologize for probably neglecting changes they proved I should make.

## 17

ROCCO J. GENNARO

# Leibniz on Consciousness and Self-consciousness

In this chapter I discuss the so-called higher-order thought theory of consciousness (the HOT theory) with special attention to how Leibnizian theses can help support it and how it can shed light on Leibniz's theory of perception, apperception, and consciousness. It will become clear how treating Leibniz as a HOT theorist can solve some of the problems he faced and some of the puzzles posed by commentators, for example, animal mentality and the role of reason and memory in self-consciousness. I do not hold Leibniz's metaphysic of immaterial simple substances (i.e., monads), but even a contemporary materialist can learn a great deal from him.

## What Is the HOT Theory?

In the absence of any plausible reductionist account of consciousness in nonmentalistic terms, the HOT theory says that the best explanation for what makes a mental state conscious is that it is accompanied by a thought (or awareness) that one is in that state.[1] The sense of "conscious state" I have in mind is the same as Nagel's; that is, there is "something it is like to be in that state" from a subjective or first-person point of view.[2] Now, when the conscious mental state is a first-order world-directed state, the HOT is not itself conscious; otherwise, circularity and an infinite regress would follow. Moreover, when the higher-order thought is itself conscious, there is a yet higher-order (or third-order) thought directed at the second-order state.

In this case, we have *introspection*, which involves a conscious HOT directed at an inner state. When one introspects, one's attention is directed "back into" one's mind.

For example, what makes my desire to finish this chapter a conscious first-order desire is that there is a (nonconscious) HOT directed at the desire. In such a case, my conscious focus is directed at the chapter. If I am introspecting my desire, however, then I have a *conscious* HOT directed at the desire itself.[3]

It is also helpful to distinguish between *momentary focused introspection*, which involves only a brief conscious HOT, and *deliberate introspection*, which involves the use of reason and a more sustained inner-directed conscious thinking over time. Sometimes we consciously think to ourselves in a deliberate manner, for example, in doing philosophy or in planning a vacation. We are also often engaged in deliberate activities (in the sense of "voluntary" or "purposeful") directed at the external world, for example, when our conscious attention is absorbed in building a model airplane. Although not all deliberate activity involves introspection, clearly some does involve sustained conscious thinking directed at one's inner states. But there is also a more modest type of introspection. One might consciously think about a mental state without deliberating in any way, for example, momentarily think about a memory or briefly consciously focus on a pain or emotion. In these cases, one is not engaged in deliberation or reasoning. Some animals seem capable of this kind of introspection even if they cannot deliberate. Like deliberate introspection, such "momentary focused introspection," as I will call it, involves having conscious HOTs.

I suggest that self-consciousness is simply having meta-psychological or higher-order thoughts, even when the HOT is not itself conscious. I have therefore argued at length[4] that consciousness entails self-consciousness, but more important here is that there are degrees or levels of self-consciousness, with introspection as its more complex form. All introspection involves self-conscious states, although not necessarily vice versa. Thinking about one's own mental states is definitive of self-consciousness, but nothing requires that the HOT itself be conscious. Just as one might have nonconscious thoughts directed at the world, one might have them directed at one's own mental states.

Some might still wonder why self-*consciousness* need not be *consciousness of* something. I offer two[5] reasons here: (1) few, if any, philosophers hold that self-consciousness is literally "consciousness of a self," especially since Hume's observation that we are not aware of an unchanging or underlying self but only a succession of mental states. Thus the "ordinary meaning" of "self-consciousness" is up for grabs since the term does not wear its meaning on its sleeve. It seems that we are somewhat free to stipulate a meaning (though not entirely arbitrarily, of course).

(2) Other philosophers have put forth even weaker criteria for what counts as "self-consciousness." For example, Van Gulick urges that it is simply the possession of meta-psychological information.[6] While I believe that his notion is too weak, my point here is that my definition is not the weakest in the literature. Owen Flanagan[7] also recognizes a "weaker" kind of self-consciousness: "All subjective experience is self-conscious in the weak sense that there is something it is like for the subject to have that experience. This involves a sense that the experience is the subject's experience, that it happens to her, occurs in her stream" (p. 194).

## Leibniz and the HOT Theory

### *Unconscious Mentality and* Petites Perceptions

Unlike Descartes, Leibniz held there to be degrees of awareness or perception. Moreover, Leibniz did not believe (as Descartes and Locke apparently did) that consciousness is essential to mentality or, at least, to each episode of thought or perception. There are *petites perceptions*, or nonconscious perceptions. Indeed, Leibniz held that all monads, the ultimate constituents of reality, perceive in the sense that they "represent" external things. We might say that all monads always have some "perceptual" or informational states with representational content, but they need not be conscious. Leibniz therefore recognized that there must be an answer to this question: what makes a perception a conscious perception? Indeed, we should ask more generally, what makes a mental state a conscious mental state? (Of course, if "perception" is used as a generic term to cover all mental states, then the questions are equivalent.) This is the fundamental question that should be answered by any theory of consciousness. The HOT theory says that what makes a mental state conscious is the presence of a suitable[8] higher-order thought directed at it. I believe that Leibniz also held this view.[9]

In connection with the idea that there are *petites perceptions*, Leibniz often speaks of perceptions that are not apperceived and says that the Cartesians made the great mistake of not accounting for them (PNG 4; AG p. 208).[10] Consider the statement that "since on being awakened from a stupor, we apperceive our perceptions, it must be the case that we had some perceptions immediately before, even though we did not apperceive them" (Mon. 23; AG p. 216). The implication is that the perception is there nonconsciously and *the apperception of it makes it conscious*. This sounds like the HOT theory: a higher-order "apperception" of the lower-order perception makes it conscious; otherwise, it would remain a nonconscious mental state. Of course, nonconscious mental states can still play a role in the production of behavior: "It would not be adding much . . . if I said that it is these minute perceptions which determine our behavior in many situations without our thinking of them . . ." (RB pp. 55–56). But, again, it is the "thinking of them" that makes them conscious.

### *The Infinite Regress Objection*

As I mentioned earlier, the HOT theorist must avoid definitional circularity and an infinte regress by explaining that the HOT need not itself be conscious when one has a first-order conscious state. Otherwise, we would be answering our basic question by appealing to consciousness, which is circular. Moreover, we would have an infinite regress because for every conscious state there would have to be a higher-order conscious state and so on ad infinitum.[11] Leibniz cleverly noticed this problem and so made room for nonconscious second-order awareness:

> It is impossible that we should always reflect explicitly on all our thoughts; [otherwise] the mind would reflect on each reflection *ad infinitum*, without ever being

able to move on to a new thought. For example, in being aware of some present feeling, I should have always to think that I think about that feeling, and further to think that I think of thinking about it, and so on *ad infinitum*. It must be that I stop reflecting on all these reflections, and that eventually some thought is allowed to occur without being thought about; otherwise I would dwell for ever on the same thing. (RB p. 118)

Presumably, the first part of this ("It is impossible that we *reflect explicitly* upon all of our thoughts") should be taken to mean that what makes our mental states conscious cannot always be higher-order *conscious* thoughts, and so instead must sometimes be higher-order nonconscious thoughts or, we might say, unconscious apperceptions. Otherwise there would be an infinite regress, and we would never "be able to move on to a new thought." However, it can be the case that we always reflect *implicitly* (i.e., nonconsciously) on our thoughts or perceptions. As Rescher[12] puts it, "The iterative piling-up of reflective awareness of reflective awareness must stop somewhere, and the conception of unconscious apperception provides a convenient means of termination" (p. 127).

I suggest that this is of a piece with the HOT theory, particularly with the idea of nonconscious second-order thoughts that are rendering lower-order states conscious. It seems reasonable to suppose that Leibniz was saying that "what makes a perception a conscious perception is the presence of a higher-order perception directed at it. However, the higher-order perception need not itself be conscious; otherwise, an infinite regress would follow." We might then use the notion of "unconscious apperception" as our lowest form of self-consciousness, that is, nonconscious meta-psychological thoughts. If we think of all apperception as higher-order inner-directed perception, then it is natural to distinguish between conscious and nonconscious apperception in the same way that Leibniz distinguishes between conscious and nonconscious first-order perception. It is therefore also reasonable to understand apperception as coming in degrees in the way that I described self-consciousness above.

### Memory

Leibniz sometimes says that what makes a mental state or perception conscious is that the subject remembers it. He speaks of "sensation" as "perception accompanied by *memory*" (PNG 4; AG p. 208) and says that "a present or immediate memory, the memory of what was taking place immediately before — or in other words, the consciousness or reflection which accompanies inner activity — cannot naturally deceive us" (RB p. 238). Notice that the mental state is already present for a short time and then it is remembered shortly thereafter. The HOT theorist can similarly say that the HOT occurs shortly after the lower-order state. This echoes Leibniz's claim in the *Monadology*, which is worth quoting again: "Since on being awakened from a stupor, we apperceive our perceptions, it must be the case that we had some perceptions immediately before, even though we did not apperceive them" (Mon. 23; AG p. 216).

But, most important, Leibniz is saying that what makes the perception conscious is a memory of it, which clearly entails that there is a higher-order state directed at the perception. If a perception occurs without the accompanying memory or higher-order state, then it will be one of our many nonconscious perceptions. On the other hand, the second-order state is a memory or "record" of a first-order state that has occurred immediately prior to it. Thus, "the immediate memory of a perception" sounds very much like "the apperception of a perception" and thus a kind of self-consciousness that makes the lower-order perception conscious.[13]

But we must be careful not to fall into the trap of the infinite regress by requiring that the memory is itself conscious. Leibniz should not be taken to hold the untenable view that the accompanying memory of every conscious perception is always itself conscious. There are, of course, various kinds of memory, some more sophisticated than others. For example, there is the rather robust "episodic" memory, which involves consciously thinking about oneself experiencing something in the past. But this kind of memory cannot be the "memory-states" Leibniz has in mind here. In this context, Leibniz seems to be using "memory" as a very unsophisticated kind of nonconscious "registering" or "tracking."[14]

### Some Support from Commentators

Mark Kulstad did not have the HOT theory in mind, although he does say the following:

> A perception which becomes . . . distinct enough to arouse a second-level mental activity, becomes thereby a sensation, or, if you like, apperceived. Whether this activity is called memory, apperception, consciousness, or reflection, is perhaps not so important, for in the end all refer to the mind's second-level or reflective awareness of its own perceptions. (p. 39)

This is clearly in the spirit of the HOT theory, although it is important not to put "consciousness" into his list because otherwise we face the infinite regress problem. As we have seen, however, the terms "apperception" and "memory" can have a nonconscious sense. The terminological problems understandably often lead Kulstad to use the more neutral term "awareness," which clearly has both a conscious and nonconscious sense. Kulstad also agrees with Rescher and says that "apperception always involves an inner directed perception: Leibniz . . . holds that consciousness is a two-tiered affair, with the thought of which we are conscious being itself perceived" (KUL 146). Again, the HOT theorist should be very sympathetic with this position.[15]

Rescher explains:

> Apperception . . . is not consciousness as such . . . but self-consciousness or self-perception generally, involving the capacity for reflexive self-revealing perception of the workings of one's own mind. The procedure of some commentators in equating apperception with *conscious perception* in general is not faithful to Leibniz' own equation: apperception = *inner-directed perception*. Leibniz' distinction between perception and apperception is in strict parallel to Locke's distinction between sensation and reflection, with consciousness present on both sides of the boundary. (pp. 119–120)

The first part of this seems right, but I do not know what to make of the Lockean analogy. Rescher cannot mean to equate Locke's sensation with Leibniz's perception per se since, according to Locke, sensation is always conscious, whereas, as Rescher knows, Leibniz makes room for unconscious perceptions. Rescher makes it sound as if "unconscious perception" is a contradiction for Leibniz, which it clearly is not.

In any case, "consciousness as such" presumably means first-order world-directed conscious states. Such states are not themselves apperceptions because they are directed at the outer world. However, first-order conscious states do entail apperceptions that render them conscious. Apperception is necessary for conscious perception, but we should not equate them.

## The Linguistic Issue

The French verb for "to perceive" was in Leibniz's time and still is *apercevoir*, and the verb for "to be aware of" was and is *'s'apercevoir de'*. The noun for the former is "perception," but there was no corresponding noun for the latter, and so Leibniz coined the technical term "apperception." Since Leibniz had the noun for (first-order) perception, it would have been unnecessary for him to create another term for it (cf. KUL pp. 21–23). This suggests that apperception is designed to cover *higher-order* perception, and just as first-order perceptions can be both unconscious and conscious, it is again reasonable to suppose that Leibniz allowed for both unconscious and conscious apperceptions

In their translation of the *New Essays*, Remnant and Bennett (RB) do not use "apperception" but instead translate Leibniz's invented term as "awareness." "To apperceive" is "to be aware of." But if apperception is only higher-order perception, then their use of "aware" can be misleading since one can also be aware of external objects. Indeed, in their note on "aware" (p. xxvii), they recognize that there are places where certain contrasts are lost. In any case, given that apperception is always higher-order, we must again note that "aware" is ambiguous between "nonconscious higher-order awareness" and "conscious higher-order awareness."

The French word *reflexion* is typically translated as "reflection" and is ambiguous between various forms of self-consciousness. The subtle distinctions we have made were perhaps not distinguished properly in the dictionary or in the minds of Leibniz's time. There is a sense in which *reflexion* means something closest to introspection and probably even the more sophisticated "deliberate introspection." Indeed, there is a cross reference to deliberation and meditation. One standard French dictionary translates *reflexion* as *Retour de la pensée sur elle-même en vue d'examiner plus à fond une idée, une situation, un problème.*[16] This can be translated as the "return of thought onto itself in order to examine more deeply an idea, a situation, or a problem." The latter part suggests deliberate introspection. Moreover, Leibniz usually uses *reflexion* when discussing reason and our ability to discover in us necessary truths and innate ideas. Thus, it is wisest to identify Leibniz's *reflexion* with our deliberate introspection and with a very sophisticated form of apperception.[17]

## The Taxonomy

So we have two kinds of perception for Leibniz: nonconscious and conscious. If I am right thus far, a nonconscious perception is a world-directed state that is not apperceived, that is, not accompanied by a HOT. On the other hand, a conscious perception *is* apperceived and so is accompanied by a HOT. Thus we have:

World-directed perceptions: (a) nonconscious and (b) conscious.

Moreover, Leibniz uses "apperception" in the way that I have described "self-consciousness" or "self-perception" generally. It comes in degrees or levels of "self-awareness" and, for the reasons given in the third section, reflection (which involves the use of reason) is best understood as the "deliberate introspection" discussed in the first section. Recalling the other two levels of self-consciousness, we can thus label our three forms of self-consciousness as follows:

Nonconscious meta-psychological thoughts = apperception$_1$
Momentary focused introspection = apperception$_2$
Deliberate introspection = apperception$_3$ = reflection

Understanding Leibniz's view about the relation among consciousness, apperception, and reflection will help us to become clearer about many of the philosophical problems he addressed.

Kulstad does distinguish between *two* kinds of reflection: simple (or mere) and focused. The former is any reflection "which does not involve a focusing of the mind's attention on what may properly be said to be in us" (KUL 24). If we read this as "mere reflection is the kind of apperception in which the mind's attention is not consciously focused on a mental state," then we would have apperception$_1$. In such a case, one's conscious attention is focused on external objects, which is precisely what the HOT theory demands. Kulstad rightly allows for this when he says that mere reflection involves attention, but "attention [is] directed towards other objects, most typically external objects" (p. 24). This is perhaps not the best fit it could be, but it seems close enough for our purposes.

However, Kulstad's "focused reflection" is often ambiguous between apperception$_2$ and apperception$_3$ since his primary description is simply "when one's attention is directed at something in oneself." Presumably, then, Kulstad's focused reflection is meant to capture the notion of *conscious* HOTs, but, as I urged earlier, having conscious HOTs can involve two kinds of ability: momentary focused introspection or the more sophisticated deliberation or reasoning ability. When discussing Leibniz's theory of innate ideas and necessary truths, Kulstad is rightly concerned with apperception$_3$. But it is unclear whether his "focused reflection" is meant to be identified with apperception$_3$. If not, then we have an ambiguity between apperception$_2$ and apperception$_3$. If so, then he does not properly account for apperception$_2$.

## Two Troublesome Passages

Some commentators (e.g., McRae)[18] have tried to support the idea that "apperception" and even "reflection" is just "consciousness" for Leibniz. As the reader will gather from the above discussion, I believe that this is far off the mark. But even those who are more sympathetic to my position must acknowledge that some passages pose problems for the interpretation of apperception as higher-order mentality. Consider the following:

> So it is well to make a distinction between perception, which is the inner state of the monad representing external things, and *apperception*, which is consciousness or the reflective knowledge of this inner state itself and which is not given to all souls or to any soul all the time. (PNG 4; L p. 637)

It seems that some commentators see "apperception, which is consciousness" and stop there in an effort to equate apperception and consciousness. But this ignores what follows, where the "or" can plausibly be read as "that is" or "in other words" so that apperception is really being identified with "reflective knowledge." My understanding is that the French gives us little help here since the word *ou* can have many meanings. But even if I am wrong, my opponents should at most have Leibniz making the disjunctive claim that apperception can either be consciousness or some kind of self-consciousness (i.e., "reflective knowledge of this inner state").

On the other hand, Rescher is so biased in my direction that he inserts "[self-]" before "consciousness" in his translation (RES p. 119). However, this move is not justified in the original French text. We should still acknowledge the ambiguity in the notion of *reflective* knowledge of the inner state. We must admit that Leibniz is simply not very clear here about whether he meant apperception$_1$, apperception$_2$, or apperception$_3$, but we need not interpret him as identifying consciousness in general with apperception.

Consider also the well-known passage from the *Monadology*: "The passing state which enfolds and represents a multitude in unity or in the simple substance is merely what is called perception. This must be distinguished from apperception or from consciousness, as what follows will make clear" (Mon. 14; L p. 644). This is probably the most problematic passage for our interpretation, but perhaps we can view the last "or" as meaning something more like "and." This rings true because of the intended contrast: perception must be distinguished from apperception and (even) from consciousness. Perception must be contrasted with both apperception and consciousness because there can be a "multitude" of perceptions that never reach the level of consciousness. So Leibniz wanted to distinguish bare perception from both (first-order) consciousness and (higher-order) apperception, and he did not merely wish to contrast perception with apperception, which just *is* consciousness. Once again, the French is not very helpful because of the ambiguity of the word *ou*. Another possibility is that Leibniz is treating apperception as higher-order states that involve consciousness. This would be to say that apperception entails consciousness (which is true), even though they are not identical. Granted that Leibniz was not very careful here, but I do not believe that this one passage should cause us to change our position.

It is also worth noting that Ariew and Garber are so biased in the other direction that it affected their translation. I quote *Monadology* 14 from Loemker because it remains more faithful to the orignial Leibnizian text ("perception . . . must be distinguished from apperception or from consciousness . . . "), whereas Ariew and Garber insert a comma after "apperception" ("perception . . . should be distinguished from apperception, or consciousness, . . . ") (AG p. 214) This makes it seem more likely that Leibniz was identifying consciousness and apperception. The comma, however, is not Leibniz's, and they should not have forced this interpretation into the text.[19]

## Do Beasts Apperceive?

I have argued at length that most animals are conscious and so are self-conscious (i.e., apperceive) in some sense,[20] but more to the point and despite what some commentators have said, I believe that Leibniz also thought so. If my interpretation of Leibniz as a HOT theorist is correct, then he must have thought that beasts (i.e., non-human animals) apperceive because (a) apperception$_1$ is necessary for conscious perception and sensation, and (b) Leibniz clearly believed that beasts are conscious. Thus, beasts are at least capable of some form of apperception.

We have already seen the evidence for (a) and how it fits in with the HOT theory. A HOT is necessary for one to have a conscious mental state. Thus, although apperception$_1$ is not identical with sensation, this helps to explain the close connection in Leibniz's use of the terms "sensation," "consciousness," and "apperception." Even McRae is forced to admit that "apperception is a necessary condition of sensation" (p. 30), but then, since he believes that *all* apperception is restricted to spirits, he accuses Leibniz of inconsistently holding that sensation is present in animals. I suggest that there is no inconsistency for Leibniz but rather a serious problem for McRae's account. Apperception$_1$ is indeed a necessary condition of all conscious states, and since both humans and animals have sensations, both humans and animals have apperception$_1$.

Moreover, there is a great deal of uncontroversial textual evidence in favor of (b). Leibniz wanted to separate himself from Descartes on animal consciousness,[21] although he did also want to maintain that there is something very special about humans. Beasts are not "simple" or "bare" monads; they are further up in Leibniz's hierarchy. Beasts have *souls*, that is, monads with conscious awareness, including distinct perceptions and memory. Leibniz does not wish to attribute "reason" to beasts, and so they are not what he calls "spirits" or "minds," that is, souls that are capable of reason and knowing necessary truths. But this does not affect his view that "beasts have souls and sensations" (RB p. 72), and he often speaks of "the souls of brutes" (AG p. 78; Letter to Arnauld). And again: "I . . . believe that beasts have some knowledge and that there is something in them . . . which can be called a soul . . . " (L pp. 275–276; Letter to Von Tschirnhaus).

So Leibniz distinguishes among (a) simple monads (monads with only unconscious perceptions), (b) souls (monads with conscious perceptions and memory), and (c) spirits or minds (monads with the capacity to reason). He says: "When these beings have sensation they are called *souls*, and when they are capable of reason they are called *minds*" (AG p. 191; Letter to Queen Sophie Charlotte of Prussia). We also have the following passages:[22]

> Since sensation is something more than a simple perception, I think that the general name of monad and entelechy is sufficient for simple substances which only have perceptions, and that we should only call those substances *souls* where perception is more distinct and accompanied by memory. (Mon. 19; AG p. 215)

> . . . *sensation*, that is, [a] perception accompanied by *memory*. . . . Such a living thing is called an *animal*, as its monad is called a *soul*. And when this soul is raised to the level of *reason*, it is something more sublime, and it is counted among the minds. (PNG 4; AG p. 208)[23]

Furthermore, as Kulstad explains, there are passages where Leibniz more directly attributes apperception to beasts (pp. 19–28). In the *New Essays*, he speaks of a boar "apperceiving impressions" (A 6.6.173; RB p. 173), which certainly sounds like a case of a second-order mental state directed at a first-order state. We also have Leibniz explaining that animals, upon death, are "reduced to a state of confusion which [suspends apperception] but which cannot last forever" (RB p. 55).[24] Kulstad rightly observes that "apperception could not be suspended in beasts if beasts never apperceived in the first place" (KUL p. 20)

Despite my argument and the above passages, some (e.g., McRae) insist on holding what Kulstad calls the "standard view," namely, that beasts do not apperceive. One has to wonder how McRae could possibly say that Leibniz "never once attributes consciousness, apperception, or reflection of any kind to animals" (MCR p. 33) In any case, Kulstad examines five arguments for the conclusion that beasts do not apperceive (KUL pp. 41–52), which is tantamount to the claim that only spirits apperceive. I will critically discuss three of them here since they are particularly relevant to my concerns in this chapter. Given the ammunition now at our disposal, we can disarm them without too much difficulty while raising some other issues.

### The Monadology Argument

(1) Apperception is consciousness (Mon. 14).
(2) Only spirits are conscious.[25]
*Therefore*, (3) Only spirits have apperceptions.

Premise (1) is clearly false as it stands because apperception is not to be understood as involving outer- or world-directed consciousness. Again, it is true that apperception$_1$ is necessary for consciousness, but that is not to say that it is identical with consciousness. Moreover, given the threefold distinction within the degrees of apperception, it is a further mistake to identify apperception *simpliciter* with consciousness (see again the preceding section).

### The Reflection-PNG 4 Argument

We might reconstruct this argument as follows:[26]

(1) Apperception entails reflection (PNG 4).

(2)  Beasts do not have the faculty of reflection.
*Therefore*, (3) Beasts do not apperceive.

We can now see that premise (1) is false since reflection is best understood as apperception₃. Thus, reflection entails apperception, but not vice versa. One can apperceive (i.e., be self-conscious) without having the capacity to reason or reflect in any deliberate way. However, Leibniz clearly believes that premise (2) is true since he repeatedly denies to animals the capacity to reason and reflect (apperception₃). Leibniz links the capacity to reflect with the ability to reason and learn necessary truths through abstraction. For example: "[Beasts] apparently recognize whiteness, and observe it in chalk as in snow; but this does not amount to abstraction, which requires attention to the general apart from the particular, and consequently involves knowledge of universal truths which beasts do not possess" (RB p. 142).

Leibniz admits to Samuel Masson that he has "denied that beasts are capable of reflection" (AG p. 228). But the real key lies in the ability to reason: "The knowledge of eternal and necessary truths is what distinguishes us from simple animals and furnishes us with *reason* and the sciences" (Mon. 29; AG p. 217; cf. L p. 588). In one place, Leibniz gives some credit to the use of language, which "enables man to reason to himself, both because words provide the means for remembering abstract thoughts and because of the usefulness of symbols" (RB p. 275). All of this is perhaps best summarized in the following portion of a letter to Queen Sophie Charlotte of Prussia:

> For since the senses and induction can never teach us truths that are fully universal, nor what is absolutely necessary . . . and since, nonetheless, we know some universal and necessary truths in the sciences, a privilege we have over the beasts, it follows that we have derived these necessary truths, in part, from what is within us. (AG p. 191; cf. L p. 325)

Even if we agree with Leibniz that beasts cannot reason in some sophisticated sense, this question still arises for us: is having apperception₃ the only way for a creature to have a concept of "I" or a "self-concept"? I do not believe so, but sometimes Leibniz seems to think so:

> It is also through the knowledge of necessary truths and through their abstractions that we rise to *reflective acts*, which enable us to think of that which is called "I" and enable us to consider that this or that is in us . . . these reflective acts furnish the principal objects of our reasonings (Mon. 30; AG p. 217)

> True reasoning depends on necessary or eternal truths . . . those who know these necessary truths are . . . properly called *rational animals*, and their souls are called *minds*. These souls are capable of performing reflective acts, and capable of considering what is called "I." (PNG 5; AG p. 209)

Leibniz is closely linking some rather sophisticated reflective capacities to having a concept of "I." But if self-consciousness comes in degrees, then we should allow that beasts can have more primitive self-concepts. Not only are animals capable of apperception₁, but it is also reasonable to attribute apperception₂ (i.e., momentary focused introspection) to beasts for several reasons:[27] (a) Leibniz agrees that beasts are capable of episodic memories of past experiences. But I suggest that if a creature C has an episodic memory of an experience, then that involves C's having a thought about itself, for example, as the previous subject of some experience. If I remember having an experience of something that happened in *my* past, then I am having a thought about myself as an enduring subject of experience. (b) We should also allow that any conscious creature can at least differentiate itself from outer objects. This entails having "I-thoughts" and being able to distinguish oneself from other objects. (c) At the very least, it seems that merely having conscious pains and feelings entails having conscious second-order thoughts. If a dog has a conscious pain or emotion, it surely has the higher-order capacity to (consciously) think about the pain or emotion, if only momentarily.

So perhaps Leibniz did not account properly for apperception$_2$ in suggesting that only minds (and not animal souls) employ self-concepts. We should not suppose that reasoning ability and knowledge of universal truths are *necessary* conditions for self-consciousness, even though they are *sufficient*. Perhaps this is all that Leibniz intended, but if so he should have been more careful and simply left open whether or not (animal) souls are also able to have I-thoughts. What is correct about Leibniz's line of thought is that in order to learn necessary truths we must reflect on our own minds and use reason in the process, which in turn involves using self-concepts. But none of this rules out animals from having more primitve forms of self-consciousness, including apperception$_2$.

### The Rationality Argument

Kulstad also discusses a related argument that explicitly mentions the capacity to reason (KUL pp. 48–51). Let us put it as follows:

(1) Only spirits are capable of reasoning.
(2) Only those souls capable of reasoning are capable of apperceiving.
*Therefore*, (3) Only spirits can apperceive.

As we have seen in our discussion of the reflection-PNG 4 argument, premise (1) is true for Leibniz. However, it should be clear by now that premise (2) is false because many apperceiving or self-conscious creatures cannot reason. That is, animals can have apperception$_1$ and even apperception$_2$ without being capable of apperception$_3$.[28]

Let us explore more fully why Leibniz thought that beasts do not reason. Perhaps the most important quotation is the following:

> Beasts are sheer empirics and are guided entirely by instances. While men are capable of demonstrative knowledge, beasts ... never manage to form necessary propositions. ... That is what makes it so easy for men to ensnare beasts, and so easy for simple empirics to make mistakes. ... The sequences of beasts are only a shadow of reasoning, that is, they are nothing but a connection in the imagination — a passage from one image to another. (RB pp. 50–51)[29]

Thus, for Leibniz, a dog's sequence of mental states is guided purely by particulars and instances. It cannot abstract from instances to grasp general or universal propositions. The dog can connect images in imagination, but this is only a "shadow of reasoning" such that the mind passes from one image to another out of expectation based on memory. Although human minds also often function in this way, Leibniz's point seems to be that animal minds *always* do:

> Memory provides a kind of sequence in souls, which imitates reason, but which must be distinguished from it. We observe that when animals have the perception of something which strikes them, and when they previously had a similar perception of that thing, then, through a representation in their memory, they expect that which was attached to the thing in the preceding perception, and are led to have sensations similar to those they had before. For example, if we show dogs a stick, they remember the pain that it caused them and they flee. (Mon. 26; AG p. 216)

> Beasts pass from one imaging to another by means of a link between them which they have previously experienced. This could be called "inference" or "reasoning" in a very broad sense. But I prefer to keep to accepted usage, reserving these words for men and restricting them to the knowledge of some *reason* for perceptions' being linked together. (RB p. 143; cf. RB p. 271)

Even if Leibniz is right about some animals, I think it is fair to say that he did underestimate the psychological capacities of many "higher" animals. For example, they often seem to be able to "figure out" what to do in an unexpected or novel situation. Leibniz's example of a dog being repeatedly hit with a stick does not address these cases. Moreover, Leibniz was clearly unaware of the degree to which animals can communicate to one another and even to us.[30]

Leibniz also does not give us any reason to rule out that some animals can grasp *general* truths (even if they are not "necessary" or "universal" in some deeper sense). Leibniz's own example could be used as evidence for the claim that the dog has grasped the general truth that "whenever someone hits me with a stick, it is going to hurt" or "whenever someone raises a stick to me, I should flee." Given that Leibniz grants to animals a fair degree of memory, it is hard to see how he rules out that some animals do at least form inductive generalizations from repeated particular instances and so are able to form more general thoughts of this kind. Thus, some animals may indeed be able to "abstract" from particular instances, even if they fall short of demonstrative knowledge. Of course, none of this may count as genuine "reasoning" or "inference" for Leibniz, but I confess that I am not sure what the "accepted usage" was or is.

In any case, I do agree with Leibniz that "expectation based on memory" does not automatically show an ability to reason or infer. I also agree that humans generally have a capacity to reason and reflect that is absent in all animals. It is interesting that when speaking of possible worlds where there are intermediate *species* between us and animals, Leibniz asserts that "nature has seen fit to keep these at a distance from us so that there will be no challenge to our superiority on our own globe" (RB p. 473). But recognizing the important objection that there are defective *individual* humans who are clearly not psychologically superior to every *individual* brute, Leibniz replies that those humans "suffer from [what] is not a lack of the faculty [of reason] but an impediment to its being exercised" (RB p. 473). The idea seems to be that, say, a mentally defective human still has the faculty of reason but simply cannot use it well or at all. Reason is thus treated as an inherent capacity of human minds even if some humans cannot manifest it because of some illness or defect. The implication is that we could ideally cure such mental defectives or correct their conditions (e.g., through medical technology) so that their capacity to reason could be manifested. Animals, on the other hand, cannot be made to have the capacity in the first place.[31] Leibniz may be right about this, but I am not sure that it warrants his rather bold claim that "the stupidest man . . . is incomparably more rational and teachable than the most intellectual of all the beasts" (RB p. 473).

In any case, we see how making a threefold distinction within apperception helps us to reply to the above arguments and shows how we can accept the view that beasts apperceive. We also can see how thinking of Leibniz as a HOT theorist sheds light on his theory of mind.[32]

My interpretation can also help to explain the following potentially troubling passages:

> Beasts have perception, [but] they don't necessarily have thought, that is, have reflection or anything which could be the object of it. (RB p. 134)

> 'Understanding' in my sense is what in Latin is called *intellectus*, and the exercise of this faculty is called 'intellection', which is a distinct perception combined with a faculty of reflection, which the beasts do not have. Any perception which is combined with this faculty is a thought, and I do not allow thought to beasts any more than I do understanding. (RB p. 173)

These passages have led some to question Leibniz's belief in animal consciousness and thought. But we now know how to reply: beasts do have higher-order thoughts that accompany conscious states; that is, they have apperception$_1$ and even apperception$_2$, but they do not have thoughts in the sense of apperception$_3$. Leibniz is not denying that beasts have thoughts; rather, he is denying that they have certain kinds of thoughts, that is, those linked with reflection. In the above passages, Leibniz is clearly linking thought to reflection and understanding.

## Infinite Perceptions and Kant's "Intensive Magnitude"

In this final section, let us return to the Leibnizian emphasis on degrees of perception. This view stems, in part, from Leibniz's commitment to the law of continuity: "Nature never makes leaps . . . any change from small to large, or vice versa, passes through something which is . . . in between" (RB p. 56). The idea is that nothing happens by jumps, and so Leibniz held a staunch gradualism about everything in nature, including minds. He then rightly recognized that this implies an *infinity* of perceptions:

> But since each distinct perception of the soul includes an infinity of confused perceptions which embrace the whole universe, the soul itself knows the things it perceives only so far as it has distinct and heightened perceptions. . . . It is like walking on the seashore and hearing the great noise of the sea: I hear the particular noises of each wave, of which the whole noise is composed, but without distinguishing them. (PNG 13; AG p. 211)

> These perceptions, however much they are multiplied, are different from one an-
> other, even though our attention cannot always distinguish them, and that is what
> makes confused perceptions, each distinct one of which contains an infinity because
> of its relation to everything external. (AG p. 229; Letter to Samuel Masson)

What is Leibniz up to here? First, he is again making room for unconscious mental
states. The idea is that a conscious mind can be conscious of or notice only so many
of its perceptions at any given time. Our minds have an infinity of perceptions of which
we obviously can have higher-order awareness of a relative few (see RB p. 53). Second,
Leibniz is recognizing his metaphysical commitment to an infinity of perceptions
within each mind. This is due to the fact that each monad "mirrors" all others, that is,
contains all of the information about every other monad. Since there are an infinity of
monads, there would need to be an infinity of perceptions. To "reflect" all of the information in the universe, each monad must "contain" an infinity of perceptions.

I wish to focus on how this might be related to Kant's notion of intensive magnitude. It is always dangerous to try to summarize *briefly* anything from Kant's
*Critique of Pure Reason*,[33] but here it goes: Kant was often concerned with the necessary conditions of conscious experience. This led him to argue for the view that
some concepts or "categories" are presupposed in consciousness. Two of the categories are Quantity (including the concepts of unity, plurality, and totality) and
Quality (including reality, negation, and limitation). Kant was then led to derive a
priori principles, which can be known antecedently to any particular experience.
The principle corresponding to the category of Quantity is the Axiom of Intuition
which says that "all intuitions are extensive magnitudes" (B202), whereas the principle derived from the category of Quality is the Anticipation of Perception, which says
that "in all appearances, the real that is an object of sensation has intensive magnitude, that is, a degree" (B207). Bennett puts the contrast as follows:

> We are concerned with extensive magnitude when we ask of an object how large it
> is, or of a process how long it lasted. We are concerned with intensive magnitude
> when we ask how acute a pain is, how loud a noise, or how sour a drink; the crucial
> idea . . . is that of the degree of intensity of some sensation.[34]

Thus, extensive magnitude has to do with parts (temporal or spatial) and is reflected in Kant's claim that "all appearances are . . . intuited as aggregates, as com-
plexes of previously given parts" (A163 = B204). On the other hand, a sensation "occupies only an instant" (A167 = B209), and so an intensive magnitude is concerned
with degrees of intensity and not with extent or parts and wholes. It is no secret that
Kant was very familiar with Leibniz's views, and I suggest that this is one place where
he incorporated a Leibnizian doctrine into his theory of mind. Kant repeatedly
speaks of the continuity of degrees of intensive magnitude; indeed, the word "degree"
is mentioned in the principle itself. He also remarks: "Corresponding to this intensity of sensation, an *intensive magnitude*, that is, a degree of influence on the sense
. . . must be ascribed to all objects of perception, in so far as the perception contains
sensation" (A166 = B208). The key Kantian idea is that we cannot know in advance
what our next sensation will be (for that is an empirical matter), but we can know a
priori that it will come in some degree on a continuum "between reality and negation."

Kant then goes on to adopt his own mental version of the law of continuity. Given any two degrees of sensation there is always an infinite range of degrees between them, and given any degree of sensation there is an infinite range of degrees down to nothing:

> Every sensation . . . is capable of diminution, so that it can decrease and gradually vanish. . . . [t]here is therefore a continuity of many possible intermediate sensations, the difference between any two of which is always smaller than the difference between the given sensation and zero or complete negation. (A168 = B210)

> Every sensation . . . has . . . an intensive magnitude which can always be diminished. Between reality and negation there is a continuity of possible realities and of possible smaller perceptions. Every color, as for instance red, has a degree which, however small it may be, is never the smallest; and so with heat . . . (A169 = B211; cf. A172 = B214)

This echoes Leibniz's belief that there is an actual infinity of perceptions within each mind and that between any two degrees of perception there must be an infinity. Once again, what is interesting is that Leibniz saw how the law of continuity was inseparable from his belief in unconscious perceptions. He speaks of it as supporting "the judgment that noticeable perceptions arise by degrees from ones which are too minute to be noticed. To think otherwise is to be ignorant of the immeasurable fineness of things, which always and everywhere involves an actual infinity" (RB p. 57).

Kant also seems committed to such a view if we are to make sense of his position. Bennett explains that Kant's view would be false "if we take it as saying that between any two degrees of intensity there is an infinite number of *noticeably* distinct intermediate degrees; for even if there is an infinite number of pain-levels between that of yesterday's toothache and that of today's, it would be absurd to claim that we can tell every pair of them apart."[35] Kant, like Leibniz, must allow for unconscious sensations or perceptions, which are, of course, nothing but perceptions of which one is not aware. That is, they are perceptions that minds have but do not notice through any form of self-consciousness. Perhaps Kant's and Leibniz's views are not identical. For example, perhaps Kant is committing himself only to the existence of a *possible* infinite number of perceptions, whereas Leibniz is more clearly committed to the presence of an *actual* infinity of perceptions. However, Kant's use of language is somewhat ambiguous on this point, and it would nonetheless be a contrast between Kant and Leibniz that is worth noting.

This adventure into Kant's theory of intensive magnitudes can perhaps help to explain Leibniz's otherwise often puzzling references (cited above) to perceptions "containing" or "including" an infinity of perceptions. We might interpret Leibniz as claiming that (a) between any two degrees of perception there is an infinity of perceptions, and (b) for any perception or sensation, there is an actual infinite between its degree and its elimination; or, to use Kant's terminology, there is an actual infinite between the "reality" of any sensation and its reduction to "negation."[36]

Perhaps this is an odd way to speak of distinct perceptions "containing" or "including" anything, but if this is not what Leibniz meant, then I have no idea what he did mean. One might understandably object that Leibniz often speaks of *each* distinct perception *at a single moment* containing an infinity of perceptions (cf. RB p.

53 and, again, the passages cited above). Leibniz's manner of speaking may cause trouble for my Kantian interpretation, but again I would then simply confess that I do not understand what he meant. However, it is tempting to adopt McRae's analysis that at least some sensible perceptions (e.g., color) "are not aggregates of insensible perceptions. Rather, they are novel emergents from a mass of insensible perceptions, emergents for an apperceptive mind which is incapable of distinguishing components" (MCR p. 38).

I suppose that more complex visual perceptions could be understood as being composed of an infinity of unconscious perceptions, whereas one's conscious mind can focus on or apperceive only a few at a time. For example, one's visual field could be broken down into an infinite number of regions, but at any moment one can only attend to a small portion of it. Perhaps one could say that my current visual perception of my office "contains" or "includes" an infinity in that sense. In any case, all of this assumes that we can make sense of an actual infinite in the first place, but I will not open that troublesome can of worms here.[37]

## Notes

1. See David Rosenthal, "Two Concepts of Consciousness," *Philosophical Studies* 49 (1986): 329–359. I have also defended the theory at great length in my *Consciousness and Self-consciousness: A Defense of the Higher-order Thought Theory of Consciousness* (Amsterdam: John Benjamins, 1996). I will hereafter refer to this book as CSC.

2. Thomas Nagel, "What Is It Like to Be a Bat?" *Philosophical Review* 83 (1974): 435–450.

3. It should be noted that I am mainly concerned here with an analysis of the locution "x (mental state) is conscious." This ought to be distinguished from "x (an organism) is conscious," as well as the two-place predicate "x is conscious of y." For some discussion of this terminological matter, see CSC 3–5.

4. In CSC.

5. See CSC 17–18 for several additional reasons.

6. Robert Van Gulick, "A Functionalist Plea for Self-consciousness," *Philosophical Review* 97 (1988): 149–181. I argue that Van Gulick's notion of self-consciousness is too weak in CSC 147–151.

7. Owen Flanagan, *Consciousness Reconsidered* (Cambridge, Mass.: MIT Press, 1992).

8. One might reasonably ask: "just what makes a higher-order thought "suitable"?" A full answer to this question would lead to a lengthy digression, which I cannot pursue here. One condition, for example, would be that the HOT must be a "momentary" and "occurrent" state, as opposed to a "dispositional" state of some kind. See CSC (chaps. 3 and 4) for my attempt at answering this question.

9. The terminology here can be a bit confusing. Sometimes thought is contrasted with perception, whereas sometimes the term "thought" is also used as a generic term, covering virtually all kinds of mental states. For our purposes, we can think of the higher-order state as some kind of higher-order awareness. For some discussion of the alleged differences between the "perceptual" and "thought" models, see CSC 95–101. Leibniz was also aware of some of the terminological difficulties (RB 171, 210). See also CSC 36–43 for at least one attempt to address them in the context of the HOT theory.

10. See RB 53–57, 77–78, 113–119, 161–162, 188. I will also abbreviate the frequently cited *Monadology* as Mon. and the *Principles of Nature and Grace* as PNG, followed by the section number.

11. For a particularly inexcusable example of this type of error, see Peter Carruthers, "Brute Experience" *Journal of Philosophy* 86 (1989): 258–269. See my reply to Carruthers in "Brute Experience and the Higher-order Thought Theory of Consciousness," *Philosophical Papers* 22 (1993): 51–69.

12. Nicholas Rescher's well-known book is *Leibniz: An Introduction to His Philosophy* (Totowa, N.J.: Rowman & Littlefield, 1979). Hereafter I will refer to it as RES, and all page references to Rescher will come from this book.

13. See also Mark Kulstad *Leibniz on Apperception, Consciousness, and Reflection* (Munich, Germany: Philosophia, 1991), pp. 33–39, 59–67. Hereafter I will refer to Kulstad's excellent book as KUL, and all page references to him will come from this book.

14. For some discussion of memory and self-consciousness, see CSC (chap. 9) or my "Consciousness, Self-consciousness, and Episodic Memory," *Philosophical Psychology* 5 (1992): 333–347.

15. Given his agreement with Rescher, it is unclear to me what to make of Kulstad's distinction between "apperception of *external* objects" and "apperception of what is in us" (KUL 133–143).

16. Paul Robert, *Dictionnaire* (Paris: Société Du Nouveau Littré, 1973).

17. I thank Stephen Voss for some help and advice on these linguistic matters.

18. See Robert McRae, *Leibniz: Perception, Apperception, and Thought* (Toronto: University of Toronto Press, 1976). I will hereafter refer to this book as MCR, and all page references to McRae will come from it.

19. I thank Jonathan Bennett for some helpful comments, especially on material in the third and fifth sections.

20. See CSC, especially chapters 1–4, 8, and 9.

21. For a critical discussion of Descartes's views, see Margaret Wilson's "Animal Ideas," *Proceedings and Addresses of the American Philosophical Association* 69 (1995): pp. 7–25. For a critical discussion of Spinoza on animal mentality, see chapter 16 in this volume.

22. I thank Jan Cover for some helpful comments on the differences among simple monads, souls, and minds or spirits.

23. See PNG 14; AG 211 and Mon. 82; AG 223.

24. The reason for the square brackets is (recall from the third section) that RB does not use the term "apperception." But see G V, 48, as an alternative source.

25. See KUL 43–44 for a discussion of this premise. I have nothing to add except that it clearly seems false given Leibniz's frequent attribution of consciousness to souls, as well as to spirits.

26. See KUL 18, 26–27, 41–42.

27. I discuss each of these at much greater length in CSC, especially chapters 4, 8, and 9.

28. Mark Kulstad ultimately replies to these arguments in a similar fashion (see, e.g., KUL 171). However, as we saw in the fourth section, it does remain a bit unclear how his twofold distinction between simple (or mere) and focused reflection fits in with my three degrees of self-consciousness. This is important because it has an effect on his list of possible responses to the standard view (KUL 19, 27). We can adopt something close to one of his possibilities; namely, that "there are [at least] two senses of "apperception" in the Leibnizian text, in [at least] one of which it is correct to say that beasts apperceive, and in one of which it is not" (KUL 19).

29. See RB 73, 81, 173, 180, 475.

30. For more on animal mentality, see CSC and Donald Griffin, *Animal Minds* (Chicago: University of Chicago Press, 1992).

31. This could be used as a way to handle the familiar charge from animal rights advo-

cates that we cannot, *based purely on psychological capacities*, grant all humans a right to life and deny such a right to all (or most) animals. I cannot delve into this ethical issue here.

32. The other two arguments for "the standard view" have to do with "personality" and the theological problem of why God would create innocent beings capable of suffering (KUL 44–48). I believe that we can respond to them in a similar fashion, that is, by properly distinguishing between degrees of apperception, but I cannot pursue a full discussion of them here.

33. Immanuel Kant *Critique of Pure Reason*, Norman Kemp Smith, trans. (New York: St. Martin's Press, [1781]1965). I will hereafter use the standard A and B edition reference system.

34. Jonathan Bennett, *Kant's Analytic* (Cambridge: Cambridge University Press, 1966), p. 167.

35. Ibid., p. 176.

36. If the reader is interested in Kant's theory of mind, see CSC, where I extensively relate his views to the HOT theory and discuss them in light of contemporary theories of consciousness.

37. Some of the work on this chapter was supported by the National Endowment for the Humanities through Jonathan Bennett's 1995 Summer Seminar; Central Themes in Descartes, Spinoza, and Leibniz. I would also like to thank Jonathan Bennett, Susanna Goodin, Eric Sotnak, and Stephen Voss for comments on an earlier draft of this chapter.

## 18

CATHERINE WILSON

# The Illusory Nature
# of Leibniz's System

Did Leibniz have a metaphysical system and, if so, what are its principal theses? Some commentators have maintained that the *Monadology* (1714) is a system; others, that there is a system already expressed in the *Discourse on Metaphysics* (1686); others, that the essential elements of a system are in place even earlier.[1] Some find that the metaphysics of the 1700s is a alternative, decadent one, which had been preceded by something more promising.[2] Another survey finds that there is a unified account that embraces all or nearly all of Leibniz's expressed claims.[3] In short, disagreement reigns. Meanwhile, the skeptic can cite historical evidence that the eighteenth-century cult of genius was created around Leibniz at the same time as it was created around the great systematists of physics and natural history, respectively, Newton and Buffon. The "systematic Leibniz" of the eighteenth century one might suspect was created from the polymathic Leibniz of the seventeenth, and Leibniz's system is a long-lasting figment of the historical imagination.[4]

The controversy is not simply about which is the right view of Leibniz but also about the nature of theories and of theories about theories. Rationalist philosophers might be defined as those who were impressed by Euclidean geometry and by the systematic interconnections that had been found in parts of the newly mathematized physics, dealing with the paths of celestial and terrestrial bodies of the seventeenth century. These philosophers hoped to find philosophical elements and axioms that might figure in deductive proofs and to identify metaphysical entities that, like the bodies of an astronomical system, were eternally and harmoniously related. By an interesting extension, it is thought, in a sense rightly, that the relationship of the commentator to the philosopher's oeuvre is like the relationship of the geometrician to lines, angles, and other mathematical concepts, or that of the natural scientist to that sector of the cosmos that he or she studies. The aim in both cases is to understand and exhibit what is being studied as a system of objects standing in abstract relations to one another.

There are two reasons that the enterprise of the philosopher to produce a system of the world or the ambition of the commentator to exhibit the philosopher's system might fail. The philosopher might prove unable to grasp the underlying order of things in the way that, for example, the Babylonians failed to grasp the underlying order and dynamics of the solar system, either because of deficiencies in the amount of evidence available or deficiencies in the philosopher's own analytic and synthetic powers. Or it might be that the set of objects being studied, for example, the class of objects consisting of stars in configurations and human characters and destinies, actually does not form a system, though it at first seemed to exhibit systematic relations. In the realm of nature, there can be subject-based failures and object-based failures to systematize. Correspondingly, in the history of philosophy as well, we might distinguish between subject-based failures (the inability of a commentator to grasp the systematicity of a philosopher's oeuvre because certain evidence is unavailable or because the commentator possesses limited powers of analysis and synthesis) and object-based failures (the fact that the statements to be found in a work do not cohere to form a systematic unit).

The view I will defend here is that Leibniz did not have a metaphysical system, if by this is meant that he envisioned a set of objects, characteristics, and properties — minds, substances, causation, animate life, and perception — about which he tells an interpretive story that is consistent, in the sense that it contains no deep and serious contradictions, and fairly complete, in the sense that it is able to answer relevant questions concerning those terms with its own resources. Nor is it the case that Leibniz detected problems with his conceptions and modified his views to solve them, finally arriving at a mature metaphysics free of gaps and conflicts. Rather, his central ideas are in active competition throughout his career.

The absence of systematicity is thus an object-based failure of Leibniz's. The prevalent impression to the contrary, which supports the notion that the failure to exhibit a system can only be a subject-based failure of some commentators, I will argue, derives in at least some cases from a misunderstanding of the Quine-Davidson principle of charity, supposed to govern the interpretation of human discourse. Although the principle of charity invites and even requires the commentator to impose order on a set of philosophical texts, it cannot require that the commentator discover a system that is the one the author intended to present.

The notions of "consistency" and "completeness" introduced here are not formal notions, for what counts as an inconsistency (or as a failure to answer relevant questions) or as resources to be found within the system is in every case a philosophically debatable question into which semantic and pragmatic considerations enter. Nevertheless, in the absence of other proposals, it appears to capture what "systematicity" refers to for historians of modern philosophy. If it turns out that it is impossible to establish agreed-on criteria for what counts as a system, then constraints on the theory of interpretation must be even more disputable than I take them to be here.

A prima facie reason for supposing that Leibniz had a system is that he refers periodically to "my system." And he encourages the impression that his monadological writings describe a metaphysical reality that is like the physical reality of the solar system, which is the basis of the set of appearances presented to our eyes. For these writings describe the activities and characteristics of objects (monads) laid out in a nondimensional, nonmetrical, as opposed to a three-dimensional and measurable, space. Like Ptolemy's or Copernicus's expositions, many of Leibniz's presentations tell us about widely separated objects that have been created in a certain harmonious and eternal pattern. At the same time, Leibniz's metaphysical writing is episodically Euclidean, for there are occasional relationships of logical dependence among his statements of doctrine. For example, from his denial of real spatial extension, the doctrine of the identity of qualitatively indiscernible entities seems to follow. Or from the principle that in all true statements the predicate is contained in the subject, the doctrine that all its future states are contained in an individual substance seems to follow. Though the length of the individual chains of deduction is short, and though they are not such tight deductions as those of logic or mathematics and are indeed not uncontroversial, they create the impression of an axiomatically ordered whole.

However, some entities that are referred to as "systems" resemble only marginally Euclidean geometry or Newtonian dynamics. The term "system" was used in the seventeenth century to mean a pedagogical scheme (e.g., a system of medicine or a system of grammar) for organizing and imparting knowledge. And the notion of a "philosophical system" originally referred to the ethical, cosmological, and theological ideas of the ancient philosophers (especially Epicurus), considered as schemes that rivaled Christian doctrine. Sometimes in the history of philosophy, "system" refers simply to a sort of innovative twist, such as Malebranche's theory of vision in God. Leibniz's references to his own theory of preestablished harmony as a "system" seem to be an example of this last usage. It is important then to establish whether systematicity in Leibniz is more than the illusion of a hidden order based on the following elements: repetition of certain characteristic patterns or figures, advice on adjusting one's attitude, short chains of deductive reasoning, and a set of twists of innovation. Add to these discursive elements the imagery of the *Monadology*, which invokes the model of the open universe with its individual stars arrayed across an unbounded sky, each offering a distinct perspective on the rest.

The order of argument will be as follows. I will identify three key ideas and a key principle in Leibniz. (This is not meant to be an exhaustive list of key ideas and principles.[5]) Next, I will show how Leibniz was drawn, as a result of his attachment to them, to three conflicting stories about perception, and so about monads, minds, souls, animals, and bodies in general. Finally, I will discuss the broader issues of interpretation connected with systematicity. It is, I will argue, the responsibility of the commentator to pinpoint the places where powerful philosophical intuitions that are inconsistent come into play and defeat even informal pretensions at systematicity. In performing this interpretive task, the commentator is bringing disorderly material into order, bringing hidden motivations and invisibly opposing forces to light to explain why a given set of objects has the structure it does. Object-level failure of systematicity on the part of the philosopher may be accompanied by successful marshaling and ordering on the part of the commentator.

## Three Metaphysical Ideas in Leibniz and a Principle

1. *The dual nature of substance.* Most philosophers have thought that the objects we see and handle daily are combinations or products of two opposing or complementary things. For Aristotle, they are form and matter; for the Neoplatonists, good and evil, light and opacity, and existence and nullity. For Leibniz, substance is also dual: variously active and passive power and being and nonbeing.[6]

2. *The continuum of animate life.* Animals, considered as organized systems, seem to be everywhere: no fraction of earth, air, or water appears on close examination to be uninhabited; no fraction of the body of an animal is uninhabited. Every cut into nature gives us more animals.[7]

3. *The priority of unextended units over extended composites.* There must be indivisible units, or else there could not be composites. These units cannot be extended, or else they would be divisible, and so composites, not units. True unities are unextended, and so invisible and intangible.[8]

In addition, Leibniz was convinced of the following principle:

4. *The equivalence of hypotheses about perception.* Experiences do not carry information about their source. My experiences do not tell me whether they arise from causal interaction with matter outside of me, or are implanted in me by God or arise from my own nature.[9]

Leibniz's primary intuitions — the duality of substance, the continuum of animate life, the priority of indivisible units — are independent: no one implies or is implied by any other. He saw it as his task to generate from these core ideas an account of the world in which physics and physiology, which discuss bodies in interaction, could be seen to contain a kind of derivative truth, without being a fundamental account. The most difficult aspect of this problem was to describe perception and embodiment, given his commitment to the equivalence of hypotheses about the external world. Here his key ideas are in active competition. The dual nature of substance (1) lends itself quite naturally to an account of soul-body composites, which supports the notion of a continuum of animals (2). However (1) cannot be reconciled with the equivalence of hypotheses (4), and the continuum of animals (2) cannot be reconciled with (3), the existence of true units. Accordingly, Leibniz has three mutually conflicting accounts of perception, each of which construes mind-body relations differently. Each operates with a different conception of an "individual substance" or "true unity" or "real being." I shall refer to these fundamental units as "monads," distinguishing them as $monads_1$, $monads_2$, and $monads_3$.

## Three Stories about Perception

### Strong Phenomenalism

In strong phenomenalism, the only truly real entities are perceiving, striving, immaterial beings, existing outside of space and time ($monads_1$).

$Monads_1$ = (Df) immaterial, unextended, striving, experiencing substances.

These beings can be said to perceive each other in the sense that their experiences (their "phenomena") are in correspondence. Each monad$_1$ perceives a "world" in which animate and inanimate objects appear outside it and appear to interact with each other and with it. But these phenomena arise in a spontaneous yet orderly manner from the depths of the subject itself. The "objects" we perceive are intentional objects: they are "our phenomena."[10]

The idea that a harmony of independent visual experiences is perceptually equivalent to the perception of a common world is one that Leibniz appears to have evolved from his earlier idea that the perceptions of created substances are partial versions of God's perception of the whole.[11] The linkage is provided by Malebranche's claim that our experience of the world in every sensory modality does not depend on causal interaction between our minds and matter; that matter exists we must anyway take on faith. It is God who bestows on us experiences, albeit in a lawlike and regular way. Although in the *Discourse on Metaphysics* Leibniz disingenuously attributes to St. Teresa the notion that, for each soul, it is as though it were alone in the world with God, the influence of Malebranche is evident. Leibniz was familiar with his *Christian Conversations* and *Search After Truth*, and the spontaneous welling up of experiences in the mind in the absence of causal interaction with matter is a figure that persists into the *Monadology*.

"My body" in strong phemomenalism is, like every other body, a phenomenon in the sense that it appears to me and appears to others. We monads$_1$ actually have no outsides or insides. Our minds are not "inside" our bodies, and our bodies and other bodies are not "outside" our minds. There are nevertheless harmonized phenomena that we refer to as causal interactions, which can be studied, for example, the effect of light particles on the eyes of animals. But these phenomena (as Berkeley claimed) exist only in some minds.

However, strong phenomenalism is not the only account of the relations among physical objects, substances, and perceptual experience to be found in Leibniz. At one point, he described Berkeley's idealism as "paradoxical"[12] and stated in his "Reply to Bayle" that God had not only created monads and their modifications but also substances, for "He finds it good that these modifications should correspond to something external."[13] Recent research has documented the persistence of the notion of "corporeal substance" and its role in giving perception an external object.[14] Other textual sites accordingly suggest that Leibniz subscribed to *weak phenomenalism*, involving monads$_2$.

### Weak Phenomenalism

In weak phenomenalism, perceiving subjects have an outside and an inside. These real beings (monads) are a unity of active and passive powers.

Monads$_2$ = (Df) fusions of active and passive powers.

Weak phenomenalism introduces the notion of "grounding." These power combinations or fusions ground the qualities we associate with materiality: extension, inertia, resistance, antitypy, and *vis viva*. Their perceptual relations also ground the spatial order we refer to as the common world, which is external to our minds, and the appearance of causal interaction.[15] Monads$_2$ are individual substances, some of which are persons. However persons, as higher monads, do not "ground" objects in the world — stones, stars, and so on. Lower monads with less clear perceptions do so.

Weak phenomenalism is "phenomenalistic" in that what are in fact loci of active and passive powers give rise to the appearance of an emergent common world of animate and inanimate beings in which mechanical interactions take place, in the same way that color emerges from or is grounded in, according to corpuscularians, colorless atoms. Whereas in both strong and weak phenomenalism it is correct to say that there are only monads and their phenomena, it is possible to say in weak phenomenalism that a set of monads$_2$ (a-n) "ground" for monad$_2$ m the ball of wax that m perceives, it being understood that this does not imply causal interaction between (a-n) and m. That is, the notion of grounding introduces a function G, which takes monads$_2$ (a-n) into object w for monad$_2$ m:

For m, G (a-n) = w.

Finally, however, there is a strain of thinking we might refer to as "very weak phenomenalism." Very weak phenomenalism is motivated by a subsidiary principle to which Leibniz attached great importance, the distinction between living things and nonliving things. The former he considered to be "true unities"; the latter, "mere aggregates." The latter, in turn, were distinguished from "mere phenomena," like the rainbow.[16] Aggregates are distinguishable from mere phenomena in virtue of the fact that they are made up of, or densely inhabited by, animalcules — monads$_3$:

## Very Weak Phenomenalism

In very weak phenomenalism, monads$_3$ are living beings, composites of soul and body, which perceive each other interactively.

Monads$_3$ = (Df) living, perceiving, active, embodied creatures of various sizes.

Sometimes the organs of monads$_3$, including those of plants and very simple or very small animals, are not constructed to enable them to form representations, and sometimes they are not constructed to enable them optically to resolve the tiny plants and animals that they encounter. In such cases, monads$_3$ perceive each other as material objects or parts of them or as air, water, and so on. Very weak phenomenalism specifies, causally and optically, the nature of the grounding relation and the grounders: monads$_3$ (a-n), ground w for m if m's perceptual apparatus cannot resolve a-n as individual living beings, with the result that m perceives the mass that they compose as inanimate mass w. These tiny living beings are like the material atoms of Epicurus or Gassendi or the corpuscles of Descartes and Boyle; they are found in functional relationships when they combine to form larger animals and plants, but in aggregated, nonhierarchical form they also make up stones, stars, and so on. With microscopes we can see some of them; with better microscopes we should be assured of finding no crevice of the world unoccupied. In this sense, monads$_3$ make up the substance of the world.[17]

Is there any way of describing monads that coherently brings together all the characteristics and roles that Leibniz ascribes to monads$_1$, monads$_2$, and monads$_3$? The pertinence of this question has been recognized ever since Bertrand Russell pointed out the conflict between Leibniz's doctrine that perceptions are produced from the subject's own depths, and thus are nonrelational, and his claim that perception gives knowledge of something external and involves relations, as well as ever since C. D. Broad confessed himself puzzled about whether monads were complete animals or only soul-like entities.[18] Perhaps the most puzzling statement of Leibniz addressed to these two problems occurs in a letter to de Volder:

> For although monads are not extended, they nevertheless have a certain kind of situation [situs] in extension, that is, they have a certain ordered relation of co-existence with others, namely, through the machine which they control. I do not think that any finite substances exist apart from a body and that they therefore lack a position or an order in relation to the other things existing in the universe. . . . Things which are simple, though they do not have extension, must yet have a position in extension.[19]

The Russell-Broad problem can be put as follows: can weak and very weak phenomenalism be given an interpretation in terms of strong phenomenalism? Although the monads$_1$ of strong phenomenalism are not themselves embodied and do not exist in space and time, can we give an interpretation to the claim that they "ground" bodies for us and for other perceiving monads$_2$ and monads$_3$? My claim is that they cannot. Moreover, Leibniz himself was aware of this aporia. He admitted that the notion of "corporeal substance" seemed to be needed to give sense to the notion of an external world for his monads. Perhaps he thought that his various statements could be accommodated within a single theory of perception. But he could not put one together — as indeed no one can.[20]

## Can Strong and Weak Phenomenalism Be Harmonized?

Unlike Russell and Broad, contemporary commentators tend to be sanguine about this possibility. Indeed, they appear more confident than Leibniz himself. Jan Cover states: "Surely nothing in the *Monadology* is inconsistent with the idea that a phenomenal aggregate is secondary matter, and that in corporeal substance there is, in the end, only a hierarchy of substantial forms."[21] Donald Rutherford similarly promises an integrated account: "To forestall [the] suggestion of a conflict within Leibniz's metaphysics, I shall demonstrate . . . how the monadic, physical, and panorganic models are integrated into a single theory of the created world."[22] Pauline Phemister says that "if no monad is ever separated from an organic body, Leibniz is at liberty to claim that there is indeed 'a world of creatures, living beings, animals, entelechies, souls, in the smallest particle of matter. . . .' He can also without any blatant inconsistency claim that the simple beings are unextended perceiving monads."[23]

But how are these claims supported? It has been pointed out that we can think of monads either as disembodied souls (like monads$_1$) or as complete animals (like monads$_3$).[24] This seems right. I can even perform the imaginative act of conceiving that the soul of this animal and of that animal should be removed from the bodies of the animals as they are moving about in three-dimensional space and "transported" to a nonspatial universe, where they exist as disembodied souls with coordinating perceptions. I can now stipulate that that universe is the ground of the familiar one. But these acts of imagination and stipulation fall short of a philosophical explication. I want now to give some basic structural arguments against the very possibility of an integrated account.

If monads$_{1-3}$ are not competing notions, and if strong, weak, and very weak phenomenalism are not competing perceptual theories, then there should be an acceptable translation for S perceives O in terms of a unitary conception of monads a, b, c, d . . . z, a′, b′, c′ . . . which will go as follows:

> Monad a is appeared to in such-and-such a way and monad b is appeared to in such-and-such a way and monad c is appeared to in such-and-such a way. . . .

This translation should make it possible to see why the following features of ordinary world-level perception hold:

1. The parts of O are near to each other, and O is (fairly) near to S.
2. S perceives O with the help of or by means of his body, that is, his eyes, ears, taste buds, and so on.
3. O appears to S like a (fairly) typical O.
4. O is the very thing that S sees.

How might this translation be constructed? Leibniz claimed that substances that can be said to be in greater proximity to one another perceive each other more distinctly than substances that are farther apart: "The soul, which naturally expresses the entire universe in a certain sense and according to the relationship which other bodies have to its own expresses more immediately the properties of the parts of its body."[25]

Let there be five monads, a, b, c, d, and e. Let the sequence $a_1, a_2, a_3, a_4, \ldots a_n$ represent a series of "appearances" of a (that is, how a "looks," not how things "look" to a) ranged from least clear to most clear. Now suppose our five monads have perceptions as follows:

$$a = \{a_9, b_8, c_7, d_2, e_1\}$$
$$b = \{b_9, a_8, c_8, d_3, e_2\}$$
$$c = \{c_9, b_8, a_7, d_4, e_3\} \qquad \text{a b c} \qquad \text{d e}$$
$$d = \{d_9, e_8, c_4, b_3, a_2\}$$
$$e = \{e_9, d_8, c_3, b_2, a_1\}$$

According to this schema,[26] a, b, and c have relatively "clear" (grades 7–9) perceptions of one another and relatively "unclear" (grades 1–3) perceptions of d and e. The scheme generates only a linear, one-dimensional ordering, but presumably an axial notation could be introduced to give the required three or even four dimensions. Thus a, b, and c are near one another and farther from d and e, which are near each other. Each monad has the clearest perception of itself and perceives it more clearly than it perceives any other monad. In this scheme, for monads (a-m) to (partially) ground one of my phenomena (say, my desk), they must perceive each other more clearly than they perceive most other monads and must be perceived by me, sitting at the desk, more clearly than objects in the next room or across the street or beyond the milky way. It should be noted that the scheme actually generates an infinite number of isomorphic object-distributions, including of course the mirror image e d　c b a. This is fully in keeping with Leibniz's relational approach to space, but it renders the grounding function G, which takes monads and their perceptions as argument and generates a spatial distribution as a value, arbitrary.[27] Moreover, there are several problems connected with the notion that monads can perceive each other more or less clearly.

1. The monads that are grounding matter are said to be lower monads. Leibniz nowhere indicates that human monads help to ground any object for other sentient beings. But lower monads are characterized as unclear perceivers. So lower monads cannot be very near each other, whereas it would follow that human monads, who are quite good perceivers, would be quite near everything. The scheme cannot explain feature 1 — why the parts of perceived objects can be said to be near each other.

2. There is no basis for an account here of feature 2, that S perceives O with the help of his body. If monad z is a part of one of my sense organs, it is presumably a subordinate monad, regulated by the dominant "I." To be dominant might then be to be able to take as argument such perceptions and to generate conscious feelings of, say, pain.

But the causal direction here is wrong: Leibniz held that superior monads are more active; inferior monads, more passive. But if my finger is in pain, the monads "composing" it or the thorn that pricks it must be active with respect to the dominant monad, which suffers pain. Conversely, the alleged regulation of my subordinate monads that are performing vital functions such as digestion or the healing of wounds is unconscious, contrary to what should be expected from active, aware, dominant monad that I am.

3. The scheme implies that there is something that it is like for a to perceive b with varying degrees of clarity, as $b_1$, $b_2$, $b_3$, $b_4$, and so on. But what? What does a monad look like and what establishes its typical appearance (feature 3)? God, it might be said, takes care of this. God makes it be the case that b has a range of appearances. However, not only does Leibniz nowhere suggest that God gives substances their own appearances, but also there is no nonarbitrary way of interpreting this statement. In an interactive theory of perception, appearances are functions determined by physical values (wavelength, electrical potential, chemical reactivity, etc.). In a noncausal or noninteractive theory, there is no principled basis for how things look. Without an interpretation for *a looks at b*, we cannot assign an interpretation to *a sees b*. Without an interpretation for *a sees b*, there is no interpretation for *a sees b more clearly than c*, and thus for *a is nearer b than it is c*.

It might be said that preestablished harmony has a role to play here. How a-n appear to each other is just how they would appear were they embodied beings in causal interaction with one another. But what bodies would God nonarbitrarily give them? It is not an illuminating answer to say that he would give them the bodies that the other monads grounding them ground.

4. What, in the relations of monads (a-m), could make O be the very thing that S perceives (feature 4)? One might try out the following: S has an O impression that is consistent with the phenomena of other perceivers; in this sense, all perceivers of O see the same thing.

Now, if I have a red car and you have the same thing, a red car, there is consistency in what we have. But there need be no *specific object* that we both have. If you have a headache, and I do too, there is again consistency in what we have. But there still need be no *thing* that we both have. You and I might share a certain red car, both be related to it as co-owners. And we might get, in a legitimate sense, the same headache if we were exposed to the same toxic chemical in an accident or an experiment. But only in a world with insides and outsides and causal relations can there be things that we both have. Only in a world with insides and outsides and causal relations can there be an object we both see.

I conclude that strong phenomenalism cannot give a nonarbitrary grounding to statements about the perception of individuals and composites.[28] What about weak and very weak phenomenalism then? Might Leibniz's alleged system be based exclusively on them? If so, might strong phenomenalism be said to belong to an early phase of Leibniz's intellectual development?

If this course is taken, we no longer have any theoretical use for the original "harmony of perceptions." And so, as relationality enters the picture through an interpretable grounding function in weak and very weak phenomenalism (a grounding function that appears to coincide with ordinary mechanical causality in very weak phenomenalism), the harmony of perceivers ceases to play a role. This should not be surprising, for the "harmony of perceptions" is simply the result of the philosopher's mental exercise of subtracting interaction and spatial distribution from perception for a class of embodied, spatially situated, interactive perceivers, whereas "grounding" is simply the name for the philosopher's action of stipulating that those perceivers are the foundation of the whole world. In the *New System*, Leibniz appears to be moving away from strong phenomenalism toward an interactive theory of perception. In the worlds of weak and very weak phenomenalism, there is no need for a harmony of perceptions. What is needed is a harmony between soul and body, or between the perceptions of creatures and what happens in their sensory organs. Leibniz indeed announces that the preestablished harmony of body and soul is the major discovery on which his new system is based. However, he still has some fondness for strong phenomenalism, as the opening sections of the *Monadology* (1714) demonstrate. As he wrote to Des Bosses in 1715:

> I fear that the things I have written to you at various times about [the monads] do not cohere very well amongst themselves, as I have not treated the question of Phenomena to be elevated to reality, or of composite substances, except when your letters suggested it.[29]

The burden of the proof here is on those who maintain, contrary to Leibniz's own admission, that he had not only thought about but also implicitly or explicitly solved the problem of "Phenomena to be elevated to reality."

## Methodological Issues in Leibniz Studies

What hangs on the answer to the question of whether Leibniz had a system? The answer is a great deal.[30] It has been suggested that proper methodology in the history of philosophy requires commentators to approach a text without imposing their own preconceptions upon it, that commentary should be a mirror of the author's intentions, and that the commentator should identify with the author and strive for a sympathetic interpretation. Rutherford, voicing this hermeneutic, states that "a systematic interpretation, as I understand it, takes an author on his own terms and seeks to reconstruct a version of his doctrines that would be recognizable to the author himself."[31] Cover says: "If we are invited to give a fragmented 'thematic' reading of Leibniz's metaphysics because he said too much, what he does say is sufficiently complex to permit and repay efforts at reading him otherwise."[32] But why does an interpretation have to reveal the existence of a system for the author to be able to recognize oneself as the subject of interpretation? Why is the complexity of a set of texts a reliable indicator of its underlying philosophical coherence? Why is it assumed that the outcome of the process of commentary, if it does not find a system, is otherwise nothing more than a certain "reading"? The implicit argument for the requirement to present systematicity seems to run as follows:

1. The author referred from time to time to "my system" or "the system of o" in a clearly proprietary way.
2. The author intended to present a system.
3. Commentators should respect the author's intentions.
4. Commentators should present the author's system for him if he did not do it.
5. Commentators who don't find a system to present fail to give a proper commentary.

There are several non sequiturs in this argument.

The inference from 1 to 2 is first of all problematic, given the various loose seventeenth-century meanings of "system" surveyed at the beginning of this chapter. In certain works, such as the *New System of the Nature and Communication of Substances*, Leibniz refers to his system and describes himself as expounding or explaining it or defending it against misunderstandings. In other, dialectically contrived works, notably the *New Essays* and the *Theodicy*, he refers to his system as capable of dealing with problems posed by others. But we have no reason to think that the text of, say, the *New System* is intended to imply an answer to every question about causation, bodies, substances, perception, and animals that can sensibly be framed, and in the dialectical works it is similarly unclear that this is what is intended.

Proposition 3 seems to be a free-standing principle. But what does it actually mean? It certainly does not imply 4. Respect for an author where merited may be exhibited in many ways: by praising his insights or deductions or the beauty of his ideas.

Proposition 4 is too ambiguous to serve as a self-evident methodological principle. What is it to "recognize" a portrayal? I can easily recognize an unflattering photograph of myself as one of me. Whether I want to have this photograph published and promulgated as a good likeness of me is another matter; I may not recognize it in the sense of authorizing and approving its use for this purpose.

Proposition 5, as a result, is simply an arbitrary and thus far ungrounded, methodological assumption.

The question of the relationship between intention and creditable interpretation, to which the above argument is addressed, was debated in aesthetics some thirty years ago, when the notion of unconscious springs of action first came into prominence. The suggestion was that behaviour, including writing behaviour, might be determined not only by the author's conscious purpose and by constraints and influences that he or she was in a position to recount, but by causes of which the writer was partially or wholly unaware: Freudian desires and antipathies, the position and social aspirations of the writer, unacknowledged influences of predecessors and contemporaries. Now, philosophy — particularly rationalist philosophy — might be held to be different from literature because it is premised on the repudiation of non-transparent reasons for belief. A rationalist is, by definition, one who seeks to recognize and free himself from contextual determinations, from the emotional power of influence and rebellion.[33] Thus, to treat a rationalist philosopher as though he were determined by darker causes is to "misunderstand" the nature of the philosophical project.

Again, however, the conclusion does not follow. One may agree that this is in a general way what rationalist philosophers (and presumably all philosophers) were trying to do. But it hardly follows that such projects are without their obscurer motivations and determinants. And there is room for skepticism over whether rationalists or empiricists for that matter, can fully succeed when they are speaking of subjects with emotional resonance — of animals, of hierarchies of excellence, of survival after death, of the true prevalence of evil — in purifying their thought from the influence of sentimental motivations: pride; fear; and hope, above all. That intentions may be dark does not show that systematicity is impossible. But the partial subordination of reasoning to the attainment of desiderata does help to explain why it is frequently not realized.

The hermeneutics of suspicion that I am advancing here is frequently contrasted with the Quine-Davidson principle of charity. Donald Davidson claimed that we are obliged to interpret another speaker so that his or her statements are in large measure true and mutually consistent: "In inferring this system [the agent's] from the evidence, we necessarily impose conditions of coherence, rationality and consistency. These conditions have no echo in physical theory."[34] There is alleged to be an incoherence involved in doing otherwise. But there is a difference between ascribing a true and coherent theory of the world to a speaker and having a coherent theory about why the speaker experiences and theorizes about the world as he does and how he experiences or theorizes about it.

Anthropology falls on the side of physical theory in the sense that we try not to impose anything but, rather, describe what we find. Thus we are well able to understand, on the basis of what a person tells us, that he holds certain religious, mythical, or even mathematical beliefs even when these beliefs, from our point of view, contain contradictions or are separated by inexplicable gaps. Some errors and inconsistencies are explicable in the way that optical illusions are explicable, while others have no evident foundation, and their holders may even assert that they are perfectly in order. The anthropologist is seeking a coherent picture of the world as his subject experiences it, and this means not that he must ascribe only true and mutually consistent beliefs to the subject but that he must report what the subject believes and must make an effort to distinguish between motivatedly false or inconsistent beliefs and accidentally false or inconsistent beliefs.

This is the role of the philosophical commentator insofar as the commentator is willing to regard philosophical assertions as expressing "beliefs" in the first place. To invoke the notion of object-based failure of consistency introduced earlier, we cannot assume that every collection with which we are faced—whether it is a collection of stars, birthdays, and characters; of native utterances; or of philosophical statements—describes an object with a real internal order. But we can assume that there are reasons that people believe and assert what they do, including reasons for failing to detect contradictions, for accepting them outright, and for believing things on the basis of questionable evidence or no evidence at all.

It is easy to imagine that failure is always subject-based failure, especially when the object we are trying to systematize embraces important mysteries. Contemporary cosmology is still unsystematized. We are still ignorant about the beginning and end of the universe, its parameters, its fundamental constants, the kinds of action and causality it contains. Here we feel that we must work harder, collect more data, and reason more brilliantly to get our knowledge to form a system. Leibniz, too, thought that there were important mysteries to be solved by metaphysics. He thought that the materialistic physics of Descartes and certain corpuscularians was full of gaps and contradictions and that the moral status and destination of the world could not be what it seemed. He thought that religion assured us of survival after death but left us no more than a few hints in chemistry and entomology about the nature of resurrection. He thought that there must exist a deterministic, multiplex harmony of striving particulars beneath and despite the appearances, and he hoped that world history would result in a convergence between the appearances and the unobserved beauty that lay beneath them. Like the natural scientist, he talked sometimes about an invisible world of tiny beings massed together; at other times, about monads spread out like stars in the heavens.

Leibniz's fascination naturally infects the commentator, who becomes convinced that Leibniz's writings contain an important mystery. To solve it, it seems, the commentator must work harder, collect more data, and reason more brilliantly. But we do not find a system in every collection of objects presented to us; rather, in making a system, it needs to be decided which objects to include and which to exclude. Including both "perceptions" qua pure experiences and "objects" qua things that found or generate appearances was one of Leibniz's basic mistakes. Including soul-body composites along with simple extensionless beings as elements to be systematically related was another basic mistake. On the commentator's level, taking the products of human efforts extending over forty years—efforts that were notoriously sporadic and reactive—as direct equivalents for the massy objects and forces that Newton described as a system or for the geometrical propositions that formed the Euclidean system is a mistake. If, however, we take turns temporarily excluding certain texts from consideration, we can ascribe to Leibniz three accounts that treat of perception, the nature of "material objects," souls, and animals, each of which is coherent considered in isolation.

A philosopher's oeuvre is, in an important respect, a sector of nature, just as the religious and magical beliefs of a culture are a sector of nature, and just as optical illusions are sectors of nature. My aim in this chapter has been to show precisely how a certain phenomenon — a large sector of Leibniz's thought and writing — though unsystematic and internally inconsistent in its own terms arises in an orderly and understandable fashion from its underlying determinants, and how the illusory impression of systematicity arises in a similarly orderly and understandable manner.

*Notes*

1. Robert M. Sleigh, Jr., *Leibniz and Arnauld* (New Haven, Conn.: Yale University Press, 1990).

2. Daniel Garber, "Leibniz and the Foundations of Physics: The Middle Years" in K. Okruhlik and J. R. Brown, eds., *The Natural Philosophy of Leibniz* (Dordrecht: Reidel, 1985), pp. 27–130.

3. Donald Rutherford, *Leibniz and the Rational Order of Nature* (Cambridge: Cambridge University Press, 1995).

4. On the role of the concept of a system, see Nicholas Rescher, "Leibniz and the Concept of a System," *Studia Leibnitiana* 13 (1981): 114–122. On the historiographic creation of Leibniz as systematist and as genius, see C. Wilson, "The Reception of Leibniz in the Eighteenth Century," in Nicholas Jolley, ed., *The Cambridge Companion to Leibniz* (Cambridge: Cambridge University Press, 1994), pp. 467–470.

5. For example, what about Leibniz's famous "containment theory" of truth, which Couturat put at the center of his thinking? Louis Couturat, "Sur la métaphysique de Leibniz," *Revue de métaphysique et de Morale* 10 (1902): 1–10. Though the principle was important for Leibniz's search for a universal calculus and for the theory of individual substance presented to Arnauld, its status is not as clear as that of the others. The reason is simply that we do not find Leibniz in the period following the correspondence with Arnauld actively propounding the containment theory; Arnauld's worried and skeptical reaction to this negative doctrine of logical fatalism seems to have persuaded Leibniz to convert the theory (which he nevertheless in some sense continued to believe and occasionally to mention) into a positive doctrine of spontaneity. As such, logical containment became incorporated into the doctrine of the equivalence of hypotheses regarding the origins of perception.

6. "*Notes on the Eucharist*" (1668): "The substance of things is an idea. Idea is the union of God and creatures, so that the action of agent and patient is one." L 118; A VI.i.153. "There is no corporeal substance in which there is nothing but extension or magnitude, figure and their variations . . . there is something in corporeal substances analogous to the soul which is form." "First Truths," L 266. "I have preferred to say that the active is incomplete without the passive, and the passive without the active, rather than to speak of matter without form and form without matter. . . ." Letter to Bernoulli (1689); L 511; G III, 551. "Body contains something dynamic, by virtue of which the laws of power are observed. It therefore contains something besides extension and antitypy, for no such thing can be proved from these two alone." Letter to de Volder, 23 June 1699; L 520; G II, 184. "I join to the entelechy in the monad or simple substance only a primitive passive force. . . ." Letter to de Volder, 20 June 1703; G II, 252 (trans. slightly modified). "Aristes: One of your friends . . . has undertaken in some essays published in the *Acta Eruditorum* . . . to show that bodies are endowed with a certain active

force and that bodies are thus composed of two natures — a primitive active force . . . and matter or primitive passive force." *Conversation of Philarete and Ariste* (c. 1711); L 624; G VI, 587–588. "The created being is said to *act*...and to *suffer*." *Monadology* 49 (1714); L 647; G VI, 615. "All creatures derive from God and from nothingness. Their self-being is of God, their non-being is of nothing." *On the true Theologia Mystica*, L 368. See also "Reflections on the Doctrine of a Single Universal Spirit" (1702); G VI, 529–538, for more such dualisms.

7. "Every small part of the universe contains a world with an infinite number of creatures." "First Truths," L 270. "All matter must be filled with animated or at least living substances . . . there is no particle of matter which does not contain a world of innumerable creatures. . . ." Letter to Arnauld, 9 October 1687; L 347; G II, 126. "There is no portion of matter, however tiny, in which there is not a world of creatures, infinite in number." "On Freedom" (1689?); L 264. "Matter is actually subdivided into infinity, so that there is in any particle of matter whatever a world of creatures." To Des Bosses, 4 August 1710; L 599; G II, 409. "Each part of matter can be thought of as a garden full of plants or as a pond full of fish. But each branch of the plant, each member of the animal, each drop of its humours, is also such a garden or such a pond." *Monadology* 67 (1714); L 650; G VI, 618.

8. "[If substance did not contain an active principle] there would always be a plurality of bodies, never one body alone, and therefore there could not, in truth, be many. By a similar argument Cordemoi proved the existence of atoms." "First Truths" L 270. "Where there is not even one thing that is a true being, there cannot be many beings . . . and every multitude presupposes a unity." Letter to Arnauld, 9 October 1687; L 342; G II, 118 "There must of necessity be simple substances everywhere, for without simple substances there would be no compounds." *Principles of Nature and of Grace* (1714), L 636; G VI, 598.

9. "By no argument can it be demonstrated absolutely that bodies exist. Nor is the argument that this makes God a deceiver, of great importance. . . . What if our nature happened to be incapable of real phenomena? Then indeed God ought not so much to be blamed as thanked, for since these phenomena could not be real, God would, by causing them at least to be in agreement, be providing us with something equally as valuable in the practices of life as would be real phenomena." "On the Method of Distinguishing Real from Imaginary Phenomena" (n.d.); L 364; G VII, 321. "The argument by which Descartes tries to prove that material things exist is weak; it would have been better not to try." "Critical Thoughts on the General Part of the Principles of Descartes" (1692); L 391; G IV, 366. "We do not have, nor ought we to hope for, any other mark of reality in phenomena than that they correspond with each other and with eternal truths as well. . . ." To de Volder, 19 January 1706; L 539; G II, 283.

10. "In themselves monads have no situation [situs] with respect to each other, that is no real order which reaches beyond the order of phenomena. Each is as it were a separate world. . . . It cannot be proved from the principle of harmony that there is anything in bodies besides phenomena. For we know on other grounds that the harmony of phenomena in souls does not arise from the influence of bodies but is pre-established." To Des Bosses, 26 May 1712; L 603; G II, 444. "Since absolute reality rests only in the monads and their perceptions, these perceptions must be well regulated." To Remond, 11 February 1715; L 659; G III, 636.

11. On the importance of "world apartness," see Sleigh, *Leibniz and Arnauld*, p. 193.

12. Leibniz, Letter to Des Bosses, 15 March 1715; L 609; G II, 492.

13. Leibniz, "Explanation of the New System" G IV, 495.

14. Glenn Hartz, "Why Corporeal Substances Keep Popping up in Leibniz's Later Philosophy," *British Journal for the History of Philosophy* 6(1998): 193–207. Hartz attributes the observation that they do to Martha Bolton.

15. "Concerning bodies I can demonstrate that not merely light, heat, color, and similar qualities are apparent but also motion, figure and extension. And that if anything is real, it is solely the force of acting and suffering." "On the Method of Distinguishing Real from Imagi-

nary Phenomena" (n.d.); L 365; G VII, 322. "Matter, taken for the mass in itself, is only a phenomenon or a well-founded appearance, as are space and time also." Letter to Arnauld, 9 October 1687; L 343; G II, 118–119. "As for the inertia of matter, since matter itself is nothing but a phenomenon — though well founded — which results from the monads, this is also true of inertia, which is a property of this phenomenon." To Remond, 11 February 1715; L 659; G III, 636.

16. This point has been made by R. M. Adams in "Phenomenalism and Corporeal Substance in Leibniz," *Midwest Studies in Philosophy*, P. A. French, T. E. Uehling, Jr., and H. K. Wettstein, eds. (Minneapolis: University of Minnesota, 1983), pp. 217–258. An exhaustive list of citations is provided by Hartz, "Why Corporeal Substances Keep Popping Up."

17. "If we assume creatures of another, infinitely small world, we will be infinite in comparison with them." "Paris Notes," 11 February 1676; L 159; A VI.iii.475. "As nothing is so solid that it has not a certain degree of fluidity, perhaps the block of marble itself is only a mass of an infinite number of living bodies like a lake full of fish, although such living bodies can ordinarily be distinguished by the eye only when the body is partially decayed." Letter to Arnauld, 30 April 1687; G II, 100–101; *Discourse on Metaphysics and Correspondence with Arnauld*, G. Montgomery, trans. (LaSalle, Ill.: Open Court, 1902), p. 194. "Those who conceive that there is, as it were, an infinity of animals in the least drop of water, as Mr. Leeuwenhoek has shown, and who do not find it strange that matter should be filled everywhere with animated substances, will not find it any more strange that there should be something animated even in ashes." To Arnauld, 9 October 1687; L 345; G II, 122. "How far a piece of flint must be divided in order to arrive at organic bodies and hence at monads, I do not know. But it is easy to see that our ignorance in these things does not prejudice the matter itself." To Bernoulli, 18 November 1698; L 512; G III, 550. "Although the earth and the air interspersed between the plants of the garden, and the water interspersed between the fish in the pond, are not themselves plants or fish, they also contain them, though frequently of a fineness imperceptible to us." *Monadology* 68 (1714); L 650; G VI, 618.

18. Bertrand Russell, *A Critical Exposition of the Philosophy of Leibniz*, 2nd ed. (London: Allen & Unwin, 1937), p. 4; C. D. Broad, *Leibniz: An Introduction* (Cambridge: Cambridge University Press, 1975), p. 88.

19. Leibniz, Letter to De Volder, 20 June 1703; L 531; G II, 253.

20. Daniel Garber's claim in "Foundations of Physics" that Leibniz moved from a robust notion of corporeal substance to idealism (= strong phenomenalism) in later life is problematic not only in the respect noted by Hartz (op cit.) but in discounting Leibniz's early attraction to strong phenomenalism. Cf. C. Wilson, *Leibniz's Metaphysics* (Princeton: Princeton University Press, 1989) pp. 65–70.

21. Jan Cover, "Review of *Leibniz's Metaphysics*," *Leibniz Society Review* 3 (1993): 7–12, at 11.

22. Rutherford, *Rational Order of Nature*, p. 212.

23. Pauline Phemister, "Review of C. Wilson, *Leibniz's Metaphysics*," *British Journal for the History of Philosophy* 4 (1996): 180–188.

24. Thus, according to Rutherford, *Rational Order of Nature*, p. 230: "There is clearly no inconsistency between Leibniz's monadic and panorganic models. They represent complementary ways of understanding the universe; one from the point of view of reality as it is in itself, a system of harmoniously related monads; the other from the point of view of the order determined by those monads' expression of themselves as embodied creatures naturally subordinated to one another."

25. Leibniz, Letter to Arnauld, 9 October 1687; L 339; G II, 111–112. The formulation is repeated in *Monadology* 60; L 649; G VI, 617. The monad's "representation is merely confused as to the details of the whole universe and can be distinct for a small part of things only, that is for those which are the nearest or the greatest in relation to each individual monad."

26. This idea was suggested by C. Huenemann, personal communication, slightly adapted by the author. I thank him for this elegant visual aid.

27. Kant however famously denied in his *Von dem ersten Grunde ds Unterschieds der Gegenden im Raum* (1756) that any set of descriptive predicates can generate a spatial distribution. In other words, though a notation could be given, it would remain a mere notation of simultaneous coexistences. It could not determine an interpretation in terms of experiences. If Kant were right, then our scheme would not even suggest a *linear* ordering to an intellectual being that was not endowed with a pure a priori form of intuition. Cf. *Critique of Pure Reason* A42/B60ff.

28. A more promising line of attack is taken by Phemister, "Review," p. 187: "When the dominant monad has perceptions-of-body, it perceives the phenomena of the subordinate monads. It perceives their body-perceptions, which are in turn also perceptions-of-body because they correspond to body-perceptions which their subordinate monads have and these in turn are perceptions-of-body because they correspond to body-perceptions of their subordinate monads, and so on to infinity."

Suppose we think accordingly of me as a pyramidal colony of monads. At the top, tier 1, is my soul; at tier 2 are monads subordinate to me but dominating others; at tier 3 are monads subordinate to tier 2 but dominating tier 4; and so on. At tier 4, let's say, there are monads with perceptions. Thinking of them as a world apart and unextended, we can nevertheless imagine that they have the "visual impressions" of particles of my blood. Phemister's suggestion is that the tier 3 monads perceive the perceptions of the tier 4 monads; they thus have visual impressions of particles of blood qualitatively different because of their different situs. Moving up to tier 1, I, too, can be said to perceive the particles of my blood, though of course confusedly and nonvisually.

Even if one is happy with the suggestion that I perceive my own blood (Leibniz seems to admit to this in the Arnauld correspondence), there are two problems: (1) what does it mean to say that the tier 1 monad perceives the perceptions (or phenomena of the tier 2 monads)? This can only mean (in a nonrelational theory of perception) that the perceptions are qualitatively similar. (I am experiencing your headache: I can't perceive a different version of your headache or experience *it* differently unless there is some "thing" independent of both our minds that your headache is.) But the dominant and subordinate monads must have qualitatively different perceptions — that is what makes them dominant and subordinate.

29. Letter to Des Bosses, 30 June 1715; G II, 499.

30. Although see the insightful methodological remarks in Sleigh, *Leibniz and Arnauld*, pp. 2–6.

31. Rutherford, *Rational Order of Nature*, p. 3.

32. Cover, "Review of *Leibniz's Metaphysics*," p. 11. Cf. C. Wilson, "Reply to Cover," *Leibniz Society Review* 4 (1994): 5–8.

33. As Leibniz was perhaps the first philosopher to call attention to unconscious motivation (in the *New Essays*, A Vi.vi.188f.), an idea that struck him as deeply charming, it is perhaps misleading to characterize him as a rationalist in this sense. (And the romantic reception of Leibniz stressed above all his aesthetic side.) But he could not have endorsed the claim that his metaphysics used acute analysis of the deficiencies of other metaphysics to generate a picture of the world in keeping with moral or other desiderata.

34. Donald Davidson, *Psychology and Philosophy* in *Essays on Actions and Events* (Oxford: Clarendon Press, 1980), p. 231.

# Index